D0948257

The Congressional System

The Congressional System:
Notes and Readings
Second Edition

Leroy N. Rieselbach
Indiana University

Duxbury Press
North Scituate, Massachusetts

The Congressional System: Notes and Readings, 2d edition, was edited and prepared for composition by Sylvia E. Stein. Interior design was provided by Elizabeth Rotchford. The cover was designed by Oliver Kline.

Duxbury Press
A Division of Wadsworth, Inc.

Library of Congress Cataloging in Publication Data

Rieselbach, Leroy N   comp.
  The congressional system.

  Bibliography: p.
  1. United States. Congress—Addresses, essays,
lectures. I. Title.
JK1061.R5   1979   328.73   78-23946

ISBN 0-87872-211-4

Printed in the United States of America
1   2   3   4   5   6   7   8   9   —   83   82   81   80   79

Contents

Preface to the Second Edition

The intent of this edition is identical to that of the first: to make available to students of Congress the best recent research on the legislature within a framework that links the selections in a meaningful fashion. Because the resurgence of scholarly interest in Congress, which stimulated the first edition, has continued unabated—indeed the events of the 1960s and 1970s, especially Vietnam and Watergate, have heightened that interest considerably—choosing the selections for the revised edition has been extraordinarily difficult. Where a decade ago there were a relatively small number of studies—then "seminal," now "classic"—that stood out in the burgeoning literature, today there exists literally a multitude of high-quality works, many of which flow directly from the earlier research. Nonetheless, I believe the selections included here not only provide a readable overview of the legislative process and congressional politics but also illustrate the variety of approaches available for understanding Congress. The references section lists some of the major studies as well as those cited in the text.

To integrate these diverse studies, I continue to find useful the "systems approach" (pioneered by David Easton and others). Admittedly, the systems framework has not "caught on" or led to decisive research findings. Yet it does clarify the interrelationships of the various facets of the legislative process, interconnections that might go unnoticed when reading the papers and essays individually. Specifically, students should be able to see the congressional institution—composed of individual members and their staffs operating within clearly defined structures and values—interacting with individuals based off "the Hill"—executives, bureaucrats, citizens, judges—to produce policy, to represent constituents, and to oversee the administration. If so, the collection will serve its purpose.

I first became interested in the systems perspective during a year as postdoctoral fellow at the Mental Health Research Institute of the University of Michigan. Although the present formulation may not satisfy the more rigorous "general systems" theorists at the institute, nonetheless it is unlikely that this collection would have been assembled or the introduction written without the stimulation and the opportunity to follow one's inclinations that the institute provided. Much of the editor's material for the first edition, some of which survives into the second, was prepared during my tenure as research associate at the Center for International Affairs, Harvard University. Over the years, Indiana University, especially its Department of Political Science, has provided a hospitable academic home, skilled staff support, and from time to time a modicum of financial aid, all of which helps its faculty substantially.

A number of individuals have also contributed aid and comfort. First and foremost, I am grateful to the scholars whose work appears in the first, second, or both editions of this book. Together they make up two generations of scholars whose work has revived, reinvigorated, and distinguished the study of Congress. I am grateful in particular to Charles S. Bullock and Michael T. Hayes for agreeing to write original papers for this edition. Richard F. Fenno, Bernard C. Hennessy, Charles O. Jones, Charles F. Levine, Morris C. Ogul, and Raymond E. Wolfinger read some or all of the editor's contributions to the first edition, and reflections of their most useful commentary shine through in the revised version. For the latter, I received beneficial suggestions from Charles S. Bullock, Roger H. Davidson, Jeff Fishel, Charles O. Jones, and David Vogler. Had my mind been more open, their invaluable ideas and suggestions might have improved the introduction and notes even more. I must record again my continuing debt to Linda Smith for her adept assistance with the permissions correspondence and flawless typing of the manuscript. As usual, Duxbury Press personnel has been both efficient and easy to work with. Finally, Frances and John Sterling have contributed mightily, if in ways indirect and unknown to them, to both editions of this collection.

It goes without saying, of course, that none of these institutions or individuals bears any responsibility for this book. I remain prepared to accept any compliments and, somewhat more reluctantly, any complaints about what appears between these covers.

Lastly, ten years ago I wrote that my work could not proceed without the patience, forbearance, encouragement, and support of my family. This is truer now than it was then, and to them—Helen and our children, Erik, Kurt, Alice, and Karen—I rededicate this book, with deepened appreciation and affection.

Part 1 Introduction: Congress as a Political System

In the aftermath of Vietnam and Watergate, those singular events that have colored and shaped so much of current American politics, much discussion has focused on the actual and the desirable relationships between the executive and legislative branches of government. Whatever the conclusions such controversies reach, it seems abundantly clear that in the final quarter of the twentieth century Congress will remain central to the operation of the national government. Virtually no federal action can be taken without the consent, explicit or implicit, of Congress; and the legislature is most unlikely to yield its authority to the executive, particularly in view of the politics of the past decade. Thus, we need to understand that complex institution, the Congress, if we are to comprehend contemporary national politics. This book, by analyzing the workings of the legislature, seeks to promote that understanding, to clarify Congress' place in the political process, and to assess the institution's strengths and weaknesses.

To understand congressional activity requires attention to more than the formal, codified rules of procedure that define how a bill becomes a law. It also requires comprehension of the informal, unwritten rules of behavior that often affect the application of the formal rules. The nature and extent of support outside the legislative halls for any particular bill and the ways that support impinges on individual legislators are important to the bill's prospects. Whether the president supports the bill, works actively to get it out of committee, or solicits votes for it may be crucial to its passage. The fate of legislation also depends on the activity of the congressional representatives; they are not merely passive occupants of positions in Congress whose behavior is determined by the workings of the institution. Rather, the attitudes and values they bring to the legislature influence their behavior, what they do to bring about the passage or the defeat of a bill. Nor does activity necessarily end when the bill is passed, for Congress must watch to see if it serves its purposes; legislators must observe critically the executive branch's administration of the bill. The bill's opponents, in Congress and outside, may organize campaigns for its amendment or repeal.

In short, to understand congressional operations necessitates taking into account not only the basic and commonly noted congressional organization and procedures but also the influence of the legislature's informal customs and the relationships of its members to a variety of people who are not members.

Recently, political scientists have employed a conceptual scheme known as systems theory or systems analysis to encompass and relate a large number of seemingly different forms of activity. Because this approach seems admirably suited to understanding congressional politics, it is used in this book.

The Systems Approach: An Overview

The System

The systems approach[1] focuses attention on what actually occurs—on the behaviors of those who are a part of the system. Institutional structures are important not because they are formally specified but because they affect individual behavior, often in ways quite unintended and unforeseen. A *system* is, in general terms, the patterned interactions among two or more actors (variables) that operate persistently over time to produce some form of result (output).[2] As Easton (1965a, pp. 27–28) suggests, there exist

> sets of interdependent actions such that a change in one part will be likely to affect what happens in another part. Included within a system will be only those actions that display a coherence and unity or constitute a whole. Modification in any part of these must have determinate repercussions on other parts. If not for this connectedness of the parts, there would be little point in identifying the behavior as a system.

The kinds of systems of interest to social scientists vary widely: They may consist of two people, say a husband and wife, or be a very large entity, such as the social system of the United States. A system is a set of interrelationships that endure over time and lead to some persistent forms of activity.

The interacting members of the system can be described as playing *roles.* Such terminology is, in general, consistent with ordinary conversational usage. We are accustomed to talking about individuals playing the role of husband, father, or citizen. We recognize that "good" citizens will act in accordance with a set of "rules" that define what kinds of actions they should take and what sorts of actions they should refrain from taking. More formally, we may define role as "*the rights and duties, the normatively approved patterns of behavior*" *for people in given positions in society.*[3]

Role thus defined has both social (or structural) and cultural attributes. A position refers to a specific place in a social structure. The rights and obligations of a position tend to be formalized and codified. Some behaviors are required or forbidden by law or by some other set of rules for the occupant of a particular position; engaging in forbidden activity will lead to the invoking of formal, legal sanctions. Culturally, a role is based upon a set of norms or expectations about how the person who takes the role should act. The members of the system learn that there are some things they are expected to do and some things they must refrain from doing; those who violate the norms, while not subject to formal sanctions, may be punished informally. They may be ignored, socially ostracized, or generally deprived of the rewards that successful role playing brings. In sum, the role concept encompasses a set of legal and extralegal, formal and informal norms, expectations, values, and beliefs about how the occupant of a given position in a system should behave in a variety of social situations.[4]

A distinction must be made between role and *role behavior*. Role defines how the role players, whoever they may be, should behave. Role behavior consists of what particular occupants of the role *actually* do. The behavior they exhibit may or may not correspond with how others expect them to play the role. Inappropriate behavior may occur for a number of reasons. In the first place, the occupants of a given role may not know what behaviors are expected of them; they may have to learn by a painful trial-and-error method. This is the process of *socialization*, the learning by the role players of the behaviors those others with whom they must deal expect them to enact. In this socialization process, the role takers may learn that there is no agreement (more formally, that *role consensus* does not exist) about how they should behave. That is, the people with whom the role occupants must interact do not agree on what is proper activity for them to engage in. Second, role players may encounter *role conflict* when they are confronted by incompatible expectations from two or more sources. That is, the role may require them to deal with two or more sets of people each of which wants them to perform different, and mutually exclusive, behaviors. Part of the socialization process involves learning how to cope with such varying expectations. Finally, role occupants may be personally incapable of meeting role demands. We are all familiar with people who seem temperamentally unsuited for marriage, group membership, or citizenship. On occasion, such individuals will be thrust into a particular role, and their personalities will render it difficult for them to behave appropriately. For all these reasons, role behavior may depart from the norms and expectations that define the role.

To summarize the discussion to this point, we can say that it facilitates understanding of the activities of a wide variety of social units if we conceive of these units as systems. The systems are comprised of sets of persistent and patterned interactions among members of the systems (actors) playing various roles. The roles are defined in terms of formal and informal rights, duties, expectations, and norms, which indicate appropriate role behavior. This discussion of system and role suggests a set of questions that must be answered if we are to understand the actions of any system: Who are the members of the system? What roles make up the system? How do these roles relate to one another? At any point, what kinds of people occupy the various roles of the system? What kinds of role behavior do they display?

Environment and System Inputs

We cannot speak of a system and the roles that compose it without noting that some things are not part of the system. This implies further that there exists a *boundary* that separates the system from all that is outside of it, its *environment*. Boundary is, at times, a difficult notion. For some purposes some actors may fall within the system; for other purposes, it will be appropriate to exclude them and to treat them as environmental in character. We generally include only those actors in whom we are interested as members of the system; that is, the analyst is free to set somewhat arbitrarily the system boundary to suit his or her research purposes.

Despite this ambiguity in definition, there exist some clues as to what to include and what to exclude from a system. The expectations and norms that define the roles will be related to one another and quite distinct from the defining roles in other systems. The members of a system will interact with each other more frequently than they interact with nonmembers. They will tend to form a group displaying solidarity and group loyalty (Easton, 1965a, pp. 68–69). In short, though delineations of system boundaries may vary, we can often establish that some people interact sufficiently often and with sufficient intensity to justify including them and excluding others as members of a system.

Simply because some things are not included in a system but are treated as environmental does not, however, eliminate them from consideration. In the social world, few if any systems are self-sufficient, that is, can survive without any interactions with environmental actors. To put the matter another way, systems of interest tend to be "open," not "closed." Thus it becomes important to look at the nature of the interchanges between elements in the environment and elements within the system's boundary. The transactions directed from the environment to the system are called *inputs* to the system. These inputs are of two forms, demands and supports. *Demands* may be defined as requests or requirements originating outside the system that the members of the system behave in given ways. The demands may create problems and cause stress for the system. The system may not have sufficient resources to deal with any given demand, or there may be too many demands from the environment for the system to cope with.[5] As the character and volume of the demands alter, the structure of the system may prove inadequate; and new processes—formal structures, new role orientations, or some combination of the two—will have to be developed if the system is to survive.

Difficulties for the system may stem from the second type of inputs, supports, as well as from demands. We define *support for a system* as the sentiments and the actions based on those sentiments that individuals hold toward the system. Support may be overt, when it is reflected in specific actions directed toward the system, or covert, when it occurs at the level of attitudes and opinions. Thus support may vary from open, positive activity on behalf of the system, through passive acquiescence or indifference, to overt antagonism toward the system. Obviously, a system cannot survive unchanged if its support falls below some minimum level. If people no longer care enough about its continued existence or openly seek its destruction, the system will be in jeopardy. Support may also, following Easton, be described as diffuse or specific. The former refers to general feelings of attachment to the system; the latter pertains to favorable responses to the system that stem from particular action (outputs) the system takes.[6]

In sum, a system, whatever its formal structures and role patterns, will interact across its boundaries with actors in its environment. These interchanges from the environment to the system, called inputs, will be of two general types: demands, requests for specific actions on the part of the system and supports, the expression of sentiments and in some cases the conversion of these sentiments into positive or negative actions toward the system. Both kinds of inputs may lead to stress on the system, which will be required to take action to respond satisfactorily to the inputs and thus to preserve its own existence.

The notion of inputs from the environment suggests a second set of questions that must be dealt with in the analysis of any system: Who are the major actors in the environment of the system? What kinds of demands do these environmental actors make on the system? What sorts of supports for the system are forthcoming from these environmental actors? What effects do these inputs have on the character of the system itself?

System Outputs

Internal adaptation is one way systems reduce the stress inputs from the environment places on them. Perhaps a more common way is to produce *outputs*, which satisfy the demands made upon the system, produce adequate levels of support for the system, or both. *Outputs* are those end results or products the system generates. Referring to the total political system, Easton refers to the outputs as "the authoritative allocations of values" for society; for less inclusive systems outputs would include decisions and articulated policies the system announces and acts upon.[7]

Outputs, like inputs, are exchanges across the boundary of the system between members of the system and actors in the environment. Outputs may serve to satisfy the demands made upon the system and thus facilitate the system's survival by reducing the level of demands upon it. Outputs may also produce support. A system decision that allocates rewards—money, favors, or prestige—to some set of individuals or groups may win in return the support of the recipients. Outputs that provide sufficient rewards for enough actors in the environment of the system may engender a good deal of support for the system.

In addition, diffuse support may linger on long after the specific output has ceased to be rewarding. It is clear that generation of support will enhance the survival potential of any system.

Any system, then, will seek, through production of outputs, to satisfy the demands made upon it and to create support for itself. To understand a particular system, we need to inquire about the kinds of outputs it produces, the effect of these outputs on demand and support levels, and the consequences of these outputs for the system itself. These sorts of inquiries constitute a third set of questions the analysis of any system must seek to answer.

Feedback

Just as inputs from the environment may affect the internal organization and activity of a system, the outputs from the system may well influence the actors in the environment. A decision that a system makes may satisfy some external actors and produce support; it thus permits the system to take additional actions on the basis of that support. A certain policy enactment may displease groups in the environment, stimulating them to make new demands or to press old demands more vigorously. This is the *feedback cycle*, or loop by which future inputs to the system reflect environmental reactions to past outputs. What the system does presently may influence, via the feedback process, what the system will be required subsequently to face.[8]

The distinction between negative (self-correcting) and positive (self-reinforcing) feedback should be noted. In the former, the responses or new inputs to the system suggest negative reactions to old outputs; and the system will attempt to adjust its behavior to take these critical reactions into account. To cite a simple example, a national system that embarks on a military buildup may stimulate countermobilization from another country and, upon learning of this, may cease its production of armaments rather than engage in an arms race that it feels it cannot win. The information that is "fed back" to the system in this instance produces a change in the system's outputs. Positive feedback, on the other hand, serves to reinforce the system's commitment to its present outputs by communicating the success of present policy. If a weapons development program does not generate counterdevelopments on the part of other nations, the first nation may decide to step up its construction of weapons in the hope of gaining a permanent military advantage vis-à-vis other countries.

The feedback process adds a dynamic element to the systems approach. Because a system seeks to survive in its environment, it will respond to external changes about which it learns through feedback. Its response may be a restructuring of the system itself, or it may take the form of an altered pattern of outputs. These new outputs may change the environmental conditions, thus stimulating still further changes in the type and intensity of the demands and supports that reach the system. Thus a continuous cycle of adaptation and readjustment is established, which, over time, may lead to fundamental changes in system character and outputs. If the feedback process fails, a system may be unable to make functional responses to its environment and may be unable to survive.

Feedback, in short, refers to what a system learns about the reactions of others to its outputs. To understand any system fully, we must attempt to answer a fourth and final set of questions: What is the environmental response to system outputs? What changes in the inputs (demands and supports) to the system does this response engender? How accurately does the system perceive these environmental changes? What alterations in the system does the new input pattern require?

To summarize, this section has sketched out, in brief and oversimplified form, the basic elements of the systems approach to the analysis of social units. A system, characterized by a particular set of formal structures and role orientations, interacts with elements in its environment. It receives inputs (demands and supports), processes them in some fashion, and produces outputs. The effects of these outputs on the relevant actors in the environment are returned to the system as new inputs through the feedback process. The interrelationships among these four sets of factors—system, inputs, outputs, and feedback—are summarized in figure I-1.

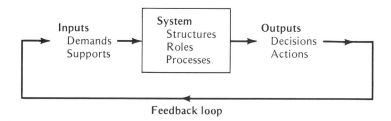

Feedback loop

Figure I-1   Schematic model of a system and its environment

Before we move on to look at the congressional system specifically, we must take note of a word of caution: This has been an oversimplified view of systems analysis. We have talked as if there were but a single system operating in an undifferentiated environment. In fact, this is not the case. What for one set of purposes may appear to be a unified system may appear, from another perspective, as only a part, a *subsystem*, of a larger system. In this book, Congress is the system on which we will focus our attention. If, however, we were to look at the entire American political system, we would discover that the legislature is merely one subsystem to be considered along with the presidential (or executive), judicial, popular, and other subsystems of the total governmental system. Similarly, when we look at the congressional system, we will find that a number of important subsystems exist within it. The committees of Congress can be treated as distinct subsystems of the legislative system, as can the party organizations.

Each of these subsystems can be analyzed as total systems, and from that perspective, we discover distinctive structures and role patterns peculiar to each committee or party. Boundary interchanges—inputs and outputs—occur between subsystems. Put another way, what is internal to a total system is environmental to some subsystem; what is a total system from one point of view may be a subsystem from another point of view. Thus, to repeat a point made earlier, every system is the analytical creation of the researcher who studies it. The true test of any formulation is, of course, the extent to which it fosters understanding of that part of social life under investigation.

The Congressional System

As the foregoing suggests, the systems framework seems well suited to analyze the U.S. Congress. This approach will permit us to see as a whole the entire range of activities in which the legislature engages. It will allow us to integrate a vast amount of recent research into as complete a picture of legislative politics as is possible. The purpose of this section is to explain how the concepts outlined in the first portion of this chapter apply to Congress.

The Congressional System

For present purposes, it seems useful to define the congressional system to include all the legislators, the senators, the representatives, and their supporting individual and committee staff facilities. Other important actors such as the executive branch, the courts, and the public will be treated as environmental factors. Drawing the boundary of the legislative system in this way is consistent with the constitutional separation of powers, which defines the independent but overlapping powers of the three branches of government. In addition, it is reasonable to believe that the members of the legislative system interact with one another more frequently than they interact with those who have been excluded from the system. Each of the environmental actors engages in substantial activity that is nonlegislative in character; members of Congress and their staff associates are involved in legislative business almost exclusively. Moreover, there exist a number of specialized norms of behavior that apply directly to those who are identified as members of the congressional system and not to actors in the environment, except as these latter take the norms into account in dealing with the legislature. Finally, in keeping with the definition of a system as the "patterned interactions among actors," and as the selections included in this volume amply illustrate, there are visible regularities in the interactions among the actors of Congress. The formal rules (for example, the regulation of debate in the House and the absence of such regulation in the Senate), the informal norms (seniority, for example), the operation of particular committees, the activities of the political parties, and other features of Congress influence outputs in predictable (or at least understandable) ways. The parties hold their adherents in line in some circumstances but not in others; patterns of advancement to positions of leadership develop; committee action reflects unwritten decision rules. Other participants in the congressional process are important, but the interactions among members of Congress and their staffs are sufficiently distinctive to justify treating the legislature as a political system, with any remaining actors considered environmental in character.

In examining the congressional system, it is important to know something about its members. Because the behavior of the legislators, like that of other people, reflects their life experiences, it is instructive to see what kinds of people are chosen to serve in Washington. The ease with which legislators learn (are socialized into) legislative roles and the way they perform those roles are often related to what they are when they arrive in the nation's capital. One facet of these life experiences can be gauged by looking at the social background characteristics of the members of Congress. Their family, their experiences—being raised in an urban or rural setting, in a rich or poor family, in a particular region of the country; their educational attainments; their occupational choices; the socioeconomic status they achieved; their religion— these and a variety of other background attributes may shape the way senators or representatives approach their jobs in Congress.[9] Though we have virtually no data to confirm our speculations, it nonetheless seems safe to suggest that representatives' personalities, presumably formed prior to their election, will influence the manner in which they act in the legislature. Common sense and casual observation permit us to recognize the introverted or shy person, the abrasive or aggressive type, or the rigid, unyielding individual; and it should come as no surprise that different personality types differ in the ways they are able to fit into the roles that make up the legislative system.[10]

A third feature of the life experiences that may influence members' legislative performance is their political background, that is, their previous involvement in politics. Have they endured the strains of many prior campaigns or are they relative newcomers to electoral politics? Did they win their congressional contests by a wide or by a narrow margin? If they have had prior exposure to politics, was it in an executive or in a legislative capacity?[11] Finally, lawmakers' behavior may reflect the nature of the constituency they represent. Members from eastern, urban, relatively poor districts may behave in committee and on the floor in a fashion quite different from those from southern, suburban, relatively well-to-do constituencies.[12] In short, role performance is likely to reflect things about legislators—social, personal, and political backgrounds, the kind of constituency they represent—that antedate their election to Congress.

The roles of a system, as noted earlier, have both structural and normative (or cultural) features. The roles of the congressional system reflect bicameralism, the central structural feature of the legislature. There are two central distinctions between the Senate and the House of Representatives that undoubtedly affect the roles played by the members of the two chambers.[13] First and most obvious is the simple matter of size—the House has more than four times as many members as the Senate. Thus the Senate can conduct its business much less formally than the House; with only one hundred members, it requires less hierarchical organization and can provide freer opportunities for individual participation in committee work and floor debate. It also allows more senators to gain access to political power. These same features, in turn, lead to much slower activity. The House, on the other hand, depends more on formal, centralized organization, minimal individual participation, and less even distribution of authority to expedite its business. Only in this more organized fashion can a body of 435 members process all the matters that come before it.

The second major difference between the two chambers lies in the types of constituencies the members represent. Senators are elected from entire, often socially heterogeneous, states; representatives tend to be selected in smaller, more homogeneous congressional districts. The wider, more diverse constituencies of the senators tend to make them more visible (they have more constituents, get more attention from the communication media, develop more prestige) and more liberal (they often have large, urban, liberal-oriented groups of constituents upon whom their reelection may depend). These differences in size and type of constituency represented and the consequences that flow from them probably create differing sets of expectations about how senators and representatives should act. Thus we may expect to find specific and contrasting roles for members of each house.

Within each house, two subsystems command immediate attention: the committees and the party organizations. The former are the main decentralizing force in Congress; each is an independent center of power that competing sources of power can control only with great difficulty. Each committee has its own specific jurisdiction and its own rules of procedure. The committee chairperson, still commonly, though not automatically, chosen on the basis of seniority (the number of years of continuous service on the committee), remains a major figure on the committee, though the powers of the chair have been circumscribed in recent years. More important, the division of nearly all congressional committees into permanent subcommittees, each of which has its own fixed jurisdiction, rules, and staff, serves to fragment power still further. In sum, the committees divide and subdivide authority within the congressional system.

Because the bulk of legislative work is performed within committee and each legislator has one or more committee assignments, members of Congress will develop a role orientation toward committee work.[14] They will decide, if they obtain a committee leadership position, how to conduct themselves as chairpersons or ranking minority members of a committee or subcommittee. They will choose whether to devote a substantial amount of time to mastery of the matters that come before the committee or whether to expend their energies elsewhere. Thus it may be possible to distinguish *committee leadership, committee specialist,* and *committee indifferent* orientations toward committee work. The committee leader attempts to run the panel from a formal leadership position; the specialist devotes much energe to mastery of the details of the committee's work in hopes of achieving leadership at some point in the future; the indifferent is not concerned with committee work beyond the minimum, preferring to expend effort on other facets of congressional activity.

What the committees rend asunder, the political parties can only partially put together. The parties employ floor leaders, whip organizations, caucuses, and policy committees in an effort to maximize the cohesion of their respective members. And although party may be the most important single influence on an individual lawmaker's behavior, rarely does a party even approach unity; legislative battles are often fought between bipartisan coalitions. In the last analysis, party lacks the sanctions required to enforce discipline among its members. Congresspersons may, willingly or unwillingly, defer to the wishes of those outside the legislative system rather than fall into line with party. In any case, senators or representatives will have to devise ways to relate to their party. Jewell and Patterson (1977, p. 350) have identified three basic orientations toward party: the *party man* who "conceives of his job as supporting the program of his party or its leaders, regardless of his own judgments or the consequences of party loyalty"; the *maverick,* who operates independent of party, often supporting the opposition; and the *party indifferent,* for whom party is of little significance.[15]

Whatever personal character they bring with them to Congress and however they choose to relate to the committee and party subsystems, legislators must operate within the framework of a formal set of rules and procedures. Among other things, these rules define the jurisdictions of the committees; the way a bill may move from committee to the floor, including its passage through the House Rules Committee; the fashion in which the proposed law may be debated and voted upon; and the mode of resolving differences between the versions of the bill passed by the two chambers.[16] The roles that members of Congress assume, then, will be shaped to an important degree by the formal rules; these rules provide the bounds beyond which legislative behavior cannot go. It should be noted that the rules profoundly influence the way Congress works. That is, rules are not neutral in their effects on legislative behavior. In general, the rules favor those who support status quo; they make more difficult the task of those lawmakers who propose changes and facilitate the job of those who resist changes. Role orientations toward the rules, then, may reflect whether the legislators seek to bring about or to inhibit change.

There are other, informal restraints that may limit the freedom of action within the legislative halls. White (1956, pp. 81–94) has characterized the Senate as a "club" with a set of norms, or folkways, that define the conditions of membership.[17] Conformity to these norms—dealing with legislative business and one's legislative colleagues in appropriate fashion—will speed lawmakers' rise to positions of influence and enhance their legislative effectiveness. The specifics of these folkways will be discussed later; for the present, the emphasis is upon Senate and House mores that impose additional constraints on individual member behavior. There may be risks to the Congress members if they chose to run counter to the norms; they will have to decide whether to be *conformists* or *nonconformists* with respect to the unwritten rules of the chamber.

To review, we have defined the congressional system to include all the senators and representatives and their supporting staffs. The roles that these men and women play in Congress, roles that may differ because of the two houses, will reflect the life experiences of the members as well as the two major subsystems of Congress—the committees and the parties. In addition, the formal rules and the informal norms will contribute to the shape of the role patterns that individual legislators develop. Role orientations may contain conflicting elements—that is, role conflict may be present. Representatives may be unable to play all their role orientations simultaneously. A role as a committee specialist may lead a member to conclusions contrary to those reached by the party leadership and thus make it impossible to assume the preferred posture of loyal party member.[18] The second part of this book will explore in some detail these elements of the legislative system, by focusing attention on the legislators, committees, parties, formal rules and informal folkways in an attempt to enhance our understanding of the congressional system.

Congressional System Inputs

If members of Congress must, as the above implies, adjust their behavior to the realities of the internal workings of the legislative system, they must also learn to deal with the inputs to that system that emanate in the environment. These inputs—demands upon and support for the congressional system—come from four major sources: the president and the executive branch, the interest (or pressure) groups, the courts, and the public.[19] With respect to public policy, the first two sources tend to be more persistent and more pervasive than the latter two; the operations of Congress will, however, reflect, to some degree, the actions of all four. Demands tend to be for three major types of congressional action: laws or policy decisions, supervision of executive branch activities, and representation of the public. Supports tend to result from these same categories of actions. These outputs will be discussed in the next section.

Without doubt, the most important single source of demands upon, and thus the chief cause of stress for, the congressional system is the executive branch—the president and the multitude of agencies under nominal (at least) presidential control. The chief executive dominates American politics and functions at the center of the political stage. Congress, like other parts of the overall political system, plays its part in support of the star. To a great extent, the legislature responds to initiatives the president takes. The president sets the agenda of Congress; the bulk of congressional activity revolves around proposals sent down from the White House. Congress may not accept what the president suggests; it may amend, modify, or even veto ideas; but it cannot escape the necessity of responding to presidential suggestions.

In addition to determining the topics on which congressional deliberations will focus, the president may well intervene in the legislative process in an effort to influence the outcome. At the president's disposal is a variety of techniques that can be used to try to affect the behavior of individual senators and representatives: positive inducements such as providing patronage appointments, public works projects, and campaign support at election time in the hopes of eliciting favorable responses from the legislators and punishments such as the withholding of favors, the opposition to a lawmaker's pet legislative project, or the withdrawal of a variety of services that the administration can perform for members of Congress. In short, the president will profoundly influence the subjects with which Congress deals and the manner in which it deals with them.[20]

It would be a serious mistake to treat the president as the entire executive branch or the speaker for it, simply because the president bears the responsibility, as "chief administrator," for supervision of the executive establishment. The organization chart that places the president neatly at the pinnacle of the executive hierarchy is not realistic; in fact, bureaucratic agencies strive for, and often attain, a good deal of independence from presidential control. Their requests for legislative action may differ markedly from the desires of the president. Frequently, for example, agencies lose out during the preparation of the budget; they dislike the treatment given to their proposals for new programs and for funds to support existing programs. In such instances they take their case, on appeal in a sense, to Congress. To the degree that the agencies find legislative allies, they may form relationships with Congress, or specifically with the congressional committees or subcommittees that handle their requests, that are far more intimate than those they establish within the executive branch.[21]

The roles the legislators assume, then, will have to relate to the executive branch. Senators and representatives will have to decide whether to be *executive oriented* or *legislative oriented*—that is, they will have to decide whether to facilitate or resist the initiatives of the president or of the executive branch agencies and bureaus. The executive-oriented legislator supports executive demands; the legislative-oriented lawmaker opposes them. When the executive agencies disagree among themselves, congresspersons may have to choose sides in an intraexecutive squabble. They may develop an *agency-oriented* role posture and act as speakers for, and defenders of, the interests of a particular agency, even if those interests run counter to the notions of the president. On the other hand, they may choose a *president-oriented* role and seek to assist the president in controlling the executive agencies. The *legislative-oriented* congressperson may prefer to impose legislative priorities on both the chief executive and the agencies.[22]

A second persistent source of inputs to the legislative system from the environment comes from the lobbyists. Hundreds of groups, including business, labor, agriculture, the professions, and a nearly infinite variety of subdivisions within these broad categories, hire representatives in Washington whose job it is to try to protect their employers' interests. These interests usually lead to efforts to encourage the enactment of beneficial legislation and to act to block passage of bills seen as detrimental to group goals. The lobbyist seeks to maintain contact with, or access to, a large number of legislators and on occasion to persuade them of the wisdom of the group's position. The classic image of interest group activity is one of unremitting pressure on lawmakers— threats of electoral reprisals, entertainment, and even bribery—in an attempt to command support for the group's position. Current research suggests that at present interest group activities include far greater efforts than have been employed in the past to earn the goodwill of legislators. Far from relying exclusively on blatant pressure, the lobbyists provide needed information to lawmakers otherwise dependent on executive branch sources; they help recruit support in response to legislative initiatives; and they seek to develop open channels of communication with members of Congress. The lobbyists hope to be able to approach the legislator in an atmosphere of trust and mutual confidence so that they can make a persuasive case on the merits of the issue. They feel that such tactful techniques, rather than threats, are likely to make them most effective.[23]

Whatever the manner of group-legislator contact, the senators and representatives have to learn to live in the constant presence of lobbyists. A study of congressional role orientations will have to take account of this virtual omnipresence. Wahlke and his associates (1962, pp. 311–342) have suggested a typology of role orientations toward interest groups that, though developed as a result of investigations at the state level, should apply to the national legislature as well. Lawmakers may be classified as pressure group *facilitators, resisters,* or *neutrals.* The facilitator is informed about and favorably disposed toward interest groups and their activities; the resister, although knowledgeable, is generally unsympathetic to lobbyists and lobbying. The neutral, as the label implies, is relatively unconcerned about pressure groups or has no consistent posture either for or against them. Role behavior may reflect these orientations.

A second set of environmental inputs to Congress may be described as intermittent because they do not impinge on legislative formulation of public policy to the same degree as do those from the executive branch and those from the lobbyists. One source of these inputs is the public—the constituents who send the lawmakers to Washington. It may seem inappropriate to characterize congressperson-constituent relations as intermittent in the light of the vast amount of time and effort legislative offices devote to handling requests that originate in the individual districts; but especially with regard to policy, Congress is not very salient to much of the electorate. About half the voters in any state or district are unable to name their representatives; in one election, 59 percent of the electorate had heard nothing about either congressional candidate; fewer than 10 percent cited issues as the basis for their vote.[24] In short, legislators seldom get policy mandates from their constituents.

This does not mean that the "folks back home" are unimportant to their representatives. On the contrary, the members of Congress, perhaps because they believe they operate in the public eye to a much greater extent than they in fact do, struggle to ascertain the views of their constituents. They scan the local press, meet the residents of their states and districts whenever possible, conduct public opinion polls, and keep tabs on the positions expressed in that issue-oriented mail they do receive. However, the messages that reach them are in all likelihood atypical of actual district sentiment, for typical citizens do not seem inclined to communicate with their representatives. Thus legislators may well not be accurately informed about the true nature of constituency opinion.

The heavy demand from constituents for services is considerably more time-consuming to legislators and their staffs. Residents of local communities have problems they believe command the attention of their representatives. They need someone to intercede with the bureaucracy, perhaps to find a lost or mislaid pension check. Some desire federal employment. Others want copies of government publications. Congressional offices, with the reelection prospects of their principals firmly in mind, strive to satisfy all such requests.[25] And indeed, the importance of this communication between citizens and their government can hardly be overstressed.

These matters will be discussed in subsequent chapters, but the important point is that lawmakers will have to decide how to relate themselves and their activities to the geographical units they represent. In the terminology employed here, the role of legislator will have to include orientations toward constituency. Three orientational patterns seem possible.[26] Congress members may focus attention on their constituency alone, that is, they may be *district (or state) oriented.* This posture suggests that the lawmakers see their tasks as promoting the interests of that geographical area from which they were elected. Alternatively, lawmakers may adopt a *nation-oriented* position; they may choose to approach policy problems from a national rather than a local perspective. Finally, the legislators may assume an in-between stance; they may be *district (state)-nation oriented*, in which case they will give roughly equal consideration to local and national interests.

A final and more clearly intermittent source of inputs to the legislative system is the judiciary, particularly the U.S. Supreme Court. Although the vast bulk of judicial activity does not concern Congress, occasionally a Court decision pertains directly to some congressional action. This direct relation of the Supreme Court to Congress has been the case more frequently in recent years as the courts have increasingly taken on a policy-making function. For instance, it is clear that Court decisions have, in recent years, enunciated public policy on educational desegregation, public school prayer, reapportionment, abortion, pornography regulation, and other matters. In each of these areas, Congress had the authority to act but for numerous reasons was unwilling or unable to do so; and the courts moved into the ensuing policy-making vacuum. In other instances the courts have overturned congressional decisions; Court decisions delayed Congress' levying an income tax, regulating child labor, and engaging in a number of New Deal-period interventions in the national economy. Whether Court action makes policy or inhibits legislative decision making, from time to time the two branches have come into open conflict; and individual legislators must decide how they will react when such clashes occur.[27]

We may distinguish two broad role orientations to such interbranch antagonism. The legislator may assume either a *pro-Court* or *anti-Court* position. The former posture reflects a disposition to accept Court rulings as binding on the legislature—to see the Court as in a sense the final arbiter of constitutional issues. The anti-Court stance is indicative of the feeling that congressional action should prevail in the event of conflict with the judiciary. The latter orientation may lead to legislative efforts to overturn Court decisions.

In discussing inputs, we have concentrated upon demands. Demands, in fact, get most attention from political researchers and observers who are concerned with the "who gets what" approach to politics. This concentration, however, should not blind us to an awareness that a system—the congressional system or any other—cannot survive unless a sufficient level of support from the environment is forthcoming. Supports are sentiments and actions in the affirmative and in the negative that actors in the environment display toward the system. Although there exists very little data about the supports directed toward the congressional system, it is clear that each set of environmental actors that makes demands upon the legislature also contributes to the continued existence of Congress by providing support for it. The president and the executive agencies work with, and through, the legislature; they do not attempt to subvert it. The president is quick to praise the legislative branch when it complies with requests; bureaucrats seek to cultivate cooperative relationships with legislators. Similarly, the interest groups support Congress; they provide information and other services to overburdened lawmakers; they respond to requests for aid from members of Congress at least as often as they try to influence them. The public continues to consider Congress a legitimate institution—that is, the public gives it diffuse support; and some segments of the populace may well give specific support in response to particular legislative enactments. Finally, support is also forthcoming from the courts. The Supreme Court upholds legislative actions far more frequently than it overturns them. The justices search for congressional "intent" in dealing with the constitutionality of statutes; their aim is to interpret a law in keeping with the purposes that prompted the lawmakers initially to pass it. On the whole, the congressional system receives sufficient support so that its place in the larger political system remains unchallenged.

In review, the congressional system receives inputs of demands and supports across its boundaries from four major sets of actors in its environment: the president and the executive agencies, interest groups, the public, and the courts. The former two tend to be more immediately involved in legislative policy making than the latter pair. The legislative role will include orientations toward these important environmental forces as well as toward the internal structural characteristics of the congressional system. The third part of this book will explore the nature of these inputs to Congress and their effects on legislative activity.

Congressional Outputs

A system, as noted earlier, exists for some purpose; some result is associated with the interactions among the system members and between those members and actors in the environment. These results, or outputs, are in a sense the products of the inputs and the internal systemic processes for converting inputs into outputs. Thus any examination of the congressional system must include some analysis of the functions the legislature performs. There are three major congressional output activities that will concern us here.

The first of these is the *lawmaking* function; Congress is expected to play its part in the enactment of public policy. Almost every policy initiative, major or minor, that the national government takes requires a congressional grant of authority, appropriation of funds, or both. Medicare, the government-financed health insurance plan for citizens over sixty-five years of age, exists only because Congress defined its coverage and enacted the tax to pay its benefits; public transportation is desegregated only because the national legislature declared it a crime to segregate transportation facilities that are involved in interstate commerce; the United States engages in a foreign aid program only as a result of congressional funding and only under conditions specified by law. Only the few decisions that are taken by the president under the commander-in-chief powers escape the necessity for congressional action; all others are scrutinized by Congress.

In addition to making policy choices, the lawmaking activities of Congress perform several useful subsidiary functions. Mere action by the legislature lends legitimacy to governmental decisions; a policy Congress has examined and debated is more likely to be considered appropriate for the nation to pursue. Legislative consideration also contributes to the process of consensus building and conflict resolution. Congressional decisions emerge from a welter of conflicting interests after each concerned group has made some concessions to the other interested parties. Thus any policy is likely to embody a compromise that provides some satisfactions for many of those involved and that helps to remove the subject from the area of most intense conflict.

Wahlke and his associates (1962, pp. 245–266) in their study of four state legislatures discovered five role orientations toward the lawmaking function that apply to the national legislature as well (Davidson, 1969, ch. 3). The first of these purposive orientations, as they have been called, is that of the *ritualist*, legislators who orient themselves "to the job of lawmaking in terms of legislative functions. . ." (Wahlke et al., 1962, p. 247). Ritualists prefer going through the appropriate motions for achieving specific goals. A second orientation, the *tribune*, aims to promote the wishes and desires of the populace; tribunes see themselves as responding to, and speaking for, public needs. A third posture, the *inventor*, seeks to find new solutions to the substantive issues confronting the country; as the name implies, the inventor is concerned with ideas more than with the process by which ideas become policies. In sharp contrast is the *broker*, the lawmaker who strives to find the acceptable solution; the broker practices the "art of the possible" and tries to compromise and coordinate diverse legislative demands. The fifth, and final, purposive role orientation is the *opportunist*, whose interests are in personal advancement and are thus nonlegislative and whose legislative activities are thereby limited to the barest minimum. Representatives will approach their lawmaking tasks from one or another of these perspectives.

A second congressional function or output activity is the exercise of *oversight* or control over the agencies of the executive branch. Congress must see whether its enactments are accomplishing their intended purposes, whether they are efficiently administered, and whether additional legislative action is needed; therefore the legislature engages in surveillance over the executive agencies. Investigations permit formal oversight. The bureaucrats testify and the legislators may question them closely about the conduct of agency affairs. More often, supervision is carried out informally through consultations between legislators and their staffs on one hand and agency personnel on the other. In addition, legislation may require the agency to submit periodic reports on its activities to the appropriate congressional committee. Using a device known as the "legislative veto," Congress often reserves the right to disapprove and block administrative rulings and regulations. These various supervisory techniques, Congress hopes, will permit the legislature to examine and control effectively current bureaucratic operations.[28]

Oversight can focus on several topics. The most important congressional control is Congress' authority to pass on the budget. Fiscal decisions are clearly policy decisions, for each set of authorization-appropriation choices determine what programs will operate and at what level they will do so; but the budget also provides interested legislators with a major opportunity to examine agency performance. At budget hearings, when the agency heads request funds for new programs as well as old ones, they must justify their use of past appropriations. They must be prepared to defend past policies and to demonstrate past efficiencies. Hearings thus provide the congresspersons with the chance to probe executive activities. Oversight also focuses on the personnel who conduct these executive activities. The Constitution requires the Senate to give "advice and consent" to presidential nominees for major administrative posts, and the upper house can use its right of confirmation as a lever to extract commitments for certain future agency or departmental behavior from the appointee. Similarly, the legislature as a whole, through its power to enact civil service requirements, can set the standards for federal employment. By determining who is eligible for government service in this way, Congress can, at least indirectly, influence the direction and the quality of agency performance. Much oversight seems to be carried out informally; bureaucrats contact the appropriate lawmaker and gain prior approval for the administrative actions they propose to take.

Thus each legislator must decide how to conduct oversight activities. Those who are *executive oriented* will see their task as assisting the president to keep control over the executive bureaus; the *legislative oriented* will seek to impose congressional control over agency performance. The lawmaker may, in addition, be *agency oriented* and attempt to exert legislative control over a particular agency or seek to protect the administrative unit from congressional intervention in its affairs. Finally, we may distinguish an *oversight-indifferent* position, the occupant of which minimizes the importance of the control function, choosing instead to spend time on other legislative duties.

The third major aspect of the congressional job is to represent the citizenry of the nation; thus we may talk about the *representative* function of Congress. It is clear that to some degree lawmakers are expected to act on behalf of constituents and to seek to promote their interests. We have already noted the very heavy demands from those in the legislators' states and districts for them to perform services, as well as the less intensive policy opinions that members of the constituency express. We suggested earlier that members of Congress must choose the geographical unit—the state or district, the nation, or some combination of the two—on which to focus attention. But such a choice is only half the problem; the lawmakers must also decide how to represent their constituents. Are they bound to follow citizen views or are they free to follow their own judgment? How are they to resolve the dilemma when constituent opinion conflicts with personal opinion?

In their study of four state legislatures, Wahlke et al. (1962, pp. 267–286) identified three basic orientations toward the legislative task of representation; these three orientations are found in Congress as well (Davidson, 1969, ch. 4). First, members of Congress may adopt a *trustee* stance, seeing themselves as free to follow the dictates of their own consciences and to act in keeping with their own notions of what is appropriate behavior. Trustees interpret their election as a vote of confidence in their judgment, not as a set of instructions to be followed slavishly. At the other extreme is the *delegate,* who assumes an obligation to adhere to constituents' desires as closely as possible. In the event of a conflict, delegates are prepared to surrender their personal views in order to act in accordance with the attitudes of those who elected them. It is possible, of course, to combine these two orientations and thus to assume a posture called the *politico.* The politicos oscillate between the trustee and delegate positions according to political conditions. They take the former position when they feel the political risks are minimal and the latter position when a disregard for district sentiment may endanger their political future. In many instances, no conflict will arise, for the preferences of congresspersons and constituents will coincide. In such cases, legislators need not make the painful choice between their own views and those of the citizens they represent.

There is another facet to the representational role of Congress members. They may not feel it is sufficient to take the positions of those whom they represent into account when they make their choices. They may, in addition, feel an obligation to explain their behavior to the residents of the district—that is, to educate them about congressional activities. Thus, through the use of "public relations" devices—newsletters, special mailings, radio and television tapes, appearances in the district—they seek to justify their legislative performance. The indirect effect of this contact may be to stimulate communication from the district so that they may be better able to gauge local sentiments and thus make the choice among representational orientations a more rational one. Moreover, by stimulating public opinion and by focusing it on particular topics and in particular ways, lawmakers hope to generate pressure for new policies. In this fashion, they may be able to use the electorate to further their own policy preferences.[29] In any event, much congressional effort goes into constituency relations.

In sum, senators and representatives as members of the congressional system produce outputs of a legislative, oversight, and representational kind; and they must assume role orientations toward each of these activities. Here, as in other aspects of their jobs, they may encounter role conflict; that is, it may be difficult, if not impossible, for them to play all their parts with equal effectiveness. There may not be time or staff resources available to be both a policy-making specialist and an efficient overseer; similarly, the necessities of policy making and representation may present choices—whether to remain in Washington or to return to the home district—where one alternative must be selected to the exclusion of the other. The lawmakers probably cannot perform all three output functions effectively at the same time, and different patterns of concern and resulting activity will emerge. The fourth part of this book will examine the output activities of Congress and the problems these activities create for the legislative system.

Feedback

Although no chapters will deal exclusively with feedback—the process by which present system outputs influence future inputs—it is essential to remember that feedback does affect many congressional operations. What Congress does today will affect what it will be asked to do tomorrow. Outputs that satisfy demands will produce support; those that do not will cause dissatisfaction and diminished support. Failure to deal with national crises may lead the public elsewhere for solutions to major problems. Inability to respond to the president's program may enhance presidential stature and domination of the total governmental system. Unwillingness to act upon public or interest group requests may lead to withdrawal of support and to increased sentiment for presidential leadership.

Total output failure, however, is unlikely; more probable is a mixed record of partial successes and failures. Congress usually manages to satisfy the demands upon it to some degree. Still, the feedback cycle operates. Passage of a medical insurance program for people over sixty-five years of age produces demands for increased benefits or for extension of the plan to the entire population or at least to some larger segment of it. These new demands may come from the executive branch, the pressure groups, the public, or some combination of the three. If the legislature does not respond to some demands, those making the requests will search for new ways to compel congressional compliance. Thus, although the substance of the demands may remain unchanged, the tactics used to support them may alter markedly and create new sorts of stressful situations for Congress.

Thus in the third and fourth parts understanding of feedback is crucial to the discussion of inputs and outputs. The demands upon and support for Congress that come from the executive branch, the pressure groups, the courts, and the public will reflect earlier congressional activity. The legislative, oversight, and representational outputs of Congress will be necessary, in part, because of earlier decisions and in turn will stimulate problems that will have to be subsequently faced. In short, though we may not have occasion repeatedly to mention it, feedback is virtually omnipresent and no one can understand the congressional system without taking it into account. Underlying much congressional behavior are calculations of the nature of environmental reaction to that behavior and of the results of such reaction.

System Change

Congress is not a static institution; rather, the congressional system changes constantly, sometimes slowly, sometimes more dramatically. Numerous new members, with new outlooks, values, and goals, may win election to the national legislature; and they may transform the assembly. They may, for instance, reshape the committee subsystems, altering their jurisdictions or revising their mode of operation. Or they may revive the political parties, committing themselves to support party programs. The newcomers may rewrite the rules of procedure to permit more efficient treatment of legislation; they may refuse to adhere to the legislative norms, thus transforming congressional folkways. Alternatively, these or similar changes may flow from sitting members shifting their stands and agreeing to structural change. In either case, the legislature will be different and the members will have to assume orientations to a new set of internal structures and processes.

Change in the environment may also induce system change in Congress. External events—a major domestic or international crisis, for instance, a new president, an aroused public, excited interest groups, or an adverse court decision—may alter the inputs directed toward Congress. New demands or supports, perhaps with new internal structures, may well lead to different outputs: Congress under such circumstances may redefine its lawmaking responsibilities, redirect its oversight efforts, or renew its representational commitments. In any event, the input-legislative process-output sequence is unlikely to remain constant, and the observer must be alert to the realities of change. Because the last several years have witnessed extraordinary changes in Congress, the fifth part of this volume will describe recent reforms and assess their impact on the congressional system.

The second section of this introduction has attempted to apply the concepts of systems analysis to the congressional system. I have defined the legislative system to include the 535 senators and representatives and their staffs. The major features of the system include bicameralism, the conduct of congressional operations through a set of highly independent committees and subcommittees, and the party organizations—all of which function within a set of formal rules and procedures. A variety of informal norms of behavior and a set of informal legislative organizations also contribute to the form of the congressional system. This system receives inputs of demands and supports from four major sources: the executive branch, the interest groups, the courts, and the public. The system responds by producing three major types of outputs: legislation, oversight, and representation. These outputs in turn are "fed back" to the environment, thus stimulating a new set of inputs with which Congress must deal. The role of congressperson includes orientations toward each of these features: the system's attributes, the inputs it receives, and the outputs it is expected to produce. These relationships are summarized in figure I-2.

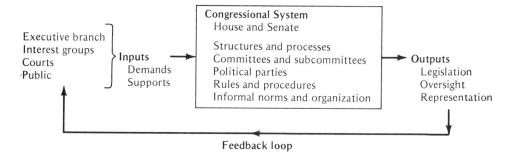

Figure I-2   Schematic model of the congressional system and its environment

All the role orientations outlined above do not actually exist as they were discussed. Rather the system-role concept suggests that they may exist, thus the conditional language employed throughout this chapter. The systems approach provides one way of looking at the complex series of relationships that make up the legislative process, but simply organizing material in this (or any other) fashion does not guarantee an accurate description or understanding of reality. It remains for research to uncover the extent to which role orientations help explain how the congressional system processes inputs to produce outputs.

We have developed a series of hypotheses about the ways members of Congress handle their roles as lawmakers. The selections included in this volume have been chosen because they both inform us about the workings of Congress and suggest the utility of the systems approach in looking at the legislative process. The notes preceding the sections attempt to make this utility clear, but much of what is presented here remains empirically undemonstrated.

The ultimate test of the value of examining Congress from a systems-role perspective is whether to do so enables us to understand, and perhaps even to predict, the operations of the legislature. We would expect to find, with respect to party role orientations, for example, that "party loyalists" vote in support of their party leaders to a high degree and "mavericks" display lower levels of party regularity. Committee "experts" are expected to participate more fully in floor debates because the nonmembers of the committee look to them for guidance; committee "indifferents" will have no need to speak on the floor and others are not likely to expect them to do so. Further, those who assume a "delegate" role orientation toward their constituents will spend more time and energy in representational activities and as a consequence have less opportunity to engage in the lawmaking function than will "trustees." Only if inquiry confirms these hypotheses can we say that the systems-role approach is useful; for then it will help us to explain how the congressional system processes inputs and produces outputs.[30]

Yet even if certain regularities are found to exist, there is no guarantee that they will continue to exist for a long time. Role orientations are seldom the result of conscious choice and will change over time. A change in presidents or the appointment of new Supreme Court justices will mean that members of Congress will have to work with, will receive inputs from, new individuals with differing expectations; new role orientations will certainly result from such changes. Likewise, inputs will alter, sometimes gradually, sometimes dramatically; and this alteration may require new behaviors to deal with altered circumstances. In short, the interactions within the system and between its members and actors in the environment are dynamic, not static; and we will be taxed to keep an accurate picture of them in our minds. Yet when the complexity of the congressional process is noted, the systems approach still seems a sound way to view the totality of congressional politics and a meaningful way to gain perspective on a complex, but crucial, feature of American political life. This collection of readings and the notes that attempt to link the papers will hopefully demonstrate the value of the systems approach.

Notes

[1]The ideas in this section are drawn, somewhat eclectically, from David Easton, William C. Mitchell, and, through them, Talcott Parsons. See Easton, 1965a, 1965b, and 1975, and Mitchell, 1962 and 1967. For other efforts to use these and related notions to analyze legislative politics, see Jewell and Patterson, 1977, and Van Der Slik, 1977.

[2]In most cases, the actors in a system are individuals; but in the international political system, nations are the unit of analysis, that is, the actors.

[3]Yinger, 1965, p. 99. Sarbin and Allen, 1968, provide a thorough overview of role and role theory; Wahlke et al., 1962, present the seminal application of these concepts to legislative politics.

[4]Talcott Parsons treats the distinctions made in previous paragraphs in a somewhat different way, using a different terminology. For a full discussion of the Parsonian alternative schema and a complete citation of Parsons' work, consult Mitchell, 1967.

[5]Easton, 1965a, pp. 114–115. Some demands may originate inside the system (Easton calls them "withinputs"), but their net effect is the same as that of the more numerous external demands.

[6]For a full treatment of these points, see Easton, 1965b, pp. 153-170.

[7]See Easton, 1965b, pp. 343-362, for a more detailed discussion of outputs.

[8]On feedback, see Easton, 1965a and 1965b, and Deutsch, 1966, especially pp. 88-97.

[9]For an example of how social background characteristics relate to legislators' roll-call votes, see Rieselbach, 1966, pp. 61-82.

[10]Surely the conspicuous differences in style and behavior between Senate Democratic leader Lyndon Johnson (1953-1961) and his successor, Mike Mansfield(1961-1977), illustrate the effects of personality. See Kearns, 1977, esp. chs. 1-4, and Huitt, 1961a, on Johnson; and Stewart, 1971, and Peabody, 1976, pp. 339-345, for comparisons of the two. Mansfield's successor, Robert Byrd, appears to occupy an intermediate position: more active, vigorous, outgoing, and flamboyant than Mansfield, but certainly less so than LBJ. For additional evidence on the relevance of personality, see Huitt, 1961b.

[11]See Matthews, 1960, pp. 102-117, on these matters.

[12]For example, see Clausen, 1973, ch. 6, and Jackson, 1974.

[13]Froman, 1967, pp. 5-15 and the table on p. 7, summarizes the distinctions between the two houses of Congress. See also Kernell, 1973.

[14]Technically speaking, each legislator plays the "role" (singular) of senator or representative. The total role, or "role set," is the sum of "role orientations" toward the "significant others" with whom the role occupant must deal. Thus the member of Congress will have orientations toward other members of the system—as a member of a party and one or more committees, for instance—and toward the relevant actors in the environment. In committee, for example, a representative who has risen to the position of chairperson will face fellow members as a leader, for the formal rules of the committee as well as the informal expectations about leadership will shape how leader and followers interact. Similarly, other committee members, because of their thorough knowledge of the substance of committee business, will be recognized as experts and as such will have characteristic patterns of interaction with others on the committee. When for purposes of explication I refer to "roles" or "orientations," I refer to the complex relationships that may exist between a legislator and some other(s) with respect to some particular segment of the total role as a member of Congress. Nor are the orientations necessarily the product of conscious choice; they may result from simple acceptance of "the way things are done." Nonetheless, the role perspective seeks to understand the various ways role players relate to those with whom they must deal. For an assessment of the value of the role concept in understanding legislatures, see Jewell, 1970.

[15]This treatment follows the pioneering Wahlke et al. 1962, pp. 343-376, study.

[16]On the rules, see Froman, 1967, and Oleszek, 1978. The texts of House and Senate rules are in Congressional Quarterly, 1976.

[17]On norms, see also Matthews, 1960, ch. 4; Fenno, 1973b; Asher, 1973; and Rohde, Ornstein, and Peabody, 1974. For a critical view, see Polsby, 1971a, pp. 52-63, and 1971b.

[18]In the language of role analysis, two types of role conflict may occur: inter- and intrarole conflict. The former refers to incompatible expectations emanating from two conflicting role orientations; the example of committee-party conflict is of this sort. Intrarole conflict occurs when inconsistent demands occur within a single role orientation, as when a committee leader is urged to follow one course by the experts on the committee and to adhere to another course by the rank-and-file membership.

[19]There will also be "withinputs," that is, demands arising within the legislative system itself. Many of these will express demands originating in the environment, and in any event, the congressional system will process all demands in similar fashion.

[20]For a summary treatment of presidential involvement with Congress, see James, 1974.

[21]For examples of the intricacies of these executive-legislative relationships, see Maass, 1951; Freeman, 1965; and Ripley and Franklin, 1976.

[22]This role pattern departs slightly from Jewell and Patterson, 1977, p. 350.

[23]On lobbying, see Congressional Quarterly, 1971; Milbrath, 1963; Bauer, Pool and Dexter, 1972. For a recent attempt at a balanced assessment of lobbying, see Hayes, 1978.

[24]Stokes and Miller, 1962. For later data, see Freedman, 1974.

[25]Mayhew, 1974a, and Fiorina, 1977a, treat in detail the connection between providing services and reelection.

[26]This classification follows Jewell and Patterson, 1977, p. 348, which adapts Wahlke et al., 1962, pp. 287–310.

[27]On the Court as policy maker, see Dahl, 1958, and Casper, 1976. On legislative-judicial conflict, consult Murphy, 1962, and Schmidhauser and Berg, 1972.

[28]For a discussion of oversight, see Harris, 1964, and Ogul, 1976.

[29]Fenno, 1977, presents an insightful analysis of these member-constituent relations.

[30]Candor requires acknowledging that research to date on role orientations and legislative politics has provided mixed results. It does seem clear that legislators in numerous systems *do* assume role orientations toward the elements of legislative politics—environmental actors, system structures and processes, and output activities (on Congress, see Davidson, 1969). The factors that predispose lawmakers to particular orientations, however, are less clear (for a summary of findings, see Jewell, 1970). On the critical question of whether role orientations relate directly to behavior, some studies (Van Der Slik, 1973; Friesema and Hedlund, 1974; and Hadley, 1977) find no link, while others (Jones, 1973; Kuklinski, with Elling, 1977; and McCrone and Kuklinski, 1977) find that role does influence behavior. Though much more research is needed, it is probably the case that there is no direct, one-to-one, relationship between role orientation and behavior. Rather, role is likely to shape behavior under certain conditions. For example, McCrone and Kuklinski, 1977, find that only when committed delegates receive consistent and unambiguous cues from their constituents does representational role orientation relate directly to roll-call behavior. The research task, of course, is to specify precisely those conditions under which knowledge of legislators' role orientations permits prediction of their behavior.

Part 2 The Nature of the Congressional System

This book, as the introduction suggests, treats Congress as a political system, a set of structures, processes, and roles that responds to inputs of demands and supports from its environment and that produces outputs of products and activities. This section pursues this line of analysis by examining the congressional system. The selections illustrate the main features of that system—committees, parties, leadership, and rules—as well as the operation of informal norms and organizations. From these readings we may gain some insights into the forces that lead members of Congress to adopt the particular role orientations they assume toward each aspect of the system.

Congressional Recruitment

Because these role orientations are in part shaped by the kinds of people recruited to the legislature, it seems useful to look briefly at the identifying characteristics of those who serve. Three general topics will be reviewed: the social backgrounds of the lawmakers, the electoral process by which they obtain and retain their jobs, and the nature of the life they lead in the nation's capital. Each of these factors contains certain experiences that influence legislators' outlook; this outlook that senators and representatives bring with them to the legislature affects their orientations toward the various features of the congressional system.

The Men and Women of Congress

What kind of people serve in Congress? Since a person acquires beliefs and commitments through the process of political socialization, it is unreasonable to expect that election to Congress will cause anyone to abandon what he or she has for long years felt to be good or bad, right or wrong, desirable or undesirable.[1] Thus an examination of the social positions that legislators occupied before they came to Washington should provide insight into how they will play their roles in Congress.

If we expect to find that members of Congress "represent" their constituents in some literal sense by possessing the same social attributes as those who vote them into office, we will be disappointed. Legislators are not typical Americans. To begin with, although senators and representatives no longer reside more often in small towns and rural areas than the general population (Rieselbach, 1970), they often remain outside the mainstream of American society. In a nation characterized by high mobility and cosmopolitanism, legislators most often are associated with the more provincial segments of society (Huntington, 1973). Nor do lawmakers come from typical families; the greatest proportion are the children of prosperous business and professional people. Few offspring of more marginal American families find their way to the halls of Congress. More specifically, incumbent lawmakers are among the best-educated groups in the United States.[2] Almost all members have attended college; fewer than half of ordinary citizens have had any higher education. In occupational terms, the majority of the senators and representatives is recruited from business and professional careers; only a few came from the ranks of organized labor and other nonmanagerial job categories. In addition, those in Congress come disproportionately from white, male, Anglo-Saxon, Protestant segments of society. In the Ninety-fifth Congress (elected in 1976), there were seventeen blacks in the House and one in the Senate (Edward Brooke, R-Mass., the first black senator since 1861 and the third in the history of the chamber). Seventeen women were elected to the Ninety-fifth House, none to the Senate (though Muriel Humphrey and Maryon Allen were appointed in 1978 to fill the seats of their late husbands, Hubert Humphrey, D-Minn., and James B. Allen, D-Ala). Finally, legislators are atypical of the population in religious and ethnic terms. Members of high-status Protestant denominations, such as Presbyterians and Episcopalians, generally win elections in greater numbers than their proportions in the population would justify; Catholics and Jews tend to be underrepresented.

The conclusion of the argument is clear—those who occupy the positions of senator and representative do not resemble a cross-section of the adult population. They tend to have benefited from more of the opportunities that American society provides than have those who elect them. Their experience in better education and better jobs lets them find room at the top of the ladder of political success. And if, as suggested, different social statuses inculcate different values, we should not be surprised to find that those who are elected to Congress bring with them attitudes and beliefs that are not necessarily typical of the attitudes and beliefs held by the general population.

The Electoral Process

Legislative role playing is influenced not only by the social backgrounds of the lawmakers but also by the electoral process that sends them to

Washington. Perhaps the most salient feature of the legislative system is its members' dependence upon the public; experiences in seeking election affect how the legislators act in office. Apportionment, district competitiveness, the primary system of nominations, and the involvement of their political party in the campaign all bear on the legislators' reelection prospects and thus on their role performance.

Opinions may differ on the extent to which there exists an effective communications link between constituents and their representatives; but there can be little doubt that most elected officials, including legislators, cannot entirely disregard the views of the "folks back home" if they wish to remain in office. What will move voters to retire an incumbent senator or representative probably differs from mid-Manhattan to rural Iowa; the issues that concern residents of such demographically dissimilar areas are, in all likelihood, not identical. Yet lawmakers believe that on some legislative questions the voters are watching them and that their legislative performance will influence voter response (Kingdon, 1967). The questions of which the electorate will be aware will vary with the nature of the district, thus members of Congress are interested in the character of their constituents.

States and districts vary widely. Alaska and New York have little in common other than statehood; their residents may well have differing expectations about how their senators should respond to pending legislative business. Similarly, the views of the constituents of East Coast industrial districts with large numbers of blacks, Puerto Ricans, Irish Catholics, or other racial or religious groups will differ considerably from the images of those views that the representatives of southern, rural, white Anglo-Saxon Protestant areas hold.[3] *Congressional Quarterly (Weekly Report,* April 22, 1978, p. 973) classifies the 435 House districts as urban (105), suburban (125), "mixed" (74), and rural (131).[4] Presumably these differences in composition are reflected by differences in the behavior of the persons who represent the districts. To the degree, then, that lawmakers are sensitive to what they perceive their constituents to believe, representatives of different kinds of districts will play their legislative roles in different ways.

Rural America, while declining as a proportion of the total population, has held more than its fair share of legislative seats. The Constitution apportions Senate seats by states and thus guarantees a large number of rural seats for the upper chamber; the state legislatures, themselves rurally dominated, perpetuated the situation in the House through their powers to set district boundaries. (The U.S. Census is used to determine the number of House seats to which each state is entitled; the state legislatures draw the district lines.) Although the disparity among the various types of constituency was never nearly so great among congressional districts as it is among state legislative units, a *Congressional Quarterly (Weekly Report,* Sept. 20, 1963, pp. 1642–1644) study found that an "ideal" apportionment based on the principle of population equality among districts would add six urban and ten suburban seats to the House of Representatives and the rural and "mixed" areas would lose twelve and four seats respectively.

A year later, in the case of *Wesberry* v. *Sanders*, the United States Supreme Court ruled that congressional districts should be as nearly equal in population as is practicable.[5] Some results of the decision are already clear. Court-induced reapportionment has moved the nation in the direction of the "one person, one vote" ideal; no longer will there be districts two or three times as large as others within a single state. Urban and suburban residents can no longer be discriminated against by state legislatures. Yet problems remain. The *gerrymander* (drawing of district lines to achieve partisan political purposes), although restricted by the equal population criterion, is still possible. And when coupled with the decline in recent years in urban population, it appears that for all the activity of the past fifteen years reapportionment has not really altered the basic contours of congressional representation to any appreciable degree (Noragon, 1972).

Yet, for obvious reasons, congressional candidates remain interested in running in a district in which they can win reelection and, in consequence, gain tenure in the House. Thus they recognize that as districts change because of population shifts or legal coercion, so too will the links between the electors and the elected. The ultimate dependence of the latter upon the former will require the representatives to pay attention to voter response to their actions. They may well feel a need to adapt their behavior accordingly, to adopt role orientations in keeping with their view of the sentiments of the constituency.

Districting will also affect the competitiveness of the constituencies. A district in which the majority party candidate can regularly count on upwards of 60 percent of the vote may well get a different sort of representation than one in which the division between the parties approximates a fifty-fifty split. Put another way, representatives' responsiveness to their constituents will be influenced by the balance of party strength in the district. The legislators' potential for influence in Congress depends on their ability to win relection, which in turn is shaped by the nature of the competition between the parties in the districts they represent. Role orientations, then, will be chosen in relation to how they will be useful in subsequent campaigns.

In Congress, as David Mayhew (1974b, reprinted as selection 1 in this collection) indicates, only a few districts are truly competitive, and, moreover, the number has been shrinking. Only a relatively few representatives win their seats with less than 60 percent of the vote; most now win comfortably and hold "safe" seats. Incumbents have become increasingly able to entrench themselves; through skillful use of available opportunities, sitting members find they have little to fear in subsequent elections. Control of the chamber hinges on the outcome in a relatively small number of constituencies.

Furthermore, rates of turnover have declined. Careers are longer, perhaps enabling incumbents to develop more professional role orientations. The elected members of Congress have at their disposal perquisites, including staff resources, mailing privileges, and travel allowances, that enable them to enter any campaign with a decided competitive advantage over their challengers.[6] Fewer and fewer seats have changed hands in recent years; in 1976, for instance, 95.8 percent of House incumbents seeking reelection were returned to office. For six House elections from 1966 through 1976, incumbent reelection success averaged 93.1 percent; in the Senate, incumbents fared less well, with slightly more than three-fourths (77.1 percent) of sitting members seeking another term emerging as victors. These figures suggest that "new blood" in Congress is far more likely to flow from the voluntary departure of current members than from transfusions the voters administer at the polls.[7] Such membership stability thus indicates that Congress is "institutionalized" (Polsby, 1968) and regularized; members' role orientations are likely to reflect these well-defined contours of the legislature.

It does not necessarily follow, however, that elected representatives need not worry about their reelection prospects. For one thing, the "safer" the district, the greater the likelihood that incumbents will face serious challenge in the primary of their own party. The nomination, when it carries with it a high probability of general election success, becomes the locus of competition. Key (1964, pp. 434–454) has shown that more primary contests occur and that these fights are closer in noncompetitive constituencies. Finally, both primary and general election campaigns are conducted by candidates without much support from the party organizations. Party leaders generally take a "hands-off" attitude toward primary contests and often give higher priority to the noncongressional races in November. Thus legislative candidates are, by necessity, on their own in many cases; they must solicit their own campaign funds, recruit their own workers, build their own coalitions. That these requirements seem to affect their orientation toward party once in office should come as no surprise.

Life in Washington

Those who survive the electoral race find themselves in a rather different world when they arrive in Washington, and the conditions of this life may affect how they perform the more narrowly legislative aspects of their jobs. Matthews (1960, pp. 68–91) has described the "way of life" of senators and suggested that all legislators share a set of common experiences that shape their responses to their work.

First of all, no matter how "safe" their seats may appear, there can be no certainty that a national crisis (like Watergate in 1974), a new challenger, or a popular opposition presidential candidate with long "coattails" will not appear and sweep incumbents out of office. Moreover, although the advantages that a sitting legislator possesses exist, they must be used; the officeholder must use these resources and work at winning reelection. Thus campaigning becomes a central preoccupation of senators and representatives. Campaigning is not restricted to election years but is virtually continuous. It is tiring and time-consuming. It is psychologically straining; the candidates must cater to the electorate, say what the people want to hear, and good-naturedly endure the abuse their opponents heap upon them. The campaign is costly; the need to win financial support may dictate campaign strategy and statements.[8] The time away from Washington precludes complete performance of congressional duties. In short, there is an insecurity that, regardless of "objective conditions" in the state or district, pervades legislators' existence. They devote great energy to ensuring as best they can that their reelection prospects remain good. The ever-present need to fill their campaign war chests may explain why so many members of Congress accepted, with no questions asked and, in most cases, no promises made, "businessman" Tongsun Park's "campaign contributions."

Life outside the congressional chamber creates other strains. The lawmakers are important persons; they become the object of much social attention and are pursued by those who seek favors or influence. Politics dominates the capital. "Washington, with its preoccupation with influence, rivalry, ambition, suspicion, and frustration, provides no respite from the extreme tensions and anxieties of the Senator's job" (Matthews, 1960, pp. 75–76). When added to the demanding legislative work load—for many at least a twelve- to fourteen-hour day, seven days a week—these social activities impose a heavy burden on the members of Congress. It is no wonder, then, that they view the foibles and failings of their legislative colleagues with a considerable tolerance. The rewards of prestige and power are great; the strains and tensions exact a high price in return.

In sum, ordinary people do not often make it to Washington. The recruitment process influences those who serve as legislators in several ways: (1) It screens out many types of Americans and permits only those of generally high social status to become members of Congress. (2) It creates pressures through the electoral process—apportionment, competitiveness, the locally based party organization—to which the lawmakers must respond. (3) It requires an extraordinary degree of energy and drive to endure the arduous life in the nation's capital. Senators and representatives, then, bring with them to legislative service values and beliefs that reflect their social positions, their experiences in successfully overcoming the electoral hurdles set up in their constituencies, and the strains the legislative life engenders. How they adjust to both the formal and informal aspects of the congressional system will depend upon the nature of those values and beliefs.

The Congressional System: Formal Attributes

Positions in Congress, of course, entitle those who hold them to participate in the lawmaking, the oversight, and the representational activities of the national legislature. As the introduction has suggested, there exist a number of alternative ways for lawmakers to relate to the formal aspects of the congressional system. The papers in this section indicate some of the factors that influence the nature of these orientations toward the committees, the political parties, and the formal rules of legislative procedure.

Committees

Perhaps the single most important feature of congressional organization is the existence of "virtually autonomous" specialized committees, each possessing jurisdiction over a specified area of legislative concern, for example, foreign affairs, appropriations, or agriculture.[9] Each committee sets its own rules, hires its own staff, establishes its own pattern and schedule of work; each dominates the legislative output within its jurisdiction; and each exercises oversight with respect to executive agencies and bureaus within its area of concern. The congressional system is a fragmented one; the chief source of this dispersion of authority is the highly independent character of the committees.[10]

Because the committees exercise substantial power over relatively limited domains, it is important to the careers of individual legislators to obtain appropriate committee assignments. The committees are not of equal stature; a lawmaker who serves on the Appropriations Committee rather than on the Post Office and Civil Service Committee is surely closer to the center of legislative activity.[11] Similarly, not all assignments are of equal relevance to constituents. A representative of a rural midwestern district would in all likelihood prefer service on the Agriculture Committee to a seat on the Merchant Marine and Fisheries Committee. The former would clearly provide opportunities that would enhance his or her reelection possibilities.

Furthermore, lawmakers' role orientations toward their committee may reflect the character of their assignments. The more satisfied they are with their committee, the more likely is the prospect that they will invest resources—time, energy, and staff—toward becoming a leader or a specialist in committee affairs. Members waiting for the opportunity to move on to a more attractive assignment may well be relatively indifferent toward their post. In any case, the politics of committee assignments becomes important for an understanding of system operation, and it is this topic that Charles Bullock explores in "House Committee Assignments," selection 2 in this collection. Bullock examines the process the political parties use to place members on committees and the criteria they employ to make the assignments. Most important, party committees on committees seek to satisfy the members—to give them the committee posts they want, the positions that will help the representatives meet their career goals. In the 1970s, nearly all members were able to secure a favorable assignment within a few years (see also Gertzog, 1976). Members, Bullock finds, seek positions from which they shape public policy in preference to those that promote reelection, though members consciously avoid assignments detrimental to their electoral situation. Party committees look to represent women and minorities on major committees—a recent development—and use seniority and party loyalty to choose among veteran members competing for a transfer to a more desirable assignment.

Once on a committee, the member begins to amass seniority, years of continuous service on the panel. Traditionally, the member of the majority party with the greatest seniority chairs the committee and the most senior member of the opposition becomes the ranking minority member. Though the seniority rule is no longer automatic, it is nonetheless almost always followed and has remained a matter of continuing controversy. Since 1971, each party in each chamber has adopted rules that permit the full party membership to vote, on the basis of criteria other than seniority, for committee chairs. Apart from the dramatic 1975 ouster of three elderly southern Democratic House chairmen, the senior member has succeeded to the committee chair. Barbara Hinckley (in selection 3) outlines and assesses the arguments surrounding seniority. The rule, she finds, is not so influential as its critics charge. On the average, it does not take members as long to achieve a chairpersonship as is commonly believed; once there, they do not hold on to their positions for excessive periods.[12] More important, although seniority "reflects and reinforces a deeper congressional conservatism," it introduces only modest regional and party distortions into legislative leadership cadres. Thus it is true that southern Democrats have held numerous House chairs, but it is also the case that southerners have been the largest component of the House Democratic party.[13]

Moreover, the chair's domination of the committees has been undercut in recent years. The chair continues to possess substantial influence—over committee agendas, as presiding officer, with respect to staff and budgetary allocations—but that authority is now exercised within specific committee rules and subject to control by the majority of the committee's members. And, because their hold on their chairs is no longer guaranteed (they must, in effect, stand for reelection at the start of each Congress), chairpersons seem to be more sensitive to the desires of their committee members. In such circumstances, the positive aspects of seniority, particularly its relatively automatic, conflict-free character, may assume a greater importance and attractiveness.

Examination of the full committees does not exhaust the forces leading to fragmentation in Congress; most committees are further divided into subcommittees, many of which, protected by a "subcommittee bill of rights" adopted in 1973, have become independent, autonomous centers of authority.[14] Subcommittee decisions will in many instances be ratified almost automatically by the full committees, which in turn can expect to see the full chamber back the committee's position. Goodwin in his discussion of subcommittees (selection 4) indicates the functions the subcommittees perform. They provide for additional specialization; the few members of a subcommittee who work at their assignment will become the only members of

Congress who qualify as experts in the area of subcommittee concern. In addition, subcommittees open additional avenues to power and influence in the legislature. Representatives with insufficient seniority to qualify as head of a full committee can find a niche for themselves by chairing an important subcommittee; here they can develop expertise, exercise influence, and promote their interests until such time as they may advance to positions of authority in the full committee. On the other hand, subcommittees contribute to further fragmentation. They create a multiplicity of independent units, each of which may be difficult to control. In some instances, subcommittee decisions may become the decisions of Congress. Such diffusion of decision making makes integrating a set of legislative policies difficult to accomplish.

Each committee and nearly all subcommittees have their own staffs; staff resources have grown enormously since 1970: 70 percent in the Senate and 165 percent in the House (Hammond, 1978). The panels have numerous employees available for a variety of duties ranging from clerical and other routine activities to highly specialized tasks such as conducting investigations and drafting legislation. The central issues in congressional staffing are the complaints that staffs are partisan and nonstaffs are political in character, dominated by members of the majority party; in some instances the chairpersons use the staff for their own purposes and deny the minority members of the committee sufficient staff aid to allow them to develop positions contrary to those the committee majority seeks to promote.[15] Whether such conditions exist or whether there is a more equitable allocation of staff resources, the staff remains an important feature of the congressional system, one that affects committee activities as well as the distribution of power within the committee.

In short, as Fenno (1973b, p. 65) puts it, "decisions of the House for the most part are decisions of its committees"; and subcommittees increasingly exercise committee power. Legislators' role orientations may well depend on access to these centers of authority. To the extent that they see a possibility to achieve status within the committee structure, they may be positively inclined to devote themselves to committee business; to the degree that such a path appears to be blocked, they may seek compensations in other parts of the legislative system. Thus, assignment to committee and subcommittee, prospects for attaining positions of leadership within these units, and availability of staff resources affect the lawmakers' decisions about their proper role vis-à-vis the committees.

Political Parties

If the committees are the centrifugal force of Congress, the political parties provide what centripetal force exists. They attempt to add some coherence to legislative activity. The parties do have some bases on which to seek to unify their members, but these are inadequate to overcome the more powerful divisive tendencies of the committees. In addition, the parties must compete with the constituencies; individual legislators often experience role conflict when party loyalty dictates one course of action while district interests seem to require a different mode of behavior.

The parties have a number of strengths. As a symbol they have meaning for their members. Republicans and Democrats in Congress would usually prefer to support the positions that their respective party leaders take. Particularly when a fellow partisan occupies the White House, legislators feel a sense of loyalty to president and party; they recognize the need to "make a record" on which all can run in the next election. Finally, because of the party basis of organization in the chambers of Congress, the parties are strategically placed to produce results.[16] They have their members on all the committees; and if those members are unified, they can exert influence at every stage of the congressional process. Thus the party is an important focus for lawmakers; it generates a "pull" on most senators and representatives to assume the role of party loyalist.

Yet this attraction of party is frequently outweighed by contrary forces. We have noted the central position of the independent committees. For many legislators, the committee provides the avenue to influence; and, if forced to choose between it and party, they will opt for loyalty to the former. This choice is made easier by the relative lack of sanctions available to the party leadership. It is far riskier for a rank-and-file lawmaker to oppose a powerful committee head than to flaunt the wishes of the party because party is not a centralized agency with the ability to punish those who defect. True *national* parties barely exist in this country; the major parties are little more than congeries of state and local organizations. These latter organizations, not the national party committees, control the nominations and campaign funds. Confronted with role conflict, legislators' choice is clear. They will probably feel compelled to avoid alienating the local interests; the voice of constituency will ring louder in their ears than the appeals of party. In some cases, other groups—state delegations, regional clusters, or ideological organizations—and personal conviction may receive individual party members' greater respect and cause them to pursue an independent course. Thus party plays a "mediate" part in the congressional system; it is important but generally not crucial to individual legislators.[17]

The parties elect a number of leaders. In the House of Representatives the Speaker of the House is the acknowledged leader of the majority party and he is assisted by the majority floor leader, who functions as the Speaker's agent on the floor. The minority floor leader leads his or her party and in all likelihood will become Speaker when the election results convert the party to the majority party. Each party has a system of whips who serve as communications channels between leaders and followers. Finally, both Republicans and Democrats maintain a set of party committees. All members of each party meet in caucus (or conference, as the House Republicans call their meeting); each party also has a policy committee formally charged with policy formulation functions. In general these committees tend to support the other leaders and often do not constitute an independent source of influence over congressional activity. The House Democratic caucus, however, has on occasion exerted a major influence on House action. Recently revivified, in part by the arrival in Washington of significant numbers of new, young, and often liberal Democrats and in part by rules changes that enhance its position, the caucus has been more forceful in the 1970s. For instance, in 1975 the caucus, using a new rule, voted to *instruct* the Rules Committee to permit an amendment repealing the oil depletion allowance (a tax break for oil producers), which had lost in the Ways and Means Committee, to be offered on the floor. Rules complied, and the full House voted to eliminate the allowance. In truth, the recent changes in congressional operations (see the fifth part of this book) have strengthened the parties in some ways and weakened them in others, and it is unclear to what extent the parties' overall influence will shift.

In the Senate a similar pattern emerges. The floor leaders are the main cogs in the party machinery. Especially among the Democrats, the leader is a powerful figure, chairing each of the major party committees (for example, the Steering Committee and the Policy Committee) as well as the conference itself. Lyndon Johnson's tenure as Majority Leader (1954–1960) indicates how effective leaders can be if they choose to exploit their leadership advantages; Johnson's successors—Mike Mansfield (D-Mont.) (1961–1977) and Robert Byrd (D-W. Va.) (1977–)—have been less forceful in employing the party leader's full range of resources. Although the Republicans disperse the powers of leadership more widely, the floor leader nonetheless tends to dominate their whip organization, party caucus, and policy committee, as does the Democratic counterpart.

These leaders, although they cannot control the legislative process, perform a number of functions. In selection 5, Peabody describes the leadership's tasks and the resources it possesses to help perform those tasks. In seeking to move the legislative program ahead, House leaders—the Speaker, the Majority Leader, and the Party Whip, in particular—can use their parliamentary powers, their legislative discretion, their primary control over the House information network, their control over the House schedule, and their ability to bargain with—to perform favors for—the rank-and-file members. Each of these resources provides levers of power that help the leaders unify their parties and overcome the existing countervailing powers. These efforts to develop party cohesion meet with differing degrees of success in varying situations. The conditions under which the leaderhsip is most likely to achieve party unity are explored (in selection 6) by Froman and Ripley. In general, the authors conclude that the parties will cohere to a greater extent on procedural rather than substantive issues and when issues are less rather than more visible to outside interests. In these circumstances, nonparty pressures from outside the legislative system will be low and the legislators will be better able to follow the lead of their party. In fact, as the Carter administration has learned so well, recent reforms have made the legislative process "operate in the sunshine," and have, in consequence, seemingly reduced the parties' ability to act cohesively.

Rules of Procedure

Both the committees and the parties operate in a legislative system that functions under a set of formal rules of procedure. Each step of a bill's existence, from its introduction through the approval of a conference report and the dispatch of completed legislation to the president, is accomplished within clearly defined procedures (see Froman, 1967, and Oleszek, 1978). These rules serve a number of uses. They serve to promote predictability in Congress; lawmakers know the rules and they know what to expect in the situations the rules cover. The rules also provide an element of stability. No matter how aroused partisan feelings may become, business will be conducted according to prescribed patterns.

We are all familiar with the major House and Senate rules. In the lower chamber, for instance, the Rules Committee presents an obstacle to any legislation. This committee screens bills, regulates debate, controls the amendment process, and generally shapes the process of deliberation on the floor. This so-called "traffic cop" power usually works well; but on occasion, as in the late 1950s and early 1960s when the committee used its authority to oppose the party leadership, it becomes a focus of controversy. In such circumstances the majority party feels a need to bring the committee into line. In 1961, three new members were added to the rules panel; the increase from twelve to fifteen converted a six-to-six deadlock into a narrow but serviceable eight-to-seven majority that would cooperate with the Democratic leadership. On two other occasions (in 1949–1950 and 1965–1966), a rule was adopted under which a bill could be removed from the Rules Committee after twenty-one days had elapsed. In the 1970s, the committee size was increased again— addition of another majority member brought the committee to sixteen members, eleven from the majority and five from the minority—and the Speaker was granted the authority personally to nominate the Democratic Rules Committee members, subject to party caucus approval. These moves, over a fifteen-year period, have substantially "tamed" the Rules Committee, converting it to a usually reliable "arm" of party leadership (see Oppenheimer, 1977a, 1977b, 1978).[18] Overall, the problems Rules Committee independence causes have been recognized; and those opposed to such independence have sought, with considerable success, to tie the committee more closely to the majority leadership.

An equally well known procedural roadblock is Senate Rule XXII, the unlimited debate or "filibuster" rule. Under this rule, there is no limit upon the length of time a bill can be considered on the Senate floor unless three-fifths (sixty members) of the full Senate vote to invoke cloture—that is, to cut off debate. It has often been extremely difficult to obtain the necessary votes for cloture and as a result many bills have been stalled in the legislative process.[19] In addition, once the nearly exclusive preserve of southerners fighting civil rights bills, the filibuster is now used by senators of varying political persuasions. In recent years conservatives have attempted to filibuster the 1975 extension of the Voting Rights Act and liberals have tried to subvert antibusing and gas deregulation measures. Moreover, if cloture is easier to obtain, those seeking to delay or kill legislation have invented new ways to do so; because all amendments introduced prior to any cloture vote may be considered, it is possible to "filibuster by amendment" even if cloture is voted.

The Rules Committee and filibuster examples underscore a fundamental point: The procedures that govern the House and Senate are not neutral. Members of Congress can exploit the intricacies of the rules to influence legislative outcomes.[20] Minorities can use the rules as weapons to frustrate the wishes of the majority. Thus, legislators' orientations toward the rules may reflect political preferences. Those who are reluctant to introduce change may insist that the rules be followed meticulously; those who favor change may assert that the rules are antiquated and that they inhibit the nation's ability to meet contemporary challenges. Because many lawmakers favor procedural niceties, the rules have an integrity of their own and their alteration is difficult to achieve. Along with the committees and the parties, the rules help to create the formal structure of the congressional system and to delineate many of the operations of the legislature.

The Congressional System: Informal Attributes

The formalities of the congressional system do not satisfactorily explain its functioning. "Behind the scenes" activities also affect congressional output. The norms or folkways—the legislative culture of the chamber—help to define appropriate behavior; adherence to these informal patterns, it is argued, is essential for the smooth functioning of the legislative system. There exist also informal groups—state delegations, "class" organizations of those elected to Congress as freshmen in a particular year, social circles—that may influence the behavior of senators and representatives.

Norms

The norms of Congress define the modes of behavior that are expected and necessary to allow individual legislators to reach positions of influence in the legislature. Conformity to these unwritten rules is usually required to gain the trust and acceptance of one's colleagues and to develop the friendships that are so important for the attainment of power. Matthews (1960) in his classic essay, "The Folkways of the United States Senate," outlines some of the norms of the upper house. Among them are the call for reciprocity, the expectation that senators will help their colleagues whenever possible, trading votes and favors with them if to do so is mutually rewarding; the norm of courtesy that urges members to cultivate friendly relations with their fellow senators; the rule of specialization that requires senators to become experts in few substantive areas and virtually to ignore other policy domains; and the injunction to "be a workhorse not a showhorse"—that is, to devote one's energies to pursuing legislative business rather than to seeking publicity. Those who accept these folkways, Matthews argues, are rewarded with an enhanced ability to get favored legislation through the Senate. Others discount the importance of this legislative culture, suggesting that nonconformists have left their marks on much legislation and in general "have often been far from powerless. . ." (Polsby, 1971a, p. 61). In short, norms do exist and do facilitate the work of the Senate, but they are not so ironclad that violators risk incurring the unending wrath of their senatorial colleagues.

Asher reaches similar conclusions about House norms (selection 7). He finds that members readily accepted such folkways as the need to develop friendly relations with other members, to observe the House rules, to trade votes, and to specialize on a limited number of substantive topics.[21] These norms appear to be obvious to most members; indeed, incoming freshmen members seemed to require little socialization because they were well aware of the general norms before they reached the capital. In sum, the legislative culture is pervasive, defining appropriate member attitudes and behaviors. The norms serve to sustain the decentralized character of Congress; they promote the division of labor among the committees, the development of expertise within the panels, and the reciprocal respect for and deference to that expertise.

The analysis of legislative norms has focused on committees as well as on the houses of Congress. Subsystems seem to develop their own customary procedures for conducting their business; different committees develop differing norm patterns (Fenno, 1973a). The House Appropriations Committee, for instance, has norms—subcommittee reciprocity, specialization, and unity, along with "minimal partisanship" on the full committee—that promote committee integration, the "working together or meshing together" of its parts; integration in turn permits the committee not only to maintain itself but also to achieve its goals (Fenno, 1962). In selection 8, Dyson and Soule assess the extent to which committee integration and minimal committee partisanship, an important aspect of integration, influence the rates at which committee legislation survives on the House floor. The more integrated committees and those that are least partisan have the highest floor success rates. Norms fostering integration and minimizing party conflict contribute to the passage of committee legislation. Committee norms may lead to potential role conflicts for some legislators. We have seen how party exerts pull on its members; yet on some committees, partisanship is to be minimized. Thus committee members may be caught between appeals from the leadership to play a partisan role and their own desires to conform to the norms of the committee in order to maintain their position on that body.

Organization

I noted earlier that informal bodies such as state delegations and social groups exert influence over individual legislators. They may supplement party or other sources of information or they may generate opposition to the appeals of party or committee leaders. The state delegation, if it is cohesive, serves its members in a number of useful ways: It performs a socializing function and reinforces the commitment of incoming members to the chamber norms; it provides companionship and the reassurance of belonging to those who might otherwise feel adrift; and it facilitates communication, providing information and giving cues to appropriate behavior (Fiellin, 1962; Deckard, 1972). The ideological organizations, the Democratic Study Group (DSG) (Ferber, 1971; Stevens, Miller, and Mann, 1974) or the liberal Republican Wednesday Group (Groennings, 1973), conduct policy research, transmit information, and in the case of the DSG seek to channel the votes of its members toward the legislation the group supports. To the extent that situations are ambiguous— where the party and committee are in conflict, where the rules are unclear, where the norms fail to provide guidance—the informal group may serve as a reference point for its members.

Summary

The papers and commentary in the second part of this book are intended to suggest the complexity of the legislative system. The recruitment process colors the outlook of those who become members of the system. The committees; the formal rules of procedure; and, to an extent, the norms of Congress create a dispersion of influence that the political parties can only partially counteract. The congressional structure these features define gives the national legislature its characteristic mode of operation: Congress makes decisions through a process of bargaining, negotiation, and compromise among numerous power holders. The committees and subcommittees are the repositories of expertise. The formal rules not only protect committee decentralization, they also impose obstacles to the passage of legislation: To become a law a bill must survive subcommittee, full committee, and floor consideration in each chamber and in all likelihood a conference to resolve House and Senate differences as well. The informal folkways—especially specialization, reciprocity, and personal courtesy—sustain the widespread sharing of influence. In combination, congressional committees, rules, and norms structure a legislative system in which majorities will be constructed most commonly through a slow and often painful process of coalition building.

The third part of this book indicates how a decentralized system interacts with environmental forces—the executive, the courts, interest groups, and the public. The fourth part suggests how fragmentation of authority affects the outputs of Congress. The point here is that there exist a number of competing foci around which lawmakers may organize their legislative role. To do so will, in all probability, require some difficult choices, for these features of the system exert conflicting pressures. Legislators will have to decide how to resolve choices between committee and party, norms and rules of procedure, and formal and informal organizations. How they decide will determine, in part at least, how they respond to the inputs of the congressional system and to what extent they affect system outputs.

Notes

[1]On political socialization, see Jaros, 1973, and Dawson, Prewitt, and Dawson, 1977.

[2]The *Congressional Quarterly Weekly Report* provides data on the backgrounds of legislators for each Congress. For the Ninety-fifth Congress, see *CQ Weekly Report,* Jan. 1, 1977, pp. 19–30. The annual *Congressional Directory* (Washington, D.C.: Government Printing Office) also presents biographical data on the members of Congress.

[3]For evidence that members from differing types of constituencies behave differently, see Deckard, 1976 (selection 14 in this book).

[4]"Mixed" districts are of a varied character—part central city, part suburban fringe, and part outlying rural areas.

[5]*Wesberry* v. *Sanders,* 376 U.S. 1 (1964). This case extended to the House of Representatives the logic already applied to the state legislators in *Baker* v. *Carr,* 369 U.S. 186 (1962).

[6]On campaigning, see Leuthold, 1968; Fishel, 1973; Mayhew, 1974a; Fiorina, 1977b; and Ferejohn, 1977.

[7]It is easy, given these data, to infer that there is little turnover in Congress. In fact, by contrast, voluntary departures—to seek other office or simply to retire—have come more frequently in recent years. The heightened scrutiny of lawmakers' ethical and financial conduct, perhaps inspired by Watergate and several instances of congressional misbehavior, seems to have encouraged more retirements in the 1970s. In any case, in 1977, at the start of the Ninety-fifth Congress, nearly one-half (48.5 percent) of the House and more than one-third (39 percent) of the Senate had been first elected to Congress in 1972 or thereafter. Thus, substantial turnover does occur, bringing numerous newcomers to the legislative halls.

[8]Matthews (1960, p. 74) quotes one senator: "When I first ran for the Senate,——told me that I would do and say things during the campaign that I would not recognize a year later. 'You

are going to be ashamed of yourself,' he warned. And he was right."

[9]The phrase "virtually autonomous" is from Clapp, 1964, p. 242.

[10]What this fragmentation means, in the language of systems analysis, is that the subsystems of the congressional system are highly autonomous—that is, are quite independent of centralizing authority. If the party leaders were able to control the subcommittee members as they can in a number of state legislatures, the subsystems could be characterized as hierarchically organized. As the subsequent paragraphs point out, the absence of a hierarchical organization has profound effects—such as creating the conditions for specialization, opening avenues for career advancement, or reducing the possibility of party discipline—on the process by which the system processes inputs into outputs.

[11]On the prestige hierarchy of congressional committees, see Goodwin, 1970; Bullock, 1973; and Jewell and Chi-Hung, 1974.

[12]The visibility and importance of such long-term chairmen as Senator John C. Stennis (D-Miss.), of the Armed Services Committee, obscures the more rapid turnover on a majority of congressional committees.

[13]The major cause of the southern advantage in congressional chairs has been the disproportionate number of "safe seats" in that region. As the states and districts of the South become somewhat more competitive and those in the rest of the nation decidedly less so, this advantage is likely to decline and disappear. See Wolfinger and Hollinger, 1971, and Ornstein and Rohde, 1975, on these projections.

[14]These "rights" include fixed jurisdictions for permanent, named subcommittees and authority to adopt their own rules, select their own leaders (though in doing so they tend to use seniority as the decisive criterion—see Wolanin, 1975), hold hearings, hire their own staff, and receive adequate funding, all independent of the full committee. On subcommittees, see Ornstein, 1975a, and Rohde, 1974.

[15]On staffing, see Kofmehl, 1977; Fox and Hammond, 1977; Price, 1971; and Patterson, 1970.

[16]Questions of House and Senate organization evoke the highest levels of party loyalty. See Froman and Ripley, 1965 (selection 6 in this book).

[17]The notion of party as a "mediate" structure appears in Truman, 1959.

[18]Even the reformed Rules Committee, however, is sometimes balky. In the fall of 1977, for instance, the panel declined to clear a bill dealing with oil drilling on the outer continental shelf, legislation that the Democratic leadership wanted for floor action; the bill was, in consequence, delayed for several months. Early in 1978, the committee refused to block floor consideration of a college tuition tax credit amendment, opposed by both the Carter administration and the House Democratic leadership.

[19]The sixty-vote requirement, the smallest number required since the original filibuster rule was adopted in 1917, has made little difference in practice. Since it was substituted (in March 1975) for the two-thirds of those present and voting standard (sixty-seven votes if all members were in attendance; more usually sixty-three or sixty-four votes), cloture has been invoked on only two occasions in which sixty or more senators, but not two-thirds of those voting, supported it.

[20]For examples of the ways in which the rules influence the substance of policy, see Shuman, 1957, and Keynes, 1969. Senator James B. Allen (D-Ala.) was the contemporary champion in the use of the rules as parliamentary tactics.

[21]Asher's (1973) study (as well as that of Rohde, Ornstein, and Peabody, 1974) suggests that the passage of time has eroded one norm, apprenticeship (the expectation that newcomers to the legislature will be "seen and not heard" while they learn their new jobs), that Matthews (1960) found to be a significant Senate folkway. Apparently, current conditions—reelection requirements or member impatience, for example—have undercut the willingness of newcomers to bide their time before entering fully into the institutional life of Congress.

Selection 1 Congressional Elections: The Case of the Vanishing Marginals

David R. Mayhew

Of the electoral instruments voters have used to influence American national government few have been more important than the biennial "net partisan swing" in United States House membership. Since Jacksonian times ups and downs in party seat holdings in the House have supplied an important form of party linkage.

The seat swing is, in practice, a two-step phenomenon. For a party to register a net gain in House seats there must occur (a) a gain (over the last election) in the national proportion of popular votes cast for House candidates of the party in question. That is, the party must be the beneficiary of a national trend in popular voting for the house.[1] But there must also occur (b) a translation of popular vote gains into seat gains.[2] Having the former without the latter might be interesting but it would not be very important.

The causes of popular vote swings have only recently been traced with any precision. There is voter behavior that produces the familiar mid-term sag for parties in control of the presidency.[3] There is the long-run close relation between changes in economic indices and changes in the House popular vote.[4] There are doubtless other matters that can give a national cast to House voting, including wars.[5]

The consequences of partisan seat swings (built on popular vote swings) have been more elusive but no less arresting. As in the case of the Great Society Congress (1965–1966), House newcomers can supply the votes to pass bills that could not have been passed without them. Presidents with ambitious domestic programs (Woodrow Wilson, Franklin Roosevelt, Lyndon Johnson) have relied heavily on the votes of temporarily augmented Democratic House majorities. No clear argument can be made, of course, that a bill-passing binge like that of 1965–1966 offers a direct conversion of popular wishes into laws. The evidence is more ambiguous. At the least a House election like the one of 1964 produces a rotation of government elites that has policy consequences; at the most there is some detectable relation between what such temporarily empowered elites do and what popular wishes are. Over time the working of the seat swing has sometimes given a dialectical cast to national policy-making, with successive elites making successive policy approximations. A case in point is the enactment of the Wagner Act in the Democratic Seventy-fourth Congress

Reprinted from *Polity* Spring 1974, Vol. 6, No. 3, pp. 295–317, by permission of the author and publisher.

followed by its Taft-Hartley revision in the Republican Eightieth. Because of all the translation uncertainties the House seat swing has been a decidedly blunt voter instrument, but it has been a noteworthy instrument nonetheless.

The foregoing is a preface to a discussion of some recent election data. The data, for the years 1956–1972, suggest strongly that the House seat swing is a phenomenon of fast declining amplitude and therefore of fast declining significance. The first task here will be to lay out the data—in nearly raw form—in order to give a sense of their shape and flow. The second task will be to speculate about causes of the pattern in the data, the third to ponder the implications of this pattern.

I.

The data are presented in figure 1–1, an array of 22 bar graphs that runs on for five pages. If the pages are turned sideways and read as if they were one long multi-page display, the graphs appear in three columns of nine, nine, and four. It will be useful to begin with an examination of the four graphs in the right-hand column.

Each of the four right-hand graphs is a frequency distribution in which congressional districts are sorted according to percentages of the major-party presidential vote cast in them in one of the four presidential elections of the years 1956–1968.[6] The districts are cumulated vertically in percentages of the total district set of 435 rather than in absolute numbers. The horizontal axis has column intervals of five percent, ranging from a far-left interval for districts where the Democratic presidential percentage was 0–4.9 to a far-right interval where the percentage was 95–100. Thus the 1956 graph shows that the Stevenson-Kefauver ticket won 50 to 54.9 percent of the major-party vote in about 7 percent of the districts (actual district N=30) and a modal 40 to 44.9 percent of the vote in about 20 percent of the districts (actual N=87).

In themselves these presidential graphs hold no surprises; they are presented for the purpose of visual comparison with the other data. The presidential mode travels well to the left of the 50 percent mark in 1956 and well to the right in 1964, but the four distributions are fundamentally alike in shape—highly peaked, unimodal, not far from normal.

The center and left columns give frequency distributions, organized on the same principles as the four presidential graphs, in which House districts are sorted according to percentages of the major-party House vote cast in them in each of the nine congressional elections in the years 1956–1972. But for each House election there are two graphs side by side. For each year the graph in the left column gives a distribution of returns for all districts in which an incumbent congressman was running, the center column a set of returns for districts with no incumbents running.[7]

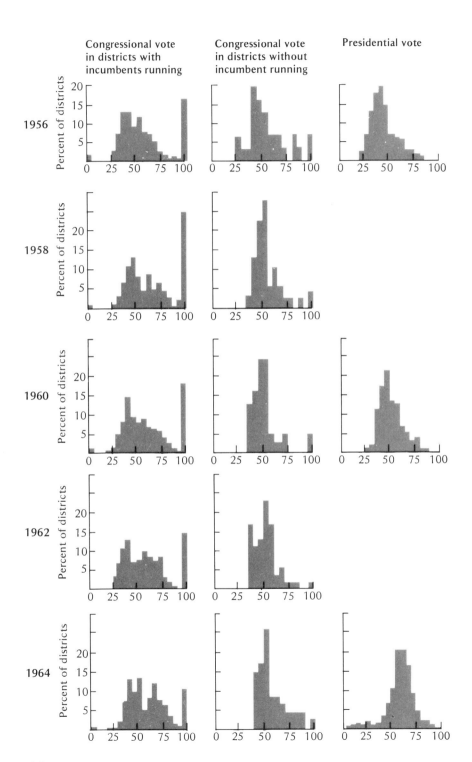

The Nature of the Congressional System

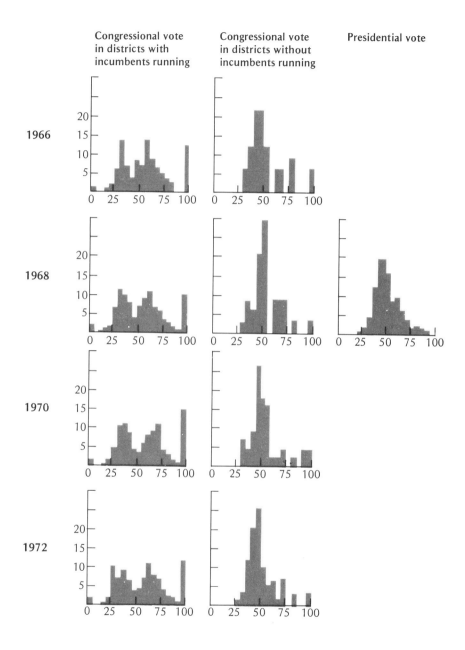

Congressional vote in districts with incumbents running

Congressional vote in districts without incumbents running

Presidential vote

Figure 1-1   Frequency distributions of Democratic percentages of the two-party vote in House districts

The center graphs, the "open seat" distributions, are erratically shaped because the N's are small. The number of House districts without incumbents running averages 43 (about a tenth of the membership) and ranges from 31 (in 1956) to 59 (in 1972); there is no discernible upward or downward trend in the series. With allowances made for erratic shape, these nine "open seat" distributions are much alike. All are highly peaked and centrally clustered. In 1958 and 1968 nearly 30 percent of the readings appear in the modal interval (in both cases the 50–54.9 percent Democratic interval). Over the set of nine elections the proportion of "open seat" outcomes falling in the 40–59.9 percent area ranges from 54.8 percent to 70.2 percent, the proportion in the 45–54.9 percent area from 29.0 percent to 50.1 percent. All of which imparts the simple and obvious message that House elections without incumbents running tend to be closely contested.

The nine graphs in the left-hand column give distributions for districts with incumbents running.[8] Thus in 1956 about 9 percent of districts with incumbents running yielded returns in the 45–49.9 percent Democratic interval. In some of these cases the incumbents were Democrats who thereby lost their seats; in any of these nine graphs the election reading for a losing incumbent will appear on what was, from his standpoint, the unfortunate side of the 50 percent line. In an Appendix the nine data sets are disaggregated to show where in fact incumbents lost.

Immediately visible on each of these incumbency graphs is the isolated mode in the 95-100 percent interval, recording the familiar phenomenon of uncontested Democratic victories—mostly in the South. But, if these right-flush modes can be ignored for a moment, what has recently been happening in the contested range is far more interesting. In 1956 and 1960 the distributions in the contested range are skewed a little to the right, but still not far from normal in shape. In the 1958 and 1962 midterm years the distributions are somewhat flatter and more jagged.[9] In 1964 and 1966 they appear only tenuously normal. In 1968, 1970, and 1972 they have become emphatically bimodal in shape. Or, to ring in the uncontested Democratic seats again, the shape of incumbency distributions has now become strikingly trimodal. Thus in the 1972 election there was a range of reasonably safe Republican seats (with the 25–29.9 percent and 35–39.5 percent intervals most heavily populated), a range of reasonably safe Democratic seats (peaked in the 60–64.9 percent interval), and a set of 44 uncontested Democratic seats.

The title of this paper includes the phrase, "The Case of the Vanishing Marginals." The "vanishing marginals" are all those congressmen whose election percentages could, but now do not, earn them places in the central range of these incumbency distributions. In the graphs for the most recent elections the trough between the "reasonably safe" Republican and Democratic modes appears in the percentage range that we are accustomed to calling "marginal." Figure 1-2 captures the point, with time series showing how many incumbent congressmen have recorded percentages in the "marginal" range in each election from 1956 through 1972.[10] The lower series on the two figure 1-2 graphs show, for comparative purposes, the number of "open seat" outcomes in the marginal range. In one graph marginality is defined narrowly (45–54.9 Democratic percentage of the major-party vote), in the other broadly (40–59.9 percent). By either definition the number of incumbents running in the marginal zone has roughly halved over the sixteen-year period.[11] For some reason, or reasons, it seems to be a lot easier now than it used to be for a sitting congressmen to win three-fifths of the November vote.

II.

Why the decline in incumbent marginality? No clear answer is available.[12] Adding complexity to the problem is the fact that the proportion of House seats won in the marginal range has been slowly declining for over a century.[13] Whatever mix of causes underlies the long-run change could account for much of the rapid current change as well. On the assumption that the contemporary decline is not ephemeral, perhaps the most useful thing to do here is to set out some hypotheses which may singly or in combination account for it. Five hypotheses are offered below. Some have a more persuasive ring than others; none is wholly implausible. The first has to do with district line-

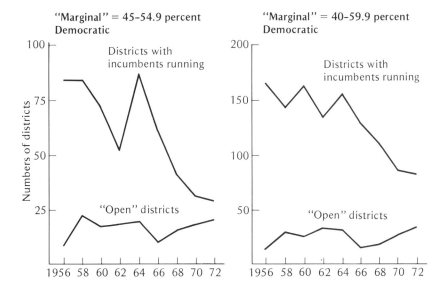

Figure 1-2   Numbers of House elections won in the "marginal" range, 1956–1972, in districts with and without incumbents running

drawing, the next three with congressmen's actions designed to attract votes, the last with voter behavior not inspired by congressmen's actions.

(1)The line-drawing explanation is easy to reach for. In the last decade of chronic redistricting the possibility of building districts to profit incumbents has not been lost on House members or others acting in their interest. With county lines less sacred than they once were, ingenious districts can be and have been drawn. And there are good examples of cross-party districting deals among congressmen of large state delegations.[14] But the problem with the line-drawing hypothesis is that it seems not to explain very much. Manipulation of the aggregate national data does not yield an impressive relation between redistricting and electoral benefit.[15] Moreover, if voters are being partitioned into safe House districts it can be argued that bimodal patterns ought to appear sooner or later in presidential and "open seat" distributions of the sort displayed in figure 1-1. Of bimodalism the relevant figure 1-1 graphs give no trace, although it must be said that the evidence is inconclusive. The evidence on redistricting generally is incomplete and inconclusive. But the odds are that it will not explain very much. If all 435 congressmen were suddenly to retire in 1974, and if elections to replace them were conducted in the 1972 district set, the odds are that a distribution of new member percentages would look like a presidential or an evened out "open seat" distribution—unimodal and roughly normal, though perhaps still with a modest isolated mode for uncontested Southerners.

The next four hypotheses hinge on the assumption that House incumbency now carries with it greater electoral advantages than it has in the past. There is evidence that it does.[16] One way to find out is to look at what happens to party fortunes in districts where congressmen die, retire, or lose primaries—to compare the last November percentages of veteran incumbents with the percentages of their successor nominees. Table 1-1 does this for the six elections in the years 1962–1972. Figures are given for transitions in which the retirees were at least two-term veterans and where the bracketing elections were both contested by both parties. It is hard to tease conclusions out of these data; the universes for the six elections are small, the districts in each inter-election set vary widely in their change percentages, national trends affect Democrats and Republicans differently, and there is the redistricting problem throughout. But these are all of the data there are on the point. Most of the columns in the table include figures on districts with line changes. Including these raises the obvious problem that redistricting itself can affect party percentages. But there is some justification for the inclusion. For one thing, no systematic difference appears here between what happens electorally in redrawn and untouched districts. For another, it is impossible to get any reading at all on the 1972 election without inspecting the redrawn districts; 25 of the 27 "succession nominations" occurred in 1972 in districts with line changes. If handled carefully the altered districts can yield information. Redrawn districts are covered here if they were treated in the press as being more or less "the same" as districts preceding them; thus for example, Paul

Cronin is commonly regarded as Bradford Morse's successor in the fifth Massachusetts district although Cronin's 1972 boundaries are somewhat different from Morse's old ones.

What to look for in table 1-1 is whether switches in party nominees bring about drops in party percentages. The bigger the drop the higher the putative value of incumbency. Inter-election changes in party percentage are calculated here by comparing party shares of the total congressional district vote in the bracketing elections.[17] The first three columns in the table give data only on districts without line changes. Thus in 1962 there were four Democratic retirements (or deaths, etc.) in districts with 1960 lines intact; the Democratic share of the total vote fell an average of 5.2 percent in these four districts between 1960 and 1962. In the four Republican retirement districts in 1962 the Republican share of the total vote fell an average of 0.2 percent. In 1964 there was an understandable party gain in the Democratic retirement districts, and an especially heavy mean loss in the Republican set. Fortuitously the numbers of retirement districts for the two parties are almost identical in each of the five elections in 1962 through 1970, so it makes sense to calculate mean change values for all retirement districts regardless of party in each year in order to try to cancel out the effects of election-specific national trends. This is done in the third column, a list of cross-party percentage change means for the six elections. (Thus in 1964 the average change in the 25 retirement seats was a negative 1.6 percent even though the average party values were far apart; Republicans generally lost more in their transitions than Democrats gained in theirs.) Here there emerges some fairly solid evidence. Mean drops in percentage were higher in 1966, 1968, and 1970 than in 1962 and 1964. (1972, with its N of 2, can be ignored.) The best evidence is for 1964 and 1970, with their large N's. Loss of incumbents cost the parties a mean of 1.6 percent in 1964, a mean of 6.5 percent in 1970.

In the fourth column figures on transitions in redrawn districts are introduced. The values are mean changes for redrawn retirement districts by year regardless of party. It will be seen that these values differ in no systematic way from the values for undisturbed districts in the third column. There is the same general trend toward bigger drops in percentage. Especially striking is the 1972 value of minus 9.5 percent, lower than any other reading in the list of values for redrawn districts. The fifth, sixth, and seventh columns of the table give mean values by year, respectively, for Democratic, Republican, and all retirement districts, with no distinctions being made between altered and unaltered districts. The eighth column gives a weighted mean for each year, a simple average of the party averages. Finally the ninth column gives a median value for the set of all readings in each year.

These readings, tenuous as they are, all point in the same direction. Incumbency does seem to have increased in electoral value, and it is reasonable to suppose that one effect of this increase has been to boost House members of both parties out of the marginal electoral range. If incumbency has risen in value, what accounts for the rise? The second, third, and fourth hypotheses

Table 1-1 Change in party percentage in House districts where incumbents have retired, died, or lost primaries

Transitions in Districts without Line Changes

	Democratic Districts		Republican Districts		All Districts		Transitions in Districts with Line Changes — All Districts	
	N	Mean	N	Mean	N	Mean	N	Mean
1962	(4)	−5.2	(4)	−0.2	(8)	−2.7	(9)	+1.3
1964	(12)	+5.5	(13)	−8.2	(25)	−1.6		
1966	(3)	−6.2	(3)	−2.5	(6)	−4.3	(7)	−7.7
1968	(4)	+1.1	(3)	−14.9	(7)	−5.8	(12)	−8.6
1970	(15)	−4.9	(17)	−7.9	(32)	−6.5	(4)	−5.7
1972	(2)	−26.7			(2)	−26.7	(25)	−9.5

Transitions in Districts with and without Line Changes

	Democratic Districts		Republican Districts		All Districts		All Districts		All Districts	
	N	Mean	N	Mean	N	Mean	N	Wghtd Mean	N	Median
1962	(5)	−6.0	(12)	+1.8	(17)	−0.5	(17)	−2.1	(17)	−13.1
1964	(12)	+5.5	(13)	−8.2	(25)	−1.6	(25)	−1.3	(25)	−3.1
1966	(8)	−8.9	(5)	−1.8	(13)	−6.2	(13)	−5.4	(13)	−8.2
1968	(10)	−1.4	(9)	−14.5	(19)	−7.6	(19)	−8.0	(19)	−4.7
1970	(19)	−5.1	(17)	−7.9	(36)	−6.4	(36)	−6.0	(36)	−5.6
1972	(12)	−13.1	(15)	−9.0	(27)	−10.8	(27)	−11.1	(27)	−10.2

below focus on electorally useful activities that House members may now be engaging in more effectively than their predecessors did ten or twenty years ago.

(2) House members may now be advertising themselves better. Simple name recognition counts for a lot in House elections, as the Survey Research Center data show.[18] A name perceived with a halo of good will around it probably counts for more. If House members have not profited from accelerated advertising in the last decade, it is not from want of trying. The time series in figure 1-3 shows, in millions of pieces, how much mail was sent out from the Capitol (by both House and Senate members) in each year from 1954 through 1970.[19] The mail includes letters, newsletters, questionnaires, child-care pamphlets, etc., some of them mailed to all district box-holders. Peak mailing months are the Octobers of even-numbered years. Mail flow more than sextupled over the sixteen-year period, with an especially steep increase between 1965 and 1966. In fact the mail-flow curve matches well any incumbency-advantage curve derivable from the data in table 1-1. There is no let-up in sight; one recent estimate has it that House members will send out about 900,000 pieces of mail per member in 1974, at a total public cost of $38.1 million.[20] So the answer to the incumbency advantage question could be a remarkably simple one: the more hundreds of thousands of messages congressmen rain down on constituents the more votes they get. Whether all this activity has significantly raised the proportion of citizens who know their congressmen's names is uncertain. There are some Gallup readings showing that the share of adults who could name their congressmen rose from 46 to 53 percent between 1966 and 1970.[21]

(3)Another possibility is that House members may be getting more political mileage out of federal programs. The number of grant-in-aid programs has risen in the last decade at something like the rate of Capitol mail flow. The more programs there are, the more chances House members have to claim credit ostentatiously for the local manifestations of them—housing grants, education grants, anti-pollution grants, etc.

(4) Yet another possibility is that House members have become more skilled at public position-taking on "issues." The point is a technological one. If more congressmen are commissioning and using scientific opinion polls to plumb district sentiment, then House members may have become, on balance, more practiced at attuning themselves to district opinion.[22] There is a possibility here, however hard it is to try to measure. There may be a greater general sophistication today about polling and its uses. In 1964, forty-nine Republican House members running for re-election signed a pre-convention statement endorsing Senator Goldwater. It was claimed that Goldwater's nomination would help the party ticket. The forty-nine suffered disproportionately in November.[23] In 1972 there was no comparable rush among House Democrats to identify themselves with Senator McGovern.

(5) The fifth and last hypothesis has to do with changes in voter

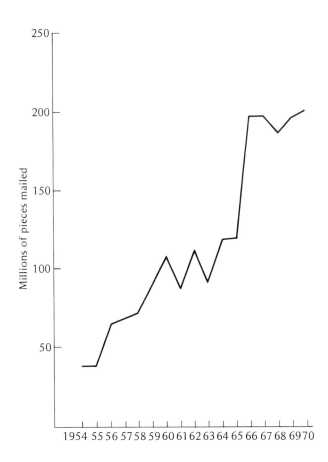

Figure 1-3   Franked mail sent out by House and Senate members, in
               millions of pieces, 1954–1970

Source: U.S. Congress, House, Committee on Appropriations, *Hearings Before a Subcommittee of the Committee on Appropriations, Legislative Branch Appropriations for 1970*, 91st Cong., 1st sess., 1969, p. 501, has 1954–1968 data. Subsequent annual hearings update estimated franking use.

behavior not inspired by changes in incumbent activities. It is possible that incumbents have been profiting not from any exertions of their own but from changes in voter attitudes. A logic suggests itself. Voters dissatisfied with party cues could be reaching for any other cues that are available in deciding how to vote. The incumbency cue is readily at hand. This hypothesis assumes a current rise in discontent with parties; it assumes nothing about changes in the cues voters have been receiving from congressmen.

There is no point in speculating further here about causes. But it is important that the subject be given further treatment, if for no other reason than that some of the variables can be legally manipulated. The congressional franking privilege comes first to mind.

III.

If fewer House members are winning elections narrowly, and if the proportion of "open seats" per election is not rising, it ought to follow that congressional seat swings are declining in amplitude. The argument requires no assumption that national swings in the House popular vote are changing in amplitude—and indeed there is no evidence in the contemporary data that they are. It does require the assumption that a congressman's percentage showing in one election supplies information on his strength as he goes into the next. That is, a House member running at the 60 percent level is less likely to be unseated by an adverse 5 percent party trend next time around than one running at the 54 percent level. It is easy to predict that a popular voting trend will cut less of a swath through a set of congressmen whose last-election percentages are arrayed like those in the 1968, 1970, and 1972 incumbency graphs of figure 1-1 than through a set whose percentages are centrally and normally distributed.

There is evidence suggesting that the flight from marginality is having its posited effect. Edward Tufte has found that a "swing ratio"—a rate of translation of votes into seats—built on data from the 1966, 1968, and 1970 elections yields an exceptionally low value when compared with ratios for other election triplets over the last century.[24] The figures in table 1-2 point in the same direction. Supplied here are data on popular vote swings, net partisan seat swings, and incumbency defeats for each and both parties in the election years from 1956 through 1972.[25] It is worth noting that the large seat swings of 1958, 1964, and 1966 were heavily dependent upon defeats of incumbents. Very few incumbents have lost since 1966. (Almost all of the 1972 losers were victims of line changes.) Especially interesting are the figures for 1970, a year in which the popular vote swing was a fairly sizable 3.3 percent. Yet only nine incumbents of the disfavored party lost and the net swing over 1968 was only twelve—of which three changed over in 1969 by-elections. Part of the explanation here is doubtless that the disfavored party had relatively few incumbents in the vulnerable range to protect. Only 47 Republicans running in 1970 had won under the 60 percent mark in 1968, whereas there had been 82 comparably exposed Republicans running in 1958, 76 Republicans in 1964, and 79 Democrats in 1966.

What general conclusions can be drawn? If the trends hold we are witnesses to the blunting of a blunt instrument. It may be too soon to say that seat swings of the 1958 or 1964 variety can be consigned to the history books, but it is hard to see how they could be equaled in the newer electoral circumstances. There is probably another manifestation here of what Walter Dean Burnham calls "electoral disaggregation"—a weakening of the peculiar links that party has supplied between electorate and government.[26] There is a concomitant triumph for the Madisonian vision; a Congress less affected by electoral tides is, on balance, one less susceptible to presidential wiles. But there is a long-run danger that a Congress that cannot supply quick electoral change is no match for a presidency that can.

Table 1-2   House vote swings and seat swings, 1956-1972

	Change in National Popular Vote over Last Election	Net Partisan Seat Swing over Last Election	Incumbent Losses to Opposite Party Challengers		
			D	R	Total
1956	1.5% D	2 D	8	7	15
1958	5.1% D	49 D	1	34	35
1960	1.1% R	20 R	22	3	25
1962	2.2% R	2 R	9	5	14
1964	4.7% D	36 D	5	39	44
1966	6.2% R	47 R	39	1	40
1968	0.4% R	5 R	5	0	5
1970	3.3% D	12 D	2	9	11
1972	1.4% R	12 R	6	3	9

Appendix

The columns of figures below are frequency distributions of Democratic percentages of the November two-party House vote recorded in districts with incumbents of either (but not both) of the parties running, in biennial elections from 1956 through 1972, with separate columns for each year for districts harboring Democratic and Republican incumbents. Thus in 1956 there were twenty-eight districts with Republican incumbents running in which Democratic percentages were in the 45–49.9 percent range. There were also eight districts with Democratic incumbents running in which Democratic percentages were in the 45–49.9 percent range; these eight Democrats thereby lost their seats.

	Numbers of Districts, by Year and by Party of Incumbent																	
Democratic % of the Two-Party Vote	1956		1958		1960		1962		1964		1966		1968		1970		1972	
	D	R	D	R	D	R	D	R	D	R	D	R	D	R	D	R	D	R
0– 4.9		3		1		3		1		1		4		9		5		7
5– 9.9																		
10– 14.9														1				
15– 19.9												3		3		2		2
20– 24.9						1				1		8		6		5		7
25– 29.9		13		1		3		11		1		24		25		15		38
30– 34.9		28		11		16		24		7		53		47		40		27
35– 39.9		54		27		33		39	2*	25	1*	26		39		41		36
40– 44.9		54		44	3*	56	2*	45	2*	47	8*	6		31		34	2*	22
45– 49.9	8*	28	1*	50	19*	19	7*	19	1*	38	30*	3	5*	10	2*	15	4*	10
50– 54.9	40	6*	4	27*	28	3*	23	4*	14	35*	28		26		8	7*	15	2*
55– 59.9	28	1*	11	7*	36		36	1*	18	4*	53	1*	38		20	1*	27	1*
60– 64.9	28		33		27		32		35		34		43		28	1*	40	
65– 69.9	21		19		26		27		45		26		24		35		30	
70– 74.9	10		26		21		31		29		20		22		42		26	
75– 79.9	7		17		16		11		24		13		12		15		16	
80– 84.9	2		10		11		4		13		9		10		12		9	
85– 89.9	4		1		4		2		4				4		4		7	
90– 94.9	1		5		3		1		2				1		1		1	
95–100.0	68		95		72		56		40		51		41		56		44	

*Values for incumbents who lost seats to opposite-party challengers.

Notes

[1]To put it yet another way, voting for House candidates must have a "national component" to it. See Donald E. Stokes, "Parties and the Nationalization of Electoral Forces," ch. 7 in William N. Chambers and Walter D. Burnham, *The American Party Systems* (New York: Oxford University Press, 1967).

[2]The best analysis of translation formulas is in Edward R. Tufte, "The Relation Between Seats and Votes in Two Party Systems," *American Political Science Review*, 67 (June, 1973), 540–554.

[3]Angus Campbell, "Surge and Decline: A Study in Electoral Change," ch. 3 in Campbell et al., *Elections and the Political Order* (New York: Wiley, 1966).

[4]Gerald H. Kramer, "Short-Term Fluctuations in U.S. Voting Behavior, 1896–1964," *American Political Science Review*, 65 (1971), 131–143.

[5]Ibid., p. 140.

[6]At the time of writing no comparable figures were yet available for the 1972 election. Dealing with the 1968 returns by calculating percentages of the major-party vote poses obvious problems—especially in the South—but so does any alternative way of dealing with them. Congressional district data used in figure 1-1 and following tables and figures were taken from *Congressional Quarterly* compilations.

[7]An incumbent is defined here as a congressman who held a seat at the time he was running in a November election, even if he had first taken the seat in a recent by-election.

[8]The center graphs cover districts with no incumbents, the left-hand graphs districts with one incumbent. This leaves no place in the diagram for districts with two opposite-party incumbents running against each other. There are 16 of these throw-in cases over the period: 7 in 1962, 1 in 1966, 4 in 1968, 1 in 1970, 3 in 1972. Republicans won in 10 of them.

[9]On balance it can be expected that distributions will be more centrally clustered in presidential than in midterm years, for the reason that presidential elections enroll expanded electorates in which disproportionate numbers of voters violate district partisan habits in their congressional voting. See Harvey Kabaker, "Estimating the Normal Vote in Congressional Elections," *Midwest Journal of Political Science*, 13 (1969), 58–83.

[10]Again, the 16 throw-in cases are not included. It should be recalled here that some of these incumbents in the marginal range moved across the 50 percent mark and lost their seats. (See the Appendix.) Of the 198 incumbents who lost elections to opposite-party challengers in the 1956–1972 period, only 4 plummeted far enough to fall outside the broadly defined (40–59.9 percent) marginal range.

[11]The decline has come in spite of Republican inroads in Southern House districts. One reason here is that, once they have gotten their seats, Southern Republican incumbents tend to win elections handily; 16 of 22 of them won with over 60 percent of the major-party vote in 1970, 18 of 22 in 1972.

[12]Albert D. Cover is conducting research at Yale on incumbency and marginality in the 1960s.

[13]I owe this point to Walter D. Burnham. On long-run decline in House turnover see Charles O. Jones, "Inter-Party Competition for Congressional Seats," *Western Political Quarterly*, 17 (1964), 461–476.

[14]Some strategies and examples are discussed in David R. Mayhew, "Congressional Representation: Theory and Practice in Drawing the Districts," ch. 7 in Nelson W. Polsby, ed., *Reapportionment in the 1970's* (Berkeley: University of California Press, 1971), pp. 274–284.

[15]On the 1966 election see Robert J. Erikson, "Malapportionment, Gerrymandering, and Party Fortunes in Congressional Elections," *American Political Science Review*, 66 (1972), 1238.

[16]Robert Erikson estimates that incumbency status was worth about 2 percent of the vote in the 1950's and early 1960's, but about 5 percent in 1966 and thereafter. Erikson, "The

Advantage of Incumbency in Congressional Elections," *Polity*, 3 (1971), 395–405. Erikson, "Malapportionment, Gerrymandering, and Party Fortunes in Congressional Elections," op. cit., 1240.

[17] Figures 1-1 and 1-2 are built on candidate percentage of the major-party vote, table 1-1 on percentages of the total vote.

[18] Donald E. Stokes and Warren E. Miller, "Party Government and the Saliency of Congress," ch. 11 in Angus Campbell, et al., *Elections and the Political Order* (New York: Wiley, 1966), pp. 204–209.

[19] Data supplied by Albert D. Cover.

[20] Norman C. Miller, "Yes, You Are Getting More Politico Mail; And It Will Get Worse," *Wall Street Journal*, March 6, 1973.

[21] Gallup survey in *Washington Post*, September 20, 1970.

[22] There is a discussion of roll-call position taking and its electoral effects in Robert Erikson, "The Electoral Impact of Congressional Roll Call Voting," *American Political Science Review*, 65 (1971), 1018–1032.

[23] Robert A. Schoenberger, "Campaign Strategy and Party Loyalty: the Electoral Relevance of Candidate Decision-Making in the 1964 Congressional Elections," *American Political Science Review*, 63 (1969), 515–520.

[24] Op. cit., pp. 549–550.

[25] The incumbency defeat figures cover only losses to opposite-party challengers. Thus once again the 16 throw-in cases are disregarded. Also ignored are the November losses of two highly visible Democrats — Brooks Hays (1958) and Louise Day Hicks (1972) — to independents who thereupon enrolled as Democrats themselves in Washington. It might be added here that some incumbents do after all lose their primaries. The figures for losses to primary challengers are: 6 in 1956, 4 in 1958, 5 in 1960, 8 in 1962, 5 in 1964, 5 in 1966, 3 in 1968, 9 in 1970, 8 in 1972. The figures for losses where redistricting has thrown incumbents into the same primary: 5 in 1962, 3 in 1964, 3 in 1966, 1 in 1968, 1 in 1970, 6 in 1972. Whatever their qualitative effects, primaries have not rivaled the larger November swings in turnover leverage.

[26] "The End of American Party Politics," *Trans-Action*, 7 (December, 1969), 18–20.

Selection 2 House
Committee Assignments

Charles S. Bullock, III

For most members of Congress committee assignments are the most important aspect of their legislative activities. Their assignments are likely to influence their choice of subject matter specialty, the benefits that they can

My thanks to Richard Fenno, Irwin Gertzog, Leroy Rieselbach, Catherine Rudder, Kenneth Shepsle, and John Stolarek, whose suggestions on an earlier draft have substantially improved this paper. This is the first publication of this article. All rights reserved. Permission to reprint must be obtained from the publisher and author.

obtain for their districts, their level of job satisfaction, and their likelihood of helping shape important legislation. Receipt of a "good" assignment early in a member's career will permit the legislator to contribute to the work of the House earlier and to lay the foundation for eventually becoming a committee leader. Those who fail to obtain a desirable initial assignment may have to mark time for several years, waiting for a chance to move to a better committee; alternatively, they may change what they perceive to be important to their career and adapt to their present assignment.

The significance of a member's assignments is partially a product of congressional norms. Norms emphasizing specialization and reciprocity discourage members from meddling in legislation before other committees and create pressures to concentrate on the subject matter of their own committees so they can become the House's expert on some aspect of these responsibilities. Dyson and Soule (1970) point out the degree to which these norms constrain the influence of nonmembers of a committee; they report that during the decade ending in 1964, approximately 90 percent of the bills House committees reported were enacted. The full House accepts with little modification most legislation as recommended by the committee responsible for it. Only on controversial topics, such as energy legislation or efforts to restrict the use of busing to promote school desegregation, is there likely to be sufficient opposition to the committee's recommendations that attempts will be mounted to amend the bill substantially on the floor.

A second consequence of the specialization norm is that members of a committee, because of their great influence, develop unique relationships with the representatives of interest groups and personnel in the executive branch concerned about the topics the committee handles. From these relationships, some perceive an ability on the part of the legislator to provide a particular set of benefits to his or her constituents. For example, serving on the Interior Committee may enhance a member's ability to obtain a new or enlarged national park in his or her district.

Aside from their importance to members, committee assignments are of great significance for party leaders. Because of the House's relatively weak party discipline, party leaders are often restricted to an indirect influence in shaping policy. The central role of committees in policy making means that if the majority party is to enact its program, members responsive to the party line must control the committees handling parts of it. Because the seniority norm guarantees members the right to remain on committees on which they sit and is also a factor in the choice of committee leaders, the appointment of party renegades to a committee may have long-lasting consequences.

These same considerations play a role in shaping congressional-executive relations. A committee with a leader or a sizable component of its membership in disagreement with the president may pursue policy objectives at variance with the administration's. Consequently, filling committee vacancies is of great significance in setting national policy.

Political scientists recognize the importance of committee assignments, giving the topic much scholarly attention since Nicholas Masters's (1961) seminal work. This article draws together what is known about the assignment process in the House of Representatives and deals with two subjects: first, the processes by which assignments are made and, second, the importance of a number of factors suggested as playing a role in determining who gets which committee assignments.

Committee Assignment Process

Making committee assignments is a very complex process in which members are fitted into vacancies. Kenneth Shepsle (1974) has shown that there are an almost incomprehensible number of possible combinations of assignments. Because this potentially monumental task must be performed every two years, it is not surprising that the process has become institutionalized.

The most difficult aspect of making assignments results from the differences in committee popularity. Some committees generally have more applicants than there are seats available, while others attract few if any members.

Democrats and Republicans in the House follow different procedures in making committee assignments. Republicans have experienced little change in recent years, but Democrats transferred the assignment responsibility from one committee to another in 1974.

The bulk of the requests for committee assignments that the Republican Committee on Committees and the Democratic Steering Committee process come from newly elected members, but these committees also have a number of requests from sitting members who want to switch assignments or who want to pick up a second assignment. For the Eighty-seventh through Ninety-fourth Congresses, 59 percent of the requests the Democratic Committee on Committees received came from first-term members (Stolarek, forthcoming).

The substantial number of the committee requests in each Congress from nonfreshmen may have either of two explanations. Some sitting members may change their minds about the committee they prefer and therefore apply for a change. Other members may continue to pursue seats they had unsuccessfully sought earlier in their careers. Gertzog (1976) reports that within five years after entering Congress, 93 percent of the Democrats first elected to the Eighty-ninth to Ninety-first Congresses had been appointed to their top-priority committee. Approximately 70 percent achieved this goal in their first term; the remainder transferred as soon as they could.

The inability of many newcomers to obtain seats on the committees of their choice points up an important constraint on the appointment process. There are a limited number of seats on each committee. After congressional elections, the Speaker and Minority Leader decide the number of seats per committee and the distribution of seats between parties. The composition of the three most prestigious committees—Appropriations, Rules, and Ways and Means—has traditionally been constant: 60 percent majority party membership on Appropriations and Ways and Means and 67 percent on Rules. The makeup of the remaining committees has closely approximated the partisan distribution in the House. For example, during the Ninety-fourth and Ninety-fifth Congresses (1975–1979), there were twice as many Democrats as Republicans; so the Democratic caucus specified that every House committee would have one more than twice as many Democrats as Republicans. In the future, partisan makeup of committees may bear less resemblance to the composition of the House because Democratic caucus rules now provide that "Committee ratios should be established to create firm working majorities on each committee. In determining the ratio on the respective standing committees, the Speaker should provide for a *minimum* of three Democrats for each two Republicans" (Democratic Caucus, 1976, p. 2). Once the party ratios on committees are fixed, applicants vie for the vacancies caused by redistribution or turnover (i.e., defeats, retirements, deaths, or relinquishing a seat on one committee to accept an appointment to another one). With rare exception, in each Congress most committee seats are filled before the session begins. The seniority norm guarantees that nonfreshmen members can retain their assignments.

A second constraint on committee assignments is party rules that limit the possible combinations of assignments available to members. Representatives are generally limited to service on a maximum of two standing committees, with the only major exceptions being the Budget Committee and the Standards of Official Conduct Committee, which handles charges of misconduct. However, the three most prestigious committees have been designated as exclusive committees; their members generally cannot hold another appointment. Exceptions are occasionally made to help a member with electoral problems. For example, in 1977 Lloyd Meeds (D-Wash.) was appointed to the Rules Committee. The previous November, Meeds had won reelection by fewer than 600 votes of 218,000 cast. He was allowed to retain his seat on the Interior Committee and the chairmanship of its Water and Resources Subcommittee, which handles legislation of great interest to his district. Another exception is the Budget Committee, on which nine members from Appropriations and Ways and Means serve as a second assignment.

Democrats classify the other standing committees as major and nonmajor (as shown in table 2-1).[1] Generally members serve on one major and one nonmajor committee or on two nonmajor committees. However, in the

Ninety-fifth Congress the Democrats had to relax this limitation and allow several members three assignments in order to find people willing to serve on the Agriculture, District of Columbia, International Relations, Judiciary, and Post Office Committees (Southwick, 1977). If interest in these committees rises, the exception may not be renewed. The Republican party does not have a major-nonmajor distinction, although it recognizes that some committees are more desirable than others.

Table 2-1   Democrats' classification of committees for assignment purposes, 95th Congress

Category	Committees	No. of Members
Exclusive	Appropriations	55
	Rules	16
	Ways and Means	37
Major	Agriculture	46
	Armed Services	40
	Banking, Finance, and Urban Affairs	46
	Education and Labor	37
	International Relations	37
	Interstate and Foreign Commerce	43
	Judiciary	34
	Public Works and Transportation	43
Non-major	Budget	25
	District of Columbia	19
	Government Operations	43
	House Administration	25
	Interior and Insular Affairs	43
	Merchant Marine and Fisheries	40
	Post Office and Civil Service	25
	Science and Technology	40
	Small Business	37
	Veterans Affairs	28
Other	Standards of Official Conduct	12

Republican Procedures

The Republican Committee on Committees formally assigns new and reassigns other members. The committee is composed of one representative from each state with a Republican in the House. Each representative has as many votes as his or her state delegation has Republicans. For example, in the Ninety-fifth Congress, Del Clawson, the California member of the committee, had fourteen votes while Thomas Coleman from Missouri had two votes and Manuel Lujan from New Mexico had one.

Table 2-2 Executive committee of the Republican Committee on Committees for the 95th Congress

Member	Represents	Votes
John Rhodes (Ariz.)	Chairman	0
Del Clawson	California	14
Samuel L. Devine	Ohio	13
Robert H. Michel	Illinois	12
Frank Horton	New York	11
Elford A Cederberg	Michigan	8
Joseph M. McDade	Pennsylvania	8
William C. Wampler	Virginia	6
Louis Frey, Jr.	Florida	5
Mathew J. Rinaldo	New Jersey	4
Albert H. Quie (Minn.)	States with 3 Republicans	3
James T. Broyhill (N.C.)	States with 2 Republicans	2
Don Young (Alas.)	States with 1 Republican	1
Willis D. Gradison, Jr. (Ohio)	94th Class	1
Eldon Rudd (Ariz.)	95th Class	1

In practice the function of the full committee is simply to ratify the recommendations of its Executive Committee (table 2-2). The Executive Committee is dominated by the representatives of the states with the largest Republican delegations. In the Ninety-fifth Congress, each of the nine largest Republican delegations was represented on the Executive Committee; these states accounted for 81 of the 143 seats the Republicans held. The party leadership has less direct influence than its Democratic counterpart but can nonetheless influence committee decisions it thinks are important. The minority leader serves as a nonvoting chairman of the Executive Committee and appoints three members, with a total of six votes.

As the fortunes of the Republican party fluctuate, the composition of the Executive Committee changes. For example, after the Goldwater presidential candidacy, Republicans lost so many seats in northern delegations that states like New Jersey and Indiana were no longer represented. Their places were taken by Alabama (where five freshmen rode to victory on Goldwater's coattails) and Kansas (where five GOP incumbents withstood the Democratic onslaught).

In addition to the members from states with larger Republican contingents, the Executive Committee includes representatives of several other groups. The minority leader appoints representatives for single-, two-, and three-member state delegations; and each of the two most recent freshman classes chooses a representative. A staff member for the Committee on Committees reports that full committee members not on the Executive Committee "usually get an Executive Committee member to 'carry water' for them, and such arrangements are based on personal friendships, geographic proximity, mutual interests, etc." However, because votes here are weighted in the same way as on the full committee, representatives from larger states are much more powerful than others, leading to some dissatisfaction among Republicans from states with small GOP delegations.

Each state delegation determines who will serve on the Committee on Committees. In delegations with only one Republican, that person automatically serves. In larger delegations the dean (i.e., the senior member of the delegation in point of service) typically holds the seat on the committee. In 1977, of thirty-one Republican delegations with more than one member, in twenty-one instances the dean served on the committee. Generally states' representatives remain on the Committee on Committees for the rest of their House careers. The members representing states with one-, two-, and three-member delegations also serve on the Executive Committee as long as they remain in the House and the size of their delegations is unchanged.

Recommendations of the Executive Committee ultimately come before the Republican conference (i.e., the total Republican House contingent) for approval. Nominations for vacancies appear to be less easily challenged in the Republican conference than in the Democratic caucus (Siff and Weil, 1977, p. 90).

Democratic Procedures

Prior to the Ninety-fourth Congress, House Democrats on the Ways and Means Committee functioned as their party's Committee on Committees, placing the committee assignment process in the hands of a group of members more senior and more conservative than the bulk of the party and limiting the influence of the elected party leadership on the process. The Speaker, Majority Leader, and Whip were not made voting members of the Committee on Committees until the Ninety-third Congress, but party leaders did have indirect influence on assignments to some committees prior to 1973 (see Manley, 1970, pp. 25–34).

In late 1974 the power to make assignments, except for the Rules Committee, was transferred to the Democratic Steering and Policy Committee. The Speaker makes apppointments to Rules to prevent the committee from refusing to report legislation the Democratic leadership favors.

The Steering Committee has twenty-four members: the Speaker, Majority Leader, Majority Whip, chairman of the caucus, eight appointees of the Speaker, and twelve regional representatives. The Democratic members of the House in a state or states in a region choose the representatives; each represents from one to ten states, and each is limited to two two-year terms. The states in a region are usually contiguous. Several of the Speaker's appointments go to deputy whips while others go to representatives of blacks, women, and newer members in the House. The personnel of the 1977 Steering Committee are listed in table 2-3.

Table 2-3   House Democratic Steering Committee, showing zone assignments for the 95th Congress

Automatic Members: Speaker—Thomas O'Neill (Mass.)
Majority Leader—Jim Wright (Tex.)
Whip—John Brademas (Ind.)
Caucus Chairman—Thomas Foley (Wash.)

Appointed by the Speaker: Don Rostenkowski (Ill.) Chief Deputy Whip
Benjamin Rosenthal (N.Y.) Deputy Whip
Bill Alexander (Ark.) Deputy Whip
George Danielson (Cal.) Deputy Whip
Barbara Jordan (Tex.) Womens Caucus
Peter Kostmayer (Pa.) 95th Class
Ralph Metcalfe (Ill.) Black Caucus
Charles Rose (N.C.) 93rd and 94th Classes

Elected by Regional Caucuses:

Region	State(s)	Member	Democrats
I	California	Henry Waxman	29
II	Arizona		2
	Colorado		3
	Hawaii		2
	Montana		1
	Nevada		1
	New Mexico		1
	Oregon		4
	Utah		1
	Washington	Lloyd Meeds	5
	Wyoming		1
III	Michigan		11
	Minnesota		4
	Wisconsin	David Obey	7
IV	Illinois	Morgan Murphy	12
	Indiana		8
	Kentucky		5
V	Arkansas		3
	Iowa		4
	Kansas		2
	Missouri	Richard Bolling	8
	Oklahoma		5
VI	Texas	Kika de la Garza	22
VII	Alabama	Walter Flowers	4
	Florida		10
	Louisiana		6
	Mississippi		3

Table 2-3   (continued)

Region	State(s)	Member	Democrats
VIII	Georgia	Dawson Mathis	10
	North Carolina		9
	South Carolina		5
	Tennessee		5
IX	Maryland		5
	New Jersey	Robert Roe	11
	Virginia		4
	West Virginia		4
X	Ohio		10
	Pennsylvania	John Dent	17
XI	New York	Johnathan Bingham	28
XII	Connecticut		4
	Massachusetts		10
	New Hampshire	Norman D'Amours	1
	Rhode Island		2
	District of Columbia		1
	Guam		1
	Puerto Rico		1
	Virgin Islands		1

Transferring responsibility for committee assignments from Ways and Means to the Steering Committee has greatly increased the influence of the party's leaders. Under the new arrangement, the Speaker names a third of the Steering Committee members. The Democratic leadership has greater influence on assignments than does the Republican leadership. Also, because half the members are chosen by regional caucuses, there is a greater likelihood of accountability to rank-and-file members in the Democratic than the Republican party. Elected regional representatives may feel a greater responsibility to their regions than Republicans on the GOP Executive Committee.

Unlike the Republican Committee, the Steering Committee does not use weighted voting. Each member has a single vote. The Steering Committee goes through the standing committees in alphabetical order. Nominations are typically made by one's regional representative, although this is not essential as it was for many years when the Ways and Means Democrats made the assignments. When nominees exceed the number of vacancies, the Steering Committee votes on the applicants, with thirteen votes needed to win a slot. Balloting continues with the person receiving the fewest votes dropped from further consideration until all vacancies are filled. The decisions of the Steering Committee are brought for approval before the full Democratic caucus, which rarely rejects them.

Requests

Legislators may do a number of things in pursuit of particular assignments. Aspirants usually visit members of the Committee on Committees as well as party leaders to voice their preferences. They may also write members of the Committee on Committees stating their desires. They will typically present their case to the dean of their state's party delegation, who may be a powerful ally and may write the Committee on Committees members on behalf of delegation members. Some aspirants visit the chairman, ranking minority member, or other influential members of the committees in which they are interested, hoping to win support or at least to neutralize any opposition. Occasionally an applicant notes that the chairman or ranking minority member approves his or her candidacy when communicating with Committee on Committees members.

In communicating committee preferences, applicants generally indicate the basis for their request. They may include a resume or discuss previous vocational or political activities that they believe prepare them for the assignment they want. Others describe how the work of a particular committee is of interest to their constituents. They may also indicate if any chamber influentials or their state delegation have endorsed their candidacies.

Other letters recommending the candidacy of an applicant may be written by the dean of the delegation, speaking either individually or on behalf of the entire delegation. Achen and Stolarek (1974) report that of 107 letters received by one Democrat on the Committee on Committees during the Eighty-eighth and Eighty-ninth Congresses, 31 came from colleagues and 3 from interest group spokespersons. An analysis of 43 letters received by a Committee on Committees Democrat in the Ninety-fourth Congress reveals that communications from people other than the aspirant are less common now. There were seven endorsements from delegation deans and one from a dean who wrote "on behalf of myself and other Democrats from the Rocky Mountain region." In all but one instance the beneficiary of these endorsements was a freshman. There were no letters from interest groups.

Although it is not uncommon for newly elected members to make a special trip to Washington to seek the support of senior members for their candidacy for coveted committee seats, some representatives begin building their case for a particular assignment during the campaign. For example, one of the issues Floyd Hicks (D-Wash.) raised when he unseated Thor Tollefson (R-Wash.) in 1964 was that the district's representative should sit on the Armed Services Committee to promote the fortunes of Boeing Aircraft, economically important to the district. (Tollefson was the ranking minority member of the Merchant Marine and Fisheries Committee, which was of some, but apparently less, interest to the district's economy.) In some contests where a challenger seems to have a good chance to take a seat from the other party,

party leaders will publicly promise during the campaign to help the challenger obtain an assignment of significance to the district.

More commonly, new members inform their deans of the committees that interest them. They may express one preference, rank order several preferences, or identify two or more committees that would be acceptable. Some freshmen make no requests, relying on their representative on the Committee on Committees to select for them. In 1974 Democratic freshmen were instructed to provide two preference schedules, one for major committees, the other for nonmajor ones.

When members with some seniority request a new assignment, they may specify either that the committee sought is to be in addition to the one they currently hold or that they are willing to relinquish one of their current assignments if their request is granted. If they seek appointment to an exclusive committee, it is usually assumed that they will forgo their current assignments.

Some sitting members are offered assignments they have not sought. Sometimes these are on the less attractive committees, e.g., House Administration or District of Columbia, where vacancies typically outnumber applicants. Even if members have no interest in such appointments, it is assumed that they will see their partisan duty and serve. The other category of unrequested assignments for nonfreshmen involves exclusive committees. Party leaders (see, e.g., Manley, 1970) recruit a number of appointees to these committees. To have these important committees responsive to the party program, the leaders may ask loyalists to allow their names to be put forward for vacancies; such requests are rarely rejected.

Assignments

The Committees on Committees weigh a number of factors in matching members with vacancies. Different members of the committees no doubt assign different weights to various factors. In this section the range of considerations deemed important in determining committee assignments will be reviewed and available empirical data presented to assess those factors important in the appointment process.

Member Preferences

Members' preferences seem to be the most important element in making assignments. Their requests to the party's Committee on Committees are the clearest indication of what they perceive to be in their best interests. If the Committees on Committees were to ignore totally such requests, they would lose legitimacy and risk rebellion in the ranks.

There is strong evidence that the Committees on Committees honor member preferences, including those of freshmen. Among both freshmen and nonfreshmen, when there is competition for an appointment, the seat usually goes to the member who ranked it higher in his or her preference schedule (Stolarek, forthcoming).

Because about 75 percent of the freshmen list multiple preferences, some flexibility is possible in making assignments. Rohde and Shepsle (1973) report that between 1959 and 1967, three-fourths of the Democratic freshmen received an appointment they wanted. Freshmen who requested only one committee were as successful as those who gave multiple preferences. Among freshmen of both parties of the Ninety-second Congress, 92 percent got an appointment they desired (Bullock, 1973b). The heightened success of freshmen in getting good assignments is partially due to the increase in the total number of seats on major and exclusive committees (Westefield, 1974).

In seeking committee assignments, members apparently pursue basic career goals. One of the most knowledgeable observers of congressional committees, Richard Fenno (1973, p. 1), asserts,

> As a congressmen he holds certain personal political goals. As a committee member he will work to further these same goals through committee activity. Committee membership, in other words, is not an end in itself for the individuals. Each member of each committee wants his committee service to bring him some benefit in terms of goals he holds as an individual congressman.

The primary goals of members are winning reelection, influencing public policy, and achieving power and prestige within the chamber. Among members there is a general consensus that some committees facilitate attaining these goals better than others.

Table 2-4 classifies committees according to the reasons freshmen of the Ninety-second Congress expressed for seeking appointments to them. The members involved here were all freshmen, so there may be a greater emphasis on reelection and less on chamber prestige than would be found among members with greater seniority. Nonetheless, table 2-4 gives a good idea of the reasons committees are desired.

Six committees were sought primarily for the potential they offered to members who felt a need to bolster their reelection chances. Some representatives saw these committees as useful because they authorize projects that benefit a member's district, e.g., irrigation and reclamation projects (Interior Committee) or public works projects (Public Works Committee). A second frequently mentioned reelection aid is that the matters the committee handles affect an important group in the legislator's constituency. Thus Agriculture attracts members representing farming districts; Merchant Marine and Fisheries, members from coastal districts; and Armed Services, members from districts with military bases (Bullock, 1976; Achen and Stolarek, 1974). A freshman seeking a seat on Armed Services explained his preference (quoted in Bullock, 1976, p. 203):

Table 2-4   Frequency of committee preference motivations[a]

	Motivations		
	Re-election	Policy-Making	Prestige
Reelection Committees			
Agriculture	10	3	0
Armed Services	5	3	1
Interior and Insular Affairs	7	4	0
Merchant Marine and Fisheries	3	0	0
Public Works and Transportation[a]	7	1	0
Veterans' Affairs	5	0	0
Policy-Making Committees			
Banking, Finance and Urban Affairs[a]	1	9	1
Education and Labor	5	7	0
International Relations[a]	1	4	0
Interstate and Foreign Commerce	3	16	1
Judiciary	0	7	0
Prestige Committees			
Appropriations	5	3	7
Rules[b]	0	0	1
Ways and Means	1	0	5
Undesired Committees			
District of Columbia[c]	0	0	0
Government Operations[c]	0	0	0
House Administration	0	0	0
Post Office and Civil Service	1	0	0
Science and Technology[a]	0	1	0
Standards of Official Conduct	0	0	0

[a]These committees are identified by their 1977 names.

[b]Appointees to Rules are selected by the leadership; therefore, it is not surprising that only one freshman requested this very prestigious committee.

[c]One member requested these committees but for reasons other than the three categorized here.

SOURCE: Reprinted with permission from Charles S. Bullock, III, "Motivations for U.S. Congressional Committee Preferences: Freshmen of the 92nd Congress," *Legislative Studies Quarterly*, 1 (May, 1976), 208.

Armed Services is the only committee of major concern to our state on which we lacked representation. It is of concern to our district because there are three military bases there and when a district is as sparsely populated as ours, anything that provides jobs and attracts people is important. We're trying to help get new units assigned to a couple of bases.

Five committees were sought primarily because they offered opportunities to become involved in shaping public policy. These committees deal with many of society's most pressing problems. Banking, Finance, and Urban Affairs handles housing legislation and authorizes many other urban-oriented programs. Education and Labor and International Relations deal with the topics their names suggest. The Commerce Committee treats energy and health care and oversees the activities of several independent regulatory commissions.

Aside from the fact that the subject matter of these committees attracts widespread attention, two other considerations lay behind some members' policy interests. Of the forty-three policy-based expressions of interest in a policy-making committee (table 2-4), eleven members were motivated by a desire to pursue interests developed while holding some other public offices. Another fifteen sought the committees because the work was related to their precongressional occupations (Bullock, 1976). A freshman interested in Education and Labor said, "I've had some experience in both fields. My first position was as a member of the city school board. And I own a business; so I understand the management point of view" (quoted in Fenno, 1973, p. 11).

Appropriations, Ways and Means, and Rules are desired largely because of their power, prestige, and influence in the House. Each has a much broader range of responsibilities than do other committees. The influence of the first two derives from their responsibilities for federal spending and taxing (Fenno, 1966; Manley, 1970). The Rules Committee, a conduit through which almost all important legislation passes on its way to the floor, exerts appreciable influence across the whole range of House legislation. One Ways and Means member illustrated the perceived significance of his committee, noting that other members "call you 'Mr.' and 'Sir'" when you serve on Ways and Means (Fenno, 1973, p. 3). The more detailed explanation of an Appropriations Committee member was that

> I thought the power would be important. . . . The process here is one where consent must be obtained before anything gets done. If you are one of those from whom consent must be obtained, then you are a more important person in the House. When you are on the Appropriations Committee you are that kind of person. That's all. It's a question of power (quoted in Fenno, 1973, p. 3).

There remain six committees in table 2-4 that freshmen of the Ninety-second Congress rarely if ever requested. During the Eighty-sixth through the Ninetieth Congresses, three of these (District of Columbia, House Administration, and Post Office) usually had fewer requests than there were seats available. The same pattern occurred, but less frequently, for Government Operations and for Science and Technology. Moreover, these committees are ones whose members are much more likely to transfer (Goodwin, 1970, 102–115; Bullock, 1973a, pp. 118–120; Jewell and Chi-hung, 1974, p. 438); they have little to attract or retain members. None is a major committee. In the past new legislators were sometimes relegated to these undesirable assignments. Now slots on these committees serve primarily as second assignments for members who also have a seat on a more desirable committee.

Representatives' primary motivations are, at least in part, a product of their electoral environment. Policy making was generally the most frequently given reason for committee requests, with reelection second; but among the least electorally secure freshmen, reelection was a much more frequent motivation (Bullock, 1976).

Concern about reelection may decline once a member gains a little seniority. A number of representatives leave committees that appear to provide excellent opportunities to advance their reelection chances. They are most likely to transfer to exclusive committees, although some move to committees that generally attract members because of their policy responsibilities (Bullock, 1973a). It appears that some members adjust their political goals once they feel electorally secure and thereafter pursue influence in the chamber (Shepsle, forthcoming) or policy-making interests.

Reelection

Not only is the desire to facilitate reelection an important consideration in determining committee preferences, but also some argue that it is an important consideration for the Committees on Committees (cf. Clapp, 1964, p. 234; Tacheron and Udall, 1966, p. 152). In his classic study of the assignment process, Masters (1961, p. 357) states, "Although a number of factors enter into committee assignments . . . the most important single consideration . . . is to provide each member with an assignment that will insure his re-election."

Assertions about the critical influence of reelection considerations have not been borne out by more systematic studies.[2] Using Democratic request books for four Congresses to look at instances where a marginal member and an electorally secure member sought the same committee seat, Achen and Stolarek (1974, p. 19) report "no support for the marginality hypothesis. For both freshmen and non-freshmen, marginally elected congressmen and safe congressmen fare about equally well in contests against one another." Other research has shown that between 1947 and 1967, narrowly elected freshmen were not more likely to receive good assignments than safe freshmen (Bullock, 1972). Thus empirical evidence does not support earlier contentions that marginal representatives are more likely to get desirable assignments (cf. Shepsle, forthcoming).

Seniority

As with reelection considerations, the influence of seniority on assignments has been debated. Because seniority plays such an important role in determining the chairs and ranking minority members of committees and subcommittees, it might also be significant in allocating seats. Certainly assignments to the exclusive committees have generally gone to members with some seniority (Fenno, 1966; Manley, 1970; Bullock, 1973a). It has been widely believed that the responsibilities of these committees are too sensitive to be entrusted to novices, although Democrats have recently placed several freshmen on exclusive committees.

Clapp (1964, p. 226), however, quotes several members who denigrate the influence of seniority. For example, "Seniority may control if all other things are equal. But other things usually are not equal. Sometimes you begin to think seniority is little more than a device to fall back on when it is convenient to do so." Rohde and Shepsle (1973) support this observation, reporting that during the four Congresses for which they had Democratic request books, freshmen received at least one of their preferences 75 percent of the time, while nonfreshmen were successful only half the time.

Using the same data, Achen and Stolarek (1974) come to the opposite conclusion. The difference reflects the fact that their study considered only instances when a freshman and a nonfreshman wanted the same committee. In such cases, senior members were successful 79 percent of the time and freshmen only 21 percent of the time. On the more desirable exclusive and major committees, nonfreshmen won 88 percent of the time in competition with freshmen. Of fifteen committees considered, senior members won most contests for seats on all but the Interior, and Post Office and Civil Service panels. On five committees no freshman ever prevailed over a nonfreshman.

Among nonfreshmen, the more senior member prevailed 57 percent of the time when there was competition for a seat (Stolarek, forthcoming). Particularly in cases involving major committees, nonfreshmen were transferring to positions that they had unsuccessfully sought earlier in their careers (Gertzog, 1976; Shepsle, forthcoming).

Seniority may help a member attain an appointment, but it may also inhibit mobility. Some members, whose initial assignment is something other than their first preference, may decide, when it becomes possible to transfer to what had been their top priority, that the costs of doing so are too great. No matter how long members have been in the House, they have no seniority on a committee to which they move. Committee seniority is important in determining the chairs of full committees and subcommittees, the members of conference committees, the order of participation in hearings, etc. Therefore those who have acquired some seniority on one committee may be reluctant to give it up. One Democrat, with six years seniority on a major committee and eight years on a nonmajor committee, acknowledged the cross-pressuring effect of seniority in a letter to Steering Committee members: "You can see that I did not make my decision to seek the Appropriations Committee without careful deliberation." Fenno (1973, p. 8) quotes an eastern Democrat on Interior who decided not to give up his seniority: "Within two and a half years I was a subcommittee Chairman and in six years I was ranking majority member. . . . I'm glad I stayed. [Later] I had a chance to go on Appropriations but I wouldn't take it." Also, after a few years on a committee members may find the work sufficiently rewarding that they decide against pursuing a transfer to a committee that initially held greater interest.

Between 1949 and 1969, more than 40 percent of all transfers came after only one term in the House and almost two-thirds occurred by the beginning of the third term (Bullock, 1973a). Within ten years of service more than 90 percent of all transfers have occurred.

In sum, acquisition of seniority may increase a member's likelihood of success in getting a coveted committee seat. At the same time, however, reluctance to transfer increases with seniority.

Party Loyalty

Because there are more applicants than vacancies on most committees, slots on heavily requested committees may go to reward the party faithful (Ripley, 1967, p. 60). Committee assignments also afford an opportunity for party leaders to increase their influence. Even before the Speaker was given the sole authority to name Democrats to the Rules Committee, the Democratic House leadership filled vacancies on this committee with an eye toward weakening the coalition of conservative southern Democrats and Republicans that kept Rules at odds with House leaders during much of the 1950s (Oppenheimer, 1977).

At times a prerequisite for committee appointment has been to pledge support for the party line. For example, during the early 1950s, Democrats who opposed constructing the St. Lawrence Seaway were excluded from the Public Works Committee (Smith, 1967). A few years later, Democratic seats on Ways and Means were restricted to representatives who favored Medicare and free trade (Manley, 1970). In late 1974, the chairman of the Democratic caucus announced that "The 'litmus test' for Ways and Means . . . will be to get a balanced membership on the committee to produce a decent and a comprehensive health bill and tax reform" (quoted in *Congressional Quarterly*, 1974, p. 3250).

Party loyalty is a common criterion in making committee assignments to nonfreshmen. Rohde and Shepsle (1973) found that 58 percent of the Democrats with above average levels of party support received their requests compared with 37 percent of those whose party support was below average. Looking at seats for which requests outnumbered vacancies, Achen and Stolarek (1974) report that 65 percent of the assignments went to the member having a higher party support score.

Region

Two considerations operate here. On the one hand, there is a general effort to see that all sections of the country are represented on each committee.

Table 2-5 Regional distribution of seats on selected committees for the 95th Congress

	Proportion of Membership* (in percent)				
	Northeast	Midwest	South	West	N
House	26.9	27.8	27.8	17.5	435
Agriculture	10.9	32.6	37.0	19.6	46
Appropriations	27.2	29.1	25.5	18.2	55
Budget	24.0	28.0	32.0	16.0	25
Commerce	32.6	25.6	27.9	14.0	43
Interior	23.3	18.6	16.3	41.9	43
Rules	25.0	25.0	31.3	18.8	16
Ways and Means	18.9	32.4	37.8	10.8	37

*Composition of the regions is as follows: *Northeast:* Conn., Del., Me., Md., Mass., N.H., N.J., N.Y., Pa., R.I., Vt., and W.Va; *Midwest:* Ill., Ind., Iowa, Kans., Mich., Minn., Mo., Nebr., N.D., Ohio, S.D., and Wis.; *South:* Ala., Ark., Fla., Ga., Ky., La., Miss., N.C., Okla., S.C., Tenn., Tx., and Va.; *West:* Alas., Ariz., Cal., Colo., Ha., Ida., Mont., Nev., N.M., Ore., Utah., Wash., and Wyo. This scheme is used by Goodwin (1970: 128–129).

On the other hand, the work of some committees is of great significance for some areas while of little interest to others. Table 2-5 shows the regional representation in the full House and on seven committees. Two of the exclusive committees (Appropriations and Rules) and the potentially very influential Budget Committee have regional compositions closely approximating the makeup of the chamber. The Commerce Committee, attractive to large numbers of members, is also fairly representative of the House, although northeasterners are slightly overrepresented. Of the five committees not designated as reelection committees (see table 2-4), only Ways and Means is badly skewed, with the South and Midwest overrepresented. Fenno (1973, p. 62) reports that, in the past, Ways and Means was very representative of House regional composition; so the present imbalance may be a recent phenomenon. Today's imbalance may be tolerated because the committee no longer makes Democratic committee assignments.

In contrast with four of the five committees with broader appeal, Agriculture and Interior are least like the House in terms of regional balance. The Interior Committee has traditionally attracted numerous westerners (Fenno, 1973). New Interior Committee activities in energy and the environment have appealed to a wider range of members; but the historic responsibilities for irrigation and reclamation, federal lands, national parks, mining, and Indians remain appealing to westerners, who still hold 41.9 percent of the seats. Agriculture also attracts members from a limited geographical area, with 70 percent of the members from the South or Midwest in 1977. Some urban northern legislators—most notably Shirley Chisholm (D-N.Y.)—have fought attempts to place them on Agriculture. Rep. Chisholm, who succeeded in having the Democratic caucus overrule the Committee on Committees, observed of the latter that, "Apparently all they know about

Brooklyn is that a tree grew there. I can think of no other reason for assigning me to the House Agriculture Committee" (quoted in Keefe and Ogul, 1977, p. 179).

Another aspect of region is the North-South split in the Democratic party. Despite efforts to represent regions on most committees, some observers have contended that southern Democrats are less successful than others in their party. Among both freshmen and nonfreshmen Democrats, nonsoutherners were more likely than southerners to have received one of their requested committees (Rohde and Shepsle, 1973). However, when southerners and non-southerners contested seats, southern freshmen won 56 percent of the contests between the Eighty-seventh and Ninety-fourth Congresses (Stolarek, forthcoming). But southern nonfreshmen won only a third of the time when competing with a nonsoutherner. The lower success rate among southern nonfreshmen may result from their generally lower level of party support.

Prescriptive Right

Some state party delegations have managed to hold seats on one or more committees for extended periods of time. For example, Missouri Democrats always hold one seat on the Agriculture Committee. Between 1947 and 1977, Texas Democrats have always been represented on thirteen committees. Once a state party delegation has established a history of representation on a committee, it may claim a prescriptive right to a seat on the committee (Bullock, 1971).[3] Therefore, when the tenure of the delegation's representative on the committee ends, the delegation will argue that the Committee on Committees should restrict the search for a replacement to their delegation. For example, a Kentuckian seeking a seat on Ways and Means wrote to the Committee on Committees: "All of my Kentucky colleagues have endorsed my candidacy. For almost 40 consecutive years prior to Representative John Watts' death in 1971, Kentucky held a seat on Ways and Means. While no state has an absolute right to any seat on any committee, Kentucky's position is not without historical weight." New York and Texas Democrats often caucus when a vacancy occurs in their representation on an important committee. The delegation seeks to unite behind a candidate for the vacancy and then urges their choice on the Committee on Committees.

Large delegations may develop prescriptive claims to seats on most committees, but smaller delegations must be much more selective. The latter are likely to concentrate efforts to claim a seat on a committee offering potential economic benefits to the state (e.g., Kansas Republicans on the Agriculture Committee) or a seat on one of the exclusive committees (e.g., Tennessee Democrats on Ways and Means).

Prescriptive seats are widespread. Between 1947 and 1968 there were 205 committee seats that members of the same state party delegation held at least twenty years (Bullock, 1971). Seats on exclusive committees are most likely to be kept within a delegation. Committees classified as generally undesirable (table 2-4) were, not surprisingly, the ones on which the smallest proportion of seats were prescriptively held.

Less frequent are instances when a committee seat is passed down from representative to representative from a single congressional district (Shepsle, forthcoming). An extraordinarily extended case of this kind of legacy involves the tenth district of Georgia. In 1977 when Doug Barnard succeeded Robert Stephens, he also took his predecessor's seat on the Banking, Finance, and Urban Affairs Committee. Barnard is the fourth congressman from the district, which has now been represented on the Banking Committee continuously since 1917, to serve on the committee.

Limitations on State Representation

The norms surrounding appointments check the ability of powerful delegations to obtain a disproportionate share of the most desirable committee seats. Generally the norms limit state party delegations to a single seat per committee. Although the rule applies to most state party delegations, it must be substantially modified for large delegations. Republicans and Democrats from California, New York, and Pennsylvania; Republicans from Ohio; and Democrats from Texas are so numerous that it is impossible to limit them to one committee seat. Consequently, to cite one example, there were two Democrats and two Republicans from New York on Appropriations in 1977. Occasionally a large state party delegation will place three or even four members on a committee, but this is the upper limit.

The constraining influence of the limit is illustrated by the extent to which the dean of the Iowa Democrats went to help two freshmen in his delegation obtain seats on the Agriculture Committee. In his letter to members of the Steering Committee, the dean enclosed a map showing grain production in the country on which he superimposed information showing where Democrats on the Agriculture Committee were from. The map documented his claim that the Midwest, which accounts for a disproportionate share of the nation's grain production, lacked a fair share of the Democratic seats on the committee.[4] The dean went on to argue that the Iowans would, in a way, be replacing a defeated South Dakotan and a Missourian who might leave the committee: One of the Iowans represented a district adjacent to South Dakota and the other one was from a district neighboring that of the Missourian. He also cited historical precedent—once before two Iowa Democrats had served together on Agriculture. The Iowa dean successfully challenged the norm, but a more common practice is for representatives from small delegations to decide among themselves who will try for the single seat that the delegation is likely to get.

Delegation Dean

A delegation's dean is the party's most senior member from a state. Democratic deans may function as brokers on behalf of their members. They may introduce freshmen to members of the Steering Committee and to the chair of the committee to which the freshman aspires. Republican deans usually represent their state on the Committee on Committees. Deans may try to guide the committee aspirations of their members, seeking to have the delegation represented on important committees and, especially, to maintain claims on prescriptive seats.

Masters (1961, p. 346) emphasizes the part played by the delegation dean: "In negotiations between the Committee-on-Committees and the applicants he plays a crucially important role in securing assignments." Masters buttresses his observations by pointing to the six 1959 Connecticut Democrats who arrived in Congress without a dean. According to Masters (1961, p. 348),

> only two of the six . . . felt that they had been given as good representation as they were entitled to. . . . The four dissatisfied Connecticut congressmen complained, two of them bitterly, that their committee positions would not help them to be re-elected—that they had received the "left over" assignments. These assignments had not been made from any desire to penalize them, but apparently because they were orphans with no dean or senior member to fight for their preferences or look after their preferences.

To put the experiences of the Connecticut freshmen in perspective, and thereby to assess the importance of a dean, comparative data are needed. To evaluate the complaints of the Connecticut representatives, their treatment was compared with that given five other large delegations of freshmen Democrats at about the same time. Because only the Connecticut contingent lacked a dean, its members should have obtained requested assignments less frequently than freshmen in the other delegations, if deans are important. Moreover, the freshmen from California (1963), Michigan (1965), and New York (1965) should have done especially well since they had senior members on the Committee on Committees.

The results of the analysis are presented in table 2-6. Half the Connecticut freshmen obtained the assignments they requested. They fared better than the six 1959 Indiana freshmen. Indeed, only the 1963 California and 1965 Iowa freshmen were more likely to be placed on desired committees than were the Connecticut newcomers.

Table 2-6 Rates at which Democratic freshmen in delegations having large numbers of freshmen received requested assignments

	All Freshmen		Excluding Those Who Made No Requests	
	%	N	%	N
Connecticut, 1959	50	6	75	4
Indiana, 1959	33	6	67	3
California, 1963*	70	10	70	10
Iowa, 1965	100	5	100	5
Michigan, 1965*	43	7	50	6
New York, 1965*	11	9	25	4

*Delegation member served on the Committee on Committees.

One reason the Connecticut freshmen did not do better is that two of them made no requests of the Committee on Committees. (A dean might have made sure that such oversights did not occur, but we cannot be certain of this because even larger proportions of the freshmen in two of the other delegations also failed to make their preferences known.) Comparing members who requested assignments, only the Iowa contingent had a higher rate of success than the Connecticut freshmen. The data (table 2-6) indicate that the lack of a dean did not handicap the Connecticut delegation. With some exceptions, such as the two Democratic freshmen from Iowa who wanted seats on Agriculture, the role of the dean does not appear to be very significant.

Delegation Representation on the Committee on Committees

This analysis of six sets of freshmen indicates that for those Democrats there was no advantage to being in a delegation represented on the Committee on Committees. Of the freshmen in the delegations without a member, 83 percent making requests were successful, compared with 65 percent in delegations with a member.

Rohde and Shepsle (1973) reached the same conclusion, looking at nonsouthern Democrats. However, southern Democrats appear to benefit from being in the same delegation as their zone's representative on the Committee on Committees. Southern freshmen in delegations lacking a member on the Committee on Committees were only half as likely to receive a requested appointment as freshmen in delegations represented on the committee. Among nonfreshmen, half of those in delegations represented on the committee got requested assignments, compared with only a quarter of the other southern nonfreshmen. Comparable data are unavailable for Republicans.

Occupation

A representative's previous occupation may influence his or her committee assignment in two ways. As noted earlier, some members seek appointments to committees responsible for subjects with which they are familiar, e.g., farmers like Robert Bergland (D-Minn.) requested Agriculture. The other aspect is that the Committee on Committees may weigh occupational experience when filling vacancies. The rules of the Democratic caucus (1976, p. 3) attempt to reduce the significance of occupation, proclaiming that "In making nominations for committee assignments the Committee on Committees shall not discriminate on the basis of prior occupation or profession in making such nominations." Nonetheless, the relationship between occupation and assignment persists, especially on the Judiciary Committee, to which only lawyers are named.

Electoral Security

Masters (1961) reported that an important prerequisite for appointment to the exclusive committees was that a member come from an electorally safe district. Fenno (1966) and Manley (1970) make similar statements about the Appropriations and Ways and Means Committees. Limiting appointments to the electorally secure seems necessary because these committees make significant decisions, and need members who can act without fear of electoral retribution. It also facilitates committee work by minimizing membership turnover.

Although it is true that the great bulk of the representatives who transfer to exclusive committees represent safe districts, the same is also true of most tranferees to other committees. Thus between 1949 and 1969, 83 percent of the members transferring to exclusive committees had safe districts; but so did 81 percent of those transferring to other committees (Bullock, 1973a, p. 108).[5] Even for the least prestigious committees, 80 percent of the transferees represented safe districts. Thus the exclusive committees are not uniquely restrictive in terms of their members' electoral security.

Responsible Legislators

Other considerations may at times influence committee assignments. In filling vacancies on the exclusive committees, aspirants' legislative styles seem to be important. Such coveted assignments are most likely to go to a responsible legislator, i.e., "one whose ability, attitudes, and relationships with his colleagues serve to enhance the prestige and importance of the House of Representatives" (Masters, 1961, p. 352). Traditionally, recruits for exclusive

The Nature of the Congressional System

committees served an apprenticeship of at least one term on another committee, during which they could demonstrate that they were able to work with party leaders and that they were not ideologues, unwilling to compromise.

In the Ninety-fourth Congress, Democrats began to relax the requirement that appointees to exclusive committees demonstrate their responsibility during an apprenticeship. Freshman Democrats have been appointed to two of these three committees at a much higher rate than previously. During the Eightieth through Ninety-third Congresses only nine first-term Democrats were appointed to Appropriations or Ways and Means; for the Ninety-fourth and Ninety-fifth Congresses alone the number was ten.

In part, the party leaders may be gambling on the extent to which these newcomers will heed their requests. In part, with a less conservative leadership, there is less need to restrict exclusive committees to people who will tolerate only gradual policy changes. The large Democratic freshman class in the Ninety-fourth Congress pushed to realign committee ratios and created fifteen more seats on the three committees. The freshmen also were able to use their numbers, in alliance with other liberals, to get some first termers named to the most prestigious committees, especially on the much enlarged Ways and Means Committee. Freshmen of the Ninety-fifth Congress were able to bargain for good seats in return for support of the competing candidates for Majority Leader. Republicans used to place freshmen on exclusive committees more often than Democrats, but this is no longer the case.

Interest Groups

Interest groups sometimes help influence committee assignments. For example, Democratic appointees to the Education and Labor Committee usually must be acceptable to organized labor. Interest groups usually do not openly work on behalf of an individual's candidacy for an assignment. No interest group tried to influence assignments in the Ninety-fourth Congress by sending letters to Democrats on the Committee on Committees. Instead, a group may express its preferences to a friendly legislator on the committee.

Race

There appears to be some concern in the Committees on Committees to have blacks on most committees, and especially on the more important ones. In the Ninety-fifth Congress, blacks served on fifteen committees. They were represented on each of the five most prestigious committees and on eight of the top eleven (see table 2-7). Nine blacks sat on the five most prestigious committees; five were on the exclusive committees. They tended to eschew com-

Table 2-7   Distributions of women and blacks on committees in the 95th Congress

	Committee Prestige by Quartiles[1]			
	1st	2nd	3rd	4th
Democratic Women				
# Committees	5	5	2	3
# of Women	7	6	4	5
Republican Women				
# Committees	3	4	0	3
# of Women	3	4	0	3
Blacks				
# Committees	5	3	4	3
# of Blacks	9	5	9	5

[1]Committee prestige is based on Bullock, 1968: 34–35. For Democrats the quartiles are as follows: 1st — Appropriations, Armed Services, International Relations Rules, and Ways and Means; 2nd — Agriculture Budget, Commerce, Judiciary, Public Works, and Science and Technology; 3rd — District of Columbia, Education and Labor, Government Operations, House Administration, and Interior; 4th — Banking and Finance, Merchant Marine, Post Office, Small Business, Standards of Official Conduct, and Veterans' Affairs.

For Republicans the quartiles are composed of the following Committees: 1st — Appropriations, Armed Services, International Relations, Rules, and Ways and Means; 2nd — Agriculture, Banking and Finance, Budget, Commerce, Education and Labor and Judiciary; 3rd — District of Columbia, House Administration, Interior, Public Works, and Science and Technology; 4th — Government Operations, Merchant Marine, Post Office, Small Business, Standards of Official Conduct, and Veterans' Affairs.

mittees of little interest to the urban black constituents whom they represented; Agriculture, Interior, and Public Works had no black members.

Sex

Women are also well represented on committees.[6] Democrats assigned women to all five of the most prestigious committees and to five of the next six. Republican women served on three of the top five. When party lines are ignored, we find women on all committees except House Administration and Interior. When seeking an assignment, women may point out that their sex is unrepresented on the committee to which they aspire, using this to advance their candidacy.

Committee Leaders

The chair, or ranking minority member, of the committee on which a person wishes to sit is also important. In the past, the chair's endorsement was often important in advancing an aspirant's candidacy. Ripley (1967, p. 61) reports, among Democrats in the Eighty-eighth Congress, that "those who received support from committee chairmen were successful in all but one case, which involved a sitting member who often opposed the administration and the leaders." Party leaders on committees now play a less central role (Gertzog, 1976), although there is some variation from chair to chair. For example, a few years ago Edward Herbert, (D-La.), chairman of the Armed Services Committee, said he would accept any black except Ron Dellums (D-Cal.). Dellums was named to the committee. Democrats with beliefs not in accord with the chairman's were also appointed to Rules, to weaken the chairman's influence.

Summary

The preceding discussion demonstrates the complexity of the committee assignment process. Both parties in the House have institutionalized the process to some degree by turning it over to small Committees on Committees. These committees are accessible to the rank and file of the party. First termers as well as nonfreshmen try to secure desired appointments by visiting and writing party leaders and Committee on Committees members. They may also use their deans as intermediaries.

Although it is not possible to rank the many factors of potential significance, some do seem to be more important than others. It appears that the single greatest consideration in making appointments is member preference. In recent years almost all freshmen have obtained one of the assignments they wanted. Thus despite the fact that requests exceed vacancies for most committees, most members serve on a committee in which they have some interest, although not all obtain their top priority. Greater consideration for freshmen began in the 1960s; by 1973 each Democrat was guaranteed a seat on an exclusive or major committee.

Reelection, while a frequent concern, is not the overriding motive among freshmen and is even less common among nonfreshmen. Both groups display great interest in committees offering opportunities to participate in shaping public policy on controversial topics. Reelection promotion is neither the overwhelming concern among committee applicants nor determinative for the Committees on Committees when making assignments. This may be because members recognize that their choice of committee need not be critical to their electoral fortunes. So long as they avoid an assignment that may be detrimental, they may find that they can promote their reelections in ways other than through committee work (e.g., through close attention to casework, as Fiorina, 1977, suggests).

Seniority does play a role; senior members generally prevail over newer members when there is competition for a seat. However, it also reduces member willingness to move to new committees. Party loyalty often determines assignments when senior members compete for limited slots.

Other elements that may be weighed in parceling out committee seats are the desire to have blacks and women on most committees and the relationship between occupational background and the work of some committees. Considerations of regional balance and claims of prescriptive right to some seats may be used to decide among applicants.

Several variables suggested as important in making assignments seem unimportant or no longer relevant. The presence of a delegation dean or a delegation representative on the Committee on Committees does not seem to get delegation members better assignments. Neither electoral security nor the need to establish a reputation as a responsible legislator seems to be a distinctive feature in recruitment to the exclusive committees any longer. Finally, interest groups do not play a large, direct role in the assignment process.

Although some factors have declined in importance, members now have a much greater likelihood of obtaining desirable appointments. Getting a good assignment early in one's career allows the recipient to participate more fully in the House sooner and to derive greater work satisfaction.

Notes

[1]Standards of Official Conduct is an exception and is not listed in any category.

[2]An exception is Rohde and Shepsle's (1973) research. "Marginal freshmen are slightly less likely to fail to receive a requested committee and are much more likely to receive their first choice than are safe freshmen. Marginal nonfreshmen are much less likely to receive no choice than are safe nonfreshmen, but they are about equally likely to receive their first choice as are safe freshmen" (p. 900). These conclusions are not supported when only contested assignments are considered, as Achens and Stolarke (1974) point out.

[3]By "prescriptive right" I mean that a state party claims a seat because it has held a slot on a committee for an extended period. This is also sometimes referred to as the "same state rule."

[4]Note that here the allegation is that midwestern Democrats were underrepresented on Agriculture. Earlier, in the section on Region, the assertion that the South and Midwest were overrepresented referred to the combined Republican and Democratic membership.

[5]Because almost all southern Democrats who transferred committees represented safe districts, they were excluded from this comparison.

[6]Placement of women on most committees may have occurred only recently. Bella Abzug charged that in the Ninety-second Congress, "Of the grand total of twelve women in the House, five have been assigned to the Education and Labor Committee. . ." (Abzug, 1972, p. 26).

References

Abzug, Bella. 1972. *Bella: Ms. Abzug Goes to Washington*. New York: Bobbs-Merrill.

Achen, Christopher H., and John S. Stolarek. 1974. "The Resolution of Congressional Committee Assignment Contests: Factors Influencing the Democratic Committee on Committees," presented at the annual meeting of the American Political Science Association, Chicago.

Bullock, Charles S., III. 1968. "The Committee Assignments of Freshmen in the House of Representatives, 1947–1967," unpublished Ph.D. dissertation, Washington University.

——. 1972. "Freshman Committee Assignments and Re-election in the United States House of Representatives," *American Political Science Review* 66 (September 1972): 996–1007.

——. 1973a. "Committee Transfers in the United States House of Representatives," *Journal of Politics* 35 (February 1973): 85–120.

——. 1973b. "Initial Committee Assignments of the 92nd Congress," presented at the annual meeting of the Southwest Political Science Association, Dallas.

——. 1976. "Motivations for U.S. Congressional Committee Preferences: Freshmen of the 92nd Congress," *Legislative Studies Quarterly* 1 (May 1976): 201–212.

Clapp, Charles. 1964. *The Congressman: His Work as He Sees It*. Garden City, N.Y.: Anchor Doubleday.

Congressional Quarterly Weekly Report 32 (December 7, 1974): 3250.

Democratic Caucus. 1976. *Preamble and Rules Adopted by the Democratic Caucus*. Washington: U.S. Government Printing Office.

Dyson, James W., and John W. Soule. 1970. "Congressional Committee Behavior on Roll Call Votes: The U.S. House of Representatives, 1955–1964," *Midwest Journal of Political Science* 14 (November 1970): 626–647.

Fenno, Richard F. 1966. *The Power of the Purse*. Boston: Little, Brown, and Co.

——. 1973. *Congressmen in Committees*. Boston: Little, Brown and Co.

Fiorina, Morris P. 1977. "The Case of the Vanishing Marginals: The Bureaucracy Did It," *American Political Science Review* 71 (February 1977): 177–181.

Gertzog, Irwin N. 1976. "The Routinization of Committee Assignments in the U.S. House of Representatives," *American Journal of Political Science* 20 (November 1976): 693–712.

Goodwin, George. 1970. *The Little Legislatures*. Amherst, Mass.: University of Massachusetts Press.

Jewell, Malcolm E., and Chu Chi-hung. 1974. "Membership Movement and Committee Attractiveness in the U.S. House of Representatives, 1963–1971," *American Journal of Political Science* 18 (May 1974): 433–441.

Keefe, William J., and Morris S. Ogul. 1977. *The American Legislative Process*, 4th ed. Englewood Cliffs, N.J.: Prentice-Hall.

Manley, John F. 1970. *The Politics of Finance: The House Committee on Ways and Means*. Boston: Little, Brown, and Co.

Masters, Nicholas A. 1961. "Committee Assignments in the House of Representatives," *American Journal of Political Science* 55 (June 1961): 345–357.

Oppenheimer, Bruce I. 1977. "The Rules Committee: New Arm of Leadership in a Decentralized House," in Lawrence C. Dodd and Bruce I. Oppenheimer (eds.), *Congress Reconsidered*, New York: Praeger.

Ripley, Randall B. 1967. *Party Leaders in the House of Representatives*. Washington: Brookings Institution.

Rohde, David W., and Kenneth A. Shepsle. 1973. "Democratic Committee Assignments in the House of Representatives: Strategic Aspects of a Social Choice Process," *American Political Science Review* 67 (September 1973): 889–905.

Shepsle, Kenneth A. 1974. "Counting the Pieces and Measuring the Effects of the Giant Jigsaw Puzzle: Committee Assignments in the House of Representatives," mimeo.

――. Forthcoming. *The Giant Jigsaw Puzzle: Committee Assignments in the Modern House.* Chicago: University of Chicago Press.

Siff, Ted, and Alan Weil (eds.). 1977. *Ruling Congress.* New York: Penguin Books.

Smith, Frank E. 1967. *Congressman from Mississippi.* New York: Capricorn Books.

Southwick, Thomas P. 1977. "Sikes Ousted as Subcommittee Head," *Congressional Quarterly Weekly Report* 35 (January 29, 1977): 159-160.

Stolarek, John S. Forthcoming. "Structure and Resolution of Democratic Committee Assignment Contests in the House of Representatives, 1960-1975," Ph.D. dissertation, Rochester University.

Tacheron, Donald G., and Morris K. Udall. 1966. *The Job of the Congressman,* 1st ed. Indianapolis: Bobbs-Merrill.

Westefield, Louis P. 1974. "Majority Party Leadership and the Committee System in the House of Representatives," *American Political Science Review* 68 (December 1974): 1593-1604.

Selection 3 The Seniority System in Congress

Barbara Hinckley

I. The Seniority System: An Introduction

The seniority system of Congress has been called by Representative Emanual Celler "as popular a target as sin itself."[1] The defects of the system have been extensively catalogued for more than two decades with each recurring plea for congressional reform. Yet the seniority system — basically a device for selecting congressional leaders — has not been systematically examined to determine the kinds of leaders it selects, its specific impact on their selection, or the way it functions within the congressional system.[2] Few institutions have been subject to so much attack and so little appraisal.

Its critics contend that the seniority rule, or "senility rule," rewards age and long service and thus builds a generation gap into congressional decision making which gives great power to those least likely to be attuned to contemporary needs.[3] By stipulating long congressional service, the seniority system, it is charged, benefits certain one-party areas of the nation at the expense of others, overrepresenting in the committee chairs rural and conervative interests, Democrats from the South and Republicans from the rural Midwest and Northeast.[4] It obstructs party cohesion in Congress by creating independent power centers, a cadre of chairmen not responsible to party leaders since those leaders do not control their selection.[5] And it reinforces this anti-party (and anti-president) tendency by favoring congressmen from safe districts, who are most likely to be out of step with current party programs.[6] In defense of the system it is argued that it avoids the organizational disruption and political in-fighting of other methods of choosing committee heads. In other words, the alternatives would be worse. . . .[7]

This body of criticism raises important questions concerning the distribution of influence in Senate and House and the functioning of a major congressional institution. Does the seniority system exert a systematic impact on the selection of leaders, overrepresenting some kinds of congressmen and some interests at the expense of others? If so, is length of *congressional* service, stressed by the critics,[8] the principal determinant of leadership? The seniority rule actually refers to length of service on the *committee*, not in Congress; hence original committee assignments, or subsequent changes in committee membership, also affect the selection of leaders. Does the seniority system distribute chairmanships according to pre-existing power alignments, and if so, what specific alignments? The answers to these questions are not necessarily mutually exclusive. Fundamentally they concern (1) to what extent and in what way the leaders selected are representative of the membership of the congressional party and (2) whether the seniority system per se, and in particular congressional seniority, exerts a systematic selective impact on leadership. . . .

Key Characteristics

The seniority system is a device for selecting the leaders of the standing committees. It is a way of ranking members, by party, according to their years of consecutive service on the committee. Parties add or drop members only at the lowest rankings. The seniority system, then, designates the top-ranking member of each party. The senior member whose party gains control of Senate or House becomes the chairman; the senior member from the other party becomes the ranking minority member.

The seniority system is unique to the United States Congress. No other national legislative assemblies, no state legislatures use seniority as the sole criterion for choosing leaders. . . .

The "seniority rule" is a custom, not a formal rule of Congress. The rules simply dictate that House or Senate shall determine committee membership and chairmen: "At the commencement of each Congress, the House shall elect as chairman of each standing committee one of the members thereof." Yet despite its lack of formal status, in recent American history exceptions have been made only in extraordinary circumstances. . . .

The rule is strongly reinforced by the tradition of respect for seniority in Congress. It is part of the "seniority-protege-apprentice system," to use Richard Fenno's phrase, for minimizing conflict over who shall exercise influence and who shall not.[9] This affects all congressmen, not merely those in line for chairmanships. Respect for seniority affects the choice of committee assignments, assignment of office space, recognition on the floor and in committee hearings, as well as committee chairmanships. . . .

Influences on the Selection of Chairmen

A number of factors, including seniority, may determine the selection of committee chairmen. First, the *distribution of members* in a congressional party may set important limits. If 50 percent of the Senate Democrats are Southerners, then Democratic committee leaders might well include 50 percent Southerners, even if the choice were by lot. Second, as much of the commentary suggests, long service in Congress—*congressional seniority*, as required by the seniority rule—might well influence the selection of chairmen. Third, *committee assignments*, both initial appointments and subsequent transfers to more desirable committees, can affect committee seniority. Finally, what Joseph Clark calls the *"luck of the seniority draw"*[10] may exert a major impact. If several senior members of a committee die, resign, or shift assignments, a relatively junior man may gain rank quickly. Similarly, a fairly senior man may have the misfortune to be ranked below one or two exceptionally hardy men with even greater seniority. Such factors as the size of the committee or the tenacity of other committee members can operate quite independently of congressional seniority. . . .

Conventional criticism of the subject usually concentrates on one factor only—the influence of congressional seniority. The seniority system, it is said, by rewarding long congressional service, effectively denies chairmanships to those states and districts that do not regularly return incumbents to office. One can see the result in the safe-seat, Southern Democratic overrepresentation in the committee chairs. This formulation is a plausible one, and well worth investigation.

Another interpretation is possible, however. . . . It may be that the seniority requirement exerts only a marginal impact on the choice of congressional leaders, given the stability over time of American voters' party loyalties, the resulting stability of congressional membership, and the variety of congressional career patterns. This suggests that (1) committee leaders may reflect in a general way the distribution of the members of their congressional party and that (2) where "misrepresentation" does occur, it may be attributable as much to patterns of committee assignment and committee changes as to congressional seniority. Therefore, the kind of chairmen selected may be the result of many causes, with the seniority rule only one of a number of influences, and in the traditional criticism its impact may have been considerably overstated.

The conventional emphasis on congressional seniority echoes the older notion of a truly competitive party system, where strong and persistent competition between parties at the state and district levels and frequent turnover of candidates is the normal situation, and one-party constituencies are abnormal. By this older notion, the seniority system rewards the abnormal minority at the expense of the majority and poses a serious conflict between the turnover encouraged by the party system and the continuity encouraged by the seniority system. But the majority of states and districts are *not* subject to frequent election overturns. American voters show marked stability in party loyalties — tending to vote for the same party for different offices over a number of elections.[11] Moreover, in elections for both the House and Senate incumbents have a decided advantage over the challengers. Senate and House incumbents of both parties over the past decade have averaged 85 percent victories in their fights for reelection.[12] Both effects combine to produce an extremely stable congressional membership. Once in office a congressman tends to stay.

In a legislative body where long service is not the exception but the rule, a stipulation for long service is not especially restrictive. It screens out only that small fraction of states and districts which, unlike the majority, are marked by frequent turnover in party control.

Second, when shifts in party fortunes at congressional elections do occur — in both presidential-year and midterm elections — they tend to occur in the same general direction in line with national trends. They may be results of a strong presidential vote in presidential-year elections, or of a derivative countertendency* at midterm elections, or of changes in party loyalties spread over an extensive regional, interest, or ideological base. In any case, they produce a clear swing for or against a party's congressional candidates rather than merely an aggregate result of many idiosyncratic contests. [13] Such large and clear trends are reflected in the membership of the congressional party — producing, for example, a relative increase in midwestern Democrats vis-à-vis Southern Democrats — and, over time, affect the chairmanships. This effect is attributable not to congressional seniority but to the fact that there are relatively more congressmen of one kind than of other kinds within a congressional party. The key to understanding how committee leaders are selected may, then, be the composition of the party's membership in Congress. The larger the number of Southern Senate Democrats in relation to Senate Democrats from other regions, the larger the relative number of committee posts they may be expected to receive.

*The automatic loss of the seats won by the help of the presidential vote two years before. See Barbara Hinckley in *American Political Science Review,* September 1967.

A third point which casts doubt on the overriding importance of congressional seniority is the variety exhibited by congressional career patterns. Many different goals can be pursued by the ambitious congressman, only one of which is a committee chairmanship. Others include a place in the party leadership, a firm interest base from which to deal with one's constituency politics, or a base allowing one to pursue the role of maverick critic of government policies.[14] It follows that rank on a specific committee would be valued differently depending on the individual's personal goal and strategy. It may suit some congressmen to stay on one committee to gain the chairmanship. Others may prefer to change committee assignments in pursuit of their individual goals or at the suggestion of the party leadership. These variations will have no necessary relationship to congressional seniority.

All this indicates that the selection of committee leaders is a much more complicated process than the usual arguments would suggest. If so, investigation should reveal (1) evidence of a variety of representational patterns for House and Senate, Democrats and Republicans, varying with differences in membership and patterns of factional strength; and (2) in cases where over-or underrepresentation is observable, evidence that it is not solely due to congressional seniority.

II. The Concept of "Seniority"

Much of the confusion surrounding the subject may stem from the vagueness of the concept of "seniority." It suggests time spent, tenure; in this context, some number of years consecutive service in Congress or on a committee. But how many years are necessary to be considered "senior"? And how much does seniority vary from one congressional party to another depending on the turnover of members? In a young party one might become a senior in six years, whereas in an old one even a ten-year man may attract little veneration. How closely related are congressional and committee seniority? A number of assumptions about the seniority system depend for their validity on answers to such simple questions. Consider the stereotype of "the little group of committee chairmen who were first elected to Congress a generation ago on issues now settled and forgotten," making decisions on legislation they can no longer understand.[15] Or consider the assertion that the system screens out a majority of states and districts from the chance at a chairmanship, which requires comparison of the average congressional service of chairmen before attaining leadership with the average length of service of all members of Congress.

I supply some substantive meaning to the word "seniority" by defining it in terms of (1) the age, tenure, and congressional careers of committee leaders (chairmen and ranking minority members); (2) the congressional seniority possessed by these leaders compared with the full membership; and (3) the relationship between congressional and committee seniority.

Age and Length of Service

To begin with a fact that will surprise no one, committee leaders are indeed "senior" in age. The median age for committee chairmen and ranking minority members for the years 1947–66 comes close to what is considered the standard retirement age in this society. The median age for Senate Democratic committee leaders is 66; for House Democrats, 65.5; for Senate Republicans, 63.5; and for House Republicans, 62.3.[16] This age level is slightly higher than the median age of all Senate and House members. The median age for Senators ranges between 55 and 60; for Representatives between 50 and 55.[17] It is interesting to note that if Congress had followed the recurring suggestion of a maximum age limit such as 70 for chairmen, a large number of committee leaders would have been disqualified. Seventeen Democratic Senators, 19 Democratic Representatives, 11 Republican Senators, and 20 Republican Representatives would have been automatically retired from their posts.

A second part of this temporal definition, however, may be much more surprising. The conventional view suggests that a chairmanship is a prize which only the hardiest—physically and electorally—can aspire to. But the number of years it takes a congressman to gain top committee rank from his first entry into the House or Senate varies considerably from one party and chamber to the other. The median years required to gain top rank for the chairmen and ranking minority members of 1947 through 1966 are as follows:[18]

Senate Democrats	10
House Democrats	16
Senate Republicans	7
House Republicans	12

Approximately this number of years is sufficient to gain top rank on the majority of committees. Committees requiring more than the median number of years include not only the more prestigious, such as Appropriations, Ways, and Means, Foreign Relations, and Armed Services, but some low-ranking committees also, such as Post Office, Labor, Government Operations, and House Un-American Activities Committees.[19] According to the Miller-Stokes six-level ranking of House committees by prestige, only Democratic chairmen of committees in the top level of prestige and those in the lowest level show any clear difference in years of previous congressional service. No clear difference is apparent for House Republican leaders.[20]

If one translates these findings into the number of elections that must be won along the way, House Democrats on the average must win nine elections and House Republicans seven to qualify for a post, whereas in the Senate, both Democrats and Republicans need win only two.

These facts suggest that the usual jump in the literature from seniority to electoral safeness may be much too hastily made. In the Senate, by this criterion of number of elections won, forty-eight states could have had at least one chairman or ranking minority member in 1947–1966. (Alaska and Hawaii would not qualify.) And in the House, although the requirement of seven to nine elections seems more severe, the number of congressional districts which could meet this requirement is rather large. In the twenty-year span, 198 Democratic congressional districts and 139 Republican districts fulfilled the minimum requirement of remaining under the same party banner for at least the nine and seven consecutive elections of the average requirement. So of the 435 present districts, only 22 percent would be automatically excluded. As operationally defined by the experience of these twenty years, the time required to gain seniority excludes only the two states new to statehood and only 22 percent of the congressional districts from Senate and House committee leadership.

A third finding may also be surprising. The number of years a chairman or ranking minority member stays in his top committee position may be shorter than is commonly thought. The median number of years for Senate Democrats is 8; for House Democrats, 6; for Senate Republicans, 4; and for House Republicans, 5. Thus committee leadership, according to Joseph Schlesinger's classification, would be called an "intermediate" office — too short to qualify as a "career" office and too long to be called a "transitory" office.[21] Any view of the venerable chairman, outlasting President after President, is not supported by these facts. Presidents, it would seem, do just as well or better than the average committee chairman or ranking minority member. A few committee chairmen, of course, correspond to the conventional image — for example, Senate Democrat George (21 years), House Republicans Taber (30 years) and Hope (24 years). The record-holder is House Democrat Carl Vinson, Committee Chairman or ranking minority member of Naval Affairs or Armed Services for 42 years. The number of years congressmen occupy top committee posts is given in table 3-1. The figures show that, although a few members serve lengthy terms — and those are the giants who come to mind — all the rest remain in office much more briefly.

To give some substance to the notion of the "time lag" built into

Table 3-1   Number of years congressmen served as committee chairmen or ranking minority members, 1947–1966[a]

No. of Years as CC or RMM	Number of Congressmen			
	Senate Dem.	House Dem.	Senate Rep.	House Rep.
More than 20	1	4	0	3
13–20	5	6	2	7
5–12	10	11	12	20
4 or less	9	11	17	25
Total no. of congressmen	25	32	31	55

[a]Only those congressmen whose terms were completed by 1965–66 are included.

Table 3-2   Rate of turnover of committee leaders by decade, 1921–1960

	Committee Leaders Who Left Office During the Decade (in percent)			
	Senate Dem.	House Dem.	Senate Rep.	House Rep.
1921–30	33	39	52	52
1931–40	39	56	47	67
1941–50	53	39	50	42
1951–60	44	42	50	58

committee leadership, one can specify the rate of turnover in committee posts per decade; i.e., what proportion of chairmen and ranking minority members who held rank at the beginning of a decade had left by the end of it. The results given in table 3-2 cover the past four decades.[22]

Roughly, more than 40 percent of the committee leaders on the average change within one decade, with the most recent ten years registering a mean turnover rate of all congressional parties of close to 50 percent. But the *variety* in the turnover rate among the four congressional parties for any one decade, and especially the variety between House and Senate leaders of the same party, should be noticed. Compare the 47 and 67 percent rates for the Republicans in the 1930's and the 39 and 56 percent rates for the Democrats in the 1930's. In view of this variety, no one average figure for time lag should be used without considerable caution. Perhaps all one can say is that it has taken about a decade or slightly more to change a majority of the committee leaders.

Such intraparty differences in the same decade suggest that a party's

Table 3-3   Interparty similarity in involuntary retirement, 1947–1966[a]

Committee Leaders	No.	No. Who Left by Election Defeat	No. Who Left by Primary Defeat	No. Who Left by Election or Primary Defeat or Death
Senate Democrats	40	1	2	10
Senate Republicans	46	7	0	9
House Democrats	51	1	3	15
House Republicans	71	6	1	15

[a]The higher incidence of primary defeat among Democrats helps to even the numbers of congressmen leaving through "involuntary retirement," but does not fully explain the similarity between parties of the numbers in the right-hand column. The similarity seems to be produced by the action of a nonpolitical variable. In this case, as the saying goes, death appears to be the "great leveler." Democrats, with lower incidence of defeat, had a higher incidence of death in the committee chairs.

It is possible that some proportion of those who retired *voluntarily* did so because they read the writing on the wall—an electoral situation which spelled defeat in the primary or election. The analysis here cannot probe this possibility. If such is the case, the higher incidence of voluntary retirement among Republicans might indicate some additional electoral vulnerability. (Those who left top committee posts by voluntary retirement are as follows: Senate Democrats, 14; Senate Republicans, 21; House Democrats, 16; and House Republicans, 36.)

electoral popularity does not significantly affect the rate of turnover. During the "Republican" 1920's, Republican chairmen in both House and Senate changed more frequently than the Democrats. In the "Democratic" 1940's, Senate Democratic chairmen changed more frequently than Senate Republicans. And the highest rate of turnover of House Democrats also came in the 1940's. In only one case did electoral defeat seem substantially to influence the rate of turnover. Seventeen Republican ranking minority members were defeated in the decade of the 1930's, producing the highest rate of turnover registered for any of the congressional parties in the four decades.

Even though Republicans have suffered more electoral defeats than Democrats, the total number of committee leaders of each party leaving involuntarily—that is, through death or defeat in a primary or general election, rather than through retirement—is almost the same, as table 3-3 makes clear.

Congressional Seniority

The impact of the seniority system may well hinge on the restrictiveness of the congressional tenure requirement—that is, on what proportion of congressmen it disqualifies from the selection process. If the requirement can be defined as the average number of consecutive elections which must be won before receiving a top committee post, the preceding section supplies data with which to investigate this alleged restrictiveness.

The range of the tenure requirement across the four congressional parties—from two consecutive elections for Senators to nine for House Democrats—obviously prohibits the use of any one measure as a definition of what constitutes a congressional "senior." But it seems suitable to take as an operational definition for each congressional party how many consecutive elections had to be won to gain a ranking position on a committee in more than half of the cases in the past two decades: two consecutive elections for Senate Democrats and Republicans; seven for House Republicans; and nine for House Democrats. . . .

This congressional seniority requirement, thus defined, should be viewed within the general context of congressional electoral patterns. As suggested earlier, the overall stability in the electorate's party attachments can be expected to produce an overall stability in congressional membership, and thus for the average congressman an expectation of considerable tenure. The normal situation, especially in House districts, is not a competitive one, as a number of writers have pointed out.[23] Incumbent candidates for both Senate and House—exhibiting an average 85 percent success rate—have a decided advantage over nonincumbents.

The Senate requirement of two consecutive victories and even the House requirement of seven to nine consecutive victories may not, therefore, be a very stiff hurdle. Of the forty-eight states examined during the twenty-year span, only four did not have at least two "senior" Senators, using the preceding definitions of a "senior" for each party. Oregon, Wyoming, and Kentucky had one senior each, and Connecticut had none. (Senator Dodd of Connecticut had won two consecutive elections, but by 1966 had not yet served ten years.) Six states had three seniors. All the remaining thirty-eight had more than three. In contradiction to the claim that the seniority system penalizes competitive states, these data suggest that at the senatorial level few states are very competitive. Parties may divide the two Senate seats, but the two seats themselves are "safe" for the incumbents.[24] In the House, despite the apparent stiffness of the requirement of seven to nine consecutive elections won, from 1947 to 1966 fifty-one separate House Democrats attained the position of committee chairman or ranking minority member, while more than twice that number (139) "qualified" by winning nine consecutive elections.[25] The seniority rule, in other words, stipulates long service from a membership where long service is not the exception but the rule.

It is, of course, true that the more congressional seniority a congressman possesses the better his chances are for receiving a top committee post. Yet some interesting discontinuities are evident. If committee leadership were strictly determined by congressional seniority, one would expect that all chairmanships would be held by the members with the longest service and, conversely, that no members would hold chairmanships while some outranking them in congressional tenure did not. Analysis of the membership of two Congresses, the 85th (1957–58) and the 88th (1963–64), illustrates the discontinuities found to exist throughout the twenty-year span. The results for the Senate are given in table 3-4 and for the House in table 3-5.

The tables show in varying degrees some relationship between the two "hierarchies," but the relationship is by no means a strict one. Considerable discontinuities are evident. To turn to the Senate first, one finds the strongest correspondence among the 1957–58 Democrats. All of the Senators who had served fifteen years or more had chairmanships. Five of the ten Senators serving ten to fifteen years had chairmanships. And only two Senators (in the five-to-nine-year category) held chairs which, if congressional seniority were strictly followed, would have gone to men in the ten-to-fourteen-year category who were not chairmen. For the Democrats in 1963–64 and the Republicans in both Congresses, the correspondence is less strong. It is true that the most senior Senators (those serving twenty years or more) all had chairmanships, but below that top category considerable discontinuity is evident, as can be seen by reading down the columns and noting the number of Senators who received top committee positions in each category while members outranking them in congressional seniority did not. . . .

The results for the House are similar to those in the Senate. Some relationship is evident between the two hierarchies, but not a particularly strong one. The House, of course, is a considerably larger body and has more members who have served more than twenty years. A category was added to the table for the House to distinguish members who had served more than twenty-four. With only nineteen or twenty committee chairs available, there were not enough chairmanships to distribute among all the veteran members. Even so, the allocation by no means closely followed congressional seniority. Some of the most senior members in the House were bypassed for the top committee posts among both Democrats and Republicans in both Congresses. Reading down the columns in table 3-5 in deceasing order of congressional seniority, one finds in both parties and in both Congresses a considerable number of Representatives without top committee posts while more junior congressmen received them. . . .

Table 3-4   Relationship between congressional seniority and committee leadership: Senate, 1957–1958, 1963–1964[a]

Congressional Seniority: No.Years Continuous Service	Democrats			Republicans		
	Sens. No.	CC's No.	CC's %	Sens. No.	RMM's No.	RMM's %
			1957–58			
20 or more	7	7	100	1	1	100
15–19	1	1	100	3	2	67
10–14	10	5	50	16	6	38
5–9	14	2	14	9	2	22
0–4	17	0	0	19	2	11
Total	49	15		48	13	
			1963–64			
20 or more	7	7	100	1	1	100
15–19	9	4	45	5	4	80
10–14	11	2	18	7	7	100
5–9	10	2	20	8	3	38
0–4	31	1	3	11	0	0
Total	68	16		32	15	

[a]Number of years of continuous service measures the seniority accumulated as of the beginning of the term in 1957 and 1963. For both Congresses, the number of Republican ranking minority members is lower than the number of Democratic chairmen because some Republicans serve as ranking minority members on more than one committee.

Committee Seniority

Can variations in committee seniority help to explain these discrepancies? In other words, does the committee seniority requirement exert an independent influence? The seniority system ranks congressmen by consecutive service on the committees. Thus a change of committee reduces a congressman to the bottom rung on the committee ladder. Perhaps some considerable number of congressmen of advanced service in Congress are disqualified for a chairmanship by such a committee change. In all subsequent discussion, a "committee senior" is a "senior" congressman who has stayed on

Table 3-5   Relationship between congressional seniority and committee leadership: House of Representatives 1957–1958, 1963–1964

Congressional Seniority: No. Years Continuous Service	Democrats			Republicans		
	Reps. No.	CC's No.	CC's %	Reps. No.	RMM's No.	RMM's %
			1957–58			
More than 24	9[a]	5	56	7	4	57
20–24	17	4	24	8	4	50
15–19	17	4	24	19	5	26
10–14	42	6	14	41	6	15
5–9	42	0	0	42	0	0
0–4	80	0	0	68	0	0
Total	207	19		185	19	
			1963–64			
More than 24	17[b]	7	41	3	2	67
20–24	24	6	25	9	6	67
15–19	24	5	21	8	4	50
10–14	48	2	4	43	5	12
5–9	36	0	0	22	1	5
0–4	91	0	0	84	0	0
Total	240	20		169	18	

[a]Two of the four representatives who were not chairmen were Speaker Rayburn and Majority Leader McCormack.

[b]One of the ten representatives who were not chairmen was Speaker McCormack.

at least one committee of initial assignment or, if elected before 1946, has stayed on the committee assigned following the Legislative Reorganization Act.

The results varied by congressional party so much that no single answer is possible. But some clarification can be offered.

First of all, changing committees is a sufficiently frequent occurrence to merit attention as a possible major influence on results. This statement holds for three of the four congressional parties—the House Democrats and Republicans—not for the Senate Democrats. Taking all congressmen who began service in or after 1947 and who stayed long enough to be considered "senior" in their congressional party, the percentage of congressmen who changed committees during that time—i.e., did not stay on at least one committee of initial appointment—is as follows:

	% Changing Committees
SD (N = 34)	15
HD (N = 35)	54
SR (N = 25)	40
HR (N = 59)	41

Only among the Senate Democrats, where only 15 percent changed committees, does it seem that "committee hopping" is an infrequent occurrence.

Second, most chairmen and ranking minority members have not changed committees; they have stayed with at least one committee of initial assignment. This may suggest that a committee change seriously hurts one's chances for a top committee post. Again, this is clearly true for three of the congressional parties, somewhat less clearly for the fourth. Investigation of the chairmen and ranking minority members from 1957 on who were "committee seniors" as previously defined—those who did not change committees—showed the following results:

CCs/RMMs	%Who Stayed with Committee of First Assignment
SD (N = 23)	91
HD (N = 27)	93
SR (N = 27)	70
HR (N = 50)	86

Democratic committee leaders in both Senate and House have stayed with their initial assignment almost without exception. In fact, the two House Democrats who switched and still became chairmen chaired only the House Un-American Activities Committee—a committee marked by frequent turnover and low congressional seniority in its chairmen. House Republicans showed a similarly high proportion. Of the seven who switched and still gained a top committee post, three headed the Un-American Activities Committee. Only for the Senate Republicans is the case not so clear, although a still substantial proportion—70 percent—were committee seniors. This congressional party, of course, suffered the most rapid electoral turnover in the predominantly Democratic years under review and showed the shortest length of congressional service necessary to gain top rank. It thus seems likely that, given the smaller membership and more frequent turnover, a Republican Senator could more easily change committee and still qualify after a short time for committee leadership.

The committee seniority requirement can, then, exert an influence of its own—most clearly for House Democrats and Republicans and, wherever the infrequent committee hopping occurred, for the Senate Democrats also. . . . But if, as with congressional seniority, there are *still* more congressmen of advanced congressional service *and* committee seniority than there are committee leadership posts, then one must look outside the seniority system— to the discretion or luck involved in the original committee assignment.

Summary

The findings clearly warn against the danger of letting the congressional party define the operation or effects of the seniority system. The average congressional seniority required to gain top committee rank varies considerably from Senate to House and from Republicans to Democrats. Senators, in fact, need win on the average only two elections to qualify for leadership. Further, by far the greatest number of committee leaders stay a relatively short time in their posts. The median number ranges between five and ten years, with a substantial proportion serving only four years or less. In light of these facts, critics who remark on the fact that chairmen were first elected "a generation ago" need to specify whether they refer to a Senate or House generation, a Democratic or Republican generation. "Seniority" as a concept implying time varies with the party and the house of Congress under discussion.

Second, committee leaders are not so distinctive a breed in advanced congressional service as to preclude a majority of congressmen from a chance at chairmanships. The congressional seniority requirement presupposed by the seniority system does not appear sufficiently restrictive to screen out of the selection process more than a fairly small minority of states and districts. Thus the traditional argument that the system benefits only the safest states and districts may have to be reversed to read that the system penalizes only the most competitive—a reversal in emphasis of considerable importance.

Third, while length of congressional service does influence who becomes a committee leader, a number of exceptions can be noted. Some can be explained by the separate influence of the committee seniority requirement, others merely by the luck or discretion involved in the initial committee assignment. These facts together point to the possibility that sheer length of service in Congress may be less crucial a determinant of committee leadership than many have supposed.

III. The Seniority System and the Congress

It should now be possible to advance further generalizations about the seniority system as a device for selecting leaders in Congress. We shall consider first its effects on the kind of leaders selected; and second, its place in the larger pattern of congressional action.

The Impact of the Seniority System

Perhaps the single most important finding of this study is that the effect of the seniority system on the kind of committee chairmen selected by Congress is at most a limited one. Democratic committee chairmen or ranking minority members, taken as a group, reflect with fair accuracy the composition of the Democratic members in Congress, and the Republican leaders even more accurately reflect their party's membership. Thus Southerners have filled more than 50 percent of the Democratic committee chairs in the past two decades, and Southerners have usually comprised more than 50 percent of the Democratic membership of the House and Senate.

The effect of the seniority system is limited because its requirement of continuous service in House or Senate can be met by a majority of congressmen. The majority of House and Senate seats are safe for the incumbents. Indeed, there are more congressmen qualified by long congressional service for committee chairs than there are chairs to be filled; hence factors other than congressional seniority, such as original committee assignments, and subsequent reassignments, can and do influence the selection of chairmen.

While the seniority system reflects the distribution of members, the reflection may be subject to some distortion. The congressional seniority requirement does screen out the small number of states and districts which switch party frequently. And at times of majority party upsets, the committee leadership may in the short run, be noticeably unrepresentative of Congress as a whole. Thus the increase of Midwestern strength in the congressional Democratic parties since the late 1950's has only recently begun to show up in the geographical redistribution of chairmanships. Because of this time lag, the seniority links congressional leadership not to the party as it is but to the party as it used to be. Actually, the difference is usually not large because of the stability of voting preferences.

The seniority system also provides a magnifying effect: it gives a bonus to the majority faction in the party, whether majorities are reckoned on a basis of North versus South, rural versus urban, or liberal versus conservative. Critics have stressed that the seniority system benefits those kinds of congressmen who have been in office longest. But in practice, the group with the longest tenure has tended also to be the largest and strongest group. The present analysis has shown that the group, geographical or other, with the largest number of members of Congress nearly always turns out to have the largest number of chairmanships (or ranking minority members). The one exception is the overrepresentation of rural districts among House Democrats.

Since the effects of congressional seniority on the selection of chairmen are marginal at most, the seniority system permits considerable variation in the way chairmanships are distributed. Republicans, but not Democrats, exhibit an extremely close fit between leaders and all members of the congressional party. The degree of unrepresentativeness within the parties also varies. This suggests that factors other than length of congressional service, such as patterns of committee assignments and reassignment, might be studied further for their influence on the selection of chairmen.

On the basis of these findings, it may be interesting to reconsider the traditional criticism of the seniority rule.

Basically, there is no evidence that application of this rule results in regional bias. The geographical distribution of the members of Congress is reproduced in the leaders on a regional and even more clearly on a state-by-state basis. Some advantage in Democratic chairmanships accrues to both the South and the West. Congressional seniority can help to explain Southern, but not Western, overrepresentation.

Democratic members from rural districts are overrepresented by committee chairmen and those from all other districts (not merely metropolitan districts) are underrepresented. But this is not true of Republicans. The rural overrepresentation among Democratic chairmen cannot be explained by the congressional seniority requirement, nor fully explained by rural-urban differences in committee changes. While committee seniority appears to play some part in benefiting the rural congressmen, again the luck or discretion involved in original committee assignments may influence the results.

Nor are small states (by population) overrepresented in the Senate. No systematic misrepresentation of states by population is observable for either party.

As to policy stands, Democratic committee chairmen show some conservative bias, and some bias against support for their party or President; Republicans do not. The Republican committee leaders followed almost exactly the same pattern as all Republican members of Congress in roll-call voting. The leaders were no more conservative than the Republican membership. The bias for conservatism and against party and President is found among Northern as well as Southern Democrats. While these effects are traceable in part to the congressional seniority requirement, all stages in the process of selecting chairmen—congressional seniority, original committee assignments, committee changes—appeared to contribute to the conservative cast of the Democratic chairmen.

The Seniority System and the Congress

How does the seniority rule affect the operation of Congress? Congress differs from many other organizations in that it does not control the selection of its own members. Members of Congress are elected by the voters. The seniority rule, then, provides a key organizational link between the party system and Congress and between the members of Congress and its leaders. Under the system, leaders are chosen from among the senior members, those who know well the organization's rules and customs. And they are chosen in a way that reinforces the main areas of strength, the established interests in the majority party in Congress. The process reflects fairly accurately the composition of the party in Congress as it has been formed over time. Where it distorts, it does so by giving the majority faction in the congressional party an increased advantage. It thus reinforces traditional areas of party strength. It helps the political parties to organize the Congress in a way that ensures that established *party* interests and established *congressional* interests will not conflict, and in a way that strengthens them both.

The seniority rule rewards age and continuous service in a body that prides itself on its long traditions and continuity. The average age in Congress is the highest in any major Western legislature.[26] The seniority rule builds a time lag into the selection of leaders of a body well known for other time lags. It gives some slight advantage to intraparty groups and factions in Congress that were already strong, and usually already dominant, in the membership. Hence, when bills are obstructed in committee, there is often reason to believe that if reported out, they would be obstructed on the floor. Graham Barden, foe of federal aid to education, used every obstructionist device available to a chairman and some improvisations of his own to stop aid bills in committee. After Barden's retirement and the elevation of liberal Adam Clayton Powell to the chairmanship of House Education and Labor, aid to education bills were stopped by the Rules Committee or defeated on the floor. The seniority system reflects and reinforces a deeper congressional conservatism.

Moreover, it helps to reinforce the decentralized character of leadership in Congress, which protects the diverse interests of the members and strengthens Congress's independence of the Presidency. Power centralized in the hands of party leaders could be more easily controlled from the outside than power dispersed among many centers. The seniority system helps Congress to defend itself against outside control by preventing lines of influence from forming between Congress and the White House. It strengthens the Congress in its well-known desire to be independent of the Presidency. As Roger Davidson and colleagues remark:

> The influence of Congress is enhanced . . . because seniority leaders represent "immovable" objects with which the executive branch must contend. . . . Many members who are troubled over the decline of Congress take comfort from the belief that, however irksome a chairman may seem to his colleagues, he may be even more so to executive branch officials.[27]

The seniority system clearly strengthens the particularistic, centrifugal tendencies in the Congress. By multiplying centers of power down to the level of committee chairmen, it contributes to the fragmentation of power which frequently makes any attempt to form a governing majority impossible.

Finally, and crucially important in a Congress which is characterized by plural, decentralized leadership and multiple interests, and in which the political process requires the forming and reforming of coalitions, the seniority system offers stability in the distribution of influence. It offers *predictability* concerning who has power in what area. Such predictability would seem a necessary prerequisite for carrying on political business. Thus the seniority system offers something valuable to leaders—both party and committee leaders—and members alike, as well as to interested parties outside Congress.

One of the most intriguing phenomena in the study of political institutions is the way systems perpetuate themselves, create and nourish subsystems that reinforce the parent system. Both leaders and ordinary members of Congress are attached to the seniority system because they profit by the stability, predictability, and maintenance of traditional power alignments which it fosters. And by contributing this stability, predictability, and support of decentralized leadership, the seniority system helps to support the larger congressional system which has produced and is nourishing it.

An exception to these remarks are, of course, the opponents of the system, who constitute a small minority of congressmen, supported by some outsiders. But these opponents seek change. They seek a more centralized distribution of influence in Congress which would be more sensitive to presidential leadership, not tendencies reinforcing decentralization and congressional independence. These opponents clearly seek a different kind of Congress, which, in view of the stable, mutually reinforcing tendencies described above, will not easily be effected. Indeed, the present study suggests that if change *is* to be effected, it will come not through altering the seniority rule or defeating Speakers of the House, but through gradual changes in the membership of Congress, brought about by the voters in elections.

For in one sense, the critics are quite correct. The seniority system is a profoundly conservative institution—not because it biases the kind of leaders selected, but because it reinforces the conservatism already present in Congress.

Notes

[1] Emanuel Celler, "The Seniority Rule in Congress," *Western Political Quarterly,* XIV (March, 1961), 160. See also Ernest S. Griffith, *Congress: Its Contemporary Role* (4th ed., New York, New York University Press, 1967), 31.

[2] Preliminary studies include George Goodwin, "The Seniority System in Congress," *American Political Science Review,* June, 1959, pp. 412–417; Donald R. Matthews, *U.S. Senators and Their World* (New York, Vintage, 1960), pp. 147–175. A work in progress by Milton Cummings, Jr., should be helpful. For the history of the seniority system, see Nelson W. Polsby, Miriam Gallaher, and Barry Spencer Rundquist, "The Growth of the Seniority System in the U.S. House of Representatives," paper presented at the American Political Science Association meeting, September, 1968, Washington, D.C.; and Michael Abram and Joseph Cooper, "The Rise of Seniority in the House of Representatives," *Polity,* Fall, 1968, 52–85.

[3] For a sample of the criticism, see Roland Young, *The American Congress* (New York, Harper, 1958), p. 108; George Galloway, *Congress at the Crossroads* (New York, Crowell, 1946), pp. 127–145; Joseph Clark, *Congress: The Sapless Branch* (rev. ed., New York, Harper & Row, 1964), p. 178; and James MacGregor Burns, *The Deadlock of Democracy* (Englewood Cliffs, N.J., Prentice-Hall, 1963), p. 244. Note also Arthur M. Schlesinger's comment on the difficulties President Kennedy faced with a Congress run by the seniority system: "The legislative process of the New Frontier was thus largely in the hands of aging

men, mostly born in another century, mostly representing rural areas in an urban nation."
A Thousand Days (Boston, Houghton Mifflin, 1965), p. 709.

[4]See for example *Congressional Quarterly Special Report*, April, 1964, p. 18; Matthews, pp. 163–165; James MacGregor Burns, *Congress on Trial* (New York, Harper & Row, 1949), p. 134; Stephen K. Bailey, *The New Congress* (New York, St. Martin's Press, 1966), p. 57.

[5]See for example Burns, *Congress on Trial*, p. 134; Griffith, p. 32; Bailey, p. 57; Douglass Cater, *Power in Washington* (New York, Random House, 1964), pp. 144–160.

[6]Matthews, pp. 163–165; Clark, p. 177; *Congressional Quarterly Special Report*, June 7, 1963, p. 878; *New York Times*, editorial, "The Tyranny of Seniority," July 15, 1966, p. 30.

[7]Galloway, pp. 189, 190; Celler, p. 190; Young, p. 110; Griffith, p. 34; Charles Clapp calls this the congressmen's characteristic defense of the system: ©*The Congressman: His Work as He Sees It* (New York, Harper, 1963), p. 257.

[8]See for example Burns, *Congress on Trial*, pp. 58, 59; and *Congressional Quarterly Weekly Report*, June 7, 1963, pp. 877, 878.

[9]Richard Fenno, Jr., "The Internal Distribution of Influence: The House," in *The Congress and America's Future*, ed. David B. Truman (Englewood Cliffs, N.J., Prentice-Hall, 1965), pp. 52–76.

[10]Clark, *Congress: The Sapless Branch*, pp. 180–181.

[11]The standard sources are V. O. Key, Jr., *Politics, Parties, and Pressure Groups* (5th ed., New York, Crowell, 1964) and "A Theory of Critical Elections," *Journal of Politics*, February, 1955, pp. 3–18; Angus Campbell, Philip E. Converse, Warren E. Miller, and Donald E. Stokes, *The American Voter* (New York, Wiley, 1960), and *Elections and the Political Order* (New York, Wiley, 1966), esp. pp. 125–135.

[12]Barbara Hinckley, "Congressional Elections Research: Some Beginnings," paper presented at the Annual Meeting of the American Political Science Association, New York, September, 1969.

[13]Key, *Politics, Parties, and Pressure Groups*; see also Charles Press, "Voting Statistics and Presidential Coattails," *American Political Science Review*, December, 1958, 1041–1050; "Presidential Coattails and Party Cohesion," *Midwest Journal of Political Science*, November, 1963, pp. 320–325; and Barbara Hinckley, "Interpreting House Midterm Elections: Toward a Measurement of the In-Party's 'Expected' Loss of Seats," *American Political Science Review*, September, 1967, pp. 694–700.

[14]See for example the analysis by Ralph K. Huitt, "The Congressional Committee: A Case Study," *American Political Science Review*, June, 1954, pp. 340–365; and Matthews, pp. 47–67.

[15]George Galloway, *Congress at the Crossroads* (New York, Crowell, 1946), p. 190. See also Richard Bolling, *House Out of Order* (New York, Dutton, 1965), p. 107. This average held fairly constant for each party and chamber throughout the twenty years.

[16]Infrequent exceptions to the overall pattern can be noted: median age of Senate Democrats climbed once into the seventies (1953–54); Senate Republicans dropped into the fifties (1965–66); and House Republicans dropped once into the fifties (1965–66). Each congressman's age was counted for each election.

[17]Cf. George Goodwin, "The Seniority System in Congress," *American Political Science Review*, June, 1959, p. 420; "Chairmen are older . . . although perhaps not as markedly so as is commonly believed."

[18]The mean was found to parallel the median closely. No trends toward shorter or longer initial service were evident through the time period. No significant regional variation was evident.

[19]That the results are not influenced by variations in committee prestige can be shown by the committees where leaders exceeded this average. Among Senate Democrats, committees where leaders won more than two consecutive elections included: Agriculture, Appropriations, Armed Services, Banking and Currency (twice), Judiciary, Labor, Post Office, and Rules (twice). Among House Democrats: Appropriations (twice), Armed

Services, Banking and Currency, Commerce (twice), Interior, Foreign Affairs (twice), Judiciary, Public Works (twice), Rules (twice), Science, Un-American Activities, and Ways and Means (three times). Ways and Means may be the only clear exception.

[20]The mean number of years chairmen served before gaining top rank for each of the six levels of committees (high prestige to low) is as follows: for House Democrats, Rank I committees, 24.3; II, 15.3; III, 18.4; IV, 18.8; V, 10.7; VI, 7.0. For House Republicans, Rank I committees, 19.3; II, 16.0; III, 13.1; IV, 14.2; V, 9.5; VI, 14.4. Warren E. Miller and Donald E. Stokes, *Representation in the American Congress*, forthcoming.

[21]Joseph A. Schlesinger, *Ambition and Politics* (Chicago, Rand McNally, 1966), p. 46.

[22]The eleven major Senate committees and twelve major House committees of the period.

[23]Raymond E. Wolfinger and Joan Heifetz, "Safe Seats, Seniority and Power in Congress," *American Political Science Review,* June, 1965, p. 346; Charles O. Jones, "Interparty Competition for Congressional Seats," *Western Political Quarterly,* September, 1964, pp. 461–476; V.O. Key, Jr., *Politics, Parties, and Political Pressure Groups* (5th ed., New York, Crowell, 1964), pp. 547, 558, 559; Julius Turner, "Primary Elections as the Alternative to Party Competition in 'Safe' Districts," *Journal of Politics,* 1953, pp. 197–199.

[24]For purposes of comparison, the House can be considered on a statewide basis. Only fourteen states did not have at least three senior Representatives,and these were states of small population and thus disadvantaged in the House to start with—except, again, Connecticut.

[25]Actually the Senate totals suggest less "competition" for committee leadership than the House totals do. There were 55 Senate Democratic seniors and 40 committee leaders; 51 Senate Republicans seniors and 46 committee leaders.

[26]For interesting comparative data on age and seniority in the United States, German, British, and French parliaments, see Gerhard Loewenberg, *Parliament in the German Political System* (Ithaca, N.Y., Cornell University Press, 1967), pp. 84–90.

[27]Roger H. Davidson, David M. Kovenock, and Michael K. O'Leary, *Congress in Crisis: Politics and Congressional Reform* (Belmont, Calif., Wadsworth Publishing Co., 1966), p. 101.

Selection 4 Subcommittees:
The Miniature Legislatures of Congress

George Goodwin, Jr.

The autonomy of the standing committees is jealously guarded. Within these standing committees a great variety of relationships exist. At one end of the spectrum there is no subcommittee organization at all, at the other end is a pattern of almost autonomous subcommittees. As one staff member described the latter extreme, "Given an active subcommittee chairman, working in a specialized field with a staff of his own, the parent committee can do no more than change the grammar of a subcommittee report."

Observers have often deplored the proliferation of subcommittees. Their persistence, however, testifies to their convenience and their congeniality to the working habits and purposes of members. When the Legislative Reorganization Act reduced the number and consolidated and rationalized jurisdictions of the standing committees, the average number of subcommittees per committee increased—as might be expected; and the trend has continued upward. In 1945 the total was 180; of these, 106 were in the House, 68 in the Senate, and 6 from joint committees.[1] By 1968 the number had grown by more than one third to a total of 258, of which 139 were in the House, 104 in the Senate and 15 from joint committees.[2] Senator Everett M. Dirksen said in describing the problem this increase has caused for some congressmen:

> I would not dare to say to the people of Illinois that I knew all the things that go on, when I serve on five subcommittees of the Committee on the Judiciary, and on three subcommittees of the Committee on Government Operations. To do so I would really need roller skates to get from one subcommittee to another, without even then knowing entirely everything about every subject matter which is considered by the various committees.[3]

A blanket condemnation of the growth of subcommittees, however, is likely to ignore their uses in a complex world. The cold war and the industrial expansion of the country since the end of World War II have created new problems. National expenditures have doubled and the executive branch has added new departments of Health, Education, and Welfare (1953), Housing and

Urban Development (1966), and Transportation (1966), as well as many other agencies. Congress, too, has reacted to these changes, most visibly by adjusting its subcommittee structure. Senate Banking and Currency, for example, dropped a subcommittee concerned with rent control and created a new one in international finance. House Foreign Affairs divided its subcommittee on the Near East and Africa in two, and Senate Foreign Relations added one on disarmament. Senate Judiciary has added a subcommittee on juvenile delinquency.

Again, some division of committee functions helps solve the ever-present problem of securing a quorum. By dividing up the work, a wisely worked out subcommittee system can also cut down the total amount of time each member is required to spend with the affairs of a given committee, and at the same time allow for a greater degree of specialization. Senator LaFollette commented in 1948: "The essential and important difference between a hodge-podge committee system and an integrated scheme is not in the relative number of subcommittees, but rather in the formalization of fixed and definite jurisdictions Congress."[4]

Further, subcommittees have often "been an outgrowth of internal friction and resentment generated by one-man rule."[5] They can, within limits, allow less senior legislators to gain prestige, to follow their interests, and to exploit their abilities as they could not in a seniority-governed committee system that tolerated no subcommittees. It is significant, for example, that Albert Rains was able to establish a subcommittee on housing of the House Banking and Currency Committee, under the chairmanship of Brent Spence, when all other subcommittees were designated by number and given no clear jurisdiction. Other examples are John E. Moss, Jr.'s subcommittee on governmental information (Government Operations, House) and Henry M. Jackson's policy machinery subcommittee (Government Operations, Senate).

Whether committees are adapting to increasingly difficult times, providing for greater specialization, or giving less senior men a position of greater importance, there comes a point of no return, and it would seem that Senator Dirksen had passed this point when he confessed his inability to keep up with his work load. This is largely a problem of the Senate and not of the House, for there are roughly one-quarter as many members to share in a task equal to that of the House of Representatives. An analysis of the number of subcommittee assignments per member in both houses shows that a representative is likely to have two subcommittee assignments at the most, while a senator is likely to have at least six.

There is a startling variety in the pattern of subcommittee organization. Some committees have no subcommittees at all; others a few, perhaps designated by number only and without clear jurisdiction; and some perform most of their important work in full committee, even though they have a well-defined subcommittee system. In the 90th Congress there were eight House and seven Senate committees that fitted into these categories (see table 4-1).

Table 4-1   Committees that have resisted subcommittee autonomy, 90th Congress

House		Senate	
There are no standing subcommittees			
Rules*		Aeronautical & Space Sciences	
Un-American Activities*		Finance*	
Ways & Means*			
Subcommittees are not given clearly defined jurisdictions			
Armed Services*			
District of Columbia			
Judiciary*			
More than half of the committee's meetings are for the full committee[†]			
House Administration	(70.4%)	Rules and Administration	(88.0%)
Banking & Currency	(54.6%)	Foreign Relations*	(85.6%)
		Agriculture & Forestry*	(75.5%)
		Post Office & Civil Service	(69.3%)
		Commerce*	(52.3%)

*Committee falls in the top half of the most coveted committees list.
†Percentages are from page 65 of the *Final Report* of the Joint Committee on the Organization of Congress (1966). They apply to the 88th Congress but are roughly similar for the 90th.

These committees include some of the most important ones of Congress. Five of the eight House and four of the seven Senate committees fall in the top half of the most coveted committees.

Other committees establish a large number of subcommittees with clear jurisdiction and grant them great autonomy. In its relatively short lifetime, the House Committee on Science and Astronautics has passed through all of these stages. What determines whether or not a committee will subdivide its work?

There is a tendency to form subcommittees when committee work involves a great deal of detail or when it includes a number of distinct subject-matter areas, the more so if the work is technical and noncontroversial, so that it matters less who handles which assignment—no one wants to be left out of a fight that matters to him. The business of the Appropriations and Judiciary Committees involves so much burdensome detail that subcommittees are inevitable, even though some of the work is controversial. The relatively noncontroversial Administration, Interior, and Public Works committees (each a consolidation of a number of different committees brought together under the Legislative Reorganization Act) have such varied tasks to perform that they inevitably work through subcommittees. On the other hand, committees are less likely to subdivide their work if it involves broad policy rather than great detail, or if it does not fall easily into categories that can be assigned to regular subcommittees. The more controversial the work, the less likely there is to be subcommittee autonomy. The activities of the House Committee on Rules (which determines the conditions under which most major legislation reaches the floor) and Un-American Activities (which is primarily an investigating committee) do not lend themselves to subcommittee organization. A somewhat better case could be made for the use of subcommittees on the two revenue-raising committees, yet they generally handle important matters that senior members are reluctant to turn over to subcommittees.[6] Even though the foreign relations committees have carefully organized subcommittee systems for study purposes, the major share of the work is done by the full committee, because of the broad nature of their work.

Beyond limits derived from the character of the committee's assigned tasks, organization reflects to a great extent the nature of the chairman—his personality, his political ideology, and his concept of his role. No recent change of chairmen has illustrated this better than the succession of Adam Clayton Powell of Harlem to the top position on the House Committee on Education and Labor in the 87th Congress. His conservative predecessor, Graham Barden of North Carolina, had succeeded in bottling up many liberal proposals in the eight years of his chairmanship. He formed only those subcommittees made necessary by the varied jurisdiction of this committee, and he saw that they were headed by trusted conservatives, passing over second-ranking Powell in the process. In 1961 Powell brought a burst of activity to the committee that was not expected by some observers, since he had not previously taken his committee work seriously. He followed a novel approach of creating three subcommittees on education and three on labor. Two of these six subcommittees were called "general," two "special," and two "select," but these titles meant nothing. By increasing the number of subcommittees he was able, without depriving existing subcommittee chairmen of their positions, to reach lower down the seniority ladder and provide chairmanships for liberals such as Edith Green, James Roosevelt, and Frank Thompson, Jr., and he channeled controversial social measures to their subcommittees. Carl D. Perkins, who succeeded Powell as chairman in 1967, continued the same pattern.

A conservative chairman usually will not want to see much development of subcommittees, especially if he heads one of the important control committees of Congress. It is significant that neither Senate Finance nor House Ways and Means has subcommittees, though there are logical subdivisions into which the work could be divided.[7] For a conservative chairman, perhaps the next best thing to having no subcommittees is to have numbered subcommittees without specified jurisdiction and to assign bills to them according to their responsiveness to his desires. The subcommittees with vague jurisdictions are all in the House. All have had chairmen of great seniority and two have had predominately conservative chairmen—the Armed Services Committee with Carl Vinson of Georgia and L. Mendel Rivers of South Carolina, and the District of Columbia Committee with John L. MacMillan of South Carolina. Judiciary has maintained numbered subcommittees, though their jurisdictions are fairly clear, out of deference to its chairman, Emanuel Celler, the senior member of the House in the 90th Congress.

Not all chairmen resist the development of subcommittees. Some may subdivide committee work from a desire for greater committee democracy. Clare Engle, when he was chairman of the House Committee on Interior and Insular Affairs, deliberately held his committee with a loose rein. He took a hand in the drawing up of rules that provided for a unique degree of democratic participation in subcommittee activities and a large measure of subcommittee autonomy. Or some chairmen may create subcommittees for some strategic reason. It may be a move to prevent a rebellion on the part of the members, which seems to have been the reason for the creation of some subcommittees on House Education and Labor by Chairman Barden; or it may be a desire to maintain friendly relations with outside groups. Lister Hill, when chairman of the Senate Committee on Labor and Public Welfare, reportedly found it advisable to divest himself of direct contact with the problems of the aging, for he wanted to remain on good terms with the American Medical Association. A subcommittee was created in the 86th Congress to handle this subject and it was given great autonomy. In the 87th Congress it was made a select committee of the Senate and thus divorced entirely from the Labor Committee.

Two other factors play a part in encouraging the creation of subcommittees: the large size of the House, and the desire of outside groups for points of contact in Congress. There is certainly pressure for the establishment of subcommittees in the House, which acts as a counterbalance to the tendency of House chairmen to maintain more centralized control. There are more members looking for something to do and more demands from them for some means of achieving public recognition. Secondly, both nongovernmental pressure groups and governmental agencies find it to their advantage to have subcommittees, preferably with permanent staffs, with which they can work. As an example, both Judiciary subcommittees on immigration have provided a point of contact for interests believing in a restrictive immigration policy. Liberal interests in the field have given strong support to the special Senate Judiciary subcommittee to investigate problems connected with refugees and escapees.

Most subcommittees are organized to handle a specific functional problem of government such as agricultural production, Indian affairs, education, flood control, or disarmament. Some committees, however, have experimented with different types of organization. The House Agriculture Committee, for example, has two sets of subcommittees, one concerned with broad agricultural problems such as farm production, and another with specific agricultural commodities. Some staff members prefer the former as a means of getting committee members to take a broader view of agricultural policy. Committee members themselves seem to prefer the commodity organization as a means of better representing their specific clientele interests.[8] It is significant that the commodity subcommittees usually win when there is a jurisdictional dispute between them and the functional subcommittees.

Both House and Senate Foreign Affairs committees have subcommittees organized on a geographical basis (Europe, Africa, etc.) as well as those organized to handle such problems as disarmament and national security. They are all called consultative subcommittees and they are used primarily as a means of liaison with the Department of State.[9] Legislative proposals are handled by the full committee or by ad hoc subcommittees, though recently the House committee has begun to assign some bills to the consultative subcommittees. This practice may lead to jurisdictional disputes as to whether a matter should be referred to a geographical or a problem subcommittee.

Subcommittee organization in the Senate is rarely identical with that of the parallel House committee. Where their jurisdiction falls into natural sub-divisions, subcommittee organization is more likely to be similar. The Interior committees are examples. They are, incidentally, the only committees to have maintained almost the same subcommittee organization since the 80th Congress. The two committees on Government Operations, on the other hand, have a far more vague jurisdiction, encompassing the entire field of government. Their subcommittees tend to reflect the interests of the chairmen and individual members.[10]

Even though the House and Senate Interior committees have almost identical subcommittee pattern, this fact does not seem to lend impetus to bicameral subcommittee cooperation. In fact, there is very little cooperation between House and Senate subcommittees. A questionnaire sent to all committees produced only four examples of joint subcommittee hearings held in recent years: The District of Columbia committees on tax problems, Government Operations committeeson intergovernmental relations, the Judiciary committees on the Immigration Act of 1952, and the Public Works committees on Niagara power. But six sets of parallel committees reported fairly close staff cooperation along subcommittee lines.[11]

Neither the House nor the Senate maintains any kind of detailed control over subcommittee organization. This may seem surprising, for subcommittee recommendations often become the law of the land without suffering major changes in the full committee or in the entire Congress. It is in keeping, however, with the general pattern of committee autonomy and the lack of any very effective party discipline.

The rules of the House and Senate do specify certain procedures that must be followed by subcommittees. For example, all subcommittee hearings, with certain exceptions, are to be open, and a subcommittee quorum may not be less than one-third of the membership except at a meeting for the purpose of taking testimony.[12]

The parent house has occasionally called for the establishment of specific subcommittees or instructed certain subcommittees to carry out a designated task, but the overwhelming practice is to leave these decisions to the committees.[13] The parent house may also specifically call for a report to be made directly to the floor without the intervening approval of the full committee.[14] Again, however, the overwhelming practice is for the full committee to approve and submit subcommittee reports. The major house control is that of granting additional funds for subcommittee staff and expenses beyond the ten positions (four professional and six clerical) automatically granted each committee by the Legislative Reorganization Act. Committees, however, are rarely denied their requested budgets.

The most effective controls over subcommittees lie clearly in the hands of the individual committees. Whether these controls are exercised by a dominant senior minority of the membership or by a majority of the full committee varies from one committee to the next. There is likely to be a tug of war between the chairman (often joined by other senior members) and the junior members. These newer members may attempt to win greater control because they do not agree with the policies of the senior members, because they are impatient with committee inactivity on a particular topic, or because they seek the publicity that can come from a skillfully timed subcommittee investigation. Chairmen are generally fearful of letting too much power slip into the hands of members. Once a system of subdivision has been established or a subcommittee chairman appointed, a chairman can rarely undo the action, though he may occasionally reorganize subcommittees as a means of decreasing the powers of particular subcommittee chairmen. Many chairmen are painfully aware of the fact that a subcommittee, especially an investigating subcommittee, can capture the limelight and severely limit the freedom of action of the parent committee.[15] Often, but by no means always, chairmen are conservatives, fearful of sharing power with the more liberal junior colleagues. Again, a chairman may hold out against delegating subcommittee powers to individual committee members because he lacks confidence in their competence or readiness to discharge committee duties adequately.

In this struggle, the chairman deals from a stacked deck of cards. He should be able to maintain control even against rank-and-file rebellion, unless he is politically inept. A strong chairman can, in most cases, establish subcommittees, determine their size, appoint the members, establish party ratios, maintain ex officio membership, control the referral of bills, and either assign or hold back staff money for subcommittee operations. In recent years, however, committee members have developed a number of limits on these powers of chairmen.

Common practice allows the chairman primary control over subcommittee structure, though he may well find it advisable to consult with other committee members.[16] As had been pointed out, he may allow no subcommittees, work primarily by means of ad hoc subcommittees, create standing subcommittees but give them numbers and assign them no continuing jurisdiction, or he may establish standing subcommittees with clearly outlined jurisdiction and some degree of autonomy.

Subcommittee members are most commonly designated by the chairman alone, or in consultation with the ranking minority member. Appointments may be designed to punish slackers and enemies and to reward friends. Often senior members will be appointed to more subcommittees than junior members as a means of preventing the newer men from gaining too much control. Membership approval of appointments is not required on a majority of committees. Those interested in limiting the powers of committee chairmen often advocate rules that subcommittee chairmen be chosen on the basis of seniority, thus removing an element of discretion, and hence influence, on the part of chairmen. The House committees on Education and Labor, Interior and Insular Affairs, and Post Office and Civil Service are the only ones with such provisions written into their rules, but the pattern is evidently widely followed. One of the major reasons for this is that senior members are often unwilling to sit under junior subcommittee chairmen in the seniority-concious Congress. In the 90th Congress there were seventeen House committees which had subcommittees, and in nine of these no senior member of the majority party had been by-passed in the choice of subcommittee chairmen. In the Senate, eight of the fourteen subdivided committees followed seniority. Interestingly, in the less party-oriented Senate, two Republicans were allowed subcommittee chairmanships in the Democratically controlled 90th Congress. George D. Aiken was chairman of the Canadian affairs subcommittee of the Committee on Foreign Relations, and Everett M. Dirksen of the federal charters, holidays, and celebrations subcommittee of the Judiciary Committee.[17]

Party ratios on subcommittees may also be controlled by the chairmen, since the full house exercises no control here. The full committee is less likely to reverse the decisions of large subcommittees, especially with a safe majority party margin. Yet under certain circumstances, a small subcommittee can serve a chairman's needs, for he may be helped by absenteeism in the minority party. The ranking Republican member of the House Committee on Armed Services asked, unsuccessfully, at its organization meeting in 1961 that the party ratio on the special investigations subcommittee be raised from 3 to 2 to 4 to 3, so that "at least two members could be present most of the time."[18] Occasional complaints reach the stage of floor debate, as in 1951 when Clare E. Hoffman called for a resolution instructing the chairman of the House Committee on Appropriations to divide subcommittee membership between Democrats and Republicans "in as near as possible the same ratio that exists in the House" instead of using this device to "punish members who voted against his pet idea of the way appropriations bills should be handled."[19] A survey of subcommittee ratios during the 89th Congress when both houses had roughly 2 to 1 party ratios shows little uniformity. Few had ratios less favorable to the minority party than 2 to 1, and the great majority were more favorably divided.

Chairmen and ranking minority members often retain ex officio membership on all subcommittees. While this may not mean that these committee leaders attend regularly, it is another means of exerting control if a need is felt. The rules of ten of the twenty House committees give ex officio membership to both chairmen and ranking minority members, while in the case of Armed Services and Judiciary, only the chairman is made a member. There is no provision for ex officio membership by ranking minority members in the Senate, but the chairman is made a member in five of the sixteen committees.

The less automatic the referral of legislative matters to subcommittees is, the greater are the chairmen's powers. In two House committees in the 90th Congress, for example (Armed Services and District of Columbia), subcommittees had no clear field of jurisdiction and referral was made entirely at the discretion of the chairman. Other committee chairmen have used this device from time to time in the past. Charles Wolverton, Republican chairman of the House Committee on Interstate and Foreign Commerce during the 80th Congress (1947–48) reportedly abolished subcommittee specialization because he was in basic disagreement with some of his senior Republican colleagues. Even the timing of referral can increase the chairman's power. Lister Hill of the Senate Labor and Public Welfare Committee did not refer important legislative matters until he had done careful preparatory groundwork, whereas in many committees, referral is handled by the clerk in routine fashion.

On the other hand, the Education and Labor, Post Office and Civil Service, and Public Works Committees have placed limitations on committee chairmen by spelling out subcommittee jurisdiction in detail and making referral as automatic as possible. Education and Labor's rules are the most detailed, since they were adopted to limit former chairman Powell's ability to delay committee action. The chairman is to notify all subcommittee chairmen of proposed referrals, which are to be made according to defined subcommittee jurisdictions and without regard for the desires of the authors of the measures involved. If, after three days, there are no objections, final referral is made, though this must be done within a week from the day on which the measure was first received. A committee majority has the power to refer a measure at any time.

Chairmen are also in a position to control committee staff assignments. Most prefer to rotate staff members and not have them permanently assigned to a subcommittee. If a subcommittee can obtain its own permanent staff it has taken a major step toward independence from the full committee. In the 90th Congress, seven House and seven Senate committees had assigned permanent staff to at least a majority of their standing committees.

Chairmen can make skillful use of the allocation of funds to subcommittees. A subcommittee appropriation with few strings attached allows great freedom in the hiring of staff and other subcommittee activities. Also, the allocation of travel funds can be used effectively to reward and punish members. At the other extreme, subcommittee chairmen of the Education and Labor Committee won complete control over these funds in the 89th Congress.

Finally, a chairman may, in the case of investigating subcommittees, withhold the subpoena power. Bernard Schwartz, recounting his experiences as staff man for the legislative oversight subcommittee of the House Committee on Interstate and Foreign Commerce, spoke to this point: "If Moulder [the subcommittee chairman] and I were given the subpoena power and the authority to secure a competent loyal staff, we would have obtained the very tools we needed to undertake a thorough probe which no one could control."[20]

Taking all these factors into consideration, which committees are the most centralized and which the least? The Finance Committee is clearly the most centralized committee in the Senate. Its chairmen have fought successfully against expansion of the size and liberalization of the membership of this important committee. Although its jurisdiction is easily divisible into such subject-matter areas as taxation, foreign trade, social security, and veterans' benefits, the committee's chairmen, not wanting to give its members "public forums for the expression of discontent," have never allowed the formation of subcommittees. Its budget has been kept low and its staff limited. Chairman Harry F. Byrd (1955–66) hired only one professional and supplemented his services with the staffs of the Legislative Reference Service and of the Joint Committee on Internal Revenue Taxation, a committee made up of the three top majority and the two top minority members of the Senate Finance and House Ways and Means committees. When Russell B. Long became chairman, he received permission to hire an additional six professional and six clerical staff people, but he had not filled all of these positions by the end of the 90th Congress. Though committee proceedings became more open and more informal under Long, the chairman continued to hold tight reins on the committee.

By most tests, Judiciary Committee Chairman James O. Eastland of Mississippi has run as decentralized a committee as any in the Senate. He has given his senior members great freedom to develop subcommittee autonomy, with the tacit understanding that they would not be too aggressively pro civil rights. Testimony as to this autonomy may be gathered from a comparison of the size of Senate committee staffs. In 1965, when the total staff for each Senate committee averaged 28, Judiciary had 137, with all but 14 employed by twelve subcommittees.[21]

On the House side there have been more examples of chairmen who keep a great deal of power in their own hands, and also more examples of committees that have revolted against the powers of their chairmen. Probably the most centralized committee is Ways and Means, the opposite number of the Senate Finance Committee. Like Finance, the work of Ways and Means lends itself to subcommittee organization, and it was organized along these lines until 1961. Wilbur D. Mills made his reputation as chairman of a subcommittee on internal revenue, but he abolished all subcommittees a short time after he succeeded to the chairmanship of the full committee. The fact that the Democrats on the Ways and Means Committee also act as a committee-on-committees for their party gives the chairman, when Democrats control the House, unique added powers.

At least two House committees, at different times, have experienced extreme decentralization. During Clare Hoffman's chairmanship of Government Operations in the Republicans 83rd Congress, committee members not only mutinied, but even more unusual, the whole affair was discussed at some length on the floor of the House.[22] Hoffman was a lone operator who had few legislative friends and who had alienated President Dwight D. Eisenhower by refusing for a long time to refer to subcommittee executive proposals to establish the Second Hoover Commission and the Commission on Intergovernmental Relations. He made great use of ad hoc subcommittees consisting of two Republicans and one Democrat, appointed minority members without consulting the ranking Democrat on the committee, and evidently, in at least one instance, failed to notify the ranking Democrat of such a subcommittee's creation. Rebellion took place on July 15, 1953, when members voted 23 to 1 (six members abstaining) to prohibit further creation of ad hoc subcommittees save by resolution of the full committee. They further voted to grant virtual autonomy to the five existing standing subcommittees, giving each the power to appoint staff members and to fix their pay, to subpoena witnesses and to hold hearings outside Washington. Throughout that Congress subcommittee chairmen signed their own expense vouchers. Even in defeat, however, Hoffman did maintain his power to refer bills to subcommittees, and to approve the printing of subcommittee hearings and reports, and he used these to harass the rest of the committee members.[23] The Democratic chairman of Government Operations, William L. Dawson, has encountered no rebellion of this sort. His subcommittees have large permanent staffs and sizeable budgets; they issue their own press releases and carry on their own mailing operations. The chairman, however, does maintain considerable quiet control over the creation, assignment of members, and reference of measures to subcommittees. He also maintains a degree of control over committee budget and staff.

In 1965 there was a rebellion against Tom Murray of Tennessee who had served as the chairman of the Post Office and Civil Service Committee since 1949, with the exception of the Republican 83rd Congress. In that liberal 89th Congress, committee members reacted against their chairman's conservative attitude toward government salaries. They adopted committee rules that severely limited his choice of subcommittee chairmen and members, his freedom of referring matters to them, and his control over budget and staff. In the 90th Congress, the rules were modified to give somewhat greater power to the new chairman, Thaddeus J. Dulski, but the committee remained one of the most decentralized in the House.

Conflicting drives for authority between chairmen and less senior members will continue to appear in the subcommittee structure. Subcommittees allow greater specialization in the legislative branch in an era that puts a premium on specialization. They also give a flexibility to the seniority system, by allowing less senior committee members to play effective legislative roles. These facts and the gradual coming to power of younger, more organization-minded chairmen must inevitably cut into the degree of centralized control that was once maintained by such chairmen as Harry Byrd and Carl Vinson.

Notes

[1]Joint Committee on the Organization of Congress, Hearings, *The Organization of Congress*, pursuant to H. Con. Res. 18, 79th Cong., 1st sess., 1945, p. 1039.

[2]*Congressional Quarterly Weekly Report*, April 12, 1968, pp. 754–781.

[3]*Congressional Record*, 83rd Cong., 2nd sess., 1954, p. 1417.

[4]*Legislative Reorganization Act of 1946*, Hearings, 1948, p. 63.

[5]Stewart L. Udall, "A Defense of the Seniority System," *New York Times Magazine*, Jan. 13, 1957, p. 64.

[6]The House Ways and Means Committee has made use of ad hoc subcommittees but has not given them power to recommend legislation to the full committee. Senator Joseph S. Clark has called for the creation of subcommittees on social security and on tax measures within the Finance Committee, claiming that it has "perhaps the most extended and complicated jurisdiction of any of the committees of the Senate" (*Congressional Record*, 88th Cong., 1st sess., 1963, p. 2664).

[7]During the period under consideration in this book the chairmen of the Finance Committee have been: Eugene D. Milliken (R., Colo., 1947–48, 1953–54), Walter F. George (D., Ga., 1949–52), Harry F. Byrd (D., Va., 1955–65), and Russell B. Long (D., La., 1965–68). Ways and Means chairmen have been: Harold Knudsen (R., Minn., 1947–48), Robert L. Doughton (D., N.C., 1949–52), Daniel A. Reed (R., N.Y., 1953–54), Jere Cooper (D., Tenn., 1955–56), and Wilbur D. Mills (D., Ark., 1958–68.)

[8]Jones found that, with three exceptions, members of the House Agriculture Committee in the 85th Congress served on subcommittees that dealt with commodities produced in their districts. See Charles O. Jones, "Representation in Congress: The Case of the House Agriculture Committee," *American Political Science Review* (June 1961): 358.

[9]The activity of these consultative subcommittees varies greatly with each chairman. Senator John F. Kennedy's African affairs subcommittee for example, was largely inactive in 1959 and 1960 because its chairman had more pressing demands on his time.

[10]In the 90th Congress, the House Committee on Government Operations had these subcommittees: executive and legislative reorganization, foreign operations and government information, government activities, intergovernmental relations, legal and monetary affairs, military operations, natural resources and power, research and technical programs, special studies, and donable property. The Senate committee had: executive reorganization, foreign aid expenditures, government research, intergovernmental relations, national security and international operations, and permanent investigations.

[11]Committees on Appropriations, Armed Services, District of Columbia, Foreign Affairs, Judiciary, and Labor.

[12]See section 133 of the Legislative Reorganization Act (Public Law 601, 79th Cong., 2nd sess.); House Rule XI; Senate Rule XXV.

[13]Charles L. Watkins and Floyd M. Riddick, *Senate Procedure* (Washington, D.C.: Government Printing Office, 1958), p. 156; and Asher Hinds and Clarence Cannon, *Precedents of the House*, 11 vols. (Washington, D.C.: Government Printing Office, 1907), 3: sec. 1754.

[14]Watkins and Riddick, *Senate Procedure*, p. 529; and Hinds and Cannon, *Precedents of the House*, 4 sec. 4551.

[15]For a fascinating example of such a situation, see Bernard Schwartz, *The Professor and the Commission* (New York: Alfred A. Knopf, 1959).

[16]The power of a chairman to establish subcommittees have been challenged in the courts on the grounds that a competent tribunal must be created by resolution of the full committee. A Federal Court of Appeals, however, stated that "it is the unvarying practice of the Senate to follow the method of creating and appointing subcommittees which was employed in this instance." See *Meyers v. United States*, 171 Federal Reporter (Second Series) 800 (1948).

[17]Prior to the 84th Congress, the Judiciary Committee had a custom, after a change in party control, of giving the previous chairman of the full committee a subcommittee chairmanship. Senator Alexander Wiley was chairman of patents in the 81st and 82nd Congresses. Senator Pat McCarran was chairman of judicial machinery in the 83rd Congress. Republican J. Glenn Beall served as chairman of the business and commerce subcommittee of District of Columbia from the 84th through the 87th Congresses.

[18]U.S. House of Representatives, Committee on Armed Services, "The Organization of the House Committee on Armed Services," committee print, February 16, 1961, p. 9.

[19]Congressional Record, 82nd Cong., 1st sess., 1951, p. 1174.

[20]Schwartz, The Professor and the Commission, p. 102.

[21]Joint Committee on the Organization of Congress, Hearings, The Organization of Congress, pursuant to S. Con. Res. 2, 89th Cong., 1st sess., 1965, p. 206.

[22]Congressional Record, 83rd Cong., 1st sess., 1953, pp. 9092–97, 9103–9107, 9242–54, 10352–82.

[23]It took great pressure from President Eisenhower to get Chairman Hoffman to refer to subcommittee proposals to establish the Second Hoover Commission and the Commission on Intergovernmental Relations.

Selection 5 House Party Leadership

Robert L. Peabody

Congressional leaders have much in common with the leaders of other large, complex organizations; yet some characteristics of their jobs are unique. Leaders cannot be understood apart from their followers, but few leaders must interact with the diversity of party, region, ideology, and subject-matter specialization characteristic of the members of legislators of modern, industrial nations. All executives must attempt to manage with scarce resources, but legislative leaders seem to operate with an especially limited supply of rewards and sanctions. All leaders confront situational constraints, internal and external, but almost none rivals the breadth and complexity of the environmental pressures imposed upon House and Senate leaders. Moreover, in common with other organizational spokesmen, the successes and failures of congressional leaders must be measured against the objectives which they and their followers set for themselves as well as the expectations of their publics, attentive and inactive.[1]

A number of further characteristics set congressional leaders apart from

From Leadership in Congress: Stability, Succession, and Change by Robert L. Peabody, Chapter 2, pp. 27–65. Copyright © 1976 by Little, Brown and Company (Inc.). Reprinted by permission. Footnotes have been renumbered for this presentation.

almost all other executives of large, complex organizations. First, they are politicians: they have to run for and be reelected to public office.[2] Second, they act as spokesmen for one or the other chamber of the national legislature. Their corporate jurisdictions may be as narrow as a question of elevator patronage or as broad as the possible impeachment of a President. Third, the breadth and complexity of the tasks they must coordinate also set them apart from all other leaders except their counterparts in other nations and the chief executive.

The highest priority tasks of any given Congress are twofold: (1) the representation of the diverse interests of their constituents and the reconciliation of these demands with national interests, and (2) policy making, in part through the checking and balancing of other branches of government, in part through use of their investigatory powers, but, most important, through the introduction, passage, and modification of bills and proposed constitutional amendments.[3] On rare occasions, a subsidiary function of Congress, such as the election of the President in the House of Representatives for lack of a majority in the electoral college or the launching of impeachment proceedings against a President may come to preoccupy its leaders and members.

The Organization of the House: Some Situational Constraints

Members of any large organization are confronted with questions of divisions of authority and of how its leaders and followers should relate to one another.[4] In an organization of any duration such questions are seldom raised explicitly; offices are created, roles are established, traditions take hold. The near 200-year-old House of Representatives is not an exception, although, of course, its organizational complexity reflects its basic nature as a legislature: a body of people who represent diverse interests brought together to decide, and, if necessary, compromise on governmental policy.[5]

To begin, each of the House's 435 members represents a unique congressional district that on the average contains some 475,000 constituents.[6] Of course, only in idealistic terms can it be said that a Representative serves as a spokesman for all his constituents. About one-third of the House districts are consistently dominated by one party, mainly Democratic districts in the big cities and the South and Republican districts in the Midwest. In these places minority interests are likely to have little voice. But even in competitive two-party districts, most Representatives identify with only a portion of the electorate, sometimes barely a majority, but seldom more than two-thirds. That is to say, they are consistently returned to office by margins of from 51 to 70 percent of the two-party vote. It is to this subset of the electorate that a Representative is most alert in terms of access and services rendered. More importantly, Representatives are most closely identified with a cluster of interests in their districts, the people they grew up and went to school with, practiced their professions or worked with in other ways. From this pool come most of the people who work in their campaigns, make financial contributions to it, and who in the process develop or improve upon their access to congressmen. However, as David Truman has noted:[7]

> The politician-legislator is not equivalent to the steel ball in a pinball game, bumping passively from post to post down an inclined plane. He is a human being involved in a variety of relationships with other human beings. In his role as legislator his accessibility to various groups is affected by the whole series of relationships that define him as a person.

In the late 18th century, and throughout most of the 19th century, House members were relatively isolated from their home districts once they arrived in the nation's Capitol. . . .[8] Congressmen's offices today are in almost constant communication with their district constituents. Most members maintain at least one district office. They may make as many as 20 or more trips to their districts in any given session. The expanding population of their districts, the growing constituency casework, the increase in the range and complexity of their legislative burdens—all have produced a need for staff assistance.[9] A congressman is no longer a "one-man band." Each must now head a sizeable staff operation and each is supported by a much larger House bureaucracy. Still, a congressman is a part of a greatly decentralized community; like one of 435 separate fiefdoms, only loosely coordinated and tied together by personal, party, and committee ties.

Obviously, no organizational chart ever fully mirrors the actual lines of authority and responsibility it is supposed to show. The boxes are always too uniform in size, the lines too straight and unbroken. More important, no organizational chart begins to capture the informal lines of communication, the by-passing of formal chains of command, the stress and flux of people interacting. Such ongoing dynamics can never be mapped completely, but figure 5-1 outlines some of the important relationships which characterize the contemporary House of.Representatives.

The Speaker

It is clear from figure 5-1 that the Speakership in the House of Representatives is of central importance. This constitutionally designated officer has as one principal duty the task of presiding over the House. Throughout the decades, by rather steady increments of power at least until 1910, the Speaker has also emerged as the majority party's top leader. The Senate has no counterpart to the Speaker of the House. The closest approximation, the Senate Majority Leader, is not a constitutionally designated officer, is not even mentioned in the Senate Rules *Manual,* and never presides in his own chamber. The Speaker's stature is enhanced further by being second

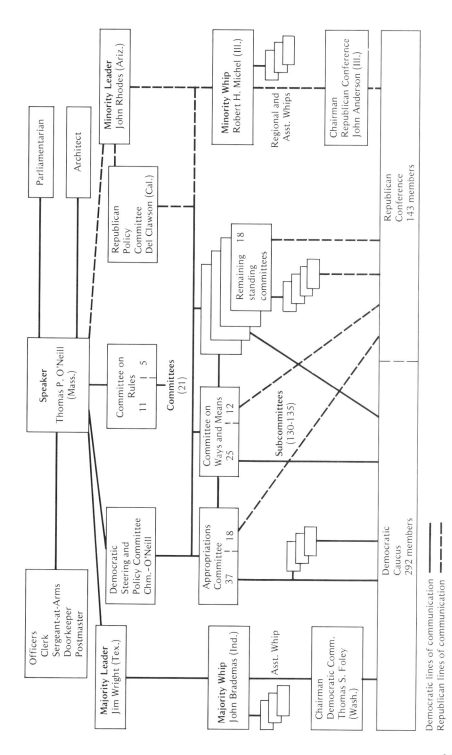

Figure 5-1   U.S. House of Representatives

(behind the Vice President) to succeed to the presidency. . . . But a most unusual set of events, the near simultaneous death, incapacity, or removal from office of both the Vice President and the President, is required before the Speaker succeeds to the presidency. (The President pro tempore of the Senate is third in succession, but his chances of becoming President are even more remote.)

Thirteen men, eight Democrats and five Republicans, have served as Speaker in the 20th century. . . . Lengthy service in the House, a minimum of eight to ten terms, is a basic prerequisite to election to this office. Further, ten of the thirteen 20th-century Speakers, and the nine most recent consecutively, have previously held the office of Majority or Minority Leader. No Speaker has come close to matching Sam Rayburn's record of 17 years' service in this high office. We shall return shortly to an in-depth analysis of the Speaker's pivotal role in the House leadership. But first, brief descriptions of the other principal party offices are in order.

Floor Leaders

The House and Senate have always made use of floor *managers* for different pieces of legislation. Usually, the chairman and ranking minority member of the committee of original jurisdiction also oversee the floor debate, maintain control over time, and have considerable voice about who will speak for or against amendments. From time to time the prime responsibility for floor management is delegated to a subcommittee chairman and, perhaps, his minority party counterpart.

The modern conception of a floor leader as a separate and independent officer charged with overall responsibility for a party's legislative program can be traced back to the period just before World War I. The curbing of Speaker Joseph Cannon in 1910, the increasing importance of party loyalty in Congress, the needs of further organization brought on by the enhanced legislative burden of the war—all contributed to the institutionalization of the floor leader's role. . . .

The Minority Leader has a somewhat longer heritage as an independent officer. Prior to 1883 the identity and role of the Minority Leader remained rather obscure. Since that date, the candidate for Speaker nominated by the minority party has generally assumed the title and function of floor leader. Thomas Reed of Maine, who alternated between Minority Leader and Speaker between 1883 and 1899, did much to give the office stature and to prepare the way for its modern development.

. . . Both parties typically have turned to people in their middle 50s with an average record of 18 years in the House prior to their first selection. Of the fourteen Majority Leaders since 1910, seven became speaker, four gave up the position because their party returned to the minority, two ran for the Senate, and one died.

The position of Minority Leader, reflecting the continuing frustrations of minority status, normally has proven less secure than its majority counterpart. Of the eleven Minority Leaders, two were ousted by their party and a third was denied the Speakership nomination. Only three Minority Leaders have advanced directly to the Speakership in this century. . . .

What preoccupies the time and interests of Majority and Minority Leaders? Their prime responsibility is marshalling their party's forces on the floor, working for majorities on key legislative votes. As is true of the Speaker, leaders seldom intervene in the drafting of legislation or interfere with a committee's initial deliberations. However, once a bill is scheduled for floor debate (agenda setting is closely coordinated through the Speaker), it is their job to see that committee-approved legislation is passed. Much depends, of course, on whether or not the party of the leader is in control of the White House. For Minority Leaders, this crucial fact determines whether their principal preoccupations are given over to bringing about the passage of the President's program, modifying it in part or more severely, or working to defeat the legislation of the opposing party.

All floor leaders, majority or minority, must deal with three broad areas of policy making; (1) internal organization, including relationships with other party and committee leaders and the supervision of their own staff; (2) legislative strategy, both the formulation of policy and its implementation, and (3) external coordination, particularly relationships with the White House and the executive branch, the national party committee, other party leaders, interest groups, the mass media, and in the broadest sense, the American electorate.[10] The three broad areas are intertwined. A congressional leader may be more adept in one area than another; he may spend some days principally preoccupied by problems in one area to the detriment of pressing needs in the other two; but, he cannot afford to ignore any one of the three areas for very long without serious consequences to the effectiveness of his party and the strength of his own leadership.

Party Whips

The whip is third in the House majority party hierarchy, a nominal second in the minority party. Unlike the Speaker and the Majority Leader, however, the Democratic whip is appointive, not elective. Therefore, he is not free to represent his party or pressure its members in the same sense as the top party leaders or even his minority counterpart. The Republican whip is elective. . . .

The tasks of the whip, majority or minority, are essentially twofold: (1)

communication by whip notices to members of the forthcoming legislative agenda; and (2) provision of information by which the party leadership decides whether to bring legislation to the floor, and/or what form amendments should take in order to ensure passage. The whips work through regional or assistant whips, each responsible for a zone of 10-20 members, on the average, in one or more states. When the leader requests, the whip conducts a poll to determine which members are for, leaning for, indifferent to, or against a proposed bill or section of a bill. By personal contact or telephone calls the whip makes a count so the leader has the best possible information to decide whether or not to move ahead, delay, or withdraw proposed legislation. A whip poll sometimes is jammed through in 24 hours or, more leisurely, in two or three days. The quality of the information gained is crucial to legislative floor strategy.[11]

Other Party Offices

Both Democrats and Republicans are organized, initially, in party caucuses or conferences held just before a new Congress convenes. . . . In recent years, both the Democratic Caucus and the Republican Conference have also played a much more regular and active role in hammering out questions of party and committee reorganization, including the reoccurring and vital issue of seniority and the election of committee chairmen and ranking minority members. The chairmen of both the Republican Conference and the Democratic Caucus have emerged as important leaders in their own right in the late 1960's and early 1970's, especially Republicans Gerald Ford (1963–64), Melvin Laird (1965–1968), and John Anderson 1969–), and Democrats Dan Rostenkowski (1967–1970) and Olin Teague (1971–1974).

Both parties in recent years have also reactivated "policy committees" as a means of thrashing out partisan positions on legislative issues and attempting to develop greater party unity. The Republican Policy Committee had a rebirth in 1959 under the initial leadership of John Byrnes (Wisc.). . . . The Democratic Steering Committee, following years of inactivity, has undergone rather sporadic revitalization since 1973, under the Speaker's chairmanship. Both policy committees have between twenty and thirty members with the core membership elected regionally, but bolstered by other party leaders.

. . . [B]oth parties also maintain active congressional campaign committees, called the Democratic National Congressional Committee and the Republican National Congressional Committee. Staffed by from three to ten professionals (Republicans have generally supported larger, better financed staff operations in attempts to overcome their minority status), the chairmen of these rather independently-run committees command considerable stature in their respective parties. It is not difficult to understand why. These senior party leaders oversee the raising of and disbursing of campaign contributions running in the several millions of dollars every two years. During the closing months of the campaign, in particular, they exercise considerable discretion about which members (and, even more important, which potentially incoming freshmen nominees) receive more than the token contributions of $3000 to $5000 dispensed to all incumbents. At least two former Republican campaign committee chairmen (Joseph Martin after 1938, Charles Halleck after 1946) utilized their success in those elections as a springboard to the floor leadership of their party.

The Committee Leaders

. . . [I]t is important to acknowledge other independent reservoirs of power in the House: the chairmen of committees, and to a lesser extent, the ranking minority leaders.[12] Usually, but not exclusively, the chairmen of the most powerful committees . . . have extended their power bases in the House beyond the jurisdictions of their own committees. The chairmen and ranking members of these three exclusive committees are almost always powerful men, especially when they work in tandem. . . .

The sources of committee chairmanship power stem from their control over committee organization resources, such as staff and space, and legislative outcomes. As one House veteran has observed:[13]

> The mortar that binds the system consists largely of what has been called inelegantly but properly "boodle" [the location of military installations, public works projects, the location of a post office, and the like].
>
> The boodle in itself is legitimate and productive. The hitch is in the way it is distributed. . . . The conservative ruling elders maintain their power by determining in large measure which House Members will get the larger portions. Generally, the stay-in-line orthodox Member will come away with the fuller plate.

Sometimes, committee leaders emerge as prospective candidates for top party leadership. . . .

The committee structure of the House, like the leadership structure, is dual in nature. The party which controls the House chooses the chairmen, sets the ratios on committees (by negotiation with the minor party leadership) and generally dominates staffing, funds for investigations, and other housekeeping matters. On the three most prestigious committees of the House—Appropriations, Ways and Means, and Rules—the ratios have traditionally been kept at 3:2, 3:2, and 2:1. However, in times of large Democratic party majorities, such as those of the 89th (1965–1966) and 94th (1975–1976) Congresses, majority party advantages in terms of numbers have been increased. The higher ratio on Rules is dictated by its status as a "leadership committee," charged with scheduling legislation for floor debate. In general, the ratio of Democrats to Republicans on the remaining 18 standing committees fluctuates with the overall House ratio, currently better than 3:2.

The Resources of the Speaker and the Majority Party

"The Speakership is not only an institution, it is an opportunity, in which men of strong character have shown their leadership."[14] So wrote Mary Parker Follett just before the turn of the century as the Speakership was nearing the apex of its formal powers. Thomas B. Reed (R., Me.) was about to be reelected Speaker and shortly to pronounce his famous rulings against "disappearing quorums," and other dilatory tactics of the minority party.[15] The revolt against Speaker Joseph G. Cannon (R., Ill.), stripping him from his chairmanship of the Committee on Rules and his powers of committee assignments, lay less than two decades away.[16] Under Reed and Cannon the formal powers of the Speaker were immeasurably strengthened. Equally important, neither hesitated to use the powers. The arbitrariness of Cannon's personality eventually led to a situation in which for the first, and probably the last, time a heavy-handed rule of the Speaker emerged.

Since the revolution against Cannon in 1910 the problem has been almost the opposite. How can any Speaker make use of his much more limited formal powers to achieve his party's legislative objectives, let alone help Congress maintain a parity with an ever-expanding executive branch? That Speakers like Nicholas Longworth (R., Ohio) and Sam Rayburn (D., Texas) from time to time have operated effectively has been attributed more to their strong personal characters and persuasive abilities rather than to the limited formal powers available to them. What seems to distinguish strong Speakers from the more mediocre ones has been a willingness to use their limited legislative powers to the hilt, at the same time exploiting other more personal forms of influence with skill and subtlety. They must initiate actions without getting too far out in front of a majority of their followers. They must operate with "controlled partisanship." A Speaker must function in two roles almost simultaneously—first, as the neutral presiding officer to protect the rights of *all* members, majority and minority alike, and second, as partisan leader of the majority party to seek ways to advance the party's policy objectives and continued control of the Congress.

Parliamentary Powers

Despite the restrictions of 1910 the formal powers of a Speaker remain considerable. Rule I of the *Rules of the House of Representatives* sets forth most of the Speaker's parliamentary duties; to preside over the House, approve the journal, preserve order and decorum, maintain general control of the House side of the Capitol (including assignment of space), sign all acts and resolutions, put all questions, vote when it would be decisive,[17] and name members to perform the duties of the chair (Speakers pro tempore). Additional rules and precedents of the House provide for the Speaker to administer the oath of office to members, to grant or refuse floor recognition, to count for quorums, to pronounce adjournments, to appoint select committees and the House members of conferences and joint committees, to appoint chairmen of the Committees of the Whole, to control admission to the floor and galleries, and to oversee the official reporters of the House (including committee stenographers and the preparation of the *Congressional Record*). If the House Judiciary Committee should report out a bill of impeachment against a President, the Speaker would preside over the floor debate and final vote.

Legislative Discretion

Many of these powers require, of course, considerable discretion on the part of the Speaker. Although not a free agent in determining who shall have control of the floor (when a particular bill is under consideration, the members of the committee with jurisdiction have priority over non-committee members), the Speaker's right to inquire — "For what purpose does the member rise?" — gives him considerable latitude, especially since there is no appeal from the Speaker's recognition or non-recognition. Speakers have utilized this power on numerous occasions to favor certain individuals, their party's position, or to postpone or block proposals.

The power of recognition frequently enters into the series of discussions which the top leaders have with committee leaders before most major legislative floor debates. The central issues usually concern the compromises to be made, in the form of one or more amendments to different provisions of the pending bill if it is to carry a majority vote on final passage. Once the committee experts have had their say and the leaders have made their strategic judgments (often after the benefit of a whip poll), then the issue is to decide which member of the committee should offer the amendment. Is Southern Democratic support needed? Should Congressman A of Georgia be asked to offer the amendment? If Congressman A proposed the amendment, then the Speaker is alert to recognize him first. The leadership meeting then takes appropriate action to shore up wavering members or to convert those in opposition. The Speaker may immediately begin to telephone key people to gain support for the amendment and the Majority Leader and whips to align support on the floor.

Information

Strategy meetings provide another valuable resource over which the leadership maintains primary control—the House information network. Each congressman has sources of communication, internal and external, but no network is spread so extensively as that of the top leadership. If the White House is controlled by the leaders' party, much information from the executive branch to the Hill is received by the Speaker and the Majority Leader. If the opposing party controls the presidency, then Minority Leaders attend White House leadership briefings on a regular weekly basis. Still, most Presidents involve the majority leadership in at least once-a-month sessions as well as in special meetings called to discuss a particular foreign or domestic crisis. Regardless of who controls the White House, the Speaker and the Majority Leader have far more communication with the executive branch than most committee chairmen or the average senior party member.

Of course, most leadership communication is general rather than specific. Agricultural committee members are in closer and more frequent communication with the Department of Agriculture Assistant Secretaries and congressional liaison people, Education and Labor committee members with their downtown departmental policy makers, and so on. However, the less technical and more politicized the message, the more likely it will filter through the House leadership offices.

Information flows out as well as in. Unlike Senators, the typical House member seldom is asked to appear on the weekly televised talk shows, "Meet the Press," "Face the Nation," and similar network presentations. Such invitations usually are reserved for House leaders. In addition, the Speaker holds a daily five-minute press conference in his office just before the House convenes. . . .

The information that dominates the Speaker's press conference— what's coming up on the floor and when—is eagerly sought by members of Congress since it affects the organization of their own work week. All, of course, on Fridays receive copies of their party's Whip's Notice which details the pending floor action for the coming week.[18] Such a schedule is notoriously unstable, and is likely to come unglued at the drop of a conference report. Only the leaders and their aides are likely to be cognizant of changes and postponements but even they cannot know that a vote scheduled for Wednesday will be delayed until Thursday. While information about scheduling is a lower-level resource compared to *control* over scheduling, it allows congressmen to plan ahead to decide whether they are able to catch a plane home, make that fund-raising dinner in Dubuque, or meet with an important district businessman or labor leader.

Scheduling

Final control over scheduling is almost exclusively a top leadership function shared by the Speaker and Majority Leader working in consultation with the minority leadership. Such control must be maintained to schedule the flow of legislation converging upon them from about twenty different directions— the standing committees of the House.

At the beginning of a session, even after an August recess, the majority leadership top aides systematically call the staff directors or chief counsel of committees to obtain legislation for floor consideration. Prior to vacation recess, before Easter or the 4th of July, and especially as the session comes to its usual frenetic wind-up, the situation is almost reversed. Committee chairmen will be hounding the Speaker, so their bills can be scheduled on the various calendars—Union, House, Consent, Private—or programmed for more extensive floor debate through a special order from the Rules Committee.[19] The ability to help members overcome the gap between the standing committees and the floor is one of the most important resources of power available to the majority leadership.

Appointments

Another resource in the arsenal of a Speaker is his power of appointment. Prior to 1910, the Speaker had exclusive committee assignment powers; since then, control rests with the Committee on Committees of the respective parties. Before reforms initiated in 1973, majority leaders had only *ex officio* status on their own party's Committee on Committees. The 15 Democratic members of the House Ways and Means Committee had control over which committee assignments freshmen members would receive and who could be transferred from a lesser committee to a more prestigious one.[20] Upon the adoption of a resolution in the opening Democratic Caucus, the Speaker, Majority Leader, and chairman of the caucus were placed on the committee, each with a zone and a vote. In reforms consolidated just before the beginning of the 94th Congress, the Democratic Caucus took committee assignment powers away from Ways and Means Committee members and lodged them, instead, with the Democratic Steering and Policy Committee, headed by the Speaker. In addition to influence over regular committee assignments, the Speaker has exclusive power to appoint members of numerous joint, select, and special committees. . . . By use of appointive power, a Speaker can reward the faithful or gain new supporters for legislative purposes.

Exchange

Majority leaders may also make use of a wide range of personal and political favors as a means of further credit-building. Numerous examples illustrate the point:

— The Speaker drops in on a downtown Washington reception a member is holding for some important constituents;
— The Leader opens his office to and spends fifteen minutes conversing with a group of high school students from a member's home town;
— The Speaker makes himself available to advise and counsel a member with domestic problems or another who confronts a tough reelection campaign;
— The Leader sends a telegram to a fund-raising dinner, emphasizing why Congressman X should be returned to Washington; or, more emphatic still, the Leader attends the dinner and makes a speech.

Rarely does a Speaker say to a member, "I did X for you; now, I want you to do Y for me." The process is far more subtle; the emphasis is on general exchange over time rather than explicit *quid-pro-quos.*

Few sanctions are available to the majority leadership other than the *withholding* of such personal, political, and legislative assistance, the refusal to support a committee assignment, the lack of intervention when help is needed. Still, as one member observed, "No one likes to cross the Speaker needlessly. You may need his help the next day or the next week. . . ."

The Resources of the Minority Party

Two obvious points about the resources of the minority party in the House of Representatives are that (1) the minority party is inherently disadvantaged as compared with the majority party in almost every conceivable resource, and (2) for more than four decades, it has been possible to equate the minority party with the Republican party in Congress.[21] Not since the 83rd Congress (1953–1954), the first Eisenhower administration Congress, have the Republicans organized the House and Senate. The only other time since 1930 that the G.O.P. held majorities in either House was the famous 80th Congress (1947–1948), which Democratic President Harry S. Truman incorrectly but effectively labeled a "Do-nothing Congress."[22]

The major resource which a minority party lacks is, of course, votes. Over the past 46 years the Republican party has fallen as low as 89 members in the 75th Congress (1937–1938), averaging about 175 members or 40 percent of the House membership over the 23 Congresses.[23]

Committee chairmen, of course, are selected from the most senior ranks of the majority. The legislative influence of a ranking minority member is highly dependent upon the closeness of his relationship with the chairmen of his committee. By and large the ratios of Democrats to Republicans on the 21 standing committees of the House reflects the overall membership composition. The minority party also is disadvantaged in terms of staff, space, and control over investigatory funds.

At the opening roll call vote of a new Congress, the minority party candidate for Speaker inevitably loses on a party-line vote to the majority candidate, and subsequently serves as the minority floor leader. Almost never will party alignments be so pure throughout the more than 300 roll-call votes in each session of the two-year period. Still, the minority party continually faces an uphill challenge both in committees and on the floor—how can they win enough majority votes to convert their minority position into a winning one? Over the years the Republican minority has been somewhat successful in forging a series of legislative alliances with southern Democrats in what has come to be known as the "conservative coalition." As John Manley concludes:[24]

> . . . [The] Conservative Coalition, born in the 1930's, has persisted as a relatively common and potent voting alliance for forty years. In both chambers, the Coalition was less successful in the late 1950's and in the 1960's than it was earlier, but as the record of the Ninetieth Congress (1967–1968) shows the Coalition was anything but a paper tiger as the 1970's dawned. In that Congress, just prior to Richard Nixon's presidency, the Coalition won 65 percent of Coalition votes in the Senate, and 59 percent in the House. With a Republican in the White House, liberals in Congress feared the worst. And, with exceptions, they got it.

The shortcomings of continued minority status for Republicans in Congress have been partially offset by the election of two contemporary Republican Presidents, Dwight D. Eisenhower (1953–1960) and Richard M. Nixon (1969–1974). In Republican administrations the tasks of Republican Minority Leaders have fluctuated from trying to build majority coalitions for Republican programs or, short of those goals, to working to sustain presidential vetoes of Democratically sponsored legislation. With the strong Democratic gains of the 1974 congressional elections, these tasks were made more difficult, but not impossible. There is no such thing as a "veto-proof" Congress, a reality which President Ford was to exploit.

If the minority party does not enjoy the multiple benefits flowing from executive branch control, three basic alternatives are available: (1) cooperation with the presidential majority, (2) partisan opposition, or (3) promotion of constructive alternatives to administrative proposals. Of course, no party practices one alternative to the exclusion of the others, but through the years different House and Senate leaders have been predominantly identified with a certain policy stance. . . .

Resources of the Minority Leader

A House Minority Leader has none of the parliamentary powers that accrue to the Speaker as presiding officer; the Minority Leader's activities are more comparable to those of the majority floor leader. The only occasion for which a Minority Leader presides over the House is to briefly congratulate his majority opponent who wins the Speakership at the opening of a Congress. Still, in common with the Speaker, a Minority Leader serves as his congressional party's prime external spokesman and principal legislative strategist. In general, similar resources to those of the Majority Leader are available, but are almost always restricted in scope and quality, even when the minority controls the presidency.

Relations, sometimes contentious, more often consultative, are always extensive between the House majority and minority leadership. At the opening of a Congress the two leaderships meet to decide upon the ratio of Democrats to Republicans on the 21 standing committees. This ratio—except in the cases of Appropriations, Rules, and Ways and Means—closely approximates the overall party division of the House of Representatives. The majority leadership retains control over the week-to-week scheduling of legislation, but frequently consults with the minority leadership. When a stalemate occurs or when a compromise is pending, the Minority Leader frequently is seen huddling with his majority counterpart on the floor or up at the Speaker's rostrum. Many parliamentary delaying tactics are available to the minority if the majority attempts to ride roughshod over its opposition. A principal responsibility of the minority leadership is to see that the rights of the minority members are continually protected.

In common with the majority leadership, a Minority Leader has command of an important information network. Some information derives from consultation with the majority leadership. When the President is of the minority party, then the Minority Leader's office becomes the central conduit for assembling and dispensing information about administration legislative programs. The House Minority Leader, accompanied by the whip, the chairmen of the conference and policy committees, and other party officials, attend weekly White House breakfasts to discuss legislative plans and other political matters. After the meetings, usually the floor leaders of the House and Senate appear before the television cameras to brief the waiting press.

A Minority Leader can easily summon a press conference of his own, or he may join with his Senate counterpart to hold monthly television programs. . . . Beyond appearances on such television shows as "Issues and Answers" or "Meet the Press," the Minority Leader has many opportunities to address party fund-raising dinners across the nation or to appear in behalf of his fellow congressmen in their home districts.

Technically, only the Speaker holds the power of appointment in the House. Routinely, however, he accepts those nominated by the Minority

Leader for Republican appointments to the many special, select, and joint committees. Moreover, the Minority Leader serves *ex officio* as chairman of his party's Committee on Committees. Although the Leader has no vote on the committee, his influence often can be persuasive in obtaining a key committee appointment for a loyal supporter.

A Minority Leader can, like his majority party counterparts, avail himself of a wide range of personal and political favors in order to generate a broader base of support among his colleagues. . . . Minority Leaders must take every advantage of positive ways to build credit, since even fewer opportunities to exercise negative sanctions are available to them as compared with their majority counterparts.

Membership Relations and Expectations of Leaders

The typical member comes to Congress, his ego inflated, ready to take on the world. He's just won out over all other competition in a district with over 400,000 people—so why shouldn't his ego be inflated?

As far as the leadership is concerned he figures he could do the job as well as anybody else. But everybody can't be Speaker, so he's willing to let McCormack or Albert or somebody else do it. You have to give up a little bit of power to get the House organized. He's willing to concede that as long as it's the bare minimum.

—Senior staff aide,
House Democratic leadership

Junior members of the House—those with fewer than three or four terms—probably hold the most ambivalent views about party leaders of any members of Congress. Almost by definition these members are the least accommodated, most frustrated and politically uneasy both about their roles in the House and about the uncertainty of their political futures. None of the majority members are likely to have a subcommittee chairmanship as yet (unlike Senate juniors). As a result of higher turnover, Republican members may soon find themselves a little higher in committee ranking, but the frustrations of minority status are hardly compensated by that mobility. Representatives into their second and third terms gain familiarity with committee and floor procedures—if they work at it. But they will lack the seniority that allows rewards in terms of legislative successes. Unless junior minority members inherit a safe seat, they must devote a great deal of time to constituency care with frequent travel to their districts.

It is particularly this junior group of members who are most likely to be critical of the workings of the House and its leadership. And why not? It is the seniority system, compounded by what is perceived primarily as a *status-quo* oriented leadership, which continues to deny them stature or meaningful impact on the legislative process. Some resentment is captured in the comment of a second-term Plains States Democrat in the process of downgrading his party's 1971 majority leadership contest:

> Frankly, I don't give a crap for titles. This whip, Majority Leader crap doesn't interest me. The sooner everybody around here realizes that we're all part of the leadership, the better off we'll be. I don't like all this scheming to get to have some worthless title that isn't worth a damn, anyway.

Paradoxically, it is precisely at this point that the party leadership has greatest control over junior members' careers. Few decisions rival the importance of the committee assignment that a freshman receives in the opening month of a new Congress. Here, and probably with even greater weight on transfers to more prestigious committees, leadership influence can be decisive.

Freshmen members in particular, and early term members in general, seldom have their names linked to major or even secondary legislation—the operations of the seniority system insure against that. To obtain passage of minor legislation, a bill which may nevertheless be highly important to their district, leadership assistance may be crucial at almost every stage. As the late Representative Clem Miller comments:[25]

> . . . This authority to refer bills, to side track them or pigeonhole them through the various calendar devices, is one of the principal power levers of the Speaker. Particularly for lesser legislation (which may be the life-blood of individual congressmen) the chasm between the standing committee and the House floor is bridged with the unchallenged power of the Speaker.

Finally, in the absence of drastic redistricting, a major election tide, or a personal scandal, the vast majority of congressmen are most vulnerable, electorally, at the beginning (and, by definition, the end) of their political careers. The value of a leader's campaign trip to the district ("The nation needs Congressman X"), the impact of a speech at an important fund-raising dinner ("Your contributions are vital to the election of Representative Y"), and even the willingness to spend a few minutes with the member and several of his constituents visiting Washington—all such political favors are likely to mean more to the younger member than the more secure, seasoned veteran.

Which is not to say that the party leadership cannot have an impact on the careers of more experienced members as well. After four or five terms in office, Representatives are coming into some power of their own. If they have not yet transferred to the prestige committees of the House—Ways and Means, Appropriations, or Rules—they are likely to have enough seniority to have secured a subcommittee of their own on their committees of original assignment. Leadership of course, has no direct control over who receives or who is passed over for an important subcommittee post. Here, the power of the chairman largely reigns supreme, although in recent years the various committees have adopted rules to protect their members from arbitrary or capricious actions of chairmen or ranking minority members.[26]

With a chairmanship (and to a lesser degree with a ranking minority position) comes control over legislation, increased opportunities to floor manage bills, enhanced stature and visibility, and in all likelihood, more space and staff. Attendant with some of these responsibilities is the chance for greater interaction with party leaders. By and large, however, the lives of these midcareer members continue to be district- and committee-centered.

What can leadership, majority or minority, do for these Representatives? With increasing frequency these members need leadership support in scheduling and implementing legislation. At this time in their careers (and in some cases even earlier) they have become eligible for the numerous joint committees, special boards, and commissions over which the Speaker (taking into consideration the recommendations of the Minority Leader) has exclusive power of appointment. Some will serve as assistant whips, other will represent their states or regions on campaign or policy committees. In short, many will be climbing the bottom steps of the "establishment" in their respective party hierarchies.

Those House members who make full use of the many advantages of incumbency are likely to carve out or maintain a fairly safe seat after two or three elections. Just about this time, as they reach their mid-40s or early 50s, many arrive at a turning point in their career. They decide whether they wish to try for a governorship, a Senate seat, or resign themselves to a full-time career in the House. . . . If members have maintained physical strength and political fortune has been kind, their late 50s or early 60s, after about eight or ten terms, may at last see them achieve a committee chairmanship. (A member of a minority party can expect to earn a ranking minority position a little earlier, say by age 50–55 and after as few as six or eight terms.)

Most mid-career House members have long since muted any strong feelings they may have about their party leaders. They can take them or leave them.[27] Except in cases of membership in the same delegation or a close friendship, party leaders can no longer effect their significant political choices. Few of these mid-career members will seek transfers to other committees. They usually can arrange for their own trips overseas. They generally are secure in their own districts. The great majority are locked into a career in the House and the long-range pursuit of a committee chairmanship. Only an active minority still explore means to other offices—a governorship, a career in the Senate, their own party leadership. Hopes of becoming a vice-presidential, let alone a presidential, candidate are all but quashed.

One small subset of this experienced, mid-seniority range of House members remains actively interested in House leadership. A few are protégés of the top leadership. . . .

From among the ranks of other, more change-oriented congressmen of mid-seniority has come the impetus for most of the contests for House party leadership as well as the primary thrusts for reform of the Republican conferences in 1965 and 1971 and the Democratic caucuses in 1971 and 1973. Sometimes their successful actions have earned them places in their own party leadership. . . . Attempts to penetrate the established pattern of majority leadership succession by middle-ranking, change-oriented Democratic congressmen . . . have generally been frustrated. . . .

Short of full committee chairmanship, much creative legislative and investigatory work must be done by subcommittee chairmen and ranking minority members. Much of the work is of a bipartisan nature. Under a weak or failing chairman, a collegial leadership of subcommittee chairmen frequently emerges. Usually the House leadership does not intervene in either committee leadership or legislative matters until the concern becomes exceedingly visible . . . or their own presidential leadership asks them to intervene. . . .

Committee Leaders and Party Leaders

. . . [T]he House leadership and their minority counterparts float in delicate and fluctuating relationships with their some twenty-one committee chairmen and ranking minority members. . . . [One] widely held view of committee leadership [is] that the leadership exists to support the committee product, that its job is to take a committee bill as a given and shepherd it through, protecting it from amendments from either side of the aisle.[28] Conversely, many ranking committee members seem to see that the job of their leadership is to help them substitute their own version of a bill, to modify unwise legislation or, indeed, to subvert it altogether through a motion to recommit.

. . . [A]nother dimension [is] what ranking minority members and committee chairmen, alike, expect in their own leadership, namely, fairness, ease of access, and openness in dealing with members of their own party. And, of course, committee minority spokesmen were particularly dependent upon fair and impartial rulings from the Speaker and his selections of seasoned Democrats to preside over the legislative deliberations in the Committee of the Whole. . . .

Several additional factors should be kept in mind in analyzing the relationships of party leaders and committee leaders, majority and minority. First, committee leaders see themselves as the substantive and technical experts; they only begrudgingly acknowledge that party leaders might excel them in techniques of floor strategy or in a commitment to broader party and national objectives. They take pride in being considered as specialists; they are reluctant to accord too much of a legislative role for the prime generalists in the House, the party leaders. . . .

A chairman, whose primary task is to bring but two or three major bills before the House in a given session, is naturally going to feel that only he and his closest committee associates are competent to know the contents of the bill and how to manage its progression through the Congress. A senior Southern Democrat talks about what is required to manage a bill on the floor (and incidentally, the limited help one could expect from the leadership).

> [First] you have to know what you're doing . . . what the implications of given pieces of the legislation are.
>
> Second, you keep your promises . . . Other members have to know that if you say something, you mean it, that there will be a follow-up on the promises you make.
>
> Third, you have to put out for the House. You can't go in half-way. Personal persuasion can be important. You can't count on the whip system to count the votes for you or for the leadership. You have to know yourself where the votes are. . . .
>
> Fourth, you have to have a feel or sense for what is going on at the moment. . . . The only way to do this was to circulate, get behind the rail, pick up the complaints and feelings of the members.

This member was typically given a free rein by the leadership when he brought a bill from his subcommittee on the floor. His more conservative chairman was not always so generous with support. For example, he would refuse to relinquish control over debate time or strategy on acceptance or rejection of amendments. A former Speaker amplifies:

> What's critical for the Speaker is how you work with the committee chairman. Some of them are great and you don't have to worry about them—Wilbur Mills, for example. But some of the others are not so smart, and I have to help them out.

"Helping out" can take a variety of forms—scheduling the legislation on an appropriate day and week, assisting in the drafting and implementation of amendments, talking to other members on behalf of the bill, coming into the well to make the rare, partisan speech in favor of the legislation.

Party leaders and committee leaders are prone to share a number of common background characteristics. If Democratic, they are likely to come from one of the two power axes of the party—northern big city districts or a southern and border base.[29] If Republican, the probability is high that both leaders and ranking members share a midwestern background.

Another common factor that tends to unite committee leaders and party leaders is the consistent "safeness" of their seats—longevity in office is essential to obtain both types of positions. Still, the relative length of service of committee chairmen as compared to the principal party leaders may ease or complicate the legislative tasks of the latter. The twenty-one chairmen in the

93rd Congress averaged 66 years in age; collectively they represented more than 600 years of service or an average of 14.3 terms in office. Almost half had served longer than the Speaker's twenty-seven years in the House; all but five chairmen had been in Congress longer than the Majority Leader (first elected in 1952).[30] "The crucial factor," observed one aspiring leader, "is whether or not they were chairmen before the Speaker became elected. His relations are almost always easier with those who became chairmen after him. . . ."

The Republican House leaders in the early 1970's by contrast have a much more advantageous relationship with their ranking minority leaders, at least in terms of comparative length of service. As a result of the higher turnover in ranking Republicans between the 92d and 93d Congresses, only one Republican outranked Minority Leader Gerald Ford in seniority; that member was Leslie Arends, the minority whip. Only four colleagues of John Rhodes of Arizona had greater seniority than he, the unanimous choice of the House Republican Conference to succeed Ford as Minority Leader in December 1973. Ranking minority members were both younger and far less senior than their Democratic counterparts. They averaged 59 years in age (as compared to 66) and had served about six fewer terms (8.4 as compared to 14.3) than Democratic chairmen.[31]

The relationship of ranking minority committee members to their leadership may be both more autonomous and less stressful than its counterpart in the majority party. Unlike the chairmen, ranking minority members do not have the prime responsibility for bringing bills to the floor. They may, however, play a stronger role as the sponsor of legislation which is being promoted by a President of their own party. If they wish to become effective legislators the main path lies through formation of a partnership with their chairman. Their satellite life is not without its frustrations:

> Our time is not our own. We're in the minority and the chairman of the committee makes the decision as to when the committee will meet. I can't go to [the chairman] and ask for a postponement when he calls one. It's a different kind of relationship, one you have to get used to.

For not a few ranking minority members their relationships with their chairmen may become more important than their ties with their own leadership. . . .

What clearly distinguishes the relationship of majority party leaders and committee chairmen is that the latter regard the former as their *peers*, not their superiors. It is for this reason that even as powerful a Speaker as Rayburn would observe: "You cannot lead people by trying to drive them. Persuasion and reason are the only ways to lead them. In that way the Speaker has influence and power in the house."[32]

Party leaders in the House of Representatives, majority and minority, operate under considerable situational constraints, especially the independence of members, the decentralized nature of the party and committee structure, and the limited personal, positional, and political resources available to them. Still, some party leaders are more successful than others both in terms of survival and the accomplishment of individual and collective objectives. . . .

Notes

[1]This chapter takes as its organizing themes those outlined in Cecil Gibb's essay on "Leadership: Psychological Aspects" in the *International Encyclopedia of the Social Sciences*, Vol. 9 (New York: Macmillan, 1968), p. 91:

> Definition of the simplest unit of analysis in leadership as the "act of leading" has led to the identification of our basic elements in the relationship: (1) the *leader*, with his "resources relevant to goal attainment . . ."; (2) the *followers*, who also have relevant abilities, personality characteristics, and resources; (3) the *situation* within which the relationship occurs; and (4) the *task* with which the interacting individuals are confronted.

[2]The President of the United States, of course, shares this risk and the unique perspective it provides. See Richard E. Neustadt's discussion of "The Common Stakes of Elective Politicians," in David B. Truman, ed., *The Congress and America's Future* (Englewood Cliffs, N.J.: Prentice-Hall 1965), p. 116–120.

[3]In his definitive analysis of *The Growth of American Law*, James W. Hurst sets forth a fourfold classification of primary legislative functions: (1) the determination of general community policy, embodied in rules, principles, or standards to govern dealings among the people or between them and the government; (2) the creation of specific executive, administrative, and judicial machinery, and the scrutiny of its operation; (3) the performance of a middleman's role between particular constituents and the executive or administrative agencies; and (4) the investigation of facts of social interest. (Boston: Little, Brown, 1950), p. 70.

[4]Harry Eckstein, "Authority Patterns: A Structural Basis for Political Inquiry," *Am. Pol. Sci. Rev.* 67 (1973), 1142–1161; Robert L. Peabody, *Organizational Authority* (New York: Atherton, 1964).

[5]"For organizations which are composed of delegated representatives of conflicting interests, whether their basis be in ideal causes, in power, or in economic advantage, may at least in external form be collegial bodies. What goes on within the body is then a process of adjustment of these conflicts of interest by compromise." Max Weber, *The Theory of Social and Economic Organization*, ed. by Talcott Parsons (Glencoe, Ill.: Free Press, 1947), p. 396.

[6]Under Article I, Section 2 and Amendment XIV, Section 2, Representatives are "apportioned among the several states . . . according to their respective numbers. . . ." Following each decennial census Representatives are reapportioned among the several states. Thus, the size of a state delegation may range from one Representative (Alaska, Delaware, Nevada, North Dakota, Vermont, and Wyoming) to as large as California's 43 members.

[7]David B. Truman, *The Governmental Process* (New York: Knopf, 1951), pp. 332–333.

[8]James S. Young, *The Washington Community. 1800–1828* (New York: Columbia University Press, 1966).

[9]Susan Webb Hammond, "Personal Staffs of Members of the U.S. House of Representatives," Ph.D dissertation, John Hopkins University, 1973.

[10]Randall B. Ripley discusses six major legislative functions performed by House leaders: "(1) organizing the party, (2) scheduling the business of the House, (3) promoting attendance of

members for important votes on the floor, (4) distributing and collecting information, (5) persuading members to act in accord with wishes, and (6) maintaining liaison with the President and his top advisors." *Party Leaders in the House of Representatives* (Washington, D.C.: Brookings Institution, 1967), pp. 54–80 at p. 54.

[11]Randall B. Ripley, "The Party Whip Organizations in the United States House of Representatives," *Am. Pol. Sci. Rev.* 58 (1964), 561–576.

[12]Richard Bolling, *House Out of Order* (New York: Dutton, 1965), esp. ch. 4; Neil MacNeil, *Forge of Democracy: The House of Representatives* (New York: McKay, 1963), esp. ch. 7.

[13]Bolling, *op. cit.*, p. 109.

[14]M. P. Follett, *The Speaker of the House of Representatives* (New York: Longmans, Green, 1896), p. 64.

[15]Samuel W. McCall, *The Life of Thomas Brackett Reed* (Boston: Houghton Mifflin, 1914), ch. 13.

[16]L. White Busbey, *Uncle Joe Cannon* (New York: Holt, 1927), ch. 12; Charles R. Atkinson, *The Committee on Rules and the Overthrow of Speaker Cannon* (New York: Columbia University Press, 1911).

[17]The Speaker may vote to make a tie and so decide a question in the negative or vote to break a tie and thus decide a question in the affirmative. Rule I, Section 6, *Constitution, Jefferson's Manual and Rules of the House of Representatives*, Lewis Deschler, Parliamentarian, 91st Congress, 2d Sess., House Document 439 (Washington, D.C.: U.S. Government Printing Office, 1971), p. 315.

[18]Somewhat paradoxically, the original Whip's Notice is *prepared* in the Office of the Majority Leader. The minority party essentially duplicates the majority version.

[19]For discussion of the uses of the various House Calendars, see Lewis A. Froman, Jr., *The Congressional Process: Strategies, Rules, and Procedures* (Boston: Little, Brown, 1967), pp. 43–52.

[20]The House Republican Committee on Committees, in contrast, is composed of one Representative from each state with Republican members in the House. Power is concentrated in the large states, since each member, save for recent class representatives, has as many votes as there are members in his delegation. Nicholas A. Masters, "Committee Assignments in the House of Representatives," *Am. Pol. Sci. Rev.* 55 (1961), 345–357; David W. Rohde and Kenneth A. Shepsle, "Democratic Committee Assignments in the House of Representatives: Strategic Aspects of a Social Choice Process," *Am. Pol. Sci. Rev.* 67 (1973), 889–905.

[21]For the definitive treatment of these problems, see Charles O. Jones, *Party and Policy-Making: The House Republican Policy Committee* (New Brunswick, N.J.: Rutgers University Press, 1964); and Jones, *The Minority Party in Congress* (Boston: Little, Brown, 1970).

[22]The 80th Congress was to pass such important measures as the Marshall Plan, the consolidation of the armed services into a single Defense Department, the Taft-Hartley Act, rent control, and tax reduction. Randall B. Ripley, *Majority Party Leadership in Congress* (Boston: Little, Brown, 1969), pp. 149–150.

[23]*Congress and the Nation*, Vol. III (Washington, D.C.: Congressional Quarterly, 1973), p. 30.

[24]John F. Manley, "The Conservative Coalition in Congress," *Am. Behav. Sci.* 17 (1973), pp. 223–247 at p. 239.

[25]Clem Miller, *Member of the House*, ed. by John W. Baker (New York: Scribner's, 1962), p. 44.

[26]Norman J. Ornstein, "Causes and Consequences of Congressional Change: Subcommittee Reforms in the House of Representatives, 1970–73," paper prepared for delivery at the 1973 APSA annual meetings, New Orleans, September 7, 1973; David W. Rohde, "Committee Reform in the House of Representatives and the Subcommittee Bill of Rights," *The Annals of the Am. Acad. Pol. & Soc. Sci.*, ed. Norman J. Ornstein, 441 (1974), pp. 39–47.

[27]A Western Democrat approaching high-ranking positions on two committees after five terms in

the House comments: "You only want two things in a leader; first, someone who will see you, and second, understand your problems. Other than that there's not much they can do for you or against you."

[28]John W. Kingdon's research generally confirms the earlier findings of David B. Truman and Donald R. Matthews that party leadership tends to vote with their ranking members of the committee reporting the bill under consideration, *Congressmen's Voting Decisions* (New York: Harper & Row, 1973), ch. 4; Truman, *The Congressional Party* (New York: Wiley, 1959), pp. 237–244; Matthews, *U.S. Senators and Their World* (Chapel Hill: University of North Carolina Press, 1960), p. 126. Of course, there is always the problem of ascertaining who goes along with whom. The Democratic party leadership was clearly dominant in terms of floor strategy in most of the some dozen meetings held with committee leaders that I was privileged to attend during the summer of 1965.

[29]The 92d Congress is fairly representative: The Democratic leaders came from Oklahoma; New Orleans, La; Cambridge, Mass.; and Texas. Nine chairmen came from southern or border states; four more from big-city districts. Of the three Republican leaders one came from Michigan and two from Illinois. Eleven of the ranking minority members came from midwestern states, including six from Ohio alone.

[30]Compiled from *Congressional Quarterly Weekly Reports* 31 (January 6, 1973, April 28, 1973), 16–26, 973–991.

[31]*Ibid.*

[32]*New York Times,* November 17, 1961, p. 28.

Selection 6 Conditions for Party Leadership

Lewis A. Froman, Jr.
Randall B. Ripley

Political power in Congress, all observers agree, is highly decentralized. The factors chiefly responsible for this are also well known: weak national parties (in the Congress this results in strong constituency ties and weak leadership sanctions over members) and a highly developed division of labor through the committee system. A leadership endowed with few opportunities to punish and reward, coupled with specialization by policy area, inevitably produces an institution with numerous and disparate centers of power. Just as inevitably the politics of such an institution is compounded of persuasion, bargaining, and logrolling.[1]

Reprinted from *The American Political Science Review* 59 (1965), pp. 52–63, by permission of the authors and publisher.

As weak as the legislative parties are, however, they still provide the major organizing force in Congress. Roll-call vote analyses have demonstrated this,[2] and a recent study of the House Whip organizations also bears it out.[3] Generally speaking, the single most important variable explaining legislative outcomes is party organization.

The extent of party leadership on the thousands of bills and resolutions which come before Congress each year, nevertheless, is itself variable. Julius Turner has provided us with documentation of this point for the inter-war years.[4] We still sense this variability in leadership control over issues when contrasting the legislative process surrounding such bills as civil rights and poverty.

An appropriate question to ask, therefore, and one heretofore left mostly unanswered, is: under what conditions is party leadership likely to be relatively strong, or relatively weak? Turner has taught us a part of the answer: party control is likely to vary with issues. Class issues generate the sharpest differences between the parties; moral and "neutral" (in the sense of not redistributing wealth) issues cut across them. But the nature of the issue is only part of the story. Even within certain classes of issues party control is likely to vary from one specific issue to the next. Even on the same issue, leadership control is likely to vary from stage to stage in the legislative process. To these consideration this paper is addressed.

Background for the Study

The data which will be brought to bear upon the question of variability of party leadership control will be a mixture of objective measures (such as roll-call votes) and more casual empiricism. All the data, however, will refer to the Democrats in the United States House of Representatives when in the majority and with a Democratic President.

The identity of the leaders in the House is for the most part institutionally established. Among House Democrats the Speaker, Majority Leader, and, to a lesser extent, the Whip are undeniably leaders in virtually all that goes on legislatively in the House. On specific pieces of legislation relevant committee and subcommittee chairmen and senior members of committees and subcommittees may also become leaders.

Conditions are sets of circumstances of two major types: those which promote and those which hinder outcomes desired by the House Democratic leaders. Six conditions have been selected for analysis. A few obvious ones, however, were purposely excluded. One is the relationship of committee chairmen to the leadership. Another is the character and personality of the leaders themselves. Most students of Congress would argue, for example, that even though any set of leaders operates within rather definite institutional boundaries, it makes a difference in legislative outcomes whether there is a forceful and dynamic personality (such as Lyndon Johnson) at the helm, or a more mild, less aggressive personality (such as Mike Mansfield). One of the differences in styles, for example, seems to be that Mansfield has an uncanny knack of cooperating with the enemy and being firm and unyielding with his friends. Hence, when trouble is brewing in the Senate it is often between Mansfield and those with whose position he is usually sympathetic. Lyndon Johnson's style, on the other hand, was to be cooperative when it paid to be cooperative, and firm when it paid to be firm, regarding almost everyone as antagonists (and hence almost everyone as friends).

The conditions we will discuss, then, will not be exhaustive. But they are important and help to provide a picture of the institutional restraints under which leaders operate. Although the conditions are not, themselves, entirely outside the control of the leaders, they are, for the most part, "givens" in the political system of Congress. This paper is an exploration of the limits on leadership in the majority party in the House of Representatives.

First Condition: Leadership Commitment, Knowledge, and Activity

First, success in leadership is likely to vary with the extent to which the leaders themselves are in agreement. It is a rare occasion when the Speaker, Majority Leader, and Whip are not one hundred percent behind a presidential program,[5] but it happens more often that an important committee member, even the chairman, does not support the President's request. A number of instances come to mind. It was long and widely felt, for example, that until Wilbur Mills, chairman of the Ways and Means Committee, supported some version of the President's medicare bill, no program of the type the President sought would be enacted. So influential is Mills in his own committee that he was able effectively to shunt aside the top-priority program until after the 1961 election returns transformed the situation. Otto Passman provides another example. A consistent opponent of foreign aid legislation, this chairman of the Appropriations Subcommittee handling funds for that purpose succeeded in cutting the Administration's program drastically, until early 1964 when he encountered a new full committee chairman who was more sympathetic with the President's wishes. We can say, then, that the more united the leadership behind a program, the greater the likelihood the program will win.

Beyond this rather obvious point, however, leadership commitment is crucial in other ways. Leaders, like other members, have a limited number of resources which they can devote to any given bill. In the Eighty-eighth Congress two of the most complete commitments were made on the cotton bill in December, 1963, and on the wheat-cotton bill in April, 1964. On these bills the leaders worked long and hard and won narrow victories both times. We may contrast with these the role of the leadership in the defeat suffered by the Administration in March, 1964, on a bill to authorize a United States contribution to the International Development Association. The bill was scheduled in a haphazard fashion at the last minute. No whip poll was started until it was too late to be useful. The Treasury, a partner in this venture with AID, was not even brought in to help lobby for the bill. These factors, along with the unpopularity of the chairman of the committee from which the bill came, helped defeat it. The latter element, however, was not decisive, as was shown two months later when the same bill was brought up again and passed by a comfortable margin, after a careful whip poll and considerably more work by the leadership. We can say, then, that the greater the leadership's commitment of its scarce resources, the greater the chances of success.

Even when the leadership is fully committed to a bill, however, there are limits on what it can do. This problem can be explored in part by reference to data stemming from the polls conducted by the Office of the Democratic Whip in the House. The bills on which these polls are conducted represent nearly all of the legislation on which the leadership is fully committed.[6] The polls sought to ascertain how every Democrat would cast his vote on the pending legislation.[7]

An effective limit on the results which the leadership can produce even when fully committed is the pattern of reliability among the membership as revealed by the whip polls. This determines, in part, the knowledge of the leaders about the members. That is, if the members report honestly through the whip organization then the leadership can quickly identify weak spots and concentrate their persuasive efforts on those spots. On the other hand, if reporting is not accurate, a good deal of effort can be wasted on members who are either hopelessly lost or already won. An analysis of the 1963 whip polls, compared with the final roll-calls on the issues on which the polls had been taken, offers some evidence on patterns of reliability among House Democrats.

Ten polls were taken during 1963.[8] The leadership won nine of the roll-calls that followed, losing only on the Area Redevelopment Act amendments in June. On each of these ten votes the Democratic Whip's Office attempted to ascertain how 256 Democratic members (excluding the Speaker) would vote. The Whip's Office was successful 90.5 percent of the time in ascertaining exactly whether a member would be present and, if so, how he would vote. In 242 cases, 9.5 percent of all votes, the Whip's Office did not have the correct information on the individual's behavior before he actually voted. These 242 cases deserve further analysis, for clues to patterns of reliability.

The leadership in 1963 always knew how 123 Democrats would vote. One hundred thirty-three (52 percent) of the Democratic members surprised the leadership one or more times.[9] Table 6-1 shows the distribution of these surprises.

Table 6-1 Frequency distribution of House Democratic voting contrary to whip poll report and leadership expectation on 10 issues, 1963

Number of Times Voting Contrary to Report	Number of Members
6	2
5	1
4	7
3	19
2	36
1	68
0	123
	256*

*Total Democratic membership, except the Speaker.

Who were more reliable and who were less? Table 6-2 shows the average Presidential Support and Presidential Opposition Scores of the members, according to their degrees of reliability, as well as their Leadership Support and Leadership Opposition Scores.[10]

Table 6-2 Presidential and leadership support and opposition scores for House Democrats by category of reliability on 10 whip polls, 1963

Number of Times Reported Inaccurately on Whip Poll	Pres. Support Score	Pres. Opposition Score	Leadership Support Score	Leadership Opposition Score
	(%)	(%)	(%)	(%)
6	59.0	36.5	65.0	35.0
5	63.0	31.0	70.0	30.0
4	59.1	26.0	58.6	32.9
3	53.8	29.5	50.5	35.8
2	57.8	26.3	58.3	31.1
1	71.3	15.2	75.7	17.1
0	82.2	5.1	94.4	1.8
Average	72	14	80	14

Evidently, members who were reported inaccurately two times or more exhibited little difference in average support and opposition scores. Those inaccurately reported only once were considerably more consistent in their party support and those who were never reported inaccurately were the most loyal of all.

Table 6-3 shows the regional breakdown by category of reliability. Southern Democrats were over-represented increasingly in categories containing larger numbers of inaccurate reports. Except for the few members in the most unreliable categories, Western Democrats were represented roughly in accordance with their numbers in all of the other categories. Northern Democrats were relatively under-represented in all categories except the one reflecting complete accuracy and reliability.[11]

Table 6-3   Regional distribution of House Democrats by category of reliability on 10 whip polls, 1963

Number of Times Reported Inaccurately on Whip Poll	Percent of All House Democrats		
	Southern (N=95) 37%	Western (N=59) 23%	Northern (N=102) 40%
	(%)	(%)	(%)
6	100.0	0	0
5	100.0	0	0
4	71.4	14.3	14.3
3	79.0	21.0	0
2	58.4	19.4	22.2
1	44.1	26.5	29.4
0	17.1	22.7	60.2

Table 6-4 demonstrates that the members most consistently opposing the leadership were more predictable and were reported more reliably and more accurately than the members who had a moderate record of support and opposition. That is, those most difficult to report prior to an actual vote tended to be ideologically uncommitted members who wavered from vote to vote with their perceptions of how much loyalty to the Democratic program their constituencies would tolerate. Table 6-4 shows the average Presidential Opposition Score of the fifty-one Democrats (one in five) who in 1963 had an Opposition score higher than 25.[12] The concentration of the most consistent Democratic opponents of the President came in categories of fairly great reliability—especially among those where only one or two mistakes were made.

Table 6-4   Distribution of strong House Democratic presidential opponents by category of reliability on whip polls, 1963

Number of Times Reported Inaccurately on Whip Polls	No. of All Democrats	No. of Strong Opponents	Percent of Strong Opponents in Category	Av. Pres. Opp. Score of Strong Opponents
6	2	2	100.0	36.5
5	1	1	100.0	31.0
4	7	5	71.4	30.2
3	19	13	68.5	38.2
2	36	14	39.0	47.2
1	68	14	20.6	49.5
0	123	2	1.6	26.0

Perhaps the most important conclusion to be drawn from this table is that the strongest opponents of the leadership can be identified and reported accurately, if the leadership wishes it. The most consistent opponents' reports can be taken at face value, if time is limited and can be devoted to only a few members. Identifying the unreliables is an economical first step for the leadership in efforts to persuade them to vote in the desired direction.

We can say, then, that the activity of leadership is limited by a ten percent unreliability in the whip polls on bills to which the leadership is fully committed, and that the unreliables in 1963 consisted predominantly of uncommitted Southern Democrats.

Once the waverers are known, how successful is the leadership in lining up votes? This question is difficult to answer by more than speculation. Data obtained on four issues in 1963, however, support some tentative conclusions. These data are of two kinds—lists of doubtful Democrats whose support for specific legislation was earnestly solicited by the Speaker and lists of those Democrats who were willing to give the Speaker a pledge to vote with him if he absolutely needed them. The four bills were those enlarging the Rules Committee permanently, in January 1963, and those involving the national debt limit in May, August and November, 1963.[13]

These data show that the Speaker seriously endeavored to change the votes of about twenty Democrats on each of the roll calls. He received varying answers from them, ranging from flat refusals to all-out promises of support. On each of the debt-limit bills he was successful in getting about eight to ten "pocket" or reserve votes, which he could call upon if absolutely needed. The members he approached were generally from the South or from the Border States, with a few lukewarm Administration supporters from the North included. They were not bitter opponents of the Administration but rather members who wanted to support the Administration when they felt their consciences and their constituencies would allow it. The Speaker did not always approach the same men. Between 35 and 40 percent of those contacted on any one impending vote were also contacted on at least one of the other four votes; or putting it the other way around, the majority on each vote was approached directly by the Speaker only on that one vote of the four.

Nor did the Speaker seem to press the same people too often for "pocket" vote commitments. Only three members gave more than one pocket vote to the Speaker on these four roll calls. These men, two Southerners and one from a border state, were among the most unreliable on the whip polls and had records of somewhat greater than average opposition to the Administration. But, apparently their feelings of party loyalty prompted them to cooperate with the party leadership when possible, or else they hoped for some future favor from the Senate in exchange.

The polls help to identify waverers, then; and when the leadership so desires it can probably change, at the minimum, ten votes. On the cotton bill in December, 1963, for example—a bill which engendered more than a usual amount of opposition—the Speaker seems to have changed as many as 40 votes in the effort to pass the bill. The cotton bill was the first major piece of legislation to come to the House under President Johnson, and the leadership was exceptionally anxious to win.

Second Condition: Procedural vs. Substantive Issues

We have already seen that party cleavages are likely to vary with issues. From the data now to be reported, it appears that party cohesion on roll-call votes depends also on whether the issue is procedural or substantive.

Most votes, of course, involve both procedural and substantive questions. Even a motion to adjourn can sometimes be partly a substantive issue, if the motion is directed at postponing action on a bill. For example, a few months before House consideration of the Civil Rights Bill in 1964 the Republicans attempted to bring the bill up for floor consideration under the procedure of Calendar Wednesday. Carl Albert immediately moved to adjourn, a motion that carried along party lines. This was a procedural motion contaminated by substantive considerations. Only at the extremes are issues either purely procedural or purely and identifiably substantive. Other motions may be viewed as on a continuum between the extremes.

The hypothesis offered here is that the Democratic leadership can count on total cohesion among Democrats in the House on the most procedural issue—the election of the Speaker—and relatively low cohesion on the votes that are most specifically and narrowly substantive—those on conference reports and on specific amendments to legislation. But in between these three categories lie at least four other types of votes which present various "mixes " of substance and procedure.

The first of the four mixed categories we have labeled "miscellaneous procedure." This includes maneuvers by the majority leader, minority leader, leaders of disgruntled blocs, and even unhappy individuals, to stall in order to prevent certain substantive actions from being taken or to affect their timing. Some of these procedural motions result merely from pique.[14] Others can be important in determining the fate of legislation, as the Calendar Wednesday adjournment example has already suggested. The second of the mixed categories comprises roll calls on rules granted by the Rules Committee for the consideration of legislation. The third category is recommittal motions— procedural motions that are almost wholly substantive in intent. Finally, there are roll calls on final passage.

The data on these seven categories of roll-call votes for the years 1961, 1962, and 1963 are presented in table 6-5. Similar data for the Republicans are also included for contrast. All roll calls taken during these three sessions are included in this analysis except those on which there were less than ten

Table 6-5 Party cohesion on all contested House roll calls, by category, 1961–1963*

Category	1961	Rank	1962	Rank	1963	Rank	Average	Rank
	(%)		(%)		(%)		(%)	
Democrats								
Election of Speaker	100.0	1	100.0	1	100.0	1	100.0	1
Rules	83.7	4	90.2	2	94.0	2	90.6	2
Misc. procedure	81.2	5	83.3	5	89.2	3	84.5	4
Final passage	84.3	3	85.9	3	85.6	5	85.2	3
Recommittal motions	86.9	2	85.6	4	80.9	6	84.1	5
Conference reports	77.2	7	82.2	6	89.2	4	82.6	6
Amendments	77.4	6	73.6	7	79.8	7	76.6	7
Republicans								
Election of Speaker	100.0	1	100.0	1	100.0	1	100.0	1
Rules	80.0	4	75.7	7	79.0	6	77.9	6
Misc. procedure	91.8	2	87.2	2	97.6	2	91.9	2
Final passage	77.9	5	77.1	4	78.8	7	78.0	5
Recommittal motions	87.7	3	85.4	3	89.9	3	87.8	3
Conference reports	76.1	6	77.0	5	81.8	5	78.1	4
Amendments	72.5	7	75.9	6	89.0	4	77.7	7

*"Contested roll calls" are those with more than ten dissenting votes. The figures in this table represent the percentage of Democrats and the percentage of Republicans voting alike on the roll calls analyzed.

dissenters. Thus, "hurrah" roll calls on matters involving defense and communism—which are taken merely for the purpose of establishing an almost unanimous record of support—are excluded because they involve no party leadership. These few exclusions leave about 100 roll-call votes per session to be examined for these three years.[15]

Analysis of the data in table 6-5 yields both findings and problems— problems because the rank order of party cohesion varied somewhat from year to year. This in itself, however, is a finding of some consequence. For the House Democrats, for example, we find cohesion on the election of the Speaker and on final passage remaining about constant, while on more nearly procedural questions of the "mixed" varieties (miscellaneous procedure, adoption of rules and conference reports) it was increasing, on recommittal motions decreasing, and on amendments low but somewhat variable. In a *post hoc* fashion we can interpret this to mean that over the course of the first three years of the new Democratic Administration the Democrats were able to increase cohesion on procedural questions.

Generally, however, the data bear out our expectations. Taking the average for the three years, as one moves from procedural to narrowly substantive questions, cohesion decreases. Election of the Speaker, adoption of rules, and miscellaneous procedures are generally the highest in cohesion, with final passage, recommittal motions, conference reports, and amendments following in descending order.

Contrasts with the Republicans are also instructive. Generally speaking, substantive alternatives proposed by the Democrats enlist higher degrees of Democratic cohesion. Thus on adoption of rules, final passage, and conference reports, Democrats obtain higher cohesion than Republicans. On the other hand, on Republican proposals of substantive alternatives to Democratic measures, and on miscellaneous procedures, we find Republicans cohering better than Democrats. Thus on recommittal motions (almost always proposed by Republicans, often with instructions incorporating a different program), and amendments (usually making the bill more "conservative") Republicans have higher rates of cohesion. This can be partly explained very simply, we feel, by looking at which party is leading at the particular time. Rules, final passage, and conference reports are motions of the majority party. Recommittal motions and, to a lesser extent, amendments, are motions of the minority party. Generally we can conclude that defections in either party are more likely to occur on motions sponsored by the opposition. On motions sponsored by their own party, defections are less likely to occur. These results may also be partly explained by a selective bias underlying the cohesion scores in roll calls demanded by the minority. The minority leadership may not press for a record vote on motions it offers or sponsors unless the prospects are good that the minority members will make a respectable showing of cohesion, or that the majority forces will be vulnerable to a split, or both.

Successes by the Democratic leadership, then, vary with the substantive nature of the issue. The more substantive the issue, the harder the leadership must work to be successful.

Third Condition: Visibility of the Issue

The effects of party leadership may also vary with the visibility of the specific matter under consideration. In general we hypothesize that as an issue becomes more visible to the general public, the chances decrease that the leadership will have its way with the members of the party. This is grounded on the proposition that the influence of party can be relatively great in the absence of contrary pressures. Most members want to support the party. It is only when party pressures run contrary to other pressures that defections are likely to occur. We would expect other pressures to increase as the visibility of the issue increases.

The major qualification that needs to be made is that the President obviously chooses to make some issues more visible than others by including them in his legislative program. He hopes that public opinion will eventually be mobilized behind these proposals and make Congressional passage easier. Whether an issue is part of the President's program or not is probably the single most important factor in determining visibility. The tax cut, civil rights, poverty, education, and other such major bills are visible because the President makes them visible. We are suggesting, however, that inside the House the popular opinion factor does not generally work to the leadership's advantage. Unless there is an overwhelming national consensus on some important proposal (and this is rare) members of the House tend to be timid about voting for something that is both controversial and highly visible. Thus the difficulty of the leadership's task is increased by greater visibility.

A second important factor in determining visibility of issues, a factor which may be independent of Presidential support, is press coverage. For example, although the proposed prayer amendment and the attempts to restrict the jurisdiction of the Supreme Court in apportionment cases were not part of the President's program, nor on the list of things that he talked about, they gained wide currency as important issues, primarily because of their nature, but also because of extended press coverage. It is worth remarking, in this respect, the way in which newspapers attempt to foment conflict. Numerous times during both the prayer amendment hearings and the reapportionment question newspapermen would gather around the important figures (such as Emanuel Celler, chairman of the House Judiciary Committee, Judge Howard W. Smith, chairman of the Committee on Rules, and others), and attempt to get them to take positions, state them strongly, and then carry these statements to opposing leaders and so "manufacture" a personal as well as an issue conflict.[16]

Another factor affecting the visibility of an issue is its complexity. Generally speaking simple issues are more visible than complex ones. One of the strategies, therefore, of those opposed to a bill is to oversimplify the issue or dramatize a single feature of it that will be understandable to the general public. A good example of this was the recent passage of a pay raise for appointed executive officials, civil servants, judges, congressional staff, and congressmen. Only a very small portion of the pay raise bill involved congressional salaries. Yet press coverage and public understanding of the issue tended to focus on this one item to the exclusion of all others. This tended to make that aspect of the bill quite visible and aided the opponents of a pay raise. Of course, the tactic of oversimplification may on occasion be available to a bill's sponsors, too; but ordinarily they carry the broader burden of explaining and justifying it in all its complexity. It is enough for the opponents to find and exploit one visible objection.

Another good example of a superficially simple and visible issue is that of keeping a limit on the national debt. This issue was voted on five times in 1962, 1963, and 1964, three times in 1963 alone. Although the issue is often characterized as "phony," the Democratic leadership had to labor very hard for passage. Making the issue simple and visible tends to work against the leadership and for the opponents.

The leadership can usually do little to control the visibility of an issue. If it strongly wants a bill, that will automatically make it visible. If the bill is part of the President's program it will by its very nature become visible. The leadership can then attempt to make the issue seem complex. In general, however, increasing the visibility of an issue is a potent weapon in the arsenal of those who oppose the leadership.[17]

Fourth Condition: Visibility of the Action

House procedures guarantee that every major piece of legislation will pass through numerous stages which vary in their visibility to the voting public, the press, the political leaders at home, and even to other members of the House. The hypothesis here is that the Democratic leadership will ordinarily have a greater chance of convincing the "followership" to act in the desired manner on matters that require less visible rather than more visible actions.

The rationale for this hypothesis is similar to the preceding one. Generally speaking, party loyalty is a strong bond. Members prefer, when possible, to go along with the party rather than court the disapproval of leadership. This is not simply a reward and punishment mechanism, primarily because the leadership has few rewards and punishments. It is also a state of mind. To invoke loyalty to the party is a strong sanction in itself.

Although party loyalty is a strong bond, in any given situation it is not necessarily the strongest. For most Southerners, for example, to vote for the civil rights bill is courting disaster at home. However, during the Judiciary Committee's deliberations on the civil rights bill in 1963 one Southerner found himself able to vote with the party leadership in committee at a crucial stage, although he later opposed the bill on the floor. What we are suggesting here is that party loyalty will vary with the visibility of the action which the party leadership expects.

The types of action about which the leaders might make specific requests are numerous. The most visible type of action is voting. But the only fully visible kind of voting is roll-call voting on final passage of measures. Roll calls on most recommittal motions are somewhat less visible because the electorate, at least, is likely to have difficulty in understanding what is involved in such a vote. Roll calls on specific amendments and on procedural questions usually attract much less attention, being interim moves. The other types of voting (usually in Committee of the Whole)—teller, division, and voice—are still less visible. The possible options for a member who does not wish to vote at all—giving a live pair, giving a regular pair on a legislative question, or purposely absenting himself with no indication of position, as well as promising the Speaker to change a vote if needed—have very low degrees of visibility. Voting in Committee, which often goes unreported, is another largely invisible activity open to leadership requests. Finally, speaking and not speaking on the floor, as well as the general line of argument to be taken there, are less visible activities subject to the requests of the leadership.

The Democratic leaders have to worry most consistently about losing substantial numbers of Democrats on the roll-call votes on recommittal motions and final passage of fairly major pieces of legislation. The reason why recommittal motions may rank relatively high in visibility is that they often carry instructions to the Committee to report back immediately a lesser bill. Conservative Democrats can thereby get credit for voting for legislation, but for a more modest program than desired by the leadership. Occasionally, the recommittal vote will become the most important House vote on a bill. The two most recent notable examples came in 1962 on the Republican motion to recommit the Trade Expansion bill with instructions simply to continue the existing reciprocal trade program for another year, and in 1963 on the Republican motion to recommit the tax bill and tie the $11 billion tax cut to reduced governmental spending.[18]

On some important votes Democratic leaders can count on a higher level of party support on the recommittal motion than on final passage. This was true, for example, of the 1964 votes on the poverty program. Even members unwilling to vote for final passage will try to retain the good will of the leadership on some recommittal motions.

Division and voice voting, because they happen so quickly, and because few members may be on the floor, or know the nature of the choice being made, are very often simply party votes. Many members scurry from the cloakrooms to the floor to vote in support of their party's side, as defined at the moment by the majority and minority floor managers from the substantive committee in charge of the bill. In informal discussions on the floor overheard by both authors, all that many members wanted to know was the position which the floor manager (usually the committee or subcommittee chairman) was taking.

Teller voting, because it takes longer (and makes it easier therefore to identify members as they queue up to vote), and because members are notified by the bell system, is subject to more strenuous efforts by the leadership to keep members in line. More members are likely to vote on teller votes, and a surprisingly large number of reversals of voice and division votes occurs because the leadership has the time to call members to the floor. These exertions are rewarded by a substantial amount of party unity on most teller votes even by members who, if forced to a roll call, would vote against the Democratic leadership.

In August, 1963, the leadership lost two relatively important teller votes on the foreign aid authorization bill. Rather than risk a rout, the leadership adjourned the House and worked much of the evening and next morning in making sure that sufficient numbers of Democrats willing to vote with the leadership would be present for the resumption of the amending process. The leadership also persuaded many Southern members who did not like the aid programs at least to avoid voting on the teller votes.[19] Similarly, on the Food Surplus bill in August, 1964, the House actually reversed itself on a number of teller votes after an intervening day in which a highly influential member was requested to, and did, change his vote. Again, in early April, 1964, the Democratic leadership held a solid party front against Republican efforts to amend by tellers a bill establishing a permanent food-stamp plan. Even when the Republicans attempted to inject the race question into the amending process the Southerners held firm. They could act with the party if they so chose because their votes would not be known at home.[20]

At times the teller votes of specific members can serve as the cues for the voting of other members. In April, 1963, for example, when the Republicans tried to insert a "Powell-type amendment" requiring non-discrimination as a prerequisite for participating in a program of loans and grants for medical and dental education, the Democratic leaders were successful in getting four of the five Negro Democrats in the House (all except Powell) to vote against the amendment on a teller vote. This made it much easier to keep other Northern, liberal Democrats with the leadership.

The success of the leadership in getting members purposely to absent themselves from the House floor varies with visibility of the action. It is rare when more than two or three Democrats can be persuaded deliberately to miss a final roll call. (Although it did happen, for example, on the second pay bill in 1964—in this case a whole committee, made up largely of opponents of the pay bill, was convinced of the wisdom of taking a trip at that particular time.) But it is not unusual for four to eight members to be so persuaded on a recommittal motion, and for many more to disappear during teller votes.

In the relatively less visible activity of speaking (or not speaking) on legislation on the floor, the leadership can control in part even some of the most recalcitrant members, as well as more moderate "mavericks" from the party position. In December, 1963, the leadership was instrumental in persuading one of the senior Southern Democrats on the Agriculture Committee (and an ultra-conservative) to keep quiet during the debate on the cotton bill because they feared his personal unpopularity in the House would jeopardize the bill (he had planned to speak in favor of the bill). In the fight to defeat the Republican recommittal motion on the 1963 tax bill the leadership was able to persuade George Mahon, then second-ranking on the Appropriations Committee and a highly respected Southerner with a moderate-to-conservative voting record, to speak against the Republican motion. This occurred shortly after the then chairman of the Appropriations Committee, Clarence Cannon, had double-crossed the leadership and spoken for the Republican motion despite an earlier commitment to Wilbur Mills to speak against it. The fact that Mahon spoke, and made such an effective argument, is credited with convincing a sufficient number of wavering Democrats to help carry the vote.

In summary, then, the less visible the action, the better the leadership's chances of holding the line against defectors. More visible actions can more easily become contaminated by other pressures which reduce the chances for leadership success.

Fifth Condition: Constituency Pressures

Perhaps the most important single factor which helps to explain why a member deviates from positions taken by the party leadership is the kind of constituency he represents. Members like to vote with the party, to be sure, but they also wish to be re-elected. For some members, on some issues, voting against the party leadership is perceived as a necessary step to re-election.

For a general measure of the extent of party bolting on roll-call votes, we may start with the 58 roll-calls in the House in 1963 in which a majority of Democrats opposed a majority of Republicans. On these votes, the average Democrat in the House supported his party 73 percent of the time, and opposed the party leadership 13 percent of the time; absenteeism, in its various forms, accounts for the remaining 14 percent. The average, however, does not tell the story; individual members varied widely in the degree of support they gave their party. For example, eight Democrats (mostly from the North) supported the party leadership at least 98 percent of the time, while five Democrats (all from the South) opposed the party leadership at least 65 percent of the time.[21]

Constituency influences show up in characteristic regional and ideological cleavages that result in many departures from the party leadership's line. For example, in 1961 Northern Democrats supported the party 92.7 percent of the time on a series of ten roll-call votes having to do with extending a larger federal role, while Southern Democrats supported these same issues, on the average, only 50.4 percent of the time.[22] A number of demographic factors, more specific to each constituency, such as percentage of owner-occupied dwelling units, percentage of non-white population, and percentage of urban population, also relate to roll-call votes and help to explain deviations from party voting.[23] The well-known affinity among conservatives on both sides of the aisle is a further manifestation of constituency influences working against party leadership. For example, of the 58 roll-call votes in 1963 mentioned above, notwithstanding that a majority of Democrats voted against a majority of Republicans, the Democrats won only 47 and lost 11. Out of the eleven lost, eight were lost to the so-called "conservative coalition" (a majority of Republicans and a majority of Southern Democrats voting against a majority of Northern Democrats).

Although the Southern wing of the Democratic party is the most troublesome area for the leadership (and is, as we saw in discussing the Whip polls earlier, well represented among those whom the leadership must aggressively pursue), a significant number of Northern Democrats also, from time to time, bolt the party position. Sometimes this is because they see their constituents as overwhelmingly opposed to the party position. Sometimes they are probably right in this, and sometimes, to their own peril, they are probably incorrect. For example, Congressman John Lesinski, from a relatively blue-collar district in Wayne County, Michigan, was the only Northern Democratic to vote against the Civil Rights Bill; he apprehended that the so-called "white-backlash" might be severe in his district. Congressman Dingell, also a Democrat from the same area, voted for the Civil Rights Bill. As it turned out, the Republican legislature in Michigan reapportioned the state's congressional districts in such a way as to throw Lesinski and Dingell into the same district in the succeeding Democratic primary. Ninety percent of the new district, however, came from Lesinski's former district. In the primary Dingell won handily. Although it is hazardous to attribute defeat to a single issue, a plausible argument can certainly be made that Lesinski seriously over-estimated the amount of white-backlash in his district.

We can say, then, that constituency factors, however useful they may be in accounting for inter-party differences, also help to differentiate among members within the Democratic party, and so to explain deviations from party leadership positions. And, since party representation in the House stems from state and local organizations, whenever a member pleads that his district will not allow him to go along with the leadership, the argument is usually understood and accepted. Constituency factors, therefore, are a powerful force in conditioning the extent of party leadership among the House Democrats.

Sixth Condition: The Activity of State Delegations

We have lately begun to learn more about the function of state delegations as informal groups in Congressional politics — and hence legislation. Alan Fiellin and John Kessel, for example, sketch out the informal relationships among members of the New York and Washington congressional delegations respectively.[24] Fiellin suggests that informal groups such as state delegations are the principal socializing agencies for the members and provide them with important cues. David Truman, on the basis of an investigation of 23 state delegations, concluded that

> the delegation thus tends to constitute a communication structure whose repeated use results in a heightened consensus and similarity of voting among its members. In short, the state party delegation in the House may be a significant alternative cue-giving mechanism within the legislative party, especially on matters whose political implications are ambiguous. Uncertainty is misery and misery loves company.[25]

One of the implications of this generalization is that state delegations provide important protective mechanisms whereby members of the same state delegation, when voting on an issue ambiguously related to their districts, can partially explain their vote, especially if they perceive their district sentiment incorrectly, as a matter important for the state. "After all," a member might say, "every congressman from this state voted that way."

The support or opposition of state delegations can be of significant help or a hindrance to the leadership. A number of examples will help to illustrate this point.

The first pay bill in 1964 contained a provision for a $10,000 increase in congressional salaries. This bill, on a roll-call vote, went down to defeat in March. The pay bill was again brought up in June with only slight changes, the most significant of which cut the increase to congressmen to $7,500. The California Democratic delegation caucused three times during this interim and voted, in each case unanimously, to oppose the bill unless it retained the original $10,000 raise. Since the California delegation is so large, and since the bill was defeated even with its support in March, to lose the California Democrats on the second bill would be a serious blow to the leadership. A compromise was worked out, however, assuring the delegation that every effort would be made to get the Senate to support a $10,000 pay increase: then the conference might accept the Senate figure. A good deal of time and effort on the part of the leadership was expended in these sets of negotiations.

Another example of the crucial activity of a state delegation occurred just before the voting on the poverty bill, early in 1964. The North Carolina delegation exacted as its price for support of the program a promise from the Administration that Adam Yarmolinsky would not be appointed to help run it. Yarmolinsky, an able and liberal-minded lawyer who had been borrowed from the Defense Department for the purpose, had been one of the President's main lieutenants in working out the details of the program. For a number of reasons, however—mainly having to do with his activity in helping to integrate southern military installations—he was not acceptable to a number of Southerners in general, and to the North Carolina delegation in particular. After the leadership promised that Yarmolinsky would not be appointed, the delegation gave its support to the program.

Much of the discussion within state delegations does not take place in formal caucus. Members from the same state tend to sit near one another on the floor, to travel together, eat together, etc. Moreover, in a situation where the natural inclination of the majority of a delegation would be to oppose the leadership on a particular piece of legislation, the delegation will not generally caucus unless its leaders think there is a chance that they will derive an advantage by voting with the House leadership after exacting some concession. On the 1962 tax bill, for instance, activity within three southern delegations was crucial in changing a possible Administration defeat into victory. One of these same delegations caucused on the farm bills (feed grains) in both 1962 and 1963 and as a result gave the leadership 75 percent of its votes, whereas the normal pattern was for only 12 percent to 50 percent of the delegation to support the leadership on most important issues.

At the other end of the spectrum are delegations that almost always support the leadership. They generally do not caucus unless they suspect a substantial feeling among them against the leadership position. The activity of the California delegation on the pay bill just discussed is a good example.

Aside, then, from the usual informal communication and cue-giving which state delegations provide for their members, they are also important as bargainers because in numbers lie strength. If the members of a large delegation can all agree on a position, and all agree on what they are willing to settle for, they may be able to get their price from the leadership in return for their support.

Summary and Conclusions

We have attempted to explore six factors which are likely to influence the success of House Democratic Party leadership: (1) leadership commitment, knowledge, and activity; (2) the nature of issues (procedural vs. substantive); (3) visibility of the issue; (4) visibility of the action; (5) constituency pressures; and (6) the activity of state delegations.

Generally, we have concluded that leadership victories are more likely to occur when (1) leadership activity is high; (2) the issue is more procedural and less substantive; (3) the visibility of the issue is low; (4) the visibility of the action is low; (5) there is little counter pressure from the constituencies; and (6) state delegations are not engaged in collective bargaining for specific demands.

Each of these conditions may range widely from high to low. The number of combinations, therefore, is potentially quite large. And as one moves along the continuum from high to low (or low to high as the case may be), it becomes increasingly more difficult for the leadership to prevail.

For analytical purposes we have considered each factor in isolation. It is not to be supposed, however, that each operates independently of the others. It is appropriate to conclude, therefore, with a few observations about their interrelationships.

The most important of these is that leadership activity is a counterweight to the other five factors: it is integrative, while the rest are divisive. Accordingly, it will be most needed, and is likely to be evoked most strongly, when one to all of the other five are actively operating against the leadership. This situation obtains when most major bills reach the floor, and continues until the vote on final passage. The leadership intervenes only intermittently prior to floor action on legislation, but floor business is leadership business and it rises to its highest intensity at the stage of recommittal and final passage.

Next, since the leadership is at the greatest advantage in dealing with procedural issues, it can afford to relax when only these are at stake; and if it runs into trouble on one of them, otherwise than from carelessness or ineptitude, the likelihood is that one or more of the countervailing factors is strongly in evidence. If it wins, that will be because fewer factors are working against the leadership than on a substantive issue. Correspondingly, when the visibility of an issue is high, it is likely to be more substantive than procedural, and to entail high activity by state delegations, constituents, and the leadership. Under this condition, the leadership is more likely to win when the visibility of the action is low. When the visibility of the action is high (on a roll-call vote), and is combined with a highly visible, substantive issue (as a major proposal of the Administration's usually is), then it will also be combined with high leadership, constituency, and state delegation activity.

Constituency influences operate irregularly, depending upon the nature and visibility of the issue and of the action. Because constituencies also vary a good deal across the country, few issues will arouse interest in every district. Hence, defections from party leadership on that account will vary considerably from one issue or action to the next. We can say, however, that widespread and intense constituency reactions are symptomatic of high visibility, and with visibility go a number of other problems for the leadership.

Finally, the bargaining power of state delegations—and hence the likelihood of their intervention—is low unless other factors in our review are high. State delegations may be quite active in gaining projects for their states, but on more general bills their appearance is a good deal less predictable. This condition seems genuinely independent of the others.

Notes

[1]See Ralph K. Huitt, "Democratic Party Leadership in the Senate," *American Political Science Review*, Vol. 55 (June, 1961), pp. 333–344, and Lewis A. Froman, Jr., *People and Politics: An Analysis of the American Political System* (Englewood Cliffs, 1962), ch. 6.

[2]Julius Turner, *Party and Constituency: Pressures on Congress* (Baltimore, The John Hopkins University Press, 1951); Duncan MacRae, Jr., *Dimensions of Congressional Voting* (Berkeley, University of California Press, 1958), I, 203–390; David B. Truman, *The Congressional Party* (New York, 1959), and Lewis A. Froman, Jr., *Congressmen and Their Constituencies* (Chicago, Rand McNally, 1963).

[3]Randall B. Ripley, "The Party Whip Organizations in the United States House of Representatives," *American Political Science Review*, Vol. 58 (September, 1964), pp. 561–576.

[4]Turner, *op cit.*, pp. 14–15, 69–70.

[5]See, for example, the stir caused when Hale Boggs, the Democratic Whip, attacked one title of the 1964 Civil Rights Bill during floor debate. *Cong. Rec.*, vol 110, no. 23 (daily ed.), Feb. 7, 1964, pp. 2406–2408.

[6]The exceptions include bills that are complex and subject to numerous amendments—like foreign aid authorization and appropriation bills. In these cases it is difficult to frame a question for polling. Another exception was the civil rights bill in February, 1964. This was a complex issue, subject to many amendments, and it was impossible to forecast how the bill would be amended. Furthermore, unlike all of the other issues polled in the 87th and 88th Congresses, this bill could not be won by Democratic votes alone. Republican votes were absolutely indispensable.

[7]See Ripley, *op cit.*, for a discussion of the role of the polling process in the work of the Democratic Whip organization.

[8]Members were polled on the following issues: (1) the permanent enlargement of the Rules Committee, (2) an amendment adding $450 million to the public works program, (3) a recommittal motion deleting student loan provisions from a Health Professions Assistance Bill, (4) final passage of the Feed Grains Bill, (5) final passage of an increase in the amount of the national debt limit, (6) final passage of a bill giving more money to the Area Redevelopment program, (7) final passage of an extension in time of the debt limit, (8) a recommittal motion on the tax bill tying it to a cut in governmental spending, (9) final passage of another increase in the amount of the debt limit, and (10) final passage of the cotton bill.

[9]"Surprises" can come for a number of reasons, including faulty work by the Assistant Whips. But the vast majority of these surprises occurred because the individual member had changed his mind, without prior notice.

[10]The first index is that used by *Congressional Quarterly*. The second is of our own devising and is based on pro-leadership votes on the ten issues which were the subject of whip polls in 1963.

[11]For our purposes the South includes all the States of the Confederacy; the West includes all States west of the Mississippi River except Arkansas, Louisiana, and Texas; the North includes the rest.

[12]This comes from *Congressional Quarterly*. An opposition score of 25 percent means that the members opposed the President on a quarter of the issues on which the latter took a position.

[13]Note that the debt limit bills all came from the Committee on Ways and Means. Chairman Wilbur Mills of this Committee is an unusually powerful and influential House member and helped the Speaker contact the doubtful members. On the Rules Committee issue Majority Leader Albert also helped make some of the contacts.

[14]For example, on April 9, 1964, after the Democratic leadership had kept the House in session until almost 1:00 A.M. the preceding day, the Republicans stalled the House for four hours, using various procedural delays.

[15]In 1961 there were 101 votes to be examined, not counting 15 "hurrah" votes. In 1962 there were 100 to be examined and 24 of the hurrah variety. In 1963 there were 105 to be examined and 14 hurrah votes.

[16]See Bernard C. Cohen, *The Press and Foreign Policy* (Princeton, Princeton University Press, 1963), pp. 54–104.

[17]For a similar point, see E. E. Schattschneider, *The Semi-Sovereign People* (New York, 1960), ch. 1.

[18]The votes on both recommittal motions were substantially closer than on final passage, although the Democratic leadership position was successful on all four roll calls.

[19]See the *Washington Post,* August 22, 1963, A1:1 and the *Wall Street Journal,* August 26, 1963, 2:3.

[20]See the *Washington Post,* April 9, 1964, A3:5, and the *Baltimore Sun,* April 9, 1964, 8:3.

[21]*Congressional Quarterly Weekly Report,* No. 14, April 3, 1964, pp. 649–653.

[22]Froman, *Congressmen and Their Constituencies, op cit.,* p. 91.

[23]*Ibid.,* chs. 7 and 9; see also Turner, *op cit.,* and MacRae, *op cit.*

[24]Alan Fiellin, "The Functions of Informal Groups: A State Delegation," in Robert L. Peabody and Nelson W. Polsby, eds., *New Perspectives on the House of Representatives* (Chicago, 1963), pp. 59–78, and John H. Kessel, "The Washington Congressional Delegation," *Midwest Journal of Political Science,* Vol. 8 (February, 1964), pp. 1–21.

[25]Truman, *op cit.,* p. 250.

Selection 7 The Learning of Legislative Norms

Herbert B. Asher

Studies of legislatures have uncovered the existence of informal norms or folkways or rules of the game that are presumed to be important for the maintenance of the legislative system.[1] It is often argued that the institution, be it the House or the Senate or a state legislature, must transmit its norms to legislative newcomers in order to insure the continued, unaltered operation of the institution, and that the member himself must learn these norms if he is to be an effective legislator. Whether or not this may be necessary, it certainly is

Reprinted from *The American Political Science Review* 67 (1973) pp. 499–513, by permission of the author and publisher. The author thanks John Kingdon, Herbert Weisberg, Richard Fenno, John Kessel, and Randall Ripley for their helpful comments and suggestions.

plausible to view freshman members of the legislative body as undergoing a socialization process which involves the learning of legislative norms. Yet previous studies have largely concentrated on the identification of legislative norms and have devoted little attention to their transmission to the newcomer. Is the freshman legislator aware of the expected types of behavior prior to taking his seat or does he learn them while in office? If he learns them in office, who actually are the agents of transmission? Or is the socialization process so informal that we cannot even speak of well-defined agents?

These questions and others have not been fully addressed, and thus the focus of this paper is on the learning of norms by freshman members of the United States House of Representatives.[2] My interest is in individual learning of legislative norms, regardless of whether the content learned is in conformity or opposition to the norms. Too often the emphasis in socialization research has been on system maintenance rather than individual adaptation, leading one to dismiss findings of deviance too readily. The data come from a broader panel study of the learning that freshman members elected to the House of Representatives in November, 1968, underwent with respect to perceptions of their job, legislative norms, and sources of voting cues.[3] Since a research interest in learning is a longitudinal concern, a two-wave panel design was employed, the first set of interviews conducted in late January and February of 1969, and the second set the following May. The purpose of the panel was to capture the changes that the 91st class members underwent in the first few months of their legislative service, a period that seemed *a priori* to be crucial in talking about learning. Of the 37 freshmen in the 91st Congress, 30 were interviewed at t_1 (late January and February) and of these 30, 24 were reinterviewed at t_2.[4]

A norm has been defined herein as a rule or standard of conduct appropriate to a person in a specified situation within a group. The norm describes the type of behavior expected by almost all of the other members of the group and often, though not necessarily, has associated with it sanctions for deviance. Since concepts such as role and norm are useful because of their normative or mutual expectations component, and since a definitional attribute of a norm is that it be shared to a high degree by the members of the group, a sample of nonfreshman members of the House was also interviewed. Certainly if incumbent representatives agreed to the norms there would be an environment more supportive of freshmen learning them. Conversely, if there were marked disagreement about the norms on the part of nonfreshmen, we might then wish to reformulate or even reject these "norms."[5]

A variety of approaches can be used to ascertain information and attitudes about legislative norms. Wahlke and his colleagues employed an open-ended question that asked the respondents to identify the rules of the game in their respective state legislatures.[6] Such an approach is particularly valuable for identifying those norms most salient to the representative, but it may fail to elicit the nascent attitudes that freshmen early in their careers are likely to possess. Hence, freshmen and nonfreshmen were queried about specific norms, the determination of which was based upon a survey of the existing literature. The main norms investigated were specialization, reciprocity, legislative work, courtesy, and aspects of apprenticeship including learning the House rules, restrained participation, and attendance on the floor and in committee.[7] A focused interview approach was selected to collect information about these norms, although this procedure raises certain problems. For example, one cannot simply ask the representative whether a norm of reciprocity exists in the House, for such a label may be without meaning to the legislator. We must attach some behavioral tag to reciprocity, and in so doing we have a wide leeway. Thus, we might ask the representative whether he thought members should do favors for one another, but unless the representative was particularly misanthropic, we would expect unanimously affirmative responses to such an item, thereby reducing the discriminatory capacity of the question to zero. Therefore, reciprocity was operationalized in this study by placing it in the context of a voting situation, with all the attendant ambiguities and pressures. The actual question was: "Would you vote a certain way on a bill that you cared little about in order to gain the vote of a fellow representative on a bill that you did care about?" The general point to be made here is that questions seeking to uncover information about norms are best framed within a fairly specific behavioral situation. If we cannot observe behavior directly (and most often we cannot), then our questions should be as behaviorally oriented as possible.

Nonfreshman and the Norms

Table 7-1 presents the level of agreement expressed by our sample of nonfreshman members of the 91st Congress to a series of items about House norms.[8] The highest level of agreement was reached on the importance of maintaining friendly relationships, with the importance of committee work running a close second, while the weakest consensus was found on the norm of apprenticeship. Some detailed analysis of the nonfreshman responses is very illuminating.

Specialization

Among the norms, specialization appeared to be adhered to largely because of certain properties of the House: Many members asserted that the heavy and varied workload of the House, as well as its large membership, made specialization mandatory. Of the eight incumbents who did not agree that Congressmen should specialize rather than generalize, six said that the

Table 7-1   Nonfreshman attitudes to the norms

	% Agreeing	N
Friendly relationships important	97	40
Important work of House done in committee	95	40
House rules important	82	40
Would not personally criticize a fellow representative	82	40
Would be likely to trade votes	81	21
Congressman should be a specialist	80	40
Freshman should serve apprenticeship	38	65

member must do both because of the interdependence of issues, while two opted for being a generalist. The two representatives who cited a generalist orientation were both extreme liberals within their party and viewed the standing committees of the House as "the hand-maidens of special interest groups."

In an attempt to learn whether their attitudes toward specialization had changed since their first term, the nonfreshmen were asked whether they had felt the same way (about specialization) when they were freshmen, and if not, what had led them to change their views. Twenty-six said yes, eleven said no, and two could not recall their earlier opinions. All eleven whose views about specialization had changed said when they entered Congress, they did not realize how necessary specialization was, but that subsequent legislative and committee experience in the House had taught them differently. Two of the eleven said they initially thought it was possible to be knowledgeable on most important issues, but that the energy and time required for this was prohibitive.

Committee Work

While 38 of the 40 incumbents interviewed claimed that most of the important work of the House was done in committee rather than on the floor, the remaining two representatives felt that neither place was crucial. Their responses revealed skepticism about the House's effectiveness as an arena for legislation.

> Most of the important work is done neither on the floor nor in committee. The most important work is done in the submission of bills to Congress by an administration when it has a majority in Congress. They get sorted and acted upon and we just screw around with them. Every time Congress tries to initiate legislation, it does a bad job—Smith Act, Taft-Hartley, Landrum-Griffin. Congress legislates in the heat of emotion as it is threatening to do now on campus unrest and did on draft resisters.

If one means by the important work of the House constituent services and the like, which I do, then it is done neither on the floor nor in committee.

Six of the incumbents who asserted the preeminence of committee work stated they they had not held that point of view when they were freshmen. A midwestern Republican claimed that his previous state legislative experience had misled him, for he "came from a state Senate where the important work was done on the floor, where the substance of bills was often changed on the floor." This suggests that in some situations previous political experience may be dysfunctional and hence may have to be unlearned. Two representatives said that it was legislative experience in general that led them to recognize the primacy of committee work. Finally, a southern Republican gave a very interesting reply as to his perception of the importance of committees where he was a freshman.

> To some extent I felt that committees were most important. It became clear to me early that if you do not have the power, then you have to go to where the power is. It is difficult for a freshman to do much on the floor, but if he goes to his committee chairman or ranking minority member and has already proven his worth to him, if he makes a suggestion and leaves it at that and does not try to grandstand, he can influence legislation from the outset through the senior member of his committee.

Friendly Relationships

The level of agreement on the importance of friendly relationships was truly impressive. One reason cited for this attitude was instrumental: friendly relationships would presumably make one more effective in getting his ideas accepted and bills passed. The other reason was the vague belief that life in general was more pleasant when friendly relationships were the rule. Some responses exemplifying these reasons were:

> Friendly relationships are important because you never know when you'll need others' help or votes. For example, I've been working on a bill on the hijacking of airplanes and got a good reception from friends while testifying at the Interstate and Foreign Commerce committee hearings.

> Friendships are extremely important; that's why the gym is so valuable. You meet guys from the other side of the aisle, people you normally would not get intimate with.

But a number of representatives qualified what was meant by friendly relationships:

> It depends on what you mean by friendly. In terms of operating as a club, I'm not attracted by the sort of thing in which the gym is the key to friendship or

advancement. But if by friendship, one means courtesy and respect, then, sure, it's important.

Friendly relationships are important, but they do not require camaraderie. There's not too much of that that bears directly on getting things passed. One should be a person one feels he can deal with, one who will keep his word. But representatives recognize that one may have to violate this, that one may have to be a demagogue on an issue important to the district. Being buddy-buddy is not as important in the Congress as it is in the state legislature which is less sophisticated.

House Rules

A fairly high consensus was attained on the importance of learning the House rules. The few cases of disagreement, however, are quite interesting. One representative well known to his colleagues for his ambition and career plans beyond the House declared that the rules were not very important to learn. He said that he had not taken the time to learn them, that he worked around the system rather than within it, and that he had not been hurt by this approach so far. It may very well be that members who do not view the House in career terms will consider the rules to be less significant. This viewpoint was expressed by another representative, who said that the importance of the rules depended on what you wanted to do; they were "damned important." Another incumbent thought that the rules were not important for freshmen:

> The rules are important, but those used most often are those used in legislative actions. If one is in a position of power, then the rules are important. Most members never come close to knowing the procedures at all, yet they can do a lot. Freshmen need know only the amenities and not the rules.

A northern Democrat thought that the rules were not all that important as the will of the majority usually prevailed; members did not use the rules against you. Another representative voiced a contrasting opinion; he said that the rules were unimportant because they were so often flouted.

Personal Criticism

While the level of agreement on the norm of refraining from personal criticism of fellow representatives was quite high, this item proved to be very difficult to answer for some members. Almost one-third of the responses were conditional or hypothetical: "I don't think I would," "I shouldn't," "It's not likely," "Not unless someone drove me to it." One representative admitted to having engaged in personal attacks, but vowed never to do it again because of the severe social consequences that he had suffered.

Reciprocity/Trading Votes

Most representatives were willing to trade votes, a manifestation of reciprocity, but many attached provisos to this type of action. Typical responses were:

> Yes, I'd trade votes, but this does not happen often. It is not a specific trade, but more a matter of good will. I never had a specific trade; this happens more in the Senate.

> It depends on the importance of the bill. On local bills, I think I would. For example, I am interested in a potato referendum bill in 48 states and I'm sure that my good friend — —— of New York couldn't care at all about the bill, but he'll probably support it because we're friends. And I'd do the same for him.

The negative responses to this item were usually spoken sharply and intensely, indicating an almost moral disapproval of this type of action. Unfortunately, the N involved here is only 21.

In summary, friendly relationships and the importance of committee work were the most commonly agreed upon norms. A somewhat lower level of consensus characterized attitudes toward specialization, reciprocity, restraint in personal criticism, and the importance of the House rules. The marked disagreement on apprenticeship calls into question the very existence of this norm.

Freshman Attitudes Toward the Norms at t_1

Table 7-2 presents the replies of the newcomers to the same norms questions asked of incumbents, as well as to some special freshman items; the nonfreshman figures are repeated as an aid to the reader.

The responses of the newcomers are quite similar to those of their more senior colleagues, suggesting a generally shared set of expectations. Both groups agree most strongly with the importance of friendly relationships; perhaps this implies that this norm, rather than being specific to the House, is carried over from general life experience. The freshmen also unanimously believed the rules to be important. The major difference between the newcomers' and incumbents' responses concerned the norm of apprenticeship; an additional 20 percent of the freshmen agreed that it is necessary. This may reflect a caution on the part of freshmen early in their incumbency.

Since the concept of norms involves shared expectations, the freshmen were queried about their perceptions of nonfreshman attitudes. They were asked whether they thought that more senior representatives favored the specialist or the generalist. All the newcomers who could answer said that senior members favored the specialist, which in effect confirmed their own

Table 7-2   Freshman attitudes to the norms at t_1

	% Freshmen Agreeing	N	% Nonfreshmen Agreeing	N
Friendly relationships important	100	30	97	40
House rules important	100	30	82	40
Important work of House done in committee	90	30	95	40
Congressman should be a specialist	73	30	80	40
Worthwhile to spend time on House floor	73	30		
Would be likely to trade votes	72	29	81	21
Senior members favor the specialist	71	28		
Would not personally criticize a fellow representative	71	28	82	40
Freshman should serve apprenticeship	57	30	38	65

earlier endorsement of specialization and committee work, but 29 percent (8 of 28) said that they did not know the preferences of senior members. And while the newcomers generally cited committee work over floor work, fully 73 percent thought it worthwhile, especially for freshmen, to spend time on the House floor. Attendance on the House floor was deemed important because it enabled the freshman representative to learn the procedures and thereby complete his apprenticeship much sooner.

Deviant Responses of the Freshmen

One can conclude from this brief outline that freshmen shared to a similar degree the norms of nonfreshmen, a situation certainly conducive to the learning of norms, but not one that automatically implies that norms were formally transmitted from senior to freshman members. It is interesting to examine some of the deviant responses given by freshmen. Numerous hypotheses were entertained about the causes of noncompliance to the norms. For example, it was thought that freshmen with prior political experience, especially in the state legislature, would be more apt to give "correct" responses. It was also thought that freshmen with a strong dedication to a career in the House would be more sensitive to the norms. These hypotheses and others were neither confirmed nor refuted because of the very small number of cases involved. The most fruitful approach to the problem is a norm-by-norm analysis of the deviant responses.

Specialization

Eight of the thirty freshmen interviewed at t_1 did not unqualifiedly opt to be specialists. Two freshmen asserted that Congressmen should be generalists, five said that it depended on the individual or that a member must be both, and one did not know. One representative who chose to be a generalist cited the heterogeneous nature of his district as the determining factor in his decision. This representative had the most extensive state legislative experience of any freshman in the 91st Congress, thereby leading one to reject the too facile linkage of state legislative service with specialization. The other generalist appeared to be motivated by two forces: a suspicion of accepting others' advice and a recognition that congressmen had to vote on a wide range of issues and should therefore be broadly informed. The theme of distrust occurred throughout this interview; the representative was very much an ideologue with little confidence in the judgment and motives of his colleagues and with a very rigid view of his job. This suspiciousness was reflected in his responses to questions on voting cues: he was very wary of members giving him wrong information and was generally expecting his votes to be uninfluenced by his colleagues. Newcomers who said that a member had to be both a specialist and a generalist argued that assignment to a committee forced one to specialize, while floor voting on a wide variety of issues compelled one to be a generalist. Another representative rejected specialization partially because of the narrowness of his committee assignment. He said:

> One has to do both. I can tell you now that I will not spend the rest of my time becoming an expert on the price of hayseed oil.

An analysis of such background variables as prior political experience uncovered no systematic differences between specialists and nonspecialists.

Committee Work

Only three of thirty freshmen did not assert that most of the important work of the House was done in committee. One member, a southern Democrat with state legislative experience and highly directed toward a career in the House, said that he did not know where the work was done since the committees had only just organized. Another freshman, our distrustful ideologue mentioned above, said without qualification that most of the important work was done on the floor, since that was where the actual passage or defeat of a piece of legislation occurred. For him, voting was the crucial aspect of the job with the events preceding any vote being of only minor importance. The third freshman who failed to assert the primacy of committee work thought, in fact, that neither the committees nor the floor was the most significant arena:

> The important work is not done in either. It is too early to say where the important work is done, if, in fact, important work is done. The important work is to stir up public opinion about the important issues.

This representative more than any other freshman had an active national constituency. His energies were constantly spread thin over a number of liberal causes that were outside the immediate context of House legislative activity. He was one of the most active and reformist freshmen, yet his behavior very much followed the traditional, accepted patterns even though he denied the importance of committee and floor work. For example, in the interview, he coupled a stinging attack on the proceedings on the House floor with a statement and explanation as to why it is important to spend time there.

> Yes, it is worthwhile to spend time on the House floor. This is where the member lobbies, where he talks to others about bills, trades information, does logrolling. People will think you are arrogant if you don't spend much time there. Debate on the floor is a sham; it's dishonest. People get things in the *Record* without saying them in debate as happened in the HUAC controversy.

And his response to the item about the importance of friendly relationships probably best typifies the difference between the activist who is careful to observe the amenities and the would-be reformer who allows personal relationships to deteriorate.

> It's very important to maintain friendly relationships. I think a big mistake is made when people who come up here hoping to change things, are frustrated and allow their frustrations to create personal animosities. I get along with everyone here; I like everyone. I even get along well with Mendel Rivers; I tease him a lot.

This same freshman's remarks on the House floor on the occasion of Speaker McCormack's announced retirement further illustrate proper, yet dissenting behavior.

> Mr. Speaker, I want especially to join in this tribute to the Speaker today because it is no secret that on some questions we have disagreed, and it is important—if this occasion is to be what it should be—that those of us who have not always agreed with him make it clear that we are no less grateful for having known him than those who have agreed with him.

> . . . I will always be grateful that we overlapped here so I could have the opportunity to know this man, generous, considerate, and fair to everyone, never vindictive no matter how great his disagreement or disappointment.

> The rules of this body continue to dismay many of us who find them neither democratic nor conducive to efficient procedures. But within these rules, the Speaker has done everything he could to protect the rights of every Member . . .[9]

Personal Criticism

There were eight freshmen out of twenty-eight who said they would personally criticize a fellow representative. For three of these representatives, this willingness to criticize their colleagues seemed to be rooted in a certain outspokenness of personality and intensity of belief that they realized would surface at some point in their congressional careers, although they did not consciously intend to make personal criticism a regular occurrence. Included among these three is our distrustful ideologue; he said that it was possible he would criticize a fellow representative "if he needed it." None of the five other freshmen had served in the state legislature, so perhaps their earlier experiences had not taught them that personal attacks were normally out of bounds. For one of these five, the lack of state legislative experience was probably less influential than the member's own weak attachment to the House. Two factors that lessened his commitment to the House were his age and his relative financial independence: he perceived himself to be too old to have any lengthy career in the House, and therefore far removed from the worries of career advancement; furthermore, as he mentioned more than once, he had a lucrative business to return to if House service ever became too compromising. Even if he were to criticize, he said that he would do it "with velvet gloves."

Reciprocity/Trading Votes

A striking similarity emerges among the freshman representatives who were not likely to trade votes: All six were Republicans. And the three members of the nonfreshman sample who unqualifiedly refused to trade votes were also Republicans. Four of the freshman responses were resounding "No's" while another was "I hope not," which seemed to imply that vote trading was wrong, but that somehow the Representative might be tempted to participate in it. The only respondent who tried to explain the negative opinion toward vote-trading stated that ten years earlier in the state legislature he had been "burned" because he did not anticipate the consequences of the bill to which he had given his vote. Perhaps what we have here is a tendency by Republicans to view politics more moralistically or ideologically so that trading votes becomes tantamount to catering to unworthy special interests and to abdicating one's own sense of right and wrong.[10]

The Usefulness of Time Spent on the House Floor

The final two norms to be investigated for deviant responses were the ones asked only of freshmen. One inquired whether they thought that senior representatives favored the specialist or the generalist. As mentioned earlier, while eight freshmen did not know the answer to this at t_1 none answered "generalist." The second item was concerned with the value of spending time on the House floor. At t_1, five representatives (four Democrats and one Republican) said that it was not worthwhile because so little was going on. Since we are interested in behavior as well as in attitudes, a crude measure of time spent on the House floor was constructed; it is simply the percentage of the quorum call votes that the member answered in the first session of the 91st Congress. This measure has severe limitations, including our expectation that members from districts relatively close to the Capitol would score low because of the extensive amount of time they would spend in their easily-reached constituencies.[11] And, obviously, members who do answer quorum calls regularly may spend very little time on the floor. Be that as it may, there was a weak, yet consistent relationship between attitudes and behavior. The 22 freshmen who felt floor-time was worthwhile missed 13 percent of the quorum calls; the 3 who were neutral missed 19 percent; and the 5 who felt floor experience was not worthwhile missed 28 percent.[12]

Forces Contributing to Deviant Responses to the Norms

From this discussion of deviant responses, we can winnow out a number of influences that promote compliance and noncompliance to the norms, but we cannot weight these influences in any quantitative fashion because of the very small N involved. Career orientation to the House appeared to be important in furthering adherence to the norms, while aspirations to other office encouraged nonadherence. Also reducing the salience of the House for the newcomer were financial security and age; older freshmen realized that they would be less likely to advance to any great degree up the House hierarchy. Finally, the extremism of the member's ideological views was related to norm compliance: The more ideological members, whether of the left or right, were somewhat more willing to violate the norms, especially those on speaking out in proper fashion. It was significant that only one representative — the distrustful ideologue — gave responses that repeatedly departed from the norms. Personality traits in combination with his view of politics seemed to account quite well for his beliefs. But for most other freshmen, deviant responses were very infrequent, so that it was impossible to talk of types of freshmen who generally did not abide by the norms. In other words, noncompliance to one norm did not predict very well attitudes toward other norms. Probably the most important finding overall is that noncompliance was minimal, implying that by one means or another, freshmen had learned the norms well, the topic to which we now turn.

Freshmen and the Learning of Norms

As already mentioned, and in contradiction to initial expectations, most of the freshmen at t_1 were giving "correct" responses to the norms items. This observation has implications for the amount of learning that the panel can uncover. If learning be defined in terms of attitude change, then we would expect little learning from t_1 to t_2 because of the correctness of the t_1 responses. While learning might come in the form of strengthening initial attitudes, the inappropriateness of Likert items for elite populations such as legislators make it difficult to get a handle on changes in attitudinal intensity. As it was, the responses to the unstructured norms questions were coded to incorporate direction and intensity of attitudes, and changes in both are reflected in the coefficients presented in table 7-3.

The low incidence of later norm learning may mean that the freshmen knew the norms before entering Congress. If this be true, it is an interesting datum in and of itself. Or perhaps freshmen learned the norms in the short interval between taking office and being interviewed by this investigator, although this possibility appears unlikely (see note 4). One way of demonstrating the minimal learning of norms from t_1 to t_2 is to cross-tabulate the t_1 and t_2 responses to each item and examine the intra-item correlations. This is done in table 7-3 for those norms questions that were coded in an ordinal fashion with at least four valid codes; the measure of association is tau-b.

Table 7-3   Intra-item correlations on the norms question (t_1 and t_2)

	Tau-B	N
Friendly relationships important	1.000	24
Would be likely to trade votes	.721	20
Freshman should serve apprenticeship	.696	24
House rules important	.693	24
Would not personally critize a fellow representative	.310	22
Worthwhile to spend time on House floor	.169	24

As one can observe, all of the items except two—personal criticism and spending time on the House floor—were very stable. Of the 22 representatives who responded to the personal criticism question at t_1 and t_2, 13 did not give identical answers at the two time points. Eight of the 13 gave answers at t_2 that made it less likely that they would engage in personal criticism, but the other five indicated a greater willingness to criticize which runs counter to the learning or reinforcement of "proper" behavior. There were no background variables that explained the changes on this item, nor did the freshmen volunteer any information that was helpful in accounting for the shifts. What we may have here is response unreliability elicited by a question whose wording left in doubt just what was meant by personal criticism.

The situation was very different on the other unstable item; here half of the 24 responses were identical from t_1 to t_2. Four of the six Republicans who changed thought it more worthwhile at t_2 to spend time on the House floor, while five of the six Democrats felt just the opposite, and each group was able to justify its own position. The Democrats were all active liberals dismayed by what they considered the scarcity of significant floor work. Republicans, however, generally cited the instructional value of being on the House floor. Thus, a part of the reason for the low intra-correlation on this item was the growing dissatisfaction on the part of some Democrats. As this discontent was basically programmatic, it did not affect the less issue-oriented Republicans, whose changes on this item in the opposite direction were less easily explained.[13]

Subdividing the freshmen according to characteristics such as party and district competitiveness does not change the tau-b's very much. There is, however, some tendency for freshmen with state legislative experience to exhibit greater stability than those without such experience, and this is especially pronounced on vote-trading. While the correlation for this item for all freshmen was .721, it rose to .792 for newcomers who had had state legislative service and plummeted to −.200 for those who had not had such service. Attitudes on vote trading, therefore, appear to be more stable if one has already had the opportunity to confront the situation in reality (as in a state legislature) and not just hypothetically. That is, members who had experienced vote trading first-hand were more consistent in their attitudes toward it, an intuitively appealing result.

Finally, let us examine the percentage agreement with each of the norms at t_1 and t_2, looking only at freshmen interviewed at both t_1 and t_2. This will indicate whether support for the norms increases or decreases (erodes) over time. The appropriate figures are presented in table 7-4.[14]

The striking point about table 7-4 is that support for the norms more commonly decreased than increased, although most of the percentage changes were small and probably mean little. The norm that suffered the greatest and most real erosion was apprenticeship; this finding will be analyzed in depth in the next section. Also suffering erosion of more than 10 percent were the items on specialization and the importance of the rules. What may be happening here is that at t_1 freshmen knew the "right" responses and uttered them automatically but that subsequent legislative experience enabled them to take a more sophisticated, knowledgeable, and qualified view of the norms. The norm showing the greatest gain in support was restraint in personal criticism, but no ready explanation comes to mind except that attendance on the House floor would indicate to the freshman, if he did not already know, that personal attacks were very rare, indeed.

The other interesting result in table 7-4 is that the t_2 freshman responses are somewhat closer to the nonfreshman replies than are the t_1 answers. This does not hold for specialization, committee work, and friendly relationships; here the t_1 answers come closer to the incumbent responses, but the differences involved are small. But for the other norms, the t_2 freshman responses are substantially closer than the t_1 responses to the nonfreshman replies. For apprenticeship, the difference between the t_1 and nonfreshman responses was 20 percent when the t_2 replies are used. Eight and 13 percent differences between the t_1 and nonfreshmen replies on House rules and personal criticism drop to six percent and zero when the t_2 responses are substituted. Thus, the freshmen were basically similar to their more senior colleagues at t_1, and by t_2 the coincidence of views toward the norms was even closer, suggesting the informal socialization to the norms was still occurring at t_2.

Table 7-4   Level of agreement to the norms at t_1 and t_2

	Freshmen				Nonfreshmen	
	% Agreeing t_1	% Agreeing t_2	Change	N	% Agreeing	N
Freshman should serve apprenticeship	58	42	−16	24	38	65
Congressman should be a specialist	83	70	−13	23	80	40
House rules important	100	88	−12	24	82	40
Important work done in committee	96	87	− 9	23	95	40
Friendly relationships important	100	92	− 8	24	97	40
Would be likely to trade votes	68	68	0	22	81	21
Worthwhile to spend time on House floor	71	75	4	24		
Senior members favor specialist	70	78	8	23		
Would not personally criticize a fellow representative	69	82	13	22	82	40

The Norm of Apprenticeship

It is the norm of apprenticeship that is most relevant to freshmen. If the traditional description of the freshman representative as unsure in his actions and ignorant to House rules and procedures is correct, then apprenticeship is obviously the crucial norm for newcomers to follow. The natural expectation is that apprenticeship would be a very commonly accepted norm given the widespread familiarity of the adage about freshmen being seen and not heard. But as table 7-5 indicates, the very existence of a norm of apprenticeship as defined herein must be called into question.[15] Almost half of the nonfreshman sample flatly denied the necessity of serving an apprenticeship, and if the qualified disagreements are added to this figure, almost two-thirds of the incumbents rejected apprenticeship. And while there was majority agreement to the norm at t_1 on the part of freshmen, a sizeable minority of 43 percent deemed it unnecessary. Those freshmen who saw the need for serving an apprenticeship were asked how long they felt it would take in their own particular cases. Four newcomers said that they could not set a specific time limit, two said a year, and only one said the full two years of his first term in office. The remaining ten all indicated that apprenticeships between two and six months would be desirable. Thus, even for freshmen who agreed to

Table 7-5   The norm of apprenticeship

	t_1 Freshman Responses	Nonfreshman Responses
	%	%
Agreement	40	24
Qualified Agreement	17	12
Qualified Disagreement	17	20
Disagreement	26	44
Total %	100	100
N	(30)	(66)

apprenticeship, the learning period was usually seen as relatively short, most often under six months. The range of freshman responses to the apprenticeship item is illustrated by the following replies:

> Yes, I'll serve an apprenticeship. Its length depends upon the individual; it will probably take me less time because of my previous legislative experience. A newcomer needs to be informed to be effective.

> Yes. The length depends, probably a few months. You can't lead the army the first day. But you do represent a district that elected you for two years and you can't just sit and do nothing.

> There is no reason for an apprenticeship. You learn best by jumping right in.

> No, you don't have to serve an apprenticeship. But one should not just jump into things. A freshman Congressman is not like a freshman in college; he is a man of some special competence. Senior people will listen to you if you have something to say.

An examination of the apprenticeship replies by party indicates some party differences, as shown in table 7-6. Seven of the nine freshman Democrats who rejected apprenticeship were urban liberals from districts with heavy constituent demands. These men were generally active and concerned with programs, and, for them, apprenticeship implied a severe restriction on the activities that they deemed most important, particularly speaking up on the floor on such issues as Vietnam, national priorities, and school desegregation. The intention to engage in specific legislative activity, shared by a number of Democratic freshmen, itself runs counter to the image of the bewildered

Table 7-6   Freshman apprenticeship responses by party

	Republicans	Democrats
"Apprenticeship Necessary"	73	40
"No Apprenticeship Necessary"	27	60
Total %	100	100
N	(15)	(15)

newcomer. For most Republicans, the idea of an apprenticeship or limited participation was not as restrictive, mainly because they were not as concerned with programs and problems. Thus, one's view of the job of the representative appears to influence one's opinions about apprenticeship.

It is reasonable therefore that freshmen who agreed to the importance of apprenticeship would be less active. Table 7-7 presents some evidence on this point using as measures of activity three simple indices constructed from the *Congressional Record*.[16] As expected, Democratic nonapprentices were substantially more active than their apprentice colleagues across all three measures. But this pattern does not hold for Republicans; here the differences between apprentices and nonapprentices are small and inconsistent. Interestingly, Republican and Democratic apprentices had comparable levels of activity, but Democratic nonapprentices were far more active than their GOP counterparts. Thus, Democratic freshmen are less likely to welcome serving an apprenticeship than Republican newcomers, and only for Democrats is the decision to choose or reject an apprenticeship reflected in varying levels of activity.

Table 7-7   Levels of activity vs. apprenticeship by party

	Republicans		Democrats	
	App.	No App.	App.	No App.
Mean Number of House Remarks	22	17	22	39
Mean Number of Extension Remarks	15	19	21	40
Mean Number of Nonprivate Bills and Resolutions Introduced	54	53	56	81
N	11	4	6	9

To help explain this finding one must recall that the Democratic party is the entrenched majority party in the House. The decision to serve an apprenticeship may be more salient for majority party members in general, since it is the majority party that sets the legislative pace, controls the committee, and the like. But more consequential for the freshman Democrat is the domination of his party by senior members, many of them Southerners, who compromise a much larger proportion of his party than senior Republicans do of the GOP.[17] The common perception of the Democratic party is that it is run by its elderly patriarchs. Hence, in making a decision about apprenticeship, the Democratic freshman is choosing a course of action that does have immediate consequences for his legislative career. He is· deciding in effect whether "to go along" as Sam Rayburn used to advise freshmen or to strike out on a more hazardous path. And the freshman Democrat is often forced to make this conscious decision about the apprenticeship because he may enter Congress with strong intentions to promote a wide range of legislative activities and at the same time realize that his position as a freshman member in a senior-dominated party works against such conduct. The question of an apprenticeship is not nearly as salient for Republican freshmen—members of a relatively junior, minority party, who early in their House careers had the vaguest legislative plans, a condition that would make serving an apprenticeship less onerous.

In addition to one's programmatic intentions, the other variable that was often cited by freshmen as influential in their apprenticeship decision was their perception of their own legislative competence. Three members specifically stated that because of their previous experience in the state legislature, their period of apprenticeship could either be shortened or be totally unnecessary. The relationship between state legislative service and attitudes toward apprenticeship is presented in table 7-8. For all freshmen, service in the state legislature does not materially affect opinions about apprenticeship. Table 7-8 further indicates that party differences with respect to apprenticeship remain even when previous state legislative experience is considered, thereby suggesting that previous experience is less important than one's own legislative goals in the decision whether or not to serve an apprenticeship. Again, Democratic freshmen were more oriented to legislation than their GOP colleagues.

Table 7-8   Apprenticeship vs. state legislative service and party

	State Service			No State Service		
	R	D	All	R	D	All
"Apprenticeship Necessary"	70	43	59	80	38	54
"No Apprenticeship Necessary"	30	57	41	20	62	46
Total %	100	100	100	100	100	100
N	(10)	(7)	(17)	(5)	(8)	(13)

The nonfreshman responses to apprenticeship are truly surprising in the extent of their disagreement with the norm. The common political lore has it that nonfreshmen, particularly the more senior among them, would be the strongest advocates of an apprenticeship norm. The nonfreshmen responses to the apprenticeship item were usually brief and to the point, indicating little difficulty in replying to the item. A few of the more detailed, qualified responses are given below:

> Apprenticeship is necessary for a period of time, but I have encouraged them [freshmen] to participate as soon as possible. I suggest that they choose as their area of expertise an area that they've had experience in previously which will let them participate earlier.

> I don't think freshman congressmen should serve a period of apprenticeship. As a matter of fact, I don't think that term can apply in Congress. Any member has an equal right with any other member. The very nature of the legislative

process does require that new members take more time to become acquainted with committee activities than those who have served for many years.

This is a difficult question to answer because of the varying backgrounds of the new members of Congress . . . Hence, it seems to me that it would be difficult to establish any rule of thumb . . . I am frank to say that I have observed instances of overenthusiastic freshman congressmen who would have done well to have been a bit more observant of the processes and legislative procedure before offering the panacea to a particular problem.

Table 7-9 presents the nonfreshman replies to the apprenticeship item by seniority and party.

The results in this table are somewhat unexpected. Overall, the more senior one is, the less likely he will say that apprenticeship is necessary. For all groups except Republicans with less than six years of service, a sizeable majority of respondents were against apprenticeship, and even for this group of Republicans the division was almost even. The reader should have greater confidence in the Republican figures than in the Democratic ones, which do not include sufficient senior representation, especially from the South and border states.

Table 7-9 seems surprising because we have been led to believe that it is senior members who keep junior men in their place. But perhaps only a subset of senior members perform this function. The probable candidates would be the senior southern and border (Democratic) members and others who also dominate the committees. After all, it was Texan Sam Rayburn who was credited with the terse description of apprenticeship as "being seen and not heard" and who advised members to go along in order to get along. There are only four southern and border Democrats in the sample with more than ten years of service in the House (in a representative sample, there would be about twice that number), and three of the four said that no apprenticeship was necessary. These figures are too small to be conclusive, especially because it is almost impossible to interview the real patriarchs of the House. We can, however, divide the sample into gross regional categories to see whether apprenticeship is more common in the South, the likely home of a disproportionate number of carriers of the creed. The results of such a division reveal no substantial regional differences; 4 of 12 southern members said that

Table 7-9   Nonfreshman apprenticeship responses by party and seniority

	6 or fewer years of service			7 to 10 years of service			More than 10 years of service		
	R	D	All	R	D	All	R	D	All
Apprenticeship	53	27	41	43	13	27	36	25	32
No Apprenticeship	47	73	59	57	87	73	64	75	68
Total %	100	100	100	100	100	100	100	100	100
N	(17)	(15)	(32)	(7)	(8)	(15)	(11)	(8)	(19)

apprenticeship was necessary as compared to 38 percent of the nonsouthern members (N=54). This conclusion must be hedged a bit because of shortcomings in the southern subsample.

Thus, apprenticeship is far from being a universally accepted norm. Indeed, one wonders why a majority of the freshmen at t_1 still subscribed to the norm, unless it represents a false anticipation. As one newcomer observed, "It may be that freshman classes have been browbeaten before they ever got here by the establishment." The browbeating may very well take place through the widespread circulation of such political lore as Speaker Rayburn's advice cited earlier. Such information about their status may be the only kind available to freshmen at first. Thus, in a sense, freshmen may have to be socialized *out of* the norm of apprenticeship. Two freshmen at t_1 said that Speaker McCormack himself had urged them to participate fully right from the outset of their service. Yet because of their prior conditioning, they were leery of such advice; they thought the Speaker was "just being nice." As noted earlier, there was erosion in support for apprenticeship from t_1 to t_2 by the 91st class; perhaps this is indicative of learning that is really unlearning. Freshmen may have seen some of their colleagues participate early, observed that no sanctions were levied, and therefore altered their views about apprenticeship. Of course, it is possible that senior members who deny the importance of apprenticeship are saying one thing and believing another. A sophomore Republican argued:

> . . . [M]any senior congressmen might say that a freshman should not serve an apprenticeship, but when it came to actual practice, the situation was quite different. I know of numerous instances of senior members grumbling when a freshman member spoke on a subject. Typical comments were: "What's he doing talking, he's a freshman," "What does he know about it, he's only a freshman."

But it seems unreasonable to consider the senior members' responses against apprenticeship as largely misstatements of the members' underlying beliefs.

This argument does not mean that apprenticeship is unnecessary or unexpected. There will be many topics about which the freshman will be uninformed because of his inexperience, and in such areas, his more senior colleagues will expect him to proceed cautiously and to learn gradually. But this type of apprenticeship is a far cry from one in which the newcomer is expected to remain silent in all situations, even when he has a contribution to make. Some years earlier, Charles Clapp came to a similar conclusion, although his evidence was incomplete since his roundtable participants tended to be disproportionately liberal, reformist, and receptive to academicians. At that time, Clapp wrote:

> The old admonition that new members should observe but not participate in debate was swept aside long ago. Apprenticeship may still precede full partnership, but the increased volume and complexity of the problems with which the Congress is compelled to cope dictate more efficient use of the membership. Freshmen are now advised to defer speaking only until the moment arrives when

they have something significant to say—indeed, colleagues counsel them not to wait too long—although they are cautioned to be sure they are well informed about their topic.[18]

Finally, it is clear that the House is not alone in its skepticism about apprenticeship; the norm of apprenticeship has fallen into bad times in the United States Senate as well, especially since 1964. The "Inner-Club" has declined in recent years and a new type of Senator, less concerned with internal Senate operations, has become more prominent.[19]

Conclusion

The main finding of this paper is that the amount of norm learning between January and May by the freshman members of the 91st Congress was unexpectedly low. As the concept of norms incorporates the notion of shared expectations, the attitudes of a sample of nonfreshmen were first analyzed to insure that we were studying genuine norms. Apprenticeship was found to be less restrictive on freshmen than originally thought, while other norms were largely adhered to. It appeared that freshmen largely knew the general House norms prior to entering Congress, which made it impossible to talk about the formal agents of socialization involved in transmitting the norms to newcomers. And the extent of change once in office was minimal.

Now this finding may be an artifact of the particular freshman class under investigation, in the sense that the 91st class was unusually well-prepared by prior political experience for House service. Of the six most recent freshman classes, the 91st class had the largest proportion of members with state legislative experience—51 percent. But an alternative explanation seems more satisfactory, that is that freshman representatives would generally know many of the norms simply because they are rules of behavior appropriate to many institutional settings. Thus, one does not have to be a member of Congress to know that personal criticism and unfriendly relationships may be dysfunctional to one's institution or group or one's own career. This argument asserts that almost any type of prior experience would make the freshman sensitive to the basic rules of behavior. Overall, it was difficult to link compliance and noncompliance to the norms to any particular characteristics because of the small number of deviant responses, but a number of plausible influences were suggested.

These data do not address the learning of committee-specific norms. These norms may not be as salient or as transferable from other contexts as the ones described above, and hence they may actually have to be learned anew by freshmen.[20] Unfortunately, the data in this article span only January to May, 1969, a time of very little legislative action, both in committee and on the floor. The 91st Congress in its early months was sharply criticized for the slowness of its legislative pace, a slowness that was due in part to the change in partisan complexion of the national administration. And this slowness of legislative pace may have retarded the learning of committee-specific norms. In their California study, Price and Bell found that the norms cited at their later interviews were most often those that concerned committee work and the handling of legislation.[21]

In summary, then, it seems as if the traditional image of the freshman congressman as ignorant and bewildered had mistakenly led us to expect substantial learning of norms on the part of supposedly ill-informed newcomers. This expectation was unwarranted on two counts: the general House norms were not so abstruse as to require formal learning, and the traditional image of the freshman Congressman was found to be out of date, a theme to be developed in a future paper.

Notes

[1]The literature on legislative norms is quite extensive. For a discussion of Senate norms, see Donald R. Matthews, *U.S. Senators and Their World* (New York: Random House, 1960) and William S. White, *Citadel: The Story of the U.S. Senate* (New York: Harper & Brothers, 1957) and two articles by Ralph Huitt, "The Outsider in the Senate: An Alternative Role," *American Political Science Review*, 55 (September, 1961), pp. 566–75 and "The Morse Committee Assignment Controversy: A Study in Senate Norms," *American Political Science Review*, 51 (June, 1957), pp. 313–29. For information on House norms, see Charles L. Clapp, *The Congressman: His Work as He Sees It* (New York: Doubleday & Company, 1963); Donald G. Tacheron and Morris K. Udall, *The Job of the Congressman* (Indianapolis and New York: The Bobbs-Merrill Company, 1966); and Clem Miller, *Member of the House: Letters of a Congressman* (New York: Charles Scribner's Sons, 1962). Also relevant to the House is the growing body of literature on committee integration and the norms that promote it. The foremost articles in this area are Richard F. Fenno, Jr., "The House Appropriations Committee as a Political System: The Problem of Integration," *American Political Science Review*, 56 (June, 1962), pp. 310–24 and John F. Manley, " The House Committee on Ways and Means: Conflict Management in a Congressional Committee," *American Political Science Review*, 59 (December, 1965), pp. 927–39. See also the broader studies by these authors: Richard F. Fenno, Jr., *The Power of the Purse: Appropriations Politics in Congress* (Boston: Little, Brown and Company, 1966) and John F. Manley, *The Politics of Finance* (Boston: Little, Brown and Company, 1970). At the state legislative level, the reader can turn to John Wahlke et al., *The Legislative System* (New York: John Wiley & Sons, 1962); Malcolm E. Jewell, *The State Legislature: Politics and Practice* (New York: Random House, 1962); and James D. Barber, *The Lawmakers: Recruitment and Adaptation to Legislative Life* (New Haven: Yale University Press, 1965). Finally, for an example of research in a non-American setting, see Allan Kornberg, "The Rules of the Game in the Canadian House of Commons," *Journal of Politics*, 26 (May, 1964), pp. 358–80.

[2]Recently, there has been a greater emphasis on the legislative newcomer and his adaptation to the institution, with one article specifically concerned with the rules of the game, although from a different perspective than employed herein. In a panel study of freshman California assemblymen, Bell and Price found that norm learning did take place. They wrote: "A whole host of 'in-house' norms were cited after legislative experience had been acquired.

Rules pertaining to committee decorum and management of bills were frequently cited in the second and third interviews; they were not often cited in the first interview." See Charles M. Price and Charles G. Bell, "The Rules of the Game: Political Fact or Academic Fancy?" *Journal of Politics,* 32 (November, 1970), p. 855. For more general discussions of freshman adaptation, see Charles G. Bell and Charles M. Price, "Pre-Legislative Sources of Representational Roles," *Midwest Journal of Political Science,* 13 (May, 1969), pp. 254–70 and Irwin N. Gertzog, "The Socialization of Freshman Congressmen: Some Agents of Organizational Continuity," Paper prepared for delivery at the 66th annual meeting of the American Political Science Association, Biltmore Hotel, Los Angeles, September 8–12, 1970, pp. 1–26.

[3]Herbert B. Asher, "The Freshman Congressman: A Developmental Analysis" (Ph.D. dissertation, University of Michigan, 1970).

[4]The selection of the times for the two waves, particularly the first, was no easy matter. Since a prime concern of my research was freshman attitudes to legislative norms, I wished to interview sufficiently early so as to ascertain these attitudes while uninfluenced by House service. But seminars for freshman representatives were held early in the session (January 8 through January 13) and at these meetings a large amount of material, some of it relevant to legislative norms, was presented to the freshmen. Thus, it would have been advantageous to talk to the newcomers before these seminars were held. But in terms of my interest in internal House voting cues, interviewing in early January would have made little sense as almost no legislative business was underway. In retrospect, the problem was not very serious as evidenced by a question included in the interview schedule designed to measure the impact of the freshman seminars. Freshmen generally indicated that the seminars were interesting and highly informative with respect to parliamentary procedures and the services available to congressmen, but generally attributed little influence to the seminars vis-à-vis House norms. Similar opinions were expressed by freshman participants in the 1959 seminars. My thanks go to Representative Morris Udall for allowing me to rummage through his files on previous freshman seminars.

There remains the possibility that substantial norm learning may have occurred in the postelection period prior to the freshman's formal entry into the House, a "waiting period" during which many freshmen took some action with regard to their future committee assignment or journeyed to Washington to handle personal business. Thus, there was certainly opportunity for norm learning to have occurred in this period, although freshmen indicated little such activity in response to questions about the waiting period. Unfortunately, resource constraints prevented a third wave of interviews shortly after the November election.

[5]The nonfreshman members of the House were stratified according to party, region, and seniority, and proportionate samples were selected randomly within these strata. The interviews obtained were very representative of Republican House membership, while they underrepresented Democrats in general and senior, southern Democrats in particular. The following figures indicate how well the nonfreshman sample matches the overall population in terms of party and seniority where a threefold classification of seniority based on the

	Republicans		Democrats	
	% of population	% of sample	% of population	% of sample
Seniority				
Low	55	49	36	48
Moderate	18	20	22	26
High	27	31	42	26
Total %	100%	100%	100%	100%
N	(174)	(35)	(224)	(31)

number of terms served prior to the start of the 91st Congress is used. Low seniority was defined as three or fewer terms, moderate as four and five terms, and high as more than five terms.

Despite the underrepresentation of senior Democrats there were no significant ideological differences between the samples selected from each stratum and the corresponding parent stratum as measured by CQ conservative coalition support scores and ADA and ACA ratings.

[6]The actual question that Wahlke and his colleagues used was: "We've been told that every legislature has its unofficial rules of the game—certain things they must do and things they must not do if they want the respect and cooperation of fellow members. What are some of these things—these 'rules of the game'—that a member must observe to hold the respect and cooperation of his fellow members?" See Wahlke et al., *The Legislative System*, p. 143.

[7]The norm of institutional patriotism was also investigated, but its operationalization was so narrow that the responses obtained were not very interesting. Members were asked whether they would ever criticize the House, and, not unexpectedly, most said that they would which presumably implies that institutional patriotism is not a viable norm. But institutional patriotism is far more complex than merely refraining from criticism so that nothing more will be said about the norm in the remainder of this paper.

[8]Some of the nonfreshman interviews were taken at t_1 and the others at t_2 There was very high agreement on some of the norms questions asked at t_1 and these were omitted at t_2 so that more attention could be devoted to other items. This accounts for the various N's on the norms questions. There was no reason to believe that the responses to the norms questions that were omitted at t_2 contained any systematic biases. The actual questions for each of the norms were: Do you think congressmen should specialize in a field or should try to be generalists? Do you think most of the important work of the House is done on the floor or in committees? How important do you think it is to maintain friendly relationships with your fellow congressmen? Do you think that freshman congressmen should serve a period of apprenticeship, that is, be more an observer than an active participant in the legislative process? How important do you think learning the House procedural rules is? Would you ever personally criticize a fellow representative on the floor of the House? Would you vote a certain way on a bill that you cared little about in order to gain the vote of a fellow congressman on a bill that you did care about?

It should be noted here that the question about where the important work of the House is done does not tap a norm in the same sense as the other items, but rather elicits a belief or opinion. Once we have found marked disagreement with certain items thought to be legislative norms, then by definition these items no longer are norms. But for simplicity of presentation, the word norm will be used in the subsequent analysis to apply to those items such as apprenticeship about which there was substantial disagreement.

[9]It is very difficult to gather systematic information on the "proper" activist who observes the rules of the game vs. the one who does not, but scattered references to various individuals in the course of interviewing suggested that these two general types were meaningful for some members of Congress. For example, specific comparisons twice were made between the "proper" liberal described above and another liberal Democratic freshman from the same region and with similar issue concerns. These comparisons were unfavorable toward the latter freshman because of his excessive behavior. He was criticized for shooting off his mouth too much and for making too many entries in the *Congressional Record*. An examination of the actual number of entries indicated that the perceptions of his behavior were accurate: he was the most verbose newcomer with nearly twice as many distinct items in the *Record* as his "proper" freshman colleague. It is noteworthy that such behavior is salient to Congressmen and that reputations, whether good or bad, can be created by such activity. In one of the rare attempts to talk in systematic and quantitative terms about the sanctions invoked against nonconformists, Wayne Swanson found that liberals, and especially anti-establishment liberals, lagged behind in advancing up the committee

hierarchy in the Senate. See Wayne R. Swanson, "Committee Assignments and the Non-Conformist Legislator: Democrats in the U.S. Senate," *Midwest Journal of Political Science,* 13 (February, 1969), pp. 84–94.

[10]There are numerous other plausible sources of party differences toward vote trading; unfortunately, we do not have adequate data to check these out. One explanation concerns the recruitment of candidates by each party. It may be that Republicans in general turn to less political types, often businessmen, who may be naive about politics and therefore not recognize the validity and usefulness of such activities as vote-trading, bargaining, compromise, and the like. While four of the six Republican freshmen in this group did not serve in the state legislature, it is interesting to note that four of the six also had as their primary occupation a business-related activity rather than the legal profession which was by far the most common occupation of the 91st class. Another explanation of this possible party difference is the position of the Democrats and Republicans as fairly permanent majority and minority parties in the House. This may mean that the responsibility for the passage of legislation is left more to the majority Democrats who must then engage in the vote trading and logrolling necessary to forge a majority coalition. It may be that Republicans tend to see this activity as illegitimate since they so often come out on the losing side, but this is purely speculative.

[11]Contrary to my expectation, it turned out that members from districts closer to Washington did not have higher absentee rates. But then one might argue that their scores would have been even higher had their districts been more distant from the Capitol.

[12]Overall, Republican freshmen missed 13 percent of the quorum votes and Democrats 17 percent. Southern freshmen in each party had the lowest absentee rates on the quorum votes—13 percent for Democrats and 8 percent for Republicans. This may be due to the fact that southern freshmen were more oriented toward the House in career terms and were therefore more likely to perform those tasks that promote a legislative career. Although I do not have data on this, there is no reason to believe that southern freshmen returned to their districts less often than their nonsouthern colleagues which then would have accounted for their higher attendance rates. In fact, five of the 11 southern districts were easily within three to five hours of Washington by car. Thus, it appears that there were regional differences in attendance rates which may reflect differing career views of the office of representative.

[12]The issue orientation of the freshmen was determined by impressionistically content-analyzing their responses to a series of questions dealing with their legislative goals, the specific pieces of legislation, if any, that they planned to introduce or work for, and the kinds of legislative matters about which their districts were most concerned.

[14]The percentages of table 7–4 are for freshmen in the aggregate. Thus, zero percent change does not necessarily mean that all the freshmen interviewed at t_1 and t_2 remained perfectly stable; shifts in one direction may have balanced out those in the other. As it was, there was general stability in the replies except for the two items discussed in the text (personal criticism and spending time on the House floor) so that the percentage differences in table 7–4 do not mask much additional shifting.

[15]As a reminder to the reader, the actual apprenticeship question was: Do you think that freshman Congressmen should serve a period of apprenticeship, that is, be more an observer than an active participant in the legislative process? In the subsequent discussion, apprenticeship will be treated as a dichotomous variable by collapsing the agreement and qualified agreement categories and by combining the disagreement and qualified disagreement categories.

[16]These measures are merely counts of the total number of entries in the *Record* and the total number of nonrelief bills and resolutions introduced. They could be refined by grouping remarks in the *Record* according to issue area or by dividing bills according to their scope of impact. But the expenditure of resources in such an endeavor seemed prohibitive. As sponsorship of bills is so prevalent in the House, the number of bills introduced may be a highly misleading measure of legislative activity. A better indicator might be the number of amendments

introduced. But since amendments from freshmen are relatively rare (only about one-fourth sponsored any), they cannot provide us with sufficient information.

[17] At the start of the 91st Congress, 21 percent of the 243 Democrats had served more than 20 years (ten terms) in the House as compared to under six percent of the 192 Republicans. Or to restate the figures, the Republicans had only eleven members with more than 20 years of service, while the Democrats had 51 such members. Furthermore, 46.4 percent of the Republicans had served three or fewer terms as opposed to 31.7 percent of the Democrats.

[18] Clapp, *The Congressman*, pp. 12–13.

[19] See Randall B. Ripley, *Power in the Senate* (New York: St. Martin's Press, 1969), p. 185 and Nelson W. Polsby, "Goodbye to the Inner Club," in *Congressional Behavior*, ed. Nelson W. Polsby (New York: Random House, 1971) pp. 105–10.

[20] A good example of such research is Fenno's treatment of apprenticeship in the context of the House Appropriations Committee. See *The Power of the Purse*, pp. 166–67.

[21] Price and Bell, "The Rules of the Game," p. 855.

Selection 8 Congressional Committee Behavior on Roll Call Votes: The U.S. House of Representatives, 1955–64

James W. Dyson
John W. Soule

Scholars have long noted the influence of Congressional committees in the legislative process. Whether committee influence is present during floor stages, or on roll calls, however, has not been explored. This study indicates that Congressional committees are highly influential on roll-call voting. Three main factors were used as explanatory variables: committee attractiveness to its members, committee integration, and the degree of partisanship on each committee. The latter two variables were related to committee success, while attractiveness was not. Highly attractive committees were not more successful, not more integrated, and as partisan as less attractive committees.

Since Woodrow Wilson[1] political scientists have recognized the considerable power and autonomy of Congressional committees. More recently committees have been carefully analyzed as discrete units from the standpoints of system theory,[2] representational theory,[3] conflict resolution,[4] and various aspects of small group theory.[5] Attempts are now underway to bring case studies on particular committees into a common theoretical framework,[6] and we view our present study as a very modest attempt toward this goal.

Most of the previous research on Congressional committees has focused on committee activity prior to the final floor stages where roll call votes are taken. No doubt committees have their most crucial impact on policies in these prior stages. Bills are submitted, written, scrutinized by subcommittees, public hearings are held, and in the final analysis committees decide what bills will and will not reach the floor and in what form. How committee norms develop and are enforced, how members perceive their work and the pressures that emanate from interested groups are all topics deserving of empirical research and, indeed, they have received a good deal of attention in regard to particular committees.

In our own study we have approached the general problem of committee influence or power from a very different standpoint. We wished to investigate the differential impact committees had upon the legislative process at the crucial

Reprinted from "Congressional Committee Behavior on Roll Call Votes: The U.S. House of Representatives, 1955–64," *Midwest Journal of Political Science* XIV (1970) by James W. Dyson and John W. Soule by permission of the Wayne State University Press. Copyright © 1970 by Wayne State University Press.

roll call stages, when Congressmen publicly voted on motions to table or recommit, on amendments, and on final passage of bills. Now debate has been present for more than ten years on the problems of making inferences from roll call votes. Similar to graduate students who facetiously ask us, "What does it all mean?" legislative scholars have been highly sensitive and prone to qualify conclusions based upon roll call data. There is no need for one to apologize for using roll call data even in analyzing the behavior of committees as long as he realizes that committees perform many tasks that cannot be analyzed or evaluated through roll call analysis. From the standpoint of Congressional committees, however, one of their primary functions is to enact legislation (with this extension being considerably less pertinent to the Rules Committee). Roll calls can, and indeed must, be used to study this function.

Congressional Committees As Small Groups

Before discussing our research design and findings, it is worthwhile to delve into some of the theoretical notions which led to the formation of our major hypotheses. Our thinking has been guided by four major concepts commonly used by students of Congress as well as experimental small group theorists—*committee success, attractiveness, integration* and *partisanship.* Congressional committees are conceived as functional subsystems of the House of Representatives. In order to perform their tasks, committees like other task-oriented small groups, must develop coping strategies to handle problems associated with tasks, member gratifications, and group integration. The tasks of Congressional committees are such that they cannot be performed by a single individual, thus the problems associated with interpersonal relationships arise. In the normal course of events, committees enjoy a high degree of operational autonomy, although in the final analysis the positive recommendations of committees are subject to the approval of the House. We shall speak of *successful* committees to the extent that they are able to realize their desires in Congress, i.e., committee recommendations are supported. Thus we have operationally defined a *committee success* as occurring when a majority of the committee is supported by a majority of the whole House on each roll call from that committee.

Since we have already indicated that committees perform important tasks other than reporting their recommendations to the floor, our treatment of committee success ignores these other aspects of committee behavior. We are only looking at the floor stages. We are assuming that committees do function to pass legislation, and that one means of determining their success is to analyze the proportion of times that their position commands support from the House.

It must be recognized that groups, including committees, are not pervasive entities. A group does not command the total person as individuals belong to more than one group. Members of a group share attitudes about relevant things.[7] Things that are not relevant to the group's attainment of goals do not require group members to behave in a cohesive way. An individual is a member of one group for one set of concerns and another group for another set of concerns. The real question is how successful is a group in commanding the loyalty of its members on relevant things.[8]

David Truman failed to specify the demands of committees on the basis of relevance. This failure led him to make an unreasonable demand on the pervasiveness of committee influence on its members. So he argued that committees are not a main source of voting cues unless the committees commanded the behavior of their members on bills outside their purview. Truman was asking in effect that a group command loyalty on irrelevant things. He said: "If the voting patterns represented something more than conscious agreement within the committee on its affairs and developed into a somewhat unconscious, generalized view of the party group on the committee as a source of voting cues, this should appear in a wide assortment of issues and not merely in those of special concern to the committee."[9] There is a twofold problem with Truman's position—one is his view that a group should command loyalty on things unrelated to the group's goals and two is the expectation that a group should have intragroup divisions that command loyalty outside of the group.

In addition to describing committee success, we have attempted to analyze why some committees are more successful than others. To do this we have employed the explanatory concepts of *attractiveness, integration,* and *partisanship.* A general view of committees is that some committees are more desirable or attractive than others. More attractive committees are often called the prestige committees, although the reasons why committees are attractive or not will not be considered here.[10]

A committee's attractiveness—as measured by who wants to join it and by the fact that very few members wish to leave it voluntarily—should predispose its members to respond to socialization in the group. Moreover, as Richard Fenno pointed out, a committee's attractiveness is a measure of its capacity to satisfy individual member needs. Thus the satisfaction associated with attractive committees increases the likelihood that members behave in such a way as to promote group success. We may hypothesize, then, that committee success will vary positively with committee attractiveness.

In addition to predicting committee success, we may expect committee attractiveness to have an impact on committee *integration.* Similar to the variable success, we have relied upon the behavior of committees on roll calls to ascertain the levels of committee integration. An integrated committee exists when members vote together on bills from that committee. It is quite possible, again, that an integrated committee on the floor is not highly integrated at stages prior to floor action, but this is unlikely. Fenno has written of the Appropriations Committee that:

On the floor, Committee members believe their power and prestige depend largely on the degree to which norms of reciprocity and unity continue to be observed. Members warn each other that if they go to the floor in disarray they will be "rolled," "jumped," or "run over" by the membership.[11]

In short, we can assume that committee integration is just as important for the functioning of committees at the roll call stage as it is in prior stages. Furthermore, this assumption can be directly tested by observing the relationship between committee integration and committee success. Should fragmented (non-integrated) committees be as successful as integrated committees, we would then have reason to doubt the importance of maintaining a unified front when facing the external environment.

Finally, we have employed the concept *partisanship* in analyzing committee success. Each committee is composed of Democratic and Republican blocs, and it is a separate empirical question as to whether a non-integrated committee is also high in partisanship. The lack of committee integration may be due to extreme partisanship, or to other factors. Partisanship occurs when both parties are cohesive in voting together, and the two blocs oppose one another.

Committees high in partisanship will, of course, be low in integration, but the relationships between attractiveness and partisanship, and success and partisanship are by no means so obvious. We shall presently examine both these relationships.

Let us summarize our own position, then, in studying Congressional committees by analyzing roll calls. A committee's attractiveness may be determined by who wants to join it and by the fact that very few members wish to leave it voluntarily. Attractiveness may result from a variety of factors peculiar to Congress not the least of which are a Congressman's constituency and the committee's subject matter. More attractive committees should experience greater integration and greater success in passing their legislation. Likewise, more integrated committees should be more successful than fragmented committees. Partisanship should be greatest in the least attractive committees, and it should contribute to committee failures.

The Study

We have utilized the roll call data compiled by the Survey Research Center at the University of Michigan which covers a ten year period (1955–1964). Studying committees over this period of time gives us much more confidence in the generalizability of our data than do previous studies of committees which are typically based on one or two sessions. In addition to these data it was necessary to compile data on committee assignments of Congressmen and to obtain data on the indications of committee attractiveness based on data from the *Congressional Quarterly Almanac* for the years studied. We used this latter source, furthermore, to discover the standing committee origin for each of the 815 roll call votes.

One further note on the roll calls used in this analysis deserves to be mentioned. *The Congressional Quarterly* publishes and we have used the results of *all* roll calls regardless of their importance. The great bulk of legislation is disposed of by voice vote. For example, Congress in 1966 passed 2,016 bills, yet recorded only 428 roll calls. On some occasions several roll calls may be taken on different amendments to the same bill. At any rate, it is important for us to make clear that we have included all roll calls. These may be taken on amendments, motions and on final passage although, in fact, most roll calls occur on final passage of bills.

Our method for assessing committee attractiveness involves the flow of members to and from committees and is spelled out more fully below. Integration and party cohesion are studied through roll call behavior. Underlying the reliance on these data is the assumption that coalitions formed on roll calls will reflect the sentiments of committee members. It is quite unlikely that a group member, who is an expert in an area, changes his mind after a bill is reported out of committee. So what is done on roll call votes should indicate what the preferences of the committee members were prior to the floor stage. There will be, of course, a handful of exceptions (if, for example, committee members agree to disagree by following party lines on the floor), but the rule that what is once on the floor of the House reflects a person's preference should be a pervasive one. Congressional acceptance, which is usually awarded through roll call votes, is the only way a committee can achieve its positive desires.

Success of Committees

The first thing we wish to record is the overwhelming success of committees. On the whole and over 10 years committees were quite successful. On nearly 90 percent of roll calls in the House on bills reported out by committees, the majority of a committee was on the winning side, i.e., the majority of the House supported the position of the committee majority. There was very little variance from Congress to Congress. Thus control of the presidency and the size of the majority party do not appear to relate to committee success to any substantial extent. For three of the Congresses the Republicans controlled the presidency and the success rate of committees was about the same as for the other two Congresses. The size of majority party's majority varied during the 10 year period, so the stability of the rate of successes of committees indicates that size of the majority party is unrelated to success.

The first table is a summary one, so it may hide differences between committees. The data in table 8-1 only indicate that on the whole committee

Table 8-1   Success of committees in enacting legislation by the House of
            Representatives: 1955-1964

	84th	85th	86th	87th	88th	Five Congresses
Successes	114	133	133	171	183	724
Failures	16	13	14	18	20	81
Percent Failures	12.3	08.9	09.5	09.5	10.4	10.1

proposals are very successful in the Congress. It may be that some committees are more successful than others. The data in table 8-1 do not indicate whether committee success depends on the posture of majority party members of the committee or the committee as a whole. We may find that on a good many issues committee success is due to partisanship rather than group integration. That is, the majority position of the committee may be representing votes on which party members of the committee differ. The remainder of the paper will examine attractiveness, committee integration, and partisanship to determine what factors relate to committee successes and to estimate how much of roll call voting behavior may reflect the hegemony of committees in the legislative process. In short, are committee successes due to the committee system or to exogeneous factors such as party memberships?

Committee Attractiveness

The first variable we wish to look at to account for the pattern of committee successes is attractiveness. We want to rank the committees on the basis of who becomes a member and whether a committee is high or low on voluntary retirements. Three indicators of these factors are used conjunctively: mean percent of freshmen per term, mean seniority per term, and mean number of voluntary retirements per term. These indicators were used over the ten year period to obtain three rankings of the committees from high to low attractiveness. The ranks were summed to obtain an overall indicator which summarized the position of each committee on each on the indicators. The complete details are presented in table 8-2.

Table 8-2 merely ranks the committees on attractiveness according to three interrelated indicators. The table shows that Rules is the most attractive committee. It ranks first overall and on each of the indicators. Ways and Means is second and Appropriations is a close third. Armed Services, Judiciary, Foreign Affairs, Un-American Activities and District of Columbia are the next cluster of attractive committees. A third cluster is made up of Agriculture, Interstate and Foreign Commerce, Science and Astronautics and House Administration. The remaining committees cluster at the bottom of the attractiveness scale.

Table 8-2   Indicators of committees attractiveness and a combined indicator of attractiveness, House of Representatives: 1955–1964 (committees are ranked by summary indication of attractiveness)

Committees	$\bar{x}$% Freshmen per Term 1	$\bar{x}$ Seniority, per Term 2	$\bar{x}$ Number of Voluntary Retirements, per Term 3	Summary Index of Ranks
Rules	.00	8.2	.000	1
Ways and Means	.01	7.0	.004	2
Appropriations	.02	7.6	.008	3
Armed Services	.10	6.6	.032	4.5
Un-American Activities	.09	5.5	.022	4.5
Judiciary	.13	5.1	.012	6
District of Columbia	.09	6.3	.080	7
Foreign Affairs	.11	4.9	.013	8
Agriculture	.15	5.7	.053	9
Interstate and Foreign Commerce	.11	4.7	.048	10
House Administration	.10	4.9	.080	11
Science and Astronautics	.16	4.5	.012	12
Public Works	.21	4.2	.065	13
Government Operations	.17	4.5	.107	14
Merchant Marines and Fisheries	.18	4.2	.084	15
Interior	.20	3.5	.098	16
Education and Labor	.21	3.8	.073	17
Banking and Currency	.27	4.7	.120	18
Post Office and Civil Service	.27	4.1	.176	19
Veterans' Affairs	.28	4.0	.150	20

Rank 1 and Rank 2, Rho = .89
Rank 1 and Rank 3, Rho = .77
Rank 2 and Rank 3, Rho = .68

$$\text{Rho} = 1 - \frac{6\,(\Sigma d^2)}{n\,(n^2 - 1)}$$

Σ Rank and Rank 1, Rho = .93
Σ Rank and Rank 2, Rho = .91
Σ Rank and Rank 3, Rho = .87

There are very few surprises in the rankings obtained. Perhaps the District of Columbia is too high and Education and Labor too low. But the results obtained are reasonable, and the rank order correlation between our ranking and that established by George Goodwin is .87.[12] Each of our indicators made a proportionate contribution to the summary indicator with mean percent freshmen per term correlating about .06 higher with the summary index than mean number of voluntary retirements. Given that the summary index does correlate very highly with each indicator only the summary index will be used as a measure of attractiveness.

Committee Integration

The index of agreement is used as the indicator of committee integration in this study. This index measures the proportion of times each committee member agrees with every other committee member on proposals from their committee.[13] Party membership is ignored in considering agreements (integration) in the whole committee. Earlier we hypothesized that the more attractive committees would be more integrated than less attractive committees.

The data in table 8-3 examine this relationship. Contrary to our initial hypothesis the two variables are not related. This lack of relationship is deter-

Table 8-3   Committee integration and number of bills reported by committee, 1955–1964 (committees listed by attractiveness ranks)

Committees	$\bar{X}$ Index of Agreement (Rank in Parenthesis)		Number of Bills
Rules	.49	(20)	06
Ways and Means	.64	(15)	81
Appropriations	.66	(13)	176
Armed Services*	.85	(02)	49
Un-American Activities*	1.00	(01)	05
Judiciary	.60	(19)	42
District of Columbia	.63	(16)	22
Foreign Affairs*	.77	(06)	52
Agriculture	.65	(14)	66
Interstate and Foreign Commerce	.71	(09)	43
House Administration	.73	(07)	07
Science and Astronautics*	.83	(04)	14
Public Works	.62	(17)	34
Government Operations	.67	(12)	15
Merchant Marines and Fisheries*	.83	(04)	08
Interior	.70	(10)	37
Education and Labor	.61	(18)	53
Banking and Currency	.71	(09)	56
Post Office and Civil Service	.69	(11)	29
Veterans' Affairs*	.83	(04)	10
Rho = −.13			
With Rules Excluded: Rho = −.06			

*Asterisks are used to note committees that attained a minimum level of agreement of .75 on the index of agreement.

mined by rho (−.13) and the slightly negative direction of the measure highlights the difference. Attractive committees do not have higher agreement scores than unattractive committees and this remains true when the Rules Committee is excluded from consideration (rho = −.06). In fact, of the highly and moderately attractive committees only Armed Services, Foreign Affairs and UnAmerican Activities have substantially high agreement scores, while two unattractive committees — Merchant Marines and Fisheries and Veterans' Affairs — also have high agreement scores.

Since a committee score of .80 on the index of agreement would mean that only a few committee members disagreed with the group, on the average, such a score would be a reasonable reflection of a highly integrated committee. In any event, a score greater than .75 is required for minimal integration as in this case there is only about a .73 percent improvement over chance agreements (which is a 50-50 split). Only six committees (the ones with asterisks after their names in table 8-3) attained an index of agreement score above .75. And of those above .80 only Armed Services and Science and Astronautics are major standing committees in Congress.

The low scores on the index of agreement indicate that committee fragmentation is more prevalent than committee integration. Since committees cannot hold members together consistently it is unlikely that noncommittee members are tacitly accepting committee judgments. The power of committees, i.e., their 90 percent success rate on all roll calls, must be structurally based rather than sociometric, viz., if the committee majorities receive support in Congress they do so mainly because of the structural roadblocks to proposing legislation and amendments on the floor of the House of Representatives. Certainly the inordinate success of committees in enacting legislation does not reflect a high level of committee integration. Moreover, since the attractive committees are not the highly integrated ones, we are led to view leadership as Alex Bavelas did:

> . . . we came close to the notion of leadership, not as a personal quality, but as an *organizational function.* Under this concept it is not sensible to ask of an organization "Who is the leader?" Rather we ask "How are the leadership functions distributed in this organization?" The distribution may be wide or narrow. It may be so narrow — so many of the leadership functions may be vested in a single person — that he is the leader in the popular sense. But in modern organization this is becoming more and more rare.[14]

Interpreting the perspective of Bavelas in terms of Congress it may be said that the prestige committees are such because they are the committees that involve Congressmen in a share of the important action. That is, these committees determine legislation in the major areas of public policy-making insofar as policy requires legislative enactments. The data presented so far show that the characteristic of leadership is distributed to the individuals who play key roles in key committees and in organization of the House itself. In this overall context our suggestion that committee success is a derivative of structural arrangements in the House of Representatives, rather than the sociometric qualities of groups, seems justifiable.

Committee Success

A more direct assessment of the relationship between attractiveness and success is shown in table 8-4. Perhaps the summary quality of the data presented in table 8-3 conceals some features of relationships that might negate our inferences. Certainly summing 815 roll calls by committees, over five Congresses may produce misleading averages. However, this possibility is simply not the case. A detailed breakdown of the data supports the interpretation that attractiveness does not determine committee success.

Of the attractive committees, Appropriations and Agriculture are less successful than the average rate of success for all committees. Conversely, a number of relatively unattractive committees are much more successful than the average rate of success for all committees. The overall pattern is indicated by rho (−.01) which points out that attractiveness and success are unrelated.

Table 8-4   Committees' defeats compared with attractiveness ranking, 1955–1964

Committee	Number of Defeats	% Defeats	Rank % Defeats, Least to Most
Rules	1	.167	18
Ways and Means	4	.049	5
Appropriations	25	.142	16
Armed Services	2	.041	4
Un-American Activities	0	.000	1
Judiciary	3	.071	9.5
District of Columbia	4	.182	20
Foreign Affairs	2	.038	3
Agriculture	9	.136	15
Interstate and Foreign Commerce	3	.070	8
House Administration	1	.143	17
Science and Aeronautics	1	.071	9.5
Public Works	2	.056	7
Government Operations	2	.133	14
Merchant Marines and Fisheries	0	.000	1
Interior	2	.054	6
Education and Labor	9	.170	19
Banking and Currency	6	.107	13
Post Office and Civil Service	3	.103	12
Veterans' Affairs	1	.100	11
Rho=−.01			
Integration and % of Victories: Rho=.58			

On the other hand when committees are ranked on integration (see table 8–3) we find that the more integrated a committee the less likely that committee will be defeated in the House of Representatives. The moderate relationship between integration and success indicated by a rho of +.58 provides further support for the hypothesis that committee power is structurally derived rather than sociometrically (attractiveness) derived.

Inter-party Agreement Within Committees

Next, we turn to the agreement of parties within the committees (table 8-5). The pattern of agreement of the two blocs within each committee also indicates that the data in table 8-3 accurately reflect committee integration. Considering the proportion of times a majority of both parties agrees (opt for the ith or jth alternative conjunctively) demonstrates a congruence between party cohesion and integration within each committee. The six committees given asterisks in table 8-3 because of high integration scores are the first six committees in proportion of interbloc agreements. The only reason the scores on the index of agreement are not higher for these six committees is a small amount of splintering within each bloc.

The data in table 8-5 also indicate that the cutoff of .75 of the index of agreement was realistic. These data show that only these six committees had a majority of each party in agreement on .75 percent of the roll call votes on bills from respective committees. Conversely, among the seven lowest ranked committees on integration, five rank lowest on the proportion of interbloc agreements. One of these seven committees, Appropriations, ranked fourteenth on integration and thirteenth on proportion of interbloc agreements. So at the two extremes the two indicators are highly congruent.

The significance of the data presented so far is that the most attractive committees are neither the most integrated nor the most successful, although a moderately strong relationship exists between success and integration. These findings *based only upon roll calls* suggest that Fenno's description[15] of the Appropriations Committee needs to be modified or at least questioned. Instead of being integrated the Appropriations Committee is high in partisanship and is one of the least successful committees in Congress. On about 46 percent of roll call votes the two blocs disagree, and the committee's majority loses about 14 percent of roll call votes. At the very least, the verbal description of committee members regarding what goes on in committees is not supported by the roll call voting behavior of committee members.

Charles Jones, on the other hand, in a study of the Committee on Agriculture found that committee members tended to think in terms of their remote environment (e.g., interests of farm regions and of constituents).[16] The interview data obtained by Jones indicate that committee integration as we have defined it is not a norm of the Agriculture Committee. As action moved

Table 8-5 Agreements and disagreements of majority of parties on votes pertaining to bills from own committee (ranked by attractiveness)

Committee	Agreements	%	Disagreements	%	Rank (most to least agreement of party majorities)
Rules	00	.000	04	1.000	20
Ways and Means	37	.507	36	.493	15
Appropriations	94	.543	79	.457	14
Armed Services	43	.896	05	.104	5
Un-American Activities	05	1.000	00	.000	1
Judiciary	26	.667	13	.333	11
District of Columbia	14	.700	06	.300	10
Foreign Affairs	41	.911	04	.089	4
Agriculture	26	.413	37	.587	17
Interstate and Foreign Commerce	31	.738	11	.262	7
House Administration	04	.571	03	.429	13
Science and Astronautics	11	.846	02	.154	6
Public Works	14	.500	14	.500	16
Government Operations	06	.400	09	.600	19
Merchant Marines and Fisheries	08	1.000	00	.000	1
Interior	24	.706	10	.294	8
Education and Labor	21	.412	30	.588	18
Banking and Currency	31	.585	22	.415	12
Post Office and Civil Service	19	.704	09	.296	9
Veterans' Affairs	09	1.000	00	.000	1
Total*	464	.60	294	.40	

Rho = −.16
Integration and % Agreements: Rho = .83
% Agreements and % Victories: Rho = .65

*Some of the 815 roll calls are not tabulated here because either or both parties failed to have a majority position, i.e., the votes were tied.

away from basic subcommittee working levels and toward the final vote, the Agriculture Committee member was more disposed to support his party's or the administration's position at the expense of committee unity. Thus the data obtained by Jones and the data reported here are congruent with regard to the Agriculture Committee. Integration is not a stipulated norm and committee fragmentation is relatively high with the majority positions of the two blocs differing on nearly 59 percent of roll-call votes pertaining to bills reported out by the committee.

Intraparty Agreement Within Committees: Partisanship

We have yet to consider the relationship of integration to partisanship or party cohesion and the relationship of attractiveness, integration and party cohesion to success in enacting legislation. Cohesion, again, is defined here as the agreement ratio of Democrats with Democrats and Republicans with Republicans (considering each bloc separately). In measuring cohesion we will again use the index of agreement, only we will hold constant party affiliation. Thus the proportion of times Democrats on a committee agree with each other, and Republicans agree with Republicans, will give a cohesion score for each bloc in each committee.

The pattern of expectations is as follows:

1. High integration requires high cohesion for each party bloc.
2. Low integration does not require partisan cohesion, hence:
   a. if integration is low and cohesion is low there are intrabloc splinters as well as partisanship.
   b. if integration is low and cohesion is high, partisanship is high.

These committess may be divided into categories in accord with the pattern of relation obtaining between integration and cohesion.

Looking first at the relationship between integration and cohesion, we find, as expected, a mixed pattern (table 8-6). However, of the five highest committees on integration four rank in the five highest committees on cohesion for Democrats. At the lowest quartile extreme on integration, three of the committees are found among the five lowest scores on cohesion by Democrats. Committee integration and cohesion for the majority party are highly related. The Republicans do not fit so nicely into the pattern. The real problem is the consistent lack of high cohesion among Republicans. For sixteen of the twenty committees, Republican cohesion is between .70 and .80. Only two committees score above .80 and only two others below .70. A greater variation in cohesion is present among Democrats. This group has one committee at 1.0, six at .90 to .99, eight between .80 and .89, three in the

Table 8-6 Index of agreement scores for committee and for Democrats and Republicans, averages (ranked from high to low integration)

Committee	Cohesion				Integration Committee	
	Democrats	Rank	Republicans	Rank	Score	Rank
Un-American Activities	1.000	(1)	1.000	(1)	1.00	(1)
Armed Services	.896	(8)	.847	(2)	.85	(2)
Science and Astronautics	.985	(2)	.761	(7)	.83	(4)
Merchant Marines and Fisheries	.933	(3)	.720	(11)	.83	(4)
Veterans' Affairs	.930	(5)	.718	(14)	.83	(4)
Foreign Affairs	.841	(10)	.719	(12)	.77	(6)
House Administration	.760	(17)	.762	(6)	.73	(7)
Banking and Currency	.909	(7)	.653	(19)	.71	(9)
Interstate and Foreign Commerce	.827	(14)	.725	(10)	.71	(9)
Interior	.823	(15)	.633	(20)	.70	(10)
Post Office and Civil Service	.837	(12)	.701	(17)	.69	(11)
Government Operations	.931	(4)	.784	(3)	.67	(12)
Appropriations	.790	(16)	.759	(8)	.66	(13)
Agriculture	.869	(9)	.771	(5)	.65	(14)
Ways and Means	.930	(5)	.718	(14)	.64	(15)
District of Columbia	.615	(20)	.718	(14)	.63	(16)
Public Works	.840	(11)	.743	(9)	.62	(17)
Education and Labor	.829	(13)	.707	(16)	.61	(18)
Judiciary	.631	(19)	.670	(18)	.60	(19)
Rules	.755	(18)	.778	(4)	.49	(20)

Dem – Rep, Rho = .33
Dem – Int., Rho = .63
Rep – Int., Rho = .30

seventies and two in the sixties. It appears that the majority party, Democrats, contributes most to whether or not a committee is integrated.

When committees are ranked on the attractiveness continuum, the most attractive committees were found to generate the most partisan conflict among both Democrats and Republicans (not shown in tabular form). For example, we compared three extremely attractive committees (Rules, Ways and Means, and Appropriations) with three others concerned with important substantive matters (Armed Services, Education, and Labor and Agriculture). We found that within the initial set of attractive committees the mean Democratic cohesion was .80 while within the less attractive committees it was .87. In short, committee attractiveness fails to account for cohesion within either party just as it earlier failed to predict committee integration.

Finally we addressed ourselves to the question of whether attractiveness or integration had greater influence on committee success in getting its recommendations accepted by Congress. Table 8-7 is addressed to this question. The data on success are distributed in accord with degree of integration and attraction. The pattern is clear: success is not varying with attractiveness, while success is varying with integration (see table 8-7, Total column). The more integrated committees are the more successful ones. In fact, the most integrated committees are three times as successful as the least integrated committees. On the other hand, the least attractive committees are only slightly less successful than the most attractive committees. Attraction is unrelated to the proportion of success a committee enjoys, while integration of a committee is a factor contributing to success.

The role that partisanship plays in determining committee success or failure can also be found in table 8-7. If the two parties disagree and the majority party's position determines the committee's position, the more integrated the committee the greater the success of the majority party. And within this subset, as with the overall pattern, attractiveness does not relate to success. The committees in the second and third quartiles are as successful as the most attractive committees. There can be little doubt that minimal partisanship on roll calls is not a function of committee attractiveness. The three most attractive committees are not the most successful, but three other attractive committees, Armed Services, Foreign Affairs, and Un-American Activities, are successful. Since these committees are also highly integrated their success may not be due to attractiveness, but to integration.

The greatest losses suffered by committees occur when a majority of both parties disagree. For all roll calls within the ten year period the majority position of the parties was in agreement 61.3 percent of the time and when this occurred the committees only lost about 5 percent of the votes. When the parties disagreed and the Democrats represented the majority position of the committee, the committees lost nearly 16 percent of the votes. The committees were even less successful when a majority of *Democrats opposed a majority of the committee*, losing about 25 percent of the votes. There can be not doubt

Table 8-7 Defeats of committees by attraction and integration separately (1955–1964)

Independent Variables	Committee Integrated [a]		Committee Fragmented Rep.Pos. Maj.[b]		Committee Fragmented Dem.Pos. Maj.[c]		Total	
	n	%	n	%	n	%	n	%
Attractiveness[d]								
First Quartile	9	(.028)	5	(.016)	18	(.057)	32	(.101)
Second Quartile	9	(.040)	2	(.009)	10	(.044)	21	(.093)
Third Quartile	1	(.011)	0	(.000)	05	(.057)	06	(.068)
Fourth Quartile	6	(.032)	2	(.011)	13	(.070)	21	(.114)
Integration[e]								
First Quartile	03	(.024)	0	(.000)	02	(.016)	05	(.040)
Second Quartile	07	(.048)	2	(.014)	04	(.028)	13	(.090)
Third Quartile	12	(.033)	5	(.014)	22	(.061)	39	(.108)
Fourth Quartile	03	(.017)	2	(.011)	18	(.103)	23	(.132)

[a]These are the defeats on the bills on which a majority of both parties agree.

[b]These are the defeats on the bills on which a majority of the committee disagrees with a majority of the Democrats.

[c]These are the defeats on the bills on which the parties disagree and the Democrats represent the majority position of committee.

[d]See Table 2 for committees in each group.

[e]See Table 7 for committees in every group.

that committee agreement across party lines contributes to committee success as party disagreements are reflected in the success ratio of committees. Even the majority party position cannot overcome committee fragmentation. On votes on which the Democrats oppose a majority of the committee the majority party is defeated about three-fourths of the time.

The pattern of success in terms of integration is quite clear: a unified committee is successful about 95 percent of the time; a Democratic party controlled committee position prevails about 84 percent of the time; a Republican party controlled committee position prevails about 75 percent of the time. Minimal partisanship is a key to committee success.

The predominance of integration over attractiveness in predicting success is shown in table 8-8. In this table the committees are grouped by two degrees of integration and attraction. The distribution indicates that regardless of the level of attractiveness, the level of integration determines the ratio of the success of committees. Integrated committees are unsuccessful about 6½ percent of the time regardless of attractiveness level. Fragmented committees are unsuccessful on slightly over 11 percent of the votes regardless of attractiveness level. Again a familiar conclusion is evident: minimal partisanship and not attractiveness accounts for the inordinate success rate of some committees.

Table 8-8   Relationship of integration and attraction to success of
             committees, 1955–1964

Integration-Fragmentation:	High Int. High Att.[1]		High Int. Low Att.[2]		High Frag. High Att.[3]		High Frag. Low Att.[4]	
Attraction:	n	%	n	%	n	%	n	%
Failures								
Defeats	11	(.064)	07	(.072)	42	(.113)	20	(.121)
Votes	171		98		371		165	

[1]Armed Services, District of Columbia, Foreign Services, Interstate and Foreign Commerce, and Un-American Activities.

[2]Interior and Insular Affairs, Merchant Marines and Fisheries, Post Office and Civil Service, Science and Astronautics, and Veterans' Affairs.

[3]Agriculture, Appropriations, Judiciary, Rules, and Ways and Means.

[4]Banking and Currency, Education and Labor, Government Operations, House Administration, and Public Works.

Conclusions

We have attempted an analysis of the behavior of Congressional committees by utilizing all 815 roll call votes taken during the ten year period, 1955–64. Standing out among the findings was the overwhelming success achieved by committees in getting Congress to accept their proposals 90 percent of the time. When party factionalism was absent on committees, success was achieved on 95 percent of the votes.

We may turn for a moment to the classical argument that pits committee government against legislative party government. Our findings regarding committee success do not necessarily preclude the Congressional party from functioning as an important cue-giving device for votes in Congress. The majority party (Democrats) in Congress defeats the majority position of the committee on 25 percent of the relevant votes. Since this circumstance can only arise when the Republicans on a committee are mostly homogeneous and the Democrats are split, this is no small feat for the majority party. Moreover, committee partisanship develops on almost 40 percent of the roll calls analyzed in this study. Such an extensive amount of fragmentation implies that party can and does function within committees, at least during roll-call stages. Only if there were a small amount of committee fragmentation would the relationship of party to roll-call voting behavior be potentially spurious. Partisanship in committees is about as pervasive as partisanship in Congress. In short, the question of party government versus committee government should not be framed as an "either-or" proposition.

When committee success, integration and partisanship are analyzed in conjunction with committee attractiveness, we found the attractive committees are not more likely to be successful, integrated or nonpartisan than unattractive committees. The finding in other small group experiments regarding the importance of group attractiveness in contributing to group harmony and task fulfillment does not appear to hold for Congressional committees.[17] Structural consideration regarding leadership in Congress, and the substantive type of legislation handled by different committees appear to override the sociometric quality of attractiveness found to be important for the functioning of other groups.

We might speculate here on why attractiveness was such a poor predictor of committee success or integration. The most attractive committees handle much of the most controversial legislation, and indeed, this factor may contribute to their attractiveness. Thus Congressmen appear to be reacting to substantive considerations rather than sociometric considerations within the committee. Furthermore, among committees that rank as unattractive on the average, it is possible that to *some* individuals they represent very attractive groups. The legislative output is low and controversial and low ranking members are biding their time to make a profitable move to another committee. So those to whom the committee is attractive get their way and the whole committee appears as low on attractiveness, high on integration and low on partisanship.

Committee integration on the floor of the house was found to be an important determinant of committee success. Fenno[18] and other scholars are correct in arguing that committees are most successful when they are able to create a united front when reporting their legislation to Congress. The particular committees that are able to remain united, however, are by no means the most attractive or prestigious.

Notes

[1]Woodrow Wilson, *Congressional Government: A Study in American Politics* (New York: Meridian Edition, 1956).

[2]Richard Fenno, "The House Appropriations Committee as a Political System: The Problems of Integration," *American Political Science Review,* LVI (June, 1962), pp. 310–324. Citation from reprint in Heinz Eulau, ed., *Political Behavior in America: New Directions* (New York: Random House, 1966).

[3]Charles O. Jones, "The Agriculture Committee and the Problem of Representation," *American Political Science Review* (June, 1961), pp. 358–367.

[4]John F. Manley, "The House Committee on Ways and Means: Conflict Management in a Congressional Committee," *American Political Science Review,* LIX (December, 1965), pp. 887–904.

[5]See Nicholas A. Masters, "Committee Assignments," *American Political Science Review,* LV (June, 1961), pp. 345–57; George Goodwin, Jr., "The Seniority System in Congress," *American Political Science Review,* LIII (June, 1959), pp. 412–36; Charles O. Jones, "The Role of the Congressional Subcommittee," *Midwest Journal of Political Science,* VI (November, 1962), pp. 327–44; James A. Robinson, *The House Rules Committee*

(Indianapolis, 1963); Ralph A. Huitt, "The Congressional Committee: A Case Study," *American Political Science Review*, XLVIII (June, 1954), pp. 340–65.

[6]Richard Fenno is presently preparing a comparative study of six Congressional committees.

[7]Joseph E. McGrath, *Social Psychology: A Brief Introduction* (New York: Holt, Rinehart and Winston, 1964), p. 107.

[8]For conceptual orientations toward groups and interaction see, for example, F. Shibutani, "Reference Groups as Perspectives," *American Journal of Sociology*, Vol. 60, 1955; Theodore M. Newcomb, "The Prediction of Interpersonal Attraction," *American Psychologist*, Vol. 11, 1956; Theodore M. Newcomb, *Social Psychology* (New York: Holt, Rinehart and Winston, 1950).

[9]David Truman, *The Congressional Party: A Case Study* (New York: John Wiley & Sons, 1959), p. 270.

[10]For one ranking of committee desirability based on the single criterion of committee transfers see George Goodwin, Jr., "The Seniority System in Congress," *American Political Science Review*, LIII (June, 1959), pp. 412–436; see also Charles Bullock and John Sprague, "A Research Note on the Committee Reassignment of Southern Democratic Congressmen," *Journal of Politics*, 31 (May, 1969), pp. 493–513.

[11]Fenno, *op. cit.*, p. 120.

[12]Goodwin, *op. cit.*

[13]We have conceptualized committee integration as a characteristic of the interpersonal relations of the group's members. Integration, then, can be appropriately operationalized by simply ascertaining how frequently committee members agree with one another. The more frequently members agree, the more integrated the committee is. An agreement is constituted by both members voting together ("Announced" or "paired" are not counted as agreements or disagreements) and the index is the proportion of times all possible pairs agree. Technically the index of agreement is:

$$\frac{2 \left[\sum\limits_{i=1}^{n-1} \sum\limits_{j=i+1}^{n} a_{ij} + \sum\limits_{n-1}^{m-1} \sum\limits_{l=k+1}^{m} a_{kl} \right]}{N \, (N-1)}$$

Where n = number selecting one alternative; m = number selecting other alternative; and N = number of maximum possible agreements.

The first extensive use of the index of agreement appeared in Herman C. Beyle, *Identification and Analysis of Attribute-Cluster-Blocs* (Chicago: University of Chicago Press, 1931). For other applications, see Truman, *op. cit.*; Arend Lijphart, "The Analysis of Bloc Voting in the General Assembly," *American Political Science Review*, 57 (December, 1963), pp. 902–917; and Lee F. Anderson, Meredith W. Watts, Jr., and Allen R. Wilcox, *Legislative Roll Call Analysis* (Evanston: Northwestern University Press, 1966), pp. 40–43.

[14]Alex Bavelas, "Leadership: Man and Function," *Administrative Science Quarterly*, Vol. 4, 1960, pp. 494–495.

[15]Fenno, *op. cit.* Let us mention again, however, that Fenno concerns himself primarily with the Appropriations Committee operations prior to the roll-call stages, whereas we have dealt with integration and cohesion only in terms of roll-call votes.

[16]Jones, *op. cit.*

[17]See all six articles reprinted in Part II of Dorwin Cartwright and Alvin Zander, eds., *Group Dynamics: Research and Theory* (Evanston, Ill.: Row, Peterson, 1960). Group attractiveness is labelled group "valence," and is found to have significant effects on the structure and performance of various kinds of task oriented groups. One of the problems in using our operational definition of attractiveness is that we cannot explore why certain committees are attractive to certain Congressmen. This would require survey work. Small group researchers have based their conception of attractiveness primarily on how

members feel about each other. We would hypothesize that attractiveness for Congressmen on committees to be based more upon task oriented considerations rather than interpersonal considerations.

[18]Fenno, *op. cit.,* p. 120.

Part 3 Pressures on the Legislative System: Inputs

The papers included in the second part treated some of the major concerns within the basic contours of the congressional system. The third part turns to the inputs to that system. Congress, operating through the processes that have been outlined, deals with inputs of demands and supports; Congress' products (outputs) are in a sense the result of the interplay of the demands and system characteristics. Inputs of demands—requests for specific actions—reach Congress from the president and the executive branch, the lobbyists, and to a lesser extent the courts and public. The same sources provide inputs of support—that is, favorable or unfavorable sentiments and actions that are directed toward the legislative system.

The role orientations legislators assume reflect the environmental forces as well as the internal organization of Congress. Members of Congress must decide how to relate to requests from the executive or from the public. Is their primary job to speak and act for external interests or should they resist such demands? Lawmakers face conflicting appeals from various external sources and decide where their primary loyalty lies, and they will in all probability have to face and reface such appeals as legislative attention shifts from issue to issue.

Demands

The President

One indisputable political fact of the twentieth century is that the president and the executive branch have assumed a central role in the legislative process. As Dahl has succinctly put it, "the president proposes, the Congress disposes."[1] Or alternatively, it is the chief executive, through his proposals to Congress, who determines the topics on which the legislature will spend the great bulk of its time. The president's program, in short, defines the work load of Congress. Moreover, executive domination of the congressional agenda has survived the skepticism about presidential leadership that Vietnam and Watergate generated. Jimmy Carter, elected in 1976 after a campaign during which he sought to play down the "imperial presidency," nonetheless provided the focus of congressional activity; his energy, welfare reform, tax, and social security proposals, to say nothing of the Panama Canal treaty, occupied the major share of Congress' time during 1977–1978. Though Congress may be more assertive than it was a decade ago, its efforts are directed largely to presidential initiatives.

The executive program is largely a product of a winnowing process that the Office of Management and Budget (OMB, formerly the Bureau of the Budget) conducts on behalf of the president. In selection 9, Gilmour (updating Neustadt's classic studies, 1954, 1955), describes the growth and evolution of this "central clearance" process. During the 1950s, these procedures produced a coordinated legislative agenda for the president to submit to Congress, using the State of the Union address, the budget speech, and other special messages as transmission channels. More recently, Gilmour suggests, the newly emerging White House staff (the president's personal aides) has also been deeply involved in the formulation of the president's program, especially with respect to highest-priority legislation. The president has, in short, substantial executive help—from OMB and his White House staff—in preparing his administration's legislative program. In addition, OMB continues its scrutiny of legislative activity after the submission of the administration program; congressional committees frequently consult with OMB to ascertain the compatibility of their thought with the program; OMB analyzes bills Congress passes for consistency with the president's positions and drafts veto messages should it deem them necessary.

Not only does the executive branch closely observe its program as it moves through the congressional system, but the president and his staff can and often do intervene in the legislative process to work for passage of specific legislative measures. The president has a number of formal and informal weapons at his disposal. His State of the Union Address and other written messages formally convey his views of what Congress should do. In addition, should the legislature pass undesirable measures, he can exercise his veto, which Congress can override only with great difficulty. Often the threat of a presidential veto will cause the lawmakers to reconsider the legislative provisions the chief executive finds objectionable.

The bulk of the president's influence, however, rests on an informal base. He can seek to recruit support for his proposals through a direct approach to individual members of Congress or more obliquely through efforts to mobilize the public—that is, to create vocal popular expression of his demands on the legislative system. His main weapon in these influence attempts is persuasion—efforts to convince legislators that their interests would be served by backing the administration program.[2] He possesses initiative and vast staff and information resources; he can, as the central figure in American politics, preempt the lawmaking stage whenever he wishes; his status guarantees attention for his policy proposals. Added to this, the state of his "professional reputation" and "public prestige" will enhance his persuasive powers. His reputation is reflected in the feeling of those whom he seeks to influence that he has the ability and the determination to employ his bargaining advantages. Prestige implies that the president will be able to rally public sentiment behind his cause. The greater the president's reputation and prestige, the more difficult it will be for members of Congress to resist White House requests, for to engage in combat with a determined and popular executive is to court disaster. Jimmy Carter's "image-building" activities during the early days of his term—his celebrated walk down Pennsylvania Avenue, his frequent press conferences, his fireside chats, his overnight stays in private homes, and so on—are consistent with this view of presidential power.

The president may deal with the entire Congress, attempting to influence legislators' views through speeches, special messages, letters to the legislative leadership that are released for publication, press conference utterances, and the reports of presidential "task forces." The president must provide a persuasive argument or at least an acceptable rationale for backing executive programs.

The president may also direct his attention to specific subgroups of Congress. He may appeal to his party colleagues in terms of partisan loyalty or the need to establish party positions. He may focus attention on the most important committee by means of letters to the members or through the testimony of executive personnel at the committee's hearings. Committee or subcommittee members may be briefed by the relevant executive agency. And, in some cases, the managers of a bill may make concessions in order to win backing from those favored by accepted amendments. Such tactics may serve both to win votes and to divide the opposition.

Special mention should be made of efforts to enlist the support of the opposition party; in the foreign policy realm these tactics are commonly identified as bipartisanship. The essence of the notion is that the president, through consultations with the leaders of the party out of power, seeks to win sufficient opposition votes to enact the desired policy. Bipartisanship can operate only when there is time for consultation, when the opposition has acknowledged policy leaders, and when these leaders are willing to work with the administration. Collaboration of this sort is likely to require permitting the opposition to get its "trademark" on the bill through participation in its drafting or by insisting on specific amendments, thus allowing it to display its impact on the shape of policy. The crucial part that Senator Everett Dirksen, the Republican leader in the Senate, played in passing the civil rights bills of the 1960s, as well as the 1977–1978 collaboration between the new Republican leader (and Dirksen's son-in-law), Howard Baker (Tenn.), and the Carter administration in support of the Panama Canal treaties illustrate the operation of bipartisanship. In short, some form of cooptation of the opposition may help the president advance his program.

The chief executive may also deal directly with legislators as individuals. The president can call them to the White House for private conferences, personally phone them to ask for support, or make favorable references to a representative in public in order to win the "goodwill" of the lawmaker and eventually to gain his or her support. Personal conversations may serve as negotiating sessions where a seldom explicit and rarely publicized "arrangement" between the chief executive and the legislator is consummated. In such situations, the bases of the president's bargaining power include his veto power, control over federal patronage, ability to provide election help, and influence on pending legislation, each of which can be employed to aid the representative.

The president may also make indirect contact with members of Congress. The departments of the executive branch maintain elaborate liaison establishments, often headed by an assistant secretary. The president's personal liaison staff operates out of the White House office and frequently (though less so in the Carter administration) includes people with considerable congressional experience as committee staff or legislative assistants. These liaison individuals may deal with congressional leaders, rank-and-file lawmakers, and the staffs of individuals and committees. They seek to represent the administration's position to the legislators and to inform the administration of congressional sentiment.[3] Beyond these formal liaison channels, the president may seek to exploit the influence of other members of the executive branch by assigning them to "lobby" for a particular policy.

Through the use of these methods, the president may seek to influence legislators directly; he may appeal to the legislature as a whole, to specific subgroups within the chambers, or to the individual members themselves. But he cannot use all these approaches simultaneously. He must select those techniques that will enable him to assemble a legislative majority.

The president can also employ many of these same techniques to operate through the legislative system. He, or other executive branch personnel acting on his behalf, can seek to influence party leaders and committee chairpersons and in turn win support from the rank-and-file lawmakers. As noted, the party leaders possess a variety of weapons they can use for the benefit, or to the detriment, of members of Congress. If the president can win the support of the party leaders, he may also be able to secure backing from others whom the leaders can persuade. Similarly, the committee and subcommittee chairpersons have perquisites they may employ to facilitate or hinder the passage of legislation. The chairpersons can, if they choose, use these bases of influence to bargain with the members of their committees for support for legislation they favor. Thus, if the president can enlist the chair in his cause, he may also win backing from the committee members. The legislative system, then, provides the president with potential methods to influence Congress. To the extent that he can win the support of those who control the levers of power within Congress, he may also be able to win the votes of those subject to the operation of that power.

In the Panama Canal fight, the Carter administration pulled out all the stops. The president personally met with a number of senators, as did Secretary of State Cyrus Vance and Carter's personal emissary and long-time Democratic party power, Robert S. Strauss. The backers of the neutrality treaty accepted three reservations to the pact to win and hold the support of wavering senators. Moreover, the administration bargained, implicitly at least, for treaty votes, using unrelated legislative matters as inducements. For instance, the *New York Times* (March 14, 1978, p. 1, col. 3) reported that "the White House . . . changed its position . . . on the $2.3 billion emergency farm bill to conform to the wishes of a Senator (Herman Talmadge, D–Ga.) whose vote it is wooing on . . . the treaties." Similarly, "The White House reversed itself and supported a plan to have the Government buy $250 million worth of copper for the nation's strategic stockpile. The reversal was at the request of Senator Dennis DeConcini, Democratic of Arizona, another of the senators who have yet to announce . . . on the treaties." One treaty supporter, Bob Packwood (R–Ore.), was reported to be so "disgusted" with the deals being made to secure votes that he was considering voting against the treaty in protest. He didn't, and the administration prevailed, sixty-eight to thirty-two, one vote in excess of the sixty-seven votes needed for ratification.

In addition to operating on legislators directly or through the legislative system, the chief executive can try to win support by mobilizing the public. He can attempt to arouse mass opinion, elite opinion, or the former through the latter. He may seek to stimulate the citizenry to communicate with their representatives in support of his position by his use of radio and television speeches, remarks at press conferences, or public appearances. If such requests stimulate a large response, the pressure on some legislators may be the decisive influence on their vote decision.[4]

The president may also try to exert influence by enlisting the support of elite opinion. If the newspapers in a state or district editorialize with near unanimity for a particular policy, the representative attuned to the press rather than to general public opinion may be led to back the president. The chief executive may also try to operate in similar fashion through other segments of elite opinion. These groups, which Rosenau (1963) has called the "opinion-makers," may be urged to arouse the average citizen. A special White House conference of these opinion makers may be convened in the hopes that the message can be transmitted to the general public via the conference participants. Similarly, the executive branch may try to coordinate the activity of interest groups to generate the maximum amount of public pressure on Congress.

Short-run presidential strategy aims at winning votes for the administration program by the most economical use of the techniques noted in the preceding paragraphs. The president may try to build his majority in a variety of ways. He may, for example, start with the bulk of his own party and attempt to add to them enough opposition votes to enact the legislation he desires. He may make legislative concessions, attempt to rally public opinion, or, if he finds votes difficult to obtain, make use of his techniques of personal persuasion. Or he may, as is so often the case with respect to civil rights issues, cast the issue in nonpartisan terms and attempt to win backing from both parties by appeals based on the merits, the national interest, or the moral necessity involved. The president will employ the methods he believes most likely to produce victory in each legislative situation.

This seemingly formidable arsenal of executive weapons is, in the last analysis, no guarantee that an unwilling Congress can be coerced to enact the president's programs. As Clausen's analysis (selection 10) indicates, only in the international sphere is presidential influence clear.[5] The chief executive can, using the techniques of persuasion available to him, secure some votes for his foreign policy. Thus, when John Kennedy succeeded Dwight Eisenhower in the White House, he was able to win support for his proposals from some, but not all, of the Democrats who had opposed similar suggestions emanating from a Republican administration. Likewise, some Republicans, freed of pressures from a president of their own party, began to vote against initiatives they had supported during the previous administration. Eight years later, in 1969, when the Republicans captured the presidency, the pattern recurred, but in reverse: In the Nixon administration, some Republican partisans began to vote for measures they had opposed under Kennedy and Johnson while some Democrats moved into opposition to the positions they had previously backed.

In the domestic political arena, in sharp contrast, Clausen finds scant evidence of presidential power to move legislators toward his positions. When the president wins—and he often does—in domestic affairs, it is more likely because his position commands a majority than through the exercise of sufficient influence on many votes on the House or Senate floor.[6] Such vote patterns demonstrate the imperfect operation of the party as a unifying device and make clear the essential coalition-building nature of presidential leadership. The chief executive seeks to get the requisite votes wherever he can find them, using whatever methods seem appropriate at the time.

The president's leadership task has been more arduous in the wake of Watergate and Vietnam. Institutionally, Congress has armed itself to challenge the executive's program and prerogatives. In 1973, the legislature passed over Richard Nixon's veto a war powers bill intended to limit the president's ability to commit American troops to an extended foreign venture (as in Vietnam) without congressional concurrence. The next year, Congress enacted the Budget and Impoundment Control Act, which provides the legislature with a procedure and the resources both to impose its own budgetary priorities and to restrain the president's authority to refuse to spend monies authorized and appropriated by Congress. Throughout the period since the mid-1960s, the legislature has moved to provide itself with more and better capacity to shape public policy. Congressional staffs, member and committee, have grown in size and skill; new information resources, for instance the Congressional Budget

Office and the Office of Technology Assessment, have strengthened Congress' position vis-à-vis the executive. Finally, apart from these institutional changes, individual members seem more inclined in the 1970s to resist presidential initiatives; they seem considerably less deferential to executive expertise.[7] In the short run at least, presidents of either political party seem fated to encounter substantially greater opposition in foreign and domestic affairs than Congress was prepared to offer only a few years ago.

In summary, demands from the president constitute a major source of inputs to the congressional system. They set the agenda of Congress; they define to a very great extent the place from which congressional activity begins. Moreover, having decided what he wants Congress to do, the president intervenes in a variety of ways in the day-to-day operations of the legislature to urge the lawmakers to act in keeping with his wishes. Demands from the White House provide much of the motive force behind congressional activity. And legislators cannot avoid taking on a particular role orientation toward the president. They must decide when and for what, if any, quid pro quo they will be executive oriented and, conversely, when they will act to resist executive blandishments.

The Lobbyists

A second major source of demands on the legislative system is the pressure or interest groups. Although interest groups are virtually omnipresent in their activities, there exists a wide divergence of opinion about their effectiveness in gaining passage of legislation that embodies their desired policy proposals. The classic image of the lobbyists holds that they in large measure determine legislative outputs, that they dictate public policy.[8] These groups are, according to this view, wielders of vast powers. They are believed to control the political futures of many lawmakers; those who fail to respond to group appeals run grave political risks because the interest group may use its great resources to defeat its enemies at the polls. This view, then, places pressure groups and their lobbyists at the very center of the legislative process.

More recently, on the basis of better empirical evidence, a more moderate "revisionist" view of the relationship of interest groups to the congressional system has emerged. This newer perspective holds that groups operate more as partners in policy-oriented coalitions than as the central determining forces in policy making. The lobbyists are in a weak position vis-à-vis Congress. They are underfinanced, understaffed, lacking in information, and short of time to perform in keeping with the classic image (Milbrath, 1963; Bauer, Pool, and Dexter, 1972).

In these circumstances, the lobby groups tend to run "service bureaus" that supply factual and interpretative information to those who will listen or to those who request them to provide needed data. Often those promoting particular policies solicit the assistance of pressure groups; they can use the information services the groups provide. The job of the lobbyist in such situations becomes one of gaining and retaining what Truman (1971, ch. 11) has called "access"—that is, the ability to present the view of the group relatively free of distortion, to a legislator. Rather than resorting to coercion, lobbyists attempt to persuade, by using sound data and low-key, inoffensive styles of presentation (Milbrath, 1963, part 3, and Ornstein and Elder, 1978). If the channels of communications are kept open to members of Congress, the pressure group may contribute to its legislative goals by providing useful data and persuasive interpretations of that data on appropriate occasions. Communication, it follows, will be directed toward allies, sympathizers, or those "on the fence," not toward those in opposition to the group's goals.

All this is not to minimize the importance or the involvement of pressure groups in the legislative process. It is only to suggest that the position of groups in congressional politics must be placed in perspective. In selection 11, Hayes details such a balanced view; interest groups, he suggests, can and do have substantial political influence, particularly in areas of "consensual" politics where they can work out accommodations with other groups, interested members of Congress, and involved bureaucrats in advance of formal legislative deliberations.[9] Where politics is "confluctual," where there is open, vigorous, and vocal policy competition among numerous competitors, clear winners and losers are harder to determine. Indeed, in such circumstances, Hayes argues, Congress will be unable to satisfy all the concerned interests and will be sorely tempted to "pass the buck" by delegating responsibility for firm decisions to those, usually in administrative agencies, outside the legislature.

The hotly contested, highly emotional abortion question provides a classic case in which Congress sought to avoid making a specific decision. Unwilling either to forbid entirely the use of federal funds, under the Medicaid program, to pay for abortions or to make abortions relatively easy to obtain, the legislature—after months of wrangling that delayed the fiscal 1978 Health, Education and Welfare-Labor Departments Appropriation Bill for many months— settled on an ambiguous formula that left the real decisions to HEW, and its secretary, Joseph Califano, in particular. Congress decreed that Medicaid funds could pay for abortions if continued pregnancy would cause a woman to suffer "severe and long-lasting physical health damage" and for "medical procedures" to treat rape and incest victims if such offenses are "promptly" reported. The term "medical procedures" and the provision for "prompt" reporting were not defined precisely. The law took on meaning only after Secretary Califano ruled that "medical procedures" could include abortion and that reports within sixty days, made by someone other than the victim to the police, a government health facility, or a crisis rape center, would satisfy the "prompt" reporting requirement. (See CQ Weekly Report, Dec. 10, 1977, p. 2547; and Jan. 28, 1978, p. 185.)

Even where they are influential, however, interest groups prefer to rely on positive inducements—services, information, and favors. From this perspective, lobbying seems far more useful than threatening. It produces needed information. Moreover, in interpreting data, the lobbyists espouse a variety of points of view, each of which is entitled to be heard. In short, lobby activity helps to resolve conflicts through its contributions to legislative decision making and through acceptance of policy choices the lobby had a hand in shaping. Interest groups are important, then, as partners in policy-centered coalitions, not as the dictators of policy decisions.

The widespread acceptance of lobbying by the members of Congress testifies to this view of interest groups. Matthews (1960, p. 177) quotes one senator: ". . . lobbies are the most valuable instrument in the legislative process." On the basis of discussions with members of Congress, Clapp (1964, p. 207) concludes that legislators believe they can "use the lobbyists' help properly without being improperly used themselves." Such responses rest on the tendencies, already noted, for contemporary interest groups to contact their allies, not their enemies, and to avoid coercion; most lawmakers will adopt a favorable or, at worst, a neutral role orientation toward the lobbyists. Because the pressure groups with which they deal seek to be helpful, there is no need for legislators to resist them.[10] Congress apparently has much to gain and little to risk from making use of interest group resources.

The Courts

The judiciary produces demands on Congress only intermittently because it passes on legislative enactments only infrequently. Demands that are made stem from court decisions that appear to challenge congressional prerogatives. Put another way, when the courts engage in policy making, as they have recently done in the areas of segregation, abortion, pornography, reapportionment, and prayer in the public school, all topics on which Congress is empowered to act, conflict usually follows. In such situations, the legislature must acquiesce to the courts' decisions or enact legislation effectively reversing those decisions. The demands from the courts are, in effect, to accept the policy implications of their decisions. For instance, the 1976 decision in Buckley v. Valeo (424 US 1 [1976]), accepting arguments raised by Senator James L. Buckley (R-Cons, N.Y.), ex-Senator Eugene McCarthy (D-Minn.), and others, overturned significant portions of the Federal Election Campaign Act of 1974. Among other things, the Court ruled that Congress cannot constitutionally limit the sums congressional candidates spend on their campaigns (but the legislature can control the amounts that individual contributors give). In addition, the Court held the Federal Election Commission, which the 1974 act established to enforce and administer the law's provisions, violated the constitutional separation of powers doctrine—because it did not consist entirely of presidential appointees—and could not, in consequence, carry out the responsibilities assigned to it. The justices, however, declined to invalidate commission rulings and gave Congress thirty days to reconstitute the commission. Confronted with this challenge, Congress complied. The legislature did not contest the ruling that invalidated the expenditure limits; it did reestablish the election commission according to the judicial specifications, taking advantage of the court-enforced reexamination to impose more stringent congressional control over the commission's activities.

Dahl (1958), treating the Supreme Court as a national policy maker, suggests that the Court is seldom "out of line" with the "lawmaking majority" as established by the presidential and congressional election returns. Moreover, when the elected branches are persistent and determined, they have generally been able to reject the demands of the courts. This was the case in the 1930s conflict over the New Deal legislation and, to a slightly lesser extent, in the struggles over segregation and internal security of the late 1950s.[11] More recently, Casper (1976) has suggested that the courts may play a more independent part in the political process than Dahl indicated. In the 1960s and 1970s, not only have the courts seemed more willing to overturn federal legislation, but also have more often left their mark on public policy through interpretation of statutes rather than through ruling laws unconstitutional. In any event, interbranch conflicts of a major sort are uncommon; the federal courts are most often a part of the dominant political alignment of the times and serve to legitimate the policy decisions of that alliance.

The problem of role-orientation choice will confront members of Congress most immediately when a judicial-legislative confrontation does occur, and their response will in all likelihood reflect their relationship to that "lawmaking majority" challenged by the courts. Whether they assume a pro-or anticourt perspective will depend on whether they find their views on the specific matter in question supported or frustrated by the court's ruling. More basically, however, because the judiciary is in effect looking over their shoulders, the representatives will have basically favorable or unfavorable dispositions toward the court; their sentiments presumably will reflect their views about the appropriateness of the court's role as at least an occasional policy maker in the larger political system.

The Public

In discussing the demands on Congress coming from the citizens of the country, a distinction needs to be made between policy demands and service demands. The former refers to requests from constituents that certain specific policy proposals be enacted or rejected; the latter consists of requests for non-legislative services such as securing information or acting as intermediary between citizens and the federal bureaucracy, as in tracing a lost social security check. Such demands for service—"casework," as members of Congress call them—are voluminous and occupy a substantial proportion of a legislator's time and staff resources. We will return to this type of activity in the fourth part when we discuss the representational outputs of Congress.

Here our concern is with policy demands. In their treatment of the salience of Congress (selection 12), Stokes and Miller indicate why it seems realistic to describe public policy demands as intermittent. Judging from off-year congressional election campaigns, issues seem unimportant to most voters. Of those citizens interviewed in a nationwide survey, few knew much about the activities of the legislative branch; only about one-half of the respondents knew which party controlled Congress; only a few indicated any awareness of the parties' legislative records; and only about 7 percent explained their votes in terms of campaign issues. Most voters cast their ballots for their own party's candidate, quite unaware of any policy implications that act might entail.

When members of Congress deviate from their party, then, it is seldom because they are responding to specific constituent demands. On the few issues about which the "folks back home" do feel strongly—for instance, civil rights questions in the old Confederacy or basic economic matters in the urban North—the legislators may feel constrained to act in keeping with their perceptions of constituency sentiment. But more often, as Stokes and Miller put it, if the lawmaker "subverts the proposals of his party," it is because he "fails to see these proposals as part of a program on which the party—and he himself—will be judged at the polls, because he knows the constituency isn't looking." From the systems perspective, this suggests that whatever weight lawmakers give to district opinion—the extent to which they assume a district (or state) or a combined national-district (or state) role orientation—will depend a good deal more on their personal preferences than on constituency pressures. This is not to say, however, that constituents have no influence. Rather, it is to suggest that their influence flows less through detailed instructions on the issues than through their more general electoral sanction—their ability to turn the incumbent out of office. Members of Congress worry; they try to anticipate when and on what issues their constituents will become concerned and active, and they try to behave in ways that will minimize potential electoral reprisals.[12] A vague but pervasive uncertainty, then, inclines numerous lawmakers to think seriously about assuming delegate and district (state) role orientations.

Supports

Demands constitute only one set of the inputs to the congressional system. Much less is known, however, about the input of support. What does seem clear is that without a certain minimum level of support—positive sentiments or an acceptance of its legitimacy—Congress could not continue to exist. Put another way, for the legislative system to continue to be accepted as an appropriate part of the total political process, it must continue to act—to produce outputs—in an acceptable way. As noted in the introduction, support may stem from particular actions Congress takes. To the extent that the legislature responds satisfactorily to at least some of their specific demands, the president, interest groups, the courts, and the public will accord it legitimacy. Underlying, in part at least, the civil rights movement of the early 1960s, the urban unrest at the end of that decade, and the Vietnam protests that continued into the early 1970s was frustration because Congress could or would not act. Even here the challenge was not to the legitimacy of the legislative branch; rather it was an effort to goad it into action. Prolonged inactivity, failure to take some steps to resolve a crisis, could lead to the rejection of Congress as a proper national policy maker. Diffuse, in contrast to specific, support generally reflects feelings that Congress is "right" or "good"; these feelings are usually independent of any actions the House or Senate may have taken.

There have been no serious recent attacks on the legitimacy of Congress, none comparable to Franklin Roosevelt's challenge to the Supreme Court that was embodied in his unsuccessful "court-packing" plan. Although it is true that there is a lack of support for the legislative branch implicit in the proposals of some reformers who want to create a "more responsible" party system, these suggestions have received scant attention outside academic circles.[13] The impatience of those who seek legislative action from Congress has been expressed most often through persuasive efforts to induce action rather than through frontal assaults on the institution or on its members.

The president, for instance, pursues a sort of "carrot and stick" strategy toward Congress. While he exhorts the lawmakers to act, his rhetoric fairly teems with references to the executive-legislative partnership. He seldom fails to heap praise on Congress when it passes the legislation he desires. Lyndon Johnson referred approvingly to the "Education Congress" or the "Conservation Congress" when the lawmakers enacted most of his programs in these areas. Bill-signing occasions tend to become mutual admiration sessions in which the ceremonial pens are freely distributed to the very visible legislators as rewards for their achievements. In these and other ways, the chief executive lends support to Congress, conferring legitimacy on it by his sustaining activities.

Similarly, the other sources of inputs to the legislature provide support as well as make demands. Like the president, the pressure groups work to induce congressional action rather than to find ways to circumvent the lawmaking branch. Their efforts attempt to make the system function effectively, not to undermine its operation. The courts, in similar fashion, seldom challenge Congress: The judiciary sustains the vast majority of congressional actions that are tested legally. A much greater number of legislative actions never find their way into the courts for review. Thus the behavior of the court serves overall to support Congress, indicating the general acceptability of the legislature's performance.

Needless to say, this does not mean that politics stops or controversy ceases. Groups that fail to win legislative victories will seek to reverse their defeats, turning to the executive or to the courts. The latter do, as noted, reverse Congress from time to time. What this reasoning does suggest is that these are "ordinary politics," not fundamental assaults on Congress' position in the political process.

Some data are available regarding the general public's support for Congress. At one level (which Easton, 1965b, pp. 190–211, calls "the regime," the constitutional structure), it is clear that Congress is a part of a widely revered political order. American citizens respect their political system, including Congress, and have not challenged it seriously since the Civil War. They tend to see the legislature as accessible and responsive, in principle, and believe they are capable of exerting influence on it (Almond and Verba, 1963, pp. 185–186; see also Wahlke, 1971).

At a more mundane level, the day-to-day public response to the incumbent authorities (the current members of Congress) and their activities, support appears far more variable, rising and falling rapidly in response to current political conditions. The lawmaking body seems to win public confidence when things are going well, when it works in harmony with the president; by contrast, when the economy is in poor shape or when the Congress clashes with the executive, the public evaluation of the legislature is less favorable (Davidson, Kovenock, and O'Leary, 1966, pp. 47–52; Davidson and Parker, 1972; Parker, 1977). Thus in 1963, when Congress blocked most of President John F. Kennedy's proposals, 33 percent of a national sample felt the legislature was doing an "excellent" or a "pretty good" job while 60 percent rated its performance as "fair" or "poor." By 1965, when the assassination of President Kennedy coupled with the 1964 Democratic landslide presidential election victory had provided the impetus for the greatest outpouring of domestic legislation since the New Deal, the comparable figures were 64 percent and 33 percent. The inevitable slowdown following the enactment of the Democratic program plus the domestic retrenchment accompanying the Vietnam War produced, by the end of 1968, a lessened public confidence in Congress. Equal segments of the population, 46 percent each, rated the legislature in the "excellent-good" and "fair-poor" categories. In the 1970s, as the Vietnam War dragged to an ambiguous conclusion and the Watergate crisis deepened, the public's assessment of Congress became still more negative. Respondents rating congressional performance as "excellent" or "good" stood at 21 percent in January 1974; 26 percent in March 1975; and, following the Wayne Hays (D-Ohio) "sex scandal" and other disclosures of congressional malfeasance, 22 percent in January 1977.[14] Support for Congress, in short, seems fragile when the focus is on the current legislature and its daily activities; but, presumably because basic commitment to the institution (diffuse support) runs deep, support for the lawmaking branch remains well above that critical level essential for continued legislative legitimacy.

Contributing to this recent decline in support is the currently fashionable tendency for political candidates, presidential and legislative alike, to run as "outsiders"—uncontaminated by contact with, much less membership in, the "insiders' establishment"—*against* the national institutions, including the Congress (see Fenno, 1978, pp. 244–247; and Vogler, 1977, pp. 73–74). It is easy to understand why, in the aftermath of Vietnam and Watergate, electoral hopefuls seek to put distance between themselves and a suspect government. Indeed, members of Congress seem to have succeeded in preserving their own popularity, as individuals, at the expense of Congress' institutional support (Fenno, 1974). As noted, this support has not yet declined to a point that threatens congressional legitimacy; but over the long run continued attacks from its own members may eventually undermine it.

In sum, the inputs to the legislative system are a mixture of demands and supports. Actors in the system's environment—executives, judges, lobbyists, and citizens—demand action and respond to congressional decisions by offering support. In this way, the legislature has continued as a legitimate participant in the making of political choices. As such, Congress is expected to continue to perform its essential functions and to produce its outputs. We turn to the question of the outputs of the legislative system in the fourth part of this book.

Notes

[1]Dahl's (1950, p. 58) comment refers to the foreign affairs area, but few would deny that presently it applies to domestic affairs as well.

[2]This discussion draws heavily on Neustadt, 1976, esp. chs. 3–5. For evidence that presidential prestige does enhance the chief executive's influence in Congress, see Edwards, 1976, 1977.

[3]On executive branch legislative liaison, see Robinson, 1967; Holtzman, 1970; and on the Carter administration, *Congressional Quarterly Weekly Report*, March 4, 1978, pp. 479–586.

[4]Though McAdams (1964, p. 198) asserts that the popular response in support of President Eisenhower's speech urging passage of the Landrum-Griffin Labor Reform Bill "was the deciding factor for a number of congressmen," mobilizing the public remains a difficult and dubious tactic. President Carter, for instance, seems to have been singularly unsuccessful in persuading Americans that the nation, in fact, faced a serious "energy crisis" or that the Panama Canal treaties were in the best interest of the country.

[5]Kesselman's two (1961, 1965) studies provide supporting evidence for presidential leadership on foreign policy.

[6]*Congressional Quarterly* calculations reveal both the proportion of presidential requests that Congress enacts and the proportion of individual roll calls in Congress on which the

president's position prevails. The former measure varies between 20 and 70 percent, the latter between 50 and 93 percent, depending on the president in office and the political circumstances of the moment. Johnson, succeeding a martyred predecessor and flushed with a landslide victory, did very well; Nixon, saddled with Vietnam and embarrassed by Watergate, did less well. Either indicator, however, makes it clear that any president can count on winning important victories in Congress. (See *CQ Weekly Report,* Jan. 7, 1978, pp. 9–15).

[7]Studies by Kingdon, 1973, and Matthews and Stimson, 1975, find that the president, though important, does not receive automatic or uncritical respect from members of Congress. They will consider the president's views and desires and then decide for themselves.

[8]As Daniel Berman, 1964, p. 104, put it: "Lobbies do not find it difficult . . . to administer one defeat after another to presidents who champion a positive legislative program." For other treatments stressing the centrality of the interest groups, see Truman, 1971; Latham, 1952; and Congressional Quarterly, 1971.

[9]See Ripley and Franklin, 1976, for a general treatment of the "subgovernment" collaborations among groups, members of Congress, and executive branch bureaucrats. Davidson, 1975, presents a clear illustration of one such subgovernment in action.

[10]For data on these points, see Davidson, 1969, pp. 162–175.

[11]For good treatments of the place of the courts in the policy process, see Schubert, 1974, Rohde and Spaeth, 1976, Wasby, 1978, and Funston, 1978. Murphy, 1962, provides a detailed account of conflict, and the accommodation reached, between the courts and Congress during the 1950s.

[12]For instance, Kingdon, 1973, p. 65, argues that both mass and elite publics constrain legislators' votes: "Even if a congressman transgresses those boundaries for isolated votes, he feels uneasy about doing so for a series of votes." Moreover, Davidson's (1969, ch. 4), findings that sizable proportions of House members take the delegate and district role orientation indicate the extent of such feelings, even in the absence of clear policy messages from constituents.

[13]Selection 12 describes the "responsible party" model.

[14]These data are from the Harris Survey, as reported in the *Louisville Courier-Journal* (Jan. 13, 1969), B 4, and Van der Slik, 1977, p. 295. The January 1977 figure is from a Harris Survey conducted for the House (Obey) Commission on Administrative Review.

Selection 9 Central Legislative Clearance: A Revised Perspective

Robert S. Gilmour

Central legislative clearance in the executive branch is widely regarded as one of the most powerful tools of the President. Under the aegis of the Office of Management and Budget (OMB, formerly the U. S. Bureau of the Budget) the hundreds of legislative proposals generated by federal departments, bureaus, and independent agencies are coordinated and reviewed to assess their acceptability as component parts of the presidential program. Here, many observers would argue, the substance of the congressional agenda is determined. Richard E. Neustadt's constantly cited history of central clearance describes legislative clearance as "by far the oldest, best intrenched, most thoroughly institutionalized of the President's coordinative instruments — always excepting the budget itself. . . ."[1] Others have reaffirmed the view that the President's program is arrived at primarily by Budget Bureau, now OMB, review of proposals "welling up" from the agencies.[2]

While accepting the importance of centralized legislative advice within the executive branch, close students of presidential policy making have not always been enthusiastic about the results of this process. For example, Arthur Maass recorded his concern more than fifteen years ago about Executive Office decision making through a process of "piecemeal review, rejection, and modification of individual proposals flowing up from the administrative units. . . ."[3] More recently Norman Thomas and Harold Wolman have reported that even "Some participants in the policy process within the Executive Office of the President have contended . . . that this pattern has resulted in the adulteration of new ideas by internal bureaucratic considerations and clientele pressures exerted through the agencies."[4]

During the 1960s, observers focused special attention on the academic community, presidential commissions, task forces, and the White House staff as the ascending stars of legislative initiation.[5] One usually unstated but implicit conclusion is that these newer presidential agents significantly augmented or supplanted traditional Budget Bureau powers over central clearance and presidential program development. Indeed, there is considerable evidence that important aspects of legislative clearance have been recentralized in the White House staff during the Kennedy and Johnson presidencies.

Reprinted from *Public Administration Review* 31 (1971), pp. 150–158, by permission of the author and publisher.

These evaluations aside, there has been surprisingly little examination of the legislative clearance process—systematic or otherwise—on which to base a firm judgment.

Our purpose here will be to consider how legislation initiated by the executive reaches the level of *central* clearance. What specific processes are involved and which actors figure most prominently at various stages in policy development? An attempt will be made, then, to re-examine the traditional conception of legislative proposals "welling up" from the bureaucracy for central clearance by the President's staff in the Executive Office.

Findings are based in part on interviews with career and political executives in eight of the eleven cabinet-rank departments and with officials in the Office of Management and Budget. Anonymity was offered all respondents, though some had no objection to being quoted or referred to as a source.

Growth of Legislative Clearance

Development of presidential oversight of the legislative ideas and views of administrative agencies is usually associated with the Budget and Accounting Act of 1921, although no provision for central legislative clearance was contained in the act, and there is certainly no record that Congress intended to invest the executive with so powerful a tool in the legislative process. Ironically, it was the suggestion of a congressional committee chairman that, according to Richard Neustadt's sleuthing, "precipitated the first presidential effort to assert central control over agency views on proposed and pending legislation. . . ."[6] A second irony was that the initial proclamation establishing the Bureau of the Budget as a legislative clearinghouse was issued and vigorously implemented by the generally "Whiggish" administration of Calvin Coolidge. As an economy move, Coolidge insisted on Budget Bureau approval of all legislation proposed by executive agencies which committed the government to future expenditures. Budget Circular 49 required reports on pending fiscal legislation to be routed through the bureau for the addition of BOB advice before they were submitted to Congress.

For reasons quite apart from those of Coolidge, President Franklin D. Roosevelt enlarged the scope of legislative clearance substantially. Acting on Roosevelt's instructions in 1935, Budget Director Daniel Bell required all agency proposals for legislation and advice on legislation pending to clear the Budget Bureau "for consideration by the President," before submission to Congress. Agency proposals subsequently sent to Congress were to include a statement that the "proposed legislation was or was not in accord with the President's program."

There is little question that the Budget Bureau took its expanded clearance role with utmost seriousness. Yet Budget apparently remained little more than a clearinghouse for sporadic, though numerous, agency proposals and reports on pending bills throughout the Roosevelt administration. Neustadt credits "The custom of compiling formal agency programs as a preliminary stage in presidential program making" to "White House requirements imposed . . . in the four years after World War II."[7]

When the Republicans returned to power in 1953, the annual Budget call for departmental and agency programs initiated during the Truman administration was continued without interruption. During mid-summer of 1953, President Eisenhower joined the Budget Bureau's call for legislative proposals in a personal letter "bearing signs of his own dictation" addressed to each cabinet officer. Neustadt notes that the cumulative response was "astonishing" to those members of the White House staff who either assumed or believed that Congress was the rightful place for legislative initiation. "For here were departmental declarations of intent to sponsor literally hundreds of measures great and small, *most of which the President was being asked to make his own by personal endorsement in a message.*"[8]

In the present study, respondents whose experience extended to the Eisenhower period agreed that the Budget Bureau exercised extremely close supervision over executive channels for legislative proposals. One suggested that it took the combination of CEA Chairman Arthur Burns and Secretary of the Treasury George Humphrey to end-play the bureau in getting legislative proposals to the President. Similarly, others indicated it was easier to risk an end-run to Congress, skirting BOB authority.

During the 1960s, the Budget Bureau's veritable monopoly over executive branch legislation built up in the Eisenhower administration appears to have eroded seriously. Nearly all "career" respondents having the perspective of relatively long tenure offered much the same view as one thirty-year veteran: "Since the Kennedy administration, the role of the White House in legislative clearance has been multiplied many times. White House staff members can operate at the highest level, hammering out programs directly with the secretary. Sometimes during the Johnson administration there was even direct communication between the White House and agency heads to develop legislative proposals."

Despite apparent changes in the relative importance of central clearance by the OMB, institutional procedures for agency submission of proposals and reports continue to operate much as they did in the Bureau of the Budget for more than twenty years. An examination of those procedures and processes should thus precede an evaluation of recent trends.

Bureaucratic Initiation

In the public mind, line bureaucrats appear to have been eclipsed as legislative innovators by presidential task forces and other outsiders to the traditional process. Nonetheless, in the business of elevating ideas as serious proposals and issues, bureaus remain well situated and prolific. To cite but one illustration, the Department of Housing and Urban Development alone proposes approximately three hundred separate bills in the space of a single legislative year, most of which are initiated by the HUD bureaucracy. Although the great bulk of these proposals are "minor amendments" or bills of "middling importance," taken collectively they can hardly be ignored as the definers of larger policy.

Legislative drafting is a continuing activity in the agencies, but most bills are generated in a hurry-up response to the annual call for legislation. Budget Circular A-19 prompts agency action with the note that "annually proposed legislative programs for the forthcoming session of Congress . . . are to be used . . . in assisting the President in the preparation of his legislative program, annual and special messages, and the annual budget."

Not surprisingly, agency-initiated bills must run the gamut of clearance channels—in the sponsoring bureau and in the departmental hierarchy above—before the process is in any way centralized by the Office of Management and Budget. Each agency has its own routing procedure for legislative proposals, yet these will normally include critical reviews by finance officers, the agency planning units, and by line divisions of the agency which have a direct interest, depending upon the substance of each proposal. Typically, centralized responsibility for the coordination of agency bills is vested in a small staff such as the U. S. Forest Service Division of Legislative Liaison and Reporting. At a later stage, and with a fair assurance of departmental support, such bills are likely to be rendered as formal drafts by the agency's legislative counsel.

Ascending the Hierarchy

Assistant secretaries and their deputies in charge of designated line bureaus normally encourage their agencies—even the field offices—to send up ideas for legislative improvement. Successful efforts of this sort have the effect of maximizing supervisory control over agency submissions, making it possible for political executives to winnow out those proposals that they believe merit departmental support. The assistant secretaries also perform an important role as mediators in ironing out the inevitable differences among bureaus' plans for legislative enactment. And once they have formally approved an agency bill— offered by a bureau immediately subordinate—they may find themselves cast as negotiators with their departmental counterparts.

The legislative counsel (assistant or associate general counsel) of a department has strong potential influence over final clearance outcomes. He is characteristically not only a routing agent, but is also expected to offer advice on the language and general desirability of each proposal. Actual influence of this position varies greatly among departments canvassed. In departments such as Commerce and Treasury, which do not generate large numbers of bills, small legislative divisions occupy most of their time with the preparation of reports on bills pending in Congress, and principally serve an "editorial function" during the clearance process. In the action departments of the 1960s, legislative attorneys have played a much more vital role. Drafting of HEW bills, for example, has been centralized in the Division of Legislation. Clearance powers of the legislative counsel are even greater in Housing and Urban Development. Preparation of HUD's "omnibus package" of legislation involves both the collection of agency proposals and the sifting of ideas recommended by HUD's architectural, construction, housing, and mortgaging clientele groups. Associate General Counsel Hilbert Fefferman recalled, "We drafted major bills on model cities, rent supplements, FHA Title 10's 'new communities,' the College Housing Act, the Housing for the Elderly Act, and a good many others."

The general counsel in most departments is not only immediately superior to his legislative attorneys and, as one respondent described him, "the final arbiter for legal language," but he is also responsible for coordinating and compiling proposals and bills originating in the agencies. Some departments additionally rely on a program review committee for this purpose, but in any case the general counsel has substantial influence over the final shape of the department's legislative package. As an appointed official, however, and quite possibly a departmental newcomer, the general counsel can hardly help but place heavy reliance on the legislative counsel and other "career" subordinates.

In addition to the general counsel's office, other staff divisions of a department, especially the finance and planning divisions, may be consulted as a part of normal clearance procedure. Indeed, the OMB formally requires that an agency ". . . shall include in its letter transmitting proposed legislation or in its report on pending legislation its best estimate of the appropriations . . . which will be needed to carry out its responsibilities under the legislation." Budget officers are necessarily consulted when proposed legislation authorizes new departmental expenditures. Drafts may also be routed to departmental program planning officers, but this consultation appears often to be the exception rather than the rule.

Most departments have at least a pro forma routing of otherwise approved proposals across the desks of the secretary and his most immediate subordinates. It is understood that the secretary may intervene at any point during the process as an initiator, advocate, or veto agent, but the typical bill will not receive the secretary's or even the undersecretary's personal attention. In effect, clearance of most departmentally-generated legislative ideas takes place in the staff offices manned by career bureaucrats. "Political" oversight is largely exercised by the assistant secretaries and the general counsels. Of course the secretary and other high officials are likely to become deeply involved in clearance when this process takes the form of policy planning to develop major departmental or presidential program thrusts.

Most respondents indicated that the secretary also performs the roles of mediator and arbiter. One strategically placed observer in HEW remarked that the "settlement of disputes between assistant secretaries, career officials, or both is about the only way he can gain any real measure of control in this circus." Another, in HUD, recalled, "When Robert Weaver was secretary during the Johnson administration, he and undersecretary Robert Wood held relatively frequent meetings to settle conflicts between assistant secretaries." If those differences were not "bargained out," then it was said that the secretary or the undersecretary "made the decision."

Interdepartmental Clearance

Before reaching the Office of Management and Budget, there is often an interdepartmental phase in the clearance process that some consider to be as important as final OMB review. One respondent in Transportation explained, "Where there's a substantial outside interest in legislation that we're drafting, we generally clear it with other agencies before going to Management and Budget." Another in Justice held, "Usually you get things worked out without the necessity of OMB negotiations."

Apparently, the points of contact between departments vary with legislative complexity and with the relative importance attached to bills by their initiators, but most are made at the operating level—one agency to another. Liaison between departments on the few major, controversial bills is likely to take place at a higher level. As a legislative attorney in Transportation put it, "Of course, if the problem were significant enough, it would go to the secretarial level."

Consultation and coordination of agency and departmental positions is not in the least secretive or inappropriate. OMB guidelines actually encourage each agency:

> . . . to consult the other agencies concerned in order that all relevant interests and points of view may be considered and accommodated, where appropriate, in the formulation of the agency's position. Such consultation is particularly important in cases of overlapping interests, and intensive efforts should be made to reach interagency agreement before proposed legislation or reports are transmitted. . . .

The Office goes further to suggest that "Interagency committees and other arrangements for joint consultation may often be useful in reaching a common understanding."

In view of Management and Budget's limited staff—twelve professionals—in its Division of Legislative Reference and the considerable technical complexity of many federal programs, OMB's formal encouragement of interdepartmental efforts to accommodate overlapping interests may be understood as a matter of practical necessity. Nonetheless, it's surprising that interdepartmental liaison in legislative policy making has drawn so little attention.

OMB Clearance

Legislative proposals cleared in the departments and sent forward to Management and Budget in response to the annual call may be seized upon for translation to presidential prose and rushed to the drafting boards, or they may be shuffled to the files of good ideas in repose. In either case, formal clearance awaits the preparation of a draft bill submitted by the sponsoring department. These are typically sent separately, following the initial proposals by weeks or months.

When each draft arrives, OMB's Division of Legislative Reference assesses its general compatibility with the President's announced program and with current budgetary projections. In making these judgments, heavy reliance is placed on presidential messages, consultation with White House staff members, and perhaps direct communication between the director and the President. "On the less important matters," as one assistant director admitted, "we rely primarily on the compromises that can be negotiated out among the departments and their respective agencies, these negotiations being within the general context of the President's objectives as he has stated them. In effect, a good portion of the President's program consists of the compromises that are struck here." Drafts deemed generally to be "in the right ballpark" are sent to the relevant line agencies for comments and deferred internally to the appropriate OMB program division where interagency negotiations over particular provisions will be held.

In dealing with each legislative proposal, Management and Budget has several alternatives. First, the Office may approve, stating with authority that the bill is "in accord with the program of the President," or appraising the bill "consistent with the objectives of the administration," or noting feebly that there is "no objection from the standpoint of the administration's program." Taking this option, OMB obviously offers varying degrees of support from strong backing to lukewarm tolerance. All the same, it here assumes a passive role which usually hinges on prior interdepartmental agreements, and it may be just those agreements that assure clearance at the lowest level of acceptance.

Secondly, Management and Budget may negotiate changes in a bill with the agencies immediately concerned to adjust differences. This course of action is much more commonly adopted, both as a means of resolving interdepartmental conflict and sometimes as a delaying tactic until a definite presidential position can be developed and enunciated. To reach agreement on points disputed in each bill, Legislative Reference may elect to act as a mediator or referee during formal meetings involving participants from departments and their agencies ranging from the assistant secretarial level downward. "The main task" of OMB, as one assistant director described it, "is that of persuading agencies to get together on proposed legislation, unless we hold strong independent views of our own. We suggest compromises and try to operate on a persuasive basis, but we stick to our guns in bargaining for the president's program."

On some occasions the OMB's efforts to "persuade" have been more direct, and the Office, as the Budget Bureau before it, takes the part of overt supervisor for legislative activities and pronouncements of line agencies. When negotiations were held over the Land and Water Conservation Fund in the early 1960s, for example, the Army Corps of Engineers and the Bureau of Reclamation (Interior Department) made known repeatedly their desire to be excluded from the fund's provisions. One member of the OMB's staff recalled, "It was necessary for us to persuade the Corps and the Bureau of Reclamation to refrain from taking an official position against their inclusion under the new conservation law." A close observer in another agency remarked, "From where we sat, that 'persuasion' looked a good deal more like a firm command." However, respondents more often criticized Management and Budget's indecisiveness and apparent inability to "take a stand."

Performance of the Office's supervisory role may also take the form of its final alternative in the clearance process, an outright block of legislation under review causing permanent rejection or at least temporary delay. It is not at all uncommon for OMB to return an agency-sponsored bill indicating that it would not be in accord with the president's program. In the past this advice has occasionally been moderated with a notation that the offending bill would not be in accord "at this time" or "at least at this time."[9]

Despite a firm prohibition against agency submission to Congress of bills which are held to be in conflict with the presidential program, it is well known that agencies frequently "get around" the confines of clearance procedures. This is accomplished through informal and nonofficial channels, most notably in the legislative drafting and information services agencies provide congressional committees and individual congressmen. Additionally, as one budget officer expressed it:

> If an agency is dissatisfied with the outcome of our negotiations, it can quite easily arrange—and they often do—to have a congressman question them at the hearings in order to bring out that our office has made them water down the bill it wanted. Certainly the people I deal with play that game, but there are disadvantages as well as advantages involved.

By implication the prime disadvantage of this latter tactic, and apparently one that is well understood by the agencies, is the notion that OMB has a "long memory" for bureaus that repeatedly employ it. An agency must therefore weigh short-term tactical gains of a successful "end run" against longer-range objectives which may be jeopardized by opposition from Management and Budget in the future.

Continuing contact between OMB and line bureaus for general management, fiscal, and legislative matters is primarily maintained by the budget examiner assigned to each agency. The examiners have also become Management and Budget's chief mediators for interdepartmental disputes centering on their agencies' programs. Stalemate of interagency negotiations will, of course, receive the attention of an OMB division chief, an assistant director, or perhaps even the director himself.

Traditionally, decisions of the director "on behalf of the President" were understood to be final, or nearly so. After a contested ruling by the director, an agency or department head was, in a formal sense, "always free to appeal to the President." But the success of this gambit was unlikely, and the logic of presidential denial in such cases seemed quite convincing. Former Budget Director Kermit Gordon has argued:

> If the President reverses his Budget director fairly frequently, the latter's usefulness to the President will be gravely impaired if not destroyed, for it will have become evident that he has failed in his effort to tune in on the President's wave length, and his desk will become only a temporary resting place for problems on the way to the President.[10]

Nonetheless, there is mounting evidence that the pattern has changed. From the standpoint of increased influence, the White House staff appears to have been the prime beneficiary.

White House Intervention

Perhaps the best illustration is that of a young OMB examiner who explained to the writer, "I'll come to work and learn that 'There was a meeting at the White House last night, and it's all settled.' The bill I've been negotiating for weeks has been pulled up from the Office by the White House staff." It is quickly learned that this is not an isolated instance. High-level Management and Budget officers have had a role in these White House sessions, but OMB no longer has the monopoly claim on clearance decisions held by the Bureau of the Budget in the 1950s. Most of us were keenly aware of the strong legislative initiatives taken by the President and White House staff during the '60s, yet few students of administration noticed that the White House staff has directly intervened in central legislative clearance.

This change has been perceived by departmental and agency

administrators throughout the executive branch. The opinion is widespread that the White House has taken over from Management and Budget on legislative matters of "any real importance." Said one respondent, "During the past ten years, especially, meetings have been called by the White House staff to hash out legislative agreements where the Department of Agriculture has been involved." The same point was made by others. In Transportation: "It is my experience that White House meetings to discuss our legislation have been called only after clearance by the secretary. These meetings usually mean, then, that there is disagreement between our department and another." In HEW: "During the last five years there have been a great many meetings called by the White House to discuss our legislative items. The Nixon administration hasn't changed that trend." A budget officer in Legislative Reference argues that the Nixon staff "has, if anything, been even more active in clearance than Johnson's or Kennedy's. The fact of the matter is that there are now many more men in the White House for this kind of work. They are better organized, and they have definite legislative and program assignments."

With this change there has apparently been a greater willingness on the parts of departmental officials to challenge the Budget director. As one respondent put it, "There has got to be a way to go over the OMB on a regular basis without going directly to the President. There is. That's the White House staff. Ted Sorensen and Joe Califano, in the Kennedy and Johnson administrations respectively, were constantly available to mediate and arbitrate between the secretary of a department and the director of the Budget." In the Department of Transportation a respondent allowed "that the Office of Management and Budget still calls negotiations to iron out agreements on legislation, but once conflict over a bill escalates to the point that the director becomes involved, the OMB is no longer in a position to act as a mediator. This is when the disagreement between parties is likely to be carried over to the White House." A Justice Department attorney in the early Nixon administration stated flatly, "[Budget Director] Mayo doesn't overrule [Attorney General] Mitchell unless Mayo represents the President." Observations of this sort were volunteered in every department interviewed, and they were intended to apply to all three administrations of the '60s.

For Presidents Kennedy and Johnson, who wished to achieve a high level of legislative accomplishment, reliance on traditional initiatory and clearance procedures were understood to be inadequate. Neither President found that the bureaucracy could supply the ideas and advice needed for a major legislative program. William Carey reports, for example, that President Johnson "spent the better part of a year badgering the Budget director to assign 'five of the best men you have' to drag advance information out of the agencies about impending decisions and actions so that he could pre-empt them and issue personal directives to carry them out, but the Budget Bureau never came anywhere near satisfying him because its own radar system was not tuned finely enough."[11]

The answer to intelligence difficulties supplied by the Kennedy and Johnson administration was, in part, the establishment of congressional liaison offices operating closely with the secretary of each cabinet-rank department. It was reasoned that this machinery would highlight major policy questions and assist the President and the secretaries in dealing effectively with Congress. According to Russell Pipe's description:

> The Johnson administration's legislative program has included many proposals affecting more than one department. Liaison officers collaborate on such legislation to see that maximum effort is expended to promote the legislation. Omnibus bills require joint liaison ventures. In addition, personal friendships, political debts, and a kind of collegial relationship growing out of shared legislative skills bring liaison officers together to work on measures requiring all-out drives for passage. Thus, a network of liaison interaction has been created.[12]

At the White House Joseph Califano's office became "a command post for directing the Great Society campaign, an operational center within the White House itself, the locus for marathon coffee-consuming sessions dedicated to knocking heads together and untangling jurisdictional and philosophical squabbles."[13] Respondents in the departments indicated repeatedly that Califano was the presidential assistant who constantly "initiated negotiations," "called us in" for conferences, and "ironed out conflicts" among the agencies.

The Nixon administration counterpart to Califano is presidential assistant John Ehrlichman, who has also become executive director of the newly established Domestic Council staff. The "Ehrlichman Operation" is considerably larger than any of its predecessors and, according to some informants, even more vigorous. The Domestic Council—functionally the cabinet without Defense and State Department components—was set in motion by President Nixon's Reorganization Plan No. 2 of 1970, and is intended to provide an "institutionally staffed group charged with advising the president on the total range of domestic policy." As yet Ehrlichman's staff shows no signs of becoming a career unit like the supporting staff of the National Security Council, but that is apparently what originators of the concept in the President's Advisory Council on Executive Organization have in mind for the future. With or without a careerist orientation, the Domestic Council staff under Ehrlichman has institutionalized the process of White House clearance for controversial or high-priority legislation beyond Management and Budget's Division of Legislative Reference.

The White House deadline is an additional structural device that has made an impact over the past decade and has had the effect of short-circuiting interdepartmental negotiations. A career attorney in Commerce commented, "It's not at all uncommon for legislative clearance to be greatly abbreviated because of short-fuse deadlines set by the White House, Management and

Budget, or both." His counterpart in another department viewed this development as "unfortunate because it means that legislative outputs are uncoordinated and often drafted in a slipshod fashion."

Still others interpreted these deadlines as a means for agencies to avoid the rigors of interdepartmental bargaining. In HEW an experienced observer noted that deadlines have "more than once facilitated a shortcut in the clearance process." He went on to suggest:

> As a department strategy for approval of its bills, specific departments have dragged their feet until the eleventh hour. Thus when the draft went in from the line departments to the OMB there was virtually no time for Budget clearance, much less for a thoughtful and coherent response from other concerned departments. In the face of a firm White House deadline, the initiating department's proposal would earn the official blessing of the President as a reward for tardiness.

A respondent in Agriculture said, "Sometimes I think agencies wait until the deadline is upon them on purpose—so they won't have to consult and coordinate with other departments." Others added that deadlines imposed by the White House have been just as firm during the first year and a half of the Nixon administration as they were under Johnson.

Conclusion

Of the approximately sixteen thousand bills annually processed by the Office of Management and Budget, probably 80 to 90 percent do come "welling up" from the agencies to be cleared in the ascending hierarchy of career bureaucrats and political overseers in the line departments and finally to be negotiated by OMB and given a grade in the President's program. Treatment of the remaining bills, those singled out for special attention by the White House, provides the most striking change in central clearance during the past decade. All three Presidents of the '60s have short-circuited normal clearance channels to put a personal stamp on high-priority legislation. On crucial new programs, the White House has imposed strict deadlines for policy development, rushing Management and Budget coodination and allowing more discretion to individual departments. When OMB clearance negotiations have dragged or stalemated, the White House has not hesitated to intervene, dealing directly with departmental program managers. Indeed, this new process appears to have been institutionalized in the Domestic Council staff. At the same time, with the encouragement of the Budget Bureau and its successor, the Office of Management and Budget, line bureaucrats may have become their own best negotiators and mediators for clearance. The result, it appears, is a substantial challenge to OMB authority for central clearance from above and below.

Notes

[1] Richard E. Neustadt, "Presidency and Legislation: The Growth of Central Clearance," *American Political Science Review* 48 (September 1954): 642.

[2] See Michael D. Reagan, "Toward Improving Presidential Level Policy Planning," *Public Administration Review* 23 (March 1963): 177; Francis E. Rourke, *Bureaucracy, Politics and Public Policy* (Boston: Little, Brown and Co., 1969), p. 49.

[3] Arthur A. Maass, "In Accord with the Program of the President?" in *Public Policy*, C. J. Friedrich and J. K. Galbraith, eds., Vol. IV (Cambridge, Mass.: Harvard University Press, 1953), p. 79.

[4] Norman C. Thomas and Harold L. Wolman, "The Presidency and Policy Formulation: The Task Force Device," *Public Administration Review* 29 (September/October 1969): 459.

[5] See especially Adam Yarmolinsky, "Ideas into Programs," *The Public Interest*, no. 2 (Winter 1966): 70–79; Daniel Bell, "Government by Commission," *The Public Interest*, no. 3 (Spring 1966): 3–9; Nathan Glazer, "On Task Forcing," *The Public Interest*, no. 15. (Spring 1969): 40–45; and William D. Carey, "Presidential Staffing in the Sixties and Seventies," *Public Administration Review* 29 (September/October 1969): 450–458.

[6] Neustadt, op. cit., pp. 643–644.

[7] Richard E. Neustadt, "Presidency and Legislation: Planning the President's Program," *American Political Science Review* 49 (December 1955): 1001.

[8] Ibid., pp. 986–987.

[9] Carl R. Sapp, "Executive Assistance in the Legislative Process," *Public Administration Review* 6 (Winter 1946): 16.

[10] Kermit Gordon, "Reflections on Spending," in *Public Policy*, J. D. Montgomery and A. Smithies, eds., Vol. XV (Cambridge, Mass.: Harvard University Press, 1966), p. 59.

[11] Carey, op. cit., p. 453.

[12] Russell B. Pipe, "Congressional Liaison: The Executive Branch Consolidates Its Relations with Congress," *Public Administration Review* 26 (March 1966): 20.

[13] Carey, op. cit., p. 454.

Selection 10 Presidential Pull up Capitol Hill

Aage R. Clausen

Presidential influence on Congress is a vast topic. It has some of the fatal allure of the female spider who kills her lovemate immediately after mating. For quite different reasons, the topic of presidential influence seems like one worth pursuing. It deals with the relation between the two branches of government most instrumental in the production of legislation, most important to the conduct of the daily business of government, and most responsible for the determination of our national commitments at home and abroad. However, the promise in the pursuit, and the potential inherent in the conquest, of this topic are, by the very nature of things, followed by the sudden death of any hope for immortality. The topic is simply too vast to be comprehended, much less researched, in any systematic and meaningful way.

The question of presidential influence on Congress, or the relative influence of each on the making of public policy, is often approached with one of two possible biases. One bias is the preference for a strong executive and a compliant Congress; the other bias is for a Congress that asserts policy leadership independent of, or in cooperation with, the president. Whatever course it follows, Congress is likely to be the object of criticism. Congressional leadership is characterized as obstructionism by proponents of executive powers; its compliance is seen by the friends of Congress as lack of initiative and political ineffectiveness.[1]

Whatever the observer's bias, the prevailing thesis appears to be that we have, today, a condition of presidential dominance, though with limitations. Consider the effects of the semiautonomous administrative agencies within the federal bureaucracy. Although most of these agencies appear in organization charts to be subordinate to the president, many operate under rules established by Congress and are beholden to Congress. Politically, most of these agencies are sensitive to the wishes of the members of Congress, particularly the relevant committees in Congress. It is not entirely clear, then, that legislation

Reprinted from Aage R. Clausen, *How Congressmen Decide: A Policy Focus* (New York: St. Martin's Press, Inc., 1973), pp. 192-212, by permission of the author and publisher.

drafted as a part of the president's program, or an appropriation request put forward by an agency and subsumed under the president's budget, is an act of executive initiative. It may have developed out of a complex pattern of communications between congressmen, administrators, and the "interest" clients who are the potential beneficiaries of the new, or modified, program. Consequently, it may be misleading to infer that congressional influence is on the wane simply because the legislative initiative appears to originate in the executive branch.

Whatever questions I might raise about the validity of the thesis of executive dominance, it is only fair to say that there is a consensus today that congressional influence is on a steady decline relative to that of the president. And the main component of this argument is that the legislative initiative has been preempted by the president.[2]

In this view, Congress is a reacting organism; it only accepts or rejects alternatives provided by the president and "his" bureaucracy. The situation is analogous to that of the American voters—they can *choose among* candidates, but few put forth candidates. This effectively limits the voters' range of choice and is an abdication of influence to the initiators. Similarly, the president assesses the country's needs, sets the agenda, and solicits a congressional response to his own liking. *The president is the chairman of the Committee on Legislation in the United States government.* Or so they say.

It is one of the blessings of scientific research that its demands for evidence, systematically assembled and cautiously interpreted, prevent one from tackling the vast topic or what some may grandly refer to as the important question. With this said, let me narrow the scope of the inquiry to the topic of *presidential influence on congressional policy positions.*

Presidential influence on policy positions is unlike the other factors considered previously; the presidential factor is a highly changeable component of the decision equation for the simple reason that presidents serve for a fairly short duration. In contrast, the other factors bearing upon the congressman's decision processes are fairly constant for periods of time probably encompassing several presidential administrations. In this work, these other factors include party, constituency, region, state, and just possibly ideology.

Although left to the last, it should be clear that *presidential influence is a fullfledged member of the set of factors that should always be included in the study of the decisions made by individual congressmen.* In terms of the very early discussion of the policy dimension theory, the president is one of those elements in the congressman's political environment that the congressman must deal with in adopting his policy position on each of the five dimensions, along with constituency, party, and so forth.

One reason for pushing the presidential component of the congressman's policy position is that I think it would be unrealistic to ignore it. Furthermore, I am emphasizing the role of presidential influence in the determination of the congressman's general policy position on each dimension in order to provide a better understanding of my earlier refusal to assess the stability of congressional policy positions in terms of positions taken during different administrations. My view is that one can expect a high degree of stability in the policy positions of congressmen during the term of a single president, since there appears to be no factor affecting the congressman's general policy positions that is subject to appreciable change. However, when a new president assumes office there is a change in one potentially important factor in the individual legislator's policy calculations. Consequently, high stability in policy positions cannot be expected across a changeover in the presidency. This is not to say that high stability across presidential terms will not occur, only that it would be perilous to take it for granted.

Expectations

Expectations concerning the depth and breadth of presidential influence on congressional policy positions are not at all well established in the literature. There is nothing matching the redundant profession of research reports on the effects of party, constituency, ideology, and region. The one policy dimension about which expectations may be held, on the the basis of solid research, is international involvement. Here clear evidence that presidential influence is operative was presented in a groundbreaking study by Mark Kesselman.[3]

Kesselman demonstrated that members of the House of Representatives move from previously held positions to support of a new president elected from their own party. The evidence is drawn from two turnovers: from Truman (Democrat) to Eisenhower (Republican) and from Eisenhower to Kennedy (Democrat). It demonstrated that representatives show more support for international involvement when the president is of their own party. This is consistent with expectations regarding the direction of presidential influence on this dimension given his role-defined responsibility for foreign policy and his need to have the tools for effective international involvement.

When we leave the field of foreign policy and enter the field of domestic policy, we are somewhat at a loss as to what to expect. It is certainly reasonable to anticipate that the president will engage the support of his fellow partisans and that he may even attract votes from the other party. The "president's position" would appear to be common knowledge in the Washington community. The *Congressional Quarterly*, the indispensable chronicler of Congress, regularly reports the president's position and publishes support scores showing each congressman's support of the man in the White House. Furthermore, congressmen are reported to have said that they like to go along with the president whenever they can. With all these indicators of the prominence of the president's wishes, our expectation would have to be that presidential influence is not restricted to the dimension of international involvement.

The Investigation

My investigation of presidential influence on congressional decision-making is a very simple operation; it consists of a measurement of the shift in congressional policy positions that accompanies a partisan turnover of the administration. Where such a shift occurs, there is a basis for inferring presidential influence.

The study embraces two partisan turnovers of the presidency, from the Republican Eisenhower administration to the Democratic Kennedy-Johnson administration, and from the latter to the Nixon administration. The mean position of each congressman in the last two Congresses of the Eisenhower administration is compared with his mean position in the first two Congresses of the Kennedy-Johnson administration to see whether there has been any change. (If the congressman has served in only one Congress of an administration, the score for that one Congress is used.) In addition, the position of each congressman in the last Congress of the Kennedy-Johnson administration (the Eighty-eighth) is compared with the one Congress of the Nixon administration for which a complete record is available at this writing (the Ninety-first). (Only the Eighty-eighth Congress was used in order to minimize the time span.)

The study skips over the Eighty-ninth and Ninetieth Congresses, since the main purpose of including the Ninety-first was to demonstrate the currency of the findings on the Eighty-third through the Eighty-eighth. I think this is no real problem, although it does mean that I am assuming no major shifts in the policy positions of congressmen during the administration beginning with Kennedy-Johnson in 1963 and ending with Johnson in 1968.

The examination of all five policy dimensions provides a broad-based test of presidential influence. It also gives us an opportunity to study relative levels of presidential influence on particular dimensions.

As it turns out, there are only two levels of presidential influence observed: some and none! The only policy dimension exhibiting any influence is international involvement; there is nothing approaching even mildly promising evidence of presidential influence on the four domestic policy dimensions. The lack of presidential influence on these four dimensions will be discussed briefly later; the discussion will undoubtedly make more sense after one has a greater familiarity with the analysis. Accordingly, we turn to a fairly searching examination of presidential influence on the international involvement dimension.

Presidential Influence: International Involvement

There is clear evidence of presidential influence in the finding that members of both the House and the Senate respond to a president *of their own party* by either retaining a constant position or moving toward a position of greater support for international involvement. For example, when a Democrat is in the White House, Democrats in the Congress are, collectively, more supportive of international involvement. Broken down to the individual level, three types of behavior are exhibited. There are (1) congressmen who are highly supportive of international involvement under *all* presidents, (2) congressmen occupying a range of positions from moderate to low support who *hold* their respective positions under different presidents, and (3) senators and representatives who *move* from a position of less to a position of more support when the new president is of their own party. In one sense, there are only two classes of congressmen, those who change their position on the international involvement dimension when there is a partisan turnover of the presidency and those who do not.

Changes in Positions of Individual Members. The closer examination and demonstration of this phenomenon begins with data that demonstrate the pattern of stability and movement just described. Data are presented for each party and each house, first for the effects of the Eisenhower to Kennedy-Johnson turnover, in figure 10–1, and second for the changes in position within each party and house during the Kennedy-Johnson to Nixon turnover in figure 10–2.

Let us look first at the effects of the turnover featuring the retirement of President Eisenhower and the installation of the black-bordered Kennedy-Johnson administration. For both parties, in both houses, the phenomenon of stability and movement described earlier is sharply illustrated by these data. The Senate and House patterns are as similar as one could possibly expect. Democrats move toward a more supportive position when a Democratic administration comes into being, and the Republicans move to a less supportive position, since they no longer need to heed the call of a president of their own party.

Moving on to the Kennedy-Johnson to Nixon turnover (figure 10–2), we see the pattern repeated. Of course, the direction of change is reversed as Democrats move toward low support positions and Republicans shift back to more support—though we must not forget that some congressmen maintain their positions through different administrations.

When one's data display such perfect order, it is difficult to avoid the temptation of displaying them in another form, thereby allowing oneself the opportunity to dwell upon them a bit longer. Such is the latent function of the next analysis; the manifest function is to obtain a more complete understanding of the workings of presidential influence on this policy dimension.

Changes in Regional Party Distributions. Distinct regional variations in policy positions on the international involvement dimension, *within*

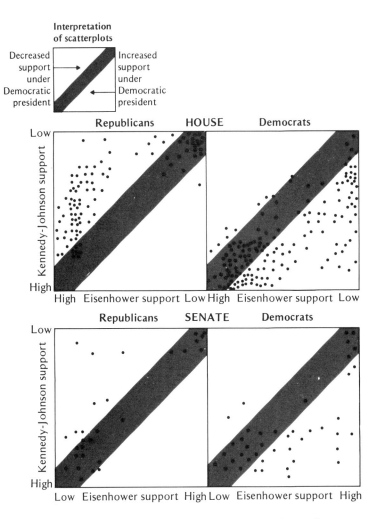

Figure 10-1   Level of support for international involvement under
Democratic Kennedy-Johnson administration as com-
pared to level under Republican Eisenhower administration

each of the parties, are found in this study as well as previous ones. Within the
Republican party the gross regional pattern is one of relatively high support for
involvement among the congressmen from the coastal states, compared with
the level of support among interior Republicans. In the Democratic party the
main difference is between northerners and southerners, the northerners being
more supportive of international involvement. With these observations in
mind, I have divided senators and representatives into four groups for the
purpose of further analysis; northern Democrats, southern Democrats, coastal
Republicans, and interior Republicans. Southern Democrats are those from the

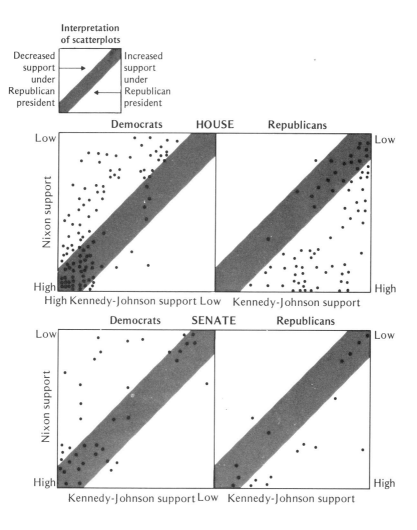

Figure 10-2   Level of support for international involvement under
Republican Nixon administration as compared to level
under Democratic Kennedy-Johnson administration

Border and Southern states; northern Democrats include the remainder.
Coastal Republicans are those from three of the eight regions — Northeast,
Middle Atlantic, Pacific; those from all other regions are considered interior
Republicans.

For another perspective on presidential influence, let us now examine,
not movements of individual members or the lack thereof, but changes in the
distribution of congressmen along the continuum from high to low support,
that occur with presidential turnovers. This will be done for each of the

regional party groupings specified above, for both the House and the Senate. Given the earlier findings, it is anticipated that the distribution of the Republican regional groupings will shift toward the high support pole when a Republican takes over from a Democrat in the White House, and vice versa. Similarly, the center of gravity of the distribution of Democrats along the international involvement dimension will be closer to the high support pole under a Democratic president.

The current demonstration of presidential influence is significantly different from the former one in two ways. (1) Regional variations within the parties are taken into account; (2) all members of each of the five relevant Congresses are brought into the analysis (the Eighty-fifth through Eighty-eighth and the Ninety-first). Up to now only those congressmen who managed to serve in at least one of the Congresses before *and* one of the Congresses after each presidential turnover have been included.

In order to simplify the review of the results of this investigation, each of the parties will be viewed separately. Thus in figure 10–3, the basis for the first description of findings, the distribution of policy positions for the two regional groupings within the Republican party is shown for the two houses. Figure 10–4 gives the same information for the Democrats. In both figures, distributions within each house's regional-party groupings are shown for the three presidential administrations, reading from left to right, Eisenhower, Kennedy-Johnson, Nixon.

Let us look first at the *Republicans.* The shifting of positions in response to presidential turnover is clearly illustrated by the interior Republicans in the House. Under the Democratic administration, nearly two-thirds of these Republicans take the least supportive position relative to international involvement, whereas only one-half occupy the low support position under the Eisenhower administration and less than a third do so under Nixon. By the same token, *none* of the interior Republicans are found at the high support pole of the dimension under the Kennedy-Johnson Administration whereas one-quarter of them move to that pole position under the two Republican administrations. Note that the same pattern of movement characterizes interior Republican Senators, only in a more subdued form.

Whereas the center of gravity of the interior Republican distribution on this dimension is clearly toward the low support end of the continuum, the center of gravity among coastal Republicans is much more towards the high support pole of the continuum. Indeed, in the Senate the coastal Republicans are massed toward the high support pole regardless which party is in the White House. However, in the House, the coastal Republicans show a very strong movement away from the high support position when a Democrat is in the White House. When the Republicans resume the White House occupancy, the coastal House Republicans join hands with their Senate fellows.

Among the *Democrats,* it is the southern contingent that displays the greatest movement from one administration to the next (figure 10–4). Southern

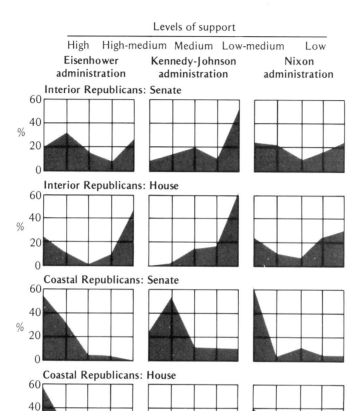

Levels of support

High   High-medium Medium Low-medium   Low

| Eisenhower administration | Kennedy-Johnson administration | Nixon administration |

Interior Republicans: Senate

Interior Republicans: House

Coastal Republicans: Senate

Coastal Republicans: House

Figure 10-3   Distribution of Republican senators and representatives on international involvement dimension (percentages taking high to low positions)

House Democrats are particularly volatile; on balance, they are high supporters of international involvement during a Democratic administration and low supporters during a Republican administration. We also see a major shift in the policy positions of southern Democratic senators between the Kennedy-Johnson and the Nixon administrations, but a much less dramatic one after the Eisenhower administration pulls down its tents.

In contrast to the southern Democrats, the northern Democrats are a bit of a bore. They tender strong support for international involvement, whichever administration is in control. However, by acting as a nearly monolithic bloc in support of international involvement under a Democratic administration, the northern Democrats manage to conform to our general expectation that the president exerts a pull on his fellow partisans in the Congress in the direction of greater support for international involvement.

Contrary to what one might expect, Democratic senators in the North are slightly less supportive of international involvement than are representatives. This is not a function of institutional differences between the Senate and the House, because the general pattern is the opposite: Senators tend to be equally or more supportive of international involvement than their colleagues in the House from the same party and region. One possible reason for the odd pattern in the northern Democratic contingent is that, relative to the House, the Midwestern, Plains and Mountain states are overrepresented in the Senate.

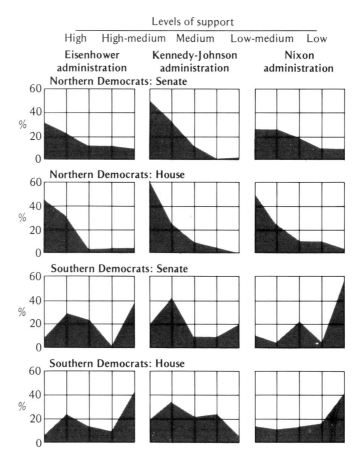

Figure 10-4   Distribution of Democratic senators and representatives on international involvement dimension (percentages taking high to low positions)

Since the latter regions tend to be somewhat less supportive of international involvement, the whole northern Democratic Senate group appears less supportive than the northern Democratic House group.

Speculations aside, the Senate-House regional-party analysis shows the strength of the evidence in support of presidential influence. This influence is effective, and demonstrably so, in all of the eight conditions I have defined: two regions within each of the two parties within each of the two houses.

Members Resisting Presidential Wishes. Throughout the greater part of this analysis and discussion of presidential influence on the policy positions of congressmen on international involvement, the emphasis has been upon the changes in policy positions accompanying a presidential turnover. There are, however, some congressmen who do not change their positions. Some of the stable types are consistently highly supportive of international involvement and would have no reason to change position in response to presidential wishes, others are stable *and* do not follow their party's president's policy lead.

Congressmen who consistently vote *against* continuing or increasing international commitments or take moderate positions fairly consistently are most interesting in comparison with those who provide little support for international involvement when their party is out of the White House but move to higher support positions when their party is in. What is the difference between these two sets of congressmen?

Although I can provide no explanation for the difference between congressmen who are responsive to presidential influence and those who are not, I can provide further information that confirms the meaningfulness of the distinction between the responsive and the resistors. This information is drawn from a study of representation conducted by Miller and Stokes on the Eighty-fifth and Eighty-sixth Congresses, 1957–1960.[4] In this study, members of the House were asked about their voting in the area of foreign affairs: "How much difference has the administration's position made to you in your roll-call votes—a great deal, a lot, some, little, or no difference?" When the answers to this question were related to the qualitative distinction between *Republicans* who persistently took low support positions on international involvement and those who moved to provide more support during the Eisenhower administration, this is what I found:

	Difference Made by Administration Position				
	Great	Lot	Some	Little	None
Responsive Republicans	6	2	3	1	3
Nonresponsive Republicans	1	1	1	1	8

Although the sample is small, being a subsample of a sample of representatives, and therefore subject to substantial sampling error, there seems to be little doubt that there is a real qualitative difference between responsive and nonresponsive Republicans. Two-thirds of the representatives whose voting behavior indicates no responsiveness to administration wishes report that the administration's position made no difference in their policy decisions on legislative notions; in contrast, only one-fifth of the representatives who change their policy positions report no administration influence.

Significantly, when the same question was asked of Democratic representatives there was an overwhelming denial of presidential influence. This is significant because these Democrats were serving under a Republican president; accordingly, there is no reason why they should be affected by the administration's position, at least not as a function of party loyalty.

The Position of the President. The presumption built into this analysis of presidential influence on the international involvement dimension is that the president himself takes a position toward the high support pole. This presumption is based on evidence. Just as congressmen can be ordered on a policy dimension according to their votes on individual roll calls associated with that dimension, so it is possible to locate the president on a dimension according to the positions he has taken on the various roll calls. When this is done for each of the three presidential administrations, the president emerges as a strong supporter of international involvement.

It may not always be the case that the president will be out front in the support of international commitments, although the fact that foreign policy is his area of responsibility makes it highly likely that such will be the general pattern. It is in his interest to push for legislation and appropriations that will give him the instruments he needs to exert influence on the international level. Such would seem to be the case for the period of eighteen years covered by this study. Much of this legislation was concerned with foreign aid of a unilateral variety, and some was supportive of international agencies such as the United Nations and the International Monetary Fund. As such it was legislation that gave the president resources useful in international negotiations, resources that are likely to be sought by any president who is concerned that this country, and he himself, should be a force in world politics.

In this light, it is understandable that the presidents in the period under study should favor international involvement. Kennedy and Nixon made it very clear that theirs was a strong interest in international relations, and the conduct of their presidencies suggests that domestic policy was certainly of no more than equal interest. Eisenhower's attentions were naturally drawn to foreign affairs because this was his area of expertise and experience in the military service during and after World War II.

Johnson is the only one of the four presidents whose capabilities and interests were domestically oriented. However, his presidency enters into our analysis only to the extent that he has an impact on the Kennedy-Johnson administration. This impact is restricted primarily to the last one of the four years, when he, as a matter of fact, gave all appearances of playing out the presidential hand of John F. Kennedy. . . .

Presidential Influence: Domestic Policy

The apparent lack of presidential influence on the policy positions of congressmen on the four domestic policy dimensions may appear a bit strange at first glance. After all, as commented earlier, there is a great deal of attention given to the president's position on a wide variety of policy questions. Yet it seems from this analysis that presidential positions on domestic policy do not alter enough votes to cause any discernible movement within the congressional ranks.

Now if the findings had been uniformly negative across all policy dimensions, it would have been possible to shrug them off as the results of an inadequate mode of analysis. Or, to the glee of some detractors of quantitative techniques, it could be just another example of the eternal verity that "if you can count it, it isn't worth counting, and what counts can't be counted." However, the counting does add up to something on the international involvement dimension; indeed the sum of the count is very impressive.

There are several objections that may be raised against my conclusion that presidential influence is either trivial or nonexistent on the domestic policy dimensions. Let me spell some of these out, doing so in the context of a clear understanding of the meaning of presidential influence as analyzed here.

Most simply, I see presidential influence as a partisan gravitational force exerted by the president on the members of Congress from his own party. This force pulls the congressman away from the position he would occupy in response to the more stable nonpresidential factors such as constituency, state, and region. When the president from the congressman's party leaves the White House, this force is removed and the congressman snaps back into his normal position, so to speak. Some congressmen somehow manage to escape the presidential gravitational field and retain their normal position. Then, of course, there are the congressmen who already occupy a position consistent with that of their party's president.

In the case of the international involvement dimension, the president's position is always at the high support pole, and his influence is always recognized as pulling congressmen in that direction. It is possible that on other dimensions Republican and Democratic presidents will be at opposite poles. No matter, this should still show up in movements in those directions as administrations change. For example, a strongly conservative Republican president taking over from a strongly liberal Democratic president should produce movement in the conservative direction among both Republicans and Democrats.

What happens if the president is a moderate in relation to his party colleagues in the Congress? Theoretically, we should see the party's congressmen converging toward the presidential position. What the members of the other party would be doing as a result of this new presidency would depend upon the character of the previous president from their party; whatever way this president had pulled them, there would be a return to their normal positions.

However, there are circumstances that diminish the importance of presidential influence on congressional policy positions. For example, if the party is highly cohesive *and the president's position is in accord with the party members' normal positions*, there is neither a need nor an occasion for the exercise of presidential influence.

The condition of party cohesion can be used as an explanation for the lack of any evidence of presidential influence on the government management dimension. The same clearly applies to the Republicans on the civil liberties dimension; and one would hardly expect a Democratic president with a liberal civil rights position to have much of an influence on the Democratic congressmen committed to the exclusion of the federal government from this field. So, for two of the four dimensions, the lack of presidential influence appears quite understandable.

Actually, the party cohesion on the two remaining dimensions, agricultural assistance and social welfare, may be high enough that few party members will be far enough out of line with their party's president to feel a strong compulsion to change their positions. The greatest opportunity for presidential influence would appear to be on the social welfare dimension among Democrats. At least a portion of the southern Democrats are clearly less supportive of social welfare than the main body of Democrats.

Even with the use of a microscope, I failed to detect any evidence of movement that went beyond the changes in scores one expects as a function of idiosyncratic factors affecting individual congressmen in individual Congresses and as a function of what has to be a very small amount of measurement error. There simply is no case that can be made for presidential influence on the social welfare dimension, even among southern Democrats. Nor is there any evidence of such influence on the agricultural assistance dimension.

The Many Facets of Presidential Influence: A Caveat

One major qualification must be presented before going on to concluding remarks. I recognize that presidential influence takes many forms that are not manifested in the current analysis. The president may, for example, "go all out" for only a few items of legislation of truly major importance, on which only a few roll calls are taken. Consequently, their effects are lost in the mass of votes on the more common, and recurring, items such as appropriations for existing programs. The president may also compel changes in legislation, formed or worked into shape in Congress, through recourse to the instruments of formal power (such as the veto) and political influence at his disposal.

But I need not go further in spelling out the limitations on my measurement of presidential influence. There are undoubtedly many willing hands more competent to do this task, both by training and inclination. I merely wanted it known that my view of presidential and congressional politics derived something from the capacity for peripheral vision.

Conclusions

Presidential influence has been recognized as a powerful factor in the determination of the policy positions of congressmen on one policy dimension. However, it appears to be effective only on congressmen of the same party as the president.

The policy dimension on which presidential influence is effective is international involvement, a dimension that the president has some reason to call his own. Let me add to this sense of proprietorship by offering the opinion that the legislation found on the international involvement dimension, in the Congresses under study, is concerned primarily with the *national interest* in international relations. The question being asked is: How can national resources best be used to maximize our political and economic advantage in a basically competitive international system? I make this point as strongly as possible to make it clear that this is not a dimension primarily concerned with the extent of United States participation in a world community.

Thus, the ordering of congressmen on the international involvement dimension does not go from the "isolationist, fortress-America-firsters" to the "antinationalist, one-world internationalists" who would prefer that the ultimate political and military power reside in some form of United Nations government. Rather it is an ordering that goes from those who seriously question the value of assisting others as a means toward helping ourselves and who prefer military strength over strong allies, since the latter may be here today and gone tomorrow, to those who feel that an active involvement in international affairs is an investment that serves the national interest.

Of course, everybody claims peace and national strength as his goals, but the proponents of international involvement are more likely to be sanguine about the possibility of avoiding conflict with the Russian bear and the Chinese dragon. It is interesting that President Nixon, an avowed anti-Communist but an international involvement *president*, is one of the relatively sanguine types, as his journeys to Peking and Moscow suggest. Perhaps the example of Richard

M. Nixon, as a supporter of international involvement in the role of president, is the clincher in the argument that to support international involvement, as measured here, does not automatically imply support for internationalism as an aspect of a humanitarian one-world philosophy.

What all this boils down to is this: The international involvement dimension is concerned with the instrumentation of a foreign policy that is premised on the need for national survival and the search for national well-being, security, and power. As such, it encompasses mainly programs, such as foreign military and economic aid, that are desired by the president to enhance his prestige, strength, and flexibility in the conduct of American foreign policy. Therefore, it is inevitable that his position will be a strongly positive one as regards the legislation he is likely to have sponsored, in one way or another. Following this same line of thought, we can expect members of the president's party in Congress to support him even though they would not necessarily support the same policies were they presented by a president of the other party. Foreign policy is the president's responsibility, and members of his party will back him because he is their president.

Congressmen of the president's party who oppose him on foreign policy requests certainly must have strong reasons for doing so. Under a Republican president they are most likely to be ones from the Midwest and the Plains and Mountain states. During a Democratic administration, it is the congressmen from the Democratic South who are most likely to hang back when the president beckons, but they are not as numerous as the interior Republicans.

The interior regions, as we have noted before, have a long tradition of opposition to "foreign entanglements," to use George Washington's words. Such deeply implanted views are difficult to uproot. Furthermore, they are sustained by a particular view of history that is not easily dismissed as irrelevant and uninformed. They can point to allies who have become enemies and enemies who have become allies, when time spans of twenty-five years, or even less, are taken into consideration. For instance, since 1900 our relationship to Russia has changed from friend, to foe, to friend, to foe again, and might possibly be turning back to friend. Observations such as this on the alternating currents of sympathy and antipathy in relations with Russia, China, Japan, Germany, Italy, and Spain are all the more difficult to discount because of the hundred-percent fervor with which we have hated our enemies and embraced our friends of the time being. If alliances and conflicts between ourselves and other nations had consistently been viewed as temporary adjustments to an international environment, the commitments of national resources in behalf of the allies of today and the enemies of tomorrow might have been borne more easily. They could have been looked upon as costs involved in deriving short-term advantages rather than as long-term investments.

I am *not* spending this much time presenting an argument for the policy of restraint in international commitments because such is my own policy view. My policy views are neither relevant nor appropriate to this work. My reason for expounding this argument is that I think it is seldom that the "isolationist" point of view is sufficiently well recognized, or even well understood, by social scientists who are preponderantly favorable to activist foreign policy. In addition, it may make it easier for the reader to understand congressmen who reject "their" president's requests.

My final words on presidential influence . . . are addressed to the finding of presidential influence on the international involvement dimension and the absence of even a trace of such influence on the four domestic policy dimensions: government management, social welfare, agricultural assistance, and civil liberties. . . . The greater part of the variation in the policy positions on the four domestic policy dimensions was found . . . to be accounted for by constituency, party, region, and state. Only about half of the variation on the international involvement dimension was explained by these factors.

The lack of success in explaining the variation in international involvement positions implies the existence of unmeasured factors that can account for an additional portion of the variation. There was good reason to believe that presidential influence would move into the existing void. Moreover, there existed the possibility that the presidential factor was counteracting the effects of the other variables. Consequently, a diminution of the influence of these other factors would occur. On the domestic policy dimensions, on the other hand, it appeared that the party and constituency roots of the congressmen's policy positions were so strong, explaining upwards of three-forths of the variation in policy positions, that there would be no opportunity for an effective exercise of presidential persuasion.

I must say that I am most strongly attracted to the proposition that presidential influence is a major force on the international involvement dimension for two reasons. First, this is an area in which the president is expected to provide leadership; and, second, foreign policy has implications sufficiently removed from the cognitive experience of the citizen that congressmen are not tightly constrained by perceptions of constituency demands. Therefore, a congressman may shift about a bit in response to executive requests without risking his political investment. And I rather suspect that those congressmen who do not respond to the president of their own party, and vote against his programs, do so more out of a personal conviction than out of concern for reprisals at the polls. This is not to deny the possibility that they are strongly influenced and supported in these convictions by political elites from their areas, such as the powerful metropolitan daily that serves their state.

Notes

[1] James M. Burns, *Deadlock of Democracy* (Englewood Cliffs, N.J.: Prentice-Hall, 1963); Ernest S. Griffith, *Congress: Its Contemporary Role*, 3rd ed. (New York: New York University Press, 1961); David B. Truman, ed., *Congress and America's Future* (Englewood Cliffs, N.J.: Prentice-Hall, 1965), see especially pieces by Neustadt, Huntington, and Mansfield.

[2] James A. Robinson, *Congress and Foreign Policy-Making*, rev. ed. (Homewood, Ill.: Dorsey, 1967).

[3] Mark Kesselman, "Presidential Leadership in Congress on Foreign Policy," *Midwest Journal of Political Science* 5 (August 1961), and "Presidential Leadership in Congress on Foreign Policy: A Replication of a Hypothesis," *Midwest Journal of Political Science* 9 (November 1965). Also highly sensitive to this possibility is Leroy N. Rieselbach, *Roots of Isolationism* (Indianapolis, Ind.: Bobbs-Merrill, 1966); Ronald C. Moe and Steven C. Teel, "Congress as Policy-Maker: A Necessary Reappraisal," *Political Science Quarterly* 85 (September 1970), pp. 443–470.

[4] Warren E. Miller and Donald E. Stokes, *Representation in Congress* (in preparation).

Selection 11 Interest Groups and Congress: Toward a Transactional Theory

Michael T. Hayes

Through most of the first half of this century, political science theory was, essentially, *group* theory. The classical works of pluralist theory regarded interest groups as the central political actors and treated Congress as little more than the arena in which the outcome of the group struggle would be ratified. According to Earl Latham, for example, Congress was little more than a referee in the group struggle: "The legislative vote on any issue thus tends to represent the composition of strength, i.e., the balance of power among the contending groups at the moment of voting."[1] Although not all scholars of the legislative process were this extreme, as late as 1964 Theodore Lowi could write that "As an argument that groups must be the major unit of analysis, pluralism excites little controversy."[2]

In the years since, however, the serious study of interest groups has ground to a virtual halt, at least among political scientists, with the onset of a new conventional wisdom that regards interest groups as peripheral actors, at best, in the legislative process. This reflects a misreading of Bauer, Pool, and Dexter's landmark study of business lobbying on the tariff issue in the 1950s, *American Business and Public Policy*, in which interest groups were observed to be underfinanced, poorly organized, and quite timid, generally approaching only those congressmen who agreed with them already.[3] Accordingly, Bauer, Pool, and Dexter, sought to correct the pressure group model of the legislative process; however, they failed to foresee that their own views would in turn become fashionable almost in caricature. Their volume is remembered less for its tentative generalizations and its call for a more sophisticated "transactional" model of the legislative role of interest groups than for its ringing denunciation of the gross oversimplifications and naiveté of the pressure group theorists.

As a correction to this new conventional wisdom, I advanced a typology of policy processes.[4] It is derived from the earlier efforts of Lowi, Edelman, Oppenheimer, and Salisbury and Heinz, specifying the circumstances under which interest groups would, and would not, play a significant role in the legislative process. This essay will attempt to move beyond that typology, focusing on the interrelationship between the underlying dimensions. A transactional theory of legislative decision making will be proposed, in response to Bauer, Pool, and Dexter, and tentatively tested against available evidence. This theory will be derived from the simple assumption that congressmen are primarily concerned with securing their own reelection; as such, it owes much to the recent efforts of Fiorina and Mayhew to develop rational choice models of congressional voting behavior.[5] It differs from these primarily in recognizing that some voters will find it rational to acquire better information than others on any given issue and that, correspondingly, some groups will be more vulnerable than others to symbolic reassurances. Once this inequality of information, and the potential for political deception it poses, are properly understood, it becomes possible to explain how interest groups can play a much more significant role in the legislative process than is implied by the new conventional wisdom while, at the same time, leaving congressmen a great deal freer than is suggested by the group theorists' metaphor of Congress as mere referee of the group struggle.

I. A Typology of Policy Processes

The first step toward transcending the new conventional wisdom lies in the recognition that there is not one single, "typical" legislative process to be explained, but rather several. Thus, I have advanced a typology of six legislative processes derived from one environmental and one output dimension, termed demand pattern and supply pattern, respectively. Demand pattern distinguishes environments in which publics seeking benefits from

Congress encounter opposition from environments where they do not. This distinction follows Fiorina's differentiation between conflictual and consensual constituencies.[6] Supply pattern, by contrast, encompasses the range of options available to congressmen faced with a given demand pattern. Essentially, Congress can respond by allocating benefits explicitly, either passing or defeating a bill, or by granting broad discretion to an administrative agency or the courts (or, in some cases, to the pressure groups themselves), thereby delegating the real responsibility for choice elsewhere.[7]

Combining these two dimensions yields a typology of six distinct policy processes:

| | | Demand Pattern | |
		Consensual	Conflictual
Supply	No Bill	Noninterference (Laissez Faire)	Nondecision (Suppression of Conflict)
Pattern	Delegation	Self-Regulation (Legitimized Autonomy)	Regulation (Extension of Group Conflict)
	Allocation	Distribution (Pork Barrel Politics)	Redistribution (Resource Transfers)

Within the realm of the politics of *noninterference*, there is a prevailing consensus against legislative action on an issue. There is no pressure for a bill, and none is passed; in this sense, this is not really an ongoing policy process at all. By its very nature, this arena is difficult to distinguish from its conflictual counterpart, the realm of *nondecisions*, first identified by Bachrach and Baratz.[8] In the arena of noninterference, an ideological consensus supports a conscious policy of nonintervention, but in the realm of nondecision, elites succeed in suppressing latent conflict by limiting the agenda of formal decision making to safe issues.

In the *self-regulatory* arena, a group or coalition seeks to legitimize its autonomy from governmental interference by obtaining the authority to regulate itself. This is distinct from the realm of noninterference, insofar as the government actively intervenes here, albeit only to guarantee the group's autonomy, enabling it to avoid unwanted competition by erecting barriers to market entry; occupational licensing is a prime example. By contrast, in the *regulatory* arena, a group or coalition approaches Congress seeking some change in the status quo with potentially redistributive consequences. However, opposition is encountered, and Congress responds with a vague and essentially symbolic bill. In this way, the group conflict is not really resolved but rather is merely passed on to a less visible administrative or judicial arena to be accommodated there. Examples abound here in the area of business regulation.

The *distributive* process is the classic realm of pork barrel politics. Here a group or coalition seeks an explicit allocation of benefits from Congress and, in the absence of aroused opposition, gets whatever it wants—dams, rivers and harbors legislation, the traditional tariff, the Sugar Act, import quotas, and subsidies of all sorts. The *redistributive* process likewise involves the explicit allocation of benefits, but it differs from its distributive counterpart primarily in the demand pattern that gives rise to the allocation. In fact, both processes involve the redistribution of resources within society. The distinction is that the losers are active and aware of the stakes involved in the redistributive arena; in the distributive realm, the losers can be kept unaware of the very existence of a conflict through the control of information and the manipulation of symbols. Thus, those actually participating in the distributive legislative process can accommodate potential conflict through logrolling at the expense of those not involved, by raising taxes or inflating the currency, for example.

II. Congressmen, Constituencies, and Information Costs

The bulk of this essay explores the interrelationship between demand and supply pattern, exploring the incentives facing congressmen confronted with different environments. In this regard, a rational choice theory of legislative decision making will be advanced; for the most part, I hypothesize, congressmen will find it rational to allocate resources directly when facing a consensual demand pattern and to avoid choice through legislative delegation when confronting a conflictual constituency. Thus, the distributive and regulative categories should be by far the most common empirically, although the circumstances contributing to self-regulatory, nondecision, or redistributive outcomes will also be reviewed.

Fiorina's theory provides the best starting point for the development of such a theory, both for what it tells us regarding congressional roll-call voting strategies and for what it fails to explain. For although he identifies a dominant electoral strategy for congressmen from homogeneous districts, he fails to find any corresponding solution for those faced with polarized constituencies. However, I will argue, the solution he provides for the consensual case is not general; at the same time, solutions for the conflictual case involve the manipulation of political symbols.

Fiorina's Theory

Fiorina assumes that congressmen are rational actors, casting their votes in an effort to secure reelection. In this regard, he distinguishes between two alternative strategies. One is simply to maximize the subjective probability of reelection; congressmen adopting this Downsian goal are termed "maximizers." The alternative goal is to maintain some aspiration level or satisfactory subjective probability of reelection; congressmen adopting such a goal are termed "maintainers." Clearly, maintainers will be much freer than maximizers; where maximizers are obsessively concerned with reelection, and thus face a determinate strategy in most instances, maintainers can exercise a bit more independence, choosing to vote, at least occasionally, to make good public policy or to gain prestige within the assembly.[9]

According to Fiorina, the environment facing the congressman from a consensual constituency is a comforting one. The optimal strategy is obvious, particularly for vote maximizers; where an issue affects all the active groups in the same way, the maximizing representative will vote with these groups, regardless of how salient the issue. Maintainers will be somewhat freer, depending upon their aspiration levels and the saliency of the issue. All in all, however, the consensual environment is highly desirable, as the intelligent representative can make his seat safe and keep it that way.[10]

The environment is more threatening when the congressman faces a conflictual constituency, as, however he votes, he must offend someone. A maintaining strategy may not exist at all, and maximizing will consist, at best, of minimizing losses. When the conflicting groups are unevenly matched in their capacity to affect the representative's reelection—in terms of resources, organization, intensity of preference, or whatever—then the optimal strategy will resemble that for the consensual constituency; maximizers will always support the stronger group, and maintainers will do so more often than not. However, this in no way enables the congressman to do more than minimize his losses. And when the contending groups are evenly matched, his dilemma is even more acute, as he cannot even trade off the support of a weak group for a strong one. There are no good options for such a representative; over time, he must inevitably forfeit the support of a majority of his constituents and be defeated.[11]

Fiorina examines abstention as a way for such congressmen to avoid choosing among conflicting groups. Ultimately, this provides no solution, however; individual congressmen may try to avoid choosing among groups on an issue, but Congress as a body cannot. Whether the bill is passed or defeated, some groups must triumph at the expense of others. The losing groups will almost surely hold the abstaining representative responsible for failing to support their cause, and the victors will owe him no corresponding debt of gratitude. It would appear, then, that there is no way out for the congressman from a conflictual constituency.[12]

Political Ignorance and Symbolic Politics

Because abstention cannot effectively shift the responsibility for choice from individual congressmen, any solution to this dilemma must somehow allow congressmen to avoid a clear-cut choice among contending groups while, at the same time, permitting them at least to appear to take a clear stand on the bill. In short, some way must be found to make both sides think they have won. The opportunity to do so is afforded by the costs associated with acquiring and interpreting information, for whenever some or all of the publics active on an issue possess imperfect information, the potential for political deception exists.

Because the expected benefit of voting is so low, most citizens will find it irrational to vote at all unless they can hold the costs of voting to an absolute minimum. As many of these costs are unavoidable (registration, time spent standing in line, etc.), the costs associated with obtaining information become a prime target. Thus, many voters will remain almost entirely ignorant on most political issues, absorbing at best only that information available to them at no cost — nightly news broadcasts, propaganda from the candidates, or an occasional headline. The vast majority of voters will never advance beyond the casually informed stage, scanning headlines and reading an occasional political piece. Such voters will vary in what catches their interest — ethnic identifications, political scandals, or editorials reinforcing preexisting biases. Thus, most voters will remain completely ignorant on most issues, attaining only a superficial understanding of most others.[13]

In this regard, Edelman has distinguished between what he terms "Pattern A" and "Pattern B" groups. Pattern A groups are characterized by a high degree of formal organization, precise information, relatively small numbers, a strong sense of political efficacy, and an interest in tangible resources. By contrast, Pattern B groups exhibit poor organization, imperfect and stereotypic information, relatively large numbers, anxieties and feelings of inefficacy, and a susceptibility to symbolic reassurances. Edelman argues that Pattern A groups will obtain tangible rewards at the expense of Pattern B groups, who will be satisfied with symbolic reassurances that their interests are being protected.[14] Thus, he observes, tangible benefits are frequently not distributed as promised in regulatory legislation, but the deprived seldom protest this. In fact, the most intensive dissemination of symbols typically attends the enactment of that legislation having the least impact on the allocation of tangible resources.[15]

III. The Calculus of Legislative Decision Making

Although Edelman's exploration of the political uses of symbols is highly suggestive, he is content to point to the pervasiveness of symbolic action in the political realm without really exploring the circumstances under which different symbolic strategies will succeed. Thus, his analysis provides a plausible explanation for the gap between rhetoric and reality in regulatory statutes but fails to explain why different types of symbolic action should be effective at different times—why, for example, some groups will be successful in obtaining and disguising outright subsidies while others will obtain licensing authority or protection from unwanted competition through regulation.

Clearly, a variety of symbolic strategies exists, each appropriate for a different set of legislative circumstances. In this regard, it will be useful to identify a variety of alternative demand patterns, distinguished by the configuration of voters and the susceptibility to political symbols characterizing those on each side. The first distinction, following Fiorina, will be that between the consensual and conflictual constituency. Although the incentives facing congressmen differ fundamentally between the two cases, as Fiorina convincingly demonstrated, both provide more potential avenues to the congressman than he implies. The conflictual constituency, in particular, will be further broken down into three distinct subcases: a pressure group opposing a mass public, counterbalanced pressure groups, and counterbalanced mass publics. A way out of the congressman's apparent no-win situation exists for each constituency configuration, but the precise nature of the dominant symbolic strategy will vary from case to case.

The Consensual Case

The distributive and self-regulatory arenas are characterized by consensual demand patterns, as the only groups active on such issues are those seeking governmental largesse. Because potential opposition has been forestalled, it is possible to keep the legislative stakes consensual. Material rewards to the participants can be drawn, almost entirely, from outside the legislative game by drawing resources from the inattentive in the form of higher taxes or higher prices. Thus, there are distinct winners and losers in both these arenas, but what makes them consensual is that the losers are not actively involved in the legislative process. Indeed, the losers may not even be aware that the legislation threatens them.

Congress will allocate freely under such circumstances. In the absence of attentive opposition groups, there are no significant political costs associated with explicit allocation. Not surprisingly, Fiorina found voting with such a consensual constituency to be the dominant strategy for both maximizers and maintainers. Moreover, significant electoral benefits may flow from such an allocation if the benefits can be tailored to specify the congressman as their source; thus, policy outcomes in the consensual case will generally take the form of what Mayhew terms "particularized benefits," and distributive policies should be much more common empirically than self-regulatory outcomes.[16] To allocate directly under such circumstances is to create a long-term dependency on the part of the beneficiaries, as they know the source of the benefits, and they have to keep returning for them year after year. To delegate under such circumstances is to forfeit these electoral advantages needlessly, as legitimizing a group's autonomy is, by its very nature, a one-shot affair, unconducive to protracted dependency and electoral gratitude.

Still, the occasional occurrence of self-regulatory policies—occupational licensing or the National Industrial Recovery Act in the 1930s—demonstrates that delegation retains some appeal in the consensual case.[17] Clearly, there is an incentive for groups to ask for self-regulatory benefits; Stigler has suggested that all groups strong enough to do so will seek to erect barriers to market entry.[18] Moreover, self-regulatory benefits often possess instrinsic symbolic appeal and thus can be more easily disguised than outright subsidies. Few people question the AMA's authority to accredit medical schools or associate its market power with rising physician costs, for example. However, as was argued above, the incentives facing congressmen to delegate under such circumstances are clearly not electoral in origin, but rather must be the classically invoked justifications for delegation: the costs of time and information. Thus, legislatures have neither the time nor the expertise to perform as licensing bureaus for the professions. Similarly, Congress shows little interest in the day-to-day administration of the price support program, although it will jealously guard its prerogative to appropriate the funds for the subsidies. Explicit allocation will be the dominant strategy for congressmen from consensual constituencies if the potential victims are inattentive or their attention can be deflected by symbolic justifications for the benefits, as with veterans' benefits or the concept of "parity" in agricultural price support legislation.[19]

Conflict: Interest Group vs. Mass Public

According to Fiorina, any conflictual demand pattern places congressmen in a no-win situation. No matter which side they choose, they must offend someone and suffer the inevitable electoral consequences. Abstention offers only a partial and unsatisfactory solution, in the dubious hope of minimizing losses. The way out, I have argued, lies in legislative delegation. To turn this bleak situation to their collective electoral advantage, congressmen must cooperate in an exercise in duplicity, passing a bill that each side can interpret as a victory. Not all delegations of discretionary authority are alike, however. Some do not resolve the legislative struggle at all, creating instead a conflictual administrative process for which the outcome is indeterminate. Others produce an administrative process almost certain to be dominated by organized interests at the expense of the unorganized. The latter outcome is particularly likely to occur whenever an organized interest is opposed by a mass public.

Although dollars and votes are both important to the reelection chances of congressmen, what is chiefly important, I would argue, is having a long memory. Constituents do occasionally become attentive, either as individuals or as members of threatened groups, and congressmen will naturally search for some way to respond to them. However, congressmen will respond to pressure groups and unorganized masses of casually informed voters in radically different ways. Members of the mass public will generally find it irrational to obtain the information necessary to identify their interests on a given issue and, moreover, will be ill equipped to interpret the information they do obtain. Consequently, they are vulnerable to symbolic reassurances that their interests are indeed being protected. By contrast, pressure group (Pattern A) voters will have a clearer understanding of their stake in the issue, will more fully understand the consequences of the congressman's stand for their position, will remain attentive to potentially adverse effects of the administration of the law, and will be quite unforgiving in both their voting and campaign activities in the next election.

Thus, consumers will receive assurances that newly created regulatory agencies have been charged to act "in the public interest" but will not receive any permanently institutionalized role in the administrative process. Rather, they will be left to depend upon their own continued, self-motivated attentiveness to the results of the administrative process for real protection of their interests—a very thin hope indeed on which to rely. In time, with the inevitable lapse of public attention, abetted by the impression that the issue has been favorably resolved, the administrative process will become consensual in form. Because this new game involves only the regulated groups and the regulators, it is hardly surprising when accommodations are worked out at the expense of the inattentive general public.

The time lag that sometimes occurs between enactment and accommodation merely reflects a period of tentative public attentiveness to the regulatory process and a cosmetic period of regulation in the consumer interest designed to provide symbolic reassurances that the intent of the statute is indeed being carried out. Lowi is not entirely correct, then, in asserting that the danger in delegation lies in the refusal of Congress to choose between conflicting groups.[20] In a very real sense, Congress does choose when it creates these consensual administrative processes insofar as the ultimate outcome is foreordained. Under such circumstances, the real effect of delegation is not so much to avoid choice as to disguise it.

A Special Case: The Politics of Innovation

The foregoing examples have portrayed congressmen as essentially reactive, employing delegation to avoid choice in a conflict thrust upon them. However, congressmen will often find it useful to contrive such conflicts, making a scapegoat of an organized interest in an effort to create a favorable image among the mass of casually informed and ignorant voters. In this vein, Galbraith has suggested that industries employ advertising to contrive synthetic consumer wants for otherwise unnecessary items.[21] Although his argument remains controversial among economists, it would seem to have considerable applicability for politicians seeking reelection. Tullock, in particular, has observed that politicians will find it rational to innovate for appearance's sake.[22] The commonly perceived function of legislators is to legislate whether new laws are needed or not. Consequently, politicians will seek to contrive synthetic preferences for some package of legislation they can claim as their own. Given that most voters never pass beyond the casually informed stage, it becomes possible to mount symbolic attacks on "vested interests" in such a way as to deceive the mass of voters without offending the organized groups so important to the congressman's reelection.

A classic instance is provided by the emergency of consumer protection as an issue in Congress in the early 1960s. The 1962 pure food and drug amendments, the 1968 truth-in-lending legislation, and the more recent automobile safety legislation were all passed ostensibly to benefit consumers. However, consumers, a quintessential Pattern B group, did not provide the primary impetus for enactment. Rather, most consumer lobbying has been instituted as a by-product activity of previously organized groups, particularly labor unions.[23] The more recent emergence of the Ralph Nader-sponsored public interest movement in no way belies this. Consumers remain unorganized, albeit not unrepresented, as a self-appointed spokesman, however dedicated, is not equivalent to a mass-based organization. Moreover, the secret of Nader's lobbying success lies not in the traditional techniques of bargaining, logrolling, or persuasion, but rather in publicity—focusing public attention on previously unperceived abuses. No prolonged attention can be given to any single problem areas as, lacking any ongoing consumer organization, Nader is forced to flit from one issue to another in quest of fresh scandals. The eventual restoration of quiescence is inevitable as Nader moves on to new issues.[24] In a very real sense, then, Nader survives by dispensing largely symbolic rewards.

The real pressure for consumer protection legislation has originated elsewhere, in the efforts of elected officials to manufacture an issue with positive electoral payoffs. President Kennedy made the first major presidential statement on consumer affairs since the New Deal in 1962, elucidating a series of consumer rights and pledging his administration to consumer protection. However, this commitment was evidently more symbolic than real, for his only intervention in consumer legislation was an attempt to weaken some sections of Senator Kefauver's original drug amendments.[25] Although the Johnson administration's legislative record on consumer protection was much stronger, its commitment appears to have been no less symbolic. President Johnson's interest stemmed chiefly from his need for a relatively inexpensive new domestic issue in the wake of the Great Society. With consumer protection, no new bureaucracies would be required, and the costs of the programs would be absorbed by consumers and industry and thus not be reflected in the federal budget. Moreover, it offered the administration a consensus issue, as opposition to the broad goal of consumer protection would be politically untenable.[26]

The electoral rewards associated with this issue were not confined to the presidency, however. Throughout the period, much of the legislation originated in Congress. A variety of congressmen cultivated images as consumer activists. Senator Magnuson of Washington, for example, used consumer protection to counteract his prevailing image as a captive of Boeing Aircraft.[27] Potential industry opposition was lessened, albeit not entirely eliminated, by the quintessentially symbolic nature of much of the legislation.

Thus, consumer protection constitutes a classic example of what Mayhew has termed a "position-taking" issue.[28] Such legislation will be tailored to suit the electoral interests of its framers and will, therefore, most profitably be symbolic. Symbolic reassurances will suffice to establish a positive image on the issue while minimizing the electoral costs associated with potential industry opposition. Moreover, consumer activists will care less that they win on a given issue than that they be clearly perceived as champions of the consumer cause. It should not be surprising, then, that there is no stable consumer coalition in Congress and little overall coordination. Rather, the emphasis is on position taking, committee specialization, and personal publicity, to the point of occasional instances of outright rivalry among members active on the same issue.[29] Indeed, the position-taking nature of the issue, with its attendant emphasis on publicity over substance, has made for a symbiotic relationship among the consumer activists in Congress, Ralph Nader, and the press, in which they cooperate in dispensing symbolic reassurances to unorganized consumers.[30]

For the most part, then, the politics of consumer protection has remained within the realm of nondecision, as fundamental changes in the relationships between buyers and sellers have been kept off the policy agenda entirely. Proposals that do reach the agenda of decision are quickly emasculated, and the legislation that has passed has been almost entirely confined to the regulative arena. Enforcement of product standards is generally delegated to an existing regulatory agency sympathetic to the industry position, and penalties for violations are mild or nonexistent. The costs of improved performance standards, where they are enforced, are imposed across the entire industry and thus in no way threaten the existing relations among competing firms. The associated costs to the industry are not excessive and, in any event, can largely be shifted to consumers in the form of higher prices. Thus, consumer protection provides a classic instance of Bachrach and Baratz's "second face of power" even as it offers politicians the opportunity to appear vigilant in their protection of the public interest.[31]

Conflict: Counterbalanced Pressure Groups

Whenever the conflict involves competing Pattern A groups, the congressman's dilemma is more acute, for the stakes will then be conflictual and clearly understood by all involved. There is thus no possibility for logrolling at the expense of unwitting spectators outside the legislative game, as affected groups are organized and attentive on both sides of the issue. As before, there is no choice but to delegate, as only by supporting a bill that seems like a victory for both sides can the congressman escape the electoral wrath of at least one of the blocs. However, because both sides are well organized and likely to remain attentive after the legislative struggle is over, both must be granted institutionalized roles in the administrative process. To do otherwise would result in an ill-concealed defeat for one of the sides and, inevitably, undesirable electoral repercussions.

Because the delegation is designed to avoid choice among the conflicting groups and because this ambiguity is reinforced by formally representing each group in the administrative process, the eventual outcome of administration will be indeterminate. Most likely, the winners and losers will vary from one round to the next. When conflict has been institutionalized through the assignment of permanent roles to the competing groups in the regulatory process, the administrators can more easily play the groups off one another and thus at least avoid appearing captured by their clientele groups.

The National Labor Relations Board provides a striking example here. Labor and management are both well organized, and both are guaranteed representation in the administrative process. Consequently, "Most analysts would agree that this is how regulation ought to operate . . ."[32] and Lowi finds in the NLRB an exception to the otherwise pervasive trend toward sweeping legislative delegation.[33] The relative independence of the NLRB is attributable to the conflictual nature of the stakes involved and to the conscious decision of the regulators to act as referees rather than as a conflict-resolving body.[34] Of course, not all regulation of conflicting groups has received comparable accolades. What frequently takes place instead is a more complex, and less recognizable, form of capture by a coalition of regulated groups at the expense of unorganized consumers. Examples here would include public utility and common carrier regulations benefiting coalitions of producer and customer groups and airline regulation that benefits both airlines and supplier groups.[35]

The regulation of air and water pollution provides an instructive case of issue movement, beginning in the realm of the politics of innovation and shifting to an instance of counterbalanced pressure groups with the maturation of the environmental movement. As Jones has persuasively demonstrated, the dramatic increase in mass public awareness of pollution as a problem in the late 1960s forced Congress to respond with "speculative augmentation" in the clean air amendments of 1970 and the federal water pollution control amendments of 1972.[36] Had public attention predictably waned in the short run, the typical pattern of regulatory capture would doubtless have ensued. However, the continued development of environmentalist groups in this period forestalled this, transforming the conflict into one of counterbalanced pressure groups. Subsequent legislation has been ambiguous by design, as congressmen have sought to avoid even a thinly disguised defeat for either side.[37]

In sum, regulatory legislation consistently benefits the organized over the unorganized. Whether an agency is captured by its clientele appears to depend upon the terms of the legislative delegation structuring the administrative process. The unorganized "public interest" will be protected, if at all, only coincidentally, when administrators are able to play off the conflicting interests of counterbalanced Pattern A groups.

Conflict: Counterbalanced Mass Publics

When few voters have passed beyond the casually informed stage on a given issue, the opportunities for political deception, particularly in the form of strategies of symbolic innovation, would appear almost unbounded. Indeed, this may account for the ability of leaders to manipulate foreign crises to bolster their popular standing at home, as foreign policy is noteworthy for its lack of organized interest group activity. Similarly, in the domestic realm, there is evidence that the war on poverty had its origins, at least in part, in President Johnson's quest for a theme around which to build his 1964 reelection campaign.[38]

Surprisingly, these innovative strategies are not devoid of risk. Although all voters are vulnerable to symbolic appeals, in such an instance, their very lack of sophistication makes them particularly resistant to "fine tuning" for electoral purposes. Ironically, the success of the innovative strategies reviewed earlier was made possible by the presence of some well-organized and attentive groups that could be made the symbolic victims of the legislative drama. Thus, these Pattern A groups could be counted upon to discount the accompanying political rhetoric even as it was accepted by the target publics. However, when none of the affected publics has advanced beyond the casually informed stage, this sophistication can no longer be assumed, and there is a very real possibility that the symbolic posturings will be believed by the ostensible victims without correspondingly deceiving the target groups.

The war on poverty provides an instance in which the groups involved were rendered more-or-less equal by their very failure to organize. Both the middle class and the poor were susceptible to symbolic reassurances. The latter thus received the assurance that the "war" was being undertaken on their behalf, while the middle class was satisfied that social disorder was being quelled while, at the same time, the undeserving poor were being controlled through restrictive eligibility and administrative standards. Both sides were reassured that the issue had been submitted to professionals for solution.

The ultimate bankruptcy of this symbolic strategy raises the question of how the war on poverty came to be enacted at all, particularly in view of the well-documented absence of organized group pressure.[39] In this regard, Piven and Cloward have convincingly interpreted the Great Society as a deliberate political strategy of the Kennedy and Johnson administrations aimed at solidifying the growing black vote in the central cities. By 1960, 90 percent of all northern blacks were concentrated in just ten of the most populous northern states, thus making them a pivotal electoral group. Their importance to the Democratic coalition was heightened by the decline of Democratic strength in the once solid South. By 1960, blacks were a key element in what remained of the Democratic coalition.[40]

Consequently, from 1961 to 1964, Democratic administrations sought new legislation explicitly aimed at problems of the inner cities: juvenile delinquency, mental health, community action, and model cities. However, the underlying intent was not to redistribute income, and the legislation can only be properly understood as regulative. The logic underlying its enactment paralleled that contributing to the enactment of the other regulatory policies reviewed above. Congressmen were faced with a conflict between unorganized mass publics. On the one hand, the poor posed the threat of social disorder in demanding some benefits, and blacks in the central cities had become a particularly well situated voting bloc. At the same time, the middle-class constituents who would bear the burden of any programs enacted tempered their compassion with a stress on the work ethic and an opposition to welfare "handouts." The solution for congressmen, just as with business regulation, was to delegate.[41]

The consequent creation of large welfare bureaucracies thus served a twofold purpose for congressmen faced with seemingly irreconcilable constituent demands. One, of course, was to avoid choice between the conflicting groups in such a way as to make both sides think they had won. The second, closely related to the first, was to defuse the welfare issue by making it appear amenable (at least eventually) to bureaucratic expertise.[42] Ultimately, however, this same logic produced the rapid expansion of a class of social welfare professionals and, in time, a growing realization that a service-oriented welfare strategy transferred income less to lower-class welfare recipients than to middle-class welfare professionals.[43]

Ironically, the strategy ultimately backfired, leaving the Democrats with the worst of both worlds. It is arguable that blacks had begun to recognize the predominantly symbolic nature of the war on poverty by the late 1960s, as evidenced by the fact that rioting in central cities took on crisis proportions only after the enactment of these programs. At the same time, survey evidence suggests that whites did not recognize the symbolic nature of the recent black gains. What whites perceived was a pattern of successive black victories in the legislative arena followed by what appeared to be an increased militance in the form of social disorder and black power movements. By the fall of 1968, this backlash was a major factor contributing to the size of the Wallace vote.[44]

The apparent failure of the war on poverty prompted the Nixon administration to attempt a major overhaul of the existing welfare system, replacing its "services strategy" with an "income strategy" that bypassed the burgeoning welfare bureaucracy. The Family Assistance Plan (FAP) proposed a form of guaranteed annual income, albeit one that rewarded work; as such, it would have had profoundly redistributive consequences. The plan reflected a decision to abandon the symbolic strategy of the 1960s while fulfilling its promises, allocating tangible rewards directly to the poor.[45]

Ironically, this decision in turn necessitated a distinct symbolic strategy of its own. The chief beneficiaries of this new strategy, particularly blacks, had voted against the president in large numbers in 1968 and could not be expected to support him under any foreseeable circumstances. At the same time, the plan involved a very serious risk of alienating the conservative core of the president's electoral coalition. Consequently, the administration set out to reassure its natural constituency that the plan was not really designed to establish the principle of income by right but rather to reinforce work incentives and family stability. According to Moynihan, who participated in the policy debate within the administration, "Symbolic rewards were devised for 'middle America' while legislative proposals were drafted for the 'other America'."[46]

Ultimately, Nixon's symbolic strategy proved to be no more successful than Johnson's. It rested on the underlying assumption that the poor, left to their own devices, would recognize their own self-interest in family assistance even as the president's middle-class constituency was being deceived regarding the true nature of the program. This assumption was ill founded, however, as conservatives very quickly recognized the plan as a guaranteed income and opposed it on those grounds, while the poor, and their traditional liberal allies, accepted the administration's rhetoric at face value. Attorney General Mitchell's attempt to make the administration's symbolic strategy explicit, by telling a group of black representatives to "watch what we do, rather than what we say," fell upon deaf ears.[47] The community action phase of the war on poverty had spawned an organization of welfare militants, the National Welfare Rights Organization, made up almost entirely of black AFDC mothers. This group was already prospering under the existing system, and its leaders had little stake in any reforms for which they could not claim credit.[48] At the same time, social welfare professionals saw in the income strategy a threat to their jobs.[49] In the end, FAP came under attack from both the left and the right and was ultimately defeated.

Thus, Nixon, like Johnson, eventually had the worst of both worlds. Faced with an environment of counterbalanced mass publics, each sought to contrive a positive electoral image through a strategy of symbolic reassurances. Ironically, although the targets of the symbolism differed in the two administrations, in both instances the targets of the symbolic appeals saw through the strategy while the real beneficiaries of the legislation mistook the symbols for reality.

IV. Semisovereign Service Bureaus? Toward a Transactional Theory of Interest Groups and Congress

Clearly, the foregoing implies a much greater role for interest groups in the legislative process than the new conventional wisdom recognizes. In the consensual arenas, organized group pressures are one-sided and overwhelming. The legislative stakes are kept consensual by "privatizing" the conflict: manipulating symbolic reassurances to keep the potential audience unaware of the real stakes.[50] Organized interests triumph at the expense of the inattentive, obtaining tangible benefits in the distributive arena and/or legitimized autonomy in the self-regulatory realm. Moreover, the advantages organized interests possess over mass publics are not confined to the consensual arenas. The prevalence of regulatory agencies "captured" by clientele groups suggests that interest groups, even when ostensibly defeated in Congress, can more than compensate by coming to dominate the administrative process. Potentially threatening reforms are rather easily deflected into the realm of nondecision, and genuinely redistributive policies are virtually nonexistent. This is well illustrated by contemporary social welfare policy, which can only be properly understood as regulative.

Although organized interests clearly possess considerable advantages over the unorganized, they by no means dominate congressmen, as implied by the naive pressure group model. Bauer, Pool, and Dexter were absolutely correct in stressing that

> . . . Congressmen have a great deal more freedom than is ordinarily attributed to them. The complexities of procedure, the chances of obfuscation, the limited attention constituents pay to any one issue, and the presence of countervailing forces all leave the congressman relatively free on most issues . . .[51]

It should be clear, however, that the presence of countervailing pressures does not, of itself, make congressmen free. Quite to the contrary, Fiorina demonstrated that such a constituency places the congressman in an impossible situation, unable to satisfy one side without alienating the other. Rather, congressmen are freed by the marginal attention constituents pay to any one issue, the very complexity of self-interest,[52] and the resulting potential for obfuscation through legislative delegation. Bauer, Pool, and Dexter recognized this potential, noting that most voters really have no idea what they want and, consequently, are satisfied merely to know their congressman "is concerned with their problem and is addressing himself effectively to it."[53] In this regard, legislative delegation allows congressmen to identify and confront perceived problems without really having to resolve them:

> A legislative enactment is seldom a clean decision of important issues. It is normally a verbal formula which the majority of congressmen find adequate as a basis for their continuing policy struggle. It sets up new ground rules within which the issue may be fought out . . .[54]

However, Bauer, Pool, and Dexter erred in assuming that this pattern of legislative delegation, which they observed for the tariff, a regulative issue, was typical of the policy process. Clearly, conflict, per se, does not make congressmen free. Rather, they are freed by the opportunity for legislative obfuscation, which is only made possible by the limited attention most constituents pay to any one issue, the complexity of self-interest, and the consequent vulnerability of most voters to symbolic reassurances.

Symbolic reassurances may be employed to the congressman's electoral advantage in both the conflictual and consensual cases. It is no accident that the outcomes in the distributive and regulative arenas bear such a striking resemblance to Mayhew's "particularized benefit" and "position-taking" issues, for these two processes are by far the most common empirically. In the distributive arena, congressmen are relatively free to "service the organized," as the conflict is kept "privatized " by the manipulation of symbolic reassurances to render the audience unaware of the real stakes. In the regulative arena, the availability of legislative delegation as an option permits congressmen to launch symbolic crusades against perceived problems while avoiding the responsibility for choice among conflicting groups.

Paradoxically, then, it appears that congressmen remain relatively free even as interest groups exercise a great deal more influence than is currently recognized. The key to resolving this paradox lies in Bauer, Pool, and Dexter's single most important, but all-too-often ignored, insight: that influence is reciprocal. In their assault on the pressure group model, they did not seek to minimize the importance of interest groups but rather merely to replace the naive conception of pressure with a more sophisticated "transactional" model of casuality, "which views all the actors in the situation as exerting continuous influence on each other. All the actors are to some extent in a situation of mutual influence and interdependence; A's influence on B is to some extent a result of B's prior influence on A."[55] However, because they focused solely on a regulatory issue, for which the outcome was rendered ambiguous by design, and because their critique of the old conventional wisdom was so devastating, the misimpression was created that interest groups are little more than service bureaus, to be used or abused by congressmen at will. This misimpression took hold as a new conventional wisdom, and their call for a transactional theory of interest groups and Congress went largely unheeded.

The theory advanced here is offered in response to that call. Following Bauer, Pool, and Dexter, it rests upon the premise that influence is reciprocal, as congressmen adjust their policy positions in an effort to secure reelection while, at the same time, remaining relatively free to manipulate these positions to create positive electoral images. Thus, congressmen retain considerable latitude to exert policy leadership, even as organized interests benefit at the expense of the inattentive. In the conflictual arenas, the availability of delegation combines with marginal attention and the complexity of self-interest to enable congressmen to avoid clear-cut choices among conflicting interests. In fact, the marginal levels of attention and information characterizing Pattern B groups provide considerable opportunities for innovation, enabling congressmen to associate themselves with particular issues without necessarily forfeiting the support of the more sophisticated Pattern A groups ostensibly under attack. Although such strategies can be risky, as was illustrated by the failures of the symbolic strategies of both Presidents Johnson and Nixon in attacking the poverty problem, it is likely that these risks will be much lower for congressmen than they were for these two presidents. The well-documented tendency of most voters to hold the president accountable for visible policy failures while returning congressional incumbents to office suggests that congressmen remain relatively free to contrive positive electoral images in this way, leaving the blame, where appropriate, for the top of the ticket to bear.[56]

Even the consensual constituency, where the relative advantage of organized groups is maximized, permits congressmen to nurture a stable and mutually beneficial alliance with the demanding groups. By channeling their demands, whenever possible, into the distributive arena, congressmen can ensure a situation of protracted dependency, as the demanding groups know the source of the particularized benefits and are forced to keep returning for them year after year. Thus, the "subgovernment" phenomenon, the cozy triangular relationships among clientele groups, executive agencies, and congressional committees characterizing a wide range of distributive issues, can be seen to rest upon a stable exchange relationship from which all the participants benefit.[57] Although Bauer, Pool, and Dexter focused solely on a regulatory issue, these distributive subgovernments would seem to constitute quintessential instances of the transactional model of causality they advanced. Congressmen do not regard such lobbying activities as attempts at "pressure," after all.[58] In this regard a consensual constituency can be easier to represent than a polarized one, as Fiorina demonstrated. If the congressman's optimal strategy is determined and, in a sense, confining, at least such a strategy exists. The consensual environment is relatively benign.

Clearly, the new conventional wisdom reflects a misreading of *American Business and Public Policy.* Although the work is flawed by its narrow focus on a regulative issue, it still represents a considerable advance over the naive pressure group model of the previous era. The authors should not be held fully accountable for the oversimplifications of their followers; for although they sought to refute the oversimplistic assertions of the pressure group model, they also sought to remind the discipline of the more sophisticated transactional underpinnings of that model, as originated by Bentley.[59] Dexter therefore characterized their effort as an exercise in "countervailing intellectual power," roughly defined as a healthy skepticism toward any notions that come to be accepted without question.[60] This essay, it is hoped, is a reflection of that skepticism.

In conclusion, organized interest groups play a much greater role in the legislative process than is commonly understood. If, as Bauer, Pool, and Dexter imply, they do perform a service bureau function, they must also be characterized as semisovereign, for they possess considerable advantages over unorganized publics in obtaining tangible benefits from government even as congressmen retain considerable latitude in defining their jobs and fashioning a reliable electoral coalition. In the consensual arenas, interest groups will often provide the only source of constituency cues available to the dedicated representative, and their dominance of the distributive and self-regulatory arenas will typically be accepted as legitimate by congressmen while provoking little challenge from deprived groups. Similarly, in the conflictual arenas, the longer attention span and greater cohesion and sophistication of the Pattern A groups better prepare them for the protracted administrative struggle that so often determines the real outcome of a seemingly inconclusive legislative conflict. Genuinely redistributive policies will be rare, as unorganized publics will be protected, if at all, only coincidentally, when policy makers are able to play off counterbalanced pressure groups. More often the vulnerability of such publics to symbolic reassurances will enable pressure groups, congressmen, and bureaucrats to "privatize" the conflict, entering into stable and mutually beneficial exchange relationships at the expense of an audience unaware of the real stakes.

Notes

[1]Earl Latham, "The Group Basis of Politics: Notes for a Theory," in H. R. Mahood (ed.), *Pressure Groups in American Politics* (New York: Charles Scribner's Sons, 1967), p. 41.

[2]Theodore Lowi, "American Business, Public Policy, Case Studies, and Political Theory," *World Politics*, 16 (July 1964), p. 679.

[3]Raymond A. Bauer, Ithiel de Sola Pool, and Lewis Anthony Dexter, *American Business and Public Policy: The Politics of Foreign Trade* (Chicago: Aldine-Atherton, Inc., 1972).

[4]Michael T. Hayes, "The Semi-Sovereign Pressure Groups: A Critique of Current Theory and an Alternative Typology," *Journal of Politics* 40 (February 1978), pp. 134–161. My typology most closely resembles two efforts by Robert Salisbury, "The Analysis of Public Policy: A Search for Theories and Roles," in Austin Ranney (ed.), *Political Science and Public*

Policy (Chicago: Markham, 1968), pp. 41–52, and (with John P. Heinz), "A Theory of Policy Analysis and Some Preliminary Applications," in Ira Sharkansky (ed.), *Policy Analysis in Political Science* (Chicago: Markham, 1970), pp. 39–59. These efforts, like my own, were stimulated by Lowi's seminal effort in "American Business." For Lowi's own subsequent efforts to elaborate his original typology, see his "Decision Making vs. Policy-Making: Toward an Antidote for Technocracy," *Public Administration Review,* 30 (May/June 1970), pp. 314–325, and "Four Systems of Policy, Politics and Choice," *Public Administration Review,* 32 (July/August 1972), pp. 298–310. My typology also draws upon the symbolic-material policy distinction advanced by Murray Edelman in *The Symbolic Uses of Politics* (Urbana: University of Illinois Press, 1964) and subsequently refined by Bruce Ian Oppenheimer in *Oil and the Congressional Process* (Lexington, Mass.: D.C. Heath, 1974).

[5]See Morris P. Fiorina, *Representatives, Roll Calls, and Constituencies* (Lexington, Mass.: D.C. Heath, 1975), and David R. Mayhew, *Congress: The Electoral Connection* (New Haven: Yale University Press, 1974).

[6]Fiorina, *Representatives,* pp. 43–67.

[7]This is analogous to Lowi's distinction between "rule-of-law" and "policy-without-law." See Theodore J. Lowi, *The End of Liberalism* (New York: Norton, 1969).

[8]Peter Bachrach and Morton S. Baratz, *Power and Poverty: Theory and Practice* (New York: Oxford University Press, 1970).

[9]Fiorina, *Representatives,* pp. 22–23.

[10]Ibid., pp. 44–49.

[11]Ibid., pp. 49–67.

[12]Ibid., p. 75.

[13]See Anthony Downs, *An Economic Theory of Democracy* (New York: Harper and Row, 1957), especially part III, "Specific Effects of Information Costs," pp. 207–276. See also Gordon Tullock, *Toward a Mathematics of Politics* (Ann Arbor: University of Michigan Press, Ann Arbor Paperbacks, 1972), especially chapter VII, "Political Ignorance," pp. 100–114.

[14]Edelman, *Symbolic Uses,* pp. 35–36.

[15]Ibid., pp. 22–23.

[16]Mayhew, *Congress,* p. 54.

[17]See Grant McConnell, *Private Power and American Democracy* (New York: Vintage Books, 1970), especially chapter 8, "Self-Regulation: The Politics of Business," pp. 246–297.

[18]George J. Stigler, "The Theory of Economic Regulation," *The Bell Journal of Economics and Management Science,* 2 (Spring 1971), pp. 3–21.

[19]Edelman, *Symbolic Uses,* p. 65.

[20]Lowi, *End of Liberalism.*

[21]John Kenneth Galbraith, *The Affluent Society,* 2nd ed., revised (Boston: Houghton Mifflin, 1969).

[22]Tullock, *Toward a Mathematics,* chapter I, "Models of Man," p. 1–17.

[23]Mark V. Nadel, *The Politics of Consumer Protection* (Indianapolis: Bobbs-Merrill, 1971), pp. 158–160.

[24]Ibid., pp. 176–191.

[25]Ibid., p. 34.

[26]Ibid., p. 41.

[27]Ibid., pp. 108–112.

[28]Mayhew, *Congress,* pp. 118–122.

[29]Nadel, *Politics,* pp. 113–114.

[30]Ibid., pp. 180–184.

[31]Ibid., pp. 224–229.

[32]Roger Noll, *Reforming Regulation* (Washington, D.C.: Brookings, 1971), p. 48.

[33]Lowi, *End of Liberalism,* p. 153.

[34]Noll, *Reforming Regulation*, pp. 48–51.

[35]Richard A. Posner, "Theories of Economic Regulation," *The Bell Journal of Economics and Management Science*, 5 (Autumn 1974), p. 351.

[36]Charles O. Jones, "Speculative Augmentation in Federal Air Pollution Policy-Making," *Journal of Politics*, 36 (May 1974), pp. 438–464. See also Walter A. Rosenbaum, *The Politics of Environmental Concern*, rev. ed. (New York: Praeger, 1977), especially chapter 5, " 'You've Got to Hit Them with a Two-by-Four': Regulating Air and Water Pollution," pp. 129–167.

[37]For example, recent amendments to the Clean Water Act "are so complex that environmentalists cannot even agree among themselves whether the alterations are good or bad." See Philip Shabecoff, "Ecologists Disagree on Clean-Water Bill," *New York Times*, November 20, 1977, p. 27, col. 1.

[38]James L. Sundquist, *Politics and Policy* (Washington, D.C.: Brookings, 1968), pp. 112–113.

[39]For a detailed case study of the legislative origins of the war on poverty that documents this absence of organized group involvement, see John C. Donovan, *The Politics of Poverty*, 2nd ed. (New York: Pegasus, 1973). For additional background, see Daniel P. Moynihan, *Maximum Feasible Misunderstanding* (New York: Free Press, 1970).

[40]Frances Fox Piven and Richard A. Cloward, *Regulating the Poor* (New York: Vintage Books, 1971), chapter 9, "The Great Society and Relief: Federal Intervention," pp. 248–284. For a sympathetic view, see Donovan, *Politics of Poverty*, pp. 106–108.

[41]Richard A. Cloward and Frances Fox Piven, "The Professional Bureaucracies: Benefit Systems as Influence Systems," in their *The Politics of Turmoil* (New York: Random House, 1974), pp. 7–27.

[42]Ibid., pp. 9–12.

[43]On this point, see Kenneth Boulding, "The Many Failures of Success," *Saturday Review*, November 23, 1968, pp. 29–31. See also Daniel P. Moynihan, *The Politics of a Guaranteed Income* (New York: Vintage Books, 1973), pp. 302–327, as well as his "The Crises in Welfare," reprinted in his volume *Coping* (New York: Vintage Books, 1975), pp. 134–166.

[44]See Richard W. Boyd, "Popular Control of Public Policy: A Normal Vote Analysis of the 1968 Election," *American Political Science Review*, 66 (June 1972), pp. 429–449. See also the various comments and rejoinders, pp. 450–470.

[45]Moynihan, *Guaranteed Income*.

[46]Ibid., p. 156.

[47]Quoted in ibid., p. 157.

[48]Ibid., pp. 158 and 327–345.

[49]Ibid., pp. 302–327.

[50] E. E. Schattschneider, *The Semi-Sovereign People* (New York: Holt, Rinehart, and Winston, 1960).

[51]Bauer, Pool, and Dexter, *American Business*, p. 478.

[52]Ibid., especially chapter 9, "The Roots of Conviction: Self-Interest and Ideology," pp. 127–153; see also pp. 472–475. On marginal attention, see Lewis Anthony Dexter, *The Sociology and Politics of Congress* (Chicago: Rand McNally, 1969), chapter VII, "Marginal Attention, 'Pressure' Politics, Political Campaigning, and Political Realities," pp. 143–150.

[53]Bauer, Pool, and Dexter, *American Business*, p. 423.

[54]Ibid., p. 426.

[55]Ibid., pp. 456–457.

[56]On presidential popularity, see John E. Mueller, *War, Presidents, and Public Opinion* (New York: Wiley, 1973). It is extremely rare, at the same time, for more than 10 percent of all incumbents seeking reelection to Congress to lose in any given year. See Randall B. Ripley, *Congress: Process and Policy* (New York: Norton, 1975), pp. 193–195.

[57]For particularly good discussions of the subgovernment phenomenon, see J. Leiper-Freeman, *The*

Political Process: Executive Bureau-Legislative Committee Relations, rev. ed. (New York: Random House, 1965), and Randall B. Ripley and Grace A. Franklin, Congress, The Bureaucracy, and Public Policy (Homewood, Ill.: Dorsey Press, 1965), especially pp. 74–95.

[58]Bauer, Pool, and Dexter, American Business, chapter 32, "Communications—Pressure, Influence, or Education?" pp. 433–443. See also Dexter, Sociology and Politics of Congress, pp. 171–174.

[59]Dexter, Sociology and Politics of Congress, especially chapter IX, "Models and Comparisons in the Study of Congress," pp. 179–183, and chapter X, "Toward an Evaluation of Analogies for Interpreting and Studying the Congress, An Effect at Historical and Anthropological Exploration," pp. 184–210. See also Dexter, "On the Use and Abuse of Social Science by Practitioners," American Behavioral Scientist, 9 (November 1965), pp. 25–29.

[60]Dexter, "Use and Abuse," p. 26.

Selection 12 Party Government and the Saliency of Congress

Donald E. Stokes
Warren E. Miller

Any mid-term congressional election raises pointed questions about party government in America. With the personality of the President removed from the ballot by at least a coat-tail, the public is free to pass judgment on the legislative record of the parties. So the civics texts would have us believe. In fact, however, an off-year election can be regarded as an assessment of the parties' record in Congress only if the electorate possesses certain minimal information about what that record is. The fact of possession needs to be demonstrated, not assumed, and the low visibility of congressional affairs to many citizens suggests that the electorate's actual information should be examined with care.

How much the people know is an important, if somewhat hidden, problem of the normative theory of representation. Implicitly at least, the

Donald E. Stokes and Warren E. Miller, "Party Government and the Saliency of Congress," Public Opinion Quarterly 26 (1962), pp. 531–546. Reprinted by permission of the authors and copyright holder. (The research from which this report is drawn was supported by grants of the Rockefeller Foundation and the Social Science Research Council.)

information the public is thought to have is one of the points on which various classical conceptions of representation divide. Edmund Burke and the liberal philosophers, for example—to say nothing of Hamilton and Jefferson—had very different views about the information the public could get or use in assessing its government. And the periods of flood tide in American democracy, especially the Jacksonian and Progressive eras, have been marked by the most optimistic assumptions as to what the people could or did know about their government. To put the matter another way: any set of representative institutions will work very differently according to the amount and quality of information the electorate has. This is certainly true of the institutional forms we associate with government by responsible parties. A necessary condition of party responsibility to the people is that the public have basic information about the parties and their legislative record. Without it, no institutional devices can make responsibility a fact.

To explore the information possessed by those who play the legislative and constituent roles in American government, the Survey Research Center of the University of Michigan undertook an interview study of Congressmen and their districts during the mid-term election of Eisenhower's second term. Immediately after the 1958 campaign the Center interviewed a nationwide sample of the electorate, clustered in 116 congressional districts, as well as the incumbent Congressmen and other major-party candidates for the House from the same collection of districts.[1] Through these direct interviews with the persons playing the reciprocal roles of representative government, this research has sought careful evidence about the perceptual ties that bind, or fail to bind, the Congressmen to his party and district. We will review some of this evidence here for the light that it throws on the problem of party cohesion and responsibility in Congress.

The Responsible-Party Model and the American Case

What the conception of government by responsible parties requires of the general public has received much less attention than what it requires of the legislative and electoral parties.[2] The notion of responsibility generally is understood to mean that the parties play a mediating role between the public and its government, making popular control effective by developing rival programs of government action that are presented to the electorate for its choice. The party whose program gains the greater support takes possession of the government and is held accountable to the public in later elections for its success in giving its program effect.

Two assumptions about the role of the public can be extracted from these ideas. *First*, in a system of party government the electorate's attitude toward the parties is based on what the party programs are and how well the parties have delivered on them. The public, in a word, gives the parties *programmatic* support. And, in view of the importance that legislative action is likely to have in any party program, such support is formed largely out of public reaction to the legislative performance of the parties, especially the party in power.

Second, under a system of party government the voters' response to the local legislative candidates is based on the candidates' identification with party programs. These programs are the substance of their appeals to the constituency, which will act on the basis of its information about the proposals and legislative record of the parties. Since the party programs are of dominant importance, the candidates are deprived of any independent basis of support. They will not be able to build in their home districts an electoral redoubt from which to challenge the leadership of their parties.[3]

How well do these assumptions fit the behavior of the American public as it reaches a choice in the off-year congressional elections? A first glance at the relation of partisan identifications to the vote might give the impression that the mid-term election is a triumph of party government. Popular allegiance to the parties is of immense importance in all our national elections, including those in which a President is chosen, but its potency in the mid-term congressional election is especially pronounced. This fact is plain—even stark—in the entries of table 12-1, which break down the vote for Congress in 1958 into its component party elements. The table makes clear, first of all, how astonishingly small a proportion of the mid-term vote is cast by political independents. Repeated electoral studies in the United States have indicated that somewhat fewer than 1 American in 10 thinks of himself as altogether independent of the two parties.[4] But in the off-year race for Congress only about a twentieth part of the vote is cast by independents, owing to their greater drop-out rate when the drama and stakes of the presidential contest are missing.

Table 12-1 also makes clear how little deviation from party there is among Republicans and Democrats voting in a mid-term year. The role of party identification in the congressional election might still be slight, whatever the size of the party followings, if partisan allegiance sat more lightly on the voting act. But almost 9 out of every 10 partisans voting in the off-year race support the parties. Indeed, something like 84 percent of *all* the votes for the House in 1958 were cast by party identifiers supporting their parties. The remaining 16 percent is not a trivial fraction of the whole—standing, as it did in this case, for 8 million people, quite enough to make and unmake a good many legislative careers. Nevertheless, the low frequency of deviation from party, together with the low frequency of independent voting, indicates that the meaning of the mid-term vote depends in large part on the nature of party voting.

Table 12-1   1958 vote for House candidates, by party identification (in percent)

| | Party Identification* | | | |
	Democratic	Independent	Republican	Total
Voted Democratic	53†	2	6	61
Voted Republican	5	3	31	39
Total	58	5	37	100

*The Democratic and Republican party identification groups include all persons who classify themselves as having some degree of party loyalty.

†Each entry of the table gives the percent of the total sample of voters having the specified combination of party identification and vote for the House in 1958.

The Saliency of the Parties' Legislative Records

If American party voting were to fit the responsible-party model it would be *programmatic* voting, that is, the giving of electoral support according to the parties' past or prospective action on programs that consist (mainly) of legislative measures. There is little question that partisan voting is one of the very few things at the bottom of our two-party system; every serious third-party movement in a hundred years has foundered on the reef of traditional Republican and Democratic loyalties. But there is also little question that this voting is largely nonprogrammatic in nature. A growing body of evidence indicates that party loyalties are typically learned early in life, free of ideological or issue content, with the family as the main socializing agency. Certainly the findings of adult interview studies show that such loyalties are extremely long-lived and, summed across the population, give rise to extraordinarily stable distributions.[5] The very persistence of party identification raises suspicion as to whether the country is responding to the parties' current legislative actions when it votes its party loyalties.

That this suspicion is fully warranted in the mid-term election is indicated by several kinds of evidence from this research. To begin with, the electorate's perceptions of the parties betray very little information about current policy issues. For the past ten years the Survey Research Center has opened its electoral interviews with a series of free-answer questions designed to gather in the positive and negative ideas that the public has about the parties. The answers, requiring on the average nearly ten minutes of conversation, are only very secondarily couched in terms of policy issues. In 1958, for example, more than six thousand distinct positive or negative comments about the parties were made by a sample of 1,700 persons. Of these, less than 12 percent by the most generous count had to do with contemporary legislative issues. As this sample of Americans pictured the reasons it liked and disliked the parties, the modern battlefields of the legislative wars—aid-to-education, farm policy, foreign aid, housing, aid to the unemployed, tariff and trade policy, social security, medical care, labor laws, civil rights, and other issues—rarely came to mind. The main themes in the public's image of the parties are not totally cut off from current legislative events; the political activist could take the group-benefit and prosperity-depression ideas that saturate the party images and connect them fairly easily with issues before Congress. The point is that the public itself rarely does so.

How little awareness of current issues is embodied in the congressional vote also is attested by the reasons people give for voting Republican or Democratic for the House. In view of the capacity of survey respondents to rationalize their acts, direct explanations of behavior should be treated with some reserve. However, rationalization is likely to increase, rather than decrease, the policy content of reasons for voting. It is therefore especially noteworthy how few of the reasons our respondents gave for their House votes in 1958 had any discernible issue content. The proportion that had—about 7 percent—was less even than the proportion of party-image references touching current issues.

Perhaps the most compelling demonstration of how hazardous it is to interpret party voting as a judgment of the parties' legislative records is furnished by the evidence about the public's knowledge of party control of Congress. When our 1958 sample was asked whether the Democrats or the Republicans had had more Congressmen in Washington during the two preceding years, a third confessed they had no idea, and an additional fifth gave control of the Eighty-fifth Congress to the Republicans. Only 47 percent correctly attributed control to the Democrats. These figures improve somewhat when nonvoters are excluded. Of those who voted in 1958, a fifth did not know which party had controlled Congress, another fifth thought the Republicans had, and the remainder (61 percent) correctly gave control to the Democrats. However, when a discount is made for guessing, the proportion of voters who really *knew* which party had controlled the Eighty-fifth Congress probably is still not more than half.[6]

It would be difficult to overstate the significance of these figures for the problem of party government. The information at issue here is not a sophisticated judgment as to what sort of coalition had *effective* control of Congress. It is simply the question of whether the country had a Democratic or a Republican Congress from 1956 to 1958. This elementary fact of political life, which any pundit would take completely for granted as he interpreted the popular vote in terms of party accountability, was unknown to something like half the people who went to the polls in 1958.

It is of equal significance to note that the parties' legislative record was no more salient to those who *deviated* from party than it was to those who voted their traditional party loyalty. It might be plausible to suppose that a floating portion of the electorate gives the parties programmatic support, even though most voters follow their traditional allegiances. If true, this difference would give the responsible-party model some factual basis, whether or not the greater part of the electorate lived in darkness. But such a theory finds very little support in these data. In 1958 neither the issue reasons given for the congressional vote nor the awareness of party control of the Eighty-fifth Congress was any higher among those who voted *against* their party identification than it was among those who voted *for* their party, as the entries of table 12-2 demonstrate. If anything, correcting perceived party control for guessing suggests that voters who deviated from their party in 1958 had poorer information about the course of political events over the preceding two years.

Table 12-2   Issue responses and awareness of which party controlled 85th Congress among party supporters and voters who deviated from party

	Party Identifiers Who	
	Voted for Own Party	Voted for Other Party
Percent aware of party control:		
Uncorrected	61	60
Corrected for guessing*	44	35
Percent giving issue reasons for House vote	6	7

*This correction deducts from the proportion attributing control to the Democrats a percentage equal to the proportion attributing control to the Republicans. See note 6.

Nor do the perceptions of party control of Congress that *are* found supply a key to understanding the congressional vote. Whatever awareness of control the electorate had in 1958 was remarkably unrelated to its support of candidates for the House. To make this point, table 12-3 analyzes deviations from party according to three perceptions held by party identifiers voting in 1958: *first*, whether they thought the country's recent domestic affairs had gone well or badly; *second* (to allow for the complication of divided government), whether they thought Congress or President had the greater influence over what the government did; and, *third*, whether they thought the Democrats or Republicans had controlled Congress. To recreate the basis on which the voter might assign credit or blame to the parties, the second and third of these perceptions may be combined; that is, partisans may be classified according to whether they thought their own party or the opposite party had controlled the more effective branch of government. Crossing this classification with perceptions of whether domestic affairs had gone well yields four groups for analysis, two of which (I and IV) might be expected to show little deviation from party, the other two (II and III) substantially more. In fact, however, the differences between these groups are almost trifling. According to the familiar lore, the groups that thought affairs had gone badly (III and IV) are the ones that should provide the clearest test of whether perceptions of party control are relevant to voting for the House. Moreover, with a recession in the immediate background, most people who could be classified into this table in 1958 fell into one of these two groups, as the frequencies indicate. But when

Table 12-3 Percentage of party identifiers voting against party in 1958, by perception of party control of government and course of domestic affairs

Thought That Domestic Affairs	Thought That More Effective Branch of Government Was Controlled by	
	Own Party	Other Party
	I	II
Had gone well	16	22
	(N=43)	(N=46)
	III	IV
Had gone badly	14	13
	(N=152)	(N=122)

the two groups that felt there had been domestic difficulties are compared, it seems not to make a particle of difference whether the Democrats or Republicans were thought to have controlled the actions of government. And when the two groups (I and II) that felt things had gone well are compared, only a slight (and statistically insignificant) difference appears. Interestingly, even this small rise in the rate of deviation from party (in cell II) is contributed mainly by Democratic identifiers who wrongly supposed that the Congress had been in Republican hands.

The conclusion to be drawn from all this certainly is not that national political forces are without *any* influence on deviations from party in the mid-term year. Clearly these forces do have an influence. Although the fluctuations of the mid-term party vote, charted over half a century or more, are very much smaller than fluctuations in the presidential vote or of the congressional vote in presidential years, there is *some* variation, and these moderate swings must be attributed to forces that have their focus at the national level.[7] Even in 1958 one party received a larger share of deviating votes than the other. Our main point is rather that the deviations that *do* result from national forces are not in the main produced by the parties' legislative records and that, in any case, the proportion of deviating votes that can be attributed to national politics is likely to be a small part of the total votes cast by persons deviating from party in a mid-term year. This was specifically true in 1958.

If the motives for deviations from party are not to be found primarily at the national level, the search moves naturally to the local congressional campaign. A third possibility—that deviations are by-products of state-wide races—can be discounted with some confidence. Despite the popular lore on the subject, evidence both from interview studies and from aggregate election statistics can be used to show that the influence of contests for Governor and Senator on the outcome of House races is light in mid-term elections, although these contests can have an immense influence on turnout for the House.[8] In our 1958 sample, a majority of those who deviated from party in voting for the House *failed* to deviate also at the state level; more often than not, what had moved them into the other party's column at the House level was dissociated from the contests for Governor or Senator in which they voted. Moreover, the fact that an elector deviates from his party in voting both for the House and some office contested on a state-wide basis is not conclusive evidence that the state race has influenced his choice for the House, rather than the other way round. When the possibility of *reverse* coat-tail effects is allowed for, the reasons for believing that the state-wide race is a potent force on the House vote seem faint indeed.[9] As we search for the motives for deviation from party, analysis of the local congressional race pays greater dividends.

The Saliency of Congressional Candidates

By the standards of the civics text, what the public knows about the candidates for Congress is as meager as what it knows about the parties' legislative records. Of the people who lived in districts where the House seat was contested in 1958, 59 percent—well over half—said that they had neither read nor heard anything about either candidate for Congress, and less than 1 in 5 felt that they knew something about both candidates. What is more, these remarkable proportions are only marginally improved by excluding nonvoters from the calculations. Of people who went to the polls and cast a vote between rival House candidates in 1958, fully 46 percent conceded that they did so without having read or heard anything about either man. What the other half *had* read or heard is illuminating; we will deal with its policy content presently. Many of our respondents said they knew something about the people contesting the House seat on the basis of very slender information indeed.

The incumbent candidate is by far the better known. In districts where an incumbent was opposed for re-election in 1958, 39 percent of our respondents knew something about the Congressman, whereas only 20 percent said they knew anything at all about his nonincumbent opponent. The incumbent's advantage of repeated exposure to the electorate is plain enough. In fact, owing to the great seniority and longer exposure of Congressmen from safe districts, the public's awareness of incumbents who were unopposed for re-election in 1958 was as great as its awareness of incumbents who had had to conduct an election campaign that year.

The saliency of a candidate is of critical importance if he is to attract support from the opposite party. However little the public may know of those seeking office, any information at all about the rival party's candidate creates the possibility of a choice deviating from party. That such a choice occurs with some frequency is shown by the entries of table 12-4, whose columns separate party identifiers in contested districts in 1958 according to whether they were aware of both candidates, the candidate of their own party or the other party only, or neither candidate. The condition of no information leads to fairly unrelieved party-line voting, and so to an even greater degree does the condition of

Table 12-4 Percentage voting for own party candidate and other party candidate for House in 1958, by saliency of candidates in contested districts

	Voter Was Aware of			
Voted for Candidate	Both Candidates (N=196)	Own Party Candidate Only (N=166)	Other Party Candidate Only (N=68)	Neither Candidate (N=368)
Of own party	83	98	60	92
Of other party	17	2	40	8
Total	100	100	100	100

information only about the candidate of the voter's own party. But if partisan voters know something about the opposition's man, substantial deviations from party appear. In fact, if such voters know *only* the opposition candidate, almost half can be induced to cast a vote contrary to their party identification. In the main, recognition carries a positive valence; to be perceived at all is to be perceived favorably. However, some *negative* perceptions are found in our interviews, and when these are taken into account the explanation of deviation from party becomes surer still. For example, if we return to table 12-4 and select from the third column only the voters who perceived the candidate of the other party *favorably*, a clear majority is found to have deviated from party allegiance in casting their votes. And if we select from the first column only the handful of voters who perceived the candidate of their own party *negatively* and of the opposite party *positively*, almost three-quarters are found to have deviated from their party loyalty in voting for the House.

What our constituent interviews show about the increment of support that accrues to the salient candidate is closely aligned to what the candidates themselves see as the roots of their electoral strength. Our interviews with incumbent and nonincumbent candidates seeking election to the House explored at length their understanding of factors aiding—or damaging—their electoral appeal. In particular, these interviews probed the candidates' assessment of four possible influences on the result: traditional party loyalties, national issues, state and local contests, and the candidates' own record and personal standing in the district. Caution is in order in dealing with answers to questions that touch the respondent's self-image as closely as these. Specifically, we may expect some overstatement of the candidate's own importance, particularly from the victors, and we may expect, too, that too large a discount will be applied to party allegiance, since this "inert" factor, having little to do with increments of strength, is so easily taken for granted.

After these allowances are made, it is still impressive how heavy a weight the incumbent assigns his personal record and standing. The Congressman's ranking of this and the other factors in the election is shown in table 12-5. As the entries of the table indicate, more than four-fifths of the incumbents re-elected in 1958 felt that the niche they had carved out in the awareness of their constituents had substantial impact on the race, a proportion that exceeds by half the percentage who gave as much weight to any of the three other factors. This difference is more than sheer puffing in the interview situation, and the perceptual facts it reveals deserve close attention. Among the forces the Representative feels may enhance his strength at the polls, he gives his personal standing with the district front rank.

In view of the way the saliency of candidates can move the electorate across party lines, great stress should be laid on the fact that the public sees individual candidates for Congress in terms of party programs scarcely at all. Our constituent interviews indicate that the popular image of the Congressman is almost barren of policy content. A long series of open-ended questions asked of those who said they had any information about the Representative produced mainly a collection of diffuse evaluative judgments; he is a good man, he is experienced, he knows the problems, he has done a good job, and the like. Beyond this, the Congressman's image consisted of a mixed bag of impressions, some of them wildly improbable, about ethnicity, the attractiveness of family, specific services to the district, and other facts in the candidate's background. By the most reasonable count, references to current legislative issues comprised not more than a thirtieth part of what the constituents had to say about their Congressmen.

The irrelevance of legislative issues to the public's knowledge of Representatives is underscored by the nature of some primary *determinants* of saliency. A full analysis of the causes of constituent awareness of candidates goes beyond the scope of this paper. Although our investigation has given a good deal of attention to communication factors and to characteristics of Congressmen and constituents themselves that determine the probability a given Congressman will be known to a given constituent, this interplay of causes cannot be explored very deeply here. However, it *is* noteworthy in the present discussion that many factors increasing the saliency of candidates are unlikely to enhance what the public knows about their stands on issues. An

Table 12-5   Relative importance of factors in re-election as seen by incumbent candidates in 1958 (in percent)

Perceived as	Personal Record and Standing	National Issues	Traditional Party Loyalties	State and Local Races
Very important	57	26	25	14
Quite important	28	20	21	19
Somewhat important	9	20	24	27
Not very important	3	27	18	19
Not important at all	3	7	12	21
Total	100	100	100	100

excellent example is sex. Both for incumbents and nonincumbents, a candidate property that is related to saliency is gender; one of the best ways for a Representative to be known is to be a Congress*woman.* How irrelevant to policy issues this property is depends on what we make of the causal relation between sex and saliency. The fact of being a woman may make a candidate more visible, but a woman may have to be unusually visible (like a Congressman's widow, say) before she can be elected to the House, or even become a serious candidate. If the first of these inferences is even partially right, the saliency of the candidate is not likely to be in terms of positions taken on legislative issues.

Given the number of women who run for Congress, the role of sex may seem a trivial example to demonstrate the irrelevance of issue stands to saliency. However, the same point can be made for a much wider set of districts by the greater saliency of candidates who live in the constituent's home community. Just as there is enormous variety in the communities that make up the American nation, so there is the widest possible variation in how well a congressional district coincides with a natural community, and the goodness of this fit is a fundamental way of typing districts. At one extreme is the constituency whose area is lost within one of the country's great metropolitan centers, comprising at best a small fraction of the whole community. At the middle of the range is the district that is itself a natural community, consisting of a single medium-sized city and its environs. At the other extreme is the district whose territory includes a great number of small communities, as well as surrounding open country that goes on, in some cases, for hundreds of miles. In all but the metropolitan districts the saliency of the candidate for the voter differs markedly according to whether candidate and voter live in the same community. The fact of common residence — of being "friends and neighbors" — stands for important facts of communication and community identification. Candidates will be joined by formal and informal communication networks to many of the voters living in the same community, and they may also be objects of considerable community pride.

The reality of this local effect is demonstrated by table 12-6. As the entries of the table show, dividing a nationwide sample of constituents according to whether they live in the same community as their Congressman or his opponent produces marked differences of saliency. The "friends and neighbors" effect made familiar by studies of primary voting in one-party areas has a counterpart in voting for Representatives throughout the country, apart from the large metropolitan areas.[10] And despite the fact that localism is found here in the context of as tightly party-determined an election as any in American politics, the irrelevance of local appeal to legislative issues is probably as great as it is in the wide-open, one-party primary.

Table 12-6 Influence of "friends and neighbors" factor on saliency of candidate for voters* (in percent)

	Incumbent Candidate Lives in		Nonincumbent Candidate Lives in	
Voter Is	Same Community as Voter (N = 269)	Other Community than Voter (N = 414)	Same Community as Voter (N = 304)	Other Community than Voter (N = 447)
Aware of candidate	67	45	47	22
Not aware of candidate	33	55	53	78
Total	100	100	100	100

*Metropolitan and large urban districts, for which the notion of the candidate living outside the voter's community has no clear meaning, are excluded from the analysis.

Conclusion

What the public knows about the legislative records of the parties and of individual congressional candidates is a principal reason for the departure of American practice from an idealized conception of party government. On the surface the legislative elections occurring in the middle of the President's term appear to be dominated by two national parties asking public support for their alternative programs. Certainly the electorate whose votes they seek responds to individual legislative candidates overwhelmingly on the basis of their party labels. Despite our kaleidoscopic electoral laws, the candidate's party is the one piece of information every voter is guaranteed. For many, it is the only information they ever get.

However, the legislative events that follow these elections diverge widely from the responsible-party model. The candidates who have presented themselves to the country under two party symbols immediately break ranks. The legislative parties speak not as two voices but as a cacophony of blocs and individuals fulfilling their own definitions of the public good. Party cohesion by no means vanishes, but it is deeply eroded by the pressures external to party to which the Congressman is subject.

The public's information about the legislative record of the parties and of members of Congress goes far toward reconciling these seemingly contradictory facts. In the congressional election, to be sure, the country votes overwhelmingly for party symbols, but the symbols have limited meaning in terms of legislative policy. The eddies and crosscurrents in Congress do not interrupt a flow of legislation that the public expects but fails to see. The electorate sees very little altogether of what goes on in the national legislature

Few judgments of legislative performance are associated with the parties, and much of the public is unaware even of which party has control of Congress. As a result, the absence of party discipline or legislative results is unlikely to bring down electoral sanctions on the ineffective party or the errant Congressman.

What the public's response to the parties lacks in programmatic support is not made up by its response to local congressional candidates. Although perceptions of individual candidates account for most of the votes cast by partisans against their parties, these perceptions are almost untouched by information about the policy stands of the men contesting the House seat. The increment of strength that some candidates, especially incumbents, acquire by being known to their constituents is almost entirely free of policy content. Were such content present, the Congressman's solidarity with his legislative party would by no means be assured. If the local constituency possessed far greater resources of information than it has, it might use the ballot to pry the Congressman away from his party quite as well as to unite him with it. Yet the fact is that, by plying his campaigning and servicing arts over the years, the Congressman is able to develop electoral strength that is almost totally dissociated from what his party wants in Congress and what he himself has done about it. The relevance of all this to the problem of cohesion and responsibility in the legislative party can scarcely be doubted.

The description of party irresponsibility in America should not be overdrawn. The American system *has* elements of party accountability to the public, although the issues on which an accounting is given are relatively few and the accounting is more often rendered by those who hold or seek the Presidency than by the parties' congressional delegations. Especially on the broad problem of government action to secure social and economic welfare it can be argued that the parties have real differences and that these have penetrated the party images to which the electorate responds at the polls.

Nevertheless, American practice does diverge widely from the model of party government, and the factors underlying the departure deserve close analysis. An implication of the analysis reported here is that the public's contribution to party irregularity in Congress is not so much a matter of encouraging or requiring its Representatives to deviate from their parties as it is of the public having so little information that the irregularity of Congressmen and the ineffectiveness of the congressional parties have scant impact at the polls. Many of those who have commented on the lack of party discipline in Congress have assumed that the Congressman votes against his party because he is forced to by the demands of one of several hundred constituencies of a superlatively heterogeneous nation. In some cases, the Representative may subvert the proposals of his party because his constituency demands it. But a more reasonable interpretation over a broader range of issues is that the Congressman fails to see these proposals as part of a program on which the party — and he himself — will be judged at the polls, because he knows the constituency isn't looking.

Notes

[1]The 116 districts are a probability sample of all constituencies, although the fact that the study was piggy-backed onto a four-year panel study of the electorate extending over the elections of 1956, 1958, and 1960 made the design of the 1958 representation sample unusually complex. In particular, since metropolitan areas and non-metropolitan counties or groups of counties, rather than congressional districts, were used as primary sampling units when the panel sample was originated in 1956, the districts represented in our 1958 sample did not have equal probability of selection and the efficiency of the sample of districts was somewhat less than that of a simple random sample of equal size. Descriptions of the sample design may be obtained from the Survey Research Center.

[2]For example, the 1950 report of the American Political Science Association's Committee on Political Parties, the closest approach to an official statement of the responsible-party view as applied to American politics, concentrates on the organization of Congress and the national parties and deals only very obliquely with the role of the public. See *Toward a More Responsible Two-party System*, New York, Rinehart, 1950. In general, theoretical and empirical treatments of party government have focused more on the nature of party *appeals*—especially the question of whether the parties present a real "choice"—than on the cognitive and motivational elements that should be found in the *response* of an electorate that is playing its correct role in a system of responsible-party government. For example, see the excellent discussion in Austin Ranney and Wilmoore Kendall, *Democracy and the American Party System*, New York, Harcourt, Brace, 1956, pp. 151–152, 384–385, 525–527.

It should be clear that the data of this report are taken from a particular election of a particular electoral era. We would expect our principal findings to apply to most recent off-year elections, but they are of course subject to modification for earlier or later periods.

[3]This assumption does not imply that pressures toward party cohesion come *only* from the mass public. Other sanctions against party irregularity are of equal or greater importance, especially those available in the nominating process and within the legislative parties themselves. To cite the most celebrated empirical case, the cohesiveness of the British parliamentary parties is not enforced primarily, if at all, by the British electorate. Nevertheless, the public ought not to give aid and comfort to the legislative party irregular; the idea of the candidate building a local bastion of strength from which he can challenge the party leadership is clearly contradictory to the party-government model.

[4]See Angus Campbell, Philip E. Converse, Warren E. Miller, and Donald E. Stokes, *The American Voter*, New York, Wiley, 1960, p. 124.

[5]For evidence on this point, see *ibid.*, pp. 120–167.

[6]Plainly, some deduction has to be made for guessing. One model of the situation would be to think of the sample as composed of three types of people: those who knew, those who didn't know and said so, and those who didn't know but guessed. Assuming that for those who guessed $p=q=\frac{1}{2}$, where p is the probability of guessing Republican, we would deduct from the Democratic answers a percentage equal to the 18 percent who guessed Republican incorrectly, hence reducing the proportion of voters who really knew which party controlled Congress to 43 percent. This model may be too severe, however, in view of the presence of the Republican President. It may be more reasonable to admit a fourth type of person, those who did not guess but were misled by Republican control of the White House. Or we might think of the guessers as following a probability law in which $p > \frac{1}{2} > q$. In either of these cases something less than 18 percent would be deducted from the Democratic answers; hence, the proportion of voters who *knew* which party controlled Congress would lie somewhere between 43 and 61 percent.

[7]A simple but persuasive comparison is this: From 1892 to 1960 the standard deviation of the two-party division of the mid-term congressional vote was 3.9 percent; of the presidential-year

congressional vote, 5.5 percent; of the presidential vote, 8.2 percent. Moreover, if the realignment of party loyalties that occurred in the early 1930's is taken into account by computing deviations from pre- and post-1932 means, rather than from a grand mean for the whole period, the standard deviation of the mid-term congressional vote is found to have been 2.4 percent, compared with a standard deviation of 7.5 percent for the presidential vote. Some of the remaining variability of the mid-term vote may be due to fluctuations of turnout that do not involve deviations from party. Yet, even ignoring this possibility, the bounds within which national political forces can have influenced the off-year vote by inducing deviations from party appear narrow indeed.

[8]A remarkable fact is that while the total vote for the House increased by 3 million between 1954 and 1958, more than 2 million of this increase was contributed by New York, where Rockefeller sought the governorship; by Ohio, where a fierce referendum battle was fought over the issue of "right-to-work"; and by California, where the fantastic Knight-Knowland-Brown free-for-all was held.

[9]This conclusion is fully supported by an analysis of the variance of turnout and party vote in the mid-term congressional elections of the 1950's. If state-wide races have a major influence on local House races, the election results for the several congressional districts of a state should vary together; similar changes of turnout and party division should be seen in the districts that are influenced by the same state-wide contests. An analysis of the variance of the differences between the 1954 and 1958 turnout level and partisan division for all congressional districts in states having at least two districts indicates that state races have a large effect on turnout; the intraclass correlation expressing the ratio of the between-state variance to the total variance of turnout was more than .45. But this analysis shows, too, that state-wide races have almost no effect whatever on the party division of the House vote; the intraclass correlation expressing the ratio of the between-state variance to the total variance of the party division was not more than .02.

[10]See V. O. Key, Jr., *Southern Politics*, New York, Knopf, 1949, pp. 37ff. We have demonstrated the "friends and neighbors" effect in terms of candidate saliency because of our interest in the policy content of candidate perceptions. However, owing to the impact of saliency on the vote, living in the same community with the candidate has a clear effect on voting as well.

Part 4 Congress in Action: Legislative Outputs

The most important aspects of the legislative system are the output activities of Congress. The character of these outputs reflects both the attributes of the congressional system and the inputs of the system; yet it is on the outputs themselves that the legislature is judged. Support, whether specific or diffuse, is forthcoming only when those who give it feel that Congress is performing its functions satisfactorily. There are, as the introduction suggests, three broad categories of outputs: lawmaking, oversight, and representation. Demands are made on Congress to perform in each of these areas; no one function can be ignored. Support will follow to the degree that specific actions of the legislature satisfy demands for particular policies or to the extent that the overall behavior of Congress leads to a general feeling that the lawmakers are doing a satisfactory job. In this part, the focus is on the ability of Congress to perform its output tasks in appropriate fashion. The selections indicate how legislative structures shape inputs into the outputs of legislation, oversight, and representation. In this sense, outputs result from the treatment of inputs by the structures and processes of the legislative system.

Lawmaking

The classic function of Congress has, of course, been that of making the laws—enacting statutes embodying the basic policy decisions of the nation. As noted in the first part of this book, senators and representatives strive to gain positions on congressional committees where they can exert influence on policy choices. They sometimes complain that representational demands take too much time and energy, making it most difficult to give sufficient attention to legislative work.[1] As we shall note, many are reluctant to invest large portions of their resources in oversight activity. In short, despite some scholarly admonitions to the contrary, members of Congress continue for the most part to feel that lawmaking ought to be the central focus of their work and to deplore any developments that they see as threats to their ability to influence the shape of public policy.[2]

Committee Deliberation

Given the fragmented, decentralized nature of Congress that its formal and informal organization creates, it is good to distinguish between policy making in the committees and on the floor. The virtually autonomous committees and, frequently, the almost completely independent subcommittees within them guarantee that in many, perhaps most, cases legislative decisions are made in committee and ratified on the floor. The committee is likely to have the congressional experts among its members; and to the extent that they remain united, the rank-and-file lawmakers may well feel constrained to accept their judgment.[3]

A newly introduced bill is automatically referred to the proper committee (as specified in the rules of the chamber); the committee controls the bill's fate, at least until such time as the committee chooses to report the bill. Hearings, usually under the control of the committee or subcommittee chair, are held and serve several purposes (Davidson and Oleszek, 1977, ch. 4). They publicize the legislation merely by being conducted, especially if the communications media choose to cover them; they permit numerous interested parties—the executive branch, interest groups, occasionally members of the general public, and often legislators not on the committee of jurisdiction—to present their views on the proposed legislation. The hearings may, but usually do not, produce new information; but they do guarantee the participants an opportunity "to have their say." Moreover, they have important political value for committee members who can elicit testimony ("make a record") for their preferred positions and attempt to gauge the relative strengths of the contending interests ("test the political waters").

The hearings completed, the committee proceeds to "mark up" the bill. The text is read, often line by line; discussed; and rewritten to the degree deemed necessary. The "mark up" is characterized by intensive negotiation and compromise. Here the competing interests, with committee members acting as their spokespersons, seek to solidify their positions. By amending the bill and modifying their stands, each side hopes to assemble a coalition that will be able to surmount the various obstacles that the rules set up and that will have the votes to pass the bill when it reaches the floor. In some cases, of course, the committee's decision is that there should be no bill; usually this decision marks the demise of the proposal in that particular Congress. Where there is to be legislation, the bill is sent to the floor accompanied by a committee report that summarizes its contents and presents the justifying arguments for (and, if the minority presents dissenting views, against) the bill.[4]

In selection 13, Fenno describes how the House Appropriations Committee makes these fundamental decisions. The Appropriations Committee must work within two conflicting sets of expectations. On one hand, the full House has passed legislation authorizing programs and it wants to see them funded. The agencies empowered to implement these policies make their demands for appropriations in the light of such expectations. On the other hand, the committee has guidelines (norms) that govern its own behavior; foremost among these is the desire to guard the federal treasury. As a way out of this dilemma—this desire to spend and to save at the same time—the committee has developed a decision rule by which it cuts agency budget requests while it simultaneously gives more money than was appropriated in the previous year. Because agencies and bureaus almost inevitably ask for more money annually, it is possible to reduce their requests while allowing them more than they had in the prior fiscal year.

These norms provide the basis on which committee unity can be created; but they are challenged directly by notions of party loyalty. Role conflict may be severe; each legislator must decide whether to follow committee norms and make incremental cuts in budget requests or to pursue party goals, which for the majority are likely to entail greater expenditures and for the minority to demand larger reductions. As Fenno suggests, committee norms tend to prevail; the Appropriations Committee cut three-fourths of all requests and raised only 8 percent. And where the committee coheres in support of its recommendations, it is likely to win at the floor stage.

Other committees display differing patterns of decision. The House Education and Labor Committee, for instance, is a policy-oriented, partisan panel (Fenno, 1973a, chs. 3, 6). Its norms (strategic premises or decision rules, as Fenno labels them) call for members to "prosecute policy partisanship" whenever possible but not at the expense of personal policy preferences—that is, Education and Labor Committee members are prepared to bolt the party traces should their own policy predilections conflict with the party's. These norms give the committee decisions their distinctive character. When Democrats control the government, the committee's activity levels increase; the liberal majority, with (or hoping for) White House backing, reports more bills. These decisions are partisan and ideological and seldom reflect intracommittee compromise. In consequence, committee bills go to the floor without the backing of an integrated, unified panel and the partisan, ideological dissension characteristic of committee deliberations often spills over and reappears on the floor, where numerous amendments may be offered and where the prospects for chamber acceptance of Education and Labor proposals diminish.

Such descriptions are possible for many House and Senate committees.[5] The essential point here is that individual committees develop their own decision-making patterns. Fenno (1973a) suggests a scheme for analysis: Members seek committee assignments that help them achieve the goals they seek from service in Congress (reelection, influence, policy); members pursue these goals within "environmental constraints" (outside forces—the executive, interest or clientele groups, constituents); committees develop norms (strategic premises), decision structures, and processes that enable them to meet their goals within the environmental restrictions; these factors—member goals, environmental conditions, committee norms, and committee organization—shape the content of committee decisions. Each committee, in other words, can be treated as a political system, as this collection treats Congress as a whole.

On the Floor

As the last section implies, policy decisions are often, but not always, settled by the time a bill reaches the floor. Most members of the chamber will have already decided how to vote; their decisions will reflect their role orientations toward the committee experts and the party leaders within Congress as well as toward those beyond the boundaries of the legislative system—the executive, the pressure groups, and segments of the public that have communicated with them. Yet it is on the floor that the ultimate decisions are ratified, if not actually made; at this stage coalitions of legislators either remain intact or disintegrate.

Floor debate is not usually aimed at winning votes but rather seeks to reinforce those already committed votes and also to get the pro and con arguments into the record for whatever political value they may have at some future occasion. In addition, the debate may serve as a channel of communications—a means by which the word may be passed about such things as the acceptability of amendments. In the Senate, debate is unlimited unless sixty senators vote to invoke cloture. Floor speeches serve the purposes of a filibuster; that is, they occupy the Senate's time rather than communicate to the members. Therefore it is not surprising that most debate is poorly attended and that even those present are inattentive to what is being said.

The amending phase of floor consideration also serves a number of purposes, not all of which are equally obvious. The first of these is to alter the policies embodied in a bill. This is seldom a simple matter. The House Rules Committee may, in the resolution defining the form in which the consideration of the bill proceeds, limit amendments severely by providing that only members of the committee originating the legislation, with the approval of a majority of the committee, may introduce amendments. Even where rank-and-file members are permitted to propose amendments, they are not likely to succeed in the face of united committee opposition. The norms of the chambers tend to promote deference toward the committees; many legislators are loath to overturn the committee experts because they desire to maintain the respect they receive as experts in their own spheres of competence. Some amendments are designed to undermine a bill's chances for passage. If the character of the legislation can be dramatically altered by changes in its content, the coalition supporting it may dissolve. Other amendments are simply efforts to get the position of a legislator or political party recorded; such a record may have political advantages later on. As with debate, the amending phase seldom alters the basic character of the legislation.

Floor consideration does entail decisions, the most important of which are taken by roll-call vote. On such occasions, the members of Congress must publicly record their positions on proposed amendments and on passage or rejection of the bill as a whole. On these same occasions, the observer can gain some insight into the nature of the coalitions backing and opposing the legislation at issue. Deckard's analysis (selection 14) of voting in the House of Representatives during the 1960s makes clear that policy coalitions do not survive over long periods of time but rather shift as the occupancy of the White House changes and as events alter the perspectives of members of Congress. In particular, over this period, clear cleavages between the two parties disintegrated as southern Democrats and eastern Republicans became "increasingly unlikely" to support the majority position in their respective parties. These changes are consistent with the premise that the two voting blocs responded to the emergence of new issues—in the areas of social welfare, civil rights and liberties, and agricultural policy—and voted *as if* they were delegates.[6] That is, the votes of southern Democrats and eastern Republicans came to mirror the characteristics of the districts they represented, leading them to vote against majorities of their own partisans more frequently.

Also, in addition to their party affiliations and the kinds of constituencies they represent, members' voting records may reflect their personal attributes (for example, their religious preferences or occupational experiences), their electoral situation (whether they represent "safe" or "marginal" districts, typical or atypical of the kind of constituency that usually elects members of one or the other political party), their status in Congress itself (their positions as leaders, as personally close to leaders, as members of a particular committee), or their relationship to environmental actors (the executive or interest groups).[7]

The floor stage also may give some clues about the role orientations of the various representatives toward the lawmaking function. We might expect to find the *tribunes,* who articulate what they see as popular desires or public needs, more active on the floor and more likely to participate in the debate and to introduce a variety of amendments than the *brokers,* who, having helped to devise a seemingly acceptable solution, will quietly work to implement the agreed-upon legislative provisions. Similarly, the *inventors* might be expected to be more active, promoting their new ideas through speeches and amendments, than other role types. Finally, we may predict that the *ritualists,* with their concern for the niceties of procedure, will have a better attendance record during the consideration of major legislation than the *opportunists,* whose attention tends to focus on the nonlegislative output activities of Congress.

Oversight

A second major category of congressional output activity is oversight — the exercise of control over the agencies of the executive branch. The legislature is to act as a "watchdog," to ensure that the bureaucrats are faithful to the intent of Congress as they administer the programs under their jurisdiction and to guarantee that programs are effectively and economically carried into effect. The chief agents of oversight are the committees: The standing committees and their subcommittees oversee the agencies administering programs within their jurisdictions; the appropriations panels watch over the expenditure of federal funds.

Oversight has not traditionally been attractive to the majority of lawmakers. A few legislators have taken advantage of the opportunities the control function has offered. The late Senator Estes Kefauver (D-Tenn.) parlayed his investigation of organized crime and his image as a sort of knight in coonskin cap tilting against the satanic figures of the criminal underworld into a vice-presidential nomination. Senator Joseph McCarthy (R-Wisc.) and a number of members of the House Un-American Activities Committee made political capital out of their search for Communist infiltration of the government. In the 1970s, Senator William Proxmire (D-Wisc.) has earned considerable attention with his "golden fleece awards," bestowed on government agencies, among others, that have, in the senator's judgment, wasted federal funds on foolish or frivolous projects. Yet the far greater numbers of legislators have preferred to expend their energies in lawmaking or representational activities.

In his paper, "Legislative Oversight: Theory and Practice" (selection 15), Ogul suggests that members of Congress avoid oversight because most commonly they believe the costs exceed the benefits to be derived from the practice. He identifies several "opportunity factors" that, if present, will encourage members of Congress to act as "watchdogs" of the administrative agencies. First, the legislators — through the committees and subcommittees — must have the legal authority to oversee. Next, they must have the staff resources, the expertise, to do so. The policies to be controlled must be comprehensible and tractable; if they are too complex or technical, oversight will be too difficult. Committee structure matters as well: A decentralized committee, with independent expert subcommittees, will be in a position to oversee; an individual member in a leadership position on such a committee will be well placed to conduct oversight. Finally, member motivation is important: Those who are concerned with bureaucratic behavior and place high priority on oversight will be inclined to act; those who are satisfied with administrative activity (perhaps because it is their party's administration) or see little value in oversight will not. Members who hope to register opposition to specific programs or seek to gain partisan advantage from oversight may commit themselves to the activity; the other members are unlikely to do so.

These and other factors influence the legislators' role orientations toward the control function.[8] Those whose sentiments are proexecutive in general or are favorable to some particular agency will be unwilling to engage in much more than routine surveillance of the bureaucracy. Rather, they will seek to protect the executive branch or some part of it from what they see as undue meddling by the lawmakers. Those who are antiexecutive or who are legislatively oriented will be more likely to try to take advantage of the opportunities that oversight offers to exert control over agency activity. Finally, those who find oversight tasks too abstruse or those who find their committee restricting the possibilities for control will adopt an indifferent view of the watchdog job and will seek their compensations from other aspects of the legislative task. Ogul concludes that more members of Congress evade oversight responsibilities than take them seriously.

The forms of oversight are varied. Provisions aimed at facilitating control may be written into statutes. Reports that detail agency actions, expenditures, and accomplishments may be required at fixed intervals. Congress may impose the "legislative veto"—that is, certain actions such as reorganization of executive agencies will go into effect only if the legislature does not veto them within a prescribed period of time. Because the individuals who run the agencies will affect what the agencies do, the control that Congress exercises over the personnel of the federal government gives the lawmakers a lever with which to influence bureaucratic behavior. The Senate, through its constitutionally granted "advice and consent" power, has a voice in the decisions about who holds many of the roughly sixty-five hundred federal posts that are generally considered patronage jobs. Few presidential nominees are rejected, but this acceptance may reflect the care with which the president clears his choices with influential senators as much as a lack of concern for oversight in this area. Although the rapid and uncritical confirmation of President Carter's nominee, Bert Lance, to head the Office of Management and Budget raised serious questions about senatorial competence (see *CQ Weekly Report*, Feb. 4, 1978, pp. 297–302), the close scrutiny given to Lyndon Johnson's nomination of Abe Fortas, Associate Justice of the Supreme Court, to be Chief Justice (the nomination was withdrawn); to Richard Nixon's choices, Clement Haynsworth and G. Harrold Carswell, for seats on the high court (both rejected); and to Jimmy Carter's selections of Theodore Sorensen to head the Central Intelligence Agency (withdrawn) and of Paul Warnke as chief negotiator for the Strategic Arms Limitation Talks (SALT) with the Soviets (narrowly confirmed) suggests what a determined Senate is capable of doing.

Perhaps the potentially most effective control device is Congress' right to appropriate all funds expended from the federal treasury. The appropriations process gives the lawmakers a broad opportunity to familiarize themselves with administrative conduct. Budget hearings give the Appropriations Committees, particularly the House Appropriations Committee, which acts first in these matters, a chance to obtain data on performance directly from the agency personnel who appear in support of their fund requests.[9] The specialized appropriations subcommittees, which are the real decision makers, can exercise control in a number of ways. They can simply criticize agency performance, calling for improvements; they can include binding restrictions in appropriations bills; they can reduce the funds for programs about which they have doubts. In general, the subcommittees can act to bring the administration of federal programs more nearly into line with their own thinking.

Investigations, too, provide oversight opportunities. Committees and subcommittees can conduct a full-scale inquiry into the behavior of some bureau or agency in order to gain information. It is beyond dispute that Congress needs reliable information if it is to perform its output functions well; it is equally true that properly conducted investigations hold promise of obtaining such data. Investigations become controversial when attempts are made to specify what constitutes proper conduct. The critics of congressional investigations assert that the process of investigation deprives those called upon to testify of the procedural safeguards guaranteed to them in a court of law. The question — To what extent should the undeniable obligation of Congress to inform itself and the public be permitted to infringe upon citizens' rights to confront their accusers, to avoid incriminating themselves, to associate freely with whomever they please, and so forth? — is more simply put than answered, particularly as it frequently applies in the delicate area of internal security matters. In any case, an investigation, or the threat of one, may serve to increase bureaucratic sensitivity to at least some segment of congressional sentiment.[10]

Finally, oversight often proceeds through informal contacts. Over the years, legislators and agency personnel develop channels of informal communication. The formal powers that Congress possesses enable those legislators interested in oversight to gain an informal hearing for their opinions. To avoid difficulties later on, bureaucrats may "clear" their proposals in advance with the proper subcommittee, legislator, or their respective staffs. The lawmaker may counter with suggestions and advice and may make oral commitments to support any agreements reached. In short, decisions that are acceptable to bureaucrat and lawmaker may be taken in advance of formal proceedings, which may serve merely to ratify earlier understandings.

In sum, to the extent that senators and representatives take oversight seriously, they have a number of channels, formal and informal, over which they can make their views known to the agencies and bureaus of the executive branch. From the bureaucratic perspective, it is good to consider legislative opinion carefully, for Congress, within limits, has opportunities to enforce its will. And inevitably a sufficient number of lawmakers will find adequate rewards in the exercise of oversight to ensure that some members of Congress, able to alert their less concerned colleagues, will be watching most facets of agency activity.

Representation

The third category of legislative output activities encompasses the various tasks that legislators undertake to represent their constituents. We have already noted that the demands for representation are of two general sorts: requests for specific policy choices—that is, for particular lawmaking outputs—and requests for services generally devoid of policy content. The former set is intermittent in terms of volume, but it is important because a wrong step on an important issue may lead to a much greater popular awareness and involvement than is customary. The latter set is constantly heavy, and most members of Congress believe they must treat this "casework" seriously and thoroughly.

Policy Representation

Policy representation refers to the belief that lawmakers should act and speak on behalf of their constituents to protect and advance citizen interests and needs (Eulau and Karps, 1977; Pitkin, 1967). Representation raises difficult questions for legislators, including, first, the nature of the districts they are to represent—that is, the issue of apportionment. Understandably, the kind of people who inhabit their districts will influence how legislators see their representative roles. Second are the problems of the focus and the style of representation. "Focus" refers to the legislators' judgment as to whether they should act in keeping with sentiment in the district; in keeping with the national interest, even if national interest runs counter to constituency demands; or in response to some combination of local and national perspectives. "Style" deals with the character of representation. Members of Congress may act as *delegates*—that is, they may mirror the sentiments of their constituents, as they perceive them, as faithfully as possible; as trustees, relying upon their own judgment rather than upon constituent opinion; or as *politicos*, responding to district views on some occasions and to conscience in other circumstances.[11]

In "Constituency Influence in Congress" (selection 16), Miller and Stokes explore these complicated interrelationships between the representatives and the residents of their districts. They suggest that for constituents to control the behavior of the individuals elected to Congress—to ensure that the legislators assume a delegate orientation—it is necessary that lawmakers' votes on pending legislation reflect their personal beliefs or their perceptions of their constituents' beliefs, that their views or perceptions correspond to the constituents' actual sentiments, and that district residents consider the issue positions of the representatives who stand for reelection. Miller and Stokes investigated the extent to which these conditions exist; they examined the legislators' voting records and interviewed them and a sample of their constituents. They found that these requisites for popular control are only imperfectly met and that they exist in different degrees with regard to different policy questions.

First of all, it is clear that representatives do vote in keeping with personal policy preferences and perceptions of constituent opinion. But it is equally clear that there often is very little correspondence between the legislators' perceptions of district beliefs and the actual distribution of district beliefs. The degree of correspondence varies with the issue in question: It is relatively high on civil rights matters, where citizens apparently feel strongly and their representatives are aware of their views; it is less close on issues of social welfare; it is virtually nonexistent in the foreign policy sphere. Finally, many voters do not consider the candidates' stands on issues in deciding for whom to cast their ballots.[12]

One cannot conclude that, on most matters, the lawmakers are uninfluenced by constituent opinion. On the contrary, they seem quite concerned with the overall impression they make on the voters of their districts; although only a few people know what their representatives are doing in Washington, these few may be enough to decide a close election contest. Similarly, it is never certain that citizens will remain largely uninformed about their representatives' behavior; and legislators may try to write a defensible record for their own protection in the event, however unlikely, that the public will be aroused by some issue. Finally, in the absence of clear information of voter opinions, the lawmaker may infer these opinions from the demographic attitudes of the district and then vote accordingly. Therefore, legislative voting does attempt to reflect constituent sentiment. But, through cultivation of a "home style"—particularly the way they present themselves and explain their Washington activities to district residents—members can shape that constituent sentiment to which they respond (Fenno, 1977, 1978). To the extent that members of Congress can win and hold the trust, confidence, and support of their constituents, they may generate considerable leeway for themselves to act in Washington as they see fit. Thus the link between citizen and representative and the role orientation of the latter toward the former, reflect a reciprocal but uncertain process of political communication.

Structural features of the congressional system also influence the extent to which legislators can represent the policy interests of their constituents; the House Agriculture Committee illustrates how a committee may be organized to facilitate the expression of district interests. Agriculture subcommittees are commodity subcommittees; for example, there are units for tobacco, cotton, rice, and grains. Members of the Agriculture Committee can choose at least one commodity subcommittee on which to serve. Virtually all committee members represent districts in which agriculture is the chief constituency interest; thus Agriculture Committee members are generally able to join a subcommittee that deals with the product of greatest concern to their particular districts. The full committee, therefore, is organized in a way that guarantees its members the opportunity to speak and act on behalf of the interests dearest to the hearts of their constituents. Agriculture bills, as a result, tend to be compromises; each subcommittee is inclined to support the work of the others in return for a relatively free hand to write the law for the products of its own concern. Representational advantages, lacking in other committees, are thus built into the structure of the Agriculture Committee (Jones, 1961; Ornstein and Rohde, 1977). Similarly, senators and House members who deal with rivers and harbors legislation, serving on the Public Works Committees and on the public works subcommittees of the appropriations panels, seem able to take advantage of their institutional vantage points to obtain more new water projects for their states and districts than do nonmembers of these committees (Ferejohn, 1974).

Constituent Services

The second representational aspect of the legislator's job is the need to perform a wide variety of services for constituents. In the view of many, sending letters of condolence and congratulation, providing information, meeting a high school class on its trip to Washington, D.C., intervening in bureaucratic affairs, and performing a myriad of similar time-consuming chores will, far more than strict attention to the lawmaking or oversight functions, provide that "decisive margin of goodwill, votes, campaign funds, and assistance which enables a member to remain in Congress."[13] This belief leads many members of Congress to commit a large proportion of their own and their staffs' resources to dealing with nonpolicy services for constituents. Every letter received must be answered; all visitors from "back home" are to be cordially greeted. Because such activities seem to produce rewards, they tend to be augmented with other "public relations" devices. Newsletters go to a vast mailing list in the district; films and tapes are offered to local television and radio stations; government publications are mailed to constituents; speeches are delivered to local organizations whenever schedules permit. To deal with all these matters, the legislators' offices—both the central office in the nation's capital and the branches in the constituency—have become highly bureaucratized. Substantial portions of the more than $250,000 yearly allowances allotted congressional offices are spent for salaries and supplies to finance these constituent services.[14]

Congressional Outputs: An Overview

There can be no doubt that Congress can and does perform the functions assigned to it; the legislature does legislate, oversee, and represent.

Major policies continue to flow from Congress: In recent years, major innovations in civil rights, environmental protection, aid to education, job training, energy policy, and a host of other fundamental programs have passed the legislature. Many of these measures have been enacted in response to presidential initiatives, but many bear the distinctive stamp of congressional involvement as well. Similarly, some oversight has been extraordinarily effective. Most dramatically, investigation of White House and executive branch abuses led to Richard Nixon's resignation, under the immediate threat of impeachment, as president; similarly, legislative vigilance uncovered substantial misconduct—illegal surveillance, unauthorized opening of mail, and attempts to assassinate foreign political leaders—on the part of the U.S. intelligence community and led directly to new congressional controls and a major administrative overhaul of intelligence gathering (CQ Weekly Report, Jan. 28, 1978, p. 173). Finally, the vast commitment of time and energy to constituent services, already noted, testifies to the continuing congressional concern for representation.

Yet problems remain. Critics of Congress are quick to point out that the legislature is often slow to act and that its policies, when passed, may be "too little and too late" to deal effectively with the problems at which they are directed. It took years, for example, for Congress to enact an energy program with any reasonable chance to reduce the growing American dependence on imported oil, which the Arab oil embargo of 1973 made graphically clear. Others suggest that a fragmented, decentralized legislature that makes policy incrementally, in small and unadventurous steps, through a process of bargaining and compromise, can never be sufficiently innovative to cope with policy problems while they remain tractable. Another line of attack (Fiorina, 1977a) argues that Congress has, in effect, abdicated its policy-making responsibilities; members prefer instead to place higher priority on retaining their own positions in Congress. Aided and abetted by the federal agencies, which provide the necessary largesse—on the basis of congressional support, of course—members entrench themselves electorally through providing goods (contracts, dams, highways) and services (casework) to their constituents. Representation, of the service not the policy variety, simply drives out concern for effective lawmaking.

Congress, of course, is not without its partisans. Orfield in selection 17 rises to the defense of the legislature. Studies of current policy making reveal "the strong continuing role of Congress in shaping domestic policies," he suggests. Particularly when a conservative or passive president occupies the White House, Congress can be highly influential and innovative. In such circumstances, during the Nixon administration, for instance, a large opposition party legislative majority may be ideally situated to exploit congressional procedures, using appropriate strategy and tactics, to add amendments to bills the president desires (and will not veto) or otherwise to maneuver new programs through the legislative maze. Under other conditions, congressional prospects are dimmer, and there certainly remain problems for policy-making efficiency in a decentralized legislature; but the record shows, Orfield believes, "that any effort to stereotype Congress as inherently passive or conservative is doomed to failure." In any case, as the debate between the critics and defenders of Congress amply demonstrates, an optimum allocation of congressional resources among the output activities of lawmaking, oversight, and representation is extremely difficult to specify or to justify.

Role Conflict

Such disagreements illustrate a central theme of this volume: The lawmaker's choices of orientations toward the various features of the legislature—its internal organization, the actors in its environment, and its output activities—cannot be made without experiencing role conflict, the perceived inability to satisfy two or more different sets of expectations simultaneously. Senators and representatives must allocate their resources among the output functions of lawmaking, oversight, and representation. No one seriously denies that each category of output is within the province of Congress or that it is reasonable to expect the legislature to perform in each area. Yet from the perspective of the individual lawmakers, it is clear that members cannot commit themselves to all three concerns to the same degree.

In the first place, there is simply no time to master the intricacies of substantive policy issues and at the same time to develop a clear understanding of the complexities of administrative agency behavior. Understanding is limited even within the specialized area of a single committee; there is just too much detailed data for one person to consume within the confines of the topics with which any single committee deals. It might be possible to develop expertise as a combined lawmaker-overseer if the full resources of a legislator's staff could be used for such a purpose; but, as noted, political survival dictates to many members of Congress that constituent services receive top priority. Reformers who argue that emphasis on local interests causes a loss of national perspective at a time when problems have long since transcended district boundaries have proposed that the burdens of rendering constituent services be removed or reduced through the use of "ombudsmen," who would answer constituent correspondence. Defenders of the present arrangements assert that no other system of representation is as likely as the present one to uncover local and regional concerns or to ensure that local citizens will have some access to their government. What is clear, regardless of one's point of view in this debate, is that legislators cannot cope satisfactorily with all three output functions; they must allocate their energies among them. Time devoted to one area cannot be spent on another.

However the representatives define their role with respect to output activities, they will face other forms of role conflict. Their party or the administration may press for particular results; their committees may have norms to which they would like to adhere; their constituents may have stakes in some issues that they must defend. Such choices must be faced in all output areas. Where legislators perceive that the constituency has substantial interests, they are likely to act to further them; where such interests are seen as negligible, they will look more often to party as a guide to action. Another way out of such conflict situations is to take advantage of the multistage character of the legislative process. Legislators may be able to satisfy one set of demands at the committee stage, another set at the point of amendment, and a third set when the roll-call vote is taken. Or alternatively, they may support authorizing a particular program but work against appropriating sufficient monies to fund it adequately.

One should not infer that role orientational choices are always "either-or" decisions. They may be explained in such terms, but they often do not occur in so clear-cut a fashion. Commitment to one activity may well yield payoffs in another. Involvement in constituent services often requires intervention in bureaucratic affairs that, in turn, may give insight into the operations of the executive branch and facilitate oversight. Listening to constituent requests may provide some clues about public needs, which legislation may be able to satisfy. The problem of role conflict is not that legislators must do one thing to the exclusion of all others but rather that they must do one (or a very few) things well while treating the others more superficially. Legislative system outputs will reflect the distribution of these choices among the individual members of Congress. So long as a significant number of senators and representatives commit themselves to each output function, the system will perform adequately in each area. To the extent that one function is neglected, a loss in support may result, with serious consequences for the future of the legislature.

Feedback

The operation of feedback provides a built-in corrective device for any imbalance that may develop among the system's outputs. Feedback refers to the process by which system outputs exert influence on the actors in the environment of the system, stimulating them to make new demand inputs and to give greater or lesser support to the system. Failure to legislate, oversee, or represent may thus be costly in systemic terms. Rejection of medicare led to increased demands for its passage and involved more groups, more legislators, and more executive branch personnel. Similarly, congressional failure to discharge adequately one of the output functions may automatically lead to demands for action in that area. Inattention may invite legislators who are looking for career opportunities to move into the area. Popular demands for action or popular dissatisfaction with past failures may have the same effect. So long as there are demands for action in all areas and support to be won for such action, apparently Congress will not long neglect any of its output functions.

This speculation should serve to remind us that the legislative system is not rigid and unchanging but is flexible and in flux. The formal and informal characteristics of the system are, though not often, dramatically modified; the actors internal to the system change with elections and with the assumption of political roles by new generations; the actors external to the system come and go, wax and wane in influence, impose new demands in keeping with new circumstances, and respond in new ways to the system's outputs. Change may not be rapid—the Congress of the 1930s bears a marked resemblance to the contemporary legislature—but it does occur. Indeed, the 1970–1977 period has been one of major reform in Congress, and in the fifth part of this book we examine these changes and their consequences in greater detail.

Notes

[1] For instance, in announcing his intention to retire at the end of the Ninety-fifth Congress, Rep. Otis Pike (D-N.Y.) declared ". . . people bug me more than they used to. They are asking their government to do more for them and are willing to do less and less for themselves" (CQ Weekly Report, Feb. 25, 1978, p. 528).

[2] Huntington, 1973, suggests that Congress, because it has remained relatively insulated from fundamental changes in American society and because of the continued dispersion of power created by its decentralized structure, may now be better suited for oversight than for lawmaking activities.

[3] Dyson and Soule (selection 8 in this book) and Fenno, 1973a, ch. 6, suggest that although there may be substantial variation among the committees, in the House at least most panels can expect to see significant proportions of the bills they report passed on the floor.

[4] In the House, of course, except for some "privileged matter" that goes directly to the floor, bills must clear the Rules Committee, which will define the conditions under which floor consideration will take place.

[5] In addition to Fenno's (1973a) study of six House committees and their Senate counterparts, see Manley, 1970; Price, 1972; Murphy, 1974; Ferejohn, 1974; and Oppenheimer, 1974.

[6] See the introduction for the distinctions among delegate, politico, and trustee role orientations.

[7] Congressional voting has been one of the most carefully studied aspects of national politics. For the major findings, consult Turner, 1970; Shannon, 1968; Kingdon, 1973; Clausen, 1973; Jackson, 1974; Fiorina, 1974; and Matthews and Stimson, 1975.

[8] For other treatments of oversight, see Scher, 1963; Bibby, 1966; Harris, 1964; Henderson, 1970; Kaiser, 1977; and Price, 1978.

[9] On the budgetary process, see selection 13 in this book; Fenno, 1966; Natchez and Bupp, 1973; Wildavsky, 1974; LeLoup, 1977; and Ippolito, 1978.

[10] Taylor, 1961, provides the history and a critical analysis of the investigatory process.

[11] Davidson, 1969, finds members of Congress taking each of these positions. With regard to the focus of representation, 42 percent of his sample saw themselves as district oriented, 28

percent as nation oriented, and 23 as district-nation oriented (with the remainder undecided or unclassifiable). On style, 23 percent were delegates, 28 percent trustees, and 46 percent politicos.

[12]This relative lack of voter concern for the issues remains the case, though some observers detect an upsurge of citizen concern for and awareness of political issues. On the question of the importance of issue voting, see the papers collected in Niemi and Weisberg, 1976.

[13]Olson, 1966, p. 341. This essay, esp. pp. 340–368, provides an excellent review of the nature of constituent service problems. Saloma, 1969, ch. 6, makes clear that members of Congress invest their own and their staff resources heavily in "education and service" activities.

[14]For a listing of the allowances and perquisites granted members of Congress, see Congressional Quarterly, 1976.

Selection 13 The House Appropriations Committee's Decisions: Patterns and Determinants

Richard F. Fenno, Jr.

The Analysis of Committee Decisions

The important results of Appropriations Committee-executive agency interaction are the Committee's decisions concerning the agency's request for money. Through its decisions, the Committee also adapts to the expectations of the parent chamber. And, through its decisions, the Committee makes its unique contribution to the sum total of congressional output. . . . The question now arises: What kinds of decisions does the Committee make? Is it possible to generalize about the substance of Committee decisions — to add to our generalizations about how they are made some generalizations about what they are? The answer is that the dollars and cents nature of appropriations decisions does make it possible to generalize, very tentatively, about Appropriations Committee decisions. The explication and explanation of some patterns is the subject of this chapter.

At the outset, certain limitations should be made clear, and they should be remembered by the reader throughout. In the first place, only one kind of Committee decision will be examined — namely, that decision which is expressed in a dollars and cents appropriation. A quick comparison between the sparse, dominantly quantitative language of an appropriation bill and the expanded, more qualitative commentary of a Committee report makes it perfectly clear that many explicit decisions of the Committee are not revealed in the dollars and cents figures. And, given the scope of informal communication between Committee and agency, it is also clear that many other Committee decisions will be hidden from public view entirely. The statutory dollars and cents decisions are supplemented and qualified by a broad range of nonstatutory decisions.

In the second place, dollars and cents figures can be compared only at the obvious cost of losing relevant information about contextual differences. The same dollars and cents figure may be subject to quite different interpretations given contextual differences. For instance, all dollars and cents appropriations figures are assumed to represent the Committee's real preferences in dealing with the agencies. As a matter of fact, we know that some Committee decisions are partly tactical decisions, made in anticipation of Senate or conference committee action. (For instance, the House sometimes grants a smaller appropriation than it "really" wants because it believes the Senate Committee will raise the appropriation and the conference committee will make a decision somewhere between that of the two committees.)

In the absence of accurate information as to what part of each appropriation figure is a tactical bargaining segment, it must be assumed that this segment is either the same or nonexistent across agencies. This is but one of the more obvious losses of information entailed in the comparison of dollars and cents figures.

A third limitation stems from the restricted sample of decisions being examined. All generalizations must be considered tentative for this reason, if for no other—that the desire of the author was to test for some patterns among a limited kind and number of executive agencies. . . . Generalizations offered here must be considered as hypotheses which remain to be tested for other departments, other program areas, and other times.

A fourth limitation stems from the fact that all the decisions being analyzed are decisions made regarding the original appropriations requests. Action taken on deficiency or supplemental budget requests is not included. Where supplementals represent the inauguration of new programs not in existence at the time of the request, their impact in the budget will be registered in the appropriations figures of the succeeding year. But where an agency returns to the Committee later in the year and is given money originally denied to it, some information will be lost by considering only the original request and the original decision.

Though the generalizations which follow cannot be considered definitive, they will furnish a more solid basis for current understanding and future investigation of appropriations output than has heretofore been available. Whatever their limitations, dollars and cents appropriations decisions are the single most important component of decision-making in this area, as any agency official will quickly acknowledge. In terms of contextual differences, some of the most obvious of these differences will be taken into account in the analysis. . . . Finally, on the testimony of Committee and bureau participants alike, the inclusion of deficiency and supplemental figures in the analysis would yield relatively minor differences in the gross patterns which will be presented. Despite limitations, therefore, a sixteen-year picture of domestic appropriations politics is rather closely approximated in the output analysis which follows.

Overall Decision Patterns

Two summary measures are mentioned most frequently by Committee members themselves in describing their dollars and cents decisions. The first is the relation between the dollars and cents agency estimates and the dollars and cents Committee recommendation. That is to say, Committee members describe their decisions as reducing, increasing, or leaving intact the budget requests of the agencies. When they speak of cutting budgets, they usually refer to decisions recommending less money for the next fiscal year than the agency asked for in its estimates. Less frequently, they speak of "giving them what they asked for" or "giving them more than they asked for." The second common measure of Committee output is the relation between the amount of money already appropriated to an agency for the current year and the amount of money recommended in the Committee's decision for the following year. Members, in other words, compare what they are recommending for next year with what the agency received at the conclusion of the appropriations process last year. During economy moods, they can sometimes demonstrate their frugality by noting that they have prevented bureaucratic growth by holding an agency to the same figure it received for the current year. Or, if they are under fire for reducing an estimate too much, they can demonstrate their support for a program by noting that they are recommending more for next year than the agency received this year. The first measure involves relationships between appropriations and estimates in a single year; the second measure involves relationships among appropriations from one year to the next. They reveal different kinds of Committee decisions, and they have quite different consequences for executive agencies. Both measures, therefore, will be used in discussing Committee decisions.

The overall pattern of Committee decisions relative to agency estimates is described in table 13-1.

The Committee does, in fact, make the kind of decisions which its members strongly believe it should make, the kind of decisions which House members less strongly believe it should make, and the kind of decisions which the Committee's own internal structure is largely designed to facilitate. In

**Table 13-1   Appropriations as related to estimates: decisions of House
Appropriations Committee, 36 bureaus, 1947 to 1962**

Committee Decisions	Number of Decisions	Percentage of Decisions
1. Increases over budget estimates	46	8.0
2. Same as budget estimates	106	18.4
3. Decreases below budget estimates	423	73.6
Total	575[a]	100

[a]In 1957, the Committee lumped the appropriations for the Soil Conservation Service in a larger total,
and the agency figures are unavailable. This accounts for all those instances where the total number
of cases is 575 rather than 576.

three-quarters of the cases, it does reduce budget estimates—thereby "protecting the power of the purse," "guarding the federal Treasury," and "reducing
unnecessary expenditures." In about two out of every ten cases, the Committee
deviates from its dominant pattern by allowing the budget estimates to stand as
the appropriation. In less than one out of every ten instances does the
Committee meet those expectations of program support or constituency service
which require increases in budget estimates. The Committee's own hierarchy
of goal expectation is reflected in the pattern of its decisions on agency budget
requests.

A breakdown of Committee decisions on the estimates reveals that a
large majority of these decisions fix on a dollars and cents figure within 5
percent of the agency estimate. The overall pattern is one of moderation rather
than of drastic action in either direction. See table 13-2.

**Table 13-2   Appropriations as a percentage of estimates: magnitude of
increases and decreases, 36 bureaus, 1947 to 1962**

Percent of Estimates Received	Number of Decisions	Percent of Decisions
Over 120	1	0.2
115.0–119.9	4	0.7
110.0–114.9	2	0.3
105.0–109.9	10	1.7
100.1–104.9	29	5.0
100	106	18.4
95.0–99.9	220	38.3
90.0–94.9	80	13.9
85.0–89.9	50	8.7
80.0–84.9	26	4.5
75.0–79.9	12	2.1
70.0–74.9	9	1.6
65.0–69.9	8	1.4
60.0–64.9	6	1.0
Below 60	12	2.1
Total	575	99.9*

*Due to rounding.

The dominant pattern is not a wholesale slashing of agency budgets. Most Committee reductions (and increases) in budget estimates are marginal ones, ranging between an increase of 5 percent and a decrease of 5 percent in budget estimates. This does not mean that they are inconsequential. Agency officials were nearly unanimous in their assertion than a 5 percent reduction in estimates would be harmful to them. And over one-third (35 percent) of all the Committee's cuts are reductions of more than 5 percent. Occasionally as the frequency distribution shows, the size of the budget reductions is of crippling proportions—the more so if it is applied to the agency's base as well as to its plans for the future. Surely the sizable number of reductions greater even than 10 percent is warning enough to the agencies that a Committee decision may hurt them very badly indeed. In one case during the 16 years, the Committee recommended no money at all for a bureau.[1] Every once in a while, on the other hand, the Committee forsakes its budget-cutting pattern to recommend appropriations greater than requested—though not of the same order of magnitude as the deepest cuts. For the agency that finds favor with the Committee, therefore, Committee decisions can also be very consequential. Whether the dominant pattern of budget reduction or the secondary patterns of decision-making are being examined, Committee decisions are primarily incremental ones. These kinds of decisions represent the logical outcome of the incrementalism which appears both in the agency's expectations about Committee action and in the Committee's perceptions of agency budgets.

The description of Committee decisions according to the second measure—the relation of this year's Committee decision to last year's final appropriation figure—accents another angle of Committee decision-making. From this perspective, the great bulk of Committee decisions involves increases over the previous year's appropriation. See table 13-3.

Table 13-3   Appropriations as related to previous year's appropriation: House Appropriations Committee decisions, 36 bureaus, 1947 to 1962

Committee Decision	Number of Decisions	Percentage of Decisions
1. Increase over last year's appropriation	398	69.2
2. Same as last year's appropriation	22	3.8
3. Decrease below last year's appropriation	155	27.0
Total	575	100

The Appropriations Committee reduces agency budgets each year; but from one year to the next they grant the agency increased appropriations. The Committee's dilemma—caught as it is between expectations (its own and others) emphasizing support for programs and expectations emphasizing economy—has been described. In the pattern of its decisions can be found, perhaps, the basic solution. On the whole, the Committee supports programs and affects economies—*both at the same time.* Agency appropriations are allowed to grow, but at a slower rate than the agencies themselves desire.

The dominant pattern of allowing increases over the previous year ought not to obscure, however, the sizable minority of cases (over 25 percent) in which the previous year's appropriation was cut back. In a great many of these instances, cutbacks mean reductions in the agency's base. And the frequency with which such drastic action does occur helps underline the possible consequences of Committee action for the executive agency.

A frequency distribution of Committee decisions relative to the previous year's appropriation reveals, again, a basic incrementalism. See table 13-4.

Table 13-4   Appropriations as related to previous year's appropriation: House Appropriations Committee decisions, 36 bureaus, 1947 to 1962

	Number of Decisions	Percentage of Decisions
Percentage increase		
Over 100.1	10	1.7
90.1–100.0	0	0
80.1–90.0	2	0.3
70.1–80.0	1	0.2
60.1–70.0	6	1.0
50.1–60.0	10	1.7
40.1–50.0	11	1.9
30.1–40.0	16	2.8
20.1–30.0	46	8.0
10.1–20.0	98	17.0
0.1–10.0	198	34.4
Same		
0	22	3.8
Percentage decrease		
−0.1–−10.0	86	15.0
−10.1–−20.0	28	4.9
−20.1–−30.0	16	2.8
Over 30.1	25	4.3
Total	575	99.8*

*Due to rounding.

The year-to-year expansion of the agencies is kept marginal by the Committee's action. A majority of the Committee's decisions (53 percent) involve no more than a 10 percent change over the previous year's appropriation. If one takes changes of 20 percent as the cutoff point, three-quarters of all the cases are included. At each 10 percent interval the number of cases drops, until a few extreme examples of growth or retardation remain at either end of the scale.

It is impossible to know what the consequences of an increase or a decrease over last year's appropriation will be unless one also knows what an agency's expectations are in each case. A decrease from last year's appropriation may not hurt the agency if, in fact, the agency had planned for and requested such a cutback. Conversely, an increase granted by the Committee may hurt an agency badly if, in fact, the agency had planned for and requested a much larger increase. (The pattern of Committee decisions just described must be related to the pattern of agency expectations. . . .) The contours of that relationship are revealed in table 13-5.

Table 13-5   House Appropriations Committee decisions in relation to agency requests: 36 bureaus, 1947 to 1962

Committee Decision (in Relation to Last Year's Appropriation)	Agency Request (in Relation to Last Year's Appropriation)	
	Increase	Decrease
Increase larger than requested by agency	32[a] (7.0%)	—
Increase same as requested by agency	72 (15.8%)	—
Increase smaller than requested by agency	287 (63.1%)	—
Decrease	64 (14.1%)	—
Decrease smaller than requested by agency	—	9 (9.9%)
Decrease same as requested by agency	—	21 (23.1%)
Decrease larger than requested by agency	—	54 (59.3%)
Increase	—	7 (7.7%)
Total	455 (100%)	91 (100%)

[a]The figures refer to number of cases. Twenty-nine cases were omitted where bureau either requested (20) or received, though requesting an increase (9), the *same* appropriation as last year.

The Appropriations Committee grants a great majority of agency requests for a dollars and cents increase over the previous appropriation. But, of the increases granted, the overwhelming number are for less than the agency requested. Some estimate of the order of magnitude of these reductions can be gleaned from table 13-2. In most cases the difference between the estimate and the appropriation is a moderate one. The modal pattern is for an agency to request an increase and for the Committee to grant it a smaller increase than requested. The Committee thereby cuts the budget but permits a conservative growth.

Table 13-5 sheds light on the sizable minority of decisions forcing cutbacks in agency appropriations. Slightly more of these cutbacks are in line with agency requests than are in opposition to them. That is to say, in 84 instances the agency requested and received a decreased appropriation, whereas in only 64 cases did the agency request an increase and receive a decrease. If, however, one combines the cases in which the agency asked for an increase and received a decrease (64) with those cases in which the agency asked for a decrease and got a bigger decrease (54), it is clear that most Committee decisions to cut back appropriations are more serious than the agencies expect. Once again, therefore, the capacity of the Committee to hurt the agency is made manifest and the seriousness with which the agencies view Committee activity is seen to be well justified. If the agency asks for an increase, it is most likely to get an increase. If it asks for the same amount as last year, it is most likely (13 out of 20 times) to get the same amount. If it asks for a decrease, it is most likely to get a decrease. But, within these broad categories, the agency may still receive a decision which it deems highly unfavorable. Its increases are most likely to be less than it wants, and, interestingly, if it asks for a decrease, it is more likely than not to receive an even greater decrease than it requested.

Appropriations Patterns and Some Environmental Variables

The decision patterns presented thus far summarize 16 years of Committee activity with regard to 36 bureaus. A breakdown of the decisions into annual patterns reveals important differences from year to year. These differences point to the existence of at least three important and interrelated environmental variables. One such variable is the complexion of party control of Congress and the Presidency. A second variable is the existence or the nonexistence of an economy mood. Since these are usually triggered by some discrete set of circumstances, their effects show up in year-to-year comparisons. A third related variable is the direction imparted by the executive branch, which, after all, holds the initiative in drawing up the budget.

Considering the appropriations decision as a percentage of agency estimates (the first measure used earlier), the average of the 36 individual bureau averages was computed for each of the 16 years. The yearly variations are presented in figure 13-1.

The years where the average percentage is low represent the years in which the Committee did the most severe budget-cutting. The years in which the average percentage is high represent the years of greatest Committee leniency in keeping appropriations close to estimates. In view of the dominantly incremental characteristic of Committee decisions, it is not surprising that the range between the Committee's most parsimonious year (1947) and its most

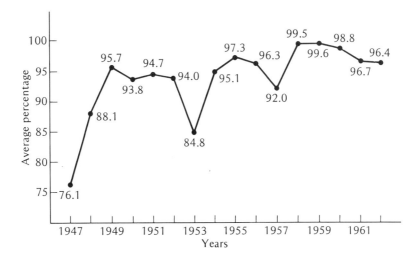

Figure 13-1   Yearly averages, appropriations as a percentage of estimates: House Appropriations Committee decisions, 36 bureaus, 1947 to 1962*

*Bureau averages are weighted equally.

profligate year (1960) is not great. Still the difference does seem significant. That is to say, it seems quite clear that decision patterns in 1947, 1948, and 1953 were substantially different from those of 1958, 1959, and 1960.

The most obvious contextual similarity linking 1947, 1948, and 1953 is the partisan complexion of Congress and the White House. The Republican party captured the Congress for the first time in 14 years and went to work reducing the budget of a Democratic President. The effect of their drive against further bureaucratic expansion and in favor of economy is reflected in the results. It hit a peak in the first year of the 80th Congress and subsided slightly in 1948. In 1953, after a hiatus of 4 years, the Republicans again took control of Congress and again confronted the executive budget. This time, the President was also a Republican—but in 1953, the budget was essentially that of the outgoing Democratic President. It was not, therefore, until 1954 that the Republicans in Congress faced the budget of a Republican President, and they acted with far greater leniency than in the previous year. Conditions for reducing budget estimates would seem to be optimal from a partisan point of view when a Republican Congress acts on a Democratic President's budget.

When party control was reversed, from 1955-1961, with the Democrats in control of Congress and the Presidency (budget-making) in the hands of a Republican, no unusual pattern of budget reduction (except in 1957) appeared. During those 6 years the Committee decisions which we have examined averaged 97.3 percent of the budget estimates, whereas in the 3 years of Republican Congresses and Democratic budgets, 1947, 1948, 1953, the average Committee decision was 83.0 percent of the budget estimates. Other things being equal, the partisan conditions most conducive to the smallest reductions in budget estimates exist when the Democrats control the Congress and the Republicans control the Presidency. The years when the executive most nearly received what it asked for were 1958, 1959, and 1960. Democratic-controlled Congresses, it appears, were more lenient with the budgets of President Eisenhower than they were with those of Presidents Truman and Kennedy.

In understanding these patterns, however, it is necessary to know what the patterns of expectations looked like, as they were expressed in the President's budget across the years. And it is also necessary to know whether, despite reductions in budget estimates, dollars and cents appropriations were increasing or decreasing. These two additional factors are presented by years in figure 13-2.

The broken line records the number of bureaus in each year which requested the same or less than their previous year's appropriation. The solid line records the number of bureaus that actually received, by Committee decision, the same or less money. To put it another way, the broken line reflects the budget-making pattern as guided by the President, and the solid line represents the Committee's response to the President's budget. And the gap between the two in any given year is a measure of conflicting expectations between the Committee and the budget-makers in the executive branch.

From the perspective of figure 13-2, the yearly variations discussed earlier become clearer and some new ones appear. The antagonisms of divided party control in 1947 and 1953 are more firmly established. In both cases, Democratic Presidents (the 1953 budget was essentially the Truman budget) presented budgets with a "normal" number of requests for cutting back or holding the line on appropriations. But the Republican-controlled Committee proceeded to reduce or hold steady large numbers of bureau appropriations. In 1948, the other year of large average reductions, the same tendency appears but not strongly. After the first year of combat, the participants seem to have brought their expectations about expansion into closer proximity. Still, however, the Congress made severe reductions in budget requests.

The circumstances of 1951, 1954, and 1958 reveal decision patterns which were obscured in the previous analyses. In these years, Committee decisions were fairly normal when considered in relation to budget estimates. Yet what happened was that the executive and the Congress agreed on the necessity for slowing down or cutting back the growth of agency appropriations. Party factors would seem to account for the agreement on cutbacks evident in 1954. This was the first time in 23 years that a Republican President had made up a budget to be considered by a Republican House Committee. Their agreement on what should be done is recorded in figure 13-2. This one case suggests the hypothesis that the optimum conditions for slowing down the dollars and cents expansion of executive agencies (as opposed to the reduction of budget estimates) occur when the Republican Party controls both ends of Pennsylvania Avenue.

The cutback years of 1951 and 1958, however, cannot be accounted for

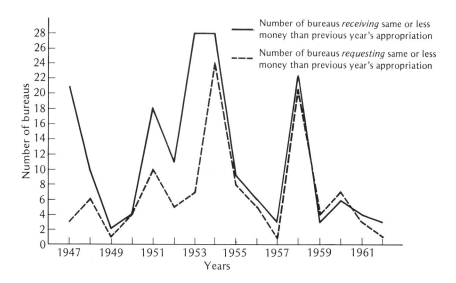

Figure 13-2   Relation of bureau requests to House Committee decisions: for bureaus requesting the same or less money than previous year, 1947 to 1962

by unified party control. Their patterns can most reasonably be accounted for by the existence of external circumstances. The Korean War began in 1950, and the reaction of both executive and Committee was to hold domestic appropriations at prewar levels. Since the budget was drawn up in 1950, the executive concern does not register quite as strongly as that of the Committee, which was making its decisions with hostilities well underway.

The 1958 pattern seems to have been a product of the ardent budget-cutting campaign waged in 1957 by President Eisenhower, Secretary of the Treasury George Humphrey ("hair curling depression"), and conservative economy-minded groups in the country. It was the size of the 1957 budget which alarmed Eisenhower, and he sought to reduce appropriations in the next budget. The 1958 budget was being made out at the time of the economy drive, and executive concern was expressed in the 21 proposals for holding down appropriations. The Committee, still responding to the economy emphasis, met the expectations of the executive. In 1957, however, the executive branch had not acted to hold agency budgets at or below the previous year's levels. Neither had the Committee. Caught between the budget estimates and Eisenhower's own statement that they should be cut, the Committee made a larger than average reduction of 8 percent in the estimates. (See figure 13-1.) Members of the House, though, caught the economy mood of 1957 even more strongly and made a number of further reductions on the floor. By 1958, the country was experiencing a slight recession, but the Committee proceeded to hold down spending in accordance with the expectations of an executive budget prepared in 1957. The recession of 1958 does account for the upswing in figure 13-1 from 1957 to 1958. And, by 1959 and 1960, both the agencies and the Committee were responding to the recession in terms of lenient treatment of budget estimates and the allowance of appropriations increases.

A larger question raised by the 1957–1958–1959 sequence involves the degree to which Committee decisions influence the obvious fluctuations in the level of appropriations. Does the Committee follow the general direction charted by the executive, or does the executive act in accordance with what it thinks Committee preferences are? As shown in figure 13-2, the levels of estimates and levels of appropriations—considered in relation to the previous year's appropriation—change in harmony with one another. Since the budgetary initiative rests with the agencies, it seems reasonable to assume that the Committee follows the general trend established by the executive branch. Given the evanescence of congressional economy moods, it seems unlikely that agencies can make budgets in anticipation of them. But it seems probable that, over a period of time, so long as dramatic external events do not intervene, the agencies and the Committee do communicate and that in the context of their constant communication the Committee does indicate what levels of appropriations it deems acceptable. Again, 1947 and 1953, and to some degree 1951, appear as exceptions—as cases in which the congressional influence on the level of appropriations was independent of agency expectations. Judging solely by the small number of years involved, it would appear that overall appropriations trends are set by the agencies. They are set, furthermore, in the light of many considerations of which anticipated Committee response is only one. Under certain conditions of party control and in the presence of unusual external events, however, the Committee may independently influence overall increases or decreases in appropriations.

Departmental Appropriations Patterns

Earlier in the chapter, we examined the gross patterns of Committee decisions. Three of the contextual variables affecting these patterns are revealed in year-by-year analysis. They are: the complexion of the party's controlling Congress and the Presidency, the inducement and the relaxation of economy moods by events external to both President and Congress, and the initiative of the executive branch. These conditions help to sort out the circumstances under which harsh and lenient treatment of the agencies (as measured in two ways) occur. A fourth rather obvious variable can also be isolated for its impact on Committee decision patterns. This factor is the type of agency involved. It is reasonable to ask whether all kinds of agencies receive the same treatment at the hands of the Committee. And it is reasonable to assume that they do not. If they do not, their differential treatments will reveal subpatterns of decision in addition to those revealed in yearly variations.

Most obviously, the 36 bureaus fall into 7 departmental clusters. And the question arises as to whether different patterns of decision appear among these clusters. In general, the answer is that they do. But, in advance, it should be understood that any generalization made about departmental patterns must be extremely tentative. The 36 bureaus were not selected randomly from the departments involved. The main criterion for their selection was that they had maintained their organizational integrity throughout the period. For some departments the bureaus are neither a good sample nor do their appropriations totals constitute a majority of the departmental budget. Since they are often the most controversial, expensive programs are apt to undergo the most frequent organizational changes. Still, some departmental patterns emerge and are suggestive enough to merit description.

When appropriations are viewed in relation to budget estimates, it seems clear that the gross patterns observed earlier have some distinct departmental origins. See table 13-6.

All departments, as would be expected, received budget cuts far more frequently than any other type of Committee decision. But beyond this general similarity, differences appear. Two departments, Agriculture and Health, Education, and Welfare accounted for the great bulk of the Committee decisions which granted the agencies more than they requested. Of the 17 cases in which agencies were granted an appropriation of 105 percent or more of their estimate (see table 13-2), 16 were agencies in these 2 departments. Similarly, 2 departments—Commerce and Interior—accounted for a disproportionate share of reductions in budget estimates. Of the 123 cases in which budget reductions of 10 percent or more were made (see table 13-2), well over half (67) involved agencies in these two departments. The difference between these two pairs of departments seems significant enough to warrant the statement that, according to this measure, the Departments of Agriculture and Health, Education, and Welfare received more favorable treatment at the hands of the House Appropriations Committee than did the Departments of Commerce and Interior. The decision pattern for each of the other 3 departments fell somewhere in between these extremes.

When the Committee's decisions are viewed in relation to the previous year's appropriation, departmental patterns are somewhat less clear. See table 13-7. All departments did receive increases over their previous appropriation more frequently than a decrease or the same appropriation. Differences among them on this score are not appreciable enough to give solid support to generalization about decision patterns. In terms of consistency in year-to-year increases, the Department of Justice fared better than the others. (One cannot, of course, judge anything about the size of increase from table 13-7.) And, again, Agriculture and Health, Education, and Welfare fared better than did Commerce and Interior—but not by so substantial a margin. By this measure too, Labor was

Table 13-6   House Appropriations Committee decisions as related to budget requests by departments, 36 bureaus, 1947 to 1962

Committee Decision on Budget Estimate	Departments						
	Agriculture (5 Bureaus)	Commerce (5 Bureaus)	HEW (5 Bureaus)	Interior (8 Bureaus)	Justice (3 Bureaus)	Labor (4 Bureaus)	Treasury (6 Bureaus)
Increase	17 (21.5%)	1 (1.2%)	18 (22.5%)	7 (5.5%)	1 (2.1%)	1 (1.6%)	1 (1.0%)
Same	15 (19.0%)	6 (7.5%)	10 (12.5%)	13 (10.1%)	15 (31.2%)	21 (32.8%)	26 (27.1%)
Decrease	47 (59.5%)	73 (91.3%)	52 (65.0%)	108 (84.4%)	32 (66.7%)	42 (65.6%)	69 (71.9%)
Total	79 (100%)	80 (100%)	80 (100%)	128 (100%)	48 (100%)	64 (100%)	96 (100%)

Table 13-7   House Committee decisions as related to previous year's appropriation: by department, 36 bureaus, 1947 to 1962

Appropriation in Relation to Previous Year's Appropriation	Departments						
	Agriculture (5 Bureaus)	Commerce (5 Bureaus)	HEW (5 Bureaus)	Interior (8 Bureaus)	Justice (3 Bureaus)	Labor (4 Bureaus)	Treasury (6 Bureaus)
Increase	59 (74.7%)	54 (67.5%)	59 (73.8%)	81 (63.3%)	41 (85.4%)	41 (64.1%)	63 (65.6%)
Same	4 (5.1%)	4 (5.0%)	1 (1.2%)	2 (1.6%)	0 (0%)	4 (6.2%)	7 (7.3%)
Decrease	16 (21.2%)	22 (27.5%)	20 (25.0%)	45 (35.1%)	7 (14.6%)	19 (29.7%)	26 (27.1%)
Total	79 (100%)	80 (100%)	80 (100%)	128 (100%)	48 (100%)	64 (100%)	96 (100%)

among the departments whose expansion was less consistent. It would appear that, in general, all departments experienced a steady growth in their appropriations. It also seems likely that when one of the contextual variables discussed earlier led to cutbacks in appropriations no department remained immune from the impact.

Where significant differences between departmental clusters appeared—such as those which separated the performance of the Interior Department bureaus from those of the Department of Health, Education, and Welfare—it seems likely that both external and internal factors were operative. The demand for expanded educational and welfare programs in recent years has been nationwide, and is felt by all members of the House. But the incidence of Interior Department programs falls in the West. The number of House members from the West, where population is relatively sparse, has been small. Correspondingly, they have enjoyed less success than education- and welfare-oriented groups in negotiating for support for their programs in the House. Surely this disparity in terms of base of support and access accounts for some of the difference in departmental success. Less obviously, however, departmental differences reflect differences in the internal legislative processes by which their appropriations decisions are made. The two appropriations subcommittees dealing with the Interior Department, the Subcommittees on Interior and on Public Works, have been deliberately and successfully weighted with non-Westerners to guard against the interest-sympathy-leniency syndrome. Neither subcommittee had a chairman or a majority of its members from west of the Mississippi River during the sixteen-year period. Furthermore, . . . Senate membership as a whole and the Senate Appropriations Subcommittees on Interior and Public Works are weighted top-heavily in favor of Westerners. The House Committee's parsimony has developed partly as a hedge against the anticipated aggressiveness and openhandedness of the Senate on behalf of the Interior Department.

By contrast, and despite the efforts of both Chairman Cannon and John Taber, the subcommittee handling the Health, Education, and Welfare appropriation has been headed for twelve of the sixteen years by a man who has consistently prodded these bureaus to develop new programs and to spend even more money in the area than they have been inclined to do. Among the many subcommittee chairmen of the period, John Fogarty has been the one least touched by the Committee's goals of budget-cutting. His disposition to loosen rather than tighten the purse strings is reflected in the performance of the five Health, Education, and Welfare bureaus. Departmental patterns can be explained, therefore, in part by subcommittee patterns.

Some Conclusions

. . . From the outset, the basic point has been made that the Committee is subject to two sets of expectations—one holding that the Committee should supply money for programs authorized by Congress and one holding that the Committee should fund these programs in as economical a manner as possible. People outside the Committee and Committee members alike hold to both sets of expectations, but the potential conflict between them is obvious. Because of their different goals and perspectives, groups outside the Committee (e.g., House members and executive agencies) tend to emphasize the positive expectation of financial support, whereas Committee members tend to place special emphasis on the more negative expectations of economy and budget reduction. If Appropriations Committee decisions are to meet the expectations of House members and executive agencies, they must be generous in response to external demands for ever-increasing funds. If Committee decisions are to meet the dominant expectations of Committee members, they must prevent the unnecessary expenditure of funds. Committee decisions, then, can be viewed as efforts to satisfy both groups—either of which could, by taking certain actions, cause radical changes in Committee activity.

In terms of an overall summary of their decisions, it appears that the Committee meets both sets of expectations. Its dominant response to bureau requests is to grant an increase over the previous year's appropriation but, at the same time, to reduce their estimates. Furthermore, in an overall sense, the Committee meets both expectations by avoiding drastic action of any kind in any direction. Its decisions are mostly marginal or incremental—whether measured by the relation of budget estimates to appropriations or by the relation of appropriations to last year's appropriation—and they tend to sustain existing relationships. These incremental responses do not come about simply as a matter of Committee choice, for the Committee acts within a set of historical, institutional, and informational restraints which circumscribe its area of discretion. Still, the Committee acts as an independent and significant influence on appropriations decisions. Viewed in the broadest perspective, Appropriations Committee decisions fall into a pattern which can be described as a balanced, conservative, incremental response to conflicting expectations.

Note

[1] The Division (now Bureau) of Labor Standards in 1947.

Selection 14 Political Upheaval and Congressional Voting: The Effects of the 1960s on Voting Patterns in the House of Representatives

Barbara Sinclair Deckard

If the U.S. House of Representatives is truly a representative body, major societal and political changes should have an effect on voting patterns in that body. The twelve-year period 1959–70 saw relative political quiescence give way to the Civil Rights Movement, then to war in Viet Nam and the peace movement, which radicalized some and led many to question old priorities at home and abroad. The political worlds of 1959 and 1970 were very different.

The purpose of this study is to show that, during this period, major changes in House voting patterns did occur and to test a number of hypotheses which could explain the change.

Changing House Voting Patterns 1959–1970

Because previous House roll call studies have found party and region to be major predictors of voting behavior, this examination of trends in voting patterns will initially concentrate on those variables.[1] All roll call votes taken during the six Congresses, 86th through 91st (1959–70), which meet the following criteria were used. (1) At least 80 percent of the membership voted. (2) At least 20 percent of those voting voted in the minority. Votes are classified in terms of the behavior of four regional party groupings — southern Democrats, northern Democrats, eastern Republicans, and non-eastern Republicans.[2] For the Republican party, the eastern-non-eastern division is used rather than the coastal-interior one because previous work has shown eastern Republicans to be the most deviant sub-grouping within the Republican party.[3]

The roll calls are classified into voting patterns on the basis of how a

Reprinted from *The Journal of Politics* 38 (1976), pp. 326–345, by permission of the author and publisher. The author would like to thank the University of California–Riverside for an intramural grant and the Inter-University Consortium for Political Research for making the roll call data available.

majority of each group voted. For example, if a majority of northern Democrats and a majority of southern Democrats voted in opposition to a majority of eastern Republicans and a majority of non-eastern Republicans, the roll call is classified as a party vote. A roll call on which a majority of northern Democrats voted against majorities of the other three groupings is called a conservative coalition vote. This procedure produces a categorization of votes into mutually exclusive and exhaustive classes.

Table 14-1 lists the possible patterns and the proportion of roll calls which fell into each category for each of the six Congresses. All of the patterns do appear but their frequency of occurrence varies greatly. Thus northern Democrats and non-eastern Republicans voted in opposition to southern Democrats and eastern Republicans only twice during this twelve-year period.

Table 14-1   Changing voting patterns 1959–1970

	Congress					
Pattern	86	87	88	89	90	91
ND,SD vs ER,n-ER	50.4[a]	47.9	54.9	38.8	28.1	16.4
(Party)	(63)	(56)	(62)	(66)	(54)	(23)
ND vs SD,ER,n-ER	16.8	18.0	8.0	24.1	27.1	30.0
(Conservative Coalition)	(21)	(21)	(9)	(41)	(52)	(42)
ND,ER vs SD,n-ER	8.0	6.8	6.2	12.4	13.0	19.3
	(10)	(8)	(7)	(21)	(25)	(24)
ND,SD,ER vs n-ER	4.8	18.8	20.4	15.3	9.4	9.3
	(6)	(22)	(23)	(26)	(18)	(13)
ND,ER,n-ER vs SD	12.0	2.6	2.7	4.7	4.7	8.6
	(15)	(3)	(3)	(8)	(9)	(12)
ND,SD,n-ER vs ER	1.6	1.7	.9	0	2.6	.7
	(2)	(2)	(1)		(5)	(1)
ND,n-ER vs SD,ER	0	0	0	0	0	1.4
						(2)
ND,SD,ER,n-ER	6.4	4.3	7.1	4.7	15.1	14.3
	(8)	(5)	(8)	(8)	(29)	(20)

[a]Top figure is percentage. N given below in parentheses.

Key: ND, northern Democrats; SD, southern Democrats; ER, eastern Republicans; n-ER, non-eastern Republicans.

An examination of the table further reveals that considerable change has taken place. During each of the first three Congresses under investigation — 86th–88th — approximately half of the roll calls were party votes. With the 89th Congress a sharp decline begins and, in the 91st, only 16.4 percent of the roll calls are party votes. In contrast conservative coalition votes increase until they make up 30 percent of the votes in the 91st Congress. The pattern of northern Democrats and eastern Republicans versus southern Democrats and non-eastern Republicans, which is infrequent in the first three Congresses, also increases from the 89th on and accounts for almost 20 percent of the roll calls during the 91st Congress.

Clearly the importance of party as a predictor of roll call voting has decreased. Yet the voting behavior of the majority segments of the two parties — northern Democrats and non-eastern Republicans — remains distinct. Majorities of these two groupings seldom vote together. If the votes on which majorities of all groups vote together are excluded, northern Democrats and non-eastern Republicans voted in opposition on 92.1 percent of the roll calls during the six Congresses and there is no trend during the period. The decrease in party voting, then, must be due to the behavior of the two minority groupings.

To show that this is the case, the frequency with which each congressman voted with a majority of northern Democrats on all votes pitting a majority of northern Democrats against a majority of non-eastern Republicans was computed. For Republicans this score is a defection rate, with a high score indicating frequent defection from the position taken by a majority of non-eastern Republicans. For Democrats, it is a cohesion or loyalty rate; a high score indicates a high frequency of voting for the position taken by a majority of northern Democrats. A defection rate can be transformed into a cohesion rate or vice versa by subtracting the score from 100.

Table 14-2 displays the means for the four regional party groupings over time. The table shows that both northern Democrats and non-eastern Republicans vote as highly cohesive groups. In contrast, the eastern Republicans' mean increases throughout the period indicate that they are more and more likely to defect from the position taken by a majority of their non-eastern party colleagues. During all six Congresses, southern Democrats frequently defected from the position taken by a majority of northern Democrats. The latter half of the period sees a further and very sharp decline in southern Democrats' voting with their northern party colleagues. In the 90th and 91st Congresses, their mean drops well below 50 percent indicating that southern Democrats were more likely to vote with the non-eastern Republicans than with the northern Democrats.

These six Congresses, then, have seen a precipitous decrease in party voting. This decrease is largely due to the behavior of southern Democrats and eastern Republicans who are increasingly unlikely to vote with the majority

Table 14-2 Changing cohesion and defection rates[a]

Congress	Northern Democrats	Southern Democrats	Eastern Republicans	Non-Eastern Republicans
86	87.9	63.0	29.0	18.3
87	91.2	65.2	31.3	16.5
88	91.6	69.1	34.8	16.1
89	89.9	54.4	38.3	13.5
90	87.8	46.9	35.4	16.6
91	81.2	38.5	46.3	25.4

[a]Score is percentage support for northern Democratic position on all votes pitting a majority of northern Democrats against a majority of non-eastern Republicans.

segments of their respective parties. During the first three Congresses under consideration — 86th–88th — the trend is only faintly evident; with the 89th it becomes extremely strong.

Development of Hypotheses

To explain changes in voting patterns a theory of how congressmen make voting decisions is needed. The delegate and trustee models of legislative voting developed by Wahlke et al.[4] will be used here to generate hypotheses which could account for the trends documented above. The hypotheses will be further elaborated and tested in the following sections.

According to the instructed delegate model, the representative votes in accordance with the wishes of the majority of his constituency. Both roll call and interview studies of congressional voting indicate that the constituency is important in voting decisions.[5] We also know, however, that the mass constituency is seldom well informed about or attentive to the congressman's voting behavior.[6] Furthermore, the congressman's knowledge about the desires of his constituency is far from perfect.[7] Previous studies, then, would indicate that some form of delegate model is reasonable but that we should expect constituency preferences to be related only to the gross direction of the vote. Knowledge of the constituency should be helpful in predicting general policy positions and perhaps the level of party loyalty but not, except in rare cases, specific voting decisions.

Within this modified delegate model, major changes in voting patterns are explained by gross changes in constituency policy preferences. Changes in constituency preferences could be due to changes in preference-related constituency characteristics, changes in the political agenda or to "pure" attitude change, that is, conversion.

We know that characteristics such as income, race and place of residence, whether urban or rural, are related to policy preferences.[8] If, through secular development or mobility, such characteristics of a district change, the representative will be faced with a changed set of constituency policy preferences. Within the model, he will either reflect these new preferences in his voting decisions or will be replaced. A change in the political agenda, that is in the issues voted upon, may result in a change in voting patterns. The same constituents faced with new stimuli may issue "directives" to their representative which result in very different voting patterns. Of course, given the mass constituency's normal inattentiveness, the change in agenda would have to be drastic to attain the saliency necessary to have such an effect. Finally, still within the delegate model, the change in voting patterns could be due to "pure" attitude change on the part of the constituency. That is, constituents might simply change their minds as to what they prefer. Conversion on such a massive scale should be traceable to factors in the socio-economic environment and one would expect such factors to be reflected in a changed political agenda. To the extent that this is not so, a test of the hypothesis cannot be undertaken here.

While the pure trustee model of congressional voting conflicts with our knowledge of the voting decision, in modified form, it does yield hypotheses worthy of consideration. Within the trustee model, the congressman votes on the basis of his own preferences or judgment regardless of the preferences of his constituency. Notions of responsibility of the welfare of the constituency and the nation as a whole are usually seen as part of the trustee model but are not relevant here and thus will be ignored.

Within the trustee model, changes in voting patterns may result from changes in personnel, changes in the political agenda or pure attitude change on the part of the congressman. Turnover in office in which congressmen with certain policy preferences are replaced by ones with different preferences could lead to changes in voting patterns. We know that congressmen have considerable, though far from absolute, leeway in how they vote. Turnover in office could, thus, account for a change in voting patterns without the turnover being the direct result of constituents' displeasure with the previous representative's voting record. If the political agenda changes, congressmen may react to the new stimuli in such a way as to produce a change in voting patterns. It might be argued that a new agenda gives congressmen greater voting freedom as their constituents will not yet have developed strong opinions on the new issues. Alternately and more convincingly, one may argue that a change in agenda sufficient to produce a major change in voting patterns would be the result of highly salient socio-economic or political factors. If such is the case, a change in agenda would make trustee voting less safe than usual. Finally, congressmen, like constituents, could simply change their minds. As was argued above, such massive conversion is unlikely to occur without an accompanying change in agenda.

Another possible explanation for voting changes is a change in the decision rule used by the congressman—from a trustee emphasis to a delegate emphasis or vice versa. Such a change would be unlikely to occur capriciously. One would expect it to be precipitated by a change in winning margin. That is, a congressman whose winning margin decreased might decide he had better pay more attention to his constituency's preferences. Conversely, if a congressman's margin increased he might feel freer to express his own preferences in his votes.

To recapitulate and summarize, a change in voting patterns may result from (1) change in preference-related constituency characteristics; (2) turnover in office; (3) change in decision rule; and (4) change in political agenda. The hypotheses are not mutually exclusive; more than one process may be at work. Thus, for example, a change in agenda, especially if it is accompanied by a heightened saliency of political matters, might well precipitate a change in decision rule.

To this point the hypotheses have been stated in terms of the individual congressman. In order for any of these hypotheses to account for the change in voting patterns documented above, the mechanism at work must be affecting groups of congressmen in systematic ways. In the following sections, the hypotheses will be restated in aggregate terms and then tested.

Constituency Change

If the decrease in party voting and the increase in cross party alliances are due to changes in preference-related constituency characteristics, then, during this period, the districts of northern Democrats and those of southern Democrats should be becoming increasingly differentiated in terms of such characteristics. The same should hold true within the Republican party. Furthermore, the districts of northern Democrats and of eastern Republicans should show increasing similarity as should those of the southern Democrats and the non-eastern Republicans.

If, in fact, this is the process at work, constituency characteristics should distinguish between regional groupings within each party increasingly well in the later Congresses. Conversely, such constituency characteristics should distinguish between cross party groupings (northern Democrats and eastern Republicans on the one hand, southern Democrats and non-eastern Republicans on the other) less well in later Congresses.

Two tests were applied. To determine how well constituency characteristics distinguish among these regional party groupings a series of regressions was run. For each Congress, constituency characteristics were used to distinguish between southern and northern Democrats, between eastern and non-eastern Republicans, between northern Democrats and eastern Republicans, between southern Democrats and non-eastern Republicans and, as a baseline, between northern Democrats and non-eastern Republicans.[9] Because this procedure violates an assumption of the regression model, the regression coefficients cannot be legitimately interpreted. The percentage of variance explained does, however, give us a notion of how well one can predict a congressman's party or region knowing only such characteristics of his district as median income, percent urban and percent black. Table 14-3 presents the results of this procedure. The R^2's for the 86th and 87th Congresses cannot be compared with those for later Congresses because different sets of independent variables were used. Much better data are available for the later Congresses.

Before examining these results for trends over time, it should be noted that these regional party groupings are distinct in terms of constituency characteristics and that the southern Democrats are by far the most distinctive grouping. To the extent that the constituency variables used are related to voting behavior, one would expect the southern Democrats to vote very differently from their northern party colleagues. The same holds true, though to a lesser extent, for the two regional groupings within the Republican party.

Table 14-3   Constituency characteristics as predictors of party/regional group membership

Congress	ND vs SD	ER vs n-ER	ND vs ER	SD vs n-ER	ND vs n-ER
86	53.1[a]	11.3	9.1	53.4	10.6
87	53.1	11.3	10.2	56.0	17.1
88	75.1	44.7	27.6	68.6	37.3
89	64.6	51.5	11.0	52.6	25.9
90	69.8	43.4	28.6	54.0	43.8
91	74.0	43.1	31.2	55.1	47.9

[a]Figures are percentage variance explained. See note 9.

While, within each party, the regional groups are distinct in terms of constituency characteristics, there is very little evidence that they have become increasingly distinct during this period. In each of the five series, R^2 jumps from the 87th and 88th Congress but this is an artifact of the independent variables used. The series for the northern Democrats and non-eastern Republicans also shows this jump, but, as demonstrated earlier, these two groupings have shown no trend in their frequency of voting together. There is also no evidence indicating that the districts of the cross party groupings which voted together more frequently in the later Congresses became more similar during that period.

As was demonstrated earlier, majorities of northern Democrats and of non-eastern Republicans opposed one another on a very large proportion of the roll calls. For these two groupings, a considerable proportion of the variance in the score based on such roll calls is explained by constituency characteristics. (See table 14-4.) The second test is based on the assumption that the more similar a congressman's district is to that of the typical northern Democrat, the more likely he will vote like the typical northern Democrat; and conversely, a district similar to that of a typical non-eastern Republican will produce voting behavior like that of a typical non-eastern Republican.

The series of equations which relate voting score to constituency characteristics for northern Democrats and non-eastern Republicans is used to compute an expected score for each congressman for each Congress.[10] These scores tell us how one would expect a given congressman to vote if he based his vote

Table 14-4   Constituency characteristics as predictors of vote

Congress	% Variance Explained-All Cases	Explained-ND and n-ER only
86	10.7	13.3
87	15.2	20.4
88	30.5	41.5
89	23.7	32.5
90	40.1	52.0
91	47.6	52.9

solely on the constituency characteristics which distinguish between the voting behavior of northern Democrats and non-eastern Republicans. If a divergence in the types of districts represented accounts for the decrease in party voting and the increase in cross party voting, the expected scores of the two regional groups within each party should be diverging. The expected scores of the cross party groups should become more similar during the period under study.

The results for the 88th through the 91st Congresses are presented in table 14-5. Unfortunately the predictive equations for the 86th and 87th Congresses are too poor to use. Since the trend which we are attempting to explain is most evident during the last three Congresses, ignoring the first two in the series does not present a major problem.

Table 14-5   Differences in expected voting scores[a]

Congress	ND-SD	ER-n-ER	ND-ER	n-ER-SD
88	30.3	22.6	5.6	2.1
89	30.9	16.6	6.2	8.1
90	35.3	24.6	6.7	4.0
91	34.2	22.0	7.9	4.3

[a]The score is that based on roll calls on which a majority of northern Democrats opposed a majority of non-eastern Republicans. For an explanation of how expected scores were computed, see text and note 10.

The scores for the two regional groupings within the Republican party do not show any tendency to diverge. Within the Democratic party some trends toward an increase in the difference between mean scores is evident but, compared with the size of the difference throughout the period, the increase is slight. The difference in mean expected scores for northern Democrats and eastern Republicans has not decreased during this period, nor has that for southern Democrats and non-eastern Republicans.

Changes in the districts represented by the four regional party groupings do not account for the change in voting behavior. A constituency basis for the sort of pattern observed during the latter part of the period under study has existed throughout. An explanation for the change must be sought elsewhere.

Turnover in Office

If the change in voting patterns is due to turnover in office, holdover congressmen should show little or no change in voting behavior. To test this proposition, scores based on party votes, on conservative coalition votes and on roll calls on which northern Democrats and eastern Republicans opposed southern Democrats and non-eastern Republicans were used. All the scores were constructed in such a way that a high score indicates a high frequency of voting with a majority of northern Democrats. The mean for each of the four party regional groupings on each of the three scores for each of the six Congresses was computed. The same procedure was then carried out using only congressmen who had served in previous Congresses.

If the hypothesis is true, holdover congressmen should show greater party loyalty than all congressmen. Thus, for example, holdover southern Democrats should have mean scores higher than the mean for all southern Democrats, while holdover eastern Republicans' scores should be lower than those of all eastern Republicans.

Of the 72 scores of holdover congressmen, only 7 differ from the scores of all congressmen by more than two percentage points. The largest difference was 4.2 percentage points and the differences were frequently of the wrong sign. Holdover congressmen do not differ in their voting behavior from new congressmen during this period. Thus, turnover in office does not explain the change in voting patterns.

Change in Decision Rule

It was hypothesized that a change in congressmen's decision rule might account for the observed change in voting patterns. If this is the case, the relationship between the congressmen's voting behavior and the policy preferences of their districts should show a change over time. For example, if congressmen increasingly emphasized the delegate role over the trustee role during the period under study, an increasingly closer relationship between congressional voting behavior and constituent preferences should be observed.

To test the hypothesis, the usual assumption that measurable constituency characteristics such as urbanism, racial composition, and median income are adequate indicators of constituency policy preferences must be made. If the hypothesis is true, our ability to predict voting behavior from a knowledge of constituency characteristics should show a trend during the period under study. A series of regressions was run. The dependent variable was the score based on all votes on which a majority of northern Democrats opposed a majority of non-eastern Republicans; selected constituency characteristics were the independent variables. For each Congress, one equation was estimated for all congressmen and another for use as a base line, for northern Democrats and non-eastern Republicans only.

Table 14-4 gives the results. First it should be noted that, from the 88th Congress on, when better data becomes available, a very substantial proportion of the variance in the voting score can be predicted from a knowledge of constituency characteristics. In every case, R^2 is larger for northern Democrats and non-eastern Republicans only than for all congressmen. That is, throughout the period, these two groupings have voted more nearly as one would expect on the basis of the characteristics of their districts. There has been a generally increasing trend in the proportion of variance explained for all congressmen and the difference between the R^2's for the two sets of equations has decreased. This indicates that southern Democrats and eastern Republicans are increasingly voting as one would predict, from knowledge of the characteristics of their districts.

It, then, does not seem unreasonable to infer that, among these two groupings, there has been a change in decision rule. Making inferences concerning the nature of the choice process from roll call data is, of course, a tenuous and tricky enterprise. Nevertheless, the findings presented above indiate that southern Democrats and eastern Republicans are increasingly voting as one would expect if they were using the delegate decision rule.

Whether or not one is fully willing to make this inference, the increasing relationship between voting behavior and constituency characteristics does require explanation. To the extent that one is willing to interpret the increase as due to a shift in decision rule, the most obvious of possible explanations lies in the congressmen's electoral fortunes. A decrease in winning margin might well precipitate a closer attention to the wishes of the constituency.

An examination of the average winning margin of each of the four groupings reveals a longitudinal trend only for southern Democrats. At the beginning of the period, the average southern Democrat received approximately 90 percent of the vote; by the end, the percentage was down to slightly over 75. While, on the average, southern Democrats are still significantly safer electorally than other congressmen, such a decrease in winning margin might have an effect on voting behavior. For congressmen accustomed to no or only token opposition, receiving "only" 75 percent of the vote may be a sobering experience.

If fear of electoral defeat accounts for the southern Democrats' and eastern Republicans' increasing defection from the majority of their respective parties, one would expect that those congressmen whose electoral margin has decreased most would be the most likely to defect. There is, however, no relationship between change in winning margin and the likelihood of defecting for any of the four groups.[11] Furthermore there is very little relationship between the size of winning margin and the likelihood of defection.

The changes in voting behavior cannot be explained by the electoral fortunes of the congressmen — at least in any simple way. While the southern Democrats' average winning margin has declined, those whose margins have declined most are not more likely to defect. The eastern Republicans' average winning margin has not declined and again there is no relationship between changes in winning margin and defection.

The anticipation of constituency sanctions may, of course, have played a role. One bit of evidence supporting this possibility is the strong relationship (.61) for southern Democrats between the 1964 Goldwater vote in their districts and their likelihood of defecting. A congressman certainly might interpret a heavy Goldwater vote as an indicator that his constituency prefers a conservative policy stance and the southern Democrats' party loyalty does decline precipitously from the 89th Congress on. For eastern Republicans, too, the 1964 election may have had a sensitizing effect. The average Johnson vote in the districts of winning eastern Republicans was 64 percent. This was over 10 percentage points higher than the comparable figure for non-eastern Republicans and only slightly below that for northern Democrats. In the two previous presidential elections, the mean Democratic vote in the districts of eastern Republicans had been much more similar to that in the districts of non-eastern Republicans. This large Democratic presidential vote combined with the defeat of a number of their colleagues may well have led the eastern Republicans to reassess their voting behavior.

There is, then, some evidence for a shift in decision rule; but this shift, especially as it was not the direct result of the congressman's own electoral fortunes, does not provide a complete explanation for the change in voting patterns. If the congressman perceives a change in his constituents' voting directives or perceives himself to have less leeway in how he votes, this also requires explanation. The following section in which the final hypothesis is tested will provide the basis for at least a partial explanation.

Agenda Change

According to the final hypothesis, the change in voting patterns is due to a change in the political agenda. To test this hypothesis, a schema for classifying votes by issue content is needed. Aage Clausen's excellent work provides such a schema. Clausen identified five issue domains which accounted for a large proportion of the roll calls taken during the period he studied—83rd–88th Congresses.[12] Within each of the policy domains a preponderant issue dimension was isolated. Clausen shows that voting behavior varies across policy dimensions, with party being a good predictor of vote for government management and agricultural policy roll calls, a poor predictor for civil liberties and international involvement roll calls, and of intermediate explanatory power for social welfare votes.[13]

A change in the political agenda which resulted in a greater proportion of roll calls being taken in the issue areas which, in the post war years were never characterized by party voting, would account for the change in voting patterns. Alternatively or simultaneously, a shift in the content of the roll calls within issue categories could account for the change.

The proportion of roll calls accounted for by each of the issue categories does not vary sufficiently to explain the change in aggregate voting patterns.[14] The next step, then, is to examine the trends in voting patterns within each of the issue categories. As table 14-6 shows, the proportion of government management, agricultural policy, and social welfare roll calls which produced party votes declined during the period under study. On civil liberties roll calls, party votes have been so rare as to be almost non-existent throughout the period. Only 2 of the 83 roll calls in this issue area produced party votes. The most frequent patterns to appear are southern Democrats opposing the other three groupings and conservative coalition. During the period, the proportion of votes accounted for by the first of these patterns has decreased while the proportion of conservative coalition votes has increased. During the 89th–91st Congresses, the pattern of northern Democrats and eastern Republicans opposing southern Democrats and non-eastern Republicans became important, accounting for a quarter to a third of the roll calls. Thus southern Democrats are increasingly being joined by Republicans, especially by non-eastern Republicans, on civil liberties votes.

Table 14-6   Decreasing percentage of party votes on government management, agricultural policy and social welfare roll calls

	Congress					
	86	87	88	89	90	91
Government Management	68.9	65.3	62.2	63.6	43.7	27.5
Agricultural Policy	80.0	66.7	77.8	80.0	45.5	28.6
Social Welfare	41.7	35.0	55.6	22.8	11.5	7.4

Voting patterns in the four issue areas examined so far do show a fairly clear trend over time. In contrast, the trend evident for international involvement roll calls seems to be a function of party control of the presidency. As it is cyclical rather than linear, it cannot contribute to an explanation of the secular change in voting patterns with which this study is concerned.

Since the other four issue areas do show a change in voting patterns over time, the next step in testing the hypothesis under consideration is to examine the content of the roll calls within each of these broad issue categories. A shift in content may explain the change in voting patterns.

The social welfare category is a broad one and various issue subsets within it have been characterized by distinctive voting patterns throughout the period. On aid to education and on labor legislation, party voting was rare during the six Congresses under study. Roll calls on housing programs, social security, minimum wage increases and other such older social welfare programs, have, throughout most of the period, been characterized by party voting. Of 34 such roll calls, 18 (52.9 percent) produced party votes. Such social welfare programs were much less frequently at the center of controversy during the last three Congresses. These older social welfare programs accounted for 31 percent of all social welfare roll calls during the 86th–88th period, but for only 10 percent during the 89th–91st period.

The center of controversy shifted during the period to programs designed to aid the very poor. The war on poverty and related programs constituted a significant change in the legislative agenda and resulted in a shift in voting alignments. Throughout the six Congress period there were 57 votes on programs to aid the very poor; 48 (84.2 percent) of these occurred during the last three Congresses. Of the total 57, 16 (28.1 percent) were party votes; of those taken after the 1964 election, only 14.6 percent were party votes.

The change in social welfare voting is largely accounted for by a change in agenda. On those social welfare programs which stem from the New Deal, a majority of southern Democrats frequently votes with a majority of their northern party colleagues. On the newer programs designed to aid the very poor, however, southern Democrats typically vote with Republicans, especially non-eastern Republicans, in opposition. And these programs dominated the social welfare domain during the 89th–91st period, accounting for 41.7 percent of all social welfare roll calls.

Civil liberties roll calls can conveniently be divided into those dealing specifically with civil rights for blacks and other civil liberties issues. An examination of voting patterns within each of these categories reveals that during the 86th through the 88th Congresses, the two types of roll calls produced distinct voting alignments (see table 14-7). On all civil rights roll calls, a majority of southern Democrats voted in opposition to majorities of the other three groupings; the conservative coalition is the dominant pattern on other civil liberties votes.

With the 89th Congress, the situation changes. On civil rights roll calls, southern Democrats are increasingly joined by Republicans especially non-eastern Republicans. This change can be attributed to a change in the content of the issues voted upon. The early civil rights bills attempted to secure blacks the right to vote through the use of the judicial process. The 1965 bill, in contrast, suspends state voter qualifications in much of the South and provides for the employment of federal registrars. The controversy over the 1966 Civil Rights Bill centered on Title IV which barred racial discrimination in the sale and rental of housing. Such federal intervention was too much for many non-eastern Republicans; they voted to weaken such bills even though they often voted for final passage.

Table 14-7   Changing voting patterns on civil liberties roll calls[a]

	Civil Rights		Civil Liberties excluding Civil Rights	
	86–88	89–91	86–88	89–91
ND, ER, n-ER vs SD	100%	33.3	9.1	7.9
ND vs SD, ER, n-ER	—	23.8	81.8	63.2
ND, ER vs SD, n-ER	—	42.9	9.1	28.9

[a]The two party votes, one of which fell into each of the two categories, are excluded from the calculations.

On other civil liberties roll calls, eastern Republicans increasingly voted with northern Democrats during the last three Congresses studied. Here also a change in the content of the roll calls accounts for the change in voting behavior. During the early Congresses this category is dominated by votes on federal criminal justice procedures and on internal security matters. Such roll calls produced the conservative coalition pattern throughout the six Congresses. The last three Congresses saw a number of votes on home rule for the District of Columbia, the seating of Adam Clayton Powell and on punishing students who participated in campus disruptions. On these issues southern Democrats and non-eastern Republicans consistently took a hard line, while a majority of eastern Republicans were more moderate and usually voted for compromise measures.

The change in voting patterns on agricultural policy can be directly traced to a change in agenda. From the 86th through the 89th Congress most of the roll calls were concerned with farm subsidies. Such roll calls most frequently produced party votes. During the 90th and 91st Congresses, farm subsidy roll calls continued to produce party votes but a new issue which resulted in quite different alignments came to the fore. On the proposal to limit the amount a farmer could receive in subsidy payments, northern Democrats and eastern Republicans consistently voted together in favor of the limitation while southern Democrats consistently opposed it. Non-eastern Republicans were split, with a majority sometimes supporting but more frequently opposing the limitation.

In the government management domain, party voting declined precipitously during the period. Yet no clear change in agenda occurred. The roll calls in this domain fall into five fairly clear subcategories: public works, government regulation of business, monetary and fiscal policy, the level of government spending (debt ceiling, across the board cuts in appropriations bills), and, what may be called subsidies to states and localities (funds for airport construction and water pollution control, for example).

The really big decrease in party voting on government management roll calls occurred in the 90th and 91st Congresses. Table 14-8 shows that each of these subcategories shows this decrease. In this case, then, voting patterns have changed without there being any clear change in agenda.

Table 14-8   Decreasing percentage of party votes on government management roll calls

	86–89	90–91
Public Works	84.6	20.0
Spending	68.0	41.4
Government Regulation	64.3	42.9
Subsidies	61.4	35.7
Monetary and Fiscal	54.5	33.3

Conclusion

During the 1959–70 period, a massive change in voting patterns took place in the House of Representatives. The decline in party voting, which is precipitous from the 89th Congress on, is largely due to increasing defections by southern Democrats and eastern Republicans from the positions taken by the majority segments of their respective parties.

Neither turnover in office nor a change in the characteristics of the constituencies represented explains this change. A constituency basis for such defections has existed throughout the period. As southern Democrats and eastern Republicans increasingly defected, the relationship between their voting behavior and the characteristics of their districts became stronger. To the extent that such district characteristics are related to constituents' policy preferences, these two groups of congressmen were increasingly voting their constituents' preferences.

In three of the five broad issue domains examined a change in the content of issues which came to a vote occurred. In a fourth issue domain no dramatic agenda shift was detected yet party voting decreased significantly.

The study, then, provides support for two of the four hypotheses tested. A change in the political agenda did occur and the voting behavior of southern Democrats and eastern Republicans conforms to what one would expect if these congressmen had shifted their decision rule towards the delegate pole on the trustee-delegate continuum.

More speculatively, I would argue that the political upheavals of the 1960s led to a new political agenda in the Congress and that the upheavals combined with the new agenda, increased the saliency of politics to the mass electorate.[15] Southern Democrats and eastern Republicans responded to the changed political climate by bringing their voting behavior into closer alignment with the perceived preferences of their constituents.

Notes

[1]See Julius Turner, *Party and Constituency: Pressures on Congress*, Revised edition by Edward V. Schneier, Jr. (Baltimore: John Hopkins Press, 1970), Aage Clausen, *How Congressmen Decide: A Policy Focus* (New York: St. Martin's Press, 1973), David R. Mayhew, *Party Loyalty among Congressmen* (Cambridge: Harvard University Press, 1966), L. N. Rieselbach, *The Roots of Isolationism* (Indianapolis: Bobbs-Merrill, 1966), L. A. Froman, *Congressmen and their Constituencies* (Chicago: Rand McNally, 1963), Gerald Marwell, "Party, Region and the Dimensions of Conflict in the House of Representatives, 1949-1954," *American Political Science Review* 61 (June 1967), David B. Truman, *The Congressional Party* (New York: Wiley, 1959).

[2]The South includes the states of the old Confederacy and the border states (SRC codes 40 through 56). The East includes New England and the middle-Atlantic states (SRC codes 1 through 14).

[3]Barbara Deckard and John Stanley, "Party Decomposition and Region: The House of Representatives, 1945–1970," *Western Political Quarterly*, 27 (June 1974).

[4]J. C. Wahlke, H. Eulau, W. Buchanan and L. C. Ferguson, *The Legislative System: Explorations in Legislative Behavior* (New York: Wiley, 1962).

[5]For roll call studies, see Turner, *Party and Constituency*, Froman, *Congressmen and their Constituencies*, Rieselbach, *Roots*. Also Duncan MacRae, *Dimensions of Congressional Voting* (Berkeley: University of California Press, 1958). For an excellent study based on interview data see John W. Kingdon, *Congressmen's Voting Decisions* (New York: Harper and Row, 1973).

[6]See Donald Stokes and Warren Miller, "Party Government and the Saliency of Congress," *Public Opinion Quarterly* 26 (Winter 1962).

[7]See Lewis Dexter, "The Representative and His District" in *New Perspectives on the House of Representatives*, ed. Robert Peabody and Nelson Polsby (Chicago: Rand McNally, 1963).

[8]See V. O. Key, Jr., *Public Opinion and American Democracy* (New York: Knopf, 1965).

[9]For each regression equation, a dichotomous variable (either party or region) was the dependent variable and various constituency characteristics obtained from the Congressional District Data Books and supplements were the independent variables. The SPSS stepwise regression program was used for all regressions reported in this paper and was always constrained so that at most six independent variables would enter the equation. See Norman Nie, Dale Bent and C. Hadlai Hull, *Statistical Package for the Social Sciences* (New York: McGraw-Hill, 1970), Ch. 15.

[10]For example, the equation estimated for the 89th Congress was

Voting Score $= 62.769 + 1.276$ (% foreign stock)

$\qquad\qquad -1.575$ (% white collar) $+ .490$ (% urban)

The expected score for any given congressman is computed by entering the values of his district into this equation.

[11]Within each group, the change in winning margin between each two succeeding elections was correlated with the congressman's voting score in the Congress following the second election. The score is based on all votes on which majorities of northern Democrats and of non-eastern Republicans voted in opposition.

[12]*How Congressmen Decide*, 38–51.

[13]*Ibid.*, 91.

[14]Space limitations prohibit including this breakdown or that of voting patterns over time within issue area. These tables are available from the author.

[15]On the increasing saliency of politics see Norman Nie with Kristi Andersen, "Mass Belief Systems Revisited: Political Change and Attitude Structure," *Journal of Politics*, 36 (August 1974).

Selection 15 Legislative Oversight: Theory and Practice

Morris S. Ogul

The question of who rules the rulers is as old as political philosophy and as new as tomorrow's newspapers headlines. The classic answer in the United States—the people rule—seems so out of accord with the realities of the twentieth century that alternative answers need to be sought. If the people do not rule directly, then perhaps the rulers restrain one another. This more realistic assessment, symbolized in American politics in such slogans as "the separation of powers" and "checks and balances," does not capture all of reality, but it does suggest topics especially worthy of attention. One of the most substantial of these is how the president and the bureaucracy relate to the Congress. For it is in these interactions that many see a primary defense against oligarchy or tyranny.

The simplest and least useful definition of executive-legislative relations holds that the Congress makes the laws and the president and his subordinates carry them out. A more complex and accurate view suggests that the administration proposes most important policies and the Congress reacts by accepting, amending, or rejecting them. The executive branch then implements them. Agenda-setting and policy initiative flow regularly from the executive. Those who assert the decline of the Congress as a viable political competitor cite this fact as evidence to support their position.

Many observers of the Congress discern legislative oversight of the bureaucracy as one means by which competitive leadership can remain a reality in American politics. Even those who question the ability of the Congress to legislate independently often believe that the Congress can perform the key function of overseeing the conduct of the national bureaucracy.

For many reasons, researchers have tended to slight this dimension of executive-legislative relations. Despite its perceived importance, oversight has remained a stepchild; a dearth of analysis is reality. As John Saloma put it, "Congressional participation in, and 'oversight' or review of, the administrative process in government is one of the least understood functions that Congress performs."[1] The significance of the topic provides ample justification for additional attention.

This [selection] attempts to shed some light on congressional oversight of the national bureaucracy. This is its broad purpose. The particular questions to be explored are: Why is it that the Congress acts as it does in its efforts to oversee? And what does the Congress accomplish by its efforts? . . .

Does the Congress Do Enough?

The Congress oversees formally and informally in many ways on a daily basis. It does this selectively. The most visible and perhaps the most effective way is through the appropriations process; the most unnoticed occurs as it considers authorizations, performs casework, and goes about business not directly labeled as oversight.

What this activity accomplishes is not as clear. Opinions about the adequacy of congressional oversight vary. Some critics assert that oversight is minimal. For others, congressional oversight is seen as so pervasive as to cripple the effective functioning of departments and agencies. Whether behavior is adequate is a complex question, for what is adequate depends on what is expected.

The clearest single statement about the oversight that the law requires the Congress to perform comes from that often quoted and seldom heeded statement in the Legislative Reorganization Act of 1946 assigning each standing committee the responsibility to "exercise continuous watchfulness of the execution by the administrative agencies concerned of any laws, the subject matter of which is within the jurisdiction of such committee." There seems to be consensus in the Congress on the principle that extensive and systematic oversight *ought* to be conducted.

That expectation is simply not met. One reason lies in the nature of the expectation. The plain but seldom acknowledged fact is that this task, at least as defined above, is impossible to perform. No amount of congressional dedication and energy, no conceivable increase in the size of committee staffs, and no extraordinary boost in committee budgets will enable the Congress to carry out its oversight obligations in a comprehensive and systematic manner. The job is too large for any combination of members and staff to master completely. Congressmen who feel obligated to obey the letter of the law are doomed to feelings of inadequacy and frustration.

Assessment of whether oversight is sufficient is tied to preferences and choices in three areas: policy preferences on substantive policy issues; definitions of what oversight is; and preferred models of legislative behavior.

Substantive Policy Preferences

Policy preferences and attitudes toward oversight frequently relate in painfully obvious ways. For some, judgments about process are routinely a function of substantive policy preferences. These persons endorse whatever structure or procedure promotes their policy desires at the moment. If a policy position draws its support from the Congress, then extensive and systematic oversight is deemed crucial; if the executive branch most adequately articulates one's policy preferences, then congressmen are deemed badgering bunglers who impose barriers to rational decision-making.

In the controversy over United States involvement in Vietnam in the 1960s, for instance, some strong supporters of presidential prerogatives in foreign affairs turned into congressional partisans as they found their policy preferences reflected more in the behavior of key senators than in the presidency. Judgments about institutions and processes are frequently functions of substantive policy positions. As Seymour Scher put it, "For the committee member there was no abstract meaning in the term 'proper' when used to describe the relationship between the independent commission and the committee. Anything was proper that served to bring the agency . . . in accord with the member's view of how the agency should act."[2]

One close observer of the Congress reached a stronger conclusion: Members seldom even reflect on questions of process outside the context of particular policies and problems. "Our impression is that members have little time and few occasions to reflect on the process. Only when the process itself becomes a policy issue as it did in the post war debates culminating in the Monroney-LaFollette Act and the reorganization of Congress, do members have opportunity to give much thought to such questions."[3]

Definitions

Assessment of oversight is conditioned also by one's perception of what oversight is. If oversight is defined only in terms of formal powers, different conclusions emerge about its adequacy than if informal relationships are taken into account. Those who view oversight as simply an attempt to influence the implementation of legislation through poststatutory investigations will reach different conclusions that will those who are sensitive to oversight performed latently.

How oversight is defined affects what oversight one finds. Writers assess oversight differently at times because they are not talking about the same thing. These differences are also mirrored in vocabulary. Thus the words scrutiny, review, inspection, control, command, supervision, watchfulness, and influence each carry connotations about what is expected.

The Joint Committee on the Organization of Congress worried at some length about appropriate terminology to describe the oversight function. Part of this groping reflected competing conceptions of reality. Their choice of "review" to replace "oversight" clarified very little.

Models of Legislative Behavior

What we expect the Congress to do conditions how we assess congressional behavior. . . . Students of legislative oversight, like most people, are in part prisoners of the pictures in their heads. What we see is partly a function of what we would like to see. What this may mean in practice is shown in table 15-1. . . . Three widely held views of how the Congress should function are set forth in the left-hand column. The column on the right shows the view of oversight that flows from each expectation.

Table 15-1   Theories of congressional functioning and their consequences

Theory of Congressional Functions	Consequences for Oversight
The president and Congress are equals with coordinate powers (Literary Theory).	Congressional oversight of the executive should be facilitated through increased use of detailed committee review of legislation, appointments, and appropriations.
The president initiates: Congress reacts and ratifies (Executive Force Theory).	Congress should grant relatively broad mandates to executive agencies and should cease such harassing tactics as one-year authorizations or required committee clearances for certain executive actions.
Executive Force Theory plus cohesive, responsible political parties (Party Government Theory).	Same as Executive Force Theory.

SOURCE: Adapted from Roger H. Davidson, David M. Kovenock, and Michael K. O'Leary, *Congress in Crisis: Politics and Congressional Reform* (Belmont, Calif.: Wadsworth Publishing Company, Inc., 1966).

In sum, policy preferences, definitions, and models of behavior all shape assessments of the adequacy of the performance of the oversight function.

Research on Legislative Oversight

Anyone attempting to understand the conduct of legislative oversight of the bureaucracy finds relatively little help in the writing about it. Two reasons may be suggested. First, there has been relatively little research on the subject. Second, most of the material published has been concerned primarily with assessing the quality of oversight or in providing descriptions of the formal procedures. . . .

A review of the analytically oriented studies reveals that oversight is neither comprehensive nor systematic. Oversight is performed intermittently. The Congress oversees essentially through its committees and subcommittees, only a few of which have been carefully studied. Moreover, oversight has been studied primarily as a manifest function—hence the conclusion that little is performed. Awareness of the performance of oversight as a latent function leads to a fuller understanding of the process. In addition to extending existing research, this study will probe into some problems in the translation of role expectations into role behavior. Finally, this study seeks to relate the growing body of studies on committees in the Congress to studies on legislative oversight.

If all oversight is conceived as an integral part of the legislative process, explained by variables relevant for other legislative behavior, then one should not treat it as an isolated phenomenon. For example, the analysis developed in this research, although organized differently, is compatible with that of Richard F. Fenno, Jr., in his trailblazing volume, *Congressmen in Committees*.[4] Fenno argues that committee behavior can be explained by attention to the goals of committee members and to the environmental constraints within which the committee functions.

A first step toward analysis is to provide an explicit statement of the subject matter. For purposes of this study, the following working definition will be used: *Legislative oversight is behavior by legislators and their staffs, individually or collectively, which results in an impact, intended or not, on bureaucratic behavior.* The focus is on what congressmen do and why. Hence conventional distinctions such as those between legislation and oversight, hearings and investigations are ignored in favor of an approach which seeks out oversight behavior wherever performed throughout the legislative process and searches for the conditions associated with its presence.

Opportunity Factors

Oversight is most likely if a series of conditioning factors is present. These are called opportunity factors because in their absence, one can predict that little oversight will occur.

Opportunity factors enhance or lessen the potential for oversight irrespective of any single, concrete situation. They establish a presumptive case for the possibility of substantial oversight. However, the presence of intervening variables will weaken attempts at establishing direct linkages between opportunity factors and behavior. Analysis of opportunity factors points to the conditions under which a high proclivity toward oversight will exist. These factors taken together provide an oversight-inducing syndrome. Opportunity factors tend to promote the potential for oversight or to limit the possibility of it. Seven such factors may be identified.

Legal Authority

Most obvious of the opportunity factors is the legal authority of the Congress and its committees. The lawmaking authority of the Congress leads by implication into attempts to oversee the implementation of the law. The authority over government expenditures may stimulate efforts to see that the money appropriated is used as intended by the Congress. The legal division of labor among congressional committees promotes the attention of subunits of the Congress to subunits of the bureaucracy. The provision of the legislative Reorganization Act of 1946 assigning each standing committee a responsibility to "exercise continuous watchfulness of the execution by the administrative agencies concerned of any laws, the subject matter of which is within the jurisdiction of such committee" provides an adequate legal base for almost any efforts at oversight.

Law legitimates substantial oversight activity by the Congress. But in a few situations, the absence of such authority can be a handicap to effective oversight.[5] In general, the legal power of legislatures to oversee is a relevant but rarely decisive factor in explaining behavior. Authority is normally larger than its exercise. What seems to matter more is the combination of a desire to oversee and resources to do so.

A Senate Committee staff member pointed out:

> In some cases, committee staff members or congressmen themselves asked for material from the General Accounting Office that they had received at some previous time and had discarded. Now, because of new sets of circumstances and new interests on their part and because of new axes to grind, they ask for the material. They ask for it again, not because it suggested things to them originally, but rather because they *now* have a use for it.

Legal capacity and a vague sense of obligation provide an inadequate explanation of oversight activities. Oversight flows more from concrete felt needs than from general obligations, legal or otherwise. . . .

Staff Resources

A second opportunity factor is that of staff resources for congressional decision makers. Access to staff and the willingness to use it are often important preconditions to substantial oversight. Oversight without effective staff work is normally impossible. But the amount of oversight performed does not depend mainly on the size of the staff available. Adequate staff is a necessary precondition to oversight but is not a sufficient one.[6] Other factors such as member priorities seem more basic. As John F. Manley notes, "They [the staff] take more cues from the formal policy makers than they give."[7]

The comments of a highly regarded staff member of a Senate committee support a related point:

> Basically the staff responds to member requests and member pressures instead of generating masses of material that might be ignored. When I first came on the committee as a staff member, I prepared many studies. Other staff people did the same. Our general idea was to do exhaustive work to prepare background materials that the members could later use for investigations and other purposes. We would work for six months on a project, spend hours and hours on it, and then it would come before the committee to be considered for investigation. One committee member would say, "Oh, there is nothing here. Let's forget it." After many experiences of this sort, the staff adopted a more passive role. The staff essentially works on the proposition that it will respond to member pressures.

Professional staff members will usually mirror the policy and process orientations of the congressmen who hire them and direct their behavior. A chairman passive about oversight is unlikely to have professional staff members who give it top priority. The senior minority member on a committee may regard the oversight function as unimportant, or he may lessen his efforts in exchange for benefits derived from the majority. The minority staff members then tend to reflect his views. Other factors can outweigh partisan opposition.

Subject Matter

A third opportunity factor is the subject matter of a policy or program. The more technical and complex the subject matter is perceived to be, the less the likelihood of oversight. Only a few members of the Congress are experts in *any* area of bureaucratic operations. Those who are, master very few. Fulfilling the obligations of a congressman requires more time than a member has available. Ease of immersion into a subject will then be one factor governing his activity. What is particularly important is how complex the subject seems to the participants involved.

How a subject area is organized within the executive branch also shapes oversight. An activity centered in one agency or department may be much easier to follow than one spread over several departments and agencies. According to one staff member:

> Beyond those factors related to the time and energy and inclinations of the congressional committees themselves, the dispersal of programs in the executive department raises problems of oversight. A committee which passes a bill concerned with a given area may find that the programs to be administered are involved in several departments separately and that serious investigation of the work involved in carrying out the legislation would involve work with several departments. This is simply too time-consuming and too complex to be undertaken without massive amounts of time and energy, and this is more than the committee staff generally has available, so oversight is not performed.

The visibility of the issue is a third aspect of subject matter relevant to oversight. Few congressmen can resist an opportunity for promoting their careers. Hence, the greater the likelihood of increased political visibility from a particular exercise of oversight, the more probable it is that oversight will be undertaken. A few members of the Congress are noted both for their impact on policy and for their anonymity, but most congressmen follow strategies that will enhance their visibility to the public.

Few issues are highly visible to most citizens. Congressmen think rather of their visibility to groups that are important to them. Which issues meet that test is related to the nature of each constituency, personal values, and career aspirations.

Committee Structure

A fourth opportunity factor is that of committee structure. Is the committee centralized or decentralized? How much latitude does the chairman permit or how much is he forced to accept? A highly centralized committee is unlikely to conduct much oversight without the active approval of the chairman. A decentralized committee — one in which power over money, staff, and program is largely in the hands of subcommittee chairmen or others — enhances the opportunity for oversight simply because decision-making is dispersed.[8]

The importance of the congressional committee in oversight is simply that almost all oversight occurs there. The Congress as a whole does not oversee, nor does the House or the Senate. The particular committee or subcommittee rather than the parent body provides the most useful focus for analysis.

Status on a Committee

A fifth opportunity factor is status on a particular committee. The higher the status of the member on a committee, the more opportunity he will have to influence oversight. Occasionally oversight flows from the efforts of junior members, but the normal correlate to oversight is high status, such as that of a committee or subcommittee chairman. The ability of a junior member to influence the conduct of oversight is tied to the preferences of his committee or subcommittee chairman.

The connections between status and opportunity pose no mystery. Access to staff illustrates the linkage. Committee chairmen, subcommittee chairmen, and ranking minority members usually have the greatest opportunity to tap staff services. In theory, the staff members work for the entire committee; in practice, the use of staff time is determined from the top.

Relations with the Executive Branch

Legislative concern with executive behavior rests on factors other than profound policy and constitutional differences. A sixth set of opportunity factors reflects this reality. As James Robinson points out, congressional attitudes about bureaucratic behavior relate to the satisfaction congressmen feel with their treatment by an executive unit.[9]

Congressional behavior is also tied to whether congressmen have confidence in key personnel of the relevant executive departments. An important factor in creating a desire for oversight is the regard, high or low, which key decision makers in the Congress have for top officials in an executive department. The actions of one executive official are grist for legislative action; the same deed in the hands of another, for legislative acquiesence or approval. Thus Allen Drury records in *A Senate Journal:*

> March 4, 1945. Fred Vinson, one of the congress darlings and an able man in his own right, has been nominated federal loan administrator to succeed Jesse [Jones]. This is greeted with great approval in the Senate, where Fred is a deservedly popular man. All talk of separating the vast, fantastic and inexcusable powers of the agency has of course automatically stopped with the appointment of a fellow everybody likes.[10]

Or, as Richard Fenno notes:

> Perhaps the most consistent thread in subcommittee decision making is the sampling they do for the purpose of deciding whether or not to tender their confidence to an agency. Given the fact that their information is imperfect and given their large zone of uncertainty about what the agency "really" needs, committee members must necessarily act on the basis of confidence, trust, or faith in agency officials. What they want to know, above all else, about an agency or administrator is "Can I believe what he tells me? Will he do what he says he will do?" So, they sample for information that will determine the degree of confidence they should have in an agency—by "sizing up" an administrator at the hearings, by asking detailed and specific questions of witnesses to see if they know their job, by checking agency performance against last year's promises, and committee directives. If subcommittee members are satisfied with the results of their sampling, they will willingly take agency statements as fact. If they are not, if the agency does not pass the test, legislators will remain extraordinarily suspicious. Confidence is the cumulative product, obviously, of countless interchanges, formal and informal, between committee and agency personnel over extended periods of time.[11]

And according to a Democratic member of the House:

> It isn't just the "Executive" that is involved; it is the plan and its spokesman. If he inspires confidence even though he is of the opposition party you trust him and feel he is not slipping a knife between your ribs or destroying something you believe in, if you think he knows what he is talking about you cooperate with him. If you don't trust him or believe he doesn't know what he is doing you treat

him with a contempt he has earned. I saw this happen to Roosevelt's executives when the Democrats had substantial majorities. He had weak executives and they couldn't carry a paper bag down the Hill.[12]

Party affiliation is a third aspect of executive-legislative relations relevant for oversight. A congressman of the president's political party is less likely to be concerned with oversight than a member of the opposition party.[13] In 1966, Representative Florence P. Dwyer (R-New Jersey), ranking minority member of the House Government Operations Committee, sponsored a bill to set up a special oversight committee controlled by the minority party when the same political party controlled both houses of the Congress. She noted:

> Although the authority of Congress to investigate the operations of the executive branch is clear and undisputed, existing procedures are demonstrably inadequate when the same party controls both branches of the government. It is unrealistic to expect the congressional members of a political party, regardless of the party, to subject executive branch officials of the same party to the kind of complete and searching scrutiny required for the proper exercise of congressional oversight activity.[14]

All legislative decisions are not party decisions. Yet, as David Truman has convincingly demonstrated, the fact that the parties are neither monolithic nor diametrically opposed on all major policy issues does not mean that party has little relevance in legislative decision-making.[15]

Member Priorities

Member priorities form a seventh opportunity factor. Each member is faced with a variety of obligations that are legitimate, important, and demanding of time and energy. In principle, he should be working hard at all of them. In fact, since he does not weigh them equally, he is unlikely to give them equal attention. He may attend to all of the areas that he is supposed to cover, but he probably will not handle all of them well. As one respected legislative assistant put it, "There is a mystique in the House of Representatives that representatives must do everything. The reality of the matter is that representatives simply can't do it. Members are caught up in this mystique themselves. This gives them the feeling that they should be doing all of these things and they talk as if they are, whereas in fact, they really can't."

In making his choices about what to do, each congressman applies his own standards of relevance. Some things count for more than other things. Problems seen as less pressing may be recognized but may remain untouched. In these calculations, oversight frequently falls into the semineglected category. Choice, not accident, governs this decision.

The crucial question is with what skill and to what subject areas the congressman will devote his major energies. In principle, a congressman is always busy; in practice, the way he responds to intrusions and pressures defines his working life. In the words of Representative William Green (D-Pennsylvania), "Each member is busy with day-to-day activities. No member has time to look out for problems or to try and create problems. We are always busy, but we can do more if we have to. The schedule is flexible, and if sensitive problems impinge on the member, the member can handle them, but he does not start a systematic search to look for problems." Representative Richard Bolling (D-Missouri) argues similarly that congressmen are pretty much free to organize their time as they wish.[16] Contemplation of what he ought to do in a pressure-free context seldom molds his daily routine.

All members of the Congress are involved in a myriad of activities. The pressures for action are often substantial. The excuses for inaction can be equally impressive. In truth, a congressman may simply lack interest in many aspects of governmental activity. He is unlikely to generate much oversight activity in such subject areas. But even where his concern is clear, choices still have to be made in the context of a shortage of time, energy, and other resources such as his status on a committee or subcommittee. The higher the priority the congressman gives to an area of bureaucratic activity, the greater the possibility that he will engage in oversight in that policy area. As Seymour Scher convincingly points out, the primary calculus is that of gains and losses to the congressman. In such a calculus, oversight often has fewer potential payoffs than other activities.[17] According to an unusually knowledgeable staff member:

> Members become concerned with the abstract obligation to oversee largely as they feel they can make political record or on occasions where they differ in policy orientation from the bureaucrats involved.
>
> The apparent abstract concern with oversight as a function of the Congress is usually only a device to gloss over personal or policy differences or the desire to build a record.

The major attention of the congressman will tend to be elsewhere. How much oversight captures his concern relates to its contribution to his political career. In the words of a sophisticated staff assistant to a senator, "Specialists in departmental interference must judge both the merits of the case and the costs in time, effort, in their own or the congressman's 'credit' with the agency, of attempting to achieve a given solution."[18]

As one study of the Senate Banking and Currency Committee concluded:

> Senior members of Banking and Currency, those in the best position to make the committee active in oversight, often yield to alternative demands on their time. . . . Non-banking and current responsibility, in conjunction with the lack of compelling interest in committee business on the part of the senior members, have restricted the committee as an oversight unit.[19]

An examination of each of these seven opportunity factors leads to the creation of hypotheses about the conduct of oversight. No single hypothesis, however, provides a sufficiently comprehensive explanation of the conditions under which the likelihood for oversight is advanced or retarded. There seems to be no single pattern which explains legislative oversight in all circumstances. There are only common factors which combine in different ways under specified sets of circumstances.

Preliminary analysis of these opportunity factors does yield an oversight-maximizing syndrome. Oversight is most likely to occur when the following are present: a legal basis for committee or individual activity, and money available; adequate staff resources defined in terms of numbers, skill, and attitudes; subject matter that is not unusually technical or complex enough to require special expertise; activities involved that are centralized in one executive department; an issue with high visibility and large political payoffs; decentralized committee operations or a chairman of the full committee who is a strong advocate of oversight in a given area; a desire of important people, usually those with committee or subcommittee chairmanships, to oversee; unhappiness of key committee members with the conduct of executive personnel, a lack of confidence in top executive personnel, or personal antipathy toward them; control of the house of the Congress involved by one political party and of the presidency by the other; poor treatment of members of the Congress, especially those on relevant committees, by executive officials; a member's strong interest in the work of his committee and the particular subject matter at hand; and committee positions highly sought by persons with more than average competence. In general, a minimizing syndrome is obtained by reversing these factors.

But what if these factors produce mixed results or indicate a high proclivity toward oversight? Does this mean that comprehensive and systematic oversight automatically results? Not necessarily. What, then, turns proclivity into behavior? Conversion factors help explain this.

Conversion Factors

Conversion factors define the most common situations in which propensities are converted into behavior. They seem to account most directly and immediately for specific oversight efforts.

What leads legislators to convert their opportunities into actual behavior? Sharp disagreement by congressmen with a new executive policy or with a substantial change in an existing policy provides strong stimuli to oversight even on subjects where scrutiny was modest previously. The more the legislator agrees with the program being implemented, the less likely he is to want to oversee; policy disagreement is a major stimulus to oversight.[20]

The most unpredictable of conversion factors is the impact of external events. A sudden crisis may stimulate attempts at oversight. A genuine scandal, or the appearance of one, may provide a stimulus sufficient to goad a congressman or a committee into action. A report by a constituent of how an agency treated him outrageously may promote congressional interest. Attention by a congressman is especially likely when the protestors are significant organized groups or constituents important to the congressman, or are supported by persons whom he respects or fears.

The impact of an external event may override legislative routines. Several pieces of legislation passed in the 1960s can be related to particular events, such as the assassinations of Senator Robert Kennedy and Martin Luther King, Jr. Just as a traumatic event can rescue stalled legislation, so can it lead to oversight efforts.

Crisis does not guarantee congressional action. No massive congressional investigation followed on the heels of the total collapse of postal service in Chicago in October 1966. In retrospect, though, the incident did precipitate pressure for reform from the executive branch which was later reflected in Congress. Congressional attention does not automatically follow any spectacular incident, but the presence of such an incident tends to convert predispositions into behavior. To paraphrase a well-worn saying, the Congress in crisis may well be the Congress at work. Still, policy by paroxysm is not the norm. . . .

Notes

[1]*Congress and the New Politics* (Boston: Little, Brown and Company, 1969), p. 130. For similar statements, see Roger H. Davidson, David M. Kovenock, and Michael K. O'Leary, *Congress in Crisis: Politics and Congressional Reform* (Belmont, Calif.: Wadsworth Publishing Company, Inc., 1966), p. 174; Ralph K. Huitt, "The Internal Distribution of Influence: The Senate," in *The Congress and America's Future,* by the American Assembly, ed., David B. Truman (Englewood Cliffs, N.J.: Prentice-Hall, Inc., 1965), p. 94; and Dale Vinyard, "The Congressional Committees on Small Business: Pattern of Legislative Committee-Executive Agency Relations," *Western Political Quarterly,* 21, no. 3 (September 1968), pp. 391, 399.

[2]"Congressional Committee Members as Independent Agency Overseers: A Case Study," *American Political Science Review,* 54, no. 4 (December 1960), p. 919.

[3]James A. Robinson, *Congress and Foreign Policy-Making: A Study in Legislative Influence and Initiative,* 1st ed. (Homewood, Ill.: The Dorsey Press, Inc., 1961), p. 229.

[4](Boston: Little, Brown and Company, 1973).

[5]For an example, see Dale Vinyard, "Congressional Committees on Small Business," *Midwest Journal of Political Science,* 10, no. 3 (August 1966), p. 376.

[6]Samuel C. Patterson related the ability of a staff to provide information more to professionalization than to size ("The Professional Staffs of Congressional Committees," *Administrative Science Quarterly,* 15, no. 1 [March 1970], p. 35).

[7]"Congressional Staff and Public Policy-Making: The Joint Committee on Internal Revenue Taxation," *Journal of Politics,* 30, no. 4 (November 1968), p. 1067.

[8]A useful discussion of subcommittees is found in George Goodwin, Jr., *The Little Legislatures: Committees of Congress* (Amherst: University of Massachusetts Press, 1970), p. 45–63.

[9]Robinson, *Congress and Foreign Policy-Making,* pp. 168–90.

[10](New York: McGraw-Hill Co., Inc., 1963), p. 375.

[11]Richard F. Fenno, Jr., "The Impact of PPBS on the Congressional Appropriation Process," in *Information Support, Program Budgeting, and the Congress,* ed. R. L. Chartran, K. Janda, and M. Hugo (New York: Spartan Books, 1968), pp. 181–82.

[12]Quoted in Charles L. Clapp, *The Congressman: His Work as He Sees It* (Washington, D.C.: The Brookings Institution, 1963), p. 278.

[13]For an example, see Thomas A. Henderson, *Congressional Oversight of Executive Agencies: A Study of the House Committee on Government Operations* (Gainesville: University of Florida Press, 1970), p. 42.

[14]Press release, July 25, 1966.

[15]*The Congressional Party* (New York: John Wiley & Sons, Inc., 1959), pp. 279–319.

[16]*Power in the House* (New York: E. P. Dutton & Co., Inc. 1968), p. 19.

[17]Seymour Scher, "Conditions for Legislation Control," *Journal of Politics,* 25, no. 3 (August 1963), pp. 528–29, 531–32.

[18]Kenneth E. Gray, "Congressional Interference in Administration," in *Cooperation and Conflict,* ed., D. J. Elazar, R. B. Carroll, E. L. Levine, and D. St. Angelo (Ithaca, Ill.: F. E. Peacock Publishers, Inc., 1969), p. 525.

[19]John Bibby and Roger Davidson, *On Capitol Hill* (New York: Holt, Rinehart and Winston, Inc., 1967), p. 189.

[20]For example, see Ira Sharkansky, "An Appropriations Subcommittee and Its Client Agencies," *American Political Science Review,* 59, no. 3 (September 1965), p. 628.

Selection 16 Constituency Influence in Congress

Warren E. Miller
Donald E. Stokes

Substantial constituency influence over the lower house of Congress is commonly thought to be both a normative principle and a factual truth of American government. From their draft constitution we may assume the Founding Fathers expected it, and many political scientists feel, regretfully, that the Framers' wish has come all too true.[1] Nevertheless, much of the evidence of constituency control rests on inference. The fact that our House of Representatives, especially by comparison with the House of Commons, has irregular party voting does not of itself indicate that Congressmen deviate from party in response to local pressure. And even more, the fact that many Congressmen *feel*

Reprinted from *The American Political Science Review* 57 (1963), pp. 45–56, by permission of the authors and publisher. (Research made possible by grants from the Rockefeller Foundation and the Social Science Research Council.)

pressure from home does not of itself establish that the local constituency is performing any of the acts that a reasonable definition of control would imply.

I. Constituency Control in the Normative Theory of Representation

Control by the local constituency is at one pole of *both* the great normative controversies about representation that have arisen in modern times. It is generally recognized that constituency control is opposite to the conception of representation associated with Edmund Burke. Burke wanted the representative to serve the constituency's *interest* but not its will, and the extent to which the representative should be compelled by electoral sanctions to follow the "mandate" of his constituents has been at the heart of the ensuing controversy as it has continued for a century and a half.[2]

Constituency control also is opposite to the conception of government by responsible national parties. This is widely seen, yet the point is rarely connected with normative discussions of representation. Indeed, it is remarkable how little attention has been given to the model of representation implicit in the doctrine of a "responsible two-party system." When the subject of representation is broached among political scientists the classical argument between Burke and his opponents is likely to come at once to mind. So great is Burke's influence that the antithesis he proposed still provides the categories of thought used in contemporary treatments of representation despite the fact that many students of politics today would advocate a relationship between the representative and the constituency that fits *neither* position of the mandate-independence controversy.

The conception of representation implicit in the doctrine of responsible parties shares the idea of popular control with the instructed-delegate model. Both are versions of popular sovereignty. But "the people" of the responsible two-party system are conceived in terms of a national rather than a local constituency. Candidates for legislative office appeal to the electorate in terms of a *national* party program and leadership, to which, if elected, they will be committed. Expressions of policy preference by the local district are reduced to endorsements of one or another of these programs, and the local district retains only the arithmetical significance that whichever party can rally to its program the greater number of supporters in the district will control its legislative seat.

No one tradition of representation has entirely dominated American practice. Elements of the Burkean, instructed-delegate, and responsible party models can all be found in our political life. Yet if the American system has elements of all three, a good deal depends on how they are combined. Especially critical is the question whether different models of representation apply to different public issues. Is the saliency of legislative action to the public so different in quality and degree on different issues that the legislator is subject to very different constraints from his constituency? Does the legislator have a single generalized mode of response to his constituency that is rooted in a normative belief about the representative's role or does the same legislator respond to his constituency differently on different issues? More evidence is needed on matters so fundamental to our system.

II. An Empirical Study of Representation

To extend what we know of representation in the American Congress the Survey Research Center of The University of Michigan interviewed the incumbent Congressman, his non-incumbent opponent (if any), and a sample of constituents in each of 116 congressional districts, which were themselves a probability sample of all districts.[3] These interviews, conducted immediately after the congressional election of 1958, explored a wide range of attitudes and perceptions held by the individuals who play the reciprocal roles of the representative relation in national government. The distinguishing feature of this research is, of course, that it sought direct information from both constituent and legislator (actual and aspiring). To this fund of comparative interview data has been added information about the roll call votes of our sample of Congressmen and the political and social characteristics of the districts they represent.

Many students of politics, with excellent reason, have been sensitive to possible ties between representative and constituent that have little to do with issues of public policy. For example, ethnic identifications may cement a legislator in the affections of his district, whatever (within limits) his stands on issues. And many Congressmen keep their tenure of office secure by skillful provision of district benefits ranging from free literature to major federal projects. In the full study of which this analysis is part we have explored several bases of constituency support that have little to do with policy issues. Nevertheless, the question how the representative should make up his mind on legislative issues is what the classical arguments over representation are all about, and we have given a central place to a comparison of the policy preferences of constituents and Representatives and to a causal analysis of the relation between the two.

In view of the electorate's scanty information about government it was not all clear in advance that such a comparison could be made. Some of the more buoyant advocates of popular sovereignty have regarded the citizen as a kind of kibitzer who looks over the shoulder of his representative at the legislative game. Kibitzer and player may disagree as to which card should be played, but they were at least thought to share a common understanding of what the alternatives are.

No one familiar with the findings of research on mass electorates could accept this view of the citizen. Far from looking over the shoulder of their Congressmen at the legislative game, most Americans are almost totally uninformed about legislative issues in Washington. At best the average citizen may be said to have some general ideas about how the country should be run, which he is able to use in responding to particular questions about what the government ought to do. For example, survey studies have shown that most people have a general (though differing) conception of how far government should go to achieve social and economic welfare objectives and that these convictions fix their response to various particular questions about actions government might take.[4]

What makes it possible to compare the policy preferences of constituents and Representatives despite the public's low awareness of legislative affairs is the fact that Congressmen themselves respond to many issues in terms of fairly broad evaluative dimensions. Undoubtedly policy alternatives are judged in the executive agencies and the specialized committees of the Congress by criteria that are relatively complex and specific to the policies at issue. But a good deal of evidence goes to show that when proposals come before the House as a whole they are judged on the basis of more general evaluative dimensions.[5] For example, most Congressmen, too, seem to have a general conception of how far government should go in the area of domestic social and economic welfare, and these general positions apparently orient their roll call votes on a number of particular social welfare issues.

It follows that such a broad evaluative dimension can be used to compare the policy preferences of constituents and Representatives despite the low state of the public's information about politics. In this study three such dimensions have been drawn from our voter interviews and from congressional interviews and roll call records. As suggested above, one of these has to do with approval of government action in the social welfare field, the primary domestic issue of the New Deal-Fair Deal (and New Frontier) eras. A second dimension has to do with support for American involvement in foreign affairs, a latter-day version of the isolationist-internationalist continuum. A third dimension has to do with approval of federal action to protect the civil rights of Negroes.[6]

Because our research focused on these three dimensions, our analysis of constituency influence is limited to these areas of policy. No point has been more energetically or usefully made by those who have sought to clarify the concepts of power and influence than the necessity of specifying the acts *with respect to which* one actor has power or influence or control over another.[7] Therefore, the scope or range of influence for our analysis is the collective legislative issues falling within our three policy domains. We are not able to say how much control the local constituency may or may not have over *all* actions of its Representative, and there may well be pork-barrel issues or other matters of peculiar relevance to the district on which the relation of Congressmen to constituency is quite distinctive. However, few observers of contemporary politics would regard the issues of government provision of social and economic welfare, of American involvement in world affairs, and of federal action in behalf of the Negro as constituting a trivial range of action. Indeed, these domains together include most of the great issues that have come before Congress in recent years.

In each policy domain we have used the procedures of cumulative scaling, as developed by Louis Guttman and others, to order our samples of Congressmen, of opposing candidates, and of voters. In each domain Congressmen were ranked once according to their roll call votes in the House and again according to the attitudes they revealed in our confidential interviews. These two orderings are by no means identical, nor are the discrepancies due simply to uncertainties of measurement.[8] Opposing candidates also were ranked in each policy domain according to the attitudes they revealed in our interviews. The nationwide sample of constituents was ordered in each domain, and by averaging the attitude scores of all constituents living in the same districts, whole constituencies were ranked on each dimension so that the views of Congressmen could be compared with those of their constituencies.[9] Finally, by considering only the constituents in each district who share some characteristic (voting for the incumbent, say) we were able to order these fractions of districts so that the opinions of Congressmen could be compared with those, for example, of the dominant electoral elements of their districts.

In each policy domain, crossing the rankings of Congressmen and their constituencies gives an empirical measure of the extent of policy agreement between legislator and district.[10] In the period of our research this procedure reveals very different degrees of policy congruence across the three issue domains. On questions of social and economic welfare there is considerable agreement between Representative and district, expressed by a correlation of approximately 0.3. The coefficient is, of course, very much less than the limiting value of 1.0, indicating that a number of Congressmen are, relatively speaking, more or less "liberal" than their districts. However, on the question of foreign involvement there is no discernible agreement between legislator and district whatever. Indeed, as if to emphasize the point, the coefficient expressing this relation is slightly negative (-0.09), although not significantly so in a statistical sense. It is in the domain of civil rights that the rankings of Congressmen and constituencies most nearly agree. When we took our measurements in the late 1950s the correlation of congressional roll call behavior with constituency opinion on questions affecting the Negro was nearly 0.6.

The description of policy agreement that these three simple correlations give can be a starting-point for a wide range of analyses. For example, the significance of party competition in the district for policy representation can be explored by comparing the agreement between district and Congressman with the agreement between the district and the Congressman's non-incumbent opponent. Alternatively, the significance of choosing Representatives from single-member districts by popular majority can be explored by comparing the agreement between the Congressman and his own supporters with the agreement between the Congressman and the supporters of his opponent. Taking *both* party competition and majority rule into account magnifies rather spectacularly some of the coefficients reported here. This is most true in the domain of social welfare, where attitudes both of candidates and of voters are most polarized along party lines. Whereas the correlation between the constituency majority and congressional role call votes is nearly +0.4 on social welfare policy, the correlation of the district majority with the non-incumbent candidate is −0.4. This difference, amounting to almost 0.8, between these two coefficients is an indicator of what the dominant electoral element of the constituency gets on the average by choosing the Congressman it has and excluding his opponent from office.[11]

These three coefficients are also the starting-point for a causal analysis of the relation of constituency to representative, the main problem of this paper. At least on social welfare and Negro rights a measurable degree of congruence is found between district and legislator. Is this agreement due to constituency influence in Congress, or is it to be attributed to other causes? If this question is to have a satisfactory answer the conditions that are necessary and sufficient to assure constituency control must be stated and compared with the available empirical evidence.

III. The Conditions of Constituency Influence

Broadly speaking, the constituency can control the policy actions of the Representative in two alternative ways. The first of these is for the district to choose a Representative who so shares its views that in following his own convictions he does his constituents' will. In this case district opinion and the Congressman's actions are connected through the Representative's own policy attitudes. The second means of constituency control is for the Congressman to follow his (at least tolerably accurate) perceptions of district attitude in order to win re-election. In this case constituency opinion and the Congressman's actions are connected through his perception of what the district wants.[12]

These two paths of constituency control are presented schematically in figure 16-1. As the figure suggests, each path has two steps, one connecting the constituency's attitude with an "intervening" attitude or perception, the other connecting this attitude or perception with the Representative's roll call behavior. Out of respect for the processes by which the human actor achieves cognitive congruence we have also drawn arrows between the two intervening factors, since the Congressman probably tends to see his district as having the same opinion as his own and also tends, over time, to bring his own opinion into line with the district's. The inclusion of these arrows calls attention to two other possible influence paths, each consisting of three steps, although these additional paths will turn out to be of relatively slight importance empirically.

Neither of the main influence paths of figure 16-1 will connect the final roll call vote to the constituency's views if either of its steps is blocked. From this,

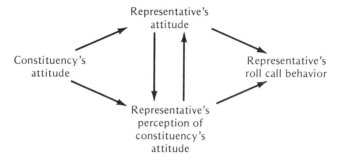

Figure 16-1   Connections between a constituency's attitude and its representative's roll call behavior

two necessary conditions of constituency influence can be stated: *first*, the Representative's votes in the House must agree substantially with his own policy views or his perceptions of the district's views, and not be determined entirely by other influences to which the Congressman is exposed; and, *second*, the attitudes or perceptions governing the Representative's acts must correspond, at least imperfectly, to the district's actual opinions. It would be difficult to describe the relation of constituency to Representative as one of control unless these conditions are met.[13]

Yet these two requirements are not sufficient to assure control. A *third* condition must also be satisfied: the constituency must in some measure take the policy views of candidates into account in choosing a Representative. If it does not, agreement between district and Congressman may arise for reasons that cannot rationally be brought within the idea of control. For example, such agreement may simply reflect the fact that a Representative drawn from a given area is likely, by pure statistical probability, to share its dominant values, without his acceptance or rejection of these ever having been a matter of consequence to his electors.

IV. Evidence of Control: Congressional Attitudes and Perceptions

How well are these conditions met in the relation of American Congressmen to their constituents? There is little question that the first is substantially satisfied; the evidence of our research indicates that members of the House do in fact vote both their own policy views and their perceptions of their constituents' views, at least on issues of social welfare, foreign involvement and civil rights. If these two intervening factors are used to predict roll call votes, the prediction is quite successful. Their multiple correlation with roll call position is 0.7 for social welfare, 0.6 for foreign involvement, and 0.9 for civil rights; the last figure is especially persuasive. What is more, both the Congressman's own convictions and his perceptions of district opinion make a distinct contribution to his roll call behavior. In each of the three domains the predictions of roll call votes is surer if it is made from both factors rather than from either alone.

Lest the strong influence that the Congressman's views and his perception of district views have on roll call behavior appear somehow foreordained—and, consequently, this finding seem a trivial one—it is worth taking a sidewise glance at the potency of possible other forces on the Representative's vote. In the area of foreign policy, for example, a number of Congressmen are disposed to follow the administration's advice, whatever they or their districts think. For those who are, the multiple correlation and roll call behavior with the Representative's own foreign policy views and his perception of district views is a mere 0.2. Other findings could be cited to support the point that the influence of the Congressman's own preferences and those he attributes to the district is extremely variable. Yet in the House as a whole over the three policy domains the influence of these forces is quite strong.

The connections of congressional attitudes and perceptions with actual constituency opinion are weaker. If policy agreement between district and Representative is moderate and variable across the policy domains, as it is, this is to be expected much more in terms of the second condition of constituency control than the first. The Representative's attitudes and perceptions most nearly match true opinion in his district on the issues of Negro rights. Reflecting the charged and polarized nature of this area, the correlation of actual district opinion with perceived opinion is greater than 0.6, and the correlation of district attitude with the Representative's own attitude is nearly 0.4, as shown by table 16-1. But the comparable correlations for foreign involvement are much smaller—indeed almost negligible. And the coefficients for social welfare are also smaller, although a detailed presentation of findings in this area would show that the Representative's perceptions and attitudes are more strongly associated with the attitude of his electoral *majority* than they are with the attitudes of the constituency as a whole.

Table 16-1   Correlations of constituency attitudes

Policy Domain	Correlation of Constituency Attitude with	
	Representative's Perception of Constituency Attitude	Representative's Own Attitude
Social welfare	.17	.21
Foreign involvement	.19	.06
Civil rights	.63	.39

Knowing this much about the various paths that may lead, directly or indirectly, from constituency attitude to roll call vote, we can assess their relative importance. Since the alternative influence chains have links of unequal strength, the full chains will not in general be equally strong, and these differences are of great importance in the relation of Representative to constituency. For the domain of civil rights figure 16-2 assembles all the intercorrelations of the variables of our system. As the figure shows, the root correlation of constituency attitude with roll call behavior in this domain is 0.57. How much of this policy congruence can be accounted for by the influence path involving the Representative's attitude? And how much by the path involving his perception of the constituency opinion? When the intercorrelations of the system are interpreted in the light of what we assume its causal structure to be, it is influence passing through the Congressman's perception of the district's views that is found to be preeminently important.[14] Under the least favorable assumption as to its importance, this path is found to account for more than twice as much of the variance of roll call behavior as the paths involving the Representative's own attitude.[15] However, when this same procedure is applied to our social welfare data, the results suggest that the direct connection of constituency and roll call through the Congressman's own attitude is the most important of the alternative paths.[16] The reversal of the relative importance of the two paths as we move from civil rights to social welfare is one of the most striking findings of this analysis.

V. Evidence of Control: Electoral Behavior

Of the three conditions of constituency influence, the requirement that the electorate take account of the policy positions of the candidates is the hardest to match with empirical evidence. Indeed, given the limited information the

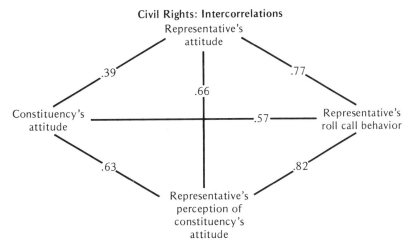

Figure 16-2   Intercorrelations of variables pertaining to civil rights

average voter carries to the polls, the public might be thought incompetent to perform any task of appraisal. Of constituents living in congressional districts where there was a contest between a Republican and a Democrat in 1958, less than one in five said they had read or heard something about both candidates, and well over half conceded they had read or heard nothing about either. And these proportions are not much better when they are based only on the part of the sample, not much more than half, that reported voting for Congress in 1958. The extent of awareness of the candidates among voters is indicated in table 16-2. As the table shows, even of the portion of the public that was sufficiently interested to vote, almost half had read or heard nothing about either candidate.

Just how low a hurdle our respondents had to clear in saying they had read or heard something about a candidate is indicated by detailed qualitative analysis of the information constituents *were* able to associate with congressional candidates. Except in rare cases, what the voters "knew" was confined to diffuse evaluative judgments about the candidate: "he's a good man," "he understands the problems," and so forth. Of detailed information about policy stands not more than a chemical trace was found. Among the comments about the candidates given in response to an extended series of free-answer questions, less than two percent had to do with stands in our three policy domains; indeed, only about three comments in every hundred had to do with legislative issues of *any* description.[17]

This evidence that the behavior of the electorate is largely unaffected by knowledge of the policy positions of the candidates is complemented by evidence about the forces that do shape the voters' choices among congressional candidates. The primary basis of voting in American congressional elections is identification with party. In 1958 only one vote in twenty was cast by persons without any sort of party loyalty. And among those who did have a party identification, only one in ten voted against their party. As a result, something like 84 percent of the vote that year was cast by party identifiers voting their usual party line. What is more, traditional party voting is seldom connected with

Table 16-2   Awareness of congressional candidates among voters, 1958

		Read or Heard Something about Incumbent[a]		
		Yes	No	
Read or Heard	Yes	24	5	29
Something about				
Non-Incumbent	No	25	46	71
		49	51	100%

[a]In order to include all districts where the House seat was contested in 1958 this table retains ten constituencies in which the incumbent Congressman did not seek re-election. Candidates of the retiring incumbent's party in these districts are treated here as if they were incumbents. Were these figures to be calculated only for constituencies in which an incumbent sought re-election, no entry in this four-fold table would differ from that given by more than two percent.

current legislative issues. As the party loyalists in a nationwide sample of voters told us what they liked and disliked about the parties in 1958, only a small fraction of the comments (about 15 percent) dealt with current issues of public policy.[18]

Yet the idea of reward or punishment at the polls for legislative stands is familiar to members of Congress, who feel that they and their records are quite visible to their constituents. Of our sample of Congressmen who were opposed for re-election in 1958, more than four-fifths said the outcome in their districts had been strongly influenced by the electorate's response to their records and personal standing. Indeed, this belief is clear enough to present a notable contradiction: Congressmen feel that their individual legislative actions may have considerable impact on the electorate, yet some simple facts about the Representative's salience to his constituents imply that this could hardly be true.

In some measure this contradiction is to be explained by the tendency of Congressmen to overestimate their visibility to the local public, a tendency that reflects the difficulties of the Representative in forming a correct judgment of constituent opinion. The communication most Congressmen have with their districts inevitably puts them in touch with organized groups and with individuals who are relatively well informed about politics. The Representative knows his constituents mostly from dealing with people who *do* write letters, who *will* attend meetings, who *have* an interest in his legislative stands. As a result, his sample of contacts with a constituency of several hundred thousand people is heavily biased: even the contacts he apparently makes at random are likely to be with people who grossly overrepresent the degree of political information and interest in the constituency as a whole.

But the contradiction is also to be explained by several aspects of the Representative's electoral situation that are of great importance to the question of constituency influence. The first of these is implicit in what has already been said. Because of the pervasive effects of party loyalties, no candidate for Congress starts from scratch in putting together an electoral majority. The Congressman is a dealer in increments and margins. He starts with a stratum of hardened party voters, and if the stratum is broad enough, he can have a measurable influence on his chance of survival simply by attracting a small additional element of the electorate — or by not losing a larger one. Therefore, his record may have a very real bearing on his electoral success or failure without most of his constituents ever knowing what that record is.

Second, the relation of Congressman to voter is not a simple bilateral one but is complicated by the presence of all manner of intermediaries: the local party, economic interests, the news media, racial and nationality organizations, and so forth. Such is the lore of American politics, as it is known to any political scientist. Very often the Representative reaches the mass public through these mediating agencies, and the information about himself and his record may be considerably transformed as it diffuses out to the electorate in two or more stages. As a result, the public — or parts of it — may get simple positive or negative cues about the Congressman which were provoked by his legislative actions but which no longer have a recognizable issue content.

Third, for most Congressmen most of the time the electorate's sanctions are potential rather than actual. Particularly the Representative from a safe district may feel his proper legislative strategy is to avoid giving opponents in his own party or outside of it material they can use against him. As the Congressman pursues this strategy he may write a legislative record that never becomes very well known to his constituents; if it doesn't win votes, neither will it lose any. This is clearly the situation of most southern Congressmen in dealing with the issue of Negro rights. By voting correctly on this issue they are unlikely to increase their visibility to constituents. Nevertheless, the fact of constituency influence, backed by potential sanctions at the polls, is real enough.

That these potential sanctions are all too real is best illustrated in the election of 1958 by the reprisal against Representative Brooks Hays in Arkansas' Fifth District.[19] Although the perception of Congressman Hays as too moderate on civil rights resulted more from his service as intermediary between the White House and Governor Faubus in the Little Rock school crisis than from his record in the House, the victory of Dale Alford as a write-in candidate was a striking reminder of what can happen to a Congressman who gives his foes a powerful issue to use against him. The extraordinary involvement of the public in this race can be seen by comparing how well the candidates were known in this constituency with the awareness of the candidates shown by table 16-2 for the country as a whole. As table 16-3 indicates, not a single voter in our sample of Arkansas' Fifth District was unaware of either candidate.[20] What is more, these interviews show that Hays was regarded both by his supporters and his opponents as more moderate than Alford on civil rights and that this perception brought his defeat. In some measure, what happened in Little Rock in 1958 can happen anywhere, and our Congressmen ought not to be entirely disbelieved in what they say about their impact at the polls. Indeed, they may be under genuine pressure from the voters even while they are the forgotten men of national elections.[21]

Table 16-3   Awareness of congressional candidates among voters in Arkansas' Fifth District, 1958

		Read or Heard Something about Hays		
		Yes	No	
Read or Heard Something about Alford	Yes	100	0	100
	No	0	0	0
		100	0	100%

V. Conclusion

Therefore, although the conditions of constituency influence are not equally satisfied, they are met well enough to give the local constituency a measure of control over the actions of its Representatives. Best satisfied is the requirement about motivational influences on the Congressman: our evidence shows that the Representative's roll call behavior is strongly influenced by his own policy preferences and by his perception of preferences held by the constituency. However, the conditions of influence that presuppose effective communication between Congressman and district are much less well met. The Representative has very imperfect information about the issue preferences of his constituency, and the constituency's awareness of the policy stands of the Representative ordinarily is slight.

The findings of this analysis heavily underscore the fact that no single tradition of representation fully accords with the realities of American legislative politics. The American system *is* a mixture, to which the Burkean, instructed-delegate, and responsible-party models all can be said to have contributed elements. Moreover, variations in the representative relation are most likely to occur as we move from one policy domain to another. No single, generalized configuration of attitudes and perceptions links Representative with constituency but rather several distinct patterns, and which of them is invoked depends very much on the issue involved.

The issue domain in which the relation of Congressman to constituency most nearly conforms to the instructed-delegate model is that of civil rights. This conclusion is supported by the importance of the influence-path passing through the Representative's perception of district opinion, although even in this domain the sense in which the constituency may be said to take the position of the candidate into account in reaching its electoral judgment should be carefully qualified.

The representative relation conforms most closely to the responsible-party model in the domain of social welfare. In this issue area, the arena of partisan conflict for a generation, the party symbol helps both constituency and Representative in the difficult process of communication between them. On the one hand, because Republican and Democratic voters tend to differ in what they would have government do, the Representative has some guide to district opinion simply by looking at the partisan division of the vote. On the other hand, because the two parties tend to recruit candidates who differ on the social welfare role of government, the constituency can infer the candidates' position with more than random accuracy from their party affiliation, even though what the constituency has learned directly about these stands is almost nothing. How faithful the representation of social welfare views is to the responsible-party model should not be exaggerated. Even in this policy domain, American practice departs widely from an ideal conception of party government.[22] But in this domain, more than any other, political conflict has become a conflict of national parties in which constituency and Representative are known to each other primarily by their party association.

It would be too pat to say that the domain of foreign involvement conforms to the third model of representation, the conception promoted by Edmund Burke. Clearly it does in the sense that the Congressman looks elsewhere than to his district in making up his mind on foreign issues. However, the reliance he puts on the President and the Administration suggests that the calculation of where the public interest lies is often passed to the Executive on matters of foreign policy. Ironically, legislative initiative in foreign affairs has fallen victim to the very difficulties of gathering and appraising information that led Burke to argue that Parliament rather than the public ought to hold the power of decision. The background information and predictive skills that Burke thought the people lacked are held primarily by the modern Executive. As a result, the present role of the legislature in foreign affairs bears some resemblance to the role that Burke had in mind for the elitist, highly restricted *electorate* of his own day.

Notes

[1] To be sure, the work of the Federal Convention has been supplemented in two critical respects. The first of these is the practice, virtually universal since the mid-19th century, of choosing Representatives from single-member districts of limited geographic area. The second is the practice, which has also become virtually universal in our own century, of selecting party nominees for the House by direct primary election.

[2] In the language of Eulau, Wahlke, *et al.* we speak here of the "style," not the "focus," of representation. See their "The Role of the Representative: Some Empirical Observations on the Theory of Edmund Burke," *American Political Science Review*, Vol. 53 (September, 1959), pp. 742–756. An excellent review of the mandate-independence controversy is given by Hanna Fenichel Pitkin, "The Theory of Representation" (unpublished doctoral dissertation, University of California, Berkeley, 1961). For other contemporary discussions of representation, see Alfred de Grazia, *Public and Republic* (New York, 1951), and John A. Fairlie, "The Nature of Political Representation," *American Political Science Review*, Vol. 34 (April–June, 1940), pp. 236–48, 456–66.

[3] The sampling aspects of this research were complicated by the fact that the study of representation was a rider midway on a four-year panel study of the electorate whose primary sampling units were not congressional districts (although there is no technical reason why they could not have been if the needs of the representation analysis had been foreseen when the design of the sample was fixed two years before). As a result, the districts in our sample had unequal probabilities of selection and unequal weights in the analysis, making the sample somewhat less efficient than an equal-probability sample of equivalent size.

It will be apparent in the discussion that follows that we have estimated characteristics of whole constituencies from our samples of constituents living in particular districts. In view of the fact that a sample of less than two thousand constituents has been divided among 116 districts, the reader may wonder about the reliability of these estimates. After considerable investigation we have concluded that their sampling error is not so severe a problem for the analysis as we had thought it would be. Several comments may indicate why it is not.

To begin with, the weighting of our sample of districts has increased the reliability of the constituency estimates. The correct theoretical weight to be assigned each district in the analysis is the inverse of the probability of the district's selection, and it can be shown that this weight is approximately proportional to the number of interviews taken in the district. The result of this is that the greatest weight is assigned the districts with the largest number of interviews and, hence, the most reliable constituency estimates. Indeed, these weights increase by half again the (weighted) mean number of interviews taken per district. To put the matter another way: the introduction of differential weights trades some of our sample of congressional districts for more reliable constituency estimates.

How much of a problem the unreliability of these estimates is depends very much on the analytic uses to which the estimates are put. If our goal were case analyses of particular districts, the constituency samples would have to be much larger. Indeed, for most case analyses we would want several hundred interviews per district (at a cost, over 116 districts, of several small nuclear reactors). However, most of the findings reported here are based not on single districts but on many or all of the districts in our sample. For analyses of this sort the number of interviews per district can be much smaller.

Our investigation of the effect of the sampling variance of the constituency estimates is quite reassuring. When statistics computed from our constituency samples are compared with corresponding parameter values for the constituencies, the agreement of the two sets of figures is quite close. For example, when the proportions voting Democratic in the 116 constituencies in 1958, as computed from our sample data, are compared with the actual proportions voting Democratic, as recorded in official election statistics, a product moment correlation of 0.93 is obtained, and this figure is the more impressive since this test throws away non-voters, almost one-half of our total sample. We interpret the Pearsonian correlation as an appropriate measure of agreement in this case, since the associated regression equations are almost exactly the identity function. The alternative intraclass correlation coefficient has almost as high a value.

Although we believe that this analysis provides a textbook illustration of how misleading intuitive ideas (including our own) about the effects of sampling error can be, these figures ought not to be too beguiling. It is clear that how close such a correlation is to 1.0 for any given variable will depend on the ratio of the between-district variance to the total variance. When this ratio is as high as it is for Republican and Democratic voting, the effect of the unreliability of our constituency estimates is fairly trivial. Although the content of the study is quite different, this sampling problem has much in common with the problem of attenuation of correlation as it has been treated in psychological testing. See, for example, J. P. Guilford, *Fundamental Statistics in Psychology and Education* (New York, 1956), pp. 475–78.

[4]See Angus Campbell, Philip E. Converse, Warren E. Miller, and Donald E. Stokes, *The American Voter* (New York, 1960), pp. 194–209.

[5]This conclusion, fully supported by our own work for later Congresses, is one of the main findings to be drawn from the work of Duncan MacRae on roll call voting in the House of Representatives. See his *Dimensions of Congressional Voting: A Statistical Study of the House of Representatives in the Eighty-First Congress* (Berkeley and Los Angeles: University of California Press, 1958). For additional evidence of the existence of scale dimensions in legislative behavior, see N. L. Gage and Ben Shimberg, "Measuring Senatorial Progressivism," *Journal of Abnormal and Social Psychology*, Vol. 44 (January 1949), pp. 112–117; George M. Belknap, "A Study of Senatorial Voting by Scale Analysis" (unpublished doctoral dissertation, University of Chicago, 1951), and "A Method for Analyzing Legislative Behavior," *Midwest Journal of Political Science*, Vol. 2. (1958), pp. 377–402; two other articles by MacRae, "The Role of the State Legislator in Massachusetts," *American Sociological Review*, Vol. 19 (April 1954), pp. 185–194, and "Roll Call Votes and Leadership," *Public Opinion Quarterly*, Vol. 20 (1956), pp. 543–558; Charles D. Farris, "A Method

of Determining Ideological Groups in Congress," *Journal of Politics*, Vol. 20 (1958), pp. 308–338; and Leroy N. Rieselbach, "Quantitative Techniques for Studying Voting Behavior in the U. N. General Assembly," *International Organization*, Vol. 14 (1960), pp. 291–306.

[6]The content of the three issue domains may be suggested by some of the roll call and interview items used. In the area of social welfare these included the issues of public housing, public power, aid to education, and government's role in maintaining full employment. In the area of foreign involvement the items included the issues of foreign economic aid, military aid, sending troops abroad, and aid to neutrals. In the area of civil rights the items included the issues of school desegregation, fair employment, and the protection of Negro voting rights.

[7]Because this point has been so widely discussed it has inevitably attracted a variety of terms. Dahl denotes the acts of *a* whose performance *A* is able to influence as the *scope* of *A*'s power. See Robert A. Dahl, "The Concept of Power," *Behavioral Science*, Vol. 2 (July 1957), pp. 201–215. This usage is similar to that of Harold D. Lasswell and Abraham Kaplan, *Power and Society* (New Haven: Yale University Press, 1950), pp. 71–73. Dorwin Cartwright, however, denotes the behavioral or psychological changes in *P* which *O* is able to induce as the *range* of *O's* power: "A Field Theoretical Conception of Power," *Studies in Social Power* (Ann Arbor: Research Center for Group Dynamics, Institute for Social Research, The University of Michigan, 1959), pp. 183–220.

[8]That the Representative's roll call votes can diverge from his true opinion is borne out by a number of findings of the study (some of which are reported here) as to the conditions under which agreement between the Congressman's roll call position and his private attitude will be high or low. However, a direct confirmation that these two sets of measurements are not simply getting at the same thing is given by differences in attitude-roll call agreement according to the Congressman's sense of how well his roll call votes have expressed his real views. In the domain of foreign involvement, for example, the correlation of our attitudinal and roll call measurements was .75 among Representatives who said that their roll call votes had expressed their real views fairly well. But this correlation was only .04 among those who said that their roll call votes had expressed their views poorly. In the other policy domains, too, attitude-roll call agreement is higher among Congressmen who are well satisfied with their roll call votes than it is among Congressmen who are not.

[9]During the analysis we have formed constituency scores out of the scores of constituents living in the same district by several devices other than calculating average constituent scores. In particular, in view of the ordinal character of our scales we have frequently used the *median* constituent score as a central value for the constituency as a whole. However, the ordering of constituencies differs very little according to which of several reasonable alternatives for obtaining constituency scores is chosen. As a result, we have preferred mean scores for the greater number of ranks they give.

[10]The meaning of this procedure can be suggested by two percentage tables standing for hypothetical extreme cases, the first that of full agreement, the second that of no agreement whatever. For convenience, these illustrative tables categorize both Congressmen and their districts in terms of only three degrees of favor and assume for both a nearly uniform distribution across the three categories. The terms "pro," "neutral," and "con" indicate a relative rather than an absolute opinion. In Case I, full agreement, all districts relatively favorable to social welfare action have Congressmen who are so too, etc.; whereas in Case II, or that of no agreement, the ordering of constituencies is independent in a statistical sense of the ranking of Congressmen: knowing the policy orientation of a district gives no clue at all to the orientation of its Congressman. Of course, it is possible for the orders of legislators and districts to be *inversely* related, and this possibility is of some importance, as indicated below, when the policy position of non-incumbent candidates as well as incumbents is taken into account. To summarize the degree of congruence between legislators and voters, a measure of correlation is introduced. Although we have used a variety of measures of association in our analysis, the values reported in this article all refer to product moment correlation coefficients. For our hypothetical Case I a measure of correlation would have the

value 1.0; for Case II, the value 0.0. When it is applied to actual data this convenient indicator is likely to have a value somewhere in between. The question is where.

Case I:
Full policy agreement

Congressmen	Constituencies			
	Pro	neutral	Con	
Pro	33	0	0	33
Neutral	0	34	0	34
Con	0	0	33	33
	33	34	33	100%

Correlation = 1.0

Case II:
No policy agreement

Congressmen	Constituencies			
	Pro	neutral	Con	
Pro	11	11	11	33
Neutral	11	12	11	34
Con	11	11	11	33
	33	34	33	100%

Correlation = 0.0

[11] A word of caution is in order, lest we compare things that are not strictly comparable. For obvious reasons, most non-incumbent candidates have no roll call record, and we have had to measure their policy agreement with the district entirely in terms of the attitudes they have revealed in interviews. However, the difference of coefficients given here is almost as great when the policy agreement between the incumbent Congressman and his district is also measured in terms of the attitudes conveyed in confidential interviews.

[12] A third type of connection, excluded here might obtain between district and Congressman if the Representative accedes to what he things the district wants because he believes that to be what a representative *ought* to do, whether or not it is necessary for re-election. We leave this type of connection out of our account here because we conceive an influence relation as one in which control is not voluntarily accepted or rejected by someone subject to it. Of course, this possible connection between district and Representative is not any the less interesting because it falls outside our definition of influence or control, and we have given a good deal of attention to it in the broader study of which this analysis is part.

[13] It scarcely needs to be said that demonstrating *some* constituency influence would not imply that the Representative's behavior is *wholly* determined by constituency pressures. The legislator acts in a complex institutional setting in which he is subject to a wide variety of influences. The constituency can exercise a genuine measure of control without driving all other influences from the Representative's life space.

[14] We have done this by a variance-component technique similar to several others proposed for dealing with problems of this type. See especially Herbert A. Simon, "Spurious Correlation: A Causal Interpretation," *Journal of the American Statistical Association*. Vol. 40 (1954), pp. 467–479; Hubert M. Blalock, Jr., "The Relative Importance of Variables," *American Sociological Review*. Vol. 26 (1961), pp. 866–874; and the almost forgotten work of Sewall

Wright, "Correlation and Causation," *Journal of Agricultural Research,* Vol. 20 (1920), pp. 557–585. Under this technique a "path coefficient" (to use Wright's terminology, although not his theory) is assigned to each of the causal arrows by solving a set of equations involving the correlations of the variables of the model. The weight assigned to a full path is then the product of its several path coefficients, and this product may be interpreted as the proportion of the variance of the dependent variable (roll call behavior, here) that is explained by a given path.

A special problem arises because influence may flow in either direction between the Congressman's attitude and his perception of district attitude (as noted above, the Representative may tend both to perceive his constituency's view selectively, as consistent with his own, and to change his own view to be consistent with the perceived constituency view). Hence, we have not a single causal model but a whole family of models, varying according to the relative importance of influence from attitude to perception and from perception to attitude. Our solution to this problem has been to calculate influence coefficients for the two extreme models in order to see how much our results could vary according to which model is chosen from our family of models. Since the systems of equations in this analysis are linear it can be shown that the coefficients we seek have their maximum and minimum values under one or the other of the limiting models. Therefore, computing any given coefficient for each of these limiting cases defines an interval in which the true value of the coefficient must lie. In fact these intervals turn out to be fairly small; our findings as to the relative importance of alternative influence paths would change little according to which model is selected.

The two limiting models with their associated systems of equations and the formulas for computing the relative importance of the three possible paths under each model are given below.

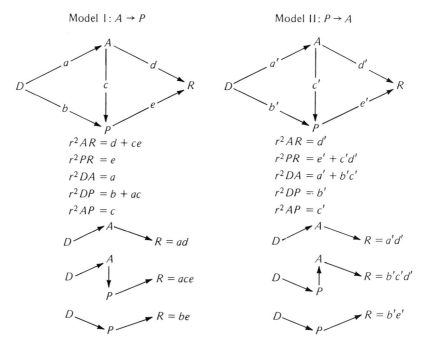

Model I: $A \to P$ Model II: $P \to A$

$r^2 AR = d + ce$ $r^2 AR = d'$

$r^2 PR = e$ $r^2 PR = e' + c'd'$

$r^2 DA = a$ $r^2 DA = a' + b'c'$

$r^2 DP = b + ac$ $r^2 DP = b'$

$r^2 AP = c$ $r^2 AP = c'$

$R = ad$ $R = a'd'$

$R = ace$ $R = b'c'd'$

$R = be$ $R = b'e'$

[15]By "least favorable" we mean the assumption that influence goes only from the Congressman's attitude to his perception of district attitude (Model I) and not the other way round. Under

this assumption, the proportions of the variance of roll call behavior accounted for by the three alternative paths, expressed as proportions of the part of the variance of roll call votes that is explained by district attitude, are these:

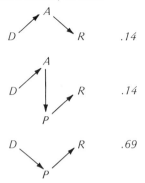

Inverting the assumed direction of influence between the Congressman's own attitude and district attitude (Model II) eliminates altogether the effect that the Representative's attitude can have had on his votes, independently of his perception of district attitude.

[16]Under both Models I and II the proportion of the variance of roll call voting explained by the influence path involving the Representative's own attitude is twice as great as the proportion explained by influence passing through his perception of district attitude.

[17]What is more, the electorate's awareness of Congress as a whole appears quite limited. A majority of the public was unable to say in 1958 which of the two parties had controlled the Congress during the preceding two years. Some people were confused by the coexistence of a Republican President and a Democratic Congress. But for most people this was simply an elementary fact about congressional affairs to which they were not privy.

[18]For a more extended analysis of forces on the congressional vote, see Donald E. Stokes and Warren E. Miller, "Party Government and the Saliency of Congress," *Public Opinion Quarterly*, Vol. 26 (Winter 1962), pp. 531–46.

[19]For an account of this episode see Corinne Silverman, "The Little Rock Story," Inter-University Case Program series, reprinted in Edwin A. Bock and Alan K. Campbell, eds., *Case Studies in American Government* (Englewood Cliffs, 1962), pp. 1–46.

[20]The sample of this constituency was limited to twenty-three persons of whom thirteen voted. However, despite the small number of cases the probability that the difference in awareness between this constituency and the country generally as the result of sampling variations is much less than one in a thousand.

[21]In view of the potential nature of the constituency's sanctions, it is relevant to characterize its influence over the Representative in terms of several distinctions drawn by recent theorists of power, especially the difference between actual and potential power, between influence and coercive power, and between influence and purposive control. Observing these distinctions, we might say that the constituency's influence is *actual* and not merely *potential* since it is the sanction behavior rather than the conforming behavior that is infrequent (Dahl). That is, the Congressman is influenced by his calculus of potential sanctions, following the "rule of anticipated reactions" (Friedrich), however oblivious of his behavior the constituency ordinarily may be. We might also say that the constituency has *power* since its influence depends partly on sanctions (Lasswell and Kaplan), although it rarely exercises *control* since its influence is rarely conscious or intended (Cartwright). In the discussion above we have of course used the terms "influence" and "control" interchangeably.

[22]The factors in American electoral behavior that encourage such a departure are discussed in Stokes and Miller, *loc. cit.*

Selection 17 Congressional Policy-Making: The Basic Patterns

Gary Orfield

Misconceptions about the Policy Process

An Old American Tradition: The Fear of Concentrated Power

The normal state of American government is one of internal division and belated response. This is no accident. Our political system was designed by people who saw government as the central threat to liberty, and who developed numerous checks and balances to limit the power of each major institution. The Founding Fathers tried to prevent tyranny by systematically fragmenting authority and building institutional competition into the heart of the government process. The solution has usually worked, but often at the price of crippling the ability of the government to deal forcefully and rapidly with the critical needs of an increasingly complex and densely settled society. In spite of these difficulties, however, the system has persisted and its basic premises enjoy wide and deep support. While people complain about inaction on individual problems, there is still a strong fear of excessively active national government. Contemporary public support for fragmentation of government power has probably been greatly expanded by President Nixon's resignation in the face of imminent Congressional impeachment.

When there is a commonly perceived sense of urgency and a broad public desire to deal forcefully with a particular problem, the obstacles built into the political system can often be overcome. When the dominant wing of either party wins efficient working control of both the White House and Congress, its program can be enacted. The problem for reformers is that this rarely happens. It is made unlikely by the great diversity of the country, by the stability of its political orientations, and by the generalized public suspicion of "big government."

While political scientists, many administrators, a number of commentators, and most reformers complain of the costs of divided, slow-moving, and unresponsive government, Americans generally continue to favor only a limited role for federal programs. In spite of serious deficiencies in some of our state and

Abridged from *Congressional Power: Congress and Social Change* by Gary Orfield. © 1975 by Harcourt Brace Jovanovich, Inc., and reprinted with their permission.

local governments, there is broad public support for keeping these institutions strong and autonomous. State and local governments dominate most areas of domestic policy and program administration, and these institutions are being strengthened by the transfer of national resources, without strings, through revenue sharing. A survey conducted in the fall of 1973 by the University of Michigan's Institute for Social Research showed, for example, that of fifteen major sets of public and private institutions, the public rated the President and the Administration lowest and the federal government next lowest. State and local governments rated higher, and local public school systems much higher. Several surveys between 1968 and 1972 showed that majorities of between 60 and 77 percent favored turning over money for revenue sharing. Although most Americans give the political system a "fair" or "poor" grade for efficiency,* the costly division of power is seen as preferable to a potentially dangerous concentration of power in the national government.[1]

Congress's Role Obscured

Many students of Congress have erred in two basic ways in describing the role of Congress in our political structure. First, because they have been insensitive to the continuing reality of fragmented power in Washington, they have often overestimated the President's power and obscured the strong continuing role of Congress in shaping domestic policies. Secondly, because they overestimated the permanence and inevitability of the political alignments crystalized in the 1930s, they assumed that there was something inherent in the nature of the modern Presidency that made the executive branch more responsive to social problems. Yet in point of fact, so long as the White House and Congress retain independent sources of power, and political coalitions continue to evolve and change across the country, the objectives of the men holding power within each major institution will continue to change, most often gradually, but sometimes with dramatic abruptness. One of those sudden changes in the roles of the national institutions came in 1968, when the Republican Party succeeded in capturing the Presidency by constructing a new and far more conservative coalition than that supporting any recent President. The change in the White House served to illuminate other, more gradual changes—in a liberal direction—within Congress. Congress, at least for a time, was clearly the more progressive institution.

Most serious scholarly studies of Congress and the Presidency have been written during recent decades of widely publicized Presidential leadership. Undeniably, the vast expansion of American government since the 1930s has

---

*Public ratings for the efficiency of the governmental system were as follows: excellent, 5%; good, 33%; fair, 50%; poor, 11%; don't know, 1%.

magnified the power of the Presidency. The growth of the office has been facilitated and publicized by the simultaneous development of national broadcast media that simplify and personalize the news, and that are best adapted to simple communication between a single leader and mass audiences. The enormous expansion of American military power, and of American influence in international affairs, has produced beliefs about Presidential leadership that have often in turn engendered assumptions about Presidential dominance of domestic policy. The result has been an unreal focus of public expectations on the President. This tendency has obscured the simultaneous development of greatly enlarged Congressional power, particularly in domestic affairs.

The longstanding inclination of observers to exaggerate the tendency toward Presidential dominance has been intensified by the Watergate scandal. Evidence of corruption, and of cynical White House efforts to manipulate other governmental institutions, tends to reinforce warnings about "Presidential dictatorship." Clearly, the Watergate scandal has revealed both the corrupting influence of private campaign financing, and the White House attempts to misuse both national security powers and a variety of federal agencies, including the Justice Department and the Internal Revenue Service. But it is extremely important to accurately assess what the scandal has shown about the Presidency.

To assume that misuse of power means that there is too much power, and to destroy that power so as to correct the abuse, is to engage in dangerous oversimplification. This was precisely the mistake made by the reformers in the House of Representatives in 1910, when they fought abuse of leadership not by removing the incumbent, but by destroying much of the power of the Speakership. The result weakened the entire House and gravely diminished its role for generations. The Watergate scandal certainly reveals the need for more Congressional overseeing of national security and the investigatory agencies, and for reform of campaign finances and techniques; yet the probable result of the scandal will be a general weakening of the Presidency, and only a desultory attempt to correct the specific abuses. We will likely respond to the misuse of office by diminishing the possibilities of leadership in office.

The reaction has grown to the point where Arthur Schlesinger, Jr., a major historian who long celebrated Presidential leadership, now condemns the "Imperial Presidency." Schlesinger claims that President Nixon was a "revolutionary" President, intently carrying to their logical extreme all the vast powers of executive dominance that had been accumulating for decades. He "aimed at reducing the power of Congress at every point along the line and moving toward rule by presidential decree." He sums up his case:

> As one examined the impressive range of Nixon's initiatives—from his appropriation of the war-making power to his interpretation of the appointing power, from his unilateral determination of social priorities to his unilateral abolition of statutory programs, from his attack on legislative privilege to his enlargement of executive privilege, from his theory of impoundment to his theory of the pocket veto, from his calculated disparagement of the cabinet and

his calculated discrediting of the press to his carefully organized concentration of federal management in the White House—from all this a larger design ineluctably emerged.[2]

This dismal view of our situation under Nixon is extremely misleading; untangling its misstatements about the past is essential to understanding the present shape of the political system. President Nixon did indeed assert many broad powers, but even before Watergate Congress had come up with some impressive answers. Presidential war powers had been limited, both by passage of legislation requiring consultation with Congress before future long-term commitments of American forces, and by Congress's unprecedented action in forcing an end to American bombing of Cambodia by cutting off funds. Congress squarely rejected the President's theory of the appointment process by handing him more defeats than any other twentieth-century President on his Supreme Court nominees. The President's claims of massive powers to impound or abolish programs were rejected both in the courts and in Congress. The very President who asserted the most sweeping version of executive privilege found himself forced by Congress and the courts to sacrifice any privacy on the most personal and degrading materials ever extracted from the White House. The President who acted as if he possessed vast powers found his modest program proposals rejected by Congress with more monotonous regularity than any other recent President.

The only alternative to the misleading global clichés that usually dominate our discussion of our major institutions is an effort to seriously examine their roles in a number of important policy decisions. When the subtleties of the policy process are sorted out and the strands of influence unwoven, it is evident that Congress is a major source of domestic policy, and often the dominant source in government. While the case studies of the earlier chapters document some of Congress's recent contributions to domestic policy, it would of course be a mistake to reach comprehensive conclusions on the basis of such a limited range of evidence. However, the general arguments set forth here are supported by the few serious scholarly efforts to systematically assess legislative contributions to a range of domestic issues.

Lawrence Chamberlain's study of the history of ninety laws from 1890 to 1940 credited Congress with initiating twice as many as the President and with sharing the responsibility for most of the rest.[3] An effort to update this analysis by looking at case studies of bills passed between 1940 and 1967 concluded that "Congress is very capable of conceptual innovation, legislation modification, and energetic oversight. . . . The evidence suggests that Congress continues to be an active innovator and very much in the legislative business. Thus the findings here tend to confirm the findings Chamberlain made a quarter of a century ago."[4] Finally, David Price's careful 1972 study of the role of three major Senate committees in shaping thirteen important recent bills concludes that, even under President Johnson, Congress's role was "more prominent and diverse than is often supposed and—what is particularly important in the current period of reduced executive creativity and leadership—that the congressional 'input' can and should become a more substantial and innovative one in the years ahead."[5] These studies of particular pieces of legislation tend to reinforce the conclusions that this book draws from examining legislative activities in certain broad areas. . . .

The Conditions for Congressional Innovation

While . . . case studies . . . have illustrated Congressional activism in the face of a conservative President, a scholar wishing to prove Congressional impotence might prepare apparently contradictory studies on Vietnam or welfare policy. Obviously, the conditions and the limitations of Congressional policy initiatives must be far more clearly specified.

The diffusion of power and the diversity of political viewpoints within Congress make it easy to support a wide range of interpretations of Congressional authority. Within an institution where great influence over the same issue may rest in one house with a reactionary Southern planter, and in the other with a very liberal New York City lawyer, a casual observer can easily become confused about Congress's position. It often is far easier to examine issues apparently supporting the thesis of dominance by a progressive Presidency than it is to sort out the net effect of the ebbs and flows of power within the complex overlapping policy systems that make up Congress. The sorting out of real policy influence is further complicated by the frequent Congressional practice of disguising real changes as "technical" alterations, or accomplishing change through private negotiations between the executive branch and powerful members of Congress.

Most existing interpretations find Presidential initiative and Presidential dominance because they focus on three types of issues: foreign policy crises, military problems, and the President's own domestic agenda. Other analysts reach conclusions about Congressional impotence based on Congress's failure to respond to national crises or critical national needs—but in so doing tend to rely on their own interpretation of national needs, rather than on the perceptions and demands of the public. Often the deadlock caused by Congress actually reflects cross-cutting public concerns and the deep uncertainty about the best policy solution.

Congress and International Affairs

The President retains a decisive initiative in diplomacy and military policy. He enjoys broad and clear grants of constitutional authority in these fields. Given the need for unity of military command and for speed and secrecy in crisis diplomacy, Congress can often do little more than respond to a White House initiative or *fait accompli.*

Even in foreign and military policy, however, Presidents are constrained by Congress, particularly in the development of long-term policies. Congress, for example, has made sharp and consistent cuts in foreign and military aid programs, denying Presidents an important policy tool. Congress has always played a very important role in shaping trade legislation — a fact underlined by its 1973 refusal to grant trade privileges to the U.S.S.R., a decision significantly impairing the President's basic policy line of détente. Presidents involved in major international negotiations do not forget the destruction of Woodrow Wilson's Administration by the Senate rejection of the Versailles Treaty.

Liberals have frequently concluded that Congress's inability to end the war in Vietnam illustrates legislative impotence. The fact is that Congress did not even try to end the war, because there was no Congressional majority opposed to the war. In the House of Representatives there was a consistent majority, including the leadership of both parties, that supported the general Presidential policy toward Vietnam. Even in the Senate the division was very close. The fact that a majority of Congress may have been wrong does not show that it was impotent, or even that it was unrepresentative. Indeed, polls show deep contradictions in public attitudes toward the war. When a particular Presidential action stirred up strong public and Congressional protests, such as the 1970 invasion of Cambodia, the threat of Congressional restrictions on the White House was sufficiently serious to bring a rapid Presidential retreat.

In the final period of U.S. military involvement in Indochina, Congress was far more responsive to war critics than was the President. The Nixon Administration found it necessary to continually fight hard against Senate attempts to legislate an end to the war. After American troops were withdrawn, it was Congress that forced an end to further U.S. bombing, and Congress that tried to restrain continued massive military aid.

In evaluating Congress's performance on the Vietnam issue, one must recognize that the American role in the war was a direct outgrowth of widely shared basic assumptions about foreign policy, and about the nature of the contest with communism in Asia. During the early phases of the war, Congressional support reflected backing by leading conservatives and liberals alike throughout the country.[6] In retrospect, we tend to blame Congress for "going along" with the war. It is hardly fair to disparage Congress as an institution for a general failure of American liberal ideology.

Although Congress did not end the war, some members and some committees did play a crucial role in reformulating the issues. By the late 1960s Congress had produced the leading figures of the opposition and provided the principal forum for their attacks. From it emerged such preeminent antiwar critics as Eugene McCarthy (D-Minn.), George McGovern (D-S. Dak.), and Paul McCloskey (R-Calif.), while the hearings of the Senate Foreign Relations Committee did more than anything else to touch off the national debate that helped persuade Lyndon Johnson, a very powerful President, to step down. After the Vietnam conflict ended, Congress moved in 1973 to extend its power with measures forcing the President to end the bombing of Cambodia and requiring advance Congressional approval of sustained military action in the future.

The Conditions of Domestic Leadership

Although Congressional helplessness in international affairs has been overstated, it is certainly true that Congressional power is vastly greater in most realms of domestic policy. Even here, however, the degree of Congressional authority varies greatly from one issue area to another. Congressional influence and innovation are most likely when the President is either conservative or passive, and when one or more of the following conditions prevails:

(1) The other party controls Congress by a substantial margin.

(2) The issue in question unites the major factions of the other party.

(3) The relevant committees are led by, or contain committed majorities of, supporters of the new program proposal.

(4) The process of innovation has already been set in motion by outside forces such as judicial decisions or administrative interpretations of existing laws, and momentum can be sustained merely by vetoing conservative proposals of the President.

(5) The innovation is not highly controversial, and supporters of change have organized constituency support from various parts of the country.

(6) The policy change can be accomplished through amendments to legislation the President cannot afford to veto.

(7) A national movement, a skillful media campaign by reformers, or a highly visible scandal has produced an insistent public demand for action.

(8) The President's public support has been so seriously eroded that he cannot maintain leadership of his own party.

(9) Legislative tactics permit proponents to present the issue for a rapid decision before existing and potential opponents have an opportunity to mobilize.

The chances of Congressional leadership diminish when one or more of the following conditions holds:

(1) The President is exercising one of his most unambiguous constitutional functions: when he is acting as Commander-in-Chief during active military operations; when he is serving as national spokesman in the conduct of international negotiations or the management of an interna-

tional crisis; or when he is exercising administrative authority over the executive branch.

(2) The President is prepared to use his veto, and can hold his party's support to sustain it.

(3) Congressional leaders of the President's party are strongly united against the proposed new program.

(4) Majority party leaders and committee chairmen seriously disagree.

(5) The issue is already highly controversial, or the President is ready to make it so through his unrivaled access to the media.

(6) The policy threatens the traditional powers of state or local governments.

(7) The policy is strongly opposed by powerful and well-organized groups or industries that have effective Washington representation, strong local branches, or major roles in providing campaign funds.

(8) Congressional advocates of change lack the technical staff resources necessary to deal with extremely complex issues.

(9) The change would require a visible tax increase.

Progressives in Congress are most successful when their goals can be accomplished by killing a conservative White House initiative, or by creating an additional, relatively noncontroversial program of federal grants or federal regulation. Congressional initiatives are frequently most important when the issues are comparatively new. Committees often develop specialists on such issues long before they appear on the President's agenda or in national political discussions, and long before the task of administering legislation has given the executive branch a reservoir of expertise. At this point—when little is known, positions are unclear, and major interests are not yet mobilized—the opportunity for legislative creativity is large. Congressional activity of this type was seen in the early phase of antipollution legislation, in the development of bilingual education programs, and in the extension of job discrimination protection to women and to state and local employees.

For a number of easily understandable reasons, Congress is far more responsive to the need for new programs than to basic fiscal or social rearrangements. Redressing general social or economic imbalances always means helping some while denying to others a portion of their goods or of their social objectives. The resulting controversy brings political trouble and a greatly increased probability that the policy will be vetoed at one of the many decision points in the Congressional process. Most new grant programs, on the other hand, give additional benefits to some groups while seldom disturbing the others. When a Senator fights for more housing or better health care for old people, or for better education benefits for veterans, he usually gains strength from a segment of his constituency without deeply offending anybody else.

Proposals to redistribute income, close big tax loopholes, break up the existing pattern of urban racial separation, or undertake other forms of basic social or economic change have very different effects. They alienate segments of the local constituency, and other members of Congress as well. By forcing members to make basic choices that are very salient, rather than mutual accommodations that pass unnoticed, they greatly increase the chances for veto. Unless there is strong and unambiguous public pressure for it, such a change is exceedingly difficult to successfully initiate within Congress.

(On the other hand, Congress is frequently important as a place where discussions of new issues can be launched. This is because of the enormous variation among districts and states represented, and the fact that problems almost always become much more acute and obvious in particular localities first. The representatives of these localities can then speak out in favor of real change without facing any personal political risk.) Presidents confront very similar difficulties and generally show similar caution.

The Influence of the Committee System

The Committees' Political Complexion

The tendency for reform supporters to concentrate on creating new federal aid programs is reinforced by the way members are often placed on committees. Most activist members see their goal as writing new laws or amendments in response to particular policy problems. They seek assignment to committees specifically responsible for measures dealing with education, housing, jobs, urban programs, and civil rights. Since these committees do not enjoy a great deal of prestige, it is often possible for a member to win assignment to one at the beginning of his Congressional career. As a result, the Democratic majorities of these key domestic policy committees tend to be more liberal ideologically and more activist politically than the party caucus as a whole.

Conservatives, on the other hand, enjoy disproportionate strength in the powerful committees controlling the budget, taxation, health and welfare policy, military policy, and the internal legislative processes of Congress. The seniority system has its most drastic impact on the character of these committees since considerable seniority is usually required for an appointment, and virtually no one leaves the committees while he remains in Congress.[7] Thus on the most important committee in the House, Ways and Means, the least senior of the Democratic members, as of 1973, had been in the House for nine years, and the average member for sixteen. The GOP minority averaged eleven years of service and contained no representation of the moderate wing of the Republican party.[8] This meant that the typical member had come to Congress in a different era, and also that the membership reflected the conservative views prevalent in the House when the appointments were made. This pattern was strikingly apparent on the powerful House Appropriations Committee, where in 1973 the six senior members of the majority party had an average service of thirty-one years. Five of these men controlling powerful subcommittees came from the South, while the other one, John Rooney, was an elderly conservative from New York.

The time lag before new trends in the parties show up on the most important committees is reinforced by the tendency of more liberal members who do win assignment to these panels to be converted to the views of older committee leaders. The most powerful committees are usually very stable social systems in which new members are judged by their acceptance of a well-established set of committee values and expectations. Members of the Ways and Means and the Appropriations committees gain reputations with their colleagues by their attention to detail, their dedication to cutting the executive-branch budget, and avoidance of "irresponsible" changes in the tax structure. By the time a member has been on a committee long enough to influence legislation strongly, his views often tend to agree with committee expectations.[9]

An Obstacle Course for Programs

The fact that the development of each federal program depends on two different sets of committees with very different memberships often deepens public confusion. Before any new program can begin operation, Congress must first pass a new law or amend an old one. This means that, before the final floor votes, the program's supporters must win majorities first in the specific subject matter subcommittees in each house, then in the committees with the appropriate jurisdiction, and finally in the House Rules Committee. These basic laws often set maximum levels of permissible spending for each part of the program, or they may just allow "such funds as necessary." Mass media coverage of the legislative process is usually limited to the climactic stages of shaping these laws.

These basic laws *authorize* the government to provide certain new services and set the fundamental framework for the programs, but they do not provide any money to carry them out. After the authorizations are enacted, then the Appropriations subcommittees and committees must decide how much money to *appropriate* each year.

Differences in membership between the program committees and the appropriating and taxing committees contribute to the confusing practice by which Congress authorizes a large new program and then allows the administrators only a fraction of the authorized funds. Democratic liberals, working from power bases on a few key legislative committees, often see their heralded legislative accomplishments eviscerated by Democratic conservatives who work from power bases further along in the legislative process. Progressives by this time have typically committed their energies to new legislative proposals, rather than fighting for resources to implement programs.

Committee differences can, of course, be exaggerated. No committee can deal with policy issues in total isolation from Congress as a whole. Committee action on visible issues where active floor debate may occur is often influenced by a desire to prevent an embarrassing floor defeat for the committee bill. Since committee power is threatened once members learn that a committee bill can be successfully challenged on the floor, committees often try to preserve their power and prestige by making the necessary accommodation to any strong and determined majority. Appropriations policy-makers also generally avoid alienating constituencies of already established programs by permitting unchallenged continuation of programs at the "base" established in previous years. This tends to limit committee power to new programs and to substantial changes in existing ones.

The process of accommodation tends to break down completely only when very sensitive social issues are involved. Thus, for example, the House Appropriations Committee tried to alter a national housing policy meant to break up ghetto concentrations by denying any money at all for enforcement of the 1968 fair-housing law, and by trying to kill a program of federal rent supplements designed to let poor people live in standard new housing. While committee resistance was eventually overcome, both programs started at a fraction of the planned level. In addition, the rent supplement program was hamstrung by an amendment requiring approval of each suburb where the money was to be spent. Thus two major elements of President Johnson's housing policy were crippled at birth. In the area of school desegregation, the Appropriations committees in both houses have similarly attempted to change the law and weaken the administrative enforcement machinery.

While major problems remain, the recent past does show a slowly diminishing role for the Appropriations committees. Both the legislative stalemate created by President Nixon's opposition to new domestic programs, and the activation of strong constituency concern as a result of the drastic Nixon cutbacks in existing programs focused unprecedented attention throughout Congress on spending decisions. Once coalitions of program supporters, such as the education groups fighting for more money, took on the House Appropriations Committee and defeated it on the floor, the committee was inclined to yield in advance rather than face further humiliation.

Meanwhile, within that same committee there were a growing number of liberals gaining seniority and influence on important subcommittees. By 1973, for example, liberals predominated in the Democratic contingents on the subcommittees controlling the budgets of HUD, HEW, the Labor Department, and the Interior Department.[10] By the beginning of the 1973 session, ten of the committee's thirty-three Democratic members had been appointed in the 1970s. The roll call votes that year show the change in the committee. According to the ratings prepared by the liberal Americans for Democratic Action (ADA), the ten newest members voted correctly an average of 57 percent of the time, while the five members with greatest seniority voted wrong 90 percent of the time.[11] The GOP, on the other hand, was continuing to name members from the extreme conservative end of the House political spectrum so that the impact of the new moderate and liberal Democrats was only beginning to be felt.

Complexity and Confusion

The different policy perspectives of the law-writing and financial committees tend to confuse and disillusion many citizens. Few realize that when Congress enacts a billion-dollar program for park land, for example, it is merely setting the *ceiling* figure for future bargaining for appropriations. Few understand the intricate game Congressmen play when they take the pose of supporting a particular constituent group by voting for its authorization, then later quietly oppose its goals by voting for a low appropriation. This way a member can claim to be both a supporter of the policy and a defender of economy in government. Members and Presidents alike often exploit this opportunity to play both sides of the issue.

The fragmentation and internal inconsistency of policy and money decisions within Congress reflect both the lack of the coherent structure of party leadership, and also the ideological deficiencies of both conservatives and liberals. There is no policy and budget coordination, because there has been no working institutional arrangement for establishing priorities and making the decision stick. The Appropriations committees were initially created to make such judgments, but they fragmented their own decisions along agency lines, and the seniority system skewed their membership in the conservative direction, creating a division between the committees and the House leadership.

Congress attempted to address this problem in June 1974 with passage of the Congressional Budget and Impoundment Control Act of 1974, potentially the most important change in Congressional organization in decades. The new law established Budget Committees in each house. The legislation also created a Congressional Budget Office to provide to Congress some of the technical expertise and staff resources available to the President through the Office of Management and Budget. Each year these committees were expected to recommend spending priority targets in the spring and ceilings in the fall. For the first time, both normal appropriations and the huge "backdoor spending" through federal contractual arrangements would come under the purview of single committees.

The legislation provided the framework for Congress to debate the relative importance of various national objectives and the general fiscal policy of the country more clearly than ever before. The Senate named a progressive committee chaired by Senator Muskie (D-Me.), while the House Democratic caucus rejected the Speaker's liberal nominee and chose instead Ways and Means Committee moderate Representative Ullman (D-Ore.).[12] Although the legislation seems likely to increase Congress's influence in the shaping of the national budget, the political consequences remain unclear.

The discontinuities of policy-making reflect blind spots in the American liberal and conservative outlooks toward the political system. Liberalism has no coherent institutional focus or set of priorities, and tends to place tremendous emphasis on the creation of new programs, leaving little time for monitoring administrative decision-making or fighting for program resources. If an old program, poorly financed and denied administrative resources, fails to solve a problem, the assumption is that creating a new program will correct the problem. Conservatism, on the other hand, is rather strongly reflected in Congress, especially among House Republicans, but has very few substantive programs. Its basic assumption is that the federal government is too big; that state or local or private business decisions are normally preferable to national public policy; that money for program administration is money wasted on bureaucrats; and that the government should not interfere with social arrangements. It frequently represents less a program to conserve certain valued aspects of the society than an uncritical hostility to the federal government itself—an attitude with deep roots in American history. The net result is often a series of sporadic, narrowly focused reform movements on the liberal side of Congress that confront a general opposition to the growth of government, and a strong resistance to new social programs from the conservative side. Similar inconsistencies frequently afflict the executive branch as well.

The ideological muddle in Congress reflects the persisting and deeply held beliefs of most Americans. Public opinion polls normally show strong support for many of the specific existing or proposed domestic programs of the federal government, but also keen opposition to "big government" or higher taxes. Gallup polls conducted in late 1972 and early 1973 revealed, for instance, that 65 percent of the public thought their income taxes were too high and that 60 percent said a balanced budget was "very important." At the same time only 38 percent supported the President's impoundment of domestic program funds "as a way of controlling the federal budget." On yet another question, 54 percent expressed support for the President's battle to "hold down government spending and taxes," and opposed Congressional attempts to "pass social programs that would give more money to the poor, the aged and to schools and the like."[13] Had the survey asked about increasing funds for particular popular programs, the confusion would doubtless have been even greater.

Each of these inconsistent positions of the public is strongly represented in the policy-making process, although the multiple vetoes built into the system produce a normal bias toward inaction. The conflict is particularly clear when Congress is controlled by one party and the Presidency by the other. Perhaps recent polls showing an actual public preference for such divided government reflect satisfaction with this clash of values, even at the price of governmental deadlock.

The Special World of Regulatory Policy

While most social program legislation is caught in the constant tension between the policy and money committees, two major kinds of social policy measures are shaped in very different environments. Policy on race, Constitutional rights, and discrimination is largely initiated in the two Judiciary committees, while another set of extremely powerful committees allocate tax benefits and liabilities, rights to retirement income and medical care, and welfare program policies.

The Judiciary Committees

Policies forbidding discrimination, or providing a legal definition or administrative support for the assertion and protection of the rights of a particular group, generally are considered by the House and Senate Judiciary committees. These policies sometimes impose sanctions on certain forms of behavior defined as illegal, and sometimes create administrative machinery to enforce the new rights, but they seldom require large expenditures. Enforcement of the sanctions requires some resources, but often depends primarily on the political judgments of the executive branch.

Civil rights legislation has been the most prominent example of massive social change through regulation. During the period between 1957 and 1972 Congress enacted six major pieces of legislation and one Constitutional amendment fundamentally affecting American race relations. In addition, there were innumerable Congressional battles in response to vigorous action for racial change by the federal courts and by the executive branch during Lyndon Johnson's Presidency. Apart from the historic struggle over civil rights, the Congress has also enacted policies against sex discrimination and granted voting rights to eighteen-year-olds.

Until recently, the House and Senate Judiciary committees reflected the polar extremes of the Democratic Party. The House committee, led for many years by New York Congressman Emanuel Celler, was a bastion of liberalism. The Senate committee, under James Eastland (D-Miss.), was the burying ground for even the most modest civil rights proposals. However, once civil rights became a constant focus for Congressional struggle in the late 1950s, the Senate Democratic leadership named a number of strong liberals to the committee, while the GOP leadership allocated some seats to the party's moderate wing. By the early 1970s the Senate committee was evenly divided, with liberals such as Philip Hart (D-Mich.), Birch Bayh (D-Ind.), and Edward Kennedy (D-Mass.) using it as an important forum for raising civil rights issues. Even so, throughout the struggle the principal point for initiating civil rights laws, and the only place for serious and systematic examination of proposed legislation, has been the

Judiciary Committee of the House. In the Senate the two most important bills were enacted, in 1964 and 1965, by bypassing the committee through direct negotiations between the Democratic and Republican Senate leadership. A third measure, the 1968 fair-housing law, began as a floor amendment to a minor bill, while in 1972 the extension of the enforcement powers and jurisdiction of the Equal Employment Opportunity Commission came through the Senate Labor and Public Welfare Committee. Thus it has been the political circumstance of liberal Democratic seniority on the House committee that has made possible a Congressional response to the movement for civil rights.

Short-circuiting Committee Power: The Role of Tactics

Two of the other major changes extending important rights to large categories of citizens came about largely independent of committee action. The extension of the suffrage to eighteen-year-olds happened suddenly in 1970, after decades of futile student demands. There was in fact little visible public demand for the change, the idea had been defeated in several state elections, and the necessary legislation had never been reported out of the Senate Judiciary Committee. Even so, Senator Edward Kennedy forced a vote on the issue through a parliamentary stratagem. When the 1970 Voting Rights bill was on the floor and the Senate was debating extending protection for the voting rights of Southern blacks for five more years, Kennedy suddenly moved to amend the bill with the unrelated measure allowing eighteen-year-olds to vote. Senate rules permit such extraneous amendments and Kennedy received the powerful support of Majority Leader Mike Mansfield. Confronted with the necessity of a public vote on the issue at a time when eighteen-year-olds were being killed in an unpopular war in Vietnam, and when the campuses were in an uproar over the invasion of Cambodia and the Kent State University shootings, a majority supported the amendment.

The Senate amendment asserted federal power to change voting-age requirements by a simple statute rather than a Constitutional amendment. This was a highly controversial theory of law, since the Constitution grants the states broad powers to regulate suffrage standards. Some liberals, including the chairman of the House Judiciary Committee, had deep reservations about the constitutionality of the measure. Since the Voting Rights Act was so terribly important to protect the political rights of Southern blacks, a reluctant House conference committee delegation accepted the eighteen-year-old amendment and sent the issue on to the courts. President Nixon was then confronted with the choice of signing the bill or vetoing a civil rights measure with broad public support. He decided to sign, but in signing, expressed his basic doubts about the constitutionality of the voting-age provision.

The issue came quickly to the Supreme Court. In a divided and confusing decision, the Court held that Congress had authority to lower the voting age for federal elections for President and Congress, but not for state and local elections. The decision threatened to produce electoral chaos. The unmanageable problems of maintaining two separate electorates led to rapid Congressional and state legislative approval of a Constitutional amendment lowering the voting age for all elections. Skillful use of legislative leverage had precipitated the extension of voting power to millions of young Americans, even before substantial public pressure had built up behind the reform movement.

Committees were almost equally unimportant in decisions to extend rights to women. The chairman of the House committee, in fact, was a leading opponent of the most important change, the Equal Rights Amendment. The key move was a discharge petition, which forced the issue to the House floor without any committee action.

In major cases of social regulatory policy, then, change has frequently come through parliamentary tactics forcing the issue to a floor vote. While opponents often pay little political price for quietly bottling up a bill in committee, the calculations change once a visible issue with a substantial local constituency comes up for a public vote on the floor. Members do not relish alienating major groups like young voters, the female majority, or the black, labor, and church groups that formed the backbone of the civil rights coalition.

Social change issues also are relatively more insulated from technical control by committee experts. While it may be a staggeringly complex job for the average Congressman to really comprehend the issues involved in a major bill amending the tax code, it requires little technical competence to reach a decision about whether the rights of blacks or students or women need more protection. For the same reason, the decisions are much more visible to the concerned public, and this puts members even more on the spot politically when a popular issue is forced to the floor. There it is far more difficult to sabotage reform legislation by making apparently "technical" changes or sending it back to committee than it would be in the case of complicated tax, appropriations, or welfare bills.

The drive for social reform legislation in the 1960s and 1970s was aided not only by success in bringing issues directly to the floor, but also by the existence of some committees that actively supported significant reforms. This was particularly true in the House, where the Judiciary Committee consistently endorsed civil rights bills.

As progressives succeeded in enacting much of the existing agenda in the 1960s, they soon discovered that another, more difficult, set of issues lay behind the regulatory changes. When the civil rights leaders came up against the hard fact that regulatory legislation could limit some forms of discrimination but still leave vast inequalities, they had to face the more arduous task of changing economic and welfare policies. This required them to shift their struggle from relatively responsive Congressional arenas to bastions of conservative power. The results were deeply discouraging.

Committee Autocracy: Taxes and the Ways and Means Committee

In sharp contrast to the committees controlling civil rights legislation, those which allocate the tax burden operate under little effective Congressional or public scrutiny, specialize in highly technical decision-making, and exhibit continuing hostility to serious reform. Although Congress has always jealously guarded its control of the power to tax, a very strong and ancient source of legislative influence, taxation decisions are very largely isolated from effective control by Congressional majorities. While virtually no Congressional actions have so immediate an impact on so many citizens as those setting tax rates and allocating retirement, medical, and welfare benefits, the social policies are obscured by incredibly complex bills amending voluminous and arcane codes understood by only a handful of specialists either inside or outside Congress.

Complexity is conducive to committee power, as is the House tradition of sending tax bills to the floor under closed rules permitting no amendment — rules intended to forestall massive efforts to write into the tax code special tax privileges for a great many local interests. The House Ways and Means Committee tends to dominate tax policy by virtue of the Constitutional requirement that the House initiate tax measures; by virtue of the greater technical mastery of House committee members; by its authority to bring bills to the floor under closed rules; and through the power it derives from its function of allocating committee assignments for the majority party. The House committee's power is further enhanced by the often bipartisan nature of its decisions, and the unusual respect enjoyed by its longtime chairman, Wilbur Mills (D-Ark.).

Ways and Means is the most prestigious committee in the House, and perhaps the most important single committee in the shaping of social policy. It is also, however, perhaps the clearest illustration of the remaining deficiencies of the Congressional process. Since no one leaves the committee once appointed, and since seniority is generally required to win a seat, the time lag before changes in the political parties are reflected on the committee is probably the greatest in Congress. Thus, for example, some of the present members were appointed by former House leaders who were concerned not about contemporary issues of national health insurance, tax reform, or welfare policy, but about the older ones of free trade and the oil depletion allowance. At a time when House Democrats were primarily Southern, committee membership was influenced by a traditional twofold commitment of the agrarian South: to low tariffs designed to hold down the costs of manufactured goods and support a free international trade for the regional farm exports; and to the special tax privileges of the powerful oil barons of Texas and Louisiana. The Democratic Party's continuing practice of allocating seats on the committee to certain states or regions further increases the obstacles to control of the committee by the party's leadership.

Until recently, Southern Democrats were vastly overrepresented on the committee, usually claiming six or seven of the fifteen majority-party seats. The panel's conservative bias was intensified by the GOP practice of naming only rock-ribbed conservatives to the ten minority seats. The committee's conservative coalition was evident, for example, when it rejected a popular 1960 medical care bill 17–8 with almost half the Democrats joining all the Republicans to destroy the chance of enacting a basic part of the party's platform during a Presidential election year. Not until 1965 did new appointments produce a slim one-vote margin for Medicare — almost two decades after President Harry Truman had made national medical insurance a part of the Democratic Party's goals.[14]

The committee's continuing role in defusing progressive efforts was very clear in the tax reform drive of the late 1960s and early 1970s. Congress was crucial in initiating this drive, but the Ways and Means Committee and the Senate Finance Committee protected the status quo. Congress helped bring the issue to public attention, directing the Johnson Administration to prepare a reform proposal and then providing the forum for the outgoing Treasury Secretary to denounce the scandalous level of tax privileges for the rich in early 1969. Under pressure, the new Nixon Administration responded with a major tax bill repealing the existing wartime 10-percent income tax surcharge, ending the business investment tax credit, and removing from the tax rolls about two million very low-income families then paying small amounts of tax. The bill included only one modest reform proposal that narrowed the use of tax shelters, and left the basic structure of tax loopholes intact.[15]

In 1969 strong public interest in reform and active pressure on the committees by unusually concerned members of the House and Senate produced some changes in a muddled bill intended to please virtually everyone. The price of this confusing compromise and the largely symbolic reforms was a permanent cut in the revenue-raising capacity of the federal government.

Congress altered the President's bill, shifting some tax relief from industry to individuals and narrowing some loopholes. The final bill, enacted in the face of a threatened Presidential veto, ended taxation of most people below the official poverty level and also raised personal exemptions for all taxpayers — this last a popular change, but one that saved the most dollars for taxpayers in the highest brackets. The bill went beyond the President's recommendations in lowering the previously sacrosanct oil depletion allowance, restricting some forms of real estate tax shelters, and closing a total of $6.6 billion in loopholes. The final bill also incorporated a large increase in Social Security benefits — one 50 percent greater than the President had asked.[16]

The Congressional change in the social impact of the White House bill was heavily influenced by pressure from outside the tax-writing committees. In the House, liberals attacked the Ways and Means Committee's draft bill shortly before it was to go to the floor; this produced additional cuts for the five lowest tax brackets, and significant relief for working families earning between $7,500 and $13,000 a year. The result was a bill that tripled the low-income exemptions proposed by the President, and provided another $2.4 billion in cuts for average wage earners. In the Senate the fight for raising the personal exemption was conducted by Senator Albert Gore (D-Tenn.).

The liberalizing amendments, however, carried a cost. The price for offering some relief to all taxpayers earning less than $100,000 and for reducing the tax rates for the highest incomes without cutting deeply into loopholes was the transformation of a tax reform bill into a large tax reduction bill. The measure sacrificed $2.5 billion in federal revenue the first year and more in succeeding years. The revenue loss limited options for new social programs. The President pointed out the problem in reluctantly signing the popular measure.[17]

President Kennedy had pioneered the idea of federal tax cuts to stimulate the economy in 1962, when the proposal was seen by economists as a strategy for putting money into the economy without confronting the Congressional deadlock over domestic programs. Congress and the President carried the approach into the Nixon period, in spite of the fact that the deadlock had been decisively broken. Tax cuts in 1969 and 1971, combined with Administration-supported cuts in corporate and excise taxes, had reduced government revenues in a full-employment economy by the staggering sum of $45 billion a year in 1972.[18]

In effect, Administration conservatives and the conservatives on the tax-writing committees had eliminated the increment of federal sources necessary to finance many of the national policy commitments made in the major Great Society bills. Since the beginning of the Johnson Administration, Congress had been financing the growth of domestic programs with annual budget increases of more than 9 percent a year—a sharp break with the pattern of the previous decade. By 1972, Great Society programs accounted for about $38 billion in federal spending, with another $32 billion added for Social Security and Medicare since the Johnson Presidency began.[19]

The Johnson programs were planned around the expectation of steadily growing federal resources. Some were still in the planning phase when Nixon took office, and there was mounting constituency and Congressional support for implementation funds. In addition, there was strong support for a range of new programs, including revenue sharing. The tax cuts and the costs of maintaining existing programs in a time of rapid inflation left very little money either for fulfillment of old commitments or for starting new ones. Few in either the White House or the Capitol weighed the long-term impact.

While a series of incremental decisions were cutting back the nation's ability to finance social programs, another series of decisions was increasing the regressive impact of the payroll tax on working-class and middle-class people. Since the tax allowed no deductions, and exempted all income above a fixed figure and all nonwage income as well, increases were a disproportionately heavy burden on lower-income families. Between 1963 and 1973, payroll tax receipts quadrupled, reaching one dollar in every twenty-five in the economy. For millions of lower-income families the net effect of cuts in income taxes, combined with the huge increase in payroll taxation, was an increase in their share of the tax burden.[20] A highly sophisticated 1974 study of the total federal, state, and local taxes paid by Americans found that the net effect of the nation's tax system was to tax almost all income groups at the same level. Families earning between $3,000 and more than $100,000 paid about the same percentage of their incomes in taxes. The very rich paid only a moderately higher level of taxes. Amazingly enough, those earning below $3,000 actually paid a significantly higher level of taxes than a great many far more affluent families.[21] The rapidly growing dependence of the federal government on Social Security payroll taxes was increasing the tax burden on millions of lower-income working families.

The payroll tax increases had been routinely passed without serious discussion. For decades most Congressmen and Senators had accepted the argument that the Social Security system was an insurance system, even though its actual functions and financing were always very different. (In actual practice, the benefits greatly outstrip typical contributions, and the size of the payment is only very imperfectly related to the amount of the contributions.) When a challenge to this assumption was made in the House in 1973, the conservative role of the Ways and Means Committee in perpetuating this regressive system became very apparent.

The House Democratic leadership, working in cooperation with the Rules Committee, bypassed the Ways and Means Committee in October 1973, authorizing liberals to try to amend a bill raising the federal debt ceiling. This tactic was intended to put the reform in a measure President Nixon couldn't afford to veto, since the government would otherwise lack authority to pay its bills. The amendment added a 7-percent boost in Social Security benefits, and obtained the necessary revenue by increasing the minimum tax on tax-sheltered earnings of companies and the rich. "It's an opportunity," said House Majority Leader Thomas O'Neill, Jr. (D-Mass.), "to raise $3 billion from people who can afford it and give some of it to senior citizens who need it." In response to the leadership initiative, however, the Ways and Means Committee rapidly cut off the reform drive by reporting out a long-stalled Social Security benefit increase financed by more payroll taxes.[22]

In spite of some stirrings of reform, and occasional grudging concessions from the tax committees, the committees retain vast power and autonomy. This power was often used to protect special interests. A study of the 1969 tax reform bill concludes:

> . . . the worst tax loopholes still remain. Percentage depletion and write-offs for intangible drilling expense for the oil and gas industry emerged from the battle virtually unscathed. A strong challenge to the tax-exempt status of state and local government bonds was successfully beaten back. . . . Proposals to eliminate entirely the preferred tax treatment of capital gains . . . were substantially softened. Many other major escape hatches . . . still remain to be dealt with.[23]

The committees have retained control for several reasons. Until recently neither committee allowed subcommittees or permitted staff aides of various members to sit in on sessions. Thus members other than the chairman could not develop expertise through running hearings, and did not have any real working access to staff experts. This put an almost impossible burden on most members:

> A final element that freezes out the average Congressman or Senator and tightens the grip of the Tax Establishment is the hideous complexity of the tax laws and the virtual unintelligibility of most of their provisions. How is the average member of Congress . . . to deal with provisions such as this one (taken at random from the Internal Revenue Code):
>
> ". . . For purposes of paragraph (3), an organization described in paragraph (2) shall be deemed to include an organization described in Section 501 (c) (4), (5) or (6) which would be described in paragraph (2) if it were an organization described in Section 501 (c) (3)."[24]

The complexity, says reformer Philip Stern, "endows the experts and the 'insiders' with unusual powers, and robs even the most vigilant Congressman or newsman of his normal powers of scrutiny. What casual observer, for example, would be able to spot a provision in a 585-page tax bill innocuously headed 'Certain New Design Products' and know that it was tailor-made to confer more than $20,000,000 in tax saving upon the Lockheed and McDonnell Douglas companies?"[25]

The power, the isolation, and the unrepresentative character of the tax-writing committees distort social policy in a conservative direction. Since it is so firmly rooted in the seniority system and the decentralized system of committee power, this distortion is difficult to rectify. Only a long series of appointments by leaders sympathetic to a contemporary party majority could turn the committee around.

While this is not likely to happen soon, there is some evidence that the committees are coming under more pressure from Congress as a whole. While the tax reform bill of 1969 was weak, it did begin the long-resisted effort to whittle down some of the least defensible deductions. Outside pressure pushed Social Security payments up far more rapidly than the committees desired in the late 1960s and early 1970s. There were efforts to challenge the committee directly on the House floor, and the House Rules Committee no longer showed a determination to forbid amendments to the major bills from the Ways and Means Committee.

Congressional Inconsistency: A Spectacularly Visible Phenomenon

The committee system, with its different political and institutional biases in various committees with overlapping responsibilities, frequently produces the appearance, and sometimes the reality, of wildly inconsistent policy decisions. The Judiciary committees may forge legislation protecting the rights of black Americans, even as the Appropriations committees starve the programs that are intended to make those rights real. The House Education and Labor Committee can shape creative new public employment programs, even as the House Ways and Means Committee forces welfare mothers to work at terrible jobs for poverty-level pay without adequate child care.

The committees distort policy development in different ways, but most of their positive decisions are at least subject to correction by the majority on the House or Senate floor. The most drastic distortions come through negative action, through refusal to take action on legislation at all, or through votes not to report measures to the floor. When the Senate Finance Committee refuses to act on tax reform at a time of great public interest, or the House Judiciary Committee stalls popular antibusing legislation, the ability of Congress to respond to strong majority wishes may be severely undermined.

The fact that Congressional policies affecting the same group often go in two different directions at the same time does not mean that Congress is either hopelessly confused, or that it is the most conservative element of the policy-making process. In fact, the internal divisions and contradictions in Congress are paralleled by less visible but very important divisions within the other branches of government. Because the executive branch is legally subject to Presidential direction, and the President approves a general set of legislative and budget priorities, there is a strong incentive to compromise disagreements into a semblance of unity. Often, however, basic differences persist. Thus, to cite one Nixon Administration example, education officials can persuade the President to announce a massive Right to Read program, only to have budget officials convince him to actually cut back on the federal share of school costs. The inconsistencies are even clearer in the simultaneous pursuit of contradictory policies toward the same clientele by a variety of executive agencies. The Public Health Service, for example, struggles against cigarette smoking, while the Agriculture Department promotes tobacco growing and exports.

Even on the Supreme Court the majority opinion is often a compromise that is unclear or even internally contradictory. To maintain unity on the landmark 1954 and 1955 school cases, for example, the Court declared that black children had an unambiguous right to a desegregated education, but then refused to give any significant enforcement to the right.

The divisions and inconsistencies in the other branches of government are generally kept private. The media usually treat the compromise statements and decisions as if they were relatively clear and rational policies, giving the President and the Court the benefit of a doubt. It is Congress's misfortune that its disunity is so painfully public and so easily publicized.

The other branches, however, at least have a recognized structure of legitimate centralized decision-making, and provide strong incentives toward quiet internal working out of conflicts. In Congress this problem is magnified by the lack of strong party leaders in recent decades. There is usually no legitimate focus for policy-making on the large divisive issues, except the total membership voting on the floor. Naturally, observers of Congress focus more on the interesting and highly visible conflicts than on the direction and significance of the legislation that eventually emerges. With so many of these conflicts to report, they pay little attention to the skillful building of consensus within committees that often precedes major legislation. And if an analyst does attempt to assess the outputs, he must weigh a complex body of laws, appropriations measures, and committee decisions to pigeonhole bills, as well as the reports and floor debates, to discern the "intent of Congress."

Congressional policy-making is often characterized by inconsistent or even contradictory policy directions. While this may well be the character of governmental decision-making in general, it is spectacularly visible in Congress. Assessment of the actual net impact of the array of Congressional policy decisions is an extremely complex undertaking, but it is essential to evaluating the real policy impact of the legislative branch. When this effort is made, the importance of Congressional policy innovation becomes far clearer. It also soon becomes evident that any effort to stereotype Congress as inherently passive or conservative is doomed to failure. Any serious attempt to describe the policy impact of Congress must obviously describe the time period, the policy areas under consideration, and the existing division of power within Congress during that period.

Notes

[1]*Washington Post,* May 9, 1974; William Watts and Lloyd A. Free, eds., *State of the Nation* (New York: Universe Books, 1973), p. 243, 246.

[2]Arthur M. Schlesinger, Jr., *The Imperial Presidency* (Boston: Houghton Mifflin, 1973), pp. 246–52.

[3]Lawrence Henry Chamberlain, *The President, Congress and Legislation* (New York: Columbia University Press, 1946).

[4]Ronald C. Moe and Steven C. Teel, "Congress as Policy-Maker: A Necessary Reappraisal," in Ronald C. Moe, ed., *Congress and the President* (Pacific Palisades, Calif.: Goodyear, 1971), p. 50.

[5]David Price, *Who Makes the Laws: Creativity and Power in Senate Committees* (New York: Schenkman Publishing, 1972), pp. 331–32.

[6]See David Halberstam, *The Best and the Brightest* (New York: Random House, 1972), for a good description of the relationship between the prevailing liberal ideology and U.S. involvement in Vietnam.

[7]Charles S. Bullock, III, "Committee Transfers in the United States House of Representatives," *Journal of Politics,* February 1973, p. 94.

[8]*Congressional Quarterly,* April 28, 1973, pp. 989, 1001–03; *Congressional Directory,* 93rd Cong., 1st Sess., 1973.

[9]Richard Fenno's *The Power of the Purse* (Boston: Little, Brown, 1966) is particularly good in explaining how this process works on the House Appropriations Committee.

[10]*Congressional Quarterly,* April 28, 1973, p. 974.

[11]*Congressional Quarterly*, March 30, 1974, pp. 816–17, contains ratings of 1973 roll calls by four organizations. Committee membership is taken from appropriate volumes of the *Congressional Directory*.

[12]*Congressional Quarterly*, August 10, 1974, p. 2163.

[13]*Gallup Opinion Index*, March 1973, pp. 4–6.

[14]John F. Manley, *The Politics of Finance: The House Committee on Ways and Means* (Boston: Little, Brown, 1970), pp. 27–29, 36–38.

[15]*Congressional Quarterly Almanac*, 1969, pp. 589, 602–03.

[16]*Ibid.*, p. 605.

[17]*Ibid.*, p. 1649.

[18]Charles L. Schultze, Edward R. Fried, Alice M. Rivlin, and Nancy H. Teeters, *Setting National Priorities: The 1973 Budget* (Washington: Brookings Institution, 1972), p. 75.

[19]*Ibid.*, pp. 398–400.

[20]Joseph A. Pechman, *Federal Tax Policy* (Washington: Brookings Institution, 1971), pp. 173–74; *Setting National Priorities: The 1973 Budget*, pp. 428–29.

[21]Joseph A. Pechman and Benjamin A. Okner, *Who Bears the Tax Burden?* (Washington: Brookings Institution, 1974), pp. 4–10.

[22]*Washington Post*, October 31 and November 2, 1973.

[23]Joseph A. Ruskay and Richard A. Osserman, *Halfway to Tax Reform* (Bloomington: Indiana University Press, 1970), p. 217.

[24]Philip M. Stern, *The Rape of the Taxpayer* (New York: Random House, 1973), pp. 393–94.

[25]*Ibid.*, pp. 394–95.

Part 5 Change in the Congressional System

The congressional system is not fixed and immutable; it is constantly changing, sometimes rapidly and dramatically, usually slowly and unobtrusively. Sometimes change is intentional and by design; when it is, we talk about congressional reform. At other times, alterations are unintentional and occur through evolution, not revolution. Indeed, if we conceive of Congress as a system—members operating within a structural context that committees, parties, rules, and norms define—that processes inputs, especially demands, but also supports, to produce outputs (policies, oversight, and representation), we should not be surprised to find that as one element changes the others alter as well. For example, as new circumstances arise—a new president, some major domestic or international crisis, or renewed public concern for some issue—the pressures on Congress will change; new members may be elected and act to alter the contours of the institution; in consequence, new and differing emphases will appear in legislative activities. In short, new demands (inputs) may require Congress to adapt (to restructure itself) to produce new, more satisfactory outputs.

In fact, just such a process has taken place in the 1970s.[1] A series of events outside Congress, the Vietnam War and the assorted scandals known collectively as Watergate in particular, provided the catalyst for a far-reaching set of changes inside the legislature. These occurrences led, in one way or another, to the election of an increasingly large contingent of new members. These newcomers joined with numerous holdover legislators to seek to revitalize congressional capacity to act vigorously and forcefully, a capacity that the events of the period suggested incontrovertibly had declined if not virtually withered away. Executive misbehavior, quite understandably, put all government in the public eye, and the scrutiny that followed uncovered congressional activities that, when not illegal, raised serious doubts about the legislators' capacity to put the national interest above personal gain.[2] The result of these happenings—and the public and governmental response to them—was that by the end of the decade Congress had changed substantially: Its members were younger and less committed to the conventional ways of doing things; its internal structures and modes of operation were significantly different; its relationships with those in its environment had shifted noticeably; and its outputs seemed likely to change in consequence of the previous changes.

What Kind of Congress?

Before turning to the specifics of these changes, it seems appropriate to raise a question that reformers often ignore. Faced with a pressing need to react to an immediate crisis, they often fail to inquire about the precise position that Congress *should* occupy in American politics. They are so busy pursuing short-run goals that they do not look to the long-term, overall effect on the legislature of the reforms they propose and seek to implement. It is, or should be, obvious that change to promote one sort of Congress may be useless, at best, if a different sort of institution appears desirable. Alternatively, a set of changes may, in effect, "cancel each other out," leaving the legislature no better off than it was in the prereform period. In short, before they prescribe for Congress, reformers need to be certain about their patient's malady and clear about the sort of health to which they wish to restore it.

Observers of Congress have envisioned at least three broad directions in which legislative reform might move; although not entirely incompatible with one another, these directions lead to quite different visions of Congress.[3] First, some see the need for a *responsible* legislature, a Congress capable of making effective public policy efficiently. Though there are variations on the theme, those who espouse the responsibility goal want Congress to be able to make, or at the very least to contribute meaningfully to the making of, sound policy. Some want Congress to dominate the policy process, to overshadow the executive branch (Burnham, 1959; de Grazia, 1965); others desire only that Congress have a greater impact on the nation's fundamental policy decisions (U.S. House, 1973); but all share the wish to see Congress' capacity to make policy enhanced and employed.

A second emphasis, on *responsiveness*, focuses less on what Congress does than on *how*, on the *process* by which, it acts. That is, those stressing the responsiveness goal believe that only Congress among the institutions of government can speak loudly and clearly on behalf of the citizens of the country. From this perspective, Congress must be organized to listen and attend to the expressed needs of the American people. Though some stress Congress as an "ombudsman," as dealing with individual problems (casework), and others see the legislature as reflecting popular policy preferences, the responsiveness criterion emphasizes that Congress must listen to, provide a clear channel of communication for, those whom it represents. Note that responsibility and responsiveness are not easily reconcilable: To the extent that Congress makes policy with speed and efficiency, it may be unable to wait for citizen viewpoints to be formulated and expressed; and conversely, to the extent that Congress waits to hear from the public, it may be unable to formulate programs promptly.

A third standard, *accountability*, is less problematic. Accountability refers to the opportunity for citizens, as voters, to judge members of Congress, retrospectively to be sure, on the basis of their conduct in office. If the legislators are found wanting, if they have failed to meet popular expectations (whether those expectations stress responsibility or responsiveness), the voters can replace them with new senators and representatives in the hopes of bringing about improved legislative performance. What is essential from this point of view is that legislative operations be visible "out in the open," so that voters can render an informed and intelligent judgment about congressional conduct.

Overall, then, the direction reformers see as desirable for Congress, the criterion they choose to apply as an evaluative standard, should suggest particular changes for the legislature. In general terms, preference for policy effectiveness (responsibility) suggests the need for centralization, most obviously through the political parties, to move legislation rapidly through to passage. A preference for representation and ease of access to Congress (responsiveness), on the other hand, indicates a need to decentralize, to open up numerous channels over which citizens can communicate with Congress. Finally, accountability requires that the legislature's actions be accessible to the public. Because such standards seldom guide legislative reform, we should not be surprised to find that changes intended to promote movement in each of these three directions have been adopted simultaneously.

Congressional Change, 1970–1978

In fact, Congress has, in the 1970–1978 period, adapted changes of a varied sort. The internal structure of the legislative system, especially the committees, but also the party organizations, has been reformed. The legislature has attempted to reshape its relationships with environmental actors—the executive in particular, but also interest groups and the public at large. These changes, moreover, seem likely to alter the outputs, especially policy and oversight, of the congressional system. In their variety, these reforms have implications for all three evaluative standards—responsibility, responsiveness, and accountability.

Reshaping the Congressional System

During the 1970s, the internal dynamics of Congress underwent great change. To begin with, the nature of electoral politics was dramatically altered with the passage, in 1974, of a Federal Election Campaign Act that imposed stringent limitations on individual and corporate campaign fund contributions. The upshot of the new law's provisions—individuals can give a maximum of $1000 and organizations no more than $5000 to any single campaign—is that members of Congress must fill their campaign coffers with many small rather than a few large donations. The intent, of course, is to reduce legislators' dependence on large donors, but the effect is to exacerbate the already onerous fund-raising chores that members face in each campaign. With inflation raising the cost of campaigns, members must now deal with a great many people to gain the necessary monies, and these numerous donors may all feel that they are entitled to the ear, if not the support, of the donee.[4] This need to devote considerable personal effort to fund raising seems to have contributed to the increased independence of the newer members, particularly in the House, who have survived the rigors of the campaign to win election.

In addition, there are significant numbers of such new members in the contemporary Congress. Often overlooked, given the frequent focus on the considerable ability of incumbents to win reelection (Burnham, 1975; Cover, 1977), is the extent to which newcomers have found their way into the hall of Congress.[5] They are younger, less tradition-bound, more independent, and John Brademas (D-Ind.), the House Majority Whip, finds them "better educated, more articulate, and more conscientious" as well as less temperamentally equipped to engage in the traditional decision-through-bargaining-and-compromise process that characterizes congressional conduct of business (Herbers, 1978).

These newcomers, and a number of holdover members as well, were quite prepared to promote congressional reform. Their first target was the power of the committee chairpersons and the venerable seniority rule that sustained that power. As already noted, the powers of the committee chair have been eroded in recent years. Each party in each chamber now permits its full membership to vote for each committee chairperson; criteria other than seniority are valid bases for this choice. Although seniority is most often observed, the ouster of three elderly, southern, conservative chairmen — W. R. Poage, seventy-five (D-Tex.), of the Agriculture Committee; F. Edward Hebert, seventy-four (D-La.), of the Armed Services Committee; and Wright Patman, eighty-one (D-Tex.), of the Banking, Currency, and Housing Committee — in 1975 makes the willingness of the new members to breach the seniority rule obvious. Hereafter, the chair will be on notice that misbehavior — real or perceived — may lead to removal from the position. Moreover, and more important, on many House and Senate committees majorities have adopted new committee rules that effectively preclude the chair from running roughshod over the rank-and-file members.

Other developments have also contributed to the changing nature of the congressional committee structure. More members now occupy a piece of committee or subcommittee "turf." In the House, no representative can chair more than one full or subcommittee; in the smaller Senate, members can chair no more than one full committee and one subcommittee on each full committee on which they serve. In addition, the members in each chamber are limited — to two in the House and three in the Senate — in the number of committees to which they can accept assignment. The effect of these changes is to open up more positions, each with some authority attached to it, to more members.

Finally, during this period, each chamber established a select committee — the House (Bolling) Committee on Committees (see U.S. House, 1974) and the Senate (Stevenson) Committee to Study the Senate Committee System (see U.S. Senate, 1977)—to analyze existing committee arrangements and procedures. The House committee's recommendations were comprehensive; they proved to be too much for the majority and were sidetracked for a more moderate set of reforms that a committee of the Democratic caucus produced (see Davidson and Oleszek, 1977). The Senate panel, after considerable give and take, produced a plan that was overwhelmingly adopted early in 1977. In both cases, the changes that were adopted tended to simplify and streamline the committee structure and, incidentally, to open up some new positions of influence.

Within these revamped committee organizational patterns, the most significant development has been the devolution of power to autonomous, independent *subcommittees.* Especially in the House, where the new developments were codified in a "subcommittee bill of rights" adopted in 1973, the subcommittees have emerged as a major locus of decision making. All House committees with twenty or more members must have at least four subcommittees (only the Rules Committee escapes this proviso); each subcommittee is to have a defined jurisdiction, to have bills on matters within that jurisdiction automatically referred to it, to have formal authority to meet and to conduct business, and to have adequate staff and financial resources. These guarantees have made many subcommittees not only the repositories of congressional expertise on the topics within their purviews but also the places where the most significant congressional decisions are made.

Finally, staff resources have been more widely distributed among the more junior members. Personal staff allowances have grown in recent years for both senators and representatives.[6] In 1975, junior senators won a significant victory, obtaining committee staff to aid them on legislative matters. All senators not already entitled to staff help—as a committee chairperson or ranking minority member—were authorized to hire one staff person, directly responsible to them, for each committee (up to three) on which they served. As noted, subcommittees were guaranteed control of their own staff and in both chambers new rules were adopted to increase the number of staff members authorized to work directly for minority party committee members. In sum, more members have access to greater staff resources, which may permit more members to develop greater expertise and make more significant contributions to the substance of legislative activity.

The thrust of all these committee changes has been to disperse influence more widely.[7] More senators and representatives are "in on the action," with institutional vantage points from which to exercise some control over at least a small segment of congressional activity. This means that Congress is more decentralized, more fragmented, than it was a decade ago. Bargaining, negotiation, and compromise are more than ever the modes by which the congressional system processes the demands on it. These changes, moreover, foster congressional responsiveness. They create and identify more points within the congressional system to which outside interests may direct their attention to be heard by those in the legislature who will ultimately make or influence congressional decisions. There are more channels open to more legislators than has been the case previously. Congress is in a better position to hear, and perhaps to act on, the views of executives, groups, and citizens.

At the same time that it has adopted these decentralizing committee changes, however, Congress has also moved to increase the possibilities for centralization. It has made the parties, at least the Democratic majority, stronger, potentially better able to move their legislative programs ahead more effectively. Both the Speaker and the party caucus have gained new powers. The former, during the 1970s, acquired new bill referral authority and now has broader power to send bills to more than one committee at a time, thus enabling the Speaker to do more to assure a measure treatment consistent with the leadership's wishes. The Democratic caucus granted the Speaker the right to nominate, subject to caucus ratification, the Democratic members of the House Rules Committee. This privilege contributed to the party's ability to hold the Rules Committee in line, to make it a partner of instead of a roadblock to the leadership.

In 1973, the caucus approved the creation of a Democratic Steering and Policy Committee, intended to aid the party leaders in planning and implementing party programs and strategy. Significantly, two years later the caucus transferred to the new committee (from the Democratic members of the Ways and Means Committee) the power to nominate members to serve on and to chair House committees, subject again to caucus approval. The shift of these committee assignment responsibilities placed them in the hands of a body both more liberal and more loyal to the Speaker than the Ways and Means Democrats.[8] In addition, the caucus asserted its authority to shape the substance of legislation. Before 1973, some legislation, mostly revenue measures from Ways and Means, reached the floor protected by a "closed rule" that effectively barred amendments the committee opposed. Under a new procedure, if fifty members propose and a majority of the caucus agrees, the Democrats on the Rules Committee are bound to allow a floor vote on a particular amendment.[9] In these ways, the Speaker and caucus are now empowered to work forcefully to define, implement, and seek to pass party programs.

There have also been some rules changes in recent years, modest in the House but more dramatic and potentially more far-reaching in the Senate, designed to reduce the ability of minorities to impede the flow of legislation through Congress. In the lower chamber, the use of a variety of dilatory tactics — for instance, repeated demands for quorum calls — was restricted. In certain circumstances, a series of votes can be clustered at the end of, rather than scattered throughout, the day to save time. An electronic voting system has shortened the time roll-call voting consumes. The most notable development, however, occurred in the Senate, where after many years of effort, reformers finally succeeded in modifying the filibuster rule. The new cloture provisions permit three-fifths of the Senate (sixty members) to cut off debate on substantive legislation; on proposals to change the rules, the old requirement of two-thirds of those present and voting (sixty-seven members if the full Senate is present) remains in force. In general, these rules changes may make Congress somewhat more efficient, more responsible, by making it a little easier to move legislation ahead.

Overall, the reformers have marched smartly in two not entirely compatible directions. On the one hand, they have restructured the committees of Congress, decentralizing them even more than was formerly the case. Greater fragmentation may encourage legislative responsiveness, by placing more legislators in positions where they can listen to and act for citizen interests; but it may also make responsible policy making more difficult, by requiring policy coalitions to encompass greater numbers of independent power wielders. On the other hand, and at the same time, the reformers have moved to strengthen the political parties. The new powers of the Speaker of the House, the revitalized House Democratic caucus, and the rules changes in the House and Senate provide some increased possibilities for more disciplined political parties, and through them, for more centralized decision making. More centralization, of course, reduces the opportunities for responsiveness. Although it is too early to determine which of these tendencies—toward responsiveness and responsibility—will prevail, as the 1970s draw to a close the indications are that the congressional system, as a result of the decade's changes, will continue to be more decentralized and individually oriented than centralized and collectively oriented.

Altered Environmental Relationships

The relationships between Congress and the actors in its environment have not been immune to change during this period. The interactions between the legislature and the executive branch, interest groups, and the public at large have all undergone substantial alteration. Most important, perhaps, in the aftermath of Vietnam and Watergate, which revealed a seemingly large decline in congressional authority relative to the presidency, Congress has made a determined effort to equip itself to play a more meaningful part in the policy process. It has sought, through a number of avenues, to move to a position of greater authority.

Congress has tried to equalize its position vis-à-vis the executive. In the foreign policy area, it passed the War Powers Resolution in 1973, limiting the president's authority to commit U.S. military forces to combat. If the chief executive sends troops into the field without a declaration of war, as he did in Korea and Vietnam, he must report the act to Congress; and if the legislature does not approve the action within sixty days, the president must withdraw them, subject to certain exceptions.[10] The utility of the resolution remains unclear; the only occasion in which it might have applied—the Cambodian seizure of an American ship, the *Mayaguez*—was too brief to permit Congress to respond to the president's use of military force.

Congressional reform has had a clearer impact in the area of budgetary politics. Long criticized for taking a piecemeal, uncoordinated approach to fiscal affairs, Congress in 1974 enacted a budget and impoundment control measure. The bill established new procedures and the Congressional Budget Office, a new legislative agency to provide budgetary expertise to rival that the Office of Management and Budget, provides the executive branch. The new scheme compels Congress to coordinate and, to some extent, centralize its budget making. Before the start of each fiscal year, Congress must specify aggregate spending levels for seventeen functional budget categories, the total federal revenues for the year, and the deficit (or surplus), the difference between spending and revenue. New Budget Committees in the House and Senate have prime responsibility for putting the congressional budget together.

The new process has worked surprisingly well during the three years since it was adopted. The Congress is no longer at the mercy of the president in budgetary politics; it has been able to produce a coherent budget, one that has reflected more legislative priorities—for example, more domestic and less defense spending—than was the case before the reforms. In addition, Title 10 of the act, through application of a "legislative veto" procedure, has enabled Congress to reduce the president's capacity to impound, that is, to refuse to spend, funds duly authorized and appropriated.[11] If the president seeks to delay spending such funds, either house can compel him to spend them by passing a simple resolution requiring him to do so. If the president desires to terminate programs or otherwise to cut spending, he must ask the legislature to rescind appropriations already voted and unless both chambers concur in the request, he must release the monies. All in all, the new budget process has provided Congress with a way to impose its own fiscal priorities, to the extent it wishes to do so, on the federal budget.

The notion of the legislative veto, embodied in the 1974 Budget Act, has gained wide currency in recent years. Dating back to the 1930s, it is now a part of more than two hundred statutes. Basically, the legislative veto delays the implementation of executive rules and regulations until Congress has had an opportunity to review them and to reject them if they are found objectionable. In the strictest form, administrative proposals cannot take effect until and unless Congress gives positive approval to them; that is, as with presidential requests for recession of funds, congressional *inaction* nullifies proposed executive actions. A more lenient and more common form of the legislative veto permits the proposed action to proceed unless Congress acts to block it; this requires one or both houses to pass a resolution disapproving the regulation within a sixty- or ninety-day period.[12] In any form, the legislative veto strengthens Congress' hand against the executive branch agencies and bureaus.

Finally, Congress has moved to reduce its "information deficit" relative to the executive branch. The newly established Congressional Budget Office gives the legislature an independent source of fiscal data and analysis. The growth, already noted, of both members' personal and committee staffs also provides the basis for enlarged analytic capacity in the Congress itself. In addition, Congress has created an Office of Technology Assessment to assess the potential impact of scientific advances; has enlarged its own research agents — the General Accounting Office and the Congressional Research Service of the Library of Congress — and has begun, in a halting fashion, to seek ways to make use of computerized information storage and retrieval and data-analysis systems. In all these ways, the legislature has moved to provide itself with independent information sources and analytic capacity that it can use to develop its own policy alternatives.

Each of these developments — the War Powers Bill, the 1974 Budget Act, the more aggressive use of the legislative veto, and an enhanced and independent informational base — has made Congress better able to challenge the executive's domination of the policy process.[13] Congress need no longer defer so readily to presumed executive expertise; it has the basis to develop a countervailing expertise of its own. These developments, then, enlarge Congress' capacity to be responsible, to formulate and enact its own effective policies. Whether the lawmakers will retain the determination to employ this capacity, especially as memories of presidential transgressions and legislative inadequacies of the Vietnam-Watergate period recede, remains to be seen; but for the moment, the Congress seems quite prepared to assert its own viewpoints forcefully.

Legislative relationships with interest groups have also been in flux. As suggested, lobbies have always been an integral part of the legislative process and members of Congress have, on the whole, felt comfortable in their presence. This still seems to be the case, and the recent changes have been more of degree than fundamental. Nonetheless, there are now more groups, somewhat better organized and financed, waging campaigns for their own particular causes. The traditional lobbies (business, labor, farm and veterans' groups) have been joined on the Washington scene by "public interest" lobbies (Berry, 1977) such as Common Cause, Ralph Nader and his associates, and a wide variety of environmental and consumer groups. The number of participants has grown and members of Congress are more likely to feel the heat from one or another of these groups. The legislative response to this increased pressure, exacerbated by the new campaign funding restrictions that require members to solicit small contributions from a greater number of sources, has been to consider seriously a more stringent lobby registration and regulation law. Proposals for such a statute have been under consideration for several years, but no consensus has emerged and no legislation has passed. In general, however, the intent of most proposals is not to restrict interest group activity but rather to expose it to public scrutiny. Debate has centered on lobbyist registration provisions and proposals to require lobbyists to report their activities. Thus when a bill is passed, as seems inevitable sooner or later, it will mandate that groups and their representatives operate in the open.

The lobby regulation bill, when it is passed, will be another step in a major effort to enhance congressional accountability by exposing a host of legislative activities to the glare of publicity. Senators and representatives moved to shore up their public reputations to overcome a scandal-induced decline in public esteem and specific (if not diffuse) support.[14] The philosophy underlying this series of reforms suggests that if Congress operates visibly—from election of the members to final decisions on legislation—the citizenry will be in a position to determine that the lawmakers are not only honest but also free of conflicts of interest and in consequence able to place the public good ahead of personal gain. Accountability—the ability to "throw the rascals out"—will also flow directly from the openness of legislative conduct.

The Federal Election Campaign Act, as amended, not only limits contributions to candidates but also requires candidates to report in detail the sources of their campaign funds and the uses to which those monies were put. In 1977, both the House and Senate adopted stringent codes of ethics that imposed financial disclosure requirements on all members. The codes obligated the legislators to reveal the source and amount of any income of $100 or more from any source; the extent and value of their financial holdings, including real estate; and the extent and value of their financial obligations and liabilities. The codes also barred members from maintaining office accounts (unofficial "slush funds" used to pay for activities not funded with regular office allowances) and limited the outside income (honoraria for speeches and articles, fees from law practices or other business activity) from all sources to 15 percent of the member's official salary.[15] Such requirements, if carefully observed, should enable concerned citizens to see from whom members receive funds and to whom they have incurred liabilities, information that should allow citizens to satisfy themselves that their elected representatives are financially beholden to no one and thus are able to apply independent judgment in carrying out their legislative activities. To the extent that voters are aware and take advantage of this information, their ability to hold members to account is enhanced.

For similar reasons and motives, Congress has also moved to open its more routine, day-to-day operations to view. Roll-call votes on House floor amendments—formerly unrecorded—and in committee are now available; new rules mandate that the position of each legislator be recorded and published.[16] Indeed the entire committee deliberation process, until recently shrouded in secrecy imposed by the tendency of many congressional committees to meet frequently in closed (executive) session, is now accessible to the mass media and interested individuals. All committee meetings, including sub- and full committee "markups" where the final versions of bills are painstakingly put together and House-Senate conference committees where interchamber disputes are resolved, are now to be open, unless the committee, meeting in public, votes to close its deliberations. In the mid-1970s, more than 95 percent of congressional committee meetings were held in public. Again, the opportunity to find out where legislators stand, what they have done, with respect to legislation and other congressional activity has grown as a result.

In sum, a series of changes has altered Congress' relationships to those important actors in its environment. The legislature has armed itself to do battle, on more favorable terrain, with the executive branch. Its ability to be responsible, to enact and sustain its own vision of wise policy, has increased. Congress has begun to reconsider the place of interest groups in the legislative process; it has sought to find formulas that will let it continue to control legislator-group interactions. And Congress has attempted, through imposing ethical standards on its members and opening its activities to public scrutiny, to reclaim the public trust and support.[17] To the degree it is successful in recapturing citizen confidence, Congress' ability to act as a responsible policy maker will grow; a respected legislature will be better able to assert and defend its views against other participants in politics.

Change and Congressional Outputs

If Congress' activities—its outputs of policy, oversight, and representation—reflect the ways its internal structures and processes work to convert inputs into outputs (as the systems perspective suggests is the case), then changes in the internal dynamics of Congress and in its relations with its environment should have altered the legislature's behavior as well. This seems to have occurred, but perhaps because there have been so many changes, so recently, that have moved Congress simultaneously toward responsibility, responsiveness, *and* accountability, the ultimate effect of reform is difficult to discern clearly. At the very least, it seems safe to say that the effects of the changes have been mixed.

This is most certainly the case with respect to policy making.[18] Some observers (Fiorina, 1977a) doubt that Congress even desires to have major policy influence; its members prefer to focus on representation, particularly of the service variety, to guarantee their own reelection and to extend their congressional careers. Fiorina deplores this situation, while Huntington (1973) suggests that because Congress is unsuited—because of its decentralized structure and its insulation from the nation's mainstream intellectual currents—to make policy, it is perhaps desirable that the legislature devote its energies to oversight and service representation. Others (Orfield, 1975) sees Congress as a far more innovative and forceful proponent of its own policy positions, particularly during periods like the Nixon-Ford administration, where the legislature confronted a White House controlled by the congressional minority party.

The record indicates that proponents of each of these views can marshal some supporting evidence. On the one hand, although the War Powers Resolution has not been (and, one hopes, will not be) tested, the new budget process—arming Congress with both more solid fiscal data and new budgetary procedures—has allowed Congress to revise the executive's budget, allocating relatively more funds to domestic and fewer to foreign affairs than the president has requested. Moreover, in the international sphere, traditionally the area of maximum legislative deference to the executive, Congress has displayed a renewed vigor. The younger members, socialized in the Vietnam period and operating from more independent power bases, have been willing to challenge presidents on foreign aid, issues relating to international financial institutions like the World Bank, arms sales overseas, and even on the structure of America's basic defense posture. On the other hand, the obvious agony Congress endured in attempting to formulate a comprehensive energy program and the slow progress made in seeking to restructure the tax and welfare systems suggest that—on controversial, emotional, and highly politicized domestic affairs at least—Congress may well find it difficult to harness the now more numerous power holders in the service of responsible policy making.[19]

A similar, uneven record emerges from examination of individual committees: Some are now more forceful and vigorous; others seem to perform as they always have, even after reform; still others seem less capable, at least temporarily, than they were previously. For instance, Kaiser (1978) finds that reform's cumulative impact on the House International Relations Committee has been to energize the panel, to stimulate it to play a more active and independent part in foreign policy formulation. By contrast, Ornstein and Rohde (1977) find both the House Agriculture and Government Operations Committees much changed by reform, but without significantly altered policy behavior as a result. The former continued to package farm bills to suit the interests of its members; the latter remained as quiescent in the postreform period as it had been previously.

On other committees change seems to have impaired policy-making efficiency. Ornstein and Rohde (1977, p. 245) quote a "thoughtful" member of the House Interstate and Foreign Commerce Committee: "Above all, reform has served to slow down the process" of legislating. Far more dramatic is the case of the House Ways and Means Committee, which change buffeted more severely than most panels (Rudder, 1977, 1978). The Democratic members lost their committee assignment authority; the panel was required to use subcommittees when it was accustomed to acting in full committee; the committee was enlarged from twenty-five to thirty-seven members, guaranteeing an influx of new members well beyond what ordinary turnover generates; the Democratic caucus took and used the power to control the conditions under which Ways and Means legislation reached the House floor; and a new chairman, Al Ullman (D-Ore.), took over in the wake of his predecessor's disgrace. These massive changes "stripped" the committee "of its power to make binding decisions"; they created circumstances in which "a legislative package cannot be developed in the committee with any assurance that it will pass intact on the floor" (Rudder,

1978, p. 86). Ways and Means failures—its 1975 energy bill was emasculated on the House floor and its decision to retain the oil depletion allowance was reversed—indicate the accuracy of this assessment.[20]

In sum, it remains unclear whether reform has improved legislative responsibility. In some ways, change has enhanced congressional policy making; in others, it has hindered it. Structural alteration is, in any case, certainly not the whole story. New members, outside events, a presidential election all contribute to legislative change; but they impinge in different ways and with varying impact on different parts of the legislative system. In some circumstances, Congress can assert its will and make its position prevail; in others, particularly when the same party that holds the presidency has the congressional majority, a policy-making partnership may develop that produces programs reflecting at least some congressional influence; in still other circumstances Congress may be unable to generate independent ideas and will be obliged to defer to the programs other actors advance. Congress has improved its capacity to shape public policy, but it is by no means easy to specify where and when it will employ this enlarged capability.

It is similarly treacherous to generalize about the impact of change on the remaining congressional outputs, oversight and representation. With regard to the first of these, the available evidence indicates that the recent period has created conditions that foster closer and more "continuous watchfulness" over the executive branch agencies; in Ogul's terms (selection 15), propensities (opportunity factors) favoring more intensive and extensive oversight have increased. Legal authority remains available; decentralization and diffusion of staff to subcommittees means that more units, suitably prepared and equipped, are in a position to act as effective overseers; executive transgressions and enlarged member policy concerns have inclined more individuals to make commitments to oversight. Yet issues remain technical and complex, potential overseers continue to be partners in legislative-administrative-clientele subgovernments, especially when their party controls both legislative and executive branches; and, most important, member priorities, reflecting the rewards available for particular kinds of activity, seem likely to lead many members to rate lawmaking and representational duties above oversight. Again, the capacity for effective oversight has grown, but the incentives to use it may not have kept pace. Some committees—the House Interstate and Foreign Commerce Committee, for example (Ornstein and Rohde, 1977), and its subcommittee on oversight and investigations (Price, 1978), and the House International Relations Committee (Kaiser, 1977)—have stepped up their oversight activities while most of the others seem to have remained less concerned with executive performance.

With respect to representation, there has probably been little change in congressional performance traceable directly to the reforms of the 1970s. Lawmakers have always been inclined to pay close attention to service representation, to the "casework" that contributes so much to their electoral fortunes; so long as so many of them continue to pursue congressional careers, there is little reason to expect them to neglect their constituents. The situation with regard to policy representation is more murky. The greater visibility of legislative activity does not seem to have led, in the short term at least, to greater public awareness of or knowledge about Congress. Greater popular concern for issues—especially economic questions—and greater involvement of more groups in the legislative process may increase congressional policy responsiveness; more points of view are being directed to the lawmakers. At the same time, however, to the extent that these louder and more numerous voices take contradictory positions, the lawmakers may have more, not less, trouble assessing the "real" constituency opinion. Even if they can determine what public opinion is, they may be in a position to play equally balanced sentiments off against one another, leaving themselves free to make choices on the basis of criteria other than the views of the "folks back home." It probably remains true that only on hotly contested questions—the abortion issue comes to mind immediately—will the legislators be in a position to know their constituents' opinions well and to feel some pressure to act consistently with them.[21]

In general, then, it is difficult to specify precisely the effect of recent legislative change inside Congress and in its relations with the executive, groups, and the public on congressional outputs. This most likely results from the movement of reform toward responsibility, responsiveness, and accountability at the same time. About all that we can say is that Congress has improved its capacity to make coherent and effective policy, even in the face of executive hostility, to oversee the executive branch, and to a somewhat lesser extent, to represent constituent policy preferences. That is, Congress—at least in some areas and under some circumstances—can be either responsible or responsive, with no sacrifice in accountability. Which it chooses to stress will, of course, reflect the commitments of time, energy, and effort that its members make. Role conflict must be faced: Senators and representatives must decide, as individuals, whether to orient themselves to lawmaking, oversight, or representation. Few, if any, can do an effective job at two, much less all, of these chores. What Congress will be in the years ahead depends on the distribution of the choices that its members make among the institutions' output obligations.

Quo Vadis Congress? The Future of the Congressional System

To suggest what Congress will be like in the future is at best highly speculative and at worst downright foolish. What party will win the next presidential election is impossible to predict. Whether cataclysmic events—at home or abroad—will alter the entire setting of American politics cannot be foretold with confidence. In short, what the environment within which Congress must operate will look like, even a short time from now, cannot be specified. And, as the environment changes, the legislative system will be compelled to adapt and adjust in ways not now clearly calculable. Nonetheless, these disclaimers to one side, some things appear more likely than others and are perhaps worth noting here.

For one thing, congressional accountability will remain possible. In the wake of the recent revelation of legislators' misconduct and the numerous instances of potential conflict of interest, any serious effort to move Congress back behind closed doors seems doomed to failure. Almost certainly, legislative activity of all kinds—electoral, committee, on the floor, and in conference committee—will continue to be conducted in public, accessible to the public and the mass media. Interested citizens will remain in a position to find out, if they choose to do so, what Congress and its members are doing and to use that information as the basis for their voting choices in congressional elections.

For another thing, the structure of the congressional system is likely to reflect decentralization and the individual concerns of senators and representatives. As long as members must endure the rigors of election campaigns for which they, not centralized national party organizations, bear the chief burdens, they will be most unwilling to alter a legislative structure that provides them with advantageous positions from which to pursue their congressional careers.[22] The policy agendas that the next decades will present to the nation seem most likely to sustain decentralization. Issues will be more, not less, technical and complex; and a division of labor, to bring appropriate expertise to bear on these questions, will remain imperative. Thus, the trend toward fragmentation will most probably triumph over the developments that give some promise of strengthening the political parties. This is more probable if, as seems likely, the Democrats cannot hold the top-heavy majorities they have had in the Ninety-fourth and Ninety-fifth Congresses. Weak parties, more nearly equal in size, seem less likely to be in a position to centralize the legislature. If so, then Congress is likely to be decentralized, to be more responsive than responsible, and to require the sort of decision through bargaining and compromise that has been its hallmark in recent years.

How this system relates to the legislature's environment is more problematic. Demands from all sources will, without doubt, continue to flow to Congress. The members are likely to show no inclination to abandon serving the very constituents on whom they depend for continuation of their careers. Groups, already ubiquitous, are unlikely to wither away; rather, they will most probably develop new methods to bring their points of view to bear on the appropriate decision-making centers. Members of Congress will continue to have to adjust to—to facilitate or resist—these group pressures. The courts will, as at present, review acts of Congress, occasionally posing challenges to which the legislature will have to respond. The most speculative environmental relationship is the most important as well: How will Congress get on with the president? The 1970s have seen Congress improve its position relative to the executive, but the important question is whether the legislature will have the determination to use its enhanced capacity. A legislative majority will be more apt to act decisively against an opposition president. The propensity to independent action, or to exact significant concessions from the executive, characteristic of the mid-seventies seems to reflect the impact of Vietnam and Watergate. A safe guess is that, as these events recede in memory and barring recurrence of similar difficulties, congressional assertiveness will wane but not disappear. Congress will probably become more inclined to cooperate with the chief executive, especially one who is not aggressive with respect to fundamental legislative prerogatives. And where the president appears wrong, Congress will remain prepared to oppose him vigorously.

Congressional outputs will reflect these possibilities. Policy will bear a congressional stamp but will be worked out, in committee and subcommittee, in consultation with executive personnel and other interests. Interbranch confrontation will decline somewhat. Oversight will continue to get short shrift unless there are clear political benefits to be derived from it. If members perceive such gains, they will find the watchdog chores attractive; if not, they will direct their attention and energy elsewhere. Representatives will continue to serve their states and districts as their electoral dependence requires them to do; they will also respond in policy matters when this same requisite demands it. Unless and until the citizens pay more heed to pending issues and communicate their views on such matters loudly, clearly, and perhaps threateningly, lawmakers will pay as little heed as necessary to their constituents' issue stands.

This speculation about Congress' future is little more than a simple and straightforward extrapolation of recent trends, particularly those toward member independence and individualism and toward institutional decentralization. Whether observers of Congress approve such a future, or any other that emerges, depends on the direction in which they prefer to see the legislature move. The vision sketched out here will please those who favor responsiveness more than those looking for a responsible policy process; it sees Congress emphasizing representation and constituent relations more than policy making. Whether or not these projections are accurate, the basic issue remains: Can Congress adapt sufficiently and rapidly enough to retain its essential strength? Those who value a strong legislative system as a counterbalance against a demonstrably powerful executive in an essentially and increasingly pluralistic political order hope that it can.

Notes

[1] The recent period has seen the greatest amount of change since the 1910–1911 revolution in the House of Representatives that gave Congress its contemporary character. For an interesting and instructive comparison of the two periods, see Jones, 1977.

[2] From the Adam Clayton Powell affair of 1967 to the allegations of Korean influence buying of a decade later, more than a dozen members of Congress, from both political parties and all parts of the country, were indicted and convicted for criminal behavior. A far larger number appeared to have conducted themselves in unseemly and unethical ways. The net result of these exposures, and much additional rumor that surrounded the Capitol during this period, was the precipitous decline in the popular standing of Congress and the wide currency given the view that the national legislature could not be trusted to serve the public good.

[3] I have described these visions in more detail in Rieselbach, 1977a.

[4] Lloyd Meeds (D-Wash.), retiring after fourteen years in the House, noted that his reelection campaign would have cost at least $250,000 and declared, "If you take that kind of dough, you're either an ingrate or obligated, and either one is an unsatisfactory position to be in" (quoted in Herbers, 1978).

[5] In 1972, sixty-nine new members were elected to the Ninety-third Congress; ninety-two freshmen were chosen to sit in the Ninety-fourth, and sixty-six first-term members won seats in the Ninety-fifth. By January 1977, when the Ninety-fifth Congress convened, 48 percent of the House, nearly half, had served four or fewer years in Congress. And, in addition, well before the start of the 1978 campaign, it was nearly clear that more than forty incumbents would retire voluntarily; when coupled with the inevitable defeat of at least a few incumbents, it seems obvious that the influx of new members will continue.

[6] In September 1977, House members were entitled to an allowance of more than $250,000 with which to hire up to eighteen staff members. In the Senate, staff allowances vary according to state population; in 1977, the average senator employed a staff of about thirty-seven persons. On staffing, see Fox and Hammond, 1977, and Hammond, 1978.

[7] For more detail on the committee reforms, see Ornstein, 1975a, 1977; and Rieselbach, 1977a. On reform more generally, see Ornstein, 1975b; Dodd and Oppenheimer, 1977b; and Congressional Quarterly, 1977, pp. 743–794.

[8] The Speaker chairs the Steering and Policy Committee. The remaining twenty-three members include the Majority Leader, the caucus chair, nine members whom the Speaker appoints, and twelve whom the caucus elects to represent geographical regions. Thus the Speaker and party leaders are clearly in a position to dominate the committee.

[9] In 1975, the new procedure was used to bring about repeal of the oil depletion allowance, a tax benefit for oil producers. Opponents of the allowance failed in Ways and Means and took their case to the caucus, which by a 153 to 98 vote instructed the Rules Democrats to permit a vote on an amendment (to a tax bill) to repeal the allowance. The amendment passed the full House.

[10] Some observers see some irony in the War Powers Resolution, suggesting that it condones what the Constitution does not confer: presidential authority to commit troops to war, for up to sixty days at least, without a declaration of war.

[11] Richard Nixon's unprecedented use of impoundment to undercut congressional programmatic goals was a major stimulus to the passage of the 1974 Act. On impoundment and the new laws impact, see Munselle, 1978. On the new law in general, see Ellwood and Thurber, 1977a and 1977b, and Thurber, 1978.

[12] The "one house" legislative veto, where either chamber acting alone can block a proposed regulation, has been challenged on constitutional grounds as contrary to the doctrine of separation of powers. In January 1978, the U.S. Supreme Court declined to decide three cases that raised clearly the issue of the legislative veto's constitutionality.

[13]It is perhaps worth noting that while aiming at increasing congressional power relative to the executive branch, these changes also reallocate intralegislative influence. Thus the Budget Act created in the Budget Committees new power centers, which challenged the traditional dominance of the appropriations and revenue (Ways and Means in the House, Finance in the Senate) committees over fiscal politics. Similarly, the diffusion of staff resources increased the authority of junior members at the expense of their seniors, the formerly exclusive managers of committee staff, at the same time it enhanced the position of the Congress as a whole relative to the executive branch.

[14]In addition to a dozen or more criminal indictments and convictions, Wayne Hays (D-Ohio) and Wilbur Mills (D-Ark.), among the most powerful members of the House, were literally driven from office for their sexual peccadilloes, involving the former's hiring his nontyping mistress as a staff typist and the latter's cavorting with an "exotic dancer."

[15]The new ethics codes are to be enforced by the Ethics Committee of the two chambers; legislation giving the codes the force of law, that is, providing criminal punishment for violations, has not yet passed. To date, then, enforcement depends on the willingness of legislators to move against their colleagues; in the past members have shown considerable reluctance to discipline others in Congress.

[16]Prior to the 1970 Legislative Reorganization Act, many amendments were handled using teller votes on which vote totals, not individual positions, were recorded. The act permitted twenty members to insist that members' stands be noted individually. In consequence, the number of roll-call votes has soared, providing clearer information about individual lawmakers' positions on a wide variety of issues.

[17]There is no evidence that the levels of public awareness of, or information about, Congress has risen since these reforms were adopted. Poll data certainly do not reveal a congressional comeback in popular standing. It is most likely that the desired effects will occur, if at all, over the long run. Only with the fading of the so-called "Koreagate" affair and a decline, not yet visible, in allegations of congressional misconduct is Congress' reputation, and its popular support, likely to rebound.

[18]On the impact of reform on policy making, see Rieselbach, 1977b, 1978, and Welch and Peters, 1977.

[19]We need to distinguish situations in which Congress cannot or will not take action—whether or not in deference to the executive branch—because of institutional barriers from those on which there simply is no agreement on the substance of policy. For example, Orfield (1975, p. 259) defends Congress against the criticism that it failed to do what was possible to end the Vietnam War on the grounds that there was no antiwar majority in Congress. Although the legislators may have been wrong, that they did not act to terminate the conflict does not mean they were either "impotent" or "unrepresentative."

[20]The contrast between this performance and that in the earlier period, ending with the Ninety-third Congress, is sharp indeed. See Manley, 1970, and Fenno, 1973a. Clymer, 1978, suggests that Ways and Means has survived a "shakedown" period, has adjusted to its new circumstances, and may be ready to reclaim a position of strength in the House.

[21]Miller and Stokes, 1963, (selection 16 in this book), identify civil rights as one such issue. Busing, its contemporary manifestation, seems to be another, as does abortion. So, at least temporarily, does Social Security taxation. In 1977, Congress "saved" the Social Security system from bankruptcy with a steep hike in Social Security tax levels and in the wage base on which the taxes are paid. There was an immediate public outcry—ironic in one sense because the tax increases that seem to occasion it were holdovers from a previous law; given the late passage of the revised tax structure, the rates that new law imposed do not take effect until 1979—and in early 1978 Congress began to consider ways to roll back the new taxes. Emotional issues that arouse the public can and do find their way onto Congress' agenda in short order.

[22]Public financing of congressional elections, a proposal that many favor to reduce external pressures on members, will buttress individual independence. Candidates will get federal funds automatically, thus eliminating their need to depend on party organizations.

References

This listing includes both the items cited in the editor's portions of the text and some recent and significant works on Congress.

Almond, G. A., and S. Verba. 1963. *The Civil Culture.* Princeton, N.J.: Princeton University Press.

Asher, H. B. 1973. "The Learning of Legislative Norms," *American Political Science Review,* 67: 449–513. Selection 7 in this volume.

———. 1975. "The Changing Status of the Freshman Representative," in N. J. Ornstein, ed., *Congress in Change: Evolution and Reform.* New York: Praeger.

Bacheller, J. M. 1977. "Lobbyists and the Legislative Process: The Impact of Environmental Constraints," *American Political Science Review,* 71: 252–263.

Bauer, R. A., I. de S. Pool, and L. A. Dexter. 1972. *American Business and Public Policy,* 2nd ed. Chicago: Aldine-Atherton.

Beard, E., and S. Horn. 1975. *Congressional Ethics: The View from the House.* Washington, D.C.: Brookings Institution.

Berman, D. 1964. *In Congress Assembled.* New York: Macmillan.

Berry, J. 1977. *Lobbying for the People.* Princeton, N.J.: Princeton University Press.

Bibby, J. F. 1966. "Committee Characteristics and Legislative Oversight of Administration," *Midwest Journal of Political Science,* 10: 78–98.

Bolling, R. 1966. *House Out of Order.* New York: Dutton.

Brezina, D. W. 1975. *Congress in Action: The Environmental Education Act.* New York: Free Press.

Bullock, C. S., III. 1973. "Committee Transfers in the United States House of Representatives," *Journal of Politics,* 35: 85–117.

———. 1976. "Motivations for U.S. Congressional Committee Preferences: Freshmen of the 92nd Congress," *Legislative Studies Quarterly,* 1: 201–212.

Burnham, J. 1959. *Congress and the American Tradition.* Chicago: Regnery.

Burnham, W. D. 1975. "Insulation and Responsiveness in Congressional Elections," *Political Science Quarterly,* 90: 411–435.

Casper, J. D. 1976. "The Supreme Court and National Policy Making," *American Political Science Review,* 70: 50–63.

Clapp, C.L. 1964. *The Congressman: His Work as He Sees It.* New York: Doubleday Anchor Books.

Clark, J. S. 1965. *Congress: The Sapless Branch.* New York: Harper and Row.

Clausen, A. R. 1973. *How Congressmen Decide: A Policy Focus.* New York: St. Martin's Press. Chapter 8 is reprinted as selection 10 in this volume.

Clymer, A. 1978. "The Chair Hasn't Been Easy for Al Ullman," *New York Times,* April 2, 1978, section 4, p. 2, col. 3.

Congressional Quarterly. 1971. *The Washington Lobby.* Washington, D.C.: Congressional Quarterly, Inc.

———. 1976. *Guide to Congress,* 2nd ed. Washington, D.C.: Congressional Quarterly, Inc.

———. 1977. *Congress and the Nation 1973–1976,* vol. 4. Washington, D.C.: Congressional Quarterly, Inc.

Cover, A. D. 1977. "One Good Term Deserves Another: The Advantages of Incumbency in Congressional Elections," *American Journal of Political Science,* 21: 523–541.

Cover, R. D., and D. R. Mayhew. 1977. "Congressional Dynamics and the Decline of Competitive Congressional Elections," in L. C. Dodd and B. I. Oppenheimer, eds., *Congress Reconsidered.* New York: Praeger.

Cronin, T. E. 1975. *The State of the Presidency.* Boston: Little, Brown.

Dahl, R. A. 1950. *Congress and Foreign Policy.* New York: Harcourt, Brace.

———. 1958. "Decision-Making in a Democracy: The Supreme Court as National Policy-Maker," *Journal of Public Law,* 6: 279–295.

Davidson, R. H. 1969. *The Role of the Congressman.* New York: Pegasus.

———. 1975. "Policy Making in the Manpower Subgovernment," in H. P. Smith et al., *Politics in America.* New York: Random House.

Davidson, R. H., D. M. Kovenock, and M. K. O'Leary. 1966. *Congress in Crisis.* Belmont, Cal.: Wadsworth.

Davidson, R. H., and G. R. Parker. 1972. "Positive Support for Political Institutions: The Case of Congress," *Western Political Quarterly,* 25: 600–612.

Davidson, R. H., and W. J. Oleszek. 1977. *Congress Against Itself.* Bloomington: Indiana University Press.

Dawson, R. E., K. Prewitt, and K. Dawson. 1977. *Political Socialization,* 2nd ed. Boston: Little, Brown.

Deckard, B. 1972. "State Party Delegations in the U.S. House of Representatives — A Comparative Study of Group Cohesion," *Journal of Politics,* 34: 199–222.

———. 1976. "Political Upheaval and Congressional Voting: The Effects of the 1960s on Voting Patterns in the House of Representatives," *Journal of Politics,* 38: 326–345. Selection 14 in this volume.

de Grazia, A. 1965. *Republic in Crisis: Congress against the Executive Force.* New York: Federal Legal Publications.

Deutsch, K. W. 1966. *The Nerves of Government.* New York: Free Press.

Dodd, L. C. 1972. "Committee Integration in the Senate: A Comparative Analysis," *Journal of Politics,* 34: 1135–1171.

———. 1977. "Congress and the Quest for Power," in L. C. Dodd and B. I. Oppenheimer, eds., *Congress Reconsidered.* New York: Praeger.

Dodd, L. C., and B. I. Oppenheimer. 1977a. "The House in Transition," in L. C. Dodd and B. I. Oppenheimer, eds., *Congress Reconsidered.* New York: Praeger.

———. eds. 1977b. *Congress Reconsidered.* New York: Praeger.

Dyson, J. W. and J. W. Soule. 1970. "Congressional Committee Behavior on Roll-Call Votes: The U.S. House of Representatives, 1955-1964," *Midwest Journal of Political Science,* 14: 626–647. Selection 8 in this volume.

Easton, D. 1965a. *A Framework for Political Analysis.* Englewood Cliffs, N.J.: Prentice-Hall.

———. 1965b. *A Systems Analysis of Political Life.* New York: Wiley.

———. 1975. "A Re-Assessment of the Concept of Political Support," *British Journal of Political Science,* 5: 435–457.

Edwards, G. C., III. 1976. "Presidential Influence in the House: Presidental Prestige as a Source of Presidential Power," *American Political Science* Review, 70: 101–113.

———. 1977. "Presidential Influence in the Senate: Presidential Prestige as a Source of Presidential Power," *American Quarterly,* 5: 481–500.

Elwood, J. W., and J. A. Thurber. 1977a. "The New Congressional Budget Process: The Hows and Whys of House-Senate Differences," in L. C. Dodd and B. I. Oppenheimer, eds., *Congress Reconsidered.* New York: Praeger.

———. 1977b. "The New Congressional Budget Process; Its Causes, Consequences, and Possible Success," in S. Welch and J. G. Peters, eds., *Legislative Reform and Public Policy.* New York: Praeger.

Erikson, R. S. 1971. "The Advantage of Incumbency in Congressional Elections," *Polity,* 3: 395–405.

Eulau, H., and P. D. Karps. 1977. "The Puzzle of Representation: Specifying the Components of Responsiveness," *Legislative Studies Quarterly,* 2: 233–354.

Fenno, R. F., Jr. 1962. "The House Appropriations Committee as a Political System: The Problem of Integration," *American Political Science Review,* 56: 310–324

——. 1966. *The Power of the Purse.* Boston: Little, Brown. An edited version of chapter 8 is reprinted as selection 13 in this volume.

——. 1973a. *Congressmen in Committees.* Boston: Little, Brown.

——. 1973b. "The Internal Distribution of Influence: The House," in D. B. Truman, ed., *The Congress and America's Future,* 2nd ed. Englewood Cliffs, N.J.: Prentice-Hall.

——. 1974. "If, as Ralph Nader Says, Congress is 'the Broken Branch,' How Come We Love Our Congressmen So Much?" in N. J. Ornstein, ed., *Congress in Change: Evolution and Reform.* New York: Praeger.

——. 1977. "U.S. House Members in Their Constituencies: An Exploration," *American Political Science Review,* 71: 883–917.

——. 1978. *Home Style: House Members in Their Districts.* Boston: Little, Brown.

Ferber, M. 1971. "The Formation of the Democratic Study Group," in N. W. Polsby, ed., *Congressional Behavior.* New York: Random House.

Ferejohn, J. A. 1974. *Pork Barrel Politics: Rivers and Harbors Legislation 1947–1968.* Stanford, Cal: Stanford University Press.

——. 1977. "On the Decline of Competition in Congressional Elections," *American Political Science Review,* 71: 166–176.

Fiellin, A. 1962. "The Functions of Informal Groups in Legislative Institutions," *Journal of Politics,* 14: 72–91.

Fiorina, M. P. 1974. *Representatives Roll Calls and Constituencies.* Lexington, Mass. Lexington Books.

——. 1977a. *Congress: Keystone of the Washington Establishment.* New Haven, Conn.: Yale University Press.

——. 1977b. "The Case of the Vanishing Marginals: The Bureaucracy Did It," *American Political Science Review,* 71: 177–181.

Fishel, J. 1973. *Party and Opposition.* New York: McKay.

Fox, D. M., and C. L. Clapp. 1970a. "The House Rules Committee and the Programs of the Kennedy and Johnson Administrations," *Midwest Journal of Political Science,* 14: 662–672.

——. 1970b. "The House Rules Committee's Agenda-Setting Function, 1961–1963," *Journal of Politics,* 32: 440–444.

Fox, H. W., Jr., and S. W. Hammond. 1977. *Congressional Staffs: The Invisible Force in American Lawmaking.* New York: Free Press.

Freedman, S. R. 1974. "The Salience of Party and Candidate in Congressional Elections," in N. R. Luttbeg, ed., *Public Opinion and Public Policy,* rev. ed. Homewood, Ill.: Dorsey Press.

Freeman, J. L. 1965. *The Political Process: Executive Bureau-Legislative Committee Relations,* rev. ed. New York: Random House.

Friesema, H. P., and R. D. Hedlund. 1974. "The Reality of Representational Roles," in N. R. Luttbeg, ed., *Public Opinion and Public Policy,* rev. ed. Homewood, Ill.: Dorsey Press.

Froman, L. A., Jr. 1967. *The Congressional Process: Strategies, Rules and Procedures.* Boston: Little, Brown.

Froman, L. A., Jr., and R. B. Ripley. 1965. "Conditions for Party Leadership," *American Political Science Review,* 59: 52–63. Selection 6 in this volume.

Funston, R. 1978. *A Vital National Seminar: The Supreme Court in American Political Life.* Palo Alto, Cal.: Mayfield.

Gertzog, I. N. 1976. "The Routinization of Committee Assignments in the U.S. House of Representatives," *American Journal of Political Science,* 20: 693–712.

Gilmour, R. S. 1971. "Central Legislative Clearance: A Revised Perspective," *Public Administration Review,* 31: 150–158. Selection 9 in this volume.

Goodwin, G., Jr. 1970. *The Little Legislatures: Committees of Congress.* Amherst: University of Massachusetts Press. Pages 27–65 are reprinted as selection 4 in this volume.

Groennings, S. 1973. "The Wednesday Group in the House of Representatives," in S. Groennings and J. P. Hawley, eds., *To Be a Congressman: The Promise and the Power.* Washington, D.C.: Acropolis Books.

Hacker, A. 1964. *Congressional Districting,* rev. ed. Washington, D.C.: Brookings Institution.

Hadley, D. J. 1977. "Legislative Role Orientations and Support for Party and Chief Executive in the Indiana House," *Legislative Studies Quarterly,* 2: 309–335.

Hammond, S. W. 1978. "Congressional Change and Reform: Staffing the Congress," in L. N. Rieselbach, ed., *Legislative Reform: The Policy Impact.* Lexington, Mass.: Lexington Books.

Harris, J. P. 1964. *Congressional Control of Administration.* Washington, D.C.: Brookings Institution.

Hayes, M. T. 1978. "The Semi-Sovereign Pressure Groups: A Critique of Current Theory and an Alternative Typology," *Journal of Politics,* 40: 134–161.

Henderson, T. A. 1970. *Congressional Oversight of Executive Agencies: A Study of the House Committee on Government Operations.* Gainesville: University of Florida Press.

Herbers, J. 1978. "Interest Groups Gaining Influence at the Expense of National Parties," *New York Times,* March 26, p. 1. col. 4.

Hinckley, B. 1971. *The Seniority System in Congress.* Bloomington: Indiana University Press. Excerpts from chapters 1, 2, and 8 are reprinted as selection 3 in this volume.

———. 1977. "Seniority 1975: Old Theories Confront New Facts," *British Journal of Political Science,* 6: 383–399.

Holtzman, A. 1970. *Legislative Liaison: Executive Leadership in Congress.* Chicago: Rand McNally.

Huitt, R. K. 1961a. "Democratic Party Leadership in the Senate," *American Political Science Review,* 55: 333–344.

———. 1961b. "The Outsider in the Senate: An Alternative Role," *American Political Science Review,* 55: 566–575.

Huntington, S. P. 1973. "Congressional Responses to the Twentieth Century," in D. B. Truman, ed., *The Congress and America's Future,* 2nd ed. Englewood Cliffs, N.J.: Prentice-Hall.

Ippolito, D. S. 1978. *The Budget and National Politics.* San Francisco: Freeman.

Jackson, J. E. 1974. *Constituencies and Leaders in Congress.* Cambridge, Mass.: Harvard University Press.

James, D. B. 1974. *The Contemporary Presidency,* 2nd ed. Indianapolis, Ind.: Pegasus.

Jaros, D. 1973. *Socialization to Politics.* New York: Praeger.

Jewell, M. E. 1970. "Attitudinal Determinants of Legislative Behavior: The Utility of Role Analysis," in A. Kornberg and L. D. Musolf, eds., *Legislatures in Developmental Perspective.* Durham, N.C.: Duke University Press.

Jewell, M. E., and C. Chi-Hung. 1974. "Membership Movement and Committee Attractiveness in the U.S. House of Representatives, 1963–1971," *American Journal of Political Science,* 18: 433–441.

Jewell, M. E., and S. C. Patterson. 1977. *The Legislative Process in the United States,* 3rd ed. New York: Random House.

Jones, B. C. 1973. "Competitiveness, Role Orientations, and Legislative Responsiveness," *Journal of Politics,* 35: 924–947.

Jones, C. O. 1961. "Representation in Congress: The Case of the House Agriculture Committee," *American Political Science Review,* 55: 358–367.

———. 1977. "How Reform Changes Congress," in S. Welch and J. G. Peters, eds., *Legislative Reform and Public Policy.* New York: Praeger.

Kaiser, F. M. 1977. "Oversight of Foreign Policy: The House Committee on International Relations," *Legislative Studies Quarterly,* 2: 255–279.

———. 1978. "Congressional Change and Foreign Policy: The House Committee on International Relations," in L. N. Rieselbach, ed., *Legislative Reform: The Policy Impact.* Lexington, Mass.: Lexington Books.

Kearns, D. 1976. *Lyndon Johnson and the American Dream.* New York: Harper and Row.

Keefe, W. J., and M. S. Ogul. 1973. *The American Legislative Process,* 3rd ed. Englewood Cliffs, N.J.: Prentice-Hall.

Kernell, S. 1973. "Is the Senate More Liberal than the House?" *Journal of Politics,* 35: 332–363.

Kesselman, M. 1961. "Presidential Leadership in Congress on Foreign Policy," *Midwest Journal of Political Science,* 5: 284–289.

———. 1965. "Presidential Leadership in Congress on Foreign Policy: A Replication of a Hypothesis," *Midwest Journal of Political Science* 9: 401–406.

Key, V. O., Jr. 1964. *Politics, Parties, and Pressure Groups,* 5th ed. New York: Crowell.

Keynes, E. 1969. "The Senate Rules and the Dirksen Amendment: A Study in Legislative Strategy and Tactics," in L. K. Pettit and E. Keynes, eds., *The Legislative Process in the U.S. Senate.* Chicago: Rand McNally.

Kingdon, J. W. 1967. "Politicians' Beliefs about Voters," *American Political Science Review* 61: 137–145.

———. 1973. *Congressmen's Voting Decisions.* New York: Harper and Row.

Kofmehl, K. 1977. *Professional Staffs of Congress,* 3rd ed. West Lafayette, Ind.: Purdue University Press.

Kostroski, W. L. 1973. "Party and Incumbency in Postwar Senate Elections: Trends, Patterns, and Models," *American Political Science Review,* 67: 1213–1234.

Kuklinski, J. H., with R. C. Elling. 1977. "Representational Role, Constituency Opinion, and Legislative Roll Call Behavior," *American Journal of Political Science,* 21: 135–147.

Latham, E. 1952. *The Group Basis of Politics.* Ithaca, N.Y.: Cornell University Press.

LeLoup, L. T. 1977. *Budgetary Politics: Dollars, Deficits, Decisions.* Brunswick, Ohio: King's Court.

Leuthold, D. A. 1968. *Electioneering in a Democracy: Campaigns for Congress.* New York: Wiley.

Lowi, T. J., and R. B. Ripley, eds. 1973. *Legislative Politics, U.S.A.,* 3rd ed. Boston: Little, Brown.

Maass, A. A. 1951. *Muddy Waters.* Cambridge, Mass.: Harvard University Press.

Manley, J. 1970. *The Politics of Finance.* Boston: Little, Brown.

Marmor, T. R. 1973. *The Politics of Medicare.* Chicago: Aldine.

Masters, N. A. 1961. "Committee Assignments in the House of Representatives," *American Political Science Review,* 55: 345–357.

Matsunaga, S. M., and P. Chen. 1976. *Rulemakers of the House.* Urbana: University of Illinois Press.

Matthews, D. R. 1960. *U. S. Senators and Their World.* Chapel Hill: University of North Carolina Press.

Matthews, D. R., and J. A. Stimson. 1975. *Yeas and Nays: Normal Decision-Making in the U.S. House of Representatives.* New York: Wiley.

Mayhew, D. R. 1974a. *Congress: The Electoral Connection.* New Haven, Conn.: Yale University Press.

———. 1974b. "Congressional Elections: The Case of the Vanishing Marginals," *Polity* 6: 295–317. Selection 1 in this volume.

McAdams, A. K. 1964. *Power and Politics in Labor Legislation.* New York: Columbia University Press.

McCrone, D. J., and J. H. Kuklinski. 1977. "The Delegate Theory of Representation," presented to the annual meeting of the American Political Science Association.

Milbrath, L. W. 1963. *The Washington Lobbyists.* Chicago: Rand McNally.

Miller, W. E., and D. E. Stokes. 1963. "Constituency Influence in Congress," *American Political Science Review,* 57: 45–57. Selection 16 in this volume.

Mitchell, W. C. 1962. *The American Polity.* New York: Free Press.

———. 1967. *Sociological Analysis and Politics: The Theories of Talcott Parsons.* Englewood Cliffs, N.J.: Prentice-Hall.

Munselle, W. G. 1978. "Presidential Impoundment and Congressional Reform," in L. N.

Rieselbach, ed., *Legislative Reform: The Policy Impact.* Lexington, Mass.: Lexington Books.

Murphy, J. T. 1974. "Political Parties and the Porkbarrel: Party Conflict and Cooperation in House Public Works Committee Decision Making," *American Political Science Review,* 68: 169–185.

Murphy, W. F. 1962. *Congress and the Court.* Chicago: University of Chicago Press.

Natchez, P. B., and I. C. Bupp. 1973. "Policy and Priority in the Budgetary Process," *American Political Science Review,* 67: 951–963.

Neustadt, R. E. 1954. "Presidency and Legislation: The Growth of Central Clearance," *American Political Science Review,* 48: 641–671.

———. 1955. "Presidency and Legislation: Planning the President's Program," *American Political Science Review,* 49: 980–1021.

———. 1976. *Presidential Power: The Politics of Leadership with Reflections on Johnson and Nixon.* New York: Wiley.

Niemi, R. G., and H. F. Weisberg, eds. 1976. *Controversies in American Voting Behavior.* San Francisco: Freeman.

Noragon, J. L. 1972. "Congressional Redistricting and Population Composition, 1964–1970," *Midwest Journal of Political Science,* 16: 295–302.

Ogul, M. S. 1976. *Congress Oversees the Bureaucracy.* Pittsburgh: University of Pittsburgh Press. An edited version of chapter 1 is reprinted as selection 15 in this volume.

Oleszek, W. J. 1978. *Congressional Procedures and the Policy Process.* Washington, D.C.: Congressional Quarterly Press.

Olson, K. G. 1966. "The Service Function of the United States Congress," in A. de Grazia, coord., *Congress: The First Branch of Government.* Washington, D.C.: American Enterprise Institute.

Oppenheimer, B. I. 1974. *Oil and the Congressional Process.* Lexington, Mass.: Lexington Books.

———. 1977a. "The Rules Committee: New Arm of the Leadership in a Decentralized House," in L. C. Dodd and B. I. Oppenheimer, eds., *Congress Reconsidered.* New York: Praeger.

———. 1977b. "The Rules Committee in the New House," presented at the annual meeting of the Midwest Political Science Association.

———. 1978. "Policy Implications of Rules Committee Reforms," in L. N. Rieselbach, ed., *Legislative Reform: The Policy Impact.* Lexington, Mass.: Lexington Books.

Orfield, G. 1975. *Congressional Power: Congress and Social Change.* New York: Harcourt Brace Jovanovich. Chapter 12 is reprinted as selection 17 in this volume.

Ornstein, N. J. 1975a. "Causes and Consequences of Congressional Change: Subcommittee Reforms in the House of Representatives, 1970–73," in N. J. Ornstein, ed., *Congress in Change: Evolution and Reform.* New York: Praeger.

———. ed. 1975b. *Congress in Change: Evolution and Reform.* New York: Praeger.

———. 1977. "The Democrats Reform Power in the House of Representatives, 1969–1975," in A. P. Sindler, ed., *America in the Seventies: Problems, Policies, and Politics.* Boston: Little, Brown.

Ornstein, N. J., and D. W. Rohde. 1975. "Seniority and Future Power in Congress," in N. J. Ornstein, ed., *Congress in Change.* New York: Praeger.

———. 1977. "Shifting Forces, Changing Rules and Political Outcomes: The Impact of Congressional Change on Four House Committees," in R. Peabody and N. W. Polsby, eds., *New Perspectives on the House of Representatives,* 3rd ed. Chicago: Rand McNally.

Ornstein, N. J., and S. Elder. 1978. *Interest Groups, Lobbying and Policymaking.* Washington, D.C.: Congressional Quarterly.

Parker, G. R. 1976. "A Note on the Impact and Salience of Congress," *American Politics Quarterly,* 4: 413–422.

———. 1977. "Some Themes in Congressional Unpopularity," *American Journal of Political Science* 21: 93–110.

Patterson, S. C. 1970. "The Professional Staffs of Congressional Committees," *Administrative Science Quarterly*, 15: 22–37.

Peabody, R. L. 1976. *Leadership in Congress*. Boston: Little, Brown. An edited version of chapter 2 is reprinted as selection 5 in this volume.

Peabody, R. L., and N. W. Polsby, eds. 1977. *New Perspectives on the House of Representatives*, 3rd ed. Chicago: Rand McNally.

Pitkin, H. F. 1967. *The Concept of Representation*. Berkeley: University of California Press.

Polsby, N. W. 1968. "The Institutionalization of the U.S. House of Representatives," *American Political Science Review*, 62: 144–168.

———. 1971a. *Congress and the Presidency*, 2nd ed. Englewood Cliffs, N.J.: Prentice-Hall.

———. 1971b. "Goodbye to the Inner Club," in N. W. Polsby, ed., *Congressional Behavior*. New York: Random House.

———. 1971c. "Strengthening Congress in National Policy-Making," in N. W. Polsby, ed., *Congressional Behavior*. New York: Random House.

Polsby, N. W., M. Gallaher, and B. S. Rundquist. 1969. "The Growth of the Seniority System in the U.S. House of Representatives," *American Political Science Review*, 63: 787–807.

Price, D. E. 1971. "Professionals and 'Entrepreneurs': Staff Orientations and Policy Making on Three Senate Committees," *Journal of Politics*, 33: 313–336.

———. 1972. *Who Makes the Laws? Creativity and Power in Senate Committees*. Cambridge, Mass.: Schenkman.

———. 1974. "The Ambivalence of Congressional Reform," *Public Administration Review*, 34: 601–608.

———. 1978. "The Impact of Reform: The House Commerce Subcommittee on Oversight and Investigations," in L. N. Rieselbach, ed., *Legislative Reform: The Policy Impact*. Lexington, Mass.: Lexington Books.

Price, H. D. 1971. "The Congressional Career—Then and Now," in N. W. Polsby, ed., *Congressional Behavior*. New York: Random House.

Redman, E. 1973. *The Dance of Legislation*. New York: Touchstone Books.

Rieselbach, L. N. 1966. *The Roots of Isolationism*. Indianapolis, Ind.: Bobbs-Merrill.

———. 1970. "Congressmen as 'Small Town Boys': A Research Note," *Midwest Journal of Political Science*, 14: 321–330.

———. 1977a. *Congressional Reform in the Seventies*. Morristown, N.J.: General Learning Press.

———. ed. 1977b. "Symposium on Legislative Reform," *Policy Studies Journal*, 5: 394–491.

———. ed. 1978. *Legislative Reform: The Policy Impact*. Lexington, Mass.: Lexington Books.

Ripley, R. B. 1967. *Party Leaders in the House of Representatives*. Washington, D.C.: Brookings Institution.

———. 1969. *Power in the Senate*. New York: St. Martin's.

———. 1975. *Congress: Process and Policy*. New York: Norton.

Ripley, R. B., and G. A. Franklin. 1976. *Congress, the Bureaucracy and Public Policy*. Homewood, Ill.: Dorsey Press.

Robinson, J. A. 1963. *The House Rules Committee*. Indianapolis, Ind.: Bobbs-Merrill.

———. 1967. *Congress and Foreign Policy-Making*, rev. ed. Homewood, Ill.: Dorsey Press.

Rohde, D. W. 1974. "Committee Reform in the House of Representatives and the Subcommittee Bill of Rights," *Annals*, 411: 39–47.

Rohde, D. W., and K. A. Shepsle. 1973. "Democratic Committee Assignments in the House of Representatives: Strategic Aspects of a Social Choice Process," *American Political Science Review*, 57: 889–905.

Rohde, D. W., N. J. Ornstein, and R. L. Peabody. 1974. "Political Change and Legislative Norms in the United States Senate," presented to the annual meeting of the American Political Science Association.

Rohde, D. W., and H. J. Spaeth. 1976. *Supreme Court Decision Making.* San Francisco: Freeman.

Rosenau, J. N. 1963. *National Leadership and Foreign Policy: A Case Study in the Mobilization of Public Support.* Princeton, N.J.: Princeton University Press.

Rudder, C. 1977. "Committee Reform and the Revenue Process," in L. C. Dodd and B. I. Oppenheimer, eds., *Congress Reconsidered.* New York: Praeger.

——. 1978. "The Policy Impact of Reform of the Committee on Ways and Means," in L. N. Rieselbach, ed., *Legislative Reform: The Policy Impact.* Lexington, Mass.: Lexington Books.

Saloma, J. S., III. 1969. *Congress and the New Politics.* Boston: Little, Brown.

Sarbin, T. R., and V. L. Allen. 1968. "Role Theory," in G. Lindzey and E. Aronson, *The Handbook of Social Psychology,* 2nd ed., vol. I. Reading, Mass.: Addison-Wesley.

Scher, S. 1963. "Conditions for Legislative Control," *Journal of Politics,* 25: 526–551.

Schmidhauser, J. R., and L. L. Berg. 1972. *The Supreme Court and Congress.* New York: Free Press.

Schubert, G. 1974. *Judicial Policy Making: The Political Role of the Courts.* Glenview, Ill.: Scott, Foresman.

Shannon, W. W. 1968. *Party, Constituency, and Congressional Voting.* Baton Rouge: Louisiana State University Press.

Shuman, H. E. 1957. "Senate Rules and the Civil Rights Bill," *American Political Science Review,* 51: 955–975.

Stevens, A. G., Jr., A. H. Miller, and T. E. Mann. 1974. "Mobilization of Liberal Strength in the House, 1955–1970: The Democratic Study Group," *American Political Science Review,* 68: 667–681.

Stewart, J. G. 1971. "Two Strategies of Leadership: Johnson and Mansfield," in N. W. Polsby, ed., *Congressional Behavior.* New York: Random House.

Stokes, D. E., and W. E. Miller. 1962. "Party Government and the Saliency of Congress," *Public Opinion Quarterly,* 26: 531–546. Selection 12 in this volume.

Strom, G. S., and B. S. Rundquist. 1977. "A Revised Theory of Winning in House-Senate Conferences," *American Political Science Review,* 71: 448–453.

Sullivan, J. L. and R. E. O'Connor. 1972. "Electoral Choice and Popular Control of Public Policy," *American Political Science Review,* 66: 1256–1268.

Taylor, T. 1961. *Grand Inquest.* New York: Ballantine Books.

Thurber, J. A. 1978. "New Powers of the Purse: An Assessment of Congressional Budget Reform," in L. N. Rieselbach, ed., *Legislative Reform: The Policy Impact.* Lexington, Mass.: Lexington Books.

Truman, D. B. 1959. *The Congressional Party: A Case Study.* New York: Wiley.

——. 1971. *The Governmental Process,* 2nd ed. New York: Knopf.

Tufte, E. R. 1975. "Determinants of the Outcomes of Midterm Congressional Elections," *American Political Science Review,* 69: 812–826.

Turner, J. 1970. *Party and Constituency: Pressures on Congress,* rev. ed., by E. V. Schneier, Jr. Baltimore: John Hopkins Press.

U. S. House of Representatives. 1973. Select Committee on Committees, *Committee Organization in the House,* vol. 2, part 3, Invited Working Papers. Washington, D.C.: Government Printing Office.

——. 1974. Select Committee on Committees, *Committee Reform Amendments of 1974.* Washington, D.C.: Government Printing Office.

U.S. Senate. 1977. Temporary Select Committee to Study the Senate Committee System. *Structure of the Senate Committee System.* Washington, D.C.: Government Printing Office.

Van Der Slik, J. R.   1973. "Role Theory and the Behavior of Representatives," *Public Affairs Bulletin*, 6, no. 2: 1–7.

——.   1977. *American Legislative Processes*. New York: Crowell.

Vogler, D. J.   1971. *The Third House: Conference Committees in the United States Congress*. Evanston, Ill.: Northwestern University Press.

——.   1977. *The Politics of Congress*, 2nd ed. Boston: Allyn and Bacon.

Wahlke, J. C.   1971. "Policy Demands and System Support: The Role of the Represented," *British Journal of Political Science*, 1: 271–290.

Wahlke, J. C., H. Eulau, W. Buchanan, and L. C. Ferguson.   1962. *The Legislative System*. New York: Wiley.

Wasby, S. L.   1978. *The Supreme Court in the Federal Judicial System*. New York: Holt, Rinehart and Winston.

Welch, S., and J. G. Peters, eds.   1977. *Legislative Reform and Public Policy*. New York: Praeger.

Westefield, L. P.   1974. "Majority Party Leadership and the Committee System in the House of Representatives," *American Political Science Review*, 68: 1593–1604.

White, W. S.   1956. *Citadel*. New York: Harper.

Wildavsky, A.   1974. *The Politics of the Budgetary Process*, 2nd ed. Boston: Little, Brown.

Wolanin, T. R.   1975. "Committee Seniority and the Choice of House Subcommittee Chairmen: 80th–91st Congresses," *Journal of Politics*, 37: 687–702.

Wolfinger, R. E., and J. H. Hollinger.   1971. "Safe Seats, Seniority, and Power in Congress," in R. E. Wolfinger, ed., *Readings on Congress*. Englewood Cliffs, N.J.: Prentice-Hall.

Yinger, J. M.   1965. *Toward a Field Theory of Behavior*. New York: McGraw-Hill.